An Introduction to
Gerontology

CW01083438

With the world's population getting increasingly older, there has never been a more pressing need for the study of old age and ageing. *An Introduction to Gerontology* provides a wide-ranging introduction to this important topic. By assuming no prior expert knowledge and avoiding jargon, this book will guide students through all the main subjects in gerontology, covering both traditional areas, such as biological and social ageing, and more contemporary areas, such as technology, the arts and sexuality. *An Introduction to Gerontology* is written by a team of international authors with multidisciplinary backgrounds who draw evidence from a variety of different traditions.

Ian Stuart-Hamilton is Professor of Developmental Psychology and Faculty Head of Research and External Activity at the University of Glamorgan. He has been teaching lifespan psychology for over twenty-five years and has written six textbooks including *The Psychology of Ageing*, which was the winner of an award from the British Medical Association and shortlisted for the British Psychological Society's Book of the Year award.

AN INTRODUCTION TO
Gerontology

Edited by

Ian Stuart-Hamilton

CAMBRIDGE UNIVERSITY PRESS
Cambridge, New York, Melbourne, Madrid, Cape Town,
Singapore, São Paulo, Delhi, Tokyo, Mexico City

Cambridge University Press
The Edinburgh Building, Cambridge CB2 8RU, UK

Published in the United States of America by Cambridge University Press, New York

www.cambridge.org
Information on this title: www.cambridge.org/9780521734950

First published 2011

Printed in the United Kingdom at the University Press, Cambridge

A catalogue record for this publication is available from the British Library

Library of Congress Cataloguing in Publication data
An introduction to gerontology / edited by Ian Stuart-Hamilton.
    p.   cm.
Includes bibliographical references and index.
ISBN 978-0-521-51330-2
1. Gerontology.   I. Stuart-Hamilton, Ian.   II. Title.
HQ1061.I5558   2011
305.26 – dc22   2011003321

ISBN 978-0-521-51330-2 Hardback
ISBN 978-0-521-73495-0 Paperback

Contents

Figures

Tables

Contributors

Kate Davidson, *University of Surrey*

Carmel Dyer, *University of Texas at Houston*

Rebecca Flyckt, *University Hospitals of Cleveland, Case Medical Center; MacDonald Women's Hospital, Cleveland*

Sheryl A. Kingsberg, *University Hospitals of Cleveland, Case Medical Center; MacDonald Women's Hospital, Cleveland*

João Pedro de Magalhães, *University of Liverpool*

Lynn McDonald, *University of Toronto*

Sean Morrison, *Mount Sinai School of Medicine, New York*

Raymond Ngan, *City University of Hong Kong*

Lynn O'Neill, *Mount Sinai School of Medicine, New York*

Sharon Ostwald, *University of Texas at Houston*

Ian Stuart-Hamilton, *University of Glamorgan*

Anthea Tinker, *King's College London*

Sandra Torres, *University of Uppsala*

Paul Verhaeghen, *Georgia Institute of Technology*

Suzanne Wait, *University College London*

Diana Wallace, *University of Glamorgan*

Bob Woods, *Bangor University*

1 Introduction

IAN STUART-HAMILTON

OVERVIEW

This chapter introduces some general concepts of ageing. First, it presents different views of what 'ageing' is and when 'old age' begins. Second, it examines changes in life expectancy and the proportion of the population that is old. Third, it considers attitudes to ageing. The final section outlines the structure of the rest of the book and its rationale.

Different views of later life

Gerontology is the study of old age and ageing. Although everyone has an intuitive sense of what 'old age' and 'ageing' are, providing a watertight objective definition is surprisingly difficult. *Ageing* could be said simply to be the process of growing older. However, pedantically speaking, we are all ageing from the moment of conception: do we really wish to say that children are 'ageing'? Hence, ageing is more sensibly described as change within old age or change that affects older people. It can thus include processes that started in earlier life but only manifest themselves in old age (e.g. a cardiovascular problem that appears in a person's sixties resulting from a poor lifestyle choice in that person's twenties). However, this begs the question of how to define 'old age'. At first the issue seems a simple one. Putting the niceties of political correctness to one side for a moment, it is intuitively obvious that most people in their seventies and teens look radically different and this is reflected in measures of fitness and health. Arguing for a distinction between older and younger people is thus reasonable. However, this raises a problem: namely, when do we decide that 'old age' begins? If we want a single 'threshold age' that marks the transition to becoming 'elderly', then this inevitably creates problems of inclusion and exclusion. For example, suppose we choose 70 years of age as marking the onset of old age. A high proportion of people aged 70 and older have the stereotypical characteristics of being 'old', but not all do. And there are many people younger than 70 who have 'elderly' characteristics. If we choose an onset age younger than 70, we are likely to include more people who lack many elderly characteristics, while choosing an older onset age will lessen this problem but increase the risk of overlooking individuals who became 'old' many years earlier.

This type of problem is sometimes likened to grading the colours of the rainbow. It is obvious that a rainbow contains bands of red, orange, yellow, green, blue, indigo and violet. It is equally obvious that when examined closely, these bands are not distinct but merge one into another. For example, there is no clear demarcation line between red and orange; instead, the red gradually changes into orange. At what point on the rainbow do we say that anything to one side is red and anything to the other is orange? The simple fact is that any demarcation line is essentially arbitrary; we have no really objective means of justifying the boundary, but for the sake of simplicity, a boundary is nonetheless created. This leads some commentators to argue that because a demarcation line is arbitrary, the entire categorization into distinct groups is wrong. However, this misses the point that although the boundaries between groups might be blurred, the groups are clear enough. Hence, even if the boundary between red and orange in a rainbow might be artificially created, nobody denies that there are distinct bands of red and orange. In a similar manner, although any threshold age marking off old age from younger ages may be arbitrary, it would be foolish in the extreme and serve no practical purpose to deny significant differences between older and younger adults in many respects. However, to return to the original question – how do we decide on what the threshold age is?

It would be possible to spend many pages of increasingly navel-gazing discussion over how to decide on a value for the threshold age. However, this would serve to do little other than obfuscate the issue. Falling on custom and practice, we can state that *old age* is defined as the final segment of the lifespan, and for those who must have a number to attach to this, it is further defined as beginning at around 60 years of age. Different gerontologists have different threshold ages for the onset, but 60 is a reasonable compromise figure. In fact, it has been accepted by the mainstream literature for nearly 200 years. The nineteenth-century Belgian statistician Adolphe Quetelet wrote a book called *Sur l'homme et le développement de ses facultés, ou, Essai de physique sociale* (Quetelet, 1836; the English translation has the more succinct title *Treatise on Man*). This was the first appreciable statistical study of human characteristics, and was hugely influential. Of especial interest here is that Quetelet defined the onset of old age as being at 60. This was because in his view, from 'sixty to sixty-five years of age viability loses much of its energy, that is to say, the probability of life then becomes very small' (Quetelet, p. 178). Once this threshold age had been thus decreed, later researchers tended to take this as an established fact and hence nearly all research from the 1840s onwards has tended to see old age as beginning at around the age of 60 (Mullan, 2002). This in turn influenced the concept of 'pensionable age': it is salient to remember that state pensions and the concept of retirement age are largely the invention of the late nineteenth century. Prior to this time, although 'old age' was identified (e.g. by exemption from payment of certain types of tax), the idea of there being an age after which one was occupied in nothing but leisure activities and 'growing old' would for nearly everybody have been an alien concept (Thane, 2000).

Thus, the concept of old age beginning at 60 (or thereabouts) might be seen as a nineteenth-century invention. Is this for the good or the bad? It is perfectly possible to argue that by having a threshold age, we lose sight of the fact that ageing is part of a continuum. We don't become 'old' overnight when we reach 60 – what we are in later life, is, as shall be seen in many of the later chapters, to a significant degree a product of what we were when younger. Similarly, having a boundary that states 'on this side you're young, on that side you're old' oversimplifies things and tends to label people as stereotypically old at the expense of their individuality. This in turn can lead to bad policy decisions (see Mullan, 2002). However, this is not the fault of having a threshold age per se. In addition, Quetelet was certainly wrong in arguing that the early sixties were a time of major decay – a quick perusal of Chapters 2 through 4 should establish that. Again, it can be questioned why the threshold age has remained so static since Quetelet's day – is what was considered 'old' in the early nineteenth century really the same as today? This leads some sociologists to question whether maintaining the threshold age is really in the interests of various authority groups (e.g. politicians) who can manipulate the concept of age categories and what is expected of each age group for their own purposes (e.g. Bourdelais, 1998). But nonetheless, it is useful, if only for *pragmatic* reasons, to have a threshold age. Provided this is employed loosely and individual variability is borne in mind, it is a useful conceptual tool. And since the established practice is to use the age of 60 (or thereabouts), this will be used here to maintain parity with earlier studies.

Having examined the bare-bones definitions of ageing and old age, we need to turn to general attitudes towards ageing. Do we see it primarily as positive or negative? Is it something that we wish to alter or are we satisfied to leave it as it is and simply act as neutral observers? For many researchers, it has been almost overwhelmingly tempting to see gerontology's subject matter purely in terms of decay, as in Peter Medawar's definition of ageing as the accumulation of changes that increase the probability of death (Medawar, 1952). More pithily making the same point, the character of Mr Bernstein in *Citizen Kane* describes old age as 'the only disease...that you don't look forward to being cured of' (Mankiewicz and Welles, 1941). Again, there are numerous examples in art and fiction of old age treated as a punishment. For example, anyone taking a guided tour of the Accademia in Venice is likely to be told the (possibly apocryphal) story behind the painting of Giorgione's *La Vecchia* ('The Old Woman'), an imposing portrait of an elderly woman in simple garb with wrinkled skin, thinning hair and signs of having suffered a stroke (and possibly dementia) clutching a scrap of paper on which is written *col tempo* ('with age'). Supposedly the painting was done as a riposte to a young woman who had spurned Giorgione's advances – in revenge he painted her as she would appear in extreme old age.

From this perspective, old age is a punishment, a time of waiting for inevitable death, the only uncertainty being when it will occur. This is in marked contrast to another, much older, set of views of ageing as a reward. For example, the *antediluvian ageing myth* argues that in the distant past people were rewarded for their great virtue by being given extremely long lifespans (cf. some of the early persons mentioned in the Bible, culminating in Methuselah, who lived to the tender age of 969 years). In contrast, the *Hyperborean ageing myth* states that there is a distant land where people live to very old age because of their virtuous lives. To some readers this may conjure thoughts of Shangri-La, a lamasery in the Himalayas containing improbably ancient monks, featured in the novel *Lost Horizon* (Hilton, 1933). A rather older legend is that of Prester John, whom Middle Ages Europe believed to be ruler of a distant Christian kingdom somewhere in Asia (or Africa – medieval knowledge was often sketchy on this point). He, too, supposedly lived an exceedingly long life, and his kingdom was a Christian paradise on Earth. A further myth is that of the *fountain of youth*, where imbibing at a magical spring or fountain or eating a special foodstuff confers long life, rejuvenation and/or immortality. We see this in numerous myths, from the apples tended by the goddess Idunn that kept the Norse gods immortal and healthy, through to such modern candy floss as *Star Trek: Insurrection*. Strictly speaking, Shangri-La also belongs in this category, since it is the food and water that hold the life-lengthening properties, not the place itself (Weil, 2005).

Although these myths are undeniably false, they indicate a deeply held wish of humankind to live long lives since they have been perpetuated across millennia and many very different cultures. How do we square this with the rather gloomier views of ageing as a time of waiting for inevitable death? If we take a closer look at the pro-ageing myths we can see that in fact they want old age, but not old age at any price. This is neatly illustrated by the ancient Greek myth of Tithonus, whose lover, Eos (goddess of the dawn), asked the gods for immortality without adding the caveat of wanting eternal youth as well. The gods, with their characteristically twisted sense of humour, duly gave Tithonus eternal life in that he was allowed to age for all eternity. This was seen as a dreadful fate and neatly illustrates that the wish for long life is for a long *physically and mentally active life*, not extreme old age just for the sake of it. The point is further amplified by Ovid's tale of Philemon and Baucis, a married couple who showed hospitality to Zeus and Hermes disguised as peasants when other members of their village had shunned them. As a reward, while the gods destroyed the rest of the village, Philemon and Baucis were spared and their humble home transformed into a temple. Of interest is that when Philemon and Baucis were granted long lives by the gods, they added a request that when one of them died, the other would die as well. So not only was a long active life seen as desirable, but also one free of grief for loss of a partner.

Thus, at the root of the various views of ageing is a clear message – give us long life, but without paying the price of suffering. This concept is more neatly expressed by *Dewey's paradox of ageing.* John Dewey, a philosopher and psychologist, wrote in the introduction to a colleague's textbook that 'we are . . . in the unpleasant and illogical condition of extolling maturity and depreciating age' (Dewey, 1939, p. iv). While the textbook has been forgotten, this phrase has remained a touchstone for the curious doublethink attitude we possess to ageing and old age. On the one hand it is a reward to be enjoyed, but if anything goes wrong, then it is a punishment.

Gerontology thus finds itself in a position of providing two sorts of answer – what the process of ageing is and how to make it as enjoyable as possible (what might be termed the 'explain' and 'improve' goals). First, let us consider providing factual information on what old age and ageing actually are. Into this category fall topics such as what happens to the ageing body, what policy decisions have been made about the welfare of older adults, and what artistic portrayals have been made of ageing and old age. These are not mere exercises in cataloguing – many models of ageing have generated vigorous debates and the area is far from theoretically dull. It also has a practical purpose, since measures of the incidence of disability in later life and similar are essential if adequate governmental planning for welfare provision is to be made in advance of an increasingly older adult population. The second type of answer concerns how we can alleviate the problems of later life so that it conforms as far as possible to the ideal of a pain and trouble-free old age. As noted in Chapter 2, many people fear that gerontologists simply want to prolong life at the expense of comfort and dignity. This is often called the *Tithonus myth* and nothing could be further from the truth. Gerontology is not and never has been about prolonging life at all costs.

So far in this chapter we have examined contrasting views of what ageing and old age are, and seen that the study of these topics is multidisciplinary and needs to be. But this does not necessarily explain why these studies are important. At a time of economic stringency, why should there be an imperative to study gerontology? The argument that it will help us to understand ourselves, while philosophically sound, is unlikely to impress those holding research funds debating whether funding the study of ageing really is more important than, for example, training more engineers or nurses. And the simple truth is that until recent times, gerontology was an academic backwater. Older people formed a minor proportion of the population, there were adequate funds to provide state pensions, and medical and nursing care largely consisted of palliative measures since, because older people by definition were going to die soon, there was little point in investing great energy into finding remedies for many of their ills. But all this was before the so-called *greying population*. Older people now form a significant proportion of the population, they are a potent economic force, and they are living longer, necessitating serious thinking about pension provision and methods of care for a group of people who can in the main expect to live for 20 years after their official retirement age. Gerontologists need to be heard because they are dealing with a significant part of the population. Not only that, but also they are dealing with a part of the lifespan that a majority of us can expect to experience, rather than the minority of a few decades ago. To explain this argument, we will need to examine population statistics.

Population trends

Let us begin by examining *life expectancy*. This is generally defined as the average time a person can expect to live. Let us start by examining what this figure means in industrialized countries with developed economies. According to the UK Office for National Statistics (www.statistics.gov.uk, accessed 29 June 2009), the life expectancy for a British boy born in 2009 is 78.3 years, and for a baby girl is 82.1 years. Women live longer than men and the reasons for this are explored in Chapter 3 (although there are suggestions the gender gap is narrowing, for which see Chapter 8). A quick perusal of the Organization for Economic Co-operation and Development (OECD) website (www.oecd.org/topicstatsportal) will reveal a similar figure for any other industrialized country. Life expectancy figures were lower in the historical past, as illustrated in Table 1.1.

In the interests of balance, it should be noted that prior to modern records, it is impossible to find totally reliable population data, but through various ingenious techniques it is possible to make a good approximation of life expectancy figures (see Acsadi and Nemeskeri, 1970) and it is these that are used here. But even allowing for measurement error, what becomes immediately apparent on looking at Table 1.1 is the vast gulf in life expectancy figures between then and now. For example, life expectancy at birth has more than doubled since 1400, and even in 1841, life expectancy was 38 years less than it is today. This increase in expectancy

Table 1.1 Life expectancy of individuals born in 1400, 1841, 1981 and 2009 in the UK

Age	1400	1841	1981	2009
0	35	40	71	78
20	48	60	72	79
40	57	67	73	80
60	69	73	76	82

Data extrapolated from Acsadi and Nemeskeri (1970) and UK Government Actuary's Department web page (www.gad.gov.uk.)

over recent historical times is truly remarkable. A study by Oeppen and Vaupel (2002) of *best practice life expectancy* (life expectancy in the country that has the longest life expectancy figure at a given time) demonstrated that the oldest age to which a human can expect to live has increased linearly from 1850 at a rate of approximately 3 months per year from 45 years in Sweden in 1840 to 85 years in Japan in 2000. The authors claim that this trend shows no sign of stopping. Is it possible that, ultimately, there will be no upper limit to how long we can live if we stay disease and accident free?

Striking as these figures are, they are potentially misleading because life expectancy figures, particularly historical ones, are poor indicators of the ages of the oldest members of the population. For example, a newcomer to the area could be forgiven for supposing that someone in 1400 who reached the age of 35 was nearing the end of their life. However, this is wrong, and a further examination of Table 1.1 will show why. It is perfectly true that at birth, there is a vast difference in life expectancy across time periods. However, look at the differences in life expectancy as people get older. If we consider people aged 60 in 1400, 1841, 1981 and 2009, we see a rather different picture. A 60-year-old in 1400 could expect to live 'only' 11 years less than someone born in 2009. This would be unlikely to have a sexagenarian of 1400 clapping their hands with glee, but it is a lot better than the 40+ years difference at birth. And the differences between the other historical times have likewise markedly diminished. For example, if we consider the difference in life expectancy for people aged 90 born in 1981 and 2009, the difference in remaining life is reduced to a mere 7 months, compared with 7 years at birth. In other words, the longer a person lives, the less extra life the modern world can give relative to historical times (though at the risk of confusing things, note that this is *relative* – there is still an increase in remaining life expectancy over time, albeit a smaller one, as will be demonstrated later in the chapter).

The principal reason why life expectancy has increased over historical time, and why the difference in expectancy decreases the older the age group considered, is that fewer people die young. This can be explained by using a contrived example. Suppose we have three groups of people called (imaginatively enough) A, B and C. Suppose also that in our imaginary world, people either die immediately after birth (so thus have an age of 0 years when they die) or live to 100 years of age and all die on their 100th birthday in the cause of simplifying the arithmetic. Suppose that in group A, everyone lives to be 100 – logically enough, the average age at death is 100 and so the life expectancy of Group A is 100. Now suppose that in group B, a quarter dies at birth and only three-quarters live to be 100. Adopting the same calculations as before, we find that the life expectancy of group B is 75. And in group C, let us suppose that half its members die at birth, and thus its life expectancy is 50. Now anyone who *only* had the life expectancy figures to view would quite reasonably suppose that group A had far more older people in it than group B, which in turn had far more older people than group C. But this would be utterly wrong – past birth, members of all three groups have the same chance of survival. However, it is the higher proportions of people dying young in groups B and C that give the erroneous impression of greater longevity for those who survive birth.

Returning to the real world, reasons for avoidance of early death in the modern world are not hard to find. Since Victorian times we have seen, *inter alia*: inoculations and the eradication of many deadly communicable diseases, improved public sanitation; antibiotics, improvements in surgery, greater food hygiene, higher quality of housing, etc. A high proportion of these innovations benefit the health of infants and children most of all, and so it is not surprising that a key component of changes in life expectancy over the last two centuries has been due to a decline in infant mortality. This also means that much of Oeppen and Vaupel's (2002) rise in best-practice life expectancy is because of a drop in infant mortality and a decline in infectious diseases, and not particularly an increase in our ability to 'age longer'. Post and Binstock (2004) accordingly advise caution in interpreting mathematical abstractions of a constant and seemingly unstoppable rise in life expectancy – it could simply be an artefact of a unique period in human history. And once infant mortality and major infectious diseases are brought under control (or at least when they reach a stable level), this particular resource for increasing life expectancy will be gone, and possibly with it the seemingly unstoppable rise in best-practice life expectancy.

There are counter-arguments to this and counter-arguments to the counter-arguments. However, the message at any point would be the same: neither side has the monopoly of the arguments, and thus future life expectancy data are uncertain. This creates a *longevity fan*, in which a graph depicting projected life expectancy fans out the further into the future the figures are extrapolated (see Dowd, Blake and Cairns, 2008, for an excellent review). Accordingly, in the UK, the Continuous Mortality Investigation, which advises actuaries, has suggested caution in projecting future life expectancies and (for want of a better phrase) predicts uncertainty in their calculation (Continuous Mortality Investigation, 2006a, b).

Discussion of life expectancy data, while interesting in its own right, tends to obscure another important fact; namely, that in developed countries and indeed many developing countries, old age is now an experience of the majority and the proportion of older adults in the population is increasing. None of this contradicts what has just been written about the deceptiveness of life expectancy figures. The fact that life expectancy figures have risen, largely because of decreased infant mortality, means that, in addition, more people reach old age. In addition, there has also been *some* improvement in the remaining years of life in older adults (albeit less impressive than in younger adults) as historical time has progressed. For example, in the UK the mortality rate for people aged over 75 has fallen from 137 deaths/1,000 in 1911–15 to 83 deaths/1,000 in 2006–7 (Office for National Statistics website www.statistics.gov.uk, accessed 1 July 2009). Similar figures can be reported for other industrialized countries.

As this growth in numbers of older adults has been matched with a fall in the number of births, this means that the proportion of older adults in the population is increasing. For example, in 2007, for the first time, there was a higher proportion of older adults than under-eighteens in the UK population (Office for National Statistics website www.statistics.gov.uk, accessed 1 July 2009). If we consider nineteenth-century industrialized nations (the first for whom arguably reliable data exist), approximately 4 per cent of the population was aged over 60 (Cowgill, 1970). In the UK today, circa 20 per cent of the population is aged 65 or older (Office for National Statistics website). This figure is expected to rise until it peaks at approximately 17 million (c.25 per cent) in 2060, before various demographic changes cause a relative decline (Shaw, 2004). Particularly noticeable is the rise in the proportion of the 'oldest old' (i.e. those aged 80 or older). Since 1981, their proportion of the total population has risen from 2.8 to 4.5 per cent (Office for National Statistics website).

This surge in proportions of older adults is in part due to lower infant mortality figures from earlier in the century working their way through to old age and partly to better health care and living conditions. It will (at the time of writing) soon be augmented by the baby boomers (those born in the 'population explosion' that occurred in the decade or so after the end of the Second World War) who will be reaching retirement age. However, whatever its causes, it means that gerontology is a study of a significant proportion of the population. More than this, it is also the study of a period of life that the overwhelming majority of people in the developed world can expect to reach. Today, approximately two-thirds of the citizens of developed countries can expect to live past 65 and about a third of these will live past 80. In contrast, in 1900, only a quarter of the population could hope to reach 65 (Brody, 1988; Sonnenschein and Brody, 2005).

Before leaving the topic of population trends, it should be noted that these changes are not uniform across all conditions. For example, as already noted, women have significantly longer lives than men (see Chapter 3). Within individual countries, there are significant differences in the proportions of older adults within its different regions (Blake, 2009). Likewise, there are regional differences in life expectancies (Griffiths and Fitzpatrick, 2001). There are also racial differences and educational differences. Members of minority racial groups and those with lower educational levels tend to have significantly lower life expectancy (Crimmins and Saito, 2001). And between countries, there is a marked division between the industrialized/high-income countries and the developing/low-income countries. However, this is not as clear-cut as might first be supposed. Life expectancy is significantly higher in industrialized countries, in no small part because of the lower levels of infant mortality and communicable diseases. These differences are projected to be still significant in 2030, by which time, the principal health burden in the developed world is anticipated to be chronic illnesses such as cancer, cardiovascular problems and similar. These are anticipated to form 90 per cent of the burden. In developing countries, the proportion is expected to be 54 per cent, with communicable diseases, nutritional problems and natal/perinatal illnesses forming 32 per cent of the burden, compared with a projected 3 per cent in developed countries (Lopez, Mathers, Ezzati et al., 2006). However, this does not mean that developing countries are automatically lagging behind. In relative terms, their improvement in life expectancy is in many cases much greater. For example, in many developing countries, the number of people aged over 65 will increase fourfold by 2050, more than double the anticipated increase in developed countries (United Nations Economic and Social Council, 2006). A confounding factor in these considerations is Africa, where the levels of AIDS/HIV infection place a serious question mark over the size of future growth (United Nations Economic and Social Council). These issues are discussed more fully in Chapter 11.

Ultimately, many of the life expectancy issues are underpinned by a single factor – money. Socio-economic status has been repeatedly shown to underpin life expectancy across time and place (e.g. Mackenbach, Stirbu, Roskam et al., 2008; Marmot, 2001; Singh and Siapush, 2006). This is not simply a matter of differences between the extremely rich and the extremely poor. Even within occupational groups that by most standards are at least financially comfortable (e.g. UK civil servants) higher-income subgroups have better life expectancies than those in middle or lower-income subgroups (see Marmot and Feeney, 1997).

Views of ageing

It might be reasonably supposed that, given the importance that ageing and old age are assuming in the modern world, not to mention the high probability that people in developed countries will experience old age for themselves, individuals would be aware of the issues concerning ageing. In fact, there seems to be a collective ignorance of issues surrounding ageing, including the holding of prejudicial stereotypes. Arguably one of the best indicators of prejudice is the ability to find a stereotyped group as intrinsically amusing. Consider the following, reputedly a real life story:

In September 1960 a resident at the Haslemere Home for the Elderly, Great Yarmouth, United Kingdom, enlivened what might have been another uneventful day by performing a striptease for the residents. Gladys Elton (aged 81) generated a rather more extreme response than she probably intended – one male resident died of a heart attack and five more residents required treatment for shock. In 1961, another resident (87 years-old Harry Meadows) dressed up as the Grim Reaper and appeared outside residents' windows beckoning them with his scythe. Three residents died as a result, and Haslemere Home for the Elderly was closed soon afterwards. (Donaldson, 2002)

The anecdote tends to strike readers as either morbidly funny or as tragic, thus perhaps reflecting Walpole's maxim that this world is a comedy to those that think, a tragedy to those that feel. However, whatever a person's reaction, it is based upon strong prior expectations of age and ageing. Consider the actions of Ms Elton. Performing a striptease in public raises questions of propriety at any age, but in most people's minds especially so in someone who is in their eighties. Almost any person in any culture will have a reaction that the elderly body is something to be covered, not flaunted. Then there is the issue of sexuality; many will feel that it is inappropriate for an older person to engage in any form of erotic or titillating behaviour. On top of this is the question of the cardiovascular health of older people. A person stripping off might have serious consequences for older people who probabilistically are less likely to endure shock than younger adults. Accordingly, Ms Elton, although perhaps motivated by an understandable desire to liven things up at the residential home, was incautious in her method of doing it. The rest of the anecdote may be dissected in a similar manner, and a useful class icebreaker for someone teaching gerontology might be to get students to see how many stereotypical beliefs about older adults are aroused in the story of Ms Elton's and Mr Meadows' activities. Notwithstanding this, the fact remains that the anecdote only works to amuse or sadden because people have strong prior expectations of what ageing is all about.

Unfortunately, for many people, stereotypes and received wisdom are the limit of their knowledge of ageing. Given that, as already stated, ageing is what happens to everyone who avoids illness and accident and is now the experience of the majority of Old World inhabitants, this ignorance is little short of amazing. Not even people whose jobs require them to work on a daily basis with older adults are immune. For example, Rust and See (2007) found that professional caregivers specializing in the care of older adults scored 40 per cent on an often-used test of knowledge of ageing (the *Palmore Facts on Aging Quiz* – Palmore, 1998). Williams and Fitzgerald (2006) found slightly better (60 per cent) but still not exactly glowing scores when assessing medical house officers. Again, Ming, Wilkerson, Reuben *et al.* (2004) found that although knowledge of ageing improved as medical students progressed through their course, 'the average scores of the student groups indicated substantial room for growth' (p. 983). In general, people who work on a regular basis with older adults, unless explicitly instructed in the matter, show a surprising ignorance of many gerontological facts (Stuart-Hamilton and Mahoney, 2003). Indeed, recent evidence points to the problem being even deeper rooted than this. Even in anonymous questionnaires such as the ones used in the studies above, participants might nonetheless be giving answers that are more socially acceptable than they actually feel. The implicit association test (Greenwald, McGhee and Schwartz, 1998) measures the speed with which participants associate pairings of a stimulus the researchers are interested in (in this case, old and young people) with either intrinsically pleasant items or unpleasant items (e.g. a pretty flower versus a cockroach). It is argued that in measures of ageism, someone with deep-rooted negative feelings about older people and ageing will be slower to associate pleasant items with images of ageing and vice versa. A study by Nash, Stuart-Hamilton and Mayer (2009) demonstrates that nursing students with regular exposure to older patients have a more negative implicit attitude to older people than a control group of psychology students. However (and perhaps more worryingly), they have a more positive *explicit* view of older people (i.e. they overtly declare support for older adults while covertly having more negative views of them). Over a year of training, this picture did not significantly change.

Views by others of later life are thus often illogical or unpleasant. However, older people's self-perceptions are not necessarily optimal either. Early research, drawing upon the psychoanalytic tradition, viewed ageing largely in terms of coming to terms with inner conflict or debate. The perceived problem was that by failing to resolve this internal battle, older adults become trapped into the wrong thought processes/attitudes to life and hence are doomed to a miserable old age. However, if this were the problem, some psychoanalytic theories hardly presented a particularly happy optimal solution. For example, as the author has noted elsewhere (Stuart-Hamilton, 2006), early Freudian theorists regarded later life as a struggle by the ego (which derives its energy from the declining nervous system) to suppress the urges of the id (which derives its energy from the relatively well-preserved smooth muscle). In order to conserve energy, the ego husbands its resources carefully and starts to rely on a limited set of very conservative attitudes. This leads to older adults becoming very hidebound and short-tempered in their ways. There is little to support this argument as studies have repeatedly shown that older adults are not, contrary to some stereotypes, curmudgeonly (see Chapter 6). However, other versions of the psychoanalytic approach have been more successful and influential, and these are not quite as depressing in their prognoses.

Perhaps best known of these is Erikson's stage theory (Erikson 1963, 1982; Wolf, 1997). Erikson took some of the elements of traditional Freudian theory and refined them, arguing that as we progress through life, we have to resolve a series of eight conflicts (i.e. unlike the traditional Freudian viewpoint, not all our problems are seen as rooted in infancy). These begin in the early years with deciding whom to trust and not to trust, and culminate in old age with resolving the conflict of *ego integrity versus despair*, which, properly resolved, will result in *ego integration* – in other words, in the acceptance that earlier conflicts and a lifetime's worth of debates and conflicts have been resolved. Without this resolution, it is argued, a person goes to the grave anxious and depressed. With this resolution, the person attains a real sense of fulfilment. A lasting appeal of Erikson's theory is that, even without accepting the tenets of psychoanalysis, the concept of conflicts that have to be resolved to lead to a more contented life has a widespread appeal. It gives clear solutions to problems that almost everyone is bound to face to some degree during a typical life. Other commentators have expanded on Erikson's model, and argued, for example, that the conflicts can be divided into substages. Peck (1968) stated that the final conflict can be segmented into three successive units: *ego differentiation versus work-role preoccupation, body transcendence versus body preoccupation* and *ego transcendence versus ego preoccupation*. In other words, individuals have first to shed concerns and preoccupations with status that belonged to their working/earlier lives. Then, they must learn to accept themselves for their minds and essential being and not be concerned with their ageing bodies (which may also by this stage be subject to ageing-probabilistic ailments such as rheumatism, angina, etc.). Finally, they must come to terms with the fact that they will die and that the self must take second place not only to spiritual considerations, but also to ensuring that what they leave behind in this world is as resolved and peaceful as it is possible to create.

Such models arguably create useful desiderata that may be appropriate in some situations (see Coleman and O'Hanlon, 2004), but they are only one aspect of a complex picture that is addressed throughout much of the rest of this book (for studies of personality in later life that are based on more empirical methods, see Chapter 6, and for studies of lifestyle in later life, see Chapters 5, 8, 9 and 12). Before leaving this topic, however, it is perhaps appropriate to consider one further model of how older people do or should behave, if only to demonstrate that deciding what is best for older adults can be fraught with problems. The topic of palliative care for the dying and very sick older person is dealt with thoroughly in Chapter 15. The topic is understandably a sensitive one since most adults have had the experience of losing an older relative and even those who have not can probably easily empathize. It therefore seems extraordinary that, in the early

1960s, two researchers proposed that a natural feature of ageing was to prepare for death by gradually withdrawing from society. This is the *disengagement theory* of Cumming and Henry (1961). Reaction against the theory was vigorous, not least because it was represented as arguing that older people 'naturally' want to die, so there is little point in being interested in their welfare. This is a gross distortion of the truth. Cumming and Henry were arguing that there was a *relative* withdrawal from society and, as Coleman and O'Hanlon (2004) point out, they were actually arguing for a greater distinctiveness for older people. At the time of the publication of Cumming and Henry's work, the prevailing view was that successful old age should be very akin to middle age. In other words, illnesses that have a high probability of appearing in old age were seen as a decline from the norm rather than a more or less inevitable feature of growing older that should be accepted and accommodated. Taken in its intended context, disengagement theory stresses that old age is not just a continuation of earlier life, but something different. It was *never* intended to state that older people should be encouraged to be lonely and die.

Cumming and Henry (1961) gathered their data from a large sample of Kansas City residents. Perhaps there was something atypical about Kansas City in the early 1960s, since later studies have failed to find disengagement as a particularly common trend in the older population. Although it is found in some older people, all other things being equal, it is typically found among those who have always been reclusive. This was first hypothesized by Maddox (1970a, b) and later supported by Barnes, Mendes de Leon, Bienios *et al.*'s (2004) longitudinal study. It is also related to economic hardship, which coincidentally means that disengagement tends to be more common among ethnic minority groups that tend to have lower average incomes (Magai, Cohen, Milburn *et al.*, 2001). For a sociological discussion of this same issue, see Chapter 8.

The link with economic hardship is important in another respect. *Activity theory*, which sprang up as a response to disengagement theory, argued that rather than allow older people to withdraw from society, active measures should be taken to increase their involvement. The theory was undoubtedly on the side of the angels. However, interventions of this type are typically only effective in lower-income groups (Larson, 1978). This implies that people who disengage in lower socio-economic groups might do so because of force of circumstance, while those who disengage in higher-income groups do so out of choice. Finally, it should be noted that in some instances, withdrawal can be an indicator of oncoming death (Bennett, 2002). Although to some extent this supports Cumming and Henry's original argument, not all illnesses lead to death if treated in time, so caution is required in treating cases of increased self-isolating behaviour.

Thus, not only is old age on the increase, not only does it require examination, but in the main people need educating about what ageing is because there are all too frequently misconceptions about not only what old age is, but also about what the best way is to address it.

The contents of this book

The intention of this book is first and foremost to provide the reader with a briefing of key findings. Because gerontology is the study of old age and the process of ageing, in theory it covers all aspects of age and ageing, and any academic discipline where ageing may have an influence is a legitimate area of study. In practice, the subject has tended to concentrate on a more circumscribed list, and following traditional practice, it will be the topics typically included in that list that are concentrated upon here. This is also convenient for a book that is intended to be a relatively concise guide. Thus, omission of a topic is not a comment on its worth, but merely a reflection of pragmatics.

In the chapters that follow, various ways of approaching the goals of *explain* and *improve* mentioned above will be explored, taking the viewpoint of a variety of key academic disciplines that have made strong inroads into gerontological research: biology, medicine, nursing, social care, education, psychology, sociology, retirement studies, studies of sexuality and relationships, government policy-making, technology, cross-cultural studies, artistic portrayals and studies of dying. Each has its own independent contribution to make to gerontology, but in combination, they produce a composite picture of ageing and old age that is greater than the sum of its parts. Each discipline/chapter has its own particular view of the subject. In part this is an obvious product of the differences in the background disciplines. Thus, different chapters utilize the views produced by their respective fields of social sciences, biological sciences, the humanities and so forth. However, there is also a radical difference in the emphasis on seeking to satisfy the *explain* and *improve* goals. In some disciplines, *explain* arguably far outweighs *improve* (the arts is a case in point); in others, the reverse. This is for a host of reasons, not least the relative maturity of different approaches, but also because, arguably, some approaches are best suited to providing explanations and others to enacting these into improvements. For example, it is no disrespect to either biology, nursing or medicine to say that in a fully realized model of gerontology, biology would largely explain old age and ageing, while medicine and nursing would enact this knowledge into providing an optimal improvement in the lives of older people.

This consideration is an important one. A criticism sometimes made of gerontology is that it is a mongrel subject, drawing together the work of distinctly different academic disciplines. This argument is weak on the a priori ground that if someone wants to learn about later life, of necessity this will involve reading in disparate disciplines addressing the same topic. However, ultimately, gerontology will come to fruition as interdisciplinary research grows and the findings in one discipline inform the others and spur them in new directions. This is already happening on a considerable scale. Although artistic portrayals of ageing remain surprisingly divorced from many of the scientific gerontological findings, it will become rapidly apparent in reading the chapters in this book that the supposedly separate disciplines rely heavily on each other for information and guidance. Thus, 'basic' biological research on cell death informs medical care and prognosis. Medical and nursing research informs planners of likely costs and benefits and likely survival rates of older patients. Survival rates and life expectancy enable psychologists to gauge likely future incidence of ageing-associated illnesses such as dementia. These in turn help planners and medical authorities to gauge future demand for nursing resources, and so on and so forth.

Although the research is interrelated, no attempt has been made to make each chapter speak in the same authorial 'voice'. The approaches of each field are still different and it was felt more important to respect this than present an ersatz uniformity. Thus, some chapters tend to be more prescriptive and factual, and others more discussion-based, reflecting the different academic traditions and enabling the subject matter to speak in its accustomed voice. The book is designed to be read in the sequence set, by presenting the reader with views of ageing within the person before moving to views of ageing in which the person interacts with others and features of the external world. If readers wish to select another sequence that makes more personal sense to them, then this should be possible as individual chapters can be read without requiring prior knowledge of the rest of the book's content. Explanatory editorial notes define terms likely to be confusing to a lay reader, and where a key expansion of an argument (or an alternative view of the same subject) is offered in another chapter, this is noted.

There is one final comment or, perhaps more accurately, a caveat. Namely, there is no one 'correct' view of gerontological issues – the interpretation one has is as much shaped by the aspect being studied at that time as any other factor. However, all are worthy of respect. Underlying all aspects of the study of ageing is the fact that we are looking at survivors. But *how* have they survived? To illustrate this, consider two contrasting quotations from the work of Alfred, Lord Tennyson. The first is from 'Ulysses' (Tennyson, 1973). Contemplating abandoning his wife and son for one last voyage (and certain death), the titular hero muses in the famous final lines:

> We are not now that strength which in old days
> Moved earth and heaven, that which we are, we are, –
> One equal temper of heroic hearts,
> Made weak by time and fate, but strong in will
> To strive, to seek, to find, and not to yield.
>
> Tennyson (1973, p. 90)

Taken at face value, the poem has a heroic quality to it of dignified acceptance of lost powers but a still unquenched spirit, and it is little surprise that quotations from it were a favourite for headstone inscriptions for decades afterwards (most notably Captain Scott's). In this sense the lines can be seen as an idealized view of ageing as a time of final consolidation. However, it is not the only view of ageing offered by Tennyson. Many who are familiar with the final lines of 'Ulysses' are unaware that Tennyson wrote a companion piece entitled 'Tithonus'. In this poem, ageing is no longer a heroic consummation but a torment to be shed, with the titular hero of this poem longing for the release of death, having (as mentioned earlier in the chapter) been cursed with everlasting ageing. At the end of this poem, there is a rather different tone, as Tithonus pleads with Eos (his former lover, who in some versions of the myth visited him each sunrise in her silver-wheeled chariot) to allow him to die:

> Release me, and restore me to the ground;
> Thou seest all things, thou wilt see my grave;
> Thou wilt renew thy beauty morn by morn;
> I earth in earth forget these empty courts,
> And thee returning on thy silver wheels.
>> Tennyson (1973, p. 91)

Should we therefore view old age as a heroic summation of all that has passed, or as an agonized brooding on all that has been lost? It is the responsibility of gerontology to address this question and ensure that in the future there is only one possible answer.

Summary

'Ageing' and 'old age' are ambiguous terms because they attempt to segment what is really a continuum, and where the dividing line is drawn is essentially arbitrary. Nonetheless, for practical purposes a threshold age of 60 (first proposed by Quetelet in the nineteenth century) or 65 is often used. Echoing this ambiguity, ideas about ageing are often contradictory and across historical time have been seen as both reward and punishment, as expressed succinctly in Dewey's paradox that 'we are ... in the unpleasant and illogical condition of extolling maturity and depreciating age'. Gerontology has become increasingly of interest as both life expectancy and the proportion of older people in the population have grown. Although mainly due to lowered early-life mortality, remaining life expectancy has also increased, questioning limits to life expectancy. Attitudes to ageing are still often negative and the degree to which older people are welcome and integrated into society (a debate arguably initiated by Cumming and Henry's disengagement theory) is questionable. It is argued that gerontology's role is both to explain ageing and improve the experiences and lives of older people, as expressed in the remaining chapters.

REFERENCES

Acsadi, G. and Nemeskeri, J. (1970) *History of human lifespan and mortality.* Budapest: Akademiai Kiado.

Barnes, L.L., Mendes de Leon, C.F., Bienios, J.L. *et al.* (2004) A longitudinal study of black–white differences in social resources, *Journals of Gerontology. Series B, Psychological Sciences and Social Sciences, 59,* 146–53.

Bennett, K.M. (2002) Low level social engagement as a precursor of mortality among people in later life, *Age and Ageing, 31,* 165–8.

Blake, S. (2009) Subnational patterns of population ageing, *Population Trends, 136,* 43–63.

Bourdelais, P. (1998) The ageing of the population: relevant question or obsolete notion?, in P. Johnson, and P. Thane (eds), *Old age from antiquity to post-modernity.* London: Routledge, 110–31.

Brody, J.A. (1988) Changing health needs of the ageing population, *Research and the ageing population.* Ciba Foundation Symposium 134. Chichester: Wiley.

Coleman, P.G. and O'Hanlon, A. (2004) *Ageing and development: theories and research.* London: Arnold.

Continuous Mortality Investigation (2006a) *The graduation of the CMI 1999–2002 mortality experience: final '00' series mortality tables – assured lives.* Working Paper 21(a).
  (2006b) *The graduation of the CMI 1999–2002 mortality experience: final '00' series mortality tables – annuitants and pensioners.* Working Paper 22(b).

Cowgill, D. (1970) The demography of aging, in A.M. Hoffman (ed.), *The daily needs and interests of older people.* Springfield, IL: C.C. Thomas, 27–69.

Crimmins, E.M. and Saito, Y. (2001) Trends in healthy life expectancy in the United States, 1970–1990: gender, racial, and educational differences, *Social Science and Medicine, 52,* 1629–41.

Cumming, E. and Henry, W.E. (1961) *Growing old.* New York: Basic Books.

Dewey, J. (1939) Introduction, in E.V. Cowdrey (ed.), *Problems of ageing.* Baltimore, MD: Williams and Wilkins, xxvi–xxxiii.

Donaldson, W. (2002) *Brewer's Rogues, villains and eccentrics.* London: Cassell.

Dowd, K., Blake, D. and Cairns, A.J.G. (2008) The facing up to uncertain life expectancy: the longevity fan charts. London: Pensions Institute, ISSN 1367–580X. www.pensions-institute.org/workingpapers/wp0703.pdf.

Erikson, E.H. (1963) *Childhood and society.* New York: Norton.
  (1982) *The life cycle completed: a review.* New York: Norton.

Greenwald, A.G., McGhee, D.E. and Schwartz, J.L.K. (1998) Measuring individual differences in implicit cognition: the Implicit Association Test, *Journal of Personality and Individual Differences, 74,* 1464–80.

Griffiths, C. and Fitzpatrick, J. (2001) Geographical inequalities in life expectancy in the United Kingdom, 1995–97, *Health Statistics Quarterly, 9,* 16–27.

Hilton, J. (1933) *Lost horizon.* London: Macmillan.

Larson, R. (1978) Thirty years of research on the subjective well-being of older Americans, *Journal of Gerontology*, *33*, 109–25.

Lopez, A., Mathers, C.D., Ezzati, M. *et al.* (2006) *Global burden of disease and risk factors*. Washington, DC: World Bank/Oxford University Press.

Mackenbach, J.P., Stirbu, I., Roskam, A.J. *et al.* (2008) Socioeconomic inequalities in morbidity and mortality in Western Europe, *New England Journal of Medicine*, *358*, 2468–81.

Maddox, G.I. (1970a) Persistence of life style among the elderly, in E. Palmore (ed.), *Normal aging*. Durham, NC: Duke University Press, 329–31.

   (1970b) Themes and issues in sociological theories of human aging, *Human Development*, *13*, 17–27.

Magai, C., Cohen, C., Milburn, N. *et al.* (2001) Attachment styles in older European American and African American adults, *Journals of Gerontology. Series B, Psychological Sciences and Social Sciences*, *56*, 28–45.

Mankiewicz, J. and Welles, O. (1941) *Citizen Kane screenplay*. Los Angeles: RKO Pictures.

Marmot, M. (2001) Inequalities in health, *New England Journal of Medicine*, *345*, 134–6.

Marmot, M. and Feeney, A. (1997) General explanations for social inequalities in health, *IARC Scientific Publications*, *138*, 207–28.

Medawar, P.B. (1952) *An unsolved problem of biology*. London: H.K. Lewis.

Ming, L., Wilkerson, L., Reuben, D.B. *et al.* (2004) Development and validation of a geriatric knowledge test for medical students, *Journal of the American Geriatrics Society*, *52*, 983–8.

Mullan, P. (2002) *The imaginary time bomb: why an ageing population is not a social problem*. New York: I.B. Tauris.

Nash, P., Stuart-Hamilton, I. and Mayer, P. (2009) The effects of specific education and direct experience on implicit and explicit measures of ageism. Paper presented at 19th World Congress of Gerontology and Geriatrics, Paris, France, 5–9 July, 2009.

Oeppen, J. and Vaupel, J.W. (2002) Broken limits to life expectancy, *Science*, *296*, 1029–31.

Palmore, E. (1998) *The facts on aging quiz*, 2nd edn. New York: Springer.

Peck, R.C. (1968) Psychological developments in the second half of life, in B.L. Neugarten (ed.), *Middle age and aging: a reader in social psychology*. University of Chicago Press, 88–92.

Post, S.G. and Binstock, R.H. (2004) *The fountain of youth: cultural, scientific and ethical perspectives on a biomedical goal*. Oxford University Press.

Quetelet, A. (1836) *Sur l'homme et le développement de ses facultés*. Brussels: Haumann.

Rust, T.B. and See, S.K. (2007) Knowledge about aging and Alzheimer disease: a comparison of professional caregivers and noncaregivers, *Educational Gerontology*, *33*, 349–64.

Shaw, C. (2004) Interim 2003-based national population projections for the United Kingdom and constituent countries, *Population Trends*, *118*, 6–16.

Singh, G.K. and Siapush, M. (2006) Widening socioeconomic inequalities in US life expectancy, 1980–2000, *International Journal of Epidemiology*, *35*, 969–79.

Sonnenschein, E. and Brody, J.A. (2005) Effect of population aging on proportionate mortality from heart disease and cancer, U.S. 2000–2050, *Journals of Gerontology. Series B, Psychological Sciences and Social Sciences*, *60*, 110–12.

Stuart-Hamilton, I. (2006) *The psychology of ageing: an introduction*, 4th edn. London: Jessica Kingsley Publishers.

Stuart-Hamilton, I. and Mahoney, B. (2003) The effect of aging awareness training on knowledge of, and attitudes towards, older adults, *Educational Gerontology*, *29*, 251–60.

Tennyson, A. (1973) *Poems and plays*, 2nd impression. Oxford University Press.

Thane, P. (2000) *Old age in English history: past experiences, present issues.* Oxford University Press.

United Nations Economic and Social Council (2006) *Major developments in the area of ageing since the Second World Assembly on Ageing.* Report of the Secretary-General, Geneva, 21 November.

Weil, A. (2005) *Healthy aging.* New York: Knopf.

Williams, B. and Fitzgerald, J.T. (2006) Brief instrument to assess geriatrics knowledge of surgical and medical subspeciality house officers, *Journal of Geriatric Medicine, 21,* 490–3.

Wolf, E.S. (1997) Self psychology and the aging self through the life curve, *Annual of Psychoanalysis, 25,* 201–15.

2 The biology of ageing
A primer

JOÃO PEDRO DE MAGALHÃES

OVERVIEW

. . . .

This chapter introduces key biological concepts of ageing. First, it defines ageing and presents the main features of human ageing, followed by a consideration of evolutionary models of ageing. Causes of variation in ageing (genetic and dietary) are reviewed, before examining biological theories of the causes of ageing.

. . . .

Introduction

Thanks to technological progress in different areas, including biomedical breakthroughs in preventing and treating infectious diseases, longevity has been increasing dramatically for decades. The life expectancy at birth in the UK for boys and girls rose, respectively, from 45 and 49 years in 1901 to 75 and 80 in 1999 with similar figures reported for other industrialized nations (see Chapter 1 for further discussion). A direct consequence is a steady increase in the proportion of people living to an age where their health and well-being are restricted by ageing. By the year 2050, it is estimated that the percentage of people in the UK over the age of 65 will rise to over 25 per cent, compared to 14 per cent in 2004 (Smith, 2004).

The greying of the population, discussed elsewhere (see Chapter 1), implies major medical and societal changes. Although ageing is no longer considered by health professionals as a direct cause of death (Hayflick, 1994), the major killers in industrialized nations are now age-related diseases like cancer, diseases of the heart and neurodegenerative diseases. The study of the biological mechanisms of ageing is thus not merely a topic of scientific curiosity, but a crucial area of research throughout the twenty-first century. In recent years, considerable progress has been made in understanding the biology of ageing. This chapter aims to describe the major observations, theories and hypotheses of *biogerontology*, the field of research that studies ageing from a biological perspective. A brief discussion on the prospects of developing therapies that delay the process of ageing and an overview of future critical areas in biogerontology are also included.

What is ageing?

Human ageing entails multiple changes at different levels. Some, like wrinkles or grey hair, are more visible than others. Age-related changes also make themselves felt at the functional and physiological level. By and large, most functions begin to decline linearly after reaching peak performance in the third decade of life (Strehler, 1999). It is common knowledge that the ability of adults to perform physical tasks declines with age. Due to loss of muscle and bone mass, ageing is also characterized by weight loss. Though there is considerable individual variability and no two people age alike, other physiological and functional hallmarks of ageing include a gradual reduction in height, a lower metabolic rate, longer reaction times and decreased sexual activity (see Chapter 10). In women, menopause or reproductive senescence is an inevitable consequence of old age. Functional declines in kidney, pulmonary and immune functions are also frequent. Lastly, as discussed in Chapter 7, a major concern of older adults is mental health since memory and cognitive impairment are associated with human ageing even in the absence of disease (Arking, 2006; Finch, 1990; Hayflick, 1994).

Although not all physiological changes lead to pathology, ultimately functional and physiological changes render people more susceptible to a number of diseases (Figure 2.1). Ageing has been defined as an intrinsic, inevitable and irreversible age-related process of loss of viability and increase in vulnerability (Comfort, 1964). Practically any system, tissue or organ can fail because of ageing (Austad, 1997b; Strehler, 1999). The heart, a critical organ with little room for error or rest, is the organ that most often fails. For people over the age of 85, diseases of the heart are the major cause of death, responsible for almost 40 per cent of all deaths, followed by cancer, cerebrovascular diseases, neurodegenerative diseases like Alzheimer's and Parkinson's disease, infectious diseases and diabetes (Heron, Hoyert, Jiaquan *et al.*, 2008). (Health issues of older adults are further discussed in the following two chapters of this book.)

It is well known that women live longer than men, even though it does not appear that women age more slowly. At virtually all ages, women have lower mortality rates for the major causes of death, including heart diseases and cancer. It is as

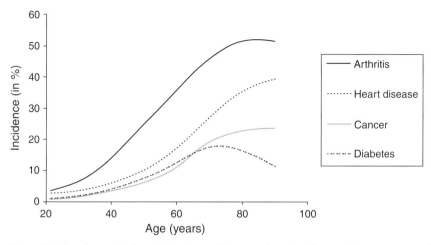

Figure 2.1 Prevalence of selected chronic conditions as a function of age. Values are expressed in percentage for the US population (2002–03 data set). *Source:* Centers for Disease Control and Prevention, 2008.

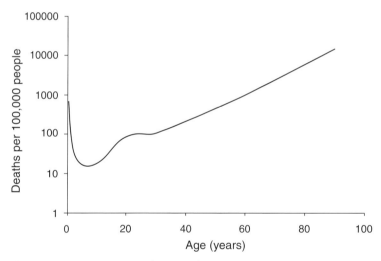

Figure 2.2 Mortality rates as a function of age. Values are expressed in deaths per 100,000 people, plotted on a logarithmic scale, for the 2002 US population. *Source:* Centers for Disease Control and Prevention, 2008.

if women were more robust than men. The causes for these gender differences remain a mystery (Austad, 2006). Paradoxically, it is conventional wisdom that women have poorer health than men, though sex differences in morbidity suggest the situation to be more complex than conventional wisdom suggests, with strong variation observed across the lifespan (Macintyre, Hunt and Sweeting, 1996).

Because ageing increases the morbidity of many diseases, one of the defining features of ageing is an increased probability of death with age (Figure 2.2). In fact, ageing has been defined as the collection of changes that render human beings progressively more likely to die (Medawar, 1952). As is clear from Figure 2.2, human mortality rates increase exponentially after about age 30. Specifically, the probability of dying for a given individual over the age of 30 doubles approximately every 8 years (Finch, 1990). The exponential increase in mortality with age is a hallmark of ageing, also observed in many other species and in animal models of biomedical research. The rate at which mortality increases with age in a given population can also be used as an estimate of the rate of ageing. For humans the 8-year mortality doubling time seems to be relatively constant across populations (Finch, 1990), though in animal models this value can vary substantially between species and even strains of the same species and can be used to test for the effects on the process of ageing of a given gene or intervention, as further discussed below.

Thus, human ageing encompasses physiological changes that typically lead to a functional decline with age, which in turn leads to a loss of the equilibrium between different physiological systems and their capacity to respond to environmental challenges, also known as *homeostasis*. As organs' functions are progressively impaired, this results in an increased susceptibility to most diseases and it is this that gives rise to the exponential increase in mortality. Ageing can thus be defined as a progressive deterioration of physiological function, accompanied by an increase in vulnerability and mortality with age. The basic process of ageing, or *senescence* as some call it, can be defined as the underlying process synchronizing the progression of the different components of ageing and is the main focus of research in biogerontology.

The evolutionary theory of ageing

As detailed above, biological ageing implies frailty, progressive functional decline and ultimately death. One puzzle of biogerontology is why, in light of evolution and the apparent disadvantage to organisms that ageing represents, is there an ageing process at all? One of the first people to address this apparent paradox was August Weismann. He proposed the hypothesis known as *group selection*, which states that ageing evolved because it benefits the species or group, even if it is detrimental to the individual (Weismann, 1891). Weismann later abandoned this concept and instead advocated that organisms that segregate *germ* and *soma* – respectively, reproductive cells and all other cells – must invest more resources to reproduce rather than to maintain the soma and ageing is the consequence of organisms renouncing the soma. Unlike group selection, which today is dismissed by most authorities, the idea of soma–germ segregation playing a role in the evolution of ageing has remained until now. It was later revised to become the *disposable soma theory*, which states that there is a trade-off between investment in soma maintenance and reproduction, such that the body declines so that reproductive capacity can be maintained (Kirkwood, 1977).

Arguably, the first model of the evolution of ageing was put forward by Peter Medawar more than half a century after Weismann's work. Inspired by earlier work from the evolutionary biologists Fisher and Haldane, Medawar assumed that, because the greatest contribution to create a new generation comes from young, not old organisms, the force of natural selection fades with age (Medawar, 1952). In the wild, the mortality of most animals is very high. Hence, if the probability of a mouse reaching age 5 is only 0.01 per cent, then there is little evolutionary pressure to select for gene variants, called *alleles*, which maintain function until age 5. Furthermore, a deleterious mutation that is harmful or even lethal at age 5 will not be selected against because few if any animals will ever reach such age, allowing late-acting hazardous alleles to persist in the population. This theory became known as the *mutation accumulation theory* (Hamilton, 1966; Kirkwood and Austad, 2000; Rose, 1991). Shortly afterwards, a complementary theory was developed by George Williams (1957). This argued that a gene that increases the chances of the survival of a mouse to reproductive age will be favoured even if the same gene produces lethal effects at age 5. As a result, genes with beneficial effects at early ages but harmful at later ones will be favoured by natural selection. Because genes with opposing effects are known as *pleiotropic*, this theory became known as the *antagonistic pleiotropy theory* (Williams, 1957).

Therefore, two main models exist for explaining the evolution of ageing: one in which harmful late-acting mutations accumulate because the force of natural selection is weaker at later ages, and the other in which harmful late-acting mutations accumulate because they are beneficial at earlier ages. Both theories, together with the mathematical models of Hamilton (1966), compose the classical evolutionary theory of ageing. The theory and models are largely supported by experimental evidence (Kirkwood and Austad, 2000; Rose, 1991). A few findings are incompatible with the theory, however. The observation that some animals might not age at all, or at least fail to exhibit the typical hallmarks of ageing even after decades of study (Finch, 1990), conflicts with the predictions of Hamilton (1966), and suggests that some refinements can still be made to the theory (Vaupel, Baudisch, Dolling *et al.*, 2004). Nonetheless, the evolutionary theory of ageing is one of the theoretical landmarks of biogerontology.

Life history theory

The evolutionary theory of ageing is part of a larger theoretical framework known as life history theory. This addresses the changes organisms undergo from conception to death, focusing particularly on the schedule of reproduction and

Table 2.1 Diversity of mammalian life histories obtained from the AnAge database (derived from: http://genomics.senescence.info/species/)

Organism (species)	Longevity (years)	Maturity (years)	Body mass (kilograms)
Human (*Homo sapiens*)	122.5	13	60
Chimpanzee (*Pan troglodytes*)	59.4	9	45
Rhesus monkey (*Macaca mulatta*)	40	5	8
Marmoset (*Callithrix jacchus*)	16.5	1.25	0.25
Mouse (*Mus musculus*)	4	0.15	0.02
Naked mole rat (*Heterocephalus glaber*)	28.3	0.75	0.03
Shrew (*Crocidura russula*)	4	0.2	0.01
Bat (*Myotis lucifugus*)	34	<1	0.01
Elephant (*Elephas maximus*)	65.5	9	3000
Sheep (*Ovis aries*)	22.8	2	110
Horse (*Equus caballus*)	57	3	250
Bowhead whale (*Balaena mysticetus*)	211	22.5	100,000
Cat (*Felis catus*)	>30	1	4
Opossum (*Didelphis virginiana*)	6.6	0.5	3

survival (Stearns, 1992). An extraordinary diversity of lifespans and ageing phenotypes – the characteristics of an organism as determined by both genes and the environment – is found among the world's species. Some organisms, like certain turtles and rockfishes, do not exhibit signs of ageing for many decades and are known as cases of *negligible senescence* (Finch, 1990). On the other hand, even vertebrates can exhibit extremely short lifespans, such as certain African annual fishes that in the laboratory do not live more than 12 weeks and exhibit signs of an extremely fast ageing process (Valdesalici and Cellerino, 2003). Intriguingly, some organisms are *semelparous*, which means they reproduce only once (also called 'big bang reproduction'), in contrast to *iteroparous* species like humans that can reproduce multiple times across the lifespan. The classical example of a semelparous species is the salmon, which dies shortly after spawning, exhibiting several pathologies. Castrated animals live longer and a hormonal cascade appears to trigger both reproduction and degeneration leading to death (Finch, 1990; Gosden, 1996; Hayflick, 1994).

Even similar species such as mammals can exhibit marked differences in longevity (Table 2.1) and ageing (Austad, 1997a, 1997b). Among mammals, only a few marsupials, like certain species of the mouse-like genus *Antechinus*, exhibit semelparity that is also triggered by hormonal changes. No mammalian species is known to avoid ageing (Finch, 1990; Gosden, 1996). Nonetheless, mammals have a wide range of lifespans from short-lived species like mice, which do not commonly live more than 4 years even in protective environments and exhibit marked signs of ageing, to the estimated 211 years one bowhead whale had lived by the time it was killed by Alaskan Inuit (George *et al.*, 1999). Humans are the second longest-lived mammal and there is abundant evidence that longevity evolved in the primate lineage leading to humans (Finch, 1990). Understanding these differences in longevity and how it evolved could provide important insights about the biology of ageing.

Life history theory provides a structure to understand these differences in *lifespan* and *longevity* – which are used herein interchangeably, though often lifespan means average lifespan while longevity represents maximum lifespan. Of interest is the concept of *r-* and *K-selections* (MacArthur and Wilson, 1967). In this model, animals in hazardous environments and thus with high mortality will maximize reproduction and thus be *r*-selected while organisms in non-hazardous environments will maximize performance under crowded conditions and be *K*-selected. In practice, *r*-selection will favour rapid development, small body size and a short lifespan while *K*-selection will favour delayed development, larger body sizes and a longer lifespan (Austad, 1997a). Humans and whales are examples of *K*-selection while mice are an example of *r*-selection (Table 2.1). Although the *r*- and *K*-selection model is now recognized as an oversimplification and more complex models exist, it can be useful to interpret life history events and strategies in the context of biogerontology.

By relating the environments under which organisms evolve to their life history, evolutionary theory provides an understanding of why different species evolve different lifespans and ageing phenotypes. There is a great interest, however, in understanding the exact genetic and physiological mechanisms underlying species differences in longevity and ageing, in particular differences between humans and related species, as these may provide clues about the human ageing process. To study species differences in ageing, researchers can compare species with different lifespans and attempt to correlate some factor or trait under study, such as the rate a given change occurs with age or potentially important functions like repair mechanisms, with the longevity of the species. Some of the mechanistic theories of ageing detailed below have been tested by such comparative approaches. Life history theory and the evolutionary theory of ageing in particular provide the theoretical framework for interpreting such experiments.

The plasticity of ageing

Ageing is thus not the immutable feature of all living things that people generally assume it to be. As mentioned above, some species appear to avoid it. Besides, differences in genes and environments can give rise to marked differences in ageing between individuals of the same species. In particular, experiments in model organisms have demonstrated that ageing can be manipulated by genetic and environmental factors. Understanding the mechanisms involved might allow human ageing to be manipulated. As such, the discoveries detailed below on the plasticity of ageing are among the most important in our understanding of the biology of ageing.

Caloric restriction

In the 1930s, Clive McCay and colleagues, guided by earlier findings, tested the idea that growth retardation could extend lifespan. They showed in a carefully conducted study that it is possible to extend the lifespan of rats by limiting the amount of calories in their diet while maintaining normal amounts of other nutrients (McCay, Crowell and Maynard, 1935). This phenomenon became known as caloric restriction (CR), or calorie restriction as some call it. Interpreting experimental results is seldom straightforward in biogerontology. In the same way that women live longer than men but do not age slower, the health, mortality and consequently average lifespan of laboratory animals can be manipulated by interventions without any effect on the ageing process. This is a crucial but often misunderstood issue in interpreting experimental results because it means that genes or interventions that affect the lifespan of animals are not necessarily influencing the process of ageing. From studies in mice and rats, not only can CR increase longevity by up to 50 per cent in certain strains but it also delays physiological ageing, postpones or diminishes the morbidity of most age-related diseases and decreases the rate of exponential increase of mortality (Masoro, 2005; Weindruch and Walford, 1988). Therefore, at least in some cases, it appears that the process of ageing is delayed by CR.

As the first robust method to extend lifespan and modulate ageing, CR has been intensively studied for decades and has been shown to increase lifespan in many organisms, including mice, rats, flies, worms and yeast. There are exceptions, however. CR does not appear to extend the lifespan of the housefly (Cooper, Mockett, Sohal *et al.*, 2004). There is also variation in the effects of CR on different strains of the same species. CR does not appear to extend average lifespan in wild-derived mice, even though it might slightly increase maximum lifespan and protect against cancer (Harper, Leathers and Austad, 2006). Because wild-derived mice are genetically more heterogeneous than laboratory strains, it could be that different individuals respond to CR in different ways and only a fraction of animals benefit from it. Also, in spite of its advantages, CR has been shown to have negative side effects, such as rendering mice more susceptible to infection (Gardner, 2005). As predicted by McCay, animals under CR are normally smaller than controls. Lastly, not much is known about the mechanisms by which CR extends lifespan, though a few mechanistic hypotheses are discussed further below.

Whether CR might delay human ageing remains a subject of intense debate. Ongoing studies in rhesus monkeys suggest that CR delays the onset of age-related diseases (Colman *et al.*, 2009). There are no long-term studies of CR in humans, however. In spite of some practitioners, CR has considerable side effects, such as mental stress and sexual dysfunctions (Dirks and Leeuwenburgh, 2006). Short-term studies have demonstrated beneficial effects of CR, such as in reducing the risk of atherosclerosis (Fontana, Meyer, Klein *et al.*, 2004). Of course, limiting calorie intake may be beneficial to health, as is conventional wisdom particularly in our societies struck by an 'obesity epidemic', without necessarily delaying the ageing process. Possibly, CR has benefits for some people, but not for all as it is unlikely that lean people will benefit from such extreme diet (Fontana and Klein, 2007). Whether CR can delay human ageing will likely generate more heat than light for years to come.

Human progeroid syndromes

One of the most fascinating observations in the biology of ageing is the accelerated ageing phenotype observed in rare patients suffering from what are known as progeroid syndromes. Many diseases can result in progeroid features (signs of early ageing such as an early greying of hair or premature cognitive impairment), but only a few diseases lead to a multitude of these features. Among such diseases are *Werner, Cockayne* and *Hutchinson–Gilford syndromes* (Martin, 1978; Martin and Oshima, 2000). Werner syndrome is the best studied of these. In spite of a short stature, patients with this disease tend to develop normally, and typically the first symptom is the absence of the normal teenage growth spurt. As the disease progresses, however, patients develop at an early age several characteristics resembling typical ageing such as cataracts, grey hair and aged skin (Martin, 1982). Patients also abnormally develop early age-related diseases like diabetes, osteoporosis, baldness and atherosclerosis, and their average lifespan is only 47–48 years (Goto, 1997; Martin and Oshima, 2000). Martin (1982), in fact, estimated that Werner syndrome patients prematurely develop roughly half of all ageing characteristics. Werner syndrome is the result of mutations in a single gene, the Werner syndrome gene (*WRN*) (Yu *et al.*, 1996), and demonstrates how disruption of a single gene can modulate multiple age-related changes and pathologies (Goto, 1997). No other known disease mimics ageing as faithfully as Werner syndrome does, though patients with Hutchinson–Gilford and Cockayne syndromes develop multiple signs of premature ageing. Contrary to patients with Werner syndrome who normally reach adulthood, patients with Hutchinson–Gilford or Cockayne syndrome are almost exclusively children.

Genetic manipulations

It is much easier to stop a machine than it is to make it work longer. A small flaw in a critical component of a large machine can break it down over time, but in order to make a machine operate longer many key components need to be made more robust. Therefore, the discovery that alterations in single genes could increase lifespan and delay ageing was not only startling but contrary to many previously held views (Johnson, 2002). Thomas Johnson and colleagues were the first to show that ageing could be regulated by single genes. Working on the roundworm nematode *Caenorhabditis elegans*, they showed that different alleles could result in worms living up to twice as long (Friedman and Johnson, 1988). They called the gene *age-1*. A few years later, Cynthia Kenyon and colleagues showed that mutations in *daf-2* could also double the lifespan of worms (Kenyon, Chang, Gensch et al., 1993). For mutations in *daf-2* to extend lifespan, the activity of a second gene, *daf-16*, is required. Both *daf-2* and *daf-16* were named because of their involvement in a developmental arrest form of worms called *dauer*, induced in times of starvation or crowding and known to be long-lived. Because *daf-2* mutants develop normally into adulthood, however, Kenyon's results indicated the existence of a regulated life extension mechanism. A few years later, Gary Ruvkun and colleagues showed that *age-1*, *daf-2* and *daf-16* encode, respectively, a signalling protein of the phosphoinositide-3-kinase family, a member of the insulin receptor family and a member of the forkhead family of transcription factors involved in development. These three genes – as well as many others – have since been shown to play roles in a pathway known as the insulin/insulin-like growth factor 1 (IGF1) signalling pathway. This pathway encompasses hormonal signals that trigger a signal transduction cascade regulating ageing not only in worms but also in flies and, as detailed below, mice (Finch and Ruvkun, 2001; Kenyon, 2010; Tatar, Bartke and Antebi, 2003).

The work of Johnson, Kenyon, Ruvkun and others opened the door for remarkable progress on the genetics of ageing. For a number of reasons outside the scope of this chapter, but including short generation times and high fecundity as well as the availability of tools for genetic manipulation, by far the four most widely used model organisms for genetic studies of ageing are yeast, fruit flies, roundworms and mice. Not surprisingly, the vast majority of genes shown to modulate ageing

Table 2.2 Genes associated with ageing and/or longevity per model organism obtained from the GenAge database (derived from: http://genomics.senescence.info/genes/)

Organism (species)	Number of genes
Roundworm (*Caenorhabditis elegans*)	555
Baker's yeast (*Saccharomyces cerevisiae*)	87
Fruit fly (*Drosophila melanogaster*)	75
Mouse (*Mus musculus*)	68
Filamentous fungus (*Podospora anserina*)	2
Golden hamster (*Mesocricetus auratus*)	1
Fission yeast (*Schizosaccharomyces pombe*)	1

and/or longevity have been identified in these organisms (Table 2.2). In worms, thanks to high-throughput technologies that allow researchers to screen for the effects on longevity of hundreds of genes simultaneously, over 500 genes have been shown to modulate longevity. Many of these ageing-associated genes appear to be related to common pathways, such as the insulin/IGF1 pathway which is the best studied pathway in the context of ageing (Guarente and Kenyon, 2000; Kenyon, 2010).

In mice, there are several genes that when individually disrupted result in a phenotype resembling accelerated ageing. Of even greater interest, a handful of genes have been shown to increase lifespan in mice, most of which are related to the mammalian equivalent of the insulin/IGF1 pathway. The first of these genes was identified somewhat serendipitously by Andrzej Bartke and colleagues. While working on a mouse strain called the Ames dwarf mouse, which has a small body size due to a lack of growth hormone, Bartke and colleagues noticed that animals were living longer than expected. Intrigued, they conducted a careful study in which they showed that indeed the Ames dwarf mice can live roughly 50 per cent longer than controls (Brown-Borg, Borg, Meliska and Bartke, 1996). Ames dwarf mice are the result of a mutation in a single gene called *Prop1*, which is essential for the production of growth hormone and prolactin in the pituitary gland. Growth hormone (GH) stimulates production of IGF1 (Hammerman, 1987), suggesting that similar endocrine pathways may regulate ageing in invertebrates and in mammals (Guarente and Kenyon, 2000; Kenyon, 2010). Several mutations in other genes that result in a disruption of what is known as the GH/IGF1 axis have since been implicated in mouse ageing (Tatar *et al.*, 2003). Because animals under CR are also smaller than controls and have decreased GH/IGF1 signalling, one emergent hypothesis is that the GH/IGF1 axis plays a causative role in CR (Bartke *et al.*, 2001; de Magalhães, 2005). Mutations in human homologues of *Prop1*, as well as in homologues of other genes in the GH/IGF1 axis, have been identified in patients. The results from human studies, however, are far less clear than those from mice, with some mutations apparently increasing lifespan and others appearing to be detrimental to health (Laron, 2005). Because mouse studies are conducted in highly controlled environments and in homogeneous genetic backgrounds, while human populations are much more diverse, it could be that mutations in the same gene have different effects on different individuals depending on environment and genetics. Supporting this notion, *Prop1* mutations in some mouse genetic backgrounds are lethal (Nasonkin *et al.*, 2004).

In addition to studying specific genetic diseases in humans, it is also possible to search for longevity effects of genes in human populations. In longevity association studies the frequency of alleles in a given population is determined. Alleles that confer an advantage to longevity will be relatively more abundant in older people, such as centenarians, than in younger individuals. One of the first of such studies focused on apolipoprotein E (*APOE*), since this gene was a known risk factor in cardiovascular disease. Indeed, an association between certain *APOE* alleles and longevity was reported (Schächter *et al.*, 1994), though because *APOE* is involved in cardiovascular diseases it might not necessarily play a causative role in the ageing process. Many other such studies have been conducted in human populations, including studies suggesting an association between alleles in the IGF1 receptor and longevity, potentially linking findings in model organisms to humans (Suh *et al.*, 2008). Though results from model organisms are not always relevant to human biology, it is plausible that some genes associated with ageing in model organisms also regulate human ageing.

Mechanistic theories of ageing

Until recently, many questioned whether there is a basic process of ageing at all (Peto and Doll, 1997). Perhaps what we call 'ageing' is merely the outcome of various debilitating diseases and processes running in parallel and overlapping each other across the body's systems (Holliday, 1995; Masoro, 2006). This notion that there is no underlying process of ageing has now been put to rest, thanks partly to the breakthroughs at the genetic level in model organisms demonstrating how the process of ageing can be regulated as a whole by manipulating single genes, as detailed above. The observation that similar species can age at remarkably different paces also suggests the existence of synchronizing mechanisms of ageing (de Magalhães, 2003). Possibly the most consensual view is that there are indeed processes capable of synchronizing and driving the progression of functional and physiological age-related debilitation as well as age-related diseases (de Magalhães, 2003; Miller, 1999). Though there could even be a single unifying process driving ageing, it also appears plausible that each individual organ system has unique degenerative processes or constraints that also contribute, with varying degrees, to its debilitation and pathological progression. At the extreme, the possibility exists that a few age-related changes progress largely independently of the process of ageing with tooth erosion as a key example of what is labelled as *mechanical senescence*, or age-related changes that are the result of worn-out body parts. One of the fundamental steps in the biology of ageing is hence the shift from describing age-related changes to understanding them and ascertaining which changes trigger which, what is the underlying mechanism or mechanisms of ageing driving this process, and synchronizing it across tissues and organs.

So far, only major physiological changes have been discussed herein. Each organ, however, is made of cells composed of smaller organelles in turn made of molecules, mostly proteins that are programmed from the genome. Multiple changes have also been observed with age on cells and molecules, including on the DNA itself (Arking, 2006; Comfort, 1964; Finch, 1990; Hayflick, 1994; Strehler, 1999). Considering this multitude of age-related changes occurring at different levels, one of the major quests in the biology of ageing has been to determine which change, process or mechanism causes the ageing process. Many hypotheses have been put forward throughout the centuries, dating back to Aristotle's treatise *On Longevity and Shortness of Life* in 350 BC, as to why we age. Medvedev (1990) catalogues these hypotheses and concluded that there are over 300 different explanations of ageing, even though many could be grouped into common themes.

There are intrinsic difficulties in testing theories of ageing. As discussed above, interpreting results is often controversial and ageing studies are expensive and time-consuming, even in animal models. It is also possible that some mechanisms of ageing are conserved across species, while others are not (Martin, Austad and Johnson, 1996). Besides, discriminating between causes and effects of a complex biological process such as ageing is problematic, even if the new genetic technologies have opened up new opportunities to move beyond correlative studies. Although the search for a causal factor in ageing remains fruitless, if indeed we could identify a unifying process of ageing it would be remarkable, and a critical step for developing anti-ageing therapies (as discussed further below). What follows is a succinct, non-exhaustive description of the most influential mechanistic theories of ageing.

Rate of living theory

The rate of living theory emerged from the work of Max Rubner, who showed in 1908 that long-lived animals are, on average, bigger and have lower metabolic rates than smaller, shorter-lived ones (Rubner, 1908). Rubner's *energy consumption hypothesis*, as it is called, states that animals are born with some form of substance or capacity and the faster they use it, the faster they will degenerate and die (Austad, 1997b; Hayflick, 1994). Raymond Pearl later extended Rubner's work to develop the rate of living theory, which is the simple idea that ageing is determined by the pace at which life is lived. The faster the metabolic rate, the faster the biochemical activity and the faster an organism will age (Pearl, 1928). The rate of living theory is intuitive as many apparent similarities can be found with machines (e.g. the higher mileage a car has, the more likely it is in poor condition). In the past decades, many researchers have tested Pearl's theory. Because CR limits energy intake, the rate of living theory has been suggested to explain the life-extending effects of CR. Some studies in rodents, however, suggest that CR can extend lifespan without reducing metabolic rate. Moreover, most experimental results have been contrary to the rate of living theory (Masoro, 2005). For example, in a classic experiment, rats kept at a cooler temperature consumed 44 per cent more food and yet did not live less long than controls (Holloszy and Smith, 1986). It has also been reported that individual mice with higher metabolic rates tend to live longer (Speakman *et al.*, 2004).

Rubner's observation that species with lower metabolic rates live longer has come under attack as well. Although it is well established that bigger species tend to have longer lifespans, this is likely due to ecological constraints such as bigger animals being less prone to predation (de Magalhães, Costa and Church, 2007; Stearns, 1992). In addition, there are notable exceptions. Bats and birds are, like mice, typically small animals with high metabolic rates and yet can live much longer than mice (Austad, 1997b). As the final nail in the coffin of the rate of living theory, studies using modern statistical methods suggested that metabolic rate does not, in fact, correlate with the longevity of mammals, including primates (de Magalhães *et al.*, 2007). Although energy metabolism might play a role in ageing, for instance as part of the GH/IGF1 axis, the rate of living theory as proposed by Rubner and Pearl has now, after a long life, been put to rest.

Damage-based theories of ageing

As the name implies, damage-based theories revolve around the notion that continuous damage accumulates throughout life and causes ageing. One or more sources of damage may exist, including by-products of metabolism. Contrary to the 'wear and tear' of inanimate objects, however, it is now largely recognized that ageing in higher organisms, which tend to have a high turnover of most cells and molecules, is not primarily the result of damage to irreplaceable body parts. Even tooth erosion, rather than the wearing out of teeth, can be seen as their lack of replacement

(Williams, 1957). Therefore, modern theories recognize that damage can often be counteracted by repair or replacement systems, even if these are imperfect.

Arguably, the most influential of the damage-based theories and perhaps the most intensively studied mechanistic theory of ageing has been the *free radical theory*. Proposed in 1956 by Denham Harman, the free radical theory argues that ageing is caused by damage from free radicals (Harman, 1956). Free radicals and oxidants, also called reactive oxygen species (ROS), are highly reactive molecules that can damage all sorts of cellular components. ROS are produced in *mitochondria*, which are the cell's powerhouses that convert oxygen and nutrients into energy and thus ROS are a normal by-product of cellular metabolism. The rate of free radical production is linked to metabolic rate and led to the association between the free radical and rate of living theories, which some authors see as one (Harman, 1981; Sohal, Mockett and Orr, 2002). Although cells possess several antioxidants (molecules that protect against oxidation such as vitamins C and E and enzymes like catalase and superoxide dismutase), oxidative damage has been shown to increase with age in several tissues, thus supporting the free radical theory (Beckman and Ames, 1998).

In the same way that oxidative damage has been hypothesized slowly to accumulate with age, evidence has been gathering against the free radical theory of ageing. Even if the outcome is not fatal yet, the free radical theory is becoming progressively more vulnerable to critics. Because certain antioxidants such as vitamins can be purified and ingested, their effects on lifespan can be tested in model systems, yet the results of decades of research have been far from convincing. The subset of studies in rodents that were able to increase average lifespan did so to a small degree (Hagen *et al.*, 2002), making the results difficult to interpret. It is widely recognized, in fact, that there is no evidence that antioxidants taken as dietary supplements influence the ageing process (Arking, 2006; Hayflick, 1994; Olshansky, Hayflick and Carnes, 2002). Furthermore, even though some studies have found correlations between antioxidant levels and species longevity, there are also contradictory findings (Finch, 1990; Sohal *et al.*, 2002).

The main reason, however, why doubts have been cast on the free radical theory is the number of contradictory results from genetic experiments. Particularly in mice, several strains have now been produced with altered levels of expression of antioxidant enzymes, yet the results have, as a rule, failed to support the free radical theory (de Magalhães, 2005; Lapointe and Hekimi, 2009; Sohal *et al.*, 2002). One strain of mice with catalase expressed in mitochondria lived 18 per cent longer but did not appear to age slower, and most likely the extended lifespan derived from a decrease in cardiac diseases across the entire lifespan (Schriner *et al.*, 2005). On the other hand, several mouse strains with altered antioxidant systems failed to support the free radical theory. In particular, one ingenious experiment raised doubts about the free radical theory. Like humans, mice have two copies of each chromosome plus two sex chromosomes. Because antioxidant enzymes are often crucial for organisms, disrupting both copies of a gene can be lethal. Arlan Richardson and colleagues created a mouse strain with only one copy of superoxide dismutase disrupted, thus lowering the enzyme's activity without completely eliminating it. The resulting heterozygous mice showed increased levels of oxidative damage with age when compared to controls but did not show differences in lifespan or ageing (Van Remmen et al., 2003). Overall, although ROS might well play a role in age-related pathologies, there is little evidence that they are at the root of the ageing process.

One crucial molecule in life is DNA. Given its central role in directing cellular functions and in the creation of the cell itself, damage to the DNA can be catas-trophic. The physicist Leo Szilard first proposed the idea that a slow build-up of damage in the DNA could gradually disrupt normal cellular functions and result in ageing (Szilard, 1959). Several studies have shown that indeed DNA mutations and lesions are observed at a higher frequency in at least some tissues of older animals, including mammals (Dolle et al., 1997; Esposito et al., 1989). A corre-lation between DNA repair and the lifespan of mammalian species has also been reported (Hart and Setlow, 1974).

The Werner syndrome gene, WRN, is involved in DNA repair. All genes asso-ciated with the three principal progeroid syndromes mentioned above, in fact, appear to have some function in DNA metabolism and repair (Martin and Oshima, 2000). To test further whether changes to the DNA are a cause or effect of ageing, a number of mouse strains with modified DNA repair pathways have been created. Many, though not all, mouse strains with disrupted DNA repair exhibit evidence of accelerated ageing, as predicted by the theory (de Magalhães, 2005; Hasty, Campisi, Hoeijmakers et al., 2003). On the other hand, it has proven difficult to extend the lifespan of mice through optimization or enhancement of DNA repair systems, an essential proof of the theory. Mice overexpressing DNA repair enzymes have in a few cases been shown to have a lower cancer incidence but not an increased lifespan (Garcia-Cao et al., 2002; Zhou et al., 2001). One study reported a 16 per cent increase in average lifespan through generation of mice with extra copies of two DNA repair genes, but it was not obvious whether ageing was delayed (Matheu et al., 2007). In conclusion, much work remains to prove this hypothesis, but it is widely accepted that changes to the DNA could play a role in the process of ageing.

In addition to the two aforementioned theories, there are many others, including variants and combinations. Because ROS can damage DNA and one major source of ROS is the mitochondrion, which possesses its own genome, an overlapping theory is the idea that ROS-inflicted damage to the mitochondrial DNA drives ageing (Harman, 1972). Interestingly, mice with a defect in mitochondrial DNA repair accumulate damage faster and exhibit signs of accelerated ageing, even if this does not appear to be related to oxidative stress (Kujoth *et al.*, 2005), and the idea that mutations to mitochondrial DNA contribute to ageing and age-related diseases remains a powerful one (Wallace, 1992).

Cellular senescence and organismal ageing

In 1961, and contradicting what was thought at the time, Leonard Hayflick and Paul Moorhead discovered that human cells can only divide a finite number of times in culture (Hayflick and Moorhead, 1961). Because studying cells *in vitro* is easier than studying animals or humans, this phenomenon, termed *replicative senescence* (RS), has been intensively studied for decades. One major hypothesis in biogerontology is that in whole organisms cells that exit the cell cycle and become senescent contribute to ageing and age-related diseases. Indeed, senescent cells have been shown to accumulate with age in certain tissues (Campisi, 2005). Moreover, many accelerated ageing diseases in mice and men, including Werner syndrome, have effects on RS, and it has been argued that senescent cells play a critical role in progeroid syndromes (Kipling, Davis, Ostler *et al.*, 2004).

At least in some cell types, RS is caused by the wearing off of the tips of chromosomes, called *telomeres*. Telomeres shorten as cells replicate and when critically short, trigger signalling pathways that result in senescence. Although other mechanisms exist, including oxidative damage from ROS, telomere shortening is considered by some authorities as the primary mechanism of RS and has been intensively studied. An enzyme called *telomerase* can elongate the telomeres and, though most human cell types do not have active telomerase, cells with telomerase activity can avoid RS (Campisi, 2005; de Magalhães, 2004; Wright and Shay, 2001). Much research has focused on RS, telomeres and telomerase. At present, their relevance to the ageing process is unclear, though there is abundant evidence that RS and telomere shortening are anti-cancer mechanisms (Campisi, 2005; de Magalhães, 2004). Mice engineered to express higher levels of telomerase have a higher cancer incidence and thus a shorter lifespan (Artandi *et al.*, 2002). In cancer-resistant genetic backgrounds, however, telomerase overexpression increased lifespan by up to 26 per cent, even if it was not clear whether ageing was delayed (Tomas-Loba *et al.*, 2008). For many decades it was thought that cells obtained from older donors could divide fewer times than cells from younger donors, an idea that has now been disproved (Cristofalo, Allen, Pignolo *et al.*, 1998). It was also thought that cells from long-lived animals could divide more times, yet it now appears that this solely reflects the fact that long-lived animals tend to be bigger (Lorenzini,

Tresini, Austad *et al.*, 2005). Humans also have relatively short telomeres when compared to other primates and mice and yet live longer (Steinert, White, Zou *et al.*, 2002).

Programmed theories of ageing

At the root of programmed theories of ageing is the idea that ageing is not a result of random or stochastic processes but rather it is driven by genetically regulated processes or predetermined mechanisms, even if these can be influenced to some degree by environmental factors and ultimately cause certain forms of damage. Semelparous species like the salmon demonstrate how the endocrine system can drive degeneration and ultimately lead to death in a well-timed, predetermined manner. Because the concentrations of key hormones like growth hormone (GH) and insulin-like growth factor 1 (IGF1) decline steadily with age (Hammerman, 1987), one influential mechanistic theory of ageing for decades has been the *endocrine theory of ageing*, the idea that hormonal changes drive ageing (Gosden, 1996). Initially, it was thought that increasing the concentration of GH at older ages would restore youthfulness. In reality, this is not the case and mice with high levels of GH tend to have shorter lifespans and maybe even age faster (Bartke, 2003). As discussed above, the results from CR and genetic mutations suggest that an attenuation of the GH/IGF1 axis increases lifespan. CR may also be, at least partly, explained by changes to the GH/IGF1 axis (Bartke *et al.*, 2001; de Magalhães, 2005; Masoro, 2005). Therefore, hormones appear to play some role in the ageing process. However, it is not clear yet how widespread this role is and which downstream mechanisms are involved.

As mentioned above, worms can enter a long-lived, developmentally arrested stage called dauer (Klass and Hirsh, 1976). There are also many other examples of delayed development leading to a longer lifespan, suggesting that at least in some species ageing can be a part of the genetic programme controlling development. In other words, as an organism progresses through its developmental stages, it triggers the process of ageing. This idea that developmental mechanisms can regulate ageing, or many aspects of it, is known as the *developmental theory of ageing* (de Magalhães and Church, 2005), an extreme form of antagonistic pleiotropy. The salmon is a good example, but the marine mollusc *Phestilla sibogae* is an even better illustration: in these animals, the length of larval life is determined by a chance encounter with a stimulus that causes metamorphosis, yet the length of post-larval life is unaffected by the length of time it takes the larva to metamorphose, as if ageing were suspended during the larval time (Miller and Hadfield, 1990). Moreover, as mentioned above, there is a robust correlation between the age at maturity and longevity (de Magalhães *et al.*, 2007). Although the developmental theory of ageing explains many observations, and may be linked to endocrine changes that regulate both development and ageing, just like the endocrine theory, it lacks concrete details of how developmental mechanisms could influence age-related changes at the cellular and molecular levels.

Other programmed theories focus on specific organs, such as the brain, from which neuroendocrine signals that could regulate ageing originate (Mattson, Duan and Maswood, 2002). Overall, programmed theories of ageing such as those based on developmental processes, like the endocrine theory, provide an alternative view to damage-based theories that manage to explain many observations in biogerontology, even if they fail fully to explain the process of ageing.

In conclusion, it is well established that cells undergo changes as humans and animals grow older that may well play a role in ageing. Though senescent cells might contribute to ageing at least in some tissues with high cellular turnover, the idea that merely lengthening telomeres with telomerase will fend off the effects of ageing has now been disproved.

Anti-ageing medicine

The greying population raises the need not only further to advance our understanding of ageing but even to develop therapies that delay the ageing process. One of the most pervasive public misconceptions about biogerontology is the idea that the goal of anti-ageing medicine is to make old people live longer by merely extending life and consequently extending age-related debilitation and suffering. This is known as the *Tithonus error*. In Greek mythology, Tithonus was a mortal to whom Zeus conceded immortality but not eternal youth, rendering Tithonus increasingly debilitated and demented as he aged. Contrary to the immortality granted to Tithonus, the goal of biogerontology is to extend healthy lifespan by postponing disease and extending the healthy period of life. Rather than focus on specific age-related diseases or changes, the goal of biogerontology is also to delay the process of ageing as a whole and not just its individual manifestations.

Historically (efforts to combat ageing date back to at least 3500 BC), anti-ageing medicine has had a poor reputation. A countless number of treatments, diets and supplements hailed as 'anti-ageing' have failed to live up to their reputation. Hormonal treatments to replenish the concentrations of key hormones to youthful levels were an early anti-ageing promise. Although much progress has been made since early last century when patients received testicular grafts from young animals as a rejuvenation method (Gosden, 1996), hormonal therapies and in particular GH supplements continue to be widely touted as anti-ageing. As mentioned above, however, higher GH concentrations seem to foster ageing in rodents, indicating that GH supplements are not the 'fountain of youth' (Olshansky *et al.*, 2002). Other anti-ageing products have been inspired by mechanistic theories of ageing. Antioxidants aim to counteract the effects of ROS and prevent the accumulation of oxidative damage and many are sold as dietary supplements. Unfortunately, even if some antioxidants such as vitamins might be healthy, they have never been shown to delay ageing in animal models (Olshansky *et al.*, 2002). Because telomere shortening can trigger cellular ageing, telomerase activators have also been suggested as a method to counter the effects of ageing. Considering that telomere shortening appears to be mostly an anti-cancer mechanism, and telomerase activation contributes to cancer in animal models, there is no evidence that elongating telomeres will delay ageing and might not even be healthy.

As aforementioned, the only intervention that might delay human ageing is CR, though because of its side effects it has failed to capture widespread public enthusiasm. One long-sought breakthrough is the development of CR mimetics, products that provide the beneficial actions of CR without its side effects. One candidate CR mimetic is *resveratrol*, a compound found in certain plants. Though resveratrol was known to have possible beneficial effects in preventing cardiovascular disease (Mizutani, Ikeda and Yamori, 2000), it came to the attention of biogerontology due to its capacity to activate a family of proteins called *sirtuins*, which had previously been shown to play a role in ageing and CR in yeast (Howitz *et al.*, 2003). Although resveratrol was reported to improve the health and survival of mice on a high-calorie diet, raising the possibility that it could be used to treat obesity-related disorders and diseases of ageing, it later failed to increase the lifespan of normal mice (Pearson *et al.*, 2008). Rapamycin – which inhibits the target of rapamycin (TOR) pathway also associated with ageing and CR in model organisms – extended the lifespan of middle-aged mice, suggesting that interventions targeting this pathway may be developed to treat or prevent age-related diseases (Harrison *et al.*, 2009). Additional compounds that modulate the activity of genes associated with CR have been and will be the subject of research for decades to come.

In conclusion, there is presently no proven way to delay, even slightly, the human ageing process. As is common knowledge, some lifestyles and diets are healthy and will increase one's chances of reaching old age, but there is no evidence that any of them will affect the process of ageing. CR might delay ageing in some people, but its effects may be less impressive than in model organisms. Nonetheless, the plasticity of ageing opens numerous opportunities for developing interventions that researchers and companies will no doubt explore. The quest for the 'fountain of youth' continues.

The post-genome future of ageing research

Technology has always driven biomedical research and many breakthroughs in the biology of ageing, such as the genetic experiments detailed above, were made possible by technological advances. At the dawn of the twenty-first century, the sequencing of genomes in particular opened a new era of biological research that is bound to lead to remarkable progress in the biology and genetics of ageing (de Magalhães, Finch and Janssens, 2010). Genetic association studies of longevity can now be done at a whole-genome level, testing all genes in the genome simultaneously for associations with longevity rather than by focusing on a few candidates, and genetic screens can be performed in model organisms in large scale to search for new genes regulating ageing. The expression of thousands of genes can also be determined in parallel thanks to post-genome technologies like microarrays, which allow changes in ageing and age-related diseases to be characterized with unprecedented accuracy. To find clues about which genes may be involved in the evolution of longevity in humans and other animals, the genomes of several organisms with different lifespans can be compared and analysed (de Magalhães *et al.*, 2010).

This scaling up in the amount of data and information that can be gathered about ageing leads to many new opportunities but also presents difficulties. One of the main challenges of post-genome research is to manage and integrate the massive amounts of data being generated to provide useful biological insights. Advances in bioinformatics allow data to be managed and archived in databases and made available online to researchers. New methods also need to be developed to integrate the different data sets. Studies of networks of genes known to impact on ageing have been used to infer how genes interact to drive ageing (de Magalhães and Toussaint, 2004). Developing integrative models of age-related changes and ageing mechanisms at different biological levels will be crucial to deepen our understanding of ageing (Arking, 2006; de Magalhães *et al.*, 2010).

Concluding remarks

Biogerontology came a long way in the twentieth century by providing accurate descriptions of multiple aspects of biological ageing, giving rise to an evolutionary explanation for the existence of ageing and showing the surprising plasticity of the ageing process and how it can be manipulated by dietary and genetic interventions. It is now established that indeed there is an ageing process and if we could understand its mechanisms and even manipulate it, this would result in unprecedented benefits to medicine and society. Unfortunately, and in spite of the many mechanistic theories that have been put forward, the mechanisms of ageing remain shrouded in mystery. It is plausible that more than one mechanistic theory of ageing is correct. Age changes to one tissue may also influence changes in another one, so it will be crucial to determine which mechanisms are essential for different tissues and how they influence each other. The challenge to biogerontology in the twenty-first century is to identify which are the most important mechanisms and genes and how they interact with each other, with the environment and with different biological levels of organization to determine the ageing phenotype.

Summary

Biogerontology is the field that studies ageing from a biological perspective. Human ageing entails numerous biological changes, which can be summarized as various physiological changes that result in functional loss or decline, leading to increased risk of disease; echoing other species, human mortality increases exponentially after 30 years of age. The evolutionary theory of ageing argues that senescence occurs because of the waning force of natural selection with age since only a small fraction of animals reach old age. Based on this premise, ageing can evolve either because mutations harmful at late ages accumulate in species (the mutation accumulation theory) or because the same mutations that are detrimental in later life confer evolutionary advantages in younger animals (the antagonistic pleiotropy theory). These theories explain much, but not all, of the evidence and inform life history (the study of changes across the lifespan, with particular reference to survival and reproduction). The latter indicates that lifespan varies considerably between species, in large part due to the evolutionary pressures placed on them by their habitat. Within species, typically biomedical model organisms but also humans, a variety of genetic and environmental factors can alter the process of ageing. Caloric restriction can increase lifespan in some (but not all) species, though often with undesirable side effects. Genes also play a key role, witnessed *in extremis* in human progeroid syndromes, but also in genes shown to modulate longevity in model organisms. Current research indicates many of these genes are concerned with the growth hormone/insulin/IGF1 pathway. Overall, the evidence supports there being processes capable of synchronizing and to a large extent regulating ageing. Models to explain this can be grouped into the rate of living theory and damage-based theories, including theories linking free radical damage and DNA mutations to ageing, models of cellular senescence and programmed theories of ageing. All have their limitations and/or lack complete supporting evidence. Likewise, biological methods of halting or retarding the ageing process have met with no lasting success. However, post-genome research promises much in this regard.

REFERENCES

Arking, R. (2006) *The biology of aging: observations and principles.* Oxford University Press.

Artandi, S.E., Alson, S., Tietze, M.K. *et al.* (2002) Constitutive telomerase expression promotes mammary carcinomas in aging mice, *Proceedings of the National Academy of Sciences of the USA*, *99*(12), 8191–6.

Austad, S.N. (1997a) Comparative aging and life histories in mammals, *Experimental Gerontology*, *32*(1–2), 23–38.

(1997b) *Why we age: what science is discovering about the body's journey through life.* New York: John Wiley & Sons.

(2006) Why women live longer than men: sex differences in longevity, *Gender Medicine*, *3*(2), 79–92.

Bartke, A. (2003) Can growth hormone (GH) accelerate aging? Evidence from GH-transgenic mice, *Neuroendocrinology*, *78*(4), 210–16.

Bartke, A., Coschigano, K., Kopchick, J. *et al.* (2001) Genes that prolong life: relationships of growth hormone and growth to aging and life span, *Journals of Gerontology. Series A, Biological Sciences and Medical Sciences*, *56*(8), B340–9.

Beckman, K.B. and Ames, B.N. (1998) The free radical theory of aging matures, *Physiological Reviews*, *78*(2), 547–81.

Brown-Borg, H.M., Borg, K.E., Meliska, C.J. *et al.* (1996) Dwarf mice and the ageing process, *Nature*, *384*(6604), 33.

Campisi, J. (2005) Senescent cells, tumor suppression, and organismal aging: good citizens, bad neighbors, *Cell*, *120*(4), 513–22.

Colman, R.J., Anderson, R.M., Johnson, S.C. *et al.* (2009) Caloric restriction delays disease onset and mortality in rhesus monkeys, *Science*, *325*(5937), 201–4.

Comfort, A. (1964) *Ageing: the biology of senescence.* London: Routledge & Kegan Paul.

Cooper, T.M., Mockett, R.J., Sohal, B.H. *et al.* (2004) Effect of caloric restriction on life span of the housefly, *Musca domestica*, *FASEB Journal*, *18*(13), 1591–3.

Cristofalo, V.J., Allen, R.G., Pignolo, R.J. *et al.* (1998) Relationship between donor age and the replicative lifespan of human cells in culture: a reevaluation, *Proceedings of the National Academy of Sciences of the USA*, *95*(18), 10614–19.

de Magalhães, J.P. (2003) Is mammalian aging genetically controlled?, *Biogerontology*, *4*(2), 119–20.

(2004) From cells to ageing: a review of models and mechanisms of cellular senescence and their impact on human ageing, *Experimental Cell Research*, *300*(1), 1–10.

(2005) Open-minded scepticism: inferring the causal mechanisms of human ageing from genetic perturbations, *Ageing Research Reviews*, *4*(1), 1–22.

de Magalhães, J.P. and Church, G.M. (2005) Genomes optimize reproduction: aging as a consequence of the developmental program, *Physiology (Bethesda)*, *20*, 252–9.

de Magalhães, J.P., Costa, J. and Church, G.M. (2007) An analysis of the relationship between metabolism, developmental schedules, and longevity using phylogenetic independent contrasts, *Journals of Gerontology. Series A, Biological Sciences and Medical Sciences*, *62*(2), 149–60.

de Magalhães, J.P., Finch, C.E. and Janssens, G. (2010) Next-generation sequencing in aging research: emerging applications, problems, pitfalls and possible solutions, *Ageing Research Reviews*, *9*(3), 315–23.

de Magalhães, J.P. and Toussaint, O. (2004) GenAge: a genomic and proteomic network map of human ageing, *FEBS Letters*, *571*(1–3), 243–7.

Dirks, A.J. and Leeuwenburgh, C. (2006) Caloric restriction in humans: potential pitfalls and health concerns, *Mechanisms of Ageing and Development*, *127*(1), 1–7.

Dolle, M.E., Giese, H., Hopkins, C.L. *et al.* (1997) Rapid accumulation of genome rearrangements in liver but not in brain of old mice, *Nature Genetics*, *17*(4), 431–4.

Esposito, D., Fassina, G., Szabo, P. *et al.* (1989) Chromosomes of older humans are more prone to aminopterine-induced breakage, *Proceedings of the National Academy of Sciences of the USA*, *86*(4), 1302–6.

Finch, C.E. (1990) *Longevity, senescence, and the genome*. University of Chicago Press.

Finch, C.E. and Ruvkun, G. (2001) The genetics of aging, *Annual Review of Genomics and Human Genetics*, *2*, 435–62.

Fontana, L. and Klein, S. (2007) Aging, adiposity, and calorie restriction, *Journal of the American Medical Association*, *297*(9), 986–94.

Fontana, L., Meyer, T.E., Klein, S. *et al.* (2004) Long-term calorie restriction is highly effective in reducing the risk for atherosclerosis in humans, *Proceedings of the National Academy of Sciences of the USA*, *101*(17), 6659–63.

Friedman, D.B. and Johnson, T.E. (1988) A mutation in the age-1 gene in *Caenorhabditis elegans* lengthens life and reduces hermaphrodite fertility, *Genetics*, *118*(1), 75–86.

Garcia-Cao, I., Garcia-Cao, M., Martin-Caballero, J. *et al.* (2002) "Super p53" mice exhibit enhanced DNA damage response, are tumor resistant and age normally, *EMBO Journal*, *21*(22), 6225–35.

Gardner, E.M. (2005) Caloric restriction decreases survival of aged mice in response to primary influenza infection, *Journals of Gerontology. Series A, Biological Sciences and Medical Sciences*, *60*(6), 688–94.

George, J.C., Bada, J., Zeh, J.W. *et al.* (1999) Age and growth estimates of bowhead whales (*Balaena mysticetus*) via aspartic acid racemization, *Canadian Journal of Zoology*, *77*, 571–80.

Gosden, R. (1996) *Cheating time*. New York: W.H. Freeman.

Goto, M. (1997) Hierarchical deterioration of body systems in Werner's syndrome: implications for normal ageing, *Mechanisms of Ageing and Development*, *98*(3), 239–54.

Guarente, L. and Kenyon, C. (2000) Genetic pathways that regulate ageing in model organisms, *Nature*, *408*(6809), 255–62.

Hagen, T.M., Liu, J., Lykkesfeldt, J. *et al.* (2002) Feeding acetyl-L-carnitine and lipoic acid to old rats significantly improves metabolic function while decreasing oxidative stress, *Proceedings of the National Academy of Sciences of the USA*, *99*(4), 1870–5.

Hamilton, W.D. (1966) The moulding of senescence by natural selection, *Journal of Theoretical Biology*, *12*(1), 12–45.

Hammerman, M.R. (1987) Insulin-like growth factors and aging, *Endocrinology and Metabolism Clinics of North America*, *16*(4), 995–1011.

Harman, D. (1956) Aging: a theory based on free radical and radiation chemistry, *Journal of Gerontology*, *11*(3), 298–300.

(1972) The biologic clock: the mitochondria?, *Journal of the American Geriatrics Society*, *20*(4), 145–7.

(1981) The aging process, *Proceedings of the National Academy of Sciences of the USA*, **78**(11), 7124–8.

Harper, J.M., Leathers, C.W. and Austad, S.N. (2006) Does caloric restriction extend life in wild mice?, *Aging Cell*, **5**(6), 441–9.

Harrison, D.E., Strong, R., Sharp, Z.D. *et al.* (2009) Rapamycin fed late in life extends lifespan in genetically heterogeneous mice, *Nature*, **460**(7253), 392–5.

Hart, R.W. and Setlow, R.B. (1974) Correlation between deoxyribonucleic acid excision-repair and life-span in a number of mammalian species, *Proceedings of the National Academy of Sciences of the USA*, **71**(6), 2169–73.

Hasty, P., Campisi, J., Hoeijmakers, J. *et al.* (2003) Aging and genome maintenance: lessons from the mouse?, *Science*, **299**(5611), 1355–9.

Hayflick, L. (1994) *How and why we age.* New York: Ballantine Books.

Hayflick, L. and Moorhead, P.S. (1961) The serial cultivation of human diploid cell strains, *Experimental Cell Research*, **25**, 585–621.

Heron, M.P., Hoyert, D.L., Jiaquan, X. *et al.* (2008) Deaths: preliminary data for 2006, *National Vital Statistics Reports*, **56**, 1–52.

Holliday, R. (1995) *Understanding ageing.* Cambridge University Press.

Holloszy, J.O. and Smith, E.K. (1986) Longevity of cold-exposed rats: a reevaluation of the "rate-of-living theory", *Journal of Applied Physiology*, **61**(5), 1656–60.

Howitz, K.T., Bitterman, K.J., Cohen, H.Y. *et al.* (2003) Small molecule activators of sirtuins extend *Saccharomyces cerevisiae* lifespan, *Nature*, **425**(6954), 191–6.

Johnson, T.E. (2002) A personal retrospective on the genetics of aging, *Biogerontology*, **3**(1–2), 7–12.

Kenyon, C., Chang, J., Gensch, E. *et al.* (1993) A *C. elegans* mutant that lives twice as long as wild type, *Nature*, **366**(6454), 461–4.

Kenyon, C.J. (2010) The genetics of ageing, *Nature*, **464**(7288), 504–12.

Kipling, D., Davis, T., Ostler, E.L. *et al.* (2004) What can progeroid syndromes tell us about human aging?, *Science*, **305**(5689), 1426–31.

Kirkwood, T.B. (1977) Evolution of ageing, *Nature*, **270**(5635), 301–4.

Kirkwood, T.B. and Austad, S.N. (2000) Why do we age?, *Nature*, **408**(6809), 233–8.

Klass, M. and Hirsh, D. (1976) Non-ageing developmental variant of *Caenorhabditis elegans*, *Nature*, **260**(5551), 523–5.

Kujoth, G.C., Hiona, A., Pugh, T.D. *et al.* (2005) Mitochondrial DNA mutations, oxidative stress, and apoptosis in mammalian aging, *Science*, **309**(5733), 481–4.

Lapointe, J. and Hekimi, S. (2009) When a theory of aging ages badly, *Cellular and Molecular Life Sciences*, **67**, 1–8.

Laron, Z. (2005) Do deficiencies in growth hormone and insulin-like growth factor-1 (IGF-1) shorten or prolong longevity?, *Mechanisms of Ageing and Development*, **126**(2), 305–7.

Lorenzini, A., Tresini, M., Austad, S.N. *et al.* (2005) Cellular replicative capacity correlates primarily with species body mass not longevity, *Mechanisms of Ageing and Development*, **126**(10), 1130–3.

MacArthur, R.H. and Wilson, E.O. (1967) *The theory of island biogeography.* Princeton University Press.

Macintyre, S., Hunt, K. and Sweeting, H. (1996) Gender differences in health: are things really as simple as they seem?, *Social Science and Medicine*, **42**(4), 617–24.

Martin, G.M. (1978) Genetic syndromes in man with potential relevance to the pathobiology of aging, *Birth Defects Original Article Series*, **14**(1), 5–39.

(1982) Syndromes of accelerated aging, *National Cancer Institute Monograph*, *60*, 241–7.

Martin, G.M., Austad, S.N. and Johnson, T.E. (1996) Genetic analysis of ageing: role of oxidative damage and environmental stresses, *Nature Genetics*, *13*(1), 25–34.

Martin, G.M. and Oshima, J. (2000) Lessons from human progeroid syndromes, *Nature*, *408*(6809), 263–6.

Masoro, E.J. (2005) Overview of caloric restriction and ageing, *Mechanisms of Ageing and Development*, *126*(9), 913–22.

(2006) Are age-associated diseases an integral part of aging?, in E.J. Masoro and S.N. Austad (eds), *Handbook of the biology of aging*, 6th edn. San Diego, CA: Academic Press, 43–62.

Matheu, A., Maraver, A., Klatt, P. *et al.* (2007) Delayed ageing through damage protection by the Arf/p53 pathway, *Nature*, *448*(7151), 375–9.

Mattson, M. P., Duan, W. and Maswood, N. (2002) How does the brain control lifespan?, *Ageing Research Reviews*, *1*(2), 155–65.

McCay, C.M., Crowell, M.F. and Maynard, L.A. (1935) The effect of retarded growth upon length of the life span and upon the ultimate body size, *Journal of Nutrition*, *10*(1), 63–75.

Medawar, P.B. (1952) *An unsolved problem of biology*. London: H.K. Lewis.

Medvedev, Z.A. (1990) An attempt at a rational classification of theories of ageing, *Biological Review*, *65*, 375–98.

Miller, R.A. (1999) Kleemeier award lecture: are there genes for aging?, *Journals of Gerontology. Series A, Biological Sciences and Medical Sciences*, *54*(7), B297–307.

Miller, S.E. and Hadfield, M.G. (1990) Developmental arrest during larval life and life-span extension in a marine mollusc, *Science*, *248*(4953), 356–8.

Mizutani, K., Ikeda, K. and Yamori, Y. (2000) Resveratrol inhibits AGEs-induced proliferation and collagen synthesis activity in vascular smooth muscle cells from stroke-prone spontaneously hypertensive rats, *Biochemical and Biophysical Research Communications*, *274*(1), 61–7.

Nasonkin, I.O., Ward, R.D., Raetzman, L.T. *et al.* (2004) Pituitary hypoplasia and respiratory distress syndrome in Prop1 knockout mice, *Human Molecular Genetics*, *13*(22), 2727–35.

Olshansky, S.J., Hayflick, L. and Carnes, B.A. (2002) No truth to the fountain of youth, *Scientific American*, *286*(6), 92–5.

Pearl, R. (1928) *The rate of living*. New York: Knopf.

Pearson, K.J., Baur, J.A., Lewis, K.N. *et al.* (2008) Resveratrol delays age-related deterioration and mimics transcriptional aspects of dietary restriction without extending life span, *Cell Metabolism*, *8*(2), 157–68.

Peto, R. and Doll, R. (1997) There is no such thing as aging, *British Medical Journal*, *315*(7115), 1030–2.

Rose, M.R. (1991) *Evolutionary biology of aging*. New York: Oxford University Press.

Schächter, F., Faure-Delanef, L., Guénot, F. *et al.* (1994) Genetic associations with human longevity at the APOE and ACE loci, *Nature Genetics*, *6*(1), 29–32.

Schriner, S.E., Linford, N.J., Martin, G.M. *et al.* (2005) Extension of murine life span by overexpression of catalase targeted to mitochondria, *Science*, *308*(5730), 1909–11.

Smith, P. (2004) Elder care, gender and work: the work–family issue of the 21st century, *Berkeley Journal of Employment and Labor Law*, *25*(2), 352–90.

Sohal, R.S., Mockett, R.J. and Orr, W.C. (2002). Mechanisms of aging: an appraisal of the oxidative stress hypothesis, *Free Radical Biology and Medicine*, *33*(5), 575–86.

Speakman, J.R., Talbot, D.A., Selman, C. *et al.* (2004) Uncoupled and surviving: individual mice with high metabolism have greater mitochondrial uncoupling and live longer, *Aging Cell*, *3*(3), 87–95.

Stearns, S.C. (1992) *The evolution of life histories.* Oxford University Press.

Steinert, S., White, D.M., Zou, Y. *et al.* (2002) Telomere biology and cellular aging in nonhuman primate cells, *Experimental Cell Research*, *272*(2), 146–52.

Strehler, B.L. (1999) *Time, cells, and aging.* Larnaca: Demetriades Brothers.

Suh, Y., Atzmon, G., Cho, M.O. *et al.* (2008) Functionally significant insulin-like growth factor I receptor mutations in centenarians, *Proceedings of the National Academy of Sciences of the USA*, *105*(9), 3438–42.

Szilard, L. (1959) On the nature of the aging process, *Proceedings of the National Academy of Sciences of the USA*, *45*(1), 30–45.

Tatar, M., Bartke, A. and Antebi, A. (2003) The endocrine regulation of aging by insulin-like signals, *Science*, *299*(5611), 1346–51.

Tomas-Loba, A., Flores, I., Fernandez-Marcos, P.J. *et al.* (2008) Telomerase reverse transcriptase delays aging in cancer-resistant mice, *Cell*, *135*(4), 609–22.

Valdesalici, S. and Cellerino, A. (2003) Extremely short lifespan in the annual fish *Nothobranchius furzeri*, *Proceedings. Biological Sciences/The Royal Society*, *270* (Suppl 2), S189–91.

Van Remmen, H., Ikeno, Y., Hamilton, M. *et al.* (2003) Life-long reduction in MnSOD activity results in increased DNA damage and higher incidence of cancer but does not accelerate aging, *Physiological Genomics*, *16*(1), 29–37.

Vaupel, J.W., Baudisch, A., Dolling, M. *et al.* (2004) The case for negative senescence, *Theoretical Population Biology*, *65*(4), 339–51.

Wallace, D.C. (1992) Mitochondrial genetics: a paradigm for aging and degenerative diseases?, *Science*, *256*(5057), 628–32.

Weindruch, R. and Walford, R.L. (1988) *The retardation of aging and disease by dietary restriction.* Springfield, IL: C.C. Thomas.

Weismann, A. (1891) *On heredity.* Oxford: Clarendon Press.

Williams, G.C. (1957) Pleiotropy, natural selection, and the evolution of senescence, *Evolution*, *11*, 398–411.

Wright, W.E. and Shay, J.W. (2001) Cellular senescence as a tumor-protection mechanism: the essential role of counting, *Current Opinion in Genetics and Development*, *11*(1), 98–103.

Yu, C.E., Oshima, J., Fu, Y.H. *et al.* (1996) Positional cloning of the Werner's syndrome gene, *Science*, *272*(5259), 258–62.

Zhou, Z.Q., Manguino, D., Kewitt, K. *et al.* (2001) Spontaneous hepatocellular carcinoma is reduced in transgenic mice overexpressing human O^6-methylguanine-DNA methyltransferase, *Proceedings of the National Academy of Sciences of the USA*, *98*(22), 12566–71.

3 Fostering resilience, promoting health and preventing disease in older adults

SHARON OSTWALD AND CARMEL DYER

OVERVIEW

This chapter examines how the health status (and with it life expectancy) of older adults can be improved through primary prevention (the use of health promotion and protection against diseases). Chapter 4 examines the same issue through secondary and tertiary prevention. Successful ageing is seen primarily in terms of resilience, and factors affecting health (e.g. environmental, cultural, gender-related and genetic) are explored.

Introduction

Living is not the good, but living well. The wise man therefore lives as long as he should, not as long as he can. He will observe where he is to live, with whom, how, and what he is to do. He will always think of life in terms of quality, not quantity.

Seneca

By 2020, the world population of people age 60 and older is expected to reach 1 billion, with over 700 million in the developing world (World Health Organization (WHO), 1999). As the world's population ages, there is increasing interest in the concept of successful ageing. However, no consensus exists on what this constitutes: although criteria usually include concepts such as low probability of disease and disease-related disability, high cognitive and physical functional capacity, and active engagement with life (Rowe and Kahn, 1987), surveys of older adults suggest they might judge success differently.

The majority of community-dwelling older adults in developed countries reported that they were successfully ageing, while fewer than 20 per cent met the criteria that Rowe and Kahn (1987) originally proposed (Montross *et al.*, 2006; Strawbridge, Wallhagen and Cohen, 2002; von Faber *et al.*, 2001). Rowe and Kahn (2000) acknowledge that even older people who are ageing successfully might have encountered serious illnesses or temporary disability in the past. They propose the concept of resilience as a way to explain the degree of rapidity and completeness with which people recover from stressful conditions. Resilience has been shown to be related to better health, health-promoting behaviours, independence in instrumental activities of daily living (IADL), positive self-ratings of health, self-esteem, competence, interpersonal control, fewer depressive symptoms and more social involvement (Hardy, Concato and Gill, 2004; Windle, Markland and Woods, 2008).

Older adults who have chronic illnesses from which they will never completely recover, and who have some functional disabilities, might view themselves as ageing successfully. Harris (2008) argues that perhaps the goal of ageing is not 'successful ageing', but resilience or that ability to 'bounce back' from adversities which is attainable by older adults who have multiple comorbidities and disabilities. Crowther and colleagues (2002) suggest that the forgotten factor in successful ageing is positive spirituality. Spirituality may be a key component of resilience and an important positive predictor of successful ageing. Positive perspectives that focus on the inner strength of older adults provide a counterbalance to the focus on loss, dysfunction, disease and death that often dominate the perspective of health care professionals.

In the 1990s, the term 'active ageing' was adopted by the World Health Organization (WHO) to convey a more inclusive message than healthy or successful ageing. It is defined as 'the process of optimizing opportunities for health, participation, and security in order to enhance quality of life as people age' (WHO, 2002a, p. 12). Active ageing moves away from viewing older adults as 'targets' of others' strategies to recognizing their rights to be autonomous with active involvement in their own heath and the policies that foster a healthy, active life. One area of focus of nursing, especially public health nursing, is wellness in old age. This chapter focuses on the promotion of health and prevention of disease and disability in older adults.

Resilience

Individuals who reach old age have demonstrated their ability to survive a variety of adverse situations. They have been able to keep or regain their health, to cope with adversities, and to adapt to the many losses that accompany the ageing process. While it is well recognized that advanced age is accompanied by increased prevalence of physical and cognitive health challenges and limitations in independent functioning, recent research has focused on some of the positive aspects of becoming old (Nygren *et al.*, 2005). It is these positive aspects of ageing that form the basis of health promotion and disease prevention in older adults.

A number of theories and models have been used to explain how older adults, especially the oldest old (85+), adapt their everyday lives and maintain a positive attitude toward their lives in spite of increasing demands and declining health. Baltes (1997) proposed a model of selective optimization with compensation, whereby older people purposefully reduce the number of demands (e.g. daily activities) on their time and use more time to achieve the activities that they select. Either by choice or by necessity, maintenance of health and management of chronic diseases demand a great deal of time and energy as people age.

Several concepts have been advanced to explain how some older adults compensate better for their losses and adapt more readily to changes in their health and function than others. These concepts include 'resilience' (Wagnild and Young, 1990), 'sense of coherence' (Antonovsky and Sagy, 1986), 'gerotranscendence' (Tornstam, 1997), 'self-transcendence' (Reed, 1991) and 'hardiness' (Maddi, 2002). These concepts, while not identical, share basic beliefs about the importance of meaning and purpose in life. In the theory of gerotranscendence, for instance, well-being in older adults is believed to be based on experiences of meaning and purpose in life and the ability to transcend or expand their boundaries, both inwardly and outwardly toward others (Tornstam, 1997). Self-transcendence has been associated with feelings of self-worth (Coward, 1990) and has been linked to spiritual connectedness (Bauer and Barron, 1995) as well as activities of daily living (ADL) (basically, the tasks that are essential in order to conduct a typical daily existence) abilities (Upchurch, 1999). Resilience is widely suggested to help explain why some people age well and others age with disability.

Resilience has been described as a personal trait, a process and a protective strength that allows individuals to have the flexibility to 'bounce back', to adapt to adverse experiences, and to maintain independence and well-being (Dyer and McGuinness, 1996; Rowe and Kahn, 2000; Staudinger, Marsiske and Baltes, 1993; Wagnild and Young, 1990). There are five interrelated characteristics that have been identified as constituting resilience (Wagnild and Young, 1990; Nygren *et al.*, 2005).

(1) equanimity (balanced perspective of one's life and experience)
(2) perseverance (a willingness and ability to remain involved)
(3) self-reliance (belief in oneself and one's capabilities)
(4) meaningfulness (an understanding that life has a purpose)
(5) existential aloneness (a realization that each person's life path is unique).

Biological research is providing new insights about processes implicated in the development of resilience. Scientists suggest that biological factors might interact with stress early in life and thus confer heightened resilience or vulnerability, which can last throughout life (Luthar and Brown, 2007). The New England Centenarian Study suggests that the oldest old are resilient because they have a higher threshold for disease and slower rates of disease progression than peers who develop chronic diseases at earlier ages. The biological connection between resilience and ageing is further enforced by the findings that siblings of centenarians also live long lives (Perls, Bubrick, Wagner *et al.*, 1998), and the longitudinal studies of Swedish twins that show heritability trends across decades (Marenberg, Risch, Berkman *et al.*, 1994). Genetics may be a major determinant in how well older persons cope with disease. Trans-disciplinary research is needed if we are to truly understand the major predictors of resilience and its relationship to health.

Self-reported health

Several studies have shown significant correlations between resilience and health in different populations of older adults (Aroian and Norris, 2000; Christopher, 2000; Klaas, 1998; Nygren *et al.*, 2005; Wagnild and Young, 1993). In their Swedish study, Nygren *et al.* (2005) found that the oldest old had higher than, or at least the same level of resilience, sense of coherence, purpose in life and self-transcendence as, younger persons. They concluded that good mental health may help persons overcome negative experiences related to declining health, physical limitations and losses. Older adults' perceptions of their own health have proved to be accurate indicators of their health status. Self-perceptions of health have been shown to be related to socio-demographic characteristics (age, income, minority status), with minority and low-income individuals consistently reporting poorer health status. For example, a US health survey found that 42 per cent of older adults aged 65–74 rated their health as excellent or very good compared to 31 per cent aged 85 and older (Centers for Disease Control and Prevention (CDC), 2005a). Older adults who have positive perceptions of their health are more likely to control their health by adopting healthier lifestyles and following disease prevention recommendations (Menec, Chipperfield and Perry, 1999). In contrast, older people who report poorer health, especially poorer functional abilities, are more likely to die in the subsequent 3 years than those who perceive their functional health to be good (Bernard *et al.*, 1997).

Life expectancy

A major goal of health-care professionals is to foster active ageing in older adults by using interventions that promote their health, prevent disease and manage chronic illnesses to prevent excess disability. Maximum age span and life expectancy are important concepts to understand. Scientists believe that humans could live at most for about 120 years (maximum lifespan) even if all diseases were eliminated (Vaupel *et al.*, 1998). Life expectancy is a probability estimate of how long individuals can expect to live, given the environmental and disease conditions currently in existence. While life expectancy varies by country, it is currently near 80 years of age in developed countries and rapidly increasing in developing countries (see Chapter 1). The process of increasing life expectancy so that it is almost the same as the maximum lifespan is termed the 'rectangularization of the survival curve' (Hayflick, 1980). While life expectancy has increased significantly, the average life expectancy is still about 40 years shorter than the maximum lifespan. Age makes older adults more prone to the development of chronic disease. However, it is not clear what changes that occur lead to the manifestations of ageing (Hayflick, 2007; see Chapter 2).

It is well accepted that health in older adults results from lifelong interactions between their genetic make-up and the social and physical environments in which they live. Over 75 per cent of the deaths in the developed world are due to chronic diseases (WHO, 2002b). However, an individual's risk of disease can be altered, even in old age. And as Rowe (1990) observes, many illnesses and disabilities arising through illness are risks, not certainties. Rowe and Kahn (1997) view people as 'ageing successfully' by lowering their risks and thus avoiding disease and disability.

Fries (1983) has proposed that attention to health promotion and disease prevention programmes can lead to a compression of morbidity; that is, a delay in the age at which people develop a chronic disease. This postponement in the onset of disease will result in fewer premature deaths, less actual time with disability, and a smaller proportion of total life spent with disease and disability. An important focus of health-care providers is on reducing the amount of time that older adults spend in dependent life expectancy. The WHO (2002a) uses the term 'disability-free life expectancy' for this concept. Active ageing ends when individuals lose their independence and need to rely on others for their ADL. It is currently estimated that about one-third of the years lived after age 65 are lived in a state of dependency (WHO, 2002a). For example, at age 65 the average woman has approximately 20 years of life left. It is estimated that 13.3 of those years will be spent in good health and 6.7 years will be spent being dependent on others. The estimates for 65-year-old men are similar, except that their life expectancy after age 65 is 17.1 years with 5.6 years estimated to be spent needing assistance from others (Administration on Aging, 2007). Fortunately, the prevalence of chronic disability has been declining among older people in developed countries, such as the USA and the UK for the last 20 years (Manton and Gu, 2001). If this trend continues, as can be seen in Figure 3.1, the number of older adults living with disability will decrease significantly over time.

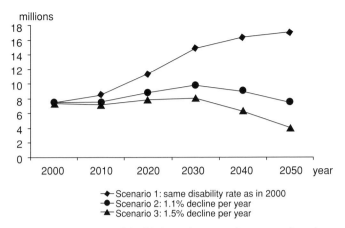

millions

- Scenario 1: same disability rate as in 2000
- Scenario 2: 1.1% decline per year
- Scenario 3: 1.5% decline per year

Figure 3.1 Projections of disabled population aged 65+ years based on actual disability figures for 1982–96 in the USA. *Source:* World Health Organization Fact Sheet, *Towards Policy for Health and Ageing* www.who.int/ageing/publications/alc_fs_ageing_policy.pdf. Reproduced by kind permission of the World Health Organization.

Prevention

Health promotion and disease prevention activities are designed to prolong active ageing and increase the quality of life of older adults. The international perspective of active ageing implies maintaining autonomy, independence and inter-generational solidarity, as a part of health promotion and disease prevention (WHO, 2002a). Throughout the world, regardless of gender, ethnicity or socio-economic status, the major causes of death and disability in populations above the age of 60 are chronic diseases. While some have questioned the importance of expending resources on promoting health and preventing disease in older people, many reasons exist to support these activities among older adults. These include: (1) prevention of premature death, (2) delay of the onset of chronic diseases, (3) postponement of disability related to chronic diseases, (4) higher quality of life, (5) greater participation in the life of the family and community in paid and unpaid roles, and (6) reduction in medical care costs, especially hospitalization and nursing home costs. Because the risks of disease and disability are higher in older people, even small increases in health can make big differences in active life expectancy and the cost of medical care (Fries, Green and Levine, 1989; WHO, 2002a). Butler (2000) sums up the argument in the statement, 'It is never too late to introduce healthy behavior and it is always too early to stop.'

Leavell and Clark (1965) articulated a broad concept of health promotion, disease and disability prevention. There are three recognized levels of prevention:

primary, secondary and tertiary. There is, however, much variation in the literature in how the terms are used (Froom and Benbassat, 2000). Leavell and Clark's original conceptualization has re-emerged as a valuable guide for physicians, nurses and public health professionals and is consistent with the recent WHO publications that include a role for governments and societies in creating and maintaining environments within which people can live healthy lives. Leavell and Clark's discussion of health promotion and protection captures the tension between personal and governmental/societal responsibility. *Primary prevention*, according to Leavell and Clark, includes generalized health promotion and specific protections against diseases. It is applied before disease emerges and includes interventions such as health education, protection against accidents and occupational hazards, risk assessments, immunizations, and policies and practices that ensure safe housing, recreation, transportation, and protections against hazards such as polluted water, air and land.

Secondary prevention emphasizes early detection and treatment of disease and maintenance of health among individuals with diseases so that they do not develop complications and excess disability. Secondary prevention strategies include screening assessments, teaching self-examination procedures, regular physical and psychological assessments, and nursing and medical care to avoid complications and excess disability (i.e. maintaining adequate nutrition, elimination, exercise, and medical and pharmacological therapies).

Tertiary prevention, according to Leavell and Clark (1965), begins after a disease or disability is present and focuses on returning the individual to maximal functioning again. Strategies include rehabilitation, self-management education, referral to support groups, and environmental and policy changes to reduce external barriers to functioning (e.g. architectural barriers). This chapter focuses on primary prevention and the early detection of disease, while Chapter 4 focuses on the assessment and management of common age-related diseases and tertiary prevention to reduce excess disability and promote maximal function.

Healthy People 2010 (US Department of Health and Human Services (USDHHS), 2000) is the third comprehensive nationwide health promotion and disease prevention agenda for improving the health of people in the USA. Similar documents have been advanced in other developed countries, such as Canada's *An Action Framework for Primary Prevention of Chronic Diseases in Canada* (Chronic Disease Prevention Alliance in Canada (CDPAC), 2006). *Healthy People 2010* proposes the achievement of two goals (increase quality and years of healthy life, and eliminate health disparities), which are addressed through 500 objectives in 26 focus areas with over 700 targets. Consistent with the work of WHO, the objectives focus not just on changes in health behaviours (diet and exercise), but also on increased access to health care (e.g. health insurance coverage, diverse health workforce), delivery of quality care (i.e. emergency, primary and long-term care), and attention to the environment (e.g. water quality, substandard housing and exposure to toxic chemicals). The focus areas are relevant to older adults, as well as to younger and middle-aged people who could improve their quality of life by entering old age with fewer chronic illnesses and disabilities. Ten health indicators, which are high-priority public health issues, are tracked as indicators of the health of people in the USA. These include physical activity, overweight and obesity, tobacco use and substance abuse, responsible sexual behaviour, mental health, injury and violence, environmental quality, immunizations and access to health care.

Screening of older adults

Chronic illnesses and accidents are the major causes of disease, disability and death in older adults. Older adults may be identified as being 'at risk' of a particular disease because of its increased prevalence in their age, gender or racial/ethnic group, family history of the disease, the existence of related diseases (e.g. diabetes), their health habits, or the social or physical environment in which they live. The national recommendations in the USA have focused on screening for risk factors related to the most common age-related diseases – cardiovascular disease, cancer and diabetes. The incidence of screening for some diseases appears to be increasing in the population. For example, in 2004, 75.1 per cent of women had received mammograms and 63.1 per cent of the population had been screened for colorectal cancer. In addition, 90.4 per cent of the US population had had their cholesterol checked within the last 5 years (CDC and Merck Company Foundation, 2007), all exceeding the targets set in *Healthy People 2010* (USDHHS, 2000). European and North American prevention guidelines are compatible for screening at-risk individuals for chronic diseases, such as cardiovascular disease (Stein, 1994).

The incidence of other important conditions (injuries, depression, alcohol or medication misuse, and elder abuse) are monitored with lower frequency. While sometimes not included in traditional lists of recommended screenings, these conditions fit the criteria that have been advanced to justify screening: (1) they have a significant effect on the length or quality of life, (2) acceptable treatment is available, (3) early treatment could reduce morbidity or mortality, (4) treating early provides a better result than a delay in treatment, (5) screening tests are available at a reasonable cost, and (6) incidence of the condition is high enough to justify the cost (Lavizzo-Mourey, Day, Diserens *et al.*, 1989).

In addition to screening for chronic illnesses and functional disabilities, the Centers for Disease Control and Prevention (CDC) recommend the use of vaccinations to protect older adults from infectious diseases. Vaccinations are recommended for influenza on a yearly basis for adults age 65 and older; the pneumococcal vaccination for pneumonia is recommended at least once for adults over the age of 65 and some authorities recommend it every 5 years. The *Healthy People 2010* target is that 90 per cent of the non-institutionalized older adults will be immunized against influenza and pneumonia by 2010 (USDHHS, 2000). By 2004, 68.1 per cent had received an influenza vaccination within the last year and 64.7 per cent had ever received a pneumococcal vaccination (CDC and Merck Company Foundation, 2007). In 2008, the CDC recommended a single vaccination for herpes zoster (shingles) for adults over the age of 60 (CDC, 2008).

Illnesses that are not identified and treated early or chronic diseases that are not controlled can lead to excess disability and reduced quality of life. Although the percentage of older adults experiencing dependence in ADL and IADL (grocery shopping, cooking, doing laundry, managing medications, paying bills, using the telephone) has declined, the actual number of older people requiring assistance has increased due to the increase in absolute numbers of older adults. While in 2004, 34 per cent of US older adults reported that they had a disability that limited their independence or required use of an assistive device, only about 6–7 per cent actually require assistance from others (Weiner, Hanley, Clark et al., 1990). Studies in different countries have consistently shown that dependence in ADL and IADL increases with age, beginning at about age 75 and is higher in women and people with low incomes (Andersen-Ranberg et al., 1999; Demura, Sato, Minami et al., 2003). The understanding of disability has changed in the latter part of the twentieth century, so that disability is no longer viewed as an individual attribute, but an interaction between the individual and the environment (Field, Jette and US Institute of Medicine (IOM), 2007). In 2001, the WHO developed a new conceptual framework to understand disability. The International Classification of Function, Disability and Health (ICF) no longer uses the word 'handicap' and does not view disability as only medical or biological. It recognizes that disability is created through interactions between physical, social and attitudinal environments and personal factors (WHO, 2001). The presence of a disability affects an older person's preventive and protective behaviours, as can be seen in Figure 3.2. While the presence of a disability is likely to increase interaction with health-care professionals and thus increase the rates of immunizations, it appears to have a deleterious effect on health-promoting behaviours, such as exercise and diet.

The identification of risk factors that underlie common health problems experienced by the older adults, such as falls, abuse or depression, requires a holistic view of the interactions between the individual and the environment. Falls are a good example of the need for multiple preventive and protective measures to reduce the high incidence of falls with related disability and death. One in three older people fall every year and the risk of falling increases with age and may differ between men and women. Falls account for 87 per cent of all fractures and 20 per cent of people who have hip fractures die within a year (CDC, 2007). Because the causes

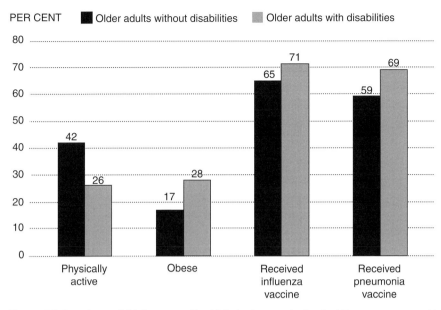

Figure 3.2 Prevalence of risk factors and health behaviours varies by disability status among older adults aged 65 or older. *Source:* Centers for Disease Control and Prevention and Merck Company Foundation (2007). The National Report Card on Healthy Aging, *The State of Aging and Health in America*, p. 11. www.cdc.gov/aging/saha.htm. Reproduced by kind permission of the Centers for Disease Control and Prevention.

are multi-factorial, primary, secondary and tertiary interventions need to be aimed at many targets. Osteoporosis is a known risk factor for fractures and it is estimated that 50 per cent of postmenopausal women are affected by it (NIH Consensus Statement, 1995). Other risk factors include poor vision, medication use, poor muscle strength and balance, and other contributing diseases, especially neuromuscular diseases. Therefore, primary prevention strategies should include screenings for vision and bone density in women; the use of vitamins and nutritional supplements to increase bone strength, if needed; evaluation of current medications that may cause confusion or dizziness; increases in physical activity to target strength, balance and flexibility; and community-based fall-prevention programmes. However, attention also needs to be directed to the environment, including evaluation of home safety; repair of home or neighbourhood hazards, such as broken sidewalks and unsafe stairwells; placement of grab bars and non-stick surfaces in tubs and showers; and the addition of night lights.

People who already have osteoporosis may need secondary prevention strategies including additional vitamin supplementation and other medications to increase bone density, physical therapy and gait training. Other contributing medical conditions need to be treated, such as poor vision or neuromuscular problems like Parkinson's disease. Emergency call systems may need to be added to the home and daily 'check-in' calls instituted by family and friends (see Chapter 13). The community is responsible for maintaining a well-trained emergency medical system.

Tertiary prevention is instituted after the person falls and sustains a fracture. This requires prompt emergency care and accessible and affordable acute-care hospitals with quality nursing and medical care so that complications of immobility, like pressure ulcers, pneumonia and contractures, do not occur. In addition, long-term care options, such as rehabilitation in either the home or a long-term care facility, must be available. If the older adult is to return to optimal function, the community will also need to consider issues such as public transportation and elimination of architectural barriers in public buildings. The most effective fall-prevention programmes combine clinical assessment, individual risk reduction and follow-up (RAND Corporation, 2003). More discussion of the assessment and management of chronic diseases and geriatric syndromes is found in Chapter 4. However, these strategies need to be accomplished within a more comprehensive framework that promotes health and prevents disease and disability by reducing risk before the disease begins but also includes rehabilitation and social supports for older adults who already have chronic diseases with attendant disability (IOM, 1990).

Decisions about the appropriateness of screening tests and preventive health care become more complex as adults get older. In addition, as Spalding and Sebesta (2008) point out, the health status, functional level and life expectancy of older adults may affect decisions. Disease-specific organizations (e.g. American Cancer Society), governmental organizations (e.g. Agency for Health Care Policy and Quality), international organizations (e.g. World Health Organization (WHO)), and professional organizations (e.g. American Academy of Family Physicians) issue guidelines that are sometimes inconsistent with each other and are frequently updated as based on the most recent research evidence. The guidelines presented in Table 3.1 are a compilation of the recommendations of these organizations, as well as the further recommendations specific to older adults suggested by Spalding and Sebesta (2008), based on life expectancy and functional impairment. They provided recommendations for four patient groups: robust, frail, moderately demented and end of life. In Table 3.1, however, we have only included recommendations for robust older adults (life expectancy greater than 5 years with independent function) and frail older adults (life expectancy less than 5 years with significant functional impairment).

Health promotion

Health promotion goes beyond the prevention of disease and disability and aims to improve a person's well-being. Positive approaches to health promotion focus on

Table 3.1 Recommendations for screening and preventive care based on functional level and life expectancy

Recommendation	Robust older person (life expectancy ≥5 years)	Frail older person (life expectancy <5 years)	Comments
Health behaviours			
Exercise	30 min/day at least 3 days per week	Individualize – adapt to ability	Include endurance, strength, balance and flexibility
Weight	Every visit	Every visit	Maintain ideal weight for age
Nutrition	*MyPyramid* adapted for older persons (>5 fruits and vegetables/day)	Individualize – consider special needs	Consider multivitamin supplements
Calcium	Counsel females about dietary intake		Consider supplement of calcium and vitamin D
Tobacco	Counsel to stop	Counsel to stop	
Alcohol	Moderate use	Moderate use	
Medications	Check at every visit	Check at every visit	Check prescription, over-the-counter (OTC) and herbal remedies
Vaccinations			
Influenza	Yearly	Yearly	
Pneumococcal	Once >65	Once >65	May repeat in 5 years if received before age 65
Tetanus and diphtheria toxoid	Primary series if not done	Primary series if not done	Repeat every 10 years
Herpes zoster	Once >60	Once >60	
Cardiovascular diseases			
Blood pressure	Every visit	Every visit	
Cholesterol	Yearly age 65–75	Yearly age 65–75 with additional risks	
Abdominal aortic aneurysm	Ultrasound once for men 65–75		AARP limits to men who have smoked
Aspirin for prevention	81 mg/daily	81 mg/daily	Discuss with men >40 and postmenopausal women
Fasting blood sugar	1–3 years over age 45 with risk factors	1–3 years with risk factors	Risk factors: hypertension, hyperlipidaemia, cardiovascular disease, overweight
Cancer			
Mammogram	Every 1–2 years for women up to age 80	Consider every 1–2 years for women up to age 75	American Cancer Society recommends yearly >50 years
Clinical breast exam	Every 1–2 years	Every 1–2 years	

(cont.)

Table 3.1 (*cont.*)

Recommendation	Robust older person (life expectancy ≥5 years)	Frail older person (life expectancy <5 years)	Comments
Self-breast exam	Monthly		
Pelvic exam and Papanicolaou (Pap) smear	1–3 Pap smears if the woman has never had a Pap smear (up to age 70)		Screening not necessary if three negative cervical cytology tests within past 10 years
Faecal occult blood	Yearly	Consider yearly	
Colonoscopy	Every 5–10 years		
Digital prostate exam	Yearly for men	Yearly for men	American Cancer Society recommends yearly over age 50
Prostate-specific antigen	Yearly for men	Yearly for men	American Cancer Society recommends yearly after age 50
Skin exam	Yearly	Yearly	American Cancer Society recommends yearly after age 40
Other preventive conditions			
Depression	Yearly	Yearly	See Chapter 4 for further discussion
Osteoporosis	Bone scan age 65+	Bone scan age 65+	
Function and Sensory			
Glaucoma	Every 3 years >55; yearly if family history	Yearly if family history	
Vision	Yearly >50	Yearly >50	
Hearing	Screen by questioning every 2–5 years	Yearly screen by questioning	
Dental exam and cleaning	Yearly	Yearly	
Gait and balance	Yearly	Every visit	
Elder abuse and neglect	Yearly	Every visit	See Chapter 4 for further discussion

AARP: American Association of Retired Persons.
Source: Adapted from American Cancer Society, *Cancer facts and figures 2008*, Atlanta, GA: American Cancer Society; revised 03/05/2008. Retrieved from www.cancer.org/docroot/ped/content/ped_2_3x_acs_cancer_detection_guidelines_36.asp.

empowerment of populations, using inner strength, building resilience and accessing resources and the political process to achieve changes in health. Much of the recent literature on health promotion, especially in the USA, has focused almost exclusively on lifestyle change, behaviour modification and personal responsibility, to the exclusion of the responsibilities of governments, societies and private-sector organizations to promote a healthy environment. Models, such as the Health Promotion Model (HPM) advanced by Pender, Murdaugh and Parsons (2006), build on previous health belief models (Becker, 1974) and have been widely used in nursing (Shin, Yun, Pender et al., 2005). These models take primarily a socio-cognitive approach to behaviour change with individual beliefs and behaviours, such as perceived benefits and barriers to health-promoting behaviours, and perceived self-efficacy, being major intervention targets. This approach to health promotion has been criticized as focusing too heavily on personal behaviour and using approaches that are almost exclusively health education (Whitehead, 2008). Although there is considerable controversy about what constitutes health promotion and how it differs from health education, the WHO makes explicit the need to focus beyond individual behaviours to the interactions between people's social and physical environments and lifestyles. This approach to lifestyle and social and physical environments can be clearly seen in the Ottawa Charter for Health Promotion (WHO, 1986, p. 1):

Health promotion is the process of enabling people to increase control over, and to improve, their health. To reach a state of complete physical, mental and social well-being, an individual or group must be able to identify and to realize aspirations, to satisfy needs, and to change or cope with the environment... Therefore, health promotion is not just the responsibility of the health sector, but goes beyond healthy life-styles to well-being.

This is further echoed in the Bangkok Charter for Health Promotion in a Globalized World (WHO, 2005), which complements and builds on the Ottawa Charter. This document focuses on the critical factors that interfere with health promotion such as social, economic and demographic changes that foster inequities within and between countries and policies that increase vulnerability and promote the exclusion of marginalized, disabled and indigenous people.

Active ageing is enhanced by health promotion and disease prevention interventions that focus on determinants of health, which are complex and interrelated, as shown in Figure 3.3. The determinants of health proposed in *Active Aging* (WHO, 2002a) have evolved from the work of LaLonde (Canadian Minister of National Health and Welfare, 1974), who originally proposed the role of national health policy in preventive health. Health promotion is beyond the purview of any one discipline, but needs the involvement of nurses, physicians, public health professionals and policymakers to be effective.

Determinants of health

Culture

Culture and gender are cross-cutting determinants of health that influence all other determinants. Culture influences how people age and the value that society

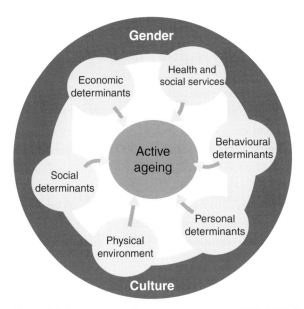

Figure 3.3 Determinants of active ageing. *Source:* WHO (2002a). *Active ageing: a policy framework.* http://whqlibdoc.who.int/hq/2002/WHO_NMH_NPH_02.8.pdf. Reproduced by kind permission of the World Health Organization.

places on older people. Some cultures may value expending resources to ensure that older people have access to public transportation and adequate food, while others believe that older people with disabilities should remain in their homes or depend on family and friends for assistance. Culture is also an important determinant of where people live; of what personal habits they pursue related to diet, exercise and smoking; and of their beliefs about the benefits or harms of medical therapies. Some cultural groups expect that older parents will live with their children and participate in the extended family life by caring for grandchildren, while others tend toward segregation of generations into independent households. Many different cultural values may exist within one country so that it is impossible to generalize individual and family expectations and obligations from one cultural group to another. Different cultural values may generate conflicts when societies, governments and private-sector organizations try to develop overarching policies about how best to use their resources to promote health. Some cultural groups may experience discrimination; perceived racial discrimination has been linked to poorer health. Older adults who are minorities and poor, or who are immigrants or refugees with different languages and customs, are more likely to experience difficulty in accessing health care (Noh, Beiser, Kaspar *et al.*, 1999; CDC and Merck Company Foundation, 2007).

Gender

Gender is a lens through which individuals view their world, and its relation to health has been an important area of study (Hunt and Annandale, 1999). The roles that men and women play in society influence their exposures to hazards and access to resources which may either promote or damage their health. Men, especially men in older age groups, have traditionally been more likely to hold jobs that expose them to environmental hazards, such as chemicals, radiation, intense temperature swings and trauma. These occupational hazards may interact with other determinants of health to increase their risk of poor health or premature death. For example, men who were exposed to asbestos at work and then smoked may die prematurely or enter old age with significant respiratory disability. In many countries, women, especially older, minority women, are viewed as less valuable to society. These prejudices may result in income inequality that limits the places where they live and their ability to access and control the resources that they need to live a healthy life. Because women often outlive men, they experience widowhood, which further increases the isolation and income inequality experienced by women in the oldest-old segment of society. Income inequality has been linked to poor health, lack of availability of health care and higher mortality rates (Lynch, Smith, Kaplan *et al.*, 2000). Furthermore, women who are widowed have been shown to have more symptoms of depression, more chronic conditions, and more functional disability than women who are not widowed (Prigerson, Maciejewski and Rosenheck, 2000).

Personal determinants

As is demonstrated throughout this book, a major myth is that 'all old people are the same'. The truth is that older people are the most heterogeneous of any segment of the population. Genetics may influence how long older people live, as suggested by studies of centenarians and Swedish twins (Marenberg *et al.*, 1994; Perls *et al.*, 1998; see Chapter 2). However, it is the behaviours and exposures that occur over a lifetime that interact with biological and psychological factors that determine whether people reach old age with good or poor health. Some personal characteristics have been found to be associated with life expectancy and health, regardless of culture. In all developed countries, women have a longer life expectancy than men (e.g. the ratio of women to men in the age group over 85 is 2:1). In all European countries (as well as the USA and Canada) the life expectancy for both males and females aged 75–84 is increasing (Kesteloot, Sans and Krombout, 2002). Women in Japan have the longest life expectancy of any country in the world (85.2 years) (Associated Press, 2007) while Russian men have the lowest life-expectancy of any developed country (59 years). A difference in sex ratio to mortality throughout the world has been attributed to lifestyle and environment, rather than genetics. Zhang, Sasaki and Kesteloot (1995) found that the differences in mortality rates among men and women were related to the different exposures and different reactions to the risk factors of cardiovascular diseases and cancer (e.g. saturated fat intake, alcohol intake and smoking habits) seen in men and women. Men have traditionally practised more risky behaviours (e.g. driving without seat belts), have been exposed to more occupational hazards (e.g. pesticides), and have practised fewer positive health habits (e.g. smoking and alcohol consumption).

Educational attainment has long been associated with good health and healthy lifestyles. Countries with high levels of educational attainment have higher life expectancies. Reactions to risk factors might partially be a function of educational level. Women tend to be better informed about nutrition and thus make better choices and have higher-quality diets than men (Variyam, Blaylock, Smallwood *et al.*, 1998). People with higher educational backgrounds are more likely to adopt healthy lifestyle behaviours (WHO, 1999).

Psychological characteristics are also important determinants of good health and good quality of life for older people. 'Inner strength' is characterized by resilience, positive spirituality and a sense of coherence, personal characteristics that influence health and an individual's ability to practise health-promoting and disease-preventing behaviours, and adapt to disease and disability in themselves and others. Attitudes, such as positive expectations, commitment, and a strong motivation or conviction to initiate and continue a behaviour, are related to maintaining healthy practices, such as exercise (WHO, 1998). Autonomy, or the ability to control factors that affect life, is valued by many older people. While older people are independent in their early years, as they age, interdependence between the individual, the family and society, becomes a more realistic goal (WHO, 1998).

Behavioural determinants

Behavioural determinants of health are the lifestyle choices that individuals make. Some believe that older adults may be too old to change their lifestyles, though performing exercise regularly, eating healthy food, avoiding tobacco, using alcohol in moderation, and correctly using medications can increase an older person's health and improve their quality of life. After studying community-dwelling adults for 35 years, Breslow and Breslow (1993) reported that disability and mortality rates were higher among people who had poor health habits (i.e. did not participate in regular physical activity, were obese, had smoked, had high alcohol intake, and did not eat breakfast or slept less than or more than 7–8 hours per night). They found that personal health practices and the strength of the social network significantly impacted life expectancy and the development of disability. Smoking, poor diet and physical inactivity were the root cause of 35 per cent of the deaths in the USA in 2000 (CDC and Merck Company Foundation, 2007).

Other countries have also reported that chronic diseases that are attributed at least in part to lifestyle choices account for up to 70 per cent of their annual mortality. Many argue that rather than focusing on many targets, as proposed in *Healthy People 2010*, progress would be made more rapidly if health-care professionals focused on the three major risk factors that contribute the most to poor health – smoking, diet and exercise (Butler, 2000). Significant progress has been made in reducing smoking among older adults in the USA (down to 9.3 per cent), although smoking still remains the number one health risk for chronic diseases in many countries (CDC and Merck Company Foundation, 2007). Alcohol abuse, another of the personal behaviours that impact quality of life, was identified as the leading cause of male disability in industrialized countries and the fourth leading cause in developing countries (WHO, 1996). Physical activity and diet are areas that need further attention if older adults are to increase their disability-free life expectancy and increase their quality of life. These two behaviours have received significant attention in developed countries, such as the USA, Canada, and the UK, as well as by the WHO.

Physical activity

Physical activity can be seen as a continuum from performing the most basic ADLs to rigorous exercise training (WHO, 1998). As people age, the amount of daily physical activity decreases, and women and people with less education report less physical activity (DiPietro, 2001). In 2004, 28 per cent of US adults between 65 and 74 were inactive, and this increased to 36 per cent over the age of 75 (CDC and Merck Company Foundation, 2007). While some of this rise in inactivity may be due to physiological changes resulting in greater disability from progressive chronic diseases, such as congestive heart failure or recurrent strokes, adapted physical activity can benefit even older adults with disabilities (Stâhle, Nordlander and Bergfeldt, 1999). Even frail adults over the age of 80, with a few weeks of regular training, have experienced increases in their ability to get out of a chair independently and walk without a cane or walker (National Institute on Aging, 2008).

Physical activity has many positive advantages for older people: (1) helping to reduce blood pressure, (2) controlling blood sugar, (3) maintaining bone density, (4) strengthening muscles and increasing balance, (5) increasing flexibility, (6) increasing stamina, (7) reducing depression, (8) preventing weight gain, and (9) decreasing the number of falls (WHO, 1998). Moderate exercise has also been shown to have a beneficial impact on the older adult's resilience by limiting the impact of stress on the immunity of chronically stressed older people (Phillips, Burns and Lord, 2007). Activities particularly well suited to older adults, such as walking, gardening, dancing, and swimming, also increase older people's interaction with a social network and can reduce depression, and lead to a higher quality of life (Hughes *et al.*, 2005).

Healthy People 2010 recommends an increase in the proportion of adults (to at least 30 per cent) who engage in regular, moderate physical activity for 30 minutes or more per day (USDHHS, 2000). However, prescribing levels of exercise necessary to achieve aerobic fitness may not be appropriate for all older adults in the community (DiPietro, 2001). Four types of exercises have demonstrated benefits to older adults: endurance, strength, balance and flexibility. Endurance or aerobic exercises (e.g. walking, swimming, dancing and climbing stairs) increase the heart rate and build stamina, while reducing the risk of diseases such as type 2 diabetes. Strengthening exercises (e.g. lifting weights) build muscle and increase an older adult's ability to do ADL such as getting out of chairs and walking without assistance. Balance exercises (e.g. standing on one foot) are important to build strength in the lower extremities and to increase coordination, a major cause of falls in older adults. Finally, flexibility exercises (e.g. stretching) help older adults to become more limber, also important in reducing falls. Older adults, including those with stable chronic illnesses, are encouraged to follow a programme of daily exercise that can be integrated into their lifestyle, is enjoyable, and includes peer support. The exercise goal for older adults is to do endurance and flexibility exercises at least three times a week and balance and strengthening exercises at least twice a week for 30 minutes per day, either sustained or in three 10-minute sessions.

Older adults who perform endurance exercises must monitor the intensity of their workouts. Traditionally, individuals monitor the intensity of their exercise by taking their pulse and aiming for a 'target heart rate (THR)'. The THR is based on age, with older people having a lower target range than younger people. For instance, the THR for a person aged 60–69 is 112–136 beats a minute, while the THR for a person 80–89 is 98–119. However, many older adults have chronic diseases or take medications that affect their heart rate and so make the THR method of measuring intensity inaccurate. For example, many older adults have hypertension and take medication (e.g. a beta blocker) that slows the heart rate, masking the actual intensity of the exercise. The National Institute on Aging (2008) recommends that older adults use the Borg Category Rating Scale to judge the intensity of their endurance exercises. The scale denotes the number of times or minutes that the older person may do an exercise to fall into a particular intensity category (e.g. very light exercise, hard exercise). However, the amount of exercise required to feel that the exercise is intense is very individualistic.

Nutrition

Good nutrition is important to maintaining health, preventing disease, and living a high-quality life, but food intake tends to decrease with age. Older adults are at

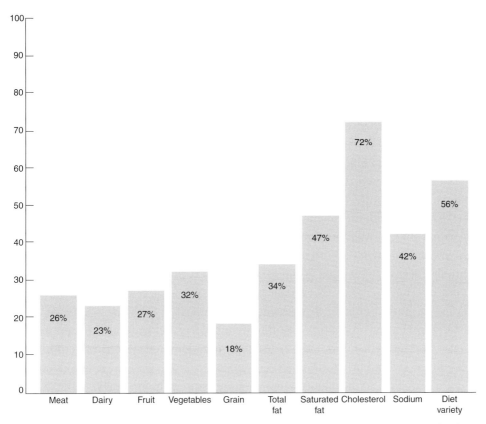

Figure 3.4 Percentage of adults 60 years of age and over meeting the dietary recommendations for the Healthy Eating Index components: USA, 1999–2002. *Source:* Ervin (2008).

risk of not meeting what have been traditionally termed the recommended dietary allowances (RDA), now referred to as the dietary reference intakes (DRI), for some nutrients (calcium; vitamins D, E and K; potassium and fibre) (Lichtenstein, Rusmussen, Yu *et al.*, 2008). A recent US National Health and Nutrition Examination Survey (NHANES) found that only 17 per cent of older adults (age 60 and over) consumed a 'good' diet, based on the Healthy Eating Index (HEI). The HEI, a tool developed to access the overall quality of a person's diet by the US Department of Agriculture's Center for Nutrition Policy and Promotion, contains 10 components (five food groups, four nutrients and a measure of variety in food intake) (Ervin, 2008). Less than one-third of US older adults were meeting recommendations for meats, dairy products, fruits, vegetables and grains (Ervin, 2008). These foods provide the building materials for healthy bones, and older adults, especially women, need encouragement to consume the DRIs of calcium and vitamins C, D, B_6 and K to prevent osteoporosis (Meunier, 1999; Weber, 1999). Figure 3.4 illustrates the percentage of older adults who met the US dietary recommendations for the 10 components in the HEI between 1999 and 2002.

Ervin (2008) reported that many socio-demographic and health characteristics were associated with dietary quality, but there were few patterns. Non-Hispanic white adults with more years of education reported better diets than non-Hispanic black adults. Smokers, older adults who were edentulous (lacking teeth), and those who rated their health as fair to poor reported a poorer-quality diet than older adults with teeth who perceived that their health was good. Men and women in their sixties reported eating more meat and vegetables than adults aged 80 and over. In general, women had higher HEI scores than men and white people had higher scores than black people.

Malnutrition, with muscle wasting, cognitive problems and impaired immunity, may be a problem for frail older adults, especially those with Alzheimer's disease, or older adults with low incomes that limit the amount or variety of food available for consumption. Malnutrition is closely related to household food insecurity in low-income countries and in some pockets of poverty in developed countries. The Chronic Disease Prevention Alliance in Canada (CDPAC) (2007) in their *Position Paper on Food Security in Canada* identified two long-term strategies that are needed to prevent chronic disease and promote health: (1) address the root cause of food insecurity – poverty – by improving safety net programmes that supply money to meet basic needs, and (2) develop a national food system that harmonizes agriculture and public health goals.

Paradoxically, in developed countries, obesity is more likely to be a concern because of the interactions between obesity and chronic disease in older people (e.g. diabetes, arthritis). Obesity, as well as malnutrition, may coexist with poor-quality diets. In 2005, the US Department of Agriculture developed a revised food pyramid, *MyPyramid,* with new Internet capabilities (US Department of Agriculture (USDA), 2005; http://nutrition.tufts.edu/docs/pdf/releases/ModifiedMyPyramid.pdf) to encourage Americans to make positive dietary behavioural changes. Lichtenstein *et al.* (2008) modified *MyPyramid* to be appropriate for older adults who might not be computer literate. *MyPyramid* is a diagrammatic representation of key foodstuffs (and the relative proportions they should form in a balanced diet) shaped in the form of a pyramid. It is based on the principles of the *Dietary Guidelines for Americans* (2005) and the WHO *Keep Fit for Life: Meeting the Nutritional Needs of Older Persons* (2002b), which stress the consumption of fruits, vegetables, whole grains, low- and non-fat dairy products, legumes, fish and lean meats. The pyramid is unique in that it includes advice on good choices of food, water consumption, and exercise recommendations in graphic design. Underlying (literally in the diagram) the foodstuffs is an emphasis on adequate fluid intake. Due to decreased thirst, chronic illnesses and medication use, many older adults become dehydrated. Approximately 1.5 per cent of community-dwelling older adults are hospitalized for dehydration every year (Reyes-Ortiz, 1997). Thus, *MyPyramid* includes 8 glasses of water to remind older adults to drink water every day. In addition, there is a row of recommended age-appropriate exercises to further emphasize the relationship between nutritional intake and energy expenditure. Finally, the flag on top of the pyramid alerts older adults that they may need additional vitamin supplements.

Older adults have some unique challenges to meeting their dietary needs. Many personal and environmental factors may influence food behaviours and health among older persons, even in developed countries. Personal factors include: (1) difficulty in chewing (e.g. loose or missing teeth), (2) medications that interact with food (e.g. Coumadin and foods high in vitamin K), (3) sensitivities to foods (e.g. lactose intolerance), (4) restrictions in ability to eat independently (e.g. stroke), (5) disease-related food restrictions (e.g. salt restrictions in hypertension), (6) mal-absorption (e.g. of vitamin B_{12}), (7) increased need for nutrients (e.g. pressure ulcer), and (8) loss of appetite (e.g. depression). Social and physical factors can also inter-fere with obtaining a high-quality diet. These include: (1) lack of adequate income, (2) lack of transportation, (3) lack of high-quality food choices in local area, (4) lack of refrigeration or cooking equipment, and (5) lack of social interac-tion during meals. Eating behaviours are influenced by very complex interactions among cultural, gender, personal and environmental determinants of health. The WHO (2002b) developed a set of principles that consider diet and health relation-ships within a cultural context (see Table 3.2).

Interventions

A panel of health-promotion experts reviewed the research on interventions that had been successful in changing health-promotion behaviours related to smoking, diet and exercise (Butler, 2000). They found that successful strategies included:

(1) self-regulatory skill training (e.g. realistic goal-setting, self-monitoring of tar-get health behaviours, use of feedback and social support, relapse prevention and preparation training)
(2) physicians who gave clear messages about the need to change behaviour with specific ways to implement change
(3) nurse-managed clinics that used proactive behavioural management strategies (e.g. collaborative patient-centred goal-setting, follow-up support, point-of-choice interventions with dietary information in grocery stores and restaurants, and policy/legislative strategies, such as no-smoking places and increased taxes on cigarettes).

The authors concluded that most research only evaluated short-term results and more information was needed about how to sustain behaviour changes over a long period of time, how to tailor interventions to age and risk, how to make health and

Table 3.2 Recommendations for food-based dietary guidelines that recognize the interactions between food and health within a social and cultural context

---

- Emphasize healthy traditional vegetable- and legume-based dishes.
- Limit traditional dishes/foods that are heavily preserved/pickled in salt and encourage the use of herbs and spices.
- Introduce healthy traditional foods or dishes from other cuisines (e.g. tofu in Europe and the tomato in Asia).
- Select nutrient-dense foods such as fish, lean meat, liver, eggs, soy products (e.g. tofu and tempeh) and low-fat dairy products, yeast-based products (e.g. spreads), fruits and vegetables, herbs and spices, whole-grain cereals, nuts and seeds.
- Consume fat from whole foods such as nuts, seeds, beans, olives and fatty fish. Where refined fats are necessary for cooking, select from a variety of liquid oils, including those high in ω-3 and ω-9 fats. Avoid fatty spreads.
- Enjoy food and eating in the company of others.
- Avoid the regular use of celebratory foods (e.g. ice cream, cakes and pastries in Western culture, confectioneries and candies in Malay culture, and crackling pork in Chinese culture).
- Encourage the food industry and fast-food chains to produce ready-made meals that are low in animal fats.
- Eat several (5–6) small non-fatty meals. This pattern appears to be associated with greater food variety and lower body fat and blood glucose and lipid levels, especially if larger meals are eaten early in the day.
- Transfer as much as possible of one's food culture, health knowledge and related skills to one's children, grandchildren and the wider community.

Source: World Health Organization (WHO) (2002b) *Keep fit for life: meeting the nutritional needs of older persons.* Geneva: WHO Press, p. 3. http://whqlibdoc.who.int/publications/9241562102.pdf. Reproduced by kind permission of the World Health Organization.

social systems more supportive of change, and how to enhance social and physical environments (Butler, 2000).

Environmental determinants (social, physical and economic)

Overall health can be influenced by multiple factors that are outside the individual older adult's control – chiefly, the physical, social and economic environments within which he or she lives. Poor social conditions, poor housing, isolation, poverty and poor education increase the likelihood of poor functional ability and increase the risk of disability and dependence on others (WHO, 1999).

Social support has been associated with reduced risk of physical disease, mental illness and mortality (Seeman, 2000). Social support includes real or perceived resources provided by others that enable a person to feel cared for, valued, and part of a network of communication and mutual obligation (Stroebe, 2000). Social support can be critical for older adults who, without the support of family, friends or organizations, would become socially isolated. Living alone, by itself, is not necessarily related to poor health. To maintain their health, older adults may need emotional support or assistance with ADL or IADL, especially as chronic diseases progress and disability increases. Older adults who are most vulnerable to poor health are those with lower levels of education, lower incomes, and poor social support. An analysis of data from agencies that provide social services to older adults found that visits with friends or relatives, having close friends for emotional support, and the perception of help being available if sick or disabled were associated with better health-related quality of life (HRQOL) and particularly with better mental health among older adults (CDC, 2005b). The sociology of ageing and social care of older persons is discussed in greater detail in Chapters 5 and 8.

Poverty is a powerful determinant of health which controls where older adults live, what they eat, where they shop, how much education they receive, their risks of chronic and infectious diseases, their access to medical care, and ultimately their physical and mental health, level of disability and life-expectancy. Lack of income can contribute to poor nutrition and homelessness, which in turn can contribute to greater poverty and ill health. Women are more likely to experience discrimination, to have lower incomes, and to be dependent on families for existence in countries where there is no social security scheme. Thus, policymakers must create supportive social and environmental conditions (WHO, 1999).

Poverty is responsible for a global housing crisis: 1.6 billion people live in substandard housing and 100 million are homeless (Kissick et al., 2006; Kothari, 2005). Thirty-two per cent of people in urban areas live in slums (with lack of water, lack of sanitation, overcrowding, non-durable structures and temporary availability) (Habitat for Humanity International, 2008). Up to 70 per cent of urban houses in sub-Saharan Africa, 50 per cent in South Asia, and 25 per cent in Latin America and the Caribbean are of poor quality and do not meet the local standards (Kissick et al., 2006). More than 14 million refugees and internally displaced people live in tents or other temporary shelters. Older adults who live in poverty are more likely to live in environmentally harmful neighbourhoods with exposure to toxic chemicals and air and water pollution. Older adults who are poor may find themselves living in overcrowded, poorly maintained houses, where they are more likely to experience falls and infections, or be victims of crimes or abuse. Clean, warm, safe housing is a prerequisite to good health and a right of all older adults (National Low Income Housing Coalition (NLIHC), 2004). Without a place to live, focusing on eating a healthy diet or increasing physical activities is futile.

Poverty is also responsible for the world hunger crisis with malnutrition at epidemic levels in developing countries. Although malnutrition is decreasing, WHO (1999) reported that 840 million people were still eating below the minimum nutritional threshold in the early 1990s. Older women are particularly vulnerable because they are likely to give their food to the children in the family (WHO, 1999). Causes of food insecurity include: (1) erratic weather, (2) rapid population growth, (3) high food prices, (4) changing agriculture practices, (5) changing eating habits, (6) poor food distribution and marketing systems, (7) low purchasing power, and (8) lack of appropriate knowledge and technology to deal with increasing needs (WHO, 2002b, p. 11). These factors, which are basic to good health and increased disability-free life expectancy, are beyond the control of individual older adults, and can only be improved through international cooperation. Public policies to ensure the production and distribution of food and a safety net to guarantee that older adults have food are essential to healthy ageing.

Health and social care determinants

To promote active ageing, health-care systems throughout the world must increase their focus on primary care that includes health promotion and disease prevention (WHO, 2002). Educating older people from every level of society about high-quality diets and increasing physical activity must occur if older adults are to experience a delay in the onset of chronic diseases (e.g. diabetes) and a reduction of excessive disability (e.g. hypertension). These changes would result in a higher quality of life and reduced costs to health-care systems. Vaccinating older people against infectious diseases can prevent suffering and save money. It is estimated that for every US$1 that is spent on influenza vaccinations, $30–60 is saved in treatment costs (USDHHS, 2000).

Most of the diseases faced by older people are chronic, and chronic diseases account for three-quarters of the total US health-care expenditures (Wagner, 2001). In developing countries, the ageing of the population places a 'double burden of disease' on health-care systems that are also trying to manage epidemics of infectious diseases and malnutrition among their populations (WHO, 2008). To be effective, health-care professionals must develop systems of care providing comprehensive, coordinated primary care that is easily accessible to older adults. The Chronic Care Model (CCM) identifies the essential elements of a health-care system that encourage high-quality chronic disease care (Wagner, 1998). In this model a chronic condition is characterized as 'any condition that requires ongoing adjustments by the affected person and interactions with the health care system'. The model has been developed to address common issues in the provision of health care to older adults – rushed practitioners, lack of evidence-based guidelines, lack of care coordination, lack of follow-up, and lack of educated, involved patients. The CCM addresses these issues through the interactions between the community, the health-care system, self-management support, delivery system design, decision support and clinical information systems (Wagner, 1998). The model has been successfully implemented in rural, underserved areas in the USA (Sixta and

Ostwald, 2008), and evaluations by RAND have demonstrated that patients have fewer risk factors for chronic illness, they have higher-quality treatment of their chronic illnesses, and the older adults are more knowledgeable about their chronic conditions (RAND Corporation, 2008).

The WHO developed an expanded CCM, designed to be more relevant to low- and middle-income countries (WHO, 2002c). The Integrative Care for Chronic Conditions (ICCC) framework is organized around a partnership between the patient, health-care team, and the community that functions within a positive policy environment. Older adults especially need primary care clinics that are easily accessible with large and easily readable signs, well-lit hallways and examination rooms, and waiting areas large enough to accommodate walking aids and additional family members. Most importantly, staff members need to be trained to be aware of the common sensory deficits experienced by older adults (particularly vision and hearing) and treat older adults with respect. Health-care facilities should be readily accessible with parking adjacent to the entry (WHO, 2004). Policies which benefit people who already have disabilities (e.g. public transport, legislation, structural changes to buildings, etc.) can do much to improve quality of life (WHO, 1999).

Promoting the health of older caregivers

In all societies of the world, women are more likely to be both caregivers and care-recipients. Men provide only about 25 per cent of the caregiving occurring within families (National Alliance for Caregiving (NAC) and AARP, 1997). Providing care to others extends throughout the life of most women, moving from caring for children, to caring for older relatives, to caring for spouses, and finally to caring for grandchildren. Grandmothers are often the primary caregivers for their grandchildren, releasing mothers and fathers to work, or in some cases replacing parents who have died from epidemics (e.g. HIV/AIDS) (WHO, 1999), or who are unavailable or unable to provide care due to illness or incarceration. Because women have greater longevity than men, they are the major caregivers for their spouses. When they become frail and need care, they often are widowed and therefore dependent on family members or institutions for their care (Velkoff and Lawson, 1998). At least 90 per cent of older adults are cared for by family members in their homes. Very small proportions of the oldest-old people (1–10 per cent) actually live in institutions in developed countries and under 1 per cent in developing countries. The ability to care for older people in the community is based on the presence of caregivers, primarily wives and adult daughters. The parent support ratio, the number of oldest old (aged 80 and over) per 100 people aged 50–64, is projected to increase, especially in developed countries, as life expectancy increases (Velkoff and Lawson, 1998).

The problems encountered by older women caregivers are well documented, with older spouses experiencing more physical and psychological distress than adult children who provide care for parents. Older caregivers are at increased risk of neglecting their own health because of their caregiving responsibilities. They are less likely to pursue health-promoting behaviours, such as getting enough sleep, exercising and taking medications, and are also less likely to take time away from caring to obtain preventive care (Burton, Newsom, Schulz *et al.*, 1997; Connell, 1994; O'Brien, 1993). In addition, older women caregivers experience high rates of depression, anxiety and physical distress, have chronic illnesses that are often exacerbated by caregiving, and are at higher risk of death than non-caregivers (Franzén-Dahlin, Larson, Murray *et al.*, 2007; Schultz and Beach, 1999; Schulz, Newsom, Mittelmark *et al.*, 1997; National Alliance for Caregiving (NAC) and AARP, 1997).

Older women caregivers are affected by all of the determinants of health that have been previously discussed. Because of their added burden of caring for others, they may experience additional personal barriers to the pursuit of health promotion and disease prevention (Ostwald, 2009). Caregivers experience competing demands for time and energy, which are exacerbated when the care demands are complex and time-consuming. O'Brien (1993) reported a significant inverse relationship between the care-recipient's level of dependency and the caregiver's health-promoting behaviours. A strong sense of obligation and responsibility to provide care for another person may result in feelings of guilt if caregivers participate in health promotion and disease prevention activities, especially if these activities entail leaving the care-recipient at home (Coombs, 2007). In normal marital relationships, spousal support has been shown to have the greatest social influence on the pursuit of a healthy lifestyle (Tucker, 2002). However, in the caregiving situation, care-receivers may be emotionally, cognitively or psychologically unable to provide support to their spouse. In addition, caregivers of older adults often have smaller social networks and less social support than caregivers of children (Ostwald, Leonard, Choi *et al.*, 1993) so there may be relatively few other individuals available for support. This makes it difficult for older caregivers to find high-quality substitute care that is available and affordable. Figure 3.5 presents a force-field analysis of the barriers and facilitators that influence an older spousal caregiver's ability to engage in health-promoting behaviours.

In spite of the difficulties faced by older women who are providing care to others, many continue in the caregiving role for long periods of time and report rewards and personal satisfaction even in difficult situations. Caregivers who are supported by their own inner strength and provide care within a supportive environment are

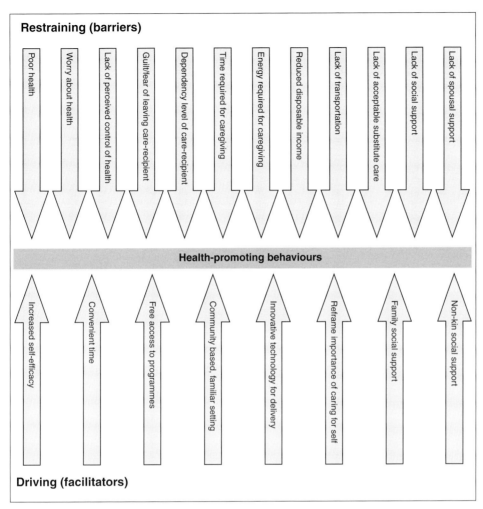

Figure 3.5 Force-field analysis of restraining and driving factors that influence an older spousal caregiver's decision to engage in health-promoting behaviours. *Source:* Ostwald (2009). Reproduced by kind permission of Wolters Kluwer Publishers.

most likely to have positive health outcomes. Resilience and a sense of coherence allow women to adapt to changing situations without losing their own self-identity. Resilient older adults are able to maintain social roles and activities that have previously brought them pleasure, rely on tried and tested coping strategies, maintain a sense of control over their lives, and have close supportive relationships with others (Hildon, Smith, Netuveli *et al.*, 2008). Resilience is strongly correlated with a sense of coherence, which has been identified as an important characteristic of caregivers who find satisfaction in the role. A sense of coherence has three dimensions, as described by Antonovsky (1987):

(1) comprehensibility (the extent to which a situation is perceived as cognitively meaningful and predictable)
(2) manageability (the degree to which resources are perceived to be sufficient to meet internal and external demands)
(3) meaningfulness (the degree to which life is viewed as emotionally meaningful and some problems are perceived as challenges rather than hindrances)

A sense of coherence has been shown to correlate positively with health (Callahan and Pincus, 1995), hope (Coward, 1996), and hardiness (Williams, 1990). Caregivers who are able to persevere in at-home caregiving roles have been shown to have resilience and are less likely to institutionalize their care-recipients (Gaugler, Kane and Newcomer, 2007).

A supportive environment has also been shown to foster positive health behaviours among older caregivers. Family and friends influence the extent to which older caregivers pursue health-promoting behaviours. Higher levels of perceived social support are associated with better health practices and better health outcomes (Monahan and Hooker, 1995). A supportive environment empowers older caregivers, provides family support and fosters choice (Hooyman and Gonyea, 1999). It thus goes beyond the role of the individual or the family. Caregiving is a complex issue that affects an older woman's health and economic security. It should not be seen as merely an individual responsibility that absolves communities and governments of any responsibility to care for the dependent segments of society, and makes caregiving an individual rather than a societal expense (Weitz and Estes, 2001).

Current interventions directed at caregivers have primarily focused on understanding and managing the behaviours of the care-recipient, not on the caregiver's health (Wright, Hickey, Buckwalter et al., 1999). Caregiving spouses, who are primarily older women, have poorer health, report more caregiving strain, have lower incomes and smaller social networks, and have not shown as positive a set of responses to traditional interventions as younger caregivers (Sörensen, Pinquart and Duberstein, 2002). Interventions need to be developed that focus on helping women integrate health promotion and preventive behaviours into their everyday lives, building supportive social networks, and accessing low-cost community resources. In addition, interventions must focus on the interplay between medical, social, and economic factors that place women caregivers in jeopardy of poor health and economic outcomes. This can only be accomplished through concerted pressure on communities and governments so that health-care problems are not solved by placing a disproportionate burden of caregiving on older women. 'Caregiving of older adults is not a private trouble nor individual stress, but a public or societal responsibility that demands a collective response for enhancing the quality of life of both the caregiver and receiver' (Hooyman and Gonyea, 1999, p. 168).

Conclusions and future trends

The population of older adults is increasing worldwide, with the increase occurring most rapidly in developing countries. The average life expectancy for women in most developed countries is approximately 80 years of age, with men lagging a few years behind. However, the average life expectancy for men is increasing faster than for women so that the gap between sexes is beginning to narrow, especially in the oldest-old populations. Nevertheless, there is still a gap between the estimated maximum lifespan (120 years) and the average life expectancy (80 years). Advances in public health and medicine resulted in impressive increases in life expectancy over the first half of the twentieth century, but the increases have slowed in spite of technological advances in health care. Little is known about whether it is possible to increase the maximum lifespan beyond approximately 120 years, or what would be the implications of such an increase in terms of the ability of the Earth to sustain a dramatically larger population.

Reaching old age in good health is an important goal for the twenty-first century. Vast differences in the prevalence of disease and disability exist among older adults throughout the world. Disease, disability and premature death are related to lifelong interactions between each individual's genetic make-up, environmental exposures, and physical and psychological reactions to those exposures. A major objective of all countries is to delay the onset of chronic disease, referred to as compression of morbidity, so that disability-free life expectancy is increased. Currently in the USA it is estimated that one-third of life expectancy after age 65 will be spent in dependency, with older adults needing to rely on others for assistance in ADL. However, the prevalence of chronic disability is decreasing in developed countries so that older adults will have more years of disability-free life expectancy over age 65. If this trend continues, older people can expect to be living longer with better health in the latter part of the twenty-first century.

The world is undergoing a rapid change in the patterns of disease. Chronic diseases account for approximately 70 per cent of the deaths in developed countries and are quickly becoming the major causes of morbidity and mortality in developing countries. The rapid shift has created a 'double burden of disease' in developing countries, which are simultaneously dealing with epidemics of infectious and chronic illnesses. The burden of chronic disease can be reduced through cost-effective primary, secondary and tertiary disease-prevention strategies. By identifying older people who are 'at risk' but do not yet have a disease, health education, immunizations and environmental safeguards can be put in place to reduce risks and keep older people healthier longer. Secondary prevention focuses on using community screenings and clinical prevention practices to identify older people who have asymptomatic disease. These diseases can be treated early and older adults can be taught to manage their chronic diseases, thus avoiding long-term disability. Even when high-quality, accessible, affordable systems of care are available to provide disease prevention services, some people will develop chronic diseases that progress and result in disability. Even at this level, there is a role for prevention. Tertiary prevention strategies are aimed at minimizing disability and restoring maximum function to the individual. This is achieved thorough the provision of quality, curative and rehabilitative care, referrals to support groups, community action to eliminate environmental barriers, and support of family caregivers.

The maintenance of health and management of chronic diseases demand a significant amount of attention, time and energy from older adults. Self-reported health perceptions have been shown to be excellent predictors of health. Older adults who are poor, uneducated, and from minority groups generally perceive their health to be worse. Perceptions of health also decrease with age. People who perceive that they have only fair to poor health are more likely to die within the following 3 years than are people who perceive their health to be very good or excellent. Older adults who perceive that their health is good are more likely to pursue good health practices and obtain preventive services.

It is estimated that approximately 50 per cent of the chronic diseases in the world could be eliminated, or at least postponed if people changed their lifestyles. Poor diet, lack of exercise, tobacco smoking and alcohol abuse are the major culprits in the cause of chronic diseases. While lifestyles are difficult to change, it is never too late for older adults to make health-promoting behavioural changes. Comprehensive health-promotion interventions that include clear messages from health professionals, self-regulatory skill training, follow-up monitoring, and peer and family support have demonstrated success in reducing risk factors in older adults, at least in the short term. Health promotion goes beyond the prevention of disease and disability and aims to improve a person's well-being by focusing on empowerment of populations, building resilience, accessing resources, and implementing political processes to support health.

Resilience is an important component of healthy ageing. It means that older people are able to maintain their integrity, view their life as one with purpose, continue involvement with others around them, and maintain their ability to adapt to changing circumstances. Resilience is not culture-bound and does not decrease with age. Resilience is one of the factors that allow older adults to persist in caring for spouses, ill relatives and grandchildren for years in spite of the personal sacrifices. It is associated with hardiness, positive spirituality and a sense of coherence that allows older adults to view life as meaningful and manageable, regardless of the circumstances. More needs to be learned about the development and maintenance of resilience. It is thought that it probably begins in early life in the interactions between biology and stress. There is a need for much more trans-disciplinary research in this area to better understand how societies may nurture resilience in their citizens.

Healthy ageing, however, does not exist in a vacuum and is not purely an individual responsibility. Social, physical and economic environments play an important role in the level of health that any population can attain. The lack of supportive environments is associated with poor physical and mental health, higher rates of disability and premature deaths. Social support from family, friends and community agencies is essential to helping older people feel loved, cared for and a part of a community. However, many factors, such as poverty, are beyond the control of any one individual or family and must be addressed through the collaborative efforts of community organizations, governments, private sector corporations, and international bodies. Poverty is a powerful determinant of health and is responsible for an epidemic of malnutrition and homelessness worldwide. Public policies are necessary to ensure that older adults live in an environment that supports independence, positive health practices and access to high-quality, affordable and accessible primary health care. As the population of the world lives longer, the quest is also to live better. At a minimum, living better means being able to care for one's own everyday needs, having a clean, safe place to live, having enough food to eat, and being involved in interesting activities with other people. Many older people in the world have not yet achieved these goals. Two directions hold promise for improving the lives of older adults in the twenty-first century – improvement of lifestyles and implementation of public policies that guarantee a safe and healthy environment in which to age.

Summary

One way of considering successful ageing is through the concept of resilience (the ability to recover from stressful conditions), which is related to many indices of health and activity in older adults. The factors underlying resilience are explored. Significantly related to this is self-reported health, which is generally well correlated with actual health status. In seeking to improve the health status of older adults, a key issue is increasing life expectancy, which still lags far behind the maximum theoretical lifespan, and factors underlying this gap are explored. Of key importance in lessening the gap is prevention (primary, secondary and tertiary); this chapter concentrates particularly on primary prevention (generalized health promotion and specific protection against diseases). Methods of doing this include screening and health promotion, which are discussed. However, older people who are the recipients of this prevention are not blank slates, and there are pre-existing factors that play a key role, such as culture, gender, personal and behavioural determinants, level and type of physical activity, and nutrition. Intervention is thus a complex issue, made yet more complicated by environmental and health and social care determinants. Informed by this information, the chapter concludes by presenting an overview and discussing future trends.

REFERENCES

Administration on Aging (2007) *Profile of older Americans: 2007*. Bethesda, MD: US Department of Health and Human Services.

Agency for Health Care Policy and Quality (AHRQ) and AARP (2006) *Staying healthy at 50+*. AHRQ Publication No. 081P003-A, AARP Publication No. C2456.

American Academy of Family Physicians (2007) *Summary of recommendations for clinical preventive services. Revision 6.4.*

American Cancer Society (2008) *Cancer facts & figures 2008*. Atlanta, GA: American Cancer Society; Revised 03/05/2008.

Andersen-Ranberg, K., Christensen, K., Jeune, B. *et al.* (1999) Declining physical abilities with age: a cross-sectional study of older twins and centenarians in Denmark, *Age and Ageing*, *28*(4), 373–7.

Antonovsky, H. (1987) *Unraveling the mystery of health: how people manage stress and stay well*. San Francisco: Jossey-Bass.

Antonovsky, H. and Sagy, S. (1986) The development of a sense of coherence and its impact on responses to stress situations, *Journal of Social Psychology*, *126*(1), 213–25.

Aroian, K.J. and Norris, A.E. (2000) Resilience, stress, and depression among Russian immigrants to Israel, *Western Journal of Nursing Research*, *22*(1), 54–67.

Associated Press (2007, March 1) *Life expectancy rises even higher in Japan: women born there can expect to live 85-plus years*. Retrieved 3 January 2009, from www.msnbc.msn.com/id/17406997/.

Baltes, P.B. (1997) On the incomplete architecture of human ontogeny. Selection, optimization, and compensation as foundation of developmental theory, *American Psychologist*, *52*(4), 366–80.

Bauer, T. and Barron, C.R. (1995) Nursing interventions for spiritual care: preferences of the community-based elderly, *Journal of Holistic Nursing*, *13*(3), 268–79.

Becker, M.H. (ed.). (1974) *The health belief model and personal health behavior*. Thorofare, NJ: Charles B. Slack.

Bernard, S.L., Kincade, J.E., Konrad, T.R. *et al.* (1997) Predicting mortality from community surveys of older adults: the importance of self-rated functional ability, *Journals of Gerontology. Series B, Psychological Sciences and Social Sciences*, *52*(3), S155–63.

Breslow, L. and Breslow, N. (1993) Health practices and disability: some evidence from Alameda County, *Preventive Medicine*, *22*(1), 86–95.

Burton, L.C., Newsom, J.T., Schulz, R. *et al.* (1997) Preventive health behaviors among spousal caregivers, *Preventive Medicine*, *26*(2), 162–9.

Butler, R.N. (2000) *Maintaining healthy lifestyles: a lifetime of choices*. Workshop Report of the International Longevity Center, USA, Ltd. Retrieved 31 December 2008 from www.ilcusa.org/media/pdfs/health.pdf.

Callahan, L.F. and Pincus, T. (1995) The Sense of Coherence Scale in patients with rheumatoid arthritis, *Arthritis Care and Research*, *8*(1), 28–35.

Canadian Minister of National Health and Welfare (1974) *A new perspective on the health of Canadians (Lalonde Report)*. Ottawa: Department of National Health and Welfare.

Centers for Disease Control and Prevention (CDC) (2005a) *Behavioral Risk Factor Surveillance System (BRFSS)*. Retrieved 28 December 2008 from www.cdc.gov/brfss/index.htm.

   (2005b) Social support and health-related quality of life among older adults – Missouri, 2000, *MMWR. Morbidity and Mortality Weekly Report*, *54*(17), 433–7.

   (2007) *Preventing injuries in America: public health action*. Retrieved 30 December 2008 from www.cdc.gov/ncipc/fact_book/Preventing%20Injuries%20in%20America%20Public%20Health%20in%20Action-2006.pdf.

   (2008) *Shingles (herpes zoster) vaccination*. Retrieved 5 January 2008 from www.cdc.gov/vaccines/vpd-vac/shingles/default.htm.

Centers for Disease Control and Prevention (CDC) and the Merck Company Foundation (2007) *The state of aging and health in America 2007*. Whitehouse Station, NJ: Merck Company Foundation.

Christopher, K.A. (2000) Determinants of psychological well-being in Irish immigrants. *Western Journal of Nursing Research*, *22*(2), 123–40.

Chronic Disease Prevention Alliance in Canada (CDPAC) (2006) *An action framework for primary prevention of chronic diseases in Canada*. Ottawa: CDPAC.

   (2007) *Food security in Canada: a leadership opportunity towards health promotion and reduction in chronic disease*. Ottawa: CDPAC.

Connell, C.M. (1994) Impact of spouse caregiving on health behaviors and physical and mental health status, *American Journal of Alzheimer's Disease and Other Dementias*, *9*(1), 26–36.

Coombs, U.E. (2007) Spousal caregiving for stroke survivors, *Journal of Neuroscience Nursing*, *39*(2), 112–19.

Coward, D.D. (1990) The lived experience of self-transcendence in women with advanced breast cancer, *Nursing Science Quarterly*, *3*(4), 162–9.

   (1996) Self-transcendence and correlates in a healthy population, *Nursing Research*, *45*(2), 116–21.

Crowther, M.R., Parker, M.W., Achenbaum, W.A. *et al.* (2002) Rowe and Kahn's model of successful aging revisited: positive spirituality – the forgotten factor, *The Gerontologist*, *42*(5), 613–20.

Demura, S., Sato, S., Minami, M. *et al.* (2003) Gender and age differences in basic ADL ability in the elderly: comparison between the independent and the dependent elderly, *Journal of Physiological Anthropology and Applied Human Science*, *22*(1), 19–27.

DiPietro, L. (2001) Physical activity in aging: changes in patterns and their relationship to health and function, *Journals of Gerontology. Series A, Biological Sciences and Medical Sciences*, *56A*(2), 13–21.

Dyer, J.G. and McGuinness, T.M. (1996) Resilience: analysis of the concept, *Archives of Psychiatric Nursing*, *10*(5), 276–82.

Ervin, R.B. (2008) Healthy Eating Index scores among adults, 60 years of age and over, by sociodemographic and health characteristics: United States, 1999–2002, *Advance Data*, *395*, 1–16.

Field, M.J., Jette, A.M. and Institute of Medicine (IOM) (2007) *The future of disability in America*. Washington, DC: National Academies Press.

Franzén-Dahlin, A., Larson, J., Murray, V. *et al.* (2007) Predictors of psychological health in spouses of persons affected by stroke, *Journal of Clinical Nursing*, *16*(5), 885–91.

Fries, J.F. (1983) The compression of morbidity, *Milbank Memorial Fund Quarterly. Health and Society*, *61*, 397–419.

Fries, J.F., Green, L.W. and Levine, S. (1989) Health promotion and the compression of morbidity, *Lancet*, *1*(8636), 481–3.

Froom, P. and Benbassat, J. (2000) Inconsistencies in the classification of preventive interventions, *Preventive Medicine*, *31*(2 Pt 1), 153–8.

Gaugler, J.E., Kane, R.L. and Newcomer, R. (2007) Resilience and transitions from dementia caregiving, *Journals of Gerontology. Series B, Psychological Sciences and Social Sciences*, *62B*(1), 38–44.

The Guardian (2008, 11 February). *No country for old men*. Retrieved 3 January 2009, from www.guardian.co.uk/world/2008/feb/11/russia.

Habitat for Humanity International (2008) *International Statistics and Research*. Retrieved 4 January 2009, from www.habitat.org/how/why/intl_stats_research.aspx.

Hardy, S.E., Concato, J. and Gill, T.N. (2004) Resilience of community-dwelling older persons, *Journal of the American Geriatrics Society*, *52*(2), 257–62.

Harris, P.B. (2008) Another wrinkle in the debate about successful aging: the undervalued concept of resilience and the lived experience of dementia, *International Journal of Aging and Human Development*, *67*(1), 43–61.

Hayflick, L. (1980) The cell biology of human aging, *Scientific American*, *242*(1), 58–65.
   (2007) Biological aging is no longer an unsolved problem, *Annals of the New York Academy of Sciences*, *1100*, 1–13.

Hildon, Z., Smith, G., Netuveli, G. *et al.*, (2008) Understanding adversity and resilience at older ages, *Sociology of Health and Illness*, *30*(5), 726–40.

Hooyman, N.R. and Gonyea, J.G. (1999) A feminist model of family care: practice and policy directions, *Journal of Women and Aging*, *11*(2–3), 149–69.

Hughes, S.L., Williams, B., Molina, L.C. *et al.* (2005) Characteristics of physical activity programs for older adults: results of a multisite survey, *The Gerontologist*, *45*(5), 667–75.

Hunt, K. and Annandale, E. (1999) Relocating gender and morbidity: examining men's and women's health in contemporary Western societies. Introduction to Special Issue on Gender and Health, *Social Science and Medicine*, *48*(1), 1–5.

Institute of Medicine (IOM) (1990) *The second fifty years: promoting health and preventing disability*. Washington, DC: National Academy Press.

Kesteloot, H., Sans, S. and Krombout, D. (2002) Evolution of all-causes and cardiovascular mortality in the age-group 75–84 years in Europe during the period 1970–1996; a comparison with worldwide changes, *European Heart Journal*, *23*(5), 384–98.

Kissick, D., Leibson, D., Kogul, M. *et al.* (2006) *Housing for all: essential for economic, social, and civic development: a 28-page manuscript prepared for the World Urban Forum III*. Vancouver: PADCO/AECOM in collaboration with the International Housing Coalition.

Klaas, D. (1998) Testing two elements of spirituality in depressed and non-depressed elders, *International Journal of Psychiatric Nursing Research*, *4*(2), 452–62.

Kothari, M. (2005, 5 November) *UN press briefing by Special Rapporteur on Right to Adequate Housing*. Retrieved 31 December 2008 from www.un.org/News/briefings/docs/2005/kotharibrf050511.doc.htm.

Lavizzo-Mourey, R., Day, S.C., Diserens, D. *et al.* (1989). *Practicing prevention for the elderly*. Philadelphia: Hanley & Belfus.

Leavell, H.R. and Clark, E.G. (1965) *Preventive medicine for the doctor in his community: an epidemiologic approach*, 3rd edn. New York: McGraw-Hill.

Lichtenstein, A.H., Rasmussen, H., Yu, W.W. *et al.* (2008) Modified *MyPyramid* for older adults, *Journal of Nutrition*, *138*(1), 5–11.

Luthar, S.S. and Brown, P.J. (2007) Maximizing resilience through diverse levels of inquiry: prevailing paradigms, possibilities, and priorities for the future, *Development and Psychopathology*, *19*(3), 931–55.

Lynch, J.W., Smith, G.D., Kaplan, G.A. *et al.* (2000) Income inequality and mortality: importance to health of individual income, psychosocial environment, or material conditions, *British Medical Journal*, *320*(7243), 1200–4.

Maddi, S.R. (2002) The story of hardiness: twenty years of theorizing, research and practice, *Consulting Psychology Journal*, *54*(3), 173–85.

Manton, K.G. and Gu X.L. (2001) Changes in the prevalence of chronic disability in the United States black and nonblack population above age 65 from 1982 to 1999, *Proceedings of the National Academy of Sciences of the USA*, *98*(11), 6354–9.

Marenberg, M.E., Risch, N., Berkman, L.F. *et al.* (1994) Genetic susceptibility to death from coronary heart disease in a study of twins, *New England Journal of Medicine. 330*(15), 1041–6.

Mayhew, M.S. and Edmunds, M. (eds) (2005) Chapter 3: Health care issues Tables 2 and 3. In *Gerontological nurse practitioner: review and resource manual*, 2nd edn. Silver Spring, MD: American Nurses Credentialing Center, Institute for Credentialing Innovation, 36–41.

Menec, V.H., Chipperfield, J.G. and Perry, R.P. (1999) Self-perceptions of health: a prospective analysis of mortality, control, and health, *Journals of Gerontology. Series B, Psychological Sciences and Social Sciences*, *54*(2), P85–93.

Meunier, P.J. (1999) Calcium, vitamin D and vitamin K in the prevention of fractures due to osteoporosis, *Osteoporosis International*, *9*(Suppl. 2), S48–52.

Monahan, D.J. and Hooker, K. (1995) Health of spouse caregivers of dementia patients: the role of personality and social support, *Social Work*, *40*(3), 305–14.

Montross, L.P., Depp, C., Daly, J. *et al.* (2006) Correlates of self-rated successful aging among community-dwelling older adults, *American Journal of Geriatric Psychiatry*, *14*(1), 43–51.

National Alliance for Caregiving (NAC) and American Association of Retired Persons (AARP) (1997) *Family caregiving in the US: findings from a national survey – final report.* Washington, DC: NAC/AARP.

National Institute on Aging (NIA) (2008) *Exercise: a guide from the National Institute on Aging.* Bethesda, MD: NIH.

National Institutes of Health (NIH) Consensus Statement (1995) Optimal calcium intake. Sponsored by National Institutes of Health Continuing Medical Education, *Nutrition, 11*(5), 409–17.

National Low Income Housing Coalition (NLIHC) (2004) *America's neighbors: the affordable housing crisis and the people it affects.* Retrieved 1 January 2008 from www.studentsagainsthunger.org/americas_neighbors.pdf.

Nesbitt, B.J. and Heidrich, S.M. (2000) Sense of coherence and illness appraisal in older women's quality of life, *Research in Nursing and Health*, *23*(1), 25–34.

Noh, S., Beiser, M., Kaspar, V. *et al.* (1999) Perceived racial discrimination, depression, and coping: a study of Southeast Asian refugees in Canada, *Journal of Health and Social Behavior*, *40*(3), 193–207.

Nygren, B., Alex, L., Jonsen, E. *et al.* (2005) Resilience, sense of coherence, purpose in life and self-transcendence in relation to perceived physical and mental health among the oldest old, *Aging and Mental Health*, *9*(4), 354–62.

O'Brien, M.T. (1993) Multiple sclerosis: health-promoting behaviors of spousal caregivers, *Journal of Neuroscience Nursing*, *25*(2), 105–12.

Ostwald, S.K. (2009) Who is caring for the caregiver? Promoting spousal caregiver's health, *Family and Community Health*, *32*(1 Suppl.), 5–14.

Ostwald, S.K., Leonard B., Choi, T. *et al.* (1993) Caregivers of frail elderly and medically fragile children: perceptions of ability to continue to provide home health care, *Home Health Care Services Quarterly*, *14*(1), 55–80.

Pender, N.J., Murdaugh, C.L. and Parsons, M.A. (2006) *Health promotion in nursing practice*, 5th edn. Upper Saddle River, NJ: Prentice-Hall.

Perls, T.T., Bubrick, E., Wagner, C.G. *et al.* (1998) Siblings of centenarians live longer, *Lancet*, *351*(9115), 1560–5.

Phillips, A.C., Burns, V.E. and Lord, J.M. (2007) Stress and exercise: getting the balance right for aging immunity, *Exercise and Sport Sciences Reviews*, *35*(1), 35–9.

Prigerson, H.G., Maciejewski, P.K. and Rosenheck, R.A. (2000) Preliminary explorations of the harmful interactive effects of widowhood and marital harmony on health, health service use, and health care costs, *The Gerontologist*, *40*(3), 349–57.

RAND Corporation (2003) Evidence report and evidence-based recommendations: falls prevention interventions in the Medicare population. Retrieved 30 December 2008 from www.rand.org/pubs/reprints/2007/RAND_RP1230.sum.pdf.

(2008) Improving illness care evaluation: a RAND health project. Retrieved 28 December 2008 from www.rand.org/health/projects/icice/findings.html.

Reed, P.G. (1991) Self-transcendence and mental health in oldest-old adults, *Nursing Research*, *40*(1), 5–11.

Reyes-Ortiz, C.A. (1997) Dehydration, delirium, and disability in elderly patients, *Journal of the American Medical Association*, *278*(4), 287–8.

Rowe, J.W. (1990) Toward successful aging: limitation of the morbidity associated with 'normal' aging, in *Principles of geriatric medicine and gerontology*, 2nd edn. New York: McGraw-Hill, 1388–1410.

Rowe, J.W. and Kahn, R.L. (1987) Human aging: usual and successful, *Science*, *237*(4811), 143–9.

(1997) Successful aging, *The Gerontologist*, *37*(4), 433–40.

(2000) Successful aging and disease prevention, *Advances in Renal Replacement Therapy*, *7*(1), 70–7.

Schulz, R. and Beach, S.R. (1999) Caregiving as a risk factor for mortality: the Caregiver Health Effects Study, *Journal of the American Medical Association*, *282*(23), 2215–19.

Schulz, R., Newsom, J., Mittelmark, M. *et al.* (1997) Health effects of caregiving: the caregiver health effects study: an ancillary study of the Cardiovascular Health Study, *Annals of Behavioral Medicine*, *19*(2), 110–16.

Seeman, T.E. (2000) Health promoting effects of friends and family on health outcomes in older adults, *American Journal of Health Promotion*, *14*(6), 362–70.

Shin, Y., Yun, S., Pender, N.J. *et al.* (2005) Test of the health promotion model as a causal model of commitment to a plan for exercise among Korean adults with chronic disease, *Research in Nursing and Health*, *28*(2), 117–25.

Sixta, C.S. and Ostwald, S.K. (2008) Strategies for implementing a promotores-led diabetes self-management program into a clinic structure, *The Diabetes Educator*, *34*(2), 285–98.

Sörensen, S., Pinquart, M. and Duberstein P. (2002) How effective are interventions with caregivers? An updated meta-analysis, *The Gerontologist*, *42*(3), 356–72.

Spalding, M.C. and Sebasta, S.C. (2008) Geriatric screening and preventive care, *American Family Physician*, *78*(2), 206–15.

Ståhle, A., Nordlander, R. and Bergfeldt, L. (1999) Aerobic group training improves exercise capacity and heart rate variability in elderly patients with a recent coronary event. A randomized controlled study, *European Heart Journal*, *20*(22), 1638–46.

Staudinger, U.M., Marsiske, M. and Baltes, P.B. (1993) Resilience and levels of reserve capacity in later adulthood: perspectives from lifespan theory, *Development and Psychopathology*, *5*(4), 541–66.

Stein, Y. (1994) Comparison of European and USA guidelines for prevention of coronary heart disease, *Atherosclerosis*, *110*, S41–4.

Strawbridge, W.J., Wallhagen, M.I. and Cohen, R.D. (2002) Successful aging and well-being: self-rated compared with Rowe and Kahn, *The Gerontologist*, *42*(6), 727–33.

Stroebe, W. (2000) Moderators of the stress–health relationship. In *Social psychology and health*. Philadelphia: Open University Press, 236–73.

Tornstam, L. (1997) Gerotranscendence: the contemplative dimension of aging, *Journal of Aging Studies*, *11*(2), 143–54.

Tucker, J.S. (2002) Health-related social control within older adults' relationships, *Journals of Gerontology. Series B, Psychological Sciences and Social Sciences*, *57B*(5), 387–95.

US Department of Agriculture (USDA) (2005) *MyPyramid tracker*. Alexandria, VA: USDA Center for Nutrition Policy and Health Promotion. Retrieved 1 January 2009 from www.mypyramidtracker.gov/.

US Department of Health and Human Services (USDHHS) (2000) *Healthy people 2010: understanding and improving health*. Retrieved 27 December 2008 from www.healthypeople.gov/.

US Department of Health and Human Services (USDHHS) and US Department of Agriculture (USDA) (2005) *Dietary guidelines for Americans*. Retrieved 31 December 2008 from www.healthierus.gov/dietaryguidelines/.

United States Preventive Services Task Force (USPSTF) *Guide to clinical preventive services*. Agency for Health Care Policy and Quality (AHRQ). Retrieved 7 January 2009 from www.ahrq.gov/clinic/cps3dix.htm.

Upchurch, S. (1999) Self-transcendence and activities of daily living. The woman with the pink slippers, *Journal of Holistic Nursing*, *17*(3), 251–66.

Variyam, J.N., Blaylock, J., Smallwood, D. *et al*. (1998) *USDA's Healthy Eating Index and nutrition information*. Washington, DC: US Department of Agriculture. Retrieved 2 January 2008 from www.ers.usda.gov/publications/TB1866/TB1866.PDF.

Vaupel, J.W., Carey, J.R., Christensen, K. *et al*. (1998) Biodemographic trajectories of longevity, *Science*, *280*(5365), 855–60.

Velkoff, V.A. and Lawson, V.A. (1998) *International brief: gender and aging – caregiving*. Washington, DC: US Department of Commerce, Economics and Statistics Administration, US Bureau of the Census.

von Faber, M., Bootsma-van der Wiel, A., van Exel, E. *et al*. (2001) Successful aging in the oldest old: who can be characterized as successfully aged?, *Archives of Internal Medicine*, *161*(22), 2694–3700.

Wagner, E. H. (1998) Chronic disease management: what will it take to improve care for chronic illness?, *Effective Clinical Practice*, *1*(1), 2–4.

(2001) Meeting the needs of chronically ill people, *British Medical Journal*, *323*(7319), 945–6.

Wagnild, G. (2003) Resilience and successful aging. Comparison among low and high income older adults, *Journal of Gerontological Nursing*, *29*(12), 42–9.

Wagnild, G. and Young, H.M. (1990) Resilience among older women, *IMAGE: Journal of Nursing Scholarship*, *22*(4), 252–5.

Weber, P. (1999) The role of vitamins in the prevention of osteoporosis – a brief status report, *International Journal for Vitamin and Nutrition Research*, *69*(3), 194–7.

Weiner, J.M., Hanley, R.J., Clark, R. *et al.* (1990) Measuring the activities of daily living: comparisons across national surveys, *Journal of Gerontology*, *45*(6), S229–37.

Weitz, T. and Estes, C.L. (2001) Adding aging and gender to the women's health agenda, *Journal of Women and Aging*, *13*(2), 3–20.

Whitehead, D. (2008) Book review of *Health Promotion in Nursing Practice*, 5th edn. *Journal of Clinical Nursing*, *17*(1), 144.

Williams, S.J. (1990) The relationship among stress, hardiness, sense of coherence, and illness in critical care nurses, *Medical Psychotherapy: An International Journal*, *3*, 171–86.

Windle, G., Markland, D.A. and Woods, R.T. (2008) Examination of a theoretical model of psychological resilience in older age, *Aging and Mental Health*, *12*(3), 285–92.

World Health Organization (1986) *The Ottawa Charter for Health Promotion*. Copenhagen, Denmark: World Health Organization Press.

World Health Organization (1996) *World health report 1996*. Geneva: World Health Organization Press.

(1998) *Growing older and staying well: ageing and physical activity in everyday life*. Geneva: World Health Organization Press.

(1999) *Ageing: exploring the myths*. Geneva: World Health Organization Press.

(2001) *The International Classification of Function, Disability and Health (ICF)*. Geneva: World Health Organization Press.

(2002a) *Active aging: a policy framework. Presented at the Second United Nations World Assembly on Aging, Madrid, Spain*. Geneva: World Health Organization Press.

(2002b) *Keep fit for life: meeting the nutritional needs of older persons*. Geneva: World Health Organization Press.

(2002c) *The Innovative Care for Chronic Conditions (ICCC) framework*. Geneva: World Health Organization Press.

(2004) *Towards age-friendly primary health care*. Geneva: World Health Organization Press.

(2005) The Bangkok Charter for Health Promotion in a Globalized World. *Health Promotion Journal of Australia*, *16*(3), 168–71.

(2008) *The global burden of disease: 2004 update*. Geneva: World Health Organization Press.

Wright, L.K., Hickey, J.V., Buckwalter, K.C. *et al.* (1999) Emotional and physical health of spouse caregivers of persons with Alzheimer's disease and stroke, *Journal of Advanced Nursing*, *30*(3), 552–63.

Zhang, X.H., Sasaki, S. and Kesteloot, H. (1995) The sex ratio of mortality and its secular trends, *International Journal of Epidemiology*, *24*(4), 720–9.

4 Ageing and health

Managing co-morbidities and functional disability in older people

CARMEL DYER AND SHARON OSTWALD

OVERVIEW

. . . .

This chapter examines common syndromes encountered in older patients, their assessment (principally using the comprehensive geriatric assessment), issues in the clinical management of older patients, the effects of vulnerability and co-morbidity, and the management of these.

. . . .

Introduction

O son, help your father in his old age, and do not grieve him as long as he lives; even if he is lacking in understanding, show forbearance; in all your strength do not despise him. For kindness to a father will not be forgotten.

Sirach 3:12–14

What is different about health in ageing people? Aren't all people simply as old as they feel? Does the approach to assessment and management differ from the approach recommended for younger people? Why are geriatric medicine specialists needed? When is care by a geriatrician appropriate and how old does one need to be before he or she should visit a geriatrician?

Chapter 2 outlined the biological changes that occur with ageing. Anyone over 40 who needs reading glasses can attest to the fact that there are physiological and functional changes that occur with advancing age. These changes occur at different rates in different individuals and can be affected by lifestyle and environment, but on average by age 75 one becomes, in the strict sense of the word, 'geriatric'. The manifestations of multiple concomitant chronic diseases and their subsequent management are different in older people and present additional challenges to the geriatricians and gerontological advanced practice professionals who care for these patients. This chapter will provide an overview of the worldwide trends in mortality and morbidity, comprehensive geriatric assessment, geriatric syndromes and disease management in older people. It will also address the consequences of vulnerability in old age and clinical approaches to improving the quality of life in frail elders. This chapter is not meant to be an exhaustive discussion of all the disorders associated with ageing, but instead an account of the most common syndromes encountered in older patients.

Trends in morbidity and mortality

Life expectancy is increasing faster in developing countries than in developed countries. The causes of mortality have shifted throughout the world from infectious to chronic diseases. The World Health Organization (WHO) (2008a) estimates that the ten leading causes of death among older people worldwide are:

(1) heart disease
(2) stroke
(3) lung cancer
(4) lower respiratory infections
(5) chronic obstructive pulmonary disease
(6) colon and rectum cancers
(7) Alzheimer's disease
(8) diabetes
(9) breast cancer
(10) stomach cancer.

Furthermore, the projections worldwide are for increases in chronic diseases (ischaemic heart disease, cancer and stroke) and a concomitant decrease in infectious diseases between 2004 and 2030 (WHO, 2008a). 'The increasing proportion of older people in the global population is contributing to the increase of age-associated chronic diseases, particularly in developing countries. Care-givers, health systems and societies need to be ready to cope with the growing needs of the elderly in every part of the world' (WHO, 2008a).

The causes of mortality, however, may be different from the major causes of morbidity and functional impairment. In the USA, the two most prevalent chronic conditions are high blood pressure and arthritis. The prevalence of chronic disease differs among older people, with African-Americans reporting higher rates of high blood pressure, arthritis, diabetes and stroke than either Hispanic or white Americans (Centers for Disease Control and Prevention and Merck Company Foundation, 2007). The number of Americans who will suffer functional disability due to arthritis, stroke, diabetes, coronary artery disease, cancer or cognitive impairment is expected to increase at least 300 per cent by 2049 (Boult, Altmann, Gilbertson *et al.*, 1996).

Comprehensive geriatric assessment

The presentation and manifestation of disease states change with age. The medical assessment that includes both a history and a physical examination must be altered to meet the needs of the patient and address the peculiarities of old age. The comprehensive geriatric assessment (CGA) is the diagnostic cornerstone of modern geriatric medicine; it has been shown in over 40 studies to be an effective approach in assessing vulnerable at-risk elders (e.g. Gammack and Paniagua, 2007; Hendriksen, Lund and Strømgard, 1984; Nikolaus, Specht-Leible, Bach *et al.*, 1999; Stuck, Aronow, Steiner *et al.*, 1995). CGA involves a multidimensional assessment and targeted interventions can be designed based on the assessment findings.

The CGA builds upon the traditional medical approach by incorporating psychosocial and functional components. It is an integrated approach to the screening and diagnosis of geriatric syndromes in a variety of domains and has been well studied. The assessment involves obtaining a comprehensive history and conducting a physical examination, as well as the use of detailed, validated instruments to quantify psychosocial health and functional abilities. Interdisciplinary teams, which generally comprise physicians, nurse practitioners, nurses and social workers who specialize in geriatric care, conduct the assessments. Psychiatrists, physical and occupational therapists, pharmacists, physiatrists and gerontologists are often called in to assist on cases where appropriate (Dyer, Hyer, Feldt *et al.*, 2003; Zeiss and Steffen, 1996).

CGA includes targeted health history and physical examinations. Because of the length of time it takes (up to 4 hours on average) it is often administered by a team that includes at least a physician, nurse and social worker. Members of other disciplines may also participate. CGA is usually coupled with an interdisciplinary team meeting where the members of the various disciplines develop a joint care plan. The components of CGA are shown in Table 4.1.

CGA has been applied successfully in a variety of settings including the hospital, nursing home, and outpatient clinics as well as patients' homes (Cohen, Feussner, Weinberger *et al.*, 2002; Engelhardt, Toseland, O'Donnell *et al.*, 1996; Fillit and Miller, 1993; Kircher, Wormstall, Müller *et al.*, 2007). CGA is a highly effective

Table 4.1 Overview of the comprehensive geriatric assessment

Component	Elements
Medical assessment	Problem list
	Co-morbid conditions and disease severity
	Medication review
	Nutritional status
Functional assessment	ADL
	IADL
	Activity/exercise status
	Gait and balance
Psychological assessment	Mental status (cognitive) testing
	Mood/depression testing
Social assessment	Information support needs and assets
	Care resource eligibility/financial assessment
Environmental assessment	Home safety
	Transportation and telehealth

Source: Wieland, D. and Hirth, V. (2003) Comprehensive geriatric assessment, *Cancer Control, 10*(6), 454–62.

procedure for diagnosing and treating co-morbid disease states and geriatric syndromes in frail elderly people. It has been used in the USA and European countries; its efficacy has been shown in at least eight successful randomized control trials in Sweden, Denmark, and the USA during the past two decades. Reported outcomes utilizing CGA include fewer nursing home placements, increased mobility and independence, and decreased mortality coupled with increased feelings of well-being and lower cost (Cohen *et al.*, 2002; Naylor, Brooten, Campbell *et al.*, 1999; Nikolaus *et al.*, 1995; Nikolaus, Specht-Leible, Bach *et al.*, 1999). In addition, studies (Boult, Boult, Morishita *et al.*, 1998; Cohen *et al.*, 2002) have demonstrated that CGA programmes have benefits such as decreased long-term costs, caregiver burden, hospitalizations and emergency room (ER) (A&E) visits; increased patient and primary-care physician satisfaction; and improved health status, function and mood.

The set of assessments that comprise the CGA are considered below. These can be grouped into patient history, physical examination and functional assessment.

Patient history

Medical history

Many aspects of the medical history are similar to that elicited in younger patients, such as history of present illness, past medical and surgical history, medications and review of symptoms. What differs in the older person is the time span that their health histories must encompass; it is difficult to recall the details of one's surgery 4 years later, let alone 40 years later (e.g. questions such as: *what was the reason for hospitalization in 1944?*). Beyond the fact that many medical problems are in the distant past, it is the sheer volume of information that can occur in a 70-, 80- or 90-year lifespan that makes history-taking more challenging.

Medication history

The medication history must include all the details including dose, frequency, and side effects. Older people often take more medicine than younger people, making this task more difficult. Clinicians must also ask about side effects, costs and ability to obtain the medication. In the USA the Joint Commission for Health Care Accreditation recently required that every medication be reviewed at admission to the hospital and at every outpatient visit (Joint Commission Resources, 2009). Geriatricians have long made medication review a part of their practices due to the serious consequences that medications can have in older patients.

Social history

Social histories in older patients are quite different from the histories elicited in younger patients. It is not sufficient only to know if the individual smokes, drinks or takes illicit drugs. There must be a detailed account of living arrangements, family and other social supports, and financial status including the extent of health-care funding for the patient. Information about living arrangements must include the type of dwelling (e.g. ground-floor house versus 15th-floor apartment), and who is living at the house. The clinician should determine how far children or family members live from the patient and who will be the spokesman should the patient need an advocate such as in the case of delirium or brain injury. Seniors should be able to describe who handles their finances, and how much money they receive or earn each month. They should be asked to detail how much is spent on medications and (in countries where this is appropriate) if an insurance plan is present to help pay for medications. Individuals who cannot describe their social support, health-care financing and other details of daily living are to be considered vulnerable and extra steps should be taken in the physical assessment to assess capacity for self-care and self-protection; this is described in greater detail below.

Collateral history

Unlike when taking a history from younger people, the clinician may need to also elicit a history from those familiar with the older patient. This is necessary in people who have dementia or depression and either cannot remember salient parts of their medical history or try to minimize problems to avoid being considered to lack capacity for self-care or to require a move to alternative accommodation.

Physical examination

The physical examination of older people contains similar components to that of younger people. Some aspects of the examination require additional attention and are detailed below.

Skin

Since older people are more prone to skin cancers as a result of cumulative sun exposure they should be evaluated for these at yearly intervals or whenever there are changes noted. Older people are also more prone to pressure ulcers and thus clinicians should examine the skin of both hospitalized patients and nursing home residents at every visit. With thinning skin and more fragile blood vessels, senile ecchymoses (bruising) and skin tears are seen commonly on the arms and legs of older people. Multiple bruises or lacerations should trigger an evaluation for elder mistreatment.

Head and neck

Older people experience multiple eye problems with ageing. The assessment should include a thorough examination of the lids, lashes and the eye itself. Glaucoma can be seen in people over the age of 40; thus, all older people should undergo yearly screening for this disorder. A commonly overlooked aspect of the physical examination is the examination of the external ear canal – accumulation of cerumen (wax) can lead to decreased auditory acuity and problems with balance. As people age and lose subcutaneous fat, the salivary glands may become more noticeable; novice clinicians often mistake these glands for tumours.

Heart

Ageing can result in calcification of many aspects of the cardiac anatomy. This can lead to arrhythmia (abnormal heart rhythm); valvular diseases, especially aortic stenosis (narrowing of the aorta); or heart failure due to problems with systolic (heart contracting) or diastolic (heart widening/filling with blood) function or both.

Lungs

Older people are prone to the same pulmonary diseases as younger persons. Very old age can lead to fibrosis of both lungs, and dry crackles can be heard at the bases of nonagenarians and centenarians. These should not be mistaken for wet rales, which are a physical examination sign of heart failure. (Wet rales is a characteristic type of 'crackling' sound heard during examination of breathing with a stethoscope.)

Table 4.2 Selected depression-screening approaches

Screening type	Description
Office screening	Can entail asking one of several questions; for example: 'During the past 4 weeks have you often felt sad or depressed?' 'Do you often feel sad, empty, or blue?' 'Do you have little interest or pleasure in doing things?'
SALSA	Mnemonic for warning signs of depression: Sleep disturbance Anhedonia Low self-esteem Appetite decreased
Geriatric Depression Scale	Long (30) or short (15) form of 'yes' and 'no' questions
Hamilton Depression Scale	21 questions (clinician interview and observation)
CES-D	20 questions with a 0–3 Likert scale

Sources: Hamilton, 1960; Maly, Hirsch and Reuben, 1997; Radoff, 1977; Yesavage, Brink, Rose *et al.*, 1983.

Central nervous system

As noted in Chapter 2, the central nervous system is prone to marked changes with ageing. Neurological assessment of memory is an essential component of the physical examination. Older people might not recognize early memory changes and family members and friends often forgive small lapses that they assume are normal changes with ageing. Therefore it is critical to formally assess mental status with a recognized test as opposed to just holding a conversation. There are a number of validated mental status tests; some are used worldwide. The commonly used instruments include clock drawing tests (Royall, Cordes and Polk, 1998), SLUMS (Tariq, Tumosa, Chibnall *et al.*, 2006), ADAS-cog (Burch and Andrews, 1987; Conner and Sabbagh, 2008), Mini-Cog (Borson, Scanlan, Chen *et al.*, 2003), and the MMSE (Folstein, Folstein and McHugh, 1975). The Mini-Mental State Examination (MMSE) has been validated in several languages in addition to English (Chandra, Ganguli, Ratcliff *et al.*, 1998; Ostrosky-Solis, Lopez-Arango and Ardila, 2000; Tiwari, Tripathi and Kumar, 2008). Central nervous system examination should also include evaluations for focal neurological signs that might indicate a prior stroke.

Psychiatric evaluation

Psychiatric examination should always include a mood assessment for depression. Depression might not be recognized by the older person or they might be ashamed of this diagnosis. Therefore standardized tests are recommended in this patient population to screen for this reversible disorder. Commonly used assessments are described in Table 4.2. This evaluation should include screening for psychosis,

Table 4.3 Triggers for IADL

Trigger	Sample question/observation
Telephone	Did the patient use the telephone to make the appointment?
Transportation	Did the patient drive to the appointment on their own or arrange their own transportation?
Medication	Did the patient have a good grasp of what the prescribed medications are and how to take them?
Grocery/food preparation	At the end of the visit, assess plans for follow-up
Finance	At the end of the visit, can the patient complete the visit with the office staff – deliver billing sheet to front desk, pay bill, make future appointments?
Housekeeping	Caregiver comments; e.g. 'The house is a mess'
Laundry	Are the patient's clothes clean?

Source: Adapted from Cape (1978).

which can be seen in older people with illnesses such as psychotic depression, dementia and bipolar disorder.

Musculoskeletal

Beyond the normal examinations for arthritis and other bone and joint abnormalities, it is important to determine how the joints and muscles work together in older people. A simple test called the Get Up and Go Test (Mathias, Nayak and Isaacs, 1986) can easily be performed in less than a minute in any setting. This test includes assessment of sitting balance, arising from chair, immediate standing balance, gait, turning balance and sitting into chair. A more detailed and standardized test, the Tinetti Gait and Balance, has been used in numerous clinical and research settings (Tinetti, 1986).

Functional assessment

The functional assessment is the third component of CGA, which lets the examiner know how the older person functions in his or her own environment.

Activities of daily living (ADL)

These are essentially routine activities that everybody engages in as a necessary part of everyday life. There are basic ADL, such as bathing, toileting, eating, dressing and walking (Katz and Akpom, 1976), and also more complex instrumental activities of daily living (IADL), shown in Table 4.3. During assessment, the patient is prompted to provide a subjective assessment of his or her ability to perform routine tasks. Since many older people may not be aware of their deficits or have such impaired memory that they forget, there are a number of validated, objective functional assessment tests. One of these is the Physical Performance Test (Reuben and Siu, 1990), which is a timed test of a series of simple tasks that are observed by the examiner.

The American Occupational Therapy Association developed the Kohlman Evaluation of Living Skills (KELS) instrument that is used throughout the USA to assess whether additional help is needed at home (Kohlman-Thomson, 1992; Morrow, 1985; Pickens, Naik, Burnett et al. 2007; Zimnavoda, Weinblatt and Katz, 2002). The KELS is a reliable and validated test that has been studied in older populations. A similar assessment can be made on a house call where the evidence of function or dysfunction can be directly observed, such as clean orderly home versus piles of laundry, old or no food in the refrigerator, etc. There are a number of house call safety check lists, and the recently developed Self-Neglect Severity Scale, a validated instrument to measure the older person's ability to provide self-care, is designed to be administered in the home setting (Dyer, Kelly, Pavlik et al., 2006; Kelly, Dyer, Pavlik et al., 2008).

Capacity assessment

Capacity is defined as the combined ability to make rational choices and act upon them. *Decisional capacity* refers to the ability to exercise good judgement in determining a course of action. A second component of capacity is executive function, which is the ability to use intention to guide one's actions (Workman, McCullough, Molinari et al., 2000). A number of disorders commonly found in older people lead to impaired capacity. These are cerebrovascular disease, dementia, depression, malnutrition, psychosis and/or substance abuse. At times, older people who lack decisional and executive capacity may unintentionally put themselves in harm's way. Therefore, it is important to determine if capacity is present to preserve the rights of those with capacity and protect those without.

Capacity assessment is a very grey area. A variety of instruments have been used when a quick capacity assessment is needed before an operation or procedure is to be performed. These include the Assessing Capacity for Everyday Decisions (ACED) instrument (Lai and Karlawish, 2007), the Capacity to Consent to Treatment Instrument (CCTI) (Marson, Ingram, Cody et al., 1995), the Executive Interview (EXIT) (Royall et al., 2005); the Hopemont Capacity Assessment Interview (HCAI) (Edelstein, 1999), and the MacArthur Competency Assessment Tool for Treatment (MACAT-T) (Appelbaum and Grisso, 2001). The reference standard in assessment for capacity is the psychiatric evaluation, a time-consuming and relatively expensive test. For particularly difficult cases, a psychiatrist may perform 4–6-hour assessments in the home of the individual. There needs to be extensive testing before a person can be declared to lack capacity because of the implications for autonomy.

Thus, the CGA provides a comprehensive overview of the past and present state of the individual older person and also can provide a good indication of their future needs. It is now time to examine some of the most frequent syndromes that are found in older adults.

Geriatric syndromes

The CGA often detects occult (present but lacking 'obvious' signs) or obvious geriatric syndromes in ageing people. Older people are afflicted with heart disease, pulmonary disease, diabetes and hypertension just like their younger counterparts. In many cases, the presentation of disease is different or altered in older people and the clinician must be extraordinarily vigilant to detect illness. For instance, pneumonia may present without fever or an elevated white blood cell count. Many older people with myocardial infarction present without chest pain. In fact, delirium may be the only manifestation of disease (see below). However, there are a number of geriatric syndromes that are multifactorial and have long been recognized as more prevalent in older people than younger people. While any one of these syndromes may be the initial presenting syndrome, often they are interconnected with one syndrome precipitating another, creating very complex assessment and management issues, as illustrated in the case of Mrs L.M.

Case study: Mrs L.M.

Mrs L.M. was a petite, well-groomed 87-year-old woman with congestive heart failure and cataracts who had been living alone until 24 hours before when she slipped and fell while picking up her medications at the local pharmacy. She was transferred to the emergency department of the local hospital by ambulance. When she was examined she was found to have a fractured femur, to be alert, and to be in severe pain. She was given meperidine for the pain, but became more agitated and was restrained. She was started on fluids and transferred to a hospital room. During the night she became very confused and tried to get out of bed. She pulled out her intravenous (IV) line. A new IV was started and her hands were restrained. She began screaming that people were in her room and was given an additional sedative. At rounds the next morning, the staff reported that an old confused woman had been admitted who was incontinent, uncooperative, and likely had dementia. No one answered the telephone number in her wallet and she could provide no history. They believed that a discharge to a nursing home was inevitable after her hip fracture was repaired. (Meperidine is better known in some countries as Demerol, a commonly prescribed painkiller; one of its potential side effects is confusion/delirium.)

Table 4.4 Types of dementia

Reversible dementia	Irreversible dementia
• Depression	• Alzheimer's disease
• Vitamin B_{12} deficiency	• Diffuse Lewy body disease
• Hyperparathyroidism	• Vascular dementia
• Alcohol-induced dementia	• Parkinson's dementia
• Hypothyroidism	• Huntington's chorea
• Normal pressure hydrocephalus	• Multiple system atrophy syndrome
• Brain tumour	• Creutzfeldt–Jakob disease (CJD)
• Subdural haematoma	• Binswanger's disease (BD)
• Neurosyphilis dementia	• Wilson's disease
• AIDS dementia	

Source: derived from Freter *et al.* (1998).

This case study illustrates the importance of being aware of the interconnectedness of the geriatric syndromes. The incorrect choice of medications, misinterpretation of symptoms, and failure to detect and diagnose geriatric syndromes may cause adverse complications leading to poor outcomes. Understanding geriatric syndromes and basic geriatric principles is essential to providing effective care to older people whose complex medical histories and atypical presentations increase the likelihood of misdiagnosis or inappropriate medical management. The prevalence, clinical signs and symptoms, evaluation and treatment of common geriatric syndromes are discussed in this section.

Dementia

Definition

Dementia is a progressive disorder characterized by problems with memory and thinking. There is a further, contrasting discussion of dementia in Chapter 7.

Prevalence

It has been estimated that over 4 million people in the USA are afflicted with dementia. This number rises to 26.6 million when one considers the worldwide incidence (Burton and Kasper, 2007). Nearly 50 per cent of people over the age of 85 have dementia. There are a number of disorders that lead to dementia and these are outlined in Table 4.4. Approximately 10 per cent of dementia is due to reversible underlying causes such as B_{12} deficiency or hypothyroidism.

Clinical signs and symptoms

Memory loss is the most pervasive symptom of dementia. Some individuals begin to forget names of people they have known all their lives, or get lost in familiar places. Some develop paranoid delusions about their spouses or neighbours. Many have unexplained weight loss. When these findings do not impair function, mild cognitive impairment (MCI) is diagnosed. About 20 per cent of people with MCI go on to develop dementia once the cognitive problems impact daily function (Ravaglia *et al.*, 2006).

Evaluation

Dementia can be detected through CGA, which includes cognitive tests. Dementia is more difficult to detect in some individuals with higher intellectual functioning or attainment. Since these individuals may be more likely to pass a dementia screening test, more complete neuropsychological testing may be required for diagnosis. In the evaluation, blood tests to detect the reversible causes of dementia should be obtained (i.e. complete blood count and chemistry panel, rapid plasma regain, B_{12} and thyroid tests, HIV). In cases where there is an abnormality in the neurological examination, brain imaging may be indicated to determine if disorders such as vascular dementia or a brain tumour are present.

Intervention

A number of medications are available for the treatment of dementia. The commonly used medications include acetyl cholinesterase inhibitors, and NMDA inhibitors. None of these medications can cure dementia, but, at the time of writing, there is strong evidence that they delay the progression of vascular dementia, Alzheimer's disease and diffuse Lewy body disease. It is estimated that if dementia could be delayed for 5 years, the incidence could be reduced by 50 per cent. Studies of the effect of an Alzheimer's vaccine on the progression of the disease are under way, but early results have shown that while it clears beta-amyloid plaques from the brain, it does not restore memory (Holmes *et al.*, 2008). However, sustained exercise has shown surprising effects in preventing the onset of dementia, slowing down the progress of Alzheimer's disease in people who already have the diagnosis, and improving health and decreasing depression when combined with caregiver behavioural techniques (Larson, Wang, Bowen *et al.*, 2006; Lautenschlager *et al.*, 2008; McCurry *et al.*, 2003; Teri, Gibbons, Toldy *et al.*, 2008).

Depression

Definition

Depression is a mood disorder characterized by withdrawal, lack of energy and feeling, or poor self-worth. For a contrasting view, see Chapter 7.

Prevalence

Depression is seen in about 12–15 per cent of older people in the community, 25 per cent of nursing home residents, 30 per cent of older people with dementia and Parkinson's disease, and nearly 50 per cent of older people with medical illnesses. The true prevalence may be much higher in older people, since many do not want to admit to a mental illness or screening does not take place. Although age is a risk factor for depression, medical disease such as diabetes or renal failure is more commonly associated with depression.

Clinical signs and symptoms

Many older people grew up in an era where it was an embarrassment to have any form of mental illness. Older people do not often recognize the depression, and family members bring it to the attention of the clinician. Moreover, older people may not have the common presenting signs of depression. There may just be unexplained weight loss or fatigue, or cognitive impairment, which can be mistaken for dementia.

Evaluation

Screening for depression is critical in older people because of the altered presentation of the disease. Table 4.2 contains a list of some commonly used screening instruments. It is important to search for disorders associated with depression such as thyroid disease or dementia. Some patients develop psychotic depression; they are often very guarded about hearing voices and this must be elicited by the examiner.

Intervention

Depression in the elderly can be effectively and safely treated. With the emergence of a number of selective serotonin reuptake inhibitors (SSRIs), symptoms of depression can be reversed in older people. These medications can be selected by their effects; some are activating (e.g. sertraline) while others are sedating (e.g. mirtazipine). Most older people require lifelong treatment since the recurrence rate is reported to be as high as 80 per cent. For patients who have multiple co-morbid diseases, electroconvulsive therapy can be very useful and it prevents adverse drug–drug reactions.

Delirium

Definition

Delirium is an acute confusional state, characterized by the inability to attend to tasks and misperception of reality.

Prevalence

Delirium is most commonly seen in older people after surgery or associated with an acute medical illness. Post-operative delirium usually lasts a day or two and the prevalence varies, based on the surgery; however, cardiovascular surgery is associated with the highest prevalence from 20–40 per cent (Chang, Tsai, Lin et al., 2008; Tan et al., 2008). When associated with medical illness, delirium is an emergency; the highest prevalence (22–89 per cent) is in people with dementia (Fick et al., 2002). Delirium is a risk factor for death (Leslie et al., 2005).

Clinical signs and symptoms

People who are delirious are often not aware of the date, where they are, or their current circumstances. They may be delusional, have altered sleep–wake cycles, and garbled or disorganized speech. There are two types of presentations of delirium – hyperactive (unusually and typically irrationally active) and hypoactive (unusually lethargic) delirium. Thus, in the hyperactive form, patients pull out their intravenous lines, toss around in the bed and yell out. In the hypoactive form, they fall asleep during the clinician's exam. The latter form is more common and more lethal (Kiely, Jones, Bergmann et al., 2007, Pandharipande et al., 2007).

Evaluation

Very florid cases of delirium are easy to detect. The hypoactive or more subtle cases can be detected by the confusion assessment method. Developed by Inouye in the 1980s, this tool has been well studied, is very sensitive (94 per cent) and specific (89 per cent), and has even been adapted for the intensive care unit by Ely and Inouye (Wei, Fearing, Sternberg et al., 2008). An electroencephalogram (EEG) can confirm delirium but is rarely necessary. In addition in delirium caused by medical illness a thorough evaluation of the underlying cause must be done. The most common causes include infections, medications, electrolyte or blood sugar disturbances, hypoxaemia or low oxygen state, and low blood pressure. Delirium may be the only presenting sign for these illnesses.

Intervention

With post-operative delirium, symptoms resolve with time. However, with delirium due to medical illness, the underlying cause must be identified and treated. The symptoms of hyperactive delirium are best treated by short-acting benzodiazepine, or haloperidol, which must be used with caution at low doses and discontinued prior to discharge from the hospital.

Falls

Definition
A fall is a sudden and unplanned change of position from sitting, lying or standing.

Prevalence
Thirty per cent of community dwelling people 75 years of age or older fall every year. After one fall, the risk of a second fall is increased. Moderate to severe injury is experienced by 20 per cent of people who fall. Falls are the sixth leading cause of death in older people in the USA.

Risk factors and outcomes
There are a number of risk factors for falling: age, dementia, depression, female gender, poor vision, poor hearing, ill-fitting footwear and environmental hazards such as rugs or electrical cords. Falls can result in problems ranging from the relatively mild (some soft-tissue injuries) to the more serious (fractures of the hip, vertebra or wrist, head injuries) ultimately resulting in loss of independence. Thirty per cent of people have a permanent disability after falling (Morley, 2008). Mrs L.M. in the case study had several of these risk factors. She was 87 years old, female, had cataracts, and wore leather-soled shoes with a small heel, increasing the chance of slipping on a polished surface.

Evaluation
Falls can be a manifestation of delirium and all the causes of delirium should be reviewed and evaluated after an acute fall. A thorough evaluation for injury including a head CT (computed tomography) scan with contrast should be done (this highlights a particular body part of interest; without contrast, this highlighting is not present). CGA can often determine risk factors for falling. Assessments to detect risk of falling include a sensory examination, examination of balance, and strength testing.

Intervention
After injuries are treated and causes of delirium excluded or treated, it is important to put preventive measures in place. There are a number of exercise interventions that have been found to be helpful such as the single-leg stance that is practised by the patient with the goal to stand unsupported on each leg for 1 minute. There is good evidence to show that t'ai chi improves balance (Wong and Lan, 2008). Lower extremity strengthening exercises and gait practice can be helpful. A home safety evaluation is in order to reduce hazards in the dwelling place.

Incontinence

Definition

Urinary incontinence (UI) is defined as the involuntary loss of urine so severe as to have social and/or hygienic consequences for individuals and/or their caregivers. UI causes significant disability and dependency. In US nursing homes alone, the costs of labour, laundry and supplies necessary to manage incontinence and its complications are more than $3 billion (Merkelj, 2001).

Prevalence

Approximately 15–50 per cent of elderly women experience some form of UI (Klausner and Vapnek, 2003).

Clinical signs and symptoms

The signs and symptoms vary according to the type of UI. Older people can have a problem with the urinary outlet or the bladder itself. The urinary outlet may be too loose as seen in stress UI, where urine leaks out of the bladder through an incompetent sphincter. People with prostatic hypertrophy have an outlet that is too tight and urine does not empty properly and then leaks out of the bladder. When the source of the incontinence is the bladder, it may be too flaccid or denervated, as seen in diabetes mellitus, or overactive, as seen with dementia. After urinating, high urinary retention is seen in flaccid bladders or tight outlets. High-volume precipitous incontinence episodes are seen in overactive bladders (DuBeau, 2007).

Evaluation

The evaluation must include screening for infection and a good history that helps determine the type of incontinence. A good external examination in both men and women, in women a pelvic and rectal examination, and in men a prostate examination are indicated.

Intervention

Intervention in older people should begin with treatment of infection if present, and thereafter treatments are based on the specific type of incontinence. For all types, simple bladder training emphasizing frequent timed voiding can decrease incontinent episodes. Many of the medications that are used to treat incontinence have anticholinergic properties and may cause confusion, constipation and dry mouth in older people. (Antichoinergic drugs suppress/inhibit nerve activity reliant on acetylcholine, a key chemical transmitter in the nervous system.) Some patients benefit from surgery. Minimally invasive therapy for women with lax urethras has become widely used and appears to be safe in older people (DuBeau, 2007).

Polypharmacy

Definition

Strictly speaking, polypharmacy is the use of multiple medications. However, the term is typically used to describe excessive prescribing of medication beyond that needed by the patient. Hence Monane (1997) offers the practical definition that polypharmacy exists whenever a patient is on a medication that he or she does not need.

Causes

The causes of polypharmacy are multifactorial and complex. In countries without a centralized health-care provision, older people may go to multiple clinicians, who may be unaware of the medications prescribed by others, but even where clinicians are fully aware of the patient's current medications, polypharmacy is still common. Older people often have multiple medical conditions that require complicated medical regimens. Some older people also take a number of complementary or alternative medications that may also interact with currently prescribed medications. Lastly, older people may be taking medications prescribed for their spouses or their friends.

Prevention

For many years, efficient geriatricians and geriatric nurses have made it a practice to review medications at every visit. These clinicians often require older adults to bring in the actual pill bottles for every medication that they take. In 2009, the Joint Commission for Hospital Accreditation in the USA began to require medication reconciliation at both inpatient and outpatient visits. Many are hopeful that the electronic medical record will help to prevent polypharmacy; however, until multiple systems can interface, these records will be less helpful. It is difficult for practising clinicians to know the effect and dosage for every possible medication. There are a number of electronic geriatric formularies that can assist in drug dosing for older people. Again, various research groups around the world have also looked at the medical evidence and provided guidelines to assist the clinician (Carey et al., 2008; Fick et al., 2003; Prudent et al., 2008).

Geriatric management principles

The geriatric medicine approach differs from that commonly applied in younger patients. Unfortunately, there are not always trials with large numbers of older people to help guide the clinician. However, there are a number of 'tricks of the trade' that can help clinicians better manage older patients. Some of them are described below.

If the brain doesn't work, the rest doesn't matter

Many older people present with complex medical histories and so many complaints that the junior clinician may have difficulty in determining which problem to tackle first. A good principle is, where possible, first to remedy the conditions that impact on cognition. Older people will not be able to remember to take their medications or to carry out other aspects of the treatment plan if their thinking and memory are impaired.

Screen for delirium

All hospitalized patients should be screened for delirium at admission and regularly throughout the hospital course. There is strong evidence that discharge from a hospital or emergency centre with delirium still present increases the risk of death within the next 6–12 months (Bellelli *et al.*, 2007; Leslie *et al.*, 2005). Screening for delirium is a high yield procedure in older people and can help the clinician diagnose occult acute illness.

Treat for depression

Other aspects of care will not be addressed by the older person if they are depressed. For example, trying to engage a depressed older person in a smoking-cessation or exercise programme will probably be fruitless if depression is present. Depression is also a risk factor for post-operative death, and in cases of elective surgery, the clinician may want to screen and treat depression prior to operation.

Treat dementia-related syndromes

Families are often willing to take care of their demented loved ones at home as long as the behaviours are tolerable. However, older people with dementia often present with psychosis, such as paranoid delusions of neighbours or loved ones stealing things. Dementia is associated with sleep disorders, and chronic behavioural problems. Although an actual psychosis requires antipsychotic medications that must be used cautiously in elders, there are a number of safe alternative medications and non-pharmacological methods for addressing behaviours. These are outlined in Table 4.5.

Table 4.5 Methods of treatment for dementia-associated behavioural problems

Non-pharmacological	Pharmacological
• Redirection (provide acceptable distraction) • Massage • Touch • Bright light therapy	• Trazodone • Propranolol (titrate to blood pressure) • Anticonvulsants (i.e. valproic acid) • Antipsychotics – if hallucinations and delusions are present (use with caution)

References: Ayalon, L., Gum, A.M., Feliciano, L. *et al.*, 2006; Viggo Hansen, N., Jørgensen, T., and Ørtenblad, L., 2006.

After the brain, the focus should be on function

Both preserving and improving function are important to the quality of life in older people. Younger individuals take performance and mobility for granted. However, restriction of either can lead to a decline in well-being and result in significant co-morbidity (to take a simple example – older people who cannot get to the pharmacy for their medications may suffer without the needed treatments). Aside from danger of weight gain through lack of exercise, immobility can result in falls, pressure ulcers and significant loss of muscle mass. Function is what allows an individual to enjoy life and both work and leisure pursuits. Once function is impaired, individuals are more prone to illness, hospitalization and the need to move from their homes to alternative living situations.

Older people and their family members often assume that loss of function is a normal part of ageing and cannot be reversed. They attribute sedentary tendencies to old age and easily become resigned to inactivity and lower expectations. At times the loss of function is so gradual that neither family members nor the older people themselves recognize the changes. It is important that self-report not be the only method of measuring function and that collateral information as well as objective tests such as the KELS and the Physical Performance Test be used to assess older people; both are described above.

It is important to maintain function through exercise; even just leaving the house daily for errands can help preserve function. Many senior centres/older persons' clubs and similar organizations have physical and mental activities to keep older people engaged and help preserve function. When there is a decline in function, occupational and physical therapy programmes can help restore lost or diminished skills. Clinicians should give priority in their treatment plans to interventions that restore function. For example, a slightly high blood sugar level is not as detrimental as loss of ability to walk – especially since glucose utilization will be improved with a sustained walking programme. Therefore in an instance like this, restoring function is more pressing than medication adjustment, which may not be needed if the functional ability is restored.

Start low and go slow

When prescribing for an older person, the dictum 'start low and go slow' is a useful approach. Because of the frequent lack of the enrolment of older people in drug trials, it is prudent when prescribing to start at very low doses and then advance the dose after observing for adverse reactions. The recommended starting dose for an older person is often half or a third that used in younger people. The effects of drugs may take longer to realize in older people. For instance, where thyroid supplementation can be adjusted in 4–5 weeks in younger people, the clinician should wait 12 weeks before assessing the effect in older people. Moreover, when making changes to medication regimens, clinicians should avoid making two changes concomitantly, since if there is an adverse event, it will not be clear which change was the culprit.

An important caveat to this is to curb the enthusiasm to use 'new' drugs. The lack of clinical trials in older people impacts daily medical care. It has been estimated that, in the USA, nearly 20 per cent of all Medicare admissions are the result of adverse drug events. (Medicare is a health care system in the USA that covers a significant proportion of health-care bills for people aged 65 years and older.) Older people with fewer physical reserves might not tolerate the adverse effects of many medications as well as younger people. It is prudent to wait until a drug has been on the market and studied in large numbers of people, including older people, before prescribing. Many older people respond to basic medications. For instance, for older people with pain, morphine may be a better choice than hydromorphone or fentanyl, because it will effectively alleviate the pain symptoms and its effect is more predictable.

In addition, there is often an argument in favour of 'less is more'. When an older person is experiencing a problem such as delirium, falls or gastrointestinal distress, the problem is more likely to be due to an excess rather than a lack of medication. When approaching delirious patients or patients with multiple medical problems, improvement is often achieved when medications are removed rather than added. In most instances a non-pharmacological approach is preferred to a pharmacological approach as in the case of incontinence where the use of a bladder-training programme is safer than some of the anticholinergic drugs used as treatment.

Avoid overmanagement and investigation of disease

Voltaire once said that 'the best is the enemy of the good'. This can apply to geriatric medicine. Some older adults have so many multiple co-morbidities that clinicians can perform countless numbers of tests to identify underlying disorders. It is always possible to perform multiple diagnostic tests in older people, but the astute clinician must always keep the goals of the person in mind. Why perform multiple invasive tests in a frail older person with nausea, for instance, if physical examination shows no abnormalities and an antacid resolves the symptom? Low heart rate in older people should not be addressed if there are no associated symptoms. The goals of older people frequently include good functional ability as opposed to living as long as possible (see discussion of the Tithonus error in Chapter 2). Thus, procedures such as cardiac catheterization and endoscopy should be carefully considered in frail elders for whom the benefit is limited. This does not mean that tests should never be done, but that investigations that could lead to improved cognition or function should take priority over testing that simply answers academic questions. Treatment can be overzealous at times. For example, many have recommended a blood pressure target of 140/80 for older people with isolated systolic hypertension, which is the same target for younger people. However, multiple studies have shown that blood pressures of less than 160/90 in people over the age of 85 are associated with increased mortality (Bulpitt *et al.*, 2003; Molander, Lövheim, Norman *et al.*, 2008; van Bemmel, Gussekloo, Westendorp *et al.*, 2006).

Similarly, caution needs to be exercised with prophylaxis. With evidence that medications like statins prevent myocardial infarction and Coumadin prevents stroke due to atrial fibrillation, many older people are taking a number of medications prophylactically. These may be indicated in some older people, but when the number of medications exceeds eight or has significant side effects, careful consideration has to be given to not prescribing just to prevent. This may seem like heresy in the current medical climate, but consider the case of the demented elder who is on Coumadin to thin his blood and then sustains a fall with fracture of the hip and the loss of several units of blood. He could go on to develop delirium, a prolonged hospital stay and a prolonged rehabilitation period or even death.

Communication is an intervention

Many older people have impaired sensory systems and cannot hear or see as well as younger people. They may have cognitive impairment and not remember the clinician's advice and recommendations. It behoves clinicians to overcome these barriers through multiple forms of communication. One strategy is to identify an additional person to whom information can be relayed if necessary. Clinicians can describe the medical instructions verbally and in written form. Translators are necessary for older people to whom English is a second language (American Geriatrics Society, 2004–9).

As more people worldwide live into old age, questions about care and normal ageing develop in the minds of older adults, their family members and their caregivers. Fear of the unknown and insecurity about change often frighten those involved. Simple explanations of the changes associated with ageing or with disease states can avert anxiety, unnecessary medication use, and unnecessary trips to the emergency centre and hospital. Clinicians should view enhanced communication as every bit as important as what they prescribe or recommend.

The hospital can be a dangerous place for older people

Hospital stays are fraught with multiple pitfalls for older people. Hospitalized older adults develop iatrogenic (created by the therapy) complications unrelated to their presenting diagnoses that can result in longer hospitalizations, functional impairment or unanticipated medical or surgical interventions. The changes associated with usual ageing when coupled with hospitalization and bed rest result in 'hazards of hospitalization' that include delirium, malnutrition, pressure ulcers, falls, restraint use, functional decline, adverse drug effects and death (Creditor, 1993; Fernandez, Callahan, Likourezos et al., 2008). The hazards of hospitalization appear to be directly related to the length of time spent in the hospital (Schimnel, 2003).

Creditor (1993) found that 31 per cent of hospitalized older patients lose the ability to perform one or more of the ADL skills at baseline, 40 per cent of these older adults remained impaired 3 months later, and 40 per cent had IADL declines at 3 months. Older people lose strength at the rate of 5 per cent per day when they are immobilized; and reconditioning takes much longer than deconditioning. Bone resorption (i.e. loss of bone) of older acutely ill people at bed rest occurs at 50 times the usual rate seen in older adults. Pressure ulcer prevalence is 20–25 per cent in hospitalized patients due to increased shearing forces. From 25 to 30 per cent of hospitalized elderly are under/malnourished. And as mentioned previously, delirium is very prevalent in hospitalized elders.

Leipzig (2009, no longer available online) has created a list of ten simple principles that decrease poor outcomes for hospitalized older patients. These are:

(1) Bed rest is for dead people and few others. GET THE PATIENT MOVING!!!
(2) The fewer drugs, the better. Review medications frequently.
(3) Get out IV lines and catheters as soon as possible.
(4) Avoid restraints whenever possible.
(5) Assess and monitor mental/cognitive status.
(6) Delirium is a medical emergency. Treat with antipsychotics only when indicated.
(7) Watch for depression.
(8) Pay attention to the amount of food consumed. Consider supplements.

(9) Involve the patient and family in decision-making and advance directives.
(10) Start discharge planning with admission.

A number of programmes can help prevent delirium and the other negative consequences of hospitalization. These include the HELP, NICHE and ACE units. ACE units are acute care of the elderly units that employ an interdisciplinary approach to the care of older hospitalized patients. These units employ the Leipzig principles in a setting that is adapted for older people, including raised toilet seats, bright lighting and grab bars, and room for family members to stay with the older person. Processes include strict attention to volume status, uninterrupted sleep and early recognition of delirium. Studies have shown decreased lengths of stay, improved function and higher rates of patient and provider satisfaction (Hartford, 2006; Haugh, 2004). The Hospital Elder Life Program (HELP) developed by Inouye is a similar approach that addresses the multiple causes of delirium in hospitalized patients and minimizes the effect. This programme includes clocks in the rooms and ensuring that all sensory assistive devices (glasses and hearing aids) are available to the older person. It includes training for volunteers to advocate for older people (Inouye, Bogardus, Charpentier *et al.*, 1999; Rubin, Williams, Lescisin *et al.*, 2006). The Nurses Improving Care for Hospitalized Elders (NICHE) was developed at New York University and has a similar focus. It trains nurses in medical and surgical units to recognize delirium and meet the special needs of older hospitalized patients (Boltz *et al.*, 2008).

Consequences of vulnerability

Vulnerability arises when the older person shows physical or mental degeneration that cannot be (or is not) compensated for through changes in the physical environment or enhanced social or medical supports. For older people, in particular, there is a very delicate balance between the person's physical or mental competence and the demands of the environment. Lawton and colleagues proposed the person–environment fit model that is a helpful way of looking at the continuous interactions between older people and their social and physical environment (Lawton and Nahemow, 1973; Robinson, Novelli, Pearson *et al.*, 2007). In this model, the environment can be broadly interpreted to refer to any external demands on the individual (i.e. society, community, home). 'Environmental press' refers to the demands that either the social or physical environment place on an older person. As discussed in Chapter 3, these demands may come in the form of lack of social support, poverty leading to lack of necessities such as food, unsafe neighbourhoods, crowded or dirty housing, or inaccessible health-care services.

Case study: Mr S.A.

Mr S.A. is an 82-year-old man with type 2 diabetes, osteoarthritis and hypertension who receives a small monthly cheque. He lives with his two daughters, travelling by bus approximately 100 miles every month to a different daughter's home. The daughters work and live in extended family households with children and grandchildren in the home. Mr S.A. sleeps on a single bed in the corner of the living room in one daughter's home and shares a bedroom with two teenage sons in the other home. He is each day responsible for his own breakfast and lunch. He complains of being tired and his blood pressure and blood glucose are both elevated. He does not have a family physician and when necessary seeks care in the local hospital emergency room. His daughters have noticed that in the last few months he has become increasingly irritable, yells at the children, complains about the noise, and sometimes seems confused.

'Personal competence' in this model refers to the upper level of a person's ability to function in areas of health, social function and cognition (Lawton and Nahemow, 1973). Personal competence is affected by many of the factors discussed in Chapter 3 – resilience, health status, lifestyle, ability to manage ADL and IADL, and self-management of chronic disease (Iwarsson, 2005). Older people function best when the environment challenges them, but does not overwhelm them. Older people who live alone with little contact with others may experience negative effects of too little stimulation. This may lead to negative affect and maladaptive behaviour, such as boredom, isolation, and sensory deprivation. On the other hand, too much environmental stimulation may also lead to negative affect and maladaptive behaviour.

Mr S.A. was clearly in a situation with too much stimulation with the demands of travel, lack of privacy, uncontrolled chronic illnesses, and a noisy, crowded environment. Overstimulation can result in negative affect and maladaptive behaviours as displayed by Mr S.A. It is imperative that social and health-care providers recognize the interactions between environments and intervene to achieve a better match between older people and their environments. Interventions may include putting resources into the home in the form of home health nurses, therapists, aides, homemakers or home-delivered meals. Alternatively, older people may receive transportation to local senior centres or become involved in support or interest groups, and eat at congregate dining sites. Social and health-care personnel may need to engage the older person and their family in a planning session to look at alternative living situations that have a low environmental pressure.

Alternative living situations

When the cognitive and functional impairments make them unable to care for themselves at home, and if family members or paid caregivers cannot provide the necessary support, older people may have to move to an alternative setting. However, many elders understandably resist these moves. They often have lived in their home for years and surrounded themselves with things that have meaning and hold memories for them. CGA is aimed at preserving function and allowing elders to stay in familiar environments. Some families and seniors are willing to risk a fall or other injury for the benefit of staying in their own home. At some point, however, for a certain number of elders, the risk to their safety and the safety of others (e.g. leaving food burning) becomes overwhelming and a move is indicated.

There are a number of independent living situations available to seniors where meal preparation and house cleaning are provided for them. When more care is needed, an assisted living facility (ALF) may be in order. In ALF, seniors must be generally able to bathe and toilet themselves and require only monitoring or medication assistance. The costs for these vary from locale to locale; however, most indigent people could not afford this form of housing without some subsidy. In the USA, often low-income people live in personal care homes, which house 3–6 seniors and provide care for them that is funded by their social security monthly income. Nursing facilities house people who can no longer perform their IADL and ADL. Approximately 5 per cent of the over-65 population in the USA live in nursing facilities (Burton and Kasper, 2007). The average length of stay is 2 years and more women than men reside in nursing facilities. The quality of care varies and vulnerable elders may be at risk of elder mistreatment in some facilities. The care of nursing home residents is extremely hard work and these facilities provide a much-needed service to the seniors and their families that are unable to deliver adequate care at home. There are independent living centres, ALFs and nursing facilities that collaborate or are built together. These are called CCRCs (continuing care retirement centres); they allow seniors to enter when they are more functional and then age in place at one location.

Motor vehicle accidents

Motor vehicle accidents are the leading cause of injury-related deaths among adults aged 65–74. The incidence of traffic fatalities may triple as the number of older drivers increases in the coming years. Worldwide, deaths from traffic accidents are predicted to increase between 2004 and 2030 (WHO, 2008). It is the opinion of the American Medical Association that physicians have a responsibility to recognize and document mental and physical impairments that may affect patients' driving safety and pose a risk to the public (American Medical Association, 2009). They must use their best judgement when reporting impairments that limit patients' driving. Elsewhere (e.g. the UK) regular medical checks of older drivers are a legal requirement if they wish to continue to drive.

Road safety analysts predict that by 2030, when all the latest baby boomers are at least 65, they will be responsible for 25 per cent of all fatal crashes. 'Drivers over the age of 65 are almost twice (1.78 times) as likely to die in car crashes as drivers age 55 to 64' (Traffic Safety Facts, retrieved on 24 January 2009 from www-nrd.nhtsa.dot.gov/Pubs/809910.PDF). Accidents that resulted in an overturn/rollover increased the likelihood of a fatality by 220 per cent for older males but only 116 per cent for middle-aged males. Such accidents increase the likelihood of injury by 133 per cent and 138 per cent for older and middle-aged males, respectively, but only 23.6 per cent for young males. When restraints (safety belts) were not used, the likelihood of injury increased 119 per cent for young females, 164 per cent for middle-aged females, and 187 per cent for older females (Islam and Mannering, 2006).

More of the US states are requiring driving assessments. Florida's requirement that drivers aged 80 and older pass a vision test resulted in the loss of a licence for about 7 per cent of elderly drivers seeking renewal, according to a study by the IIHS (Insurance Institute for Highway Safety). Other studies include the dynamic visual acuity test (DVA), which assesses impairments in a patient's ability to perceive objects accurately while actively moving the head. In normal individuals, losses in visual acuity are minimized during head movements by the vestibular ocular reflex (VOR) system that maintains the direction of gaze on an external target by driving the eyes in the opposite direction of the head movement. When the VOR system is impaired, visual acuity degrades during head movements. Another study is the gaze stabilization test (GST), which quantifies the head movement velocities over which the patient is able to maintain an acceptable level of visual acuity (McGwin, Sarrels, Griffin *et al.*, 2008). The American Association of Neurology recommends that anyone diagnosed with dementia should stop driving (Dubinsky, Stein and Lyons, 2000). A prior study suggested that a 22 on the MMSE (normal is 24 or above for high-school graduates) was an appropriate cutoff for driving, but this has been difficult to validate. Neurocognitive testing can often be helpful or a simple driving test by the department that issues driving licences. Older people must have both intact decision-making and executive capacity to drive safely (see references to driving in Chapter 6 for further discussion).

To fulfil this ethical responsibility, physicians must possess specific knowledge and skill to recognize and evaluate unsafe driving risk and counsel patients and their families (Carr, Duchek, Meuser *et al.*, 2006) More awareness for health-care professionals is in order. A number of recommendations are being proposed. These include mandating physicians to inform authorities of patients who fail to match criteria, increased awareness for the general public, occupational and physical therapy interventions to improve strength and coordination, driver evaluation programmes by the Department of Motor Vehicles, and a focus on function rather than age as a strict criterion. Note that these are for the USA. Many other countries already have such regulations or similar in place.

Elder mistreatment

As people age, they face a variety of biological changes due to ageing or disease states. They may lose decision-making and executive capacity. As a result, elders are less able to care for and protect themselves. As the need for social and medical support from others increases, so does the risk of mistreatment. Although sometimes further subdivided, there are generally considered to be three broad types of elder mistreatment: abuse, neglect, and exploitation. Elder abuse is defined as the infliction of physical harm on a senior and includes sexual assault. Lacerations and bruises are often seen in these cases. Neglect is the failure to provide the goods or services needed to meet basic needs (food, shelter, medical care) and can be perpetrated by a caregiver or by the vulnerable individual on him- or herself (self-neglect). Unexplained weight loss or untreated medical conditions are often seen in cases of neglect. Exploitation is use of an older adult's money or resources by caregivers for their own purposes (National Center on Elder Abuse, 2005).

The National Elder Abuse Incidence Study estimated that, in 1996 in the USA, at least 500,000 community-dwelling elders experienced abuse, neglect and/or self-neglect (National Center on Elder Abuse, 1998). A longitudinal study of a large cohort of community-dwelling older adults revealed an incidence of Adult Protective Service cases of 6.4 per cent over an 11-year period (Lachs, Williams, O'Brian *et al.*, 1996). Experts have estimated that only 20 per cent of elder mistreatment cases are ever reported and thus elder mistreatment remains a largely hidden problem. Lachs *et al.* demonstrated that older people who are reported to APS (Adult Protective Services; see below) for physical abuse or caregiver neglect have a mortality rate three times that of seniors never reported to APS (Lachs, Williams, O'Brien *et al.*, 1998).

Elders in the community often experience a deterioration of their social network that may contribute to cognitive and functional decline (Yeh and Liu, 2003), factors linked to elder abuse and neglect. The NCEA Incidence Study (1998) found that elders unable to care for themselves were at greater risk of abuse; approximately

Table 4.6 Forensic markers

Forensic markers of abuse	Forensic markers of neglect
• Fractures, especially rib and sites that differ from sites of fractures seen with osteoporosis • Lacerations and abrasions • Bruises regardless of coloration • Evidence of use of restraints • Toxic levels of medication • Burns	• Dehydration • Malnutrition • Pressure ulcers • Contractures • Poor hygiene • Insect infestations

Sources: Dyer, Connolly and McFeeley, 2002; Mosqueda, Burnight and Liao, 2005.

60 per cent of victims of substantiated elder mistreatment had some degree of mental impairment. Other risk factors for elder mistreatment in the community include poor social functioning such as conflict with family or friends, social isolation, alcohol abuse and psychiatric illness (Shugarman, Fries, Wolf *et al.*, 2003).

The above arguments drawn from North American studies are illustrative of a wider phenomenon. In 2002, the World Health Organization declared elder mistreatment a worldwide problem (WHO, 2002). But how do we gain a more accurate picture of its actual prevalence? Although a number of screening tools exist, they are cumbersome and have mainly been used for research (Fulmer, 2008). CGA is probably the best procedure for detecting elder mistreatment; however, it, too, is lengthy and requires a team of people. In most emergency centres or outpatient settings, it is most practical simply to ask if mistreatment is taking place. Some older people are embarrassed about the mistreatment, do not remember, or want to protect the perpetrators (who are likely to be family members). Clinicians can ask three simple questions to help determine the presence of mistreatment: (1) do you feel safe at home? (2) who prepares your meals? and (3) who handles your finances? Unsatisfactory or vague answers to these questions should provoke a further evaluation (Fulmer, Dyer, Connolly *et al.*, 2004). There are also a number of recognized forensic markers that can increase the clinician's index of suspicion for mistreatment (see Table 4.6).

In every jurisdiction in the USA, there is an agency responsible for accepting reports and protecting older people. In 46 of 50 states, there are mandatory reporting laws for health professionals. These protective agencies provide more or less social interventions based on budgetary constraints. Local social service agencies also minister to mistreated elders, bringing food, supplying medications and helping with home repair. Medical intervention teams in the USA and the UK help address the medical and social needs. Legal services are often needed to separate elders from perpetrators, help handle finances and enact guardianships where appropriate. To date there have been no clinical trials on interventions in cases of elder mistreatment.

The special case of self-neglect

Self-neglect is the commonest type of case received by state and county APS agencies (Lachs *et al.*, 1996; Pavlik, Festa, Hyman *et al.*, 2001). (APS refers to (US) Adult Protective Services, designed to protect adults at a potentially higher degree of risk such as older adults and adults with atypical physical and/or mental status.) Seniors who neglect themselves often live in squalor and/or dangerous environments such as homes with gas leaks, vermin, and animal and human faeces. Self-neglect almost always involves medical issues, such as co-morbid disease states that affect cognition and function (Dyer, Goodwin, Pickens-Pace, *et al.*, 2007). Self-neglect is often viewed as a benign condition that is the result of poor choices by cognitively intact elders. However, in a study of people with self-neglecting behaviours, Tierney and colleagues designed a study to measure harm in 131 people (Tierney, Charles, Naglie *et al.*, 2004). They defined harm as physical injury, property loss or damage, or an incident requiring emergency community intervention, as was experienced in 21 per cent of the self-neglecting study subjects. Dyer and colleagues reported on serious consequences of self-neglect, which included the absence of utilities, the presence of spoiled or rotting food, living with untreated advanced medical disease, or lying in excrement (Dyer, Pickens and Burnett 2007).

Addressing vulnerability

Seniors and their families must make concerted efforts to protect their interests and desires before they become too impaired to participate in their own decision-making. There are a number of vehicles to help one prepare. Unfortunately, many older people do not recognize or are unwilling to admit that they may become physically and/or cognitively disabled.

Wills

These legal documents can outline the wishes of an older person to be enacted at the time of his or her death. The concern is that as some older people become cognitively impaired, unscrupulous individuals befriend them and have the elder alter their will to benefit the new friend. Offspring also participate in this form of financial exploitation. It behoves lawyers who participate in this type of probate work to be sure that there is not undue influence exerted on the senior who wishes to change his or her will and that they have decision-making capacity (American Bar Association, 2005).

Advanced directives

These documents are often completed at the time that a will is made. They vary according to the laws of the individual locales. Advanced directives generally are enacted when the senior becomes too impaired to participate in rational decision-making. The medical power of attorney is duty-bound to honour the wishes of the senior.

Long-term care insurance

These policies may be helpful to some seniors, especially when home health services are covered. Alas, there are not enough data to determine if these policies are helpful to the majority of beneficiaries.

Family discussions

These discussions can be helpful to offspring or spouses left to care for an impaired elder. They must go beyond advanced directives to better elucidate the wishes of the senior regarding living situation, how to handle grey areas of decision-making (e.g. if the person is still physically functional, but has a dementing illness – what would the wishes be then?).

Guardianship

In some instances there are no family members to care for a senior or the family members are unable to provide the necessary care. In some other instances family members are abusing or neglecting the elder. In these cases guardianship may be a solution (note that the precise term used differs between places – e.g. it is called *conservatorship* in California, USA, and *ward of court* in the UK). Details vary according to the locale, but, in essence, a court-appointed body (either a single person or a committee) is appointed to take care of the financial and welfare needs of the person concerned. Decisions about guardianship should always require much thought and extensive evaluation on the part of the medical and legal teams. Guardianship strips older people of all rights and relegates him or her to the level of decision-making of a child and should never be entered into lightly.

Conclusion

This chapter has described some trends in mortality and morbidity that will affect the ageing population and the specialized assessment that is a standard of care for older people. The most common geriatric syndromes have been discussed and several management issues that differ in older patients from younger patients have been addressed. Finally, some of the consequences of co-morbid disease and vulnerability in ageing people have been described. Geriatricians, gerontological nurse practitioners and gerontological social workers have the training and experience to recognize these disorders and address the needs of vulnerable elders. Colleagues at Saint Louis University Geriatric Education Center (Morley, 2008) answer the question posed in the introduction: 'When is care by a geriatrician appropriate and how old does one need to be before he or she should visit a geriatrician?' They posit the following 10 reasons to see a geriatrician:

(1) memory problems
(2) falls
(3) polypharmacy
(4) sadness not being treated
(5) incontinence not being treated
(6) unexplained fatigue
(7) unexplained weight loss
(8) pain inadequately treated
(9) unsatisfactory experience with a physician's explanation
(10) at age 70 to check for potential geriatric problems and advice on health promotion and disease prevention.

Work force needed!

The management of co-morbidities and functional disabilities in older people will require a health-care workforce that is trained in the peculiarities and special needs of older people. These health professionals will need the skill sets and knowledge base that are broadly addressed in this chapter and other chapters in this book. In a 2008 Institute of Medicine report entitled *Retooling for an Ageing America: Building the Health Care Workforce*, the panel described the state of the health-care workforce and issued several recommendations. They noted that the health-care system often failed to deliver high-quality services tailored to the needs of older people. The education and training of the entire health-care workforce was deemed 'woefully inadequate'. The panel cautioned that immediate action was necessary to increase the numbers and skill sets of the health-care workforce so that they may competently meet the demographic shift and the health-care challenges it brings. The committee proposed the following approach:

- enhance the competence of all individuals in the delivery of geriatric care
- increase the recruitment and retention of geriatric specialists and caregivers
- redesign models of care and broaden provider and patient roles to achieve greater flexibility.

The WHO in collaboration with the ministries of health from the developed and developing countries developed a Primary Health Care Toolkit (WHO, 2005, 2008b). The purpose of this document is to sensitize and educate primary-care clinicians about the care of older people. The toolkit is a resource for:

- comprehensive and integrated care
- continuum of care
- physical and social environment
- primary-health-care core competencies.

The WONCA (World Organization of National Colleges and Academic Associations of General Practitioners/Family Physicians), the IAGG (International Association of Gerontology and Geriatrics), the IFA (International Federation on Ageing), the HAI (HelpAge International), the NYAM (New York Academy of Medicine), and others endorsed this document.

This population ageing can be seen as a success story for public health policies and for socio-economic development, but it also challenges society to adapt, in order to maximize the health and functional capacity of older people as well as their social participation and security. Along with this positive trend, however, come special health challenges for the twenty-first century. Preparing health providers and societies to meet the needs of elderly people is essential: this includes training for health professionals on old-age care, preventing and managing age-associated chronic diseases, designing sustainable policies on long-term care, and developing age-friendly services and settings (WHO, 2009).

Summary

The chapter examines the commonest syndromes encountered in older patients. Following an examination of trends in morbidity and mortality, it presents a very widely used method of geriatric medical assessment, the comprehensive geriatric assessment (CGA), the components of which are described in detail, but broadly are categorized as patient history, physical examination and functional assessment. Syndromes commonly found in older patients are then examined: dementia, depression, delirium, falls, incontinence and problems associated with polypharmacy. Clinical care of these and other problems often require techniques different from those required in younger patients, and a series of geriatric management principles are outlined. These are in essence 'tricks of the trade' designed to facilitate clinicians' management and care of older patients. These at times run counter to what would intuitively be considered good practice in younger patients. The chapter then considers the consequences of vulnerability, which arises when a person's physical or mental state cannot be, or is not, compensated for by the environment and/or medical support. Dealing with vulnerability often requires a delicate balance of intervention strategies. Several problems that arise from the consequences of co-morbid disease and vulnerability are then considered – alternative living situations, motor vehicle accidents, elder mistreatment and self-neglect. Finally, how to address vulnerability is critically discussed.

REFERENCES

American Bar Association Commission on Law and Aging and American Psychological Association Assessment of Capacity in Older Adults Project Working Group (2005) *Assessment of older adults with diminished capacity: a handbook for lawyers.*

American Geriatrics Society (2004–9) *Doorway thoughts: cross-cultural health care for older adults* (vols 1–3). Sudbury, MA: Jones and Bartlett.

American Medical Association (AMA) (2009) *Physician's guide to assessing and counseling older drivers.* Retrieved 7 January 2009 from www.ama-assn.org/ama/pub/category/10791.html.

Appelbaum, P.S. and Grisso, T. (2001) MacArthur Competence Assessment Tool for Clinical Research (MacCAT-CR). Sarasota, FL: Professional Resource Press.

Ayalon, L., Gum, A.M., Feliciano, L. *et al.* (2006) Effectiveness of nonpharmacological interventions for the management of neuropsychiatric symptoms in patients with dementia. A systematic review, *Archives of Internal Medicine, 18,* 166, 2182–8.

Bellelli, G., Frisoni, G.B., Turco, R. *et al.* (2007) Delirium superimposed on dementia predicts 12-month survival in elderly patients discharged from a postacute rehabilitation facility, *Journals of Gerontology. Series A, Biological Sciences and Medical Sciences, 62*(11), 1306–9.

Boltz, M., Capezuti, E., Bowar-Ferres, S. *et al.* (2008) Changes in the geriatric care environment associated with NICHE (Nurses Improving Care for Health System Elders), *Geriatric Nursing, 29*(3), 176–85.

Borson, S., Scanlan, J.M., Chen, P. *et al.* (2003) The Mini-Cog as a screen for dementia: validation in a population-based sample, *Journal of the American Geriatrics Society, 51*(10), 1451–4.

Boult, C., Altmann, M., Gilbertson, D. *et al.* (1996) Decreasing disability in the 21st century: the future effects of controlling six fatal and nonfatal conditions, *American Journal of Public Health, 86*(1), 1388–93.

Boult, C., Boult, L., Morishita, L. *et al.* (1998) Outpatient geriatric evaluation and management, *Journal of the American Geriatrics Society, 46*(3), 296–302.

Bulpitt, C.J., Beckett, N.S., Cooke, J. *et al.* (2003) Hypertension in the Very Elderly Trial Working Group, *Journal of Hypertension, 21*(12), 2409–17.

Burch, E.A. and Andrews, S.R. (1987) Comparison of two cognitive rating scales in medically ill patients, *International Journal of Psychiatry and Medicine, 17*(2), 193–200.

Burton, L. and Kasper, J.D. (2007) Demography, in P. Pompei and J.B. Murphy (eds), *Geriatrics Review Syllabus: a core curriculum in geriatric medicine,* 6th edn. New York: American Geriatrics Society, 229–32.

Cape, R. (1978) *Aging: its complex management.* Hagerstown, MD: Harper & Row.

Carey, I.M., De Wilde, S., Harris, T. *et al.* (2008) What factors predict potentially inappropriate primary care prescribing in older people? Analysis of UK primary care patient record database, *Drugs and Aging, 25*(8), 693–706.

Carr, D.B., Duchek, J.M., Meuser, T.M. *et al.* (2006) Older adult drivers with cognitive impairment, *American Family Physician*, *73*(6), 1029–34.

Centers for Disease Control and Prevention (CDC) and Merck Company Foundation. (2007) *The state of aging and health in America 2007*. Whitehouse Station, NJ: Merck Company Foundation. Retrieved 27 December 2008 from www.cdc.gov/aging/pdf/saha_2007.pdf.

Chandra, V., Ganguli, M., Ratcliff, G. *et al.* (1998) Practical issues in cognitive screening of elderly illiterate populations in developing countries. The Indo-US Cross-National Dementia Epidemiology Study, *Aging (Milan, Italy)*, *10*(5), 349–57.

Chang, Y.L., Tsai, Y.F., Lin, P.J. *et al.* (2008) Prevalence and risk factors for postoperative delirium in a cardiovascular intensive care unit, *American Journal of Critical Care*, *17*(6), 567–75.

Cohen, H.J., Feussner, J.R., Weinberger, M. *et al.* (2002) A controlled trial of inpatient and outpatient geriatric evaluation and management, *New England Journal of Medicine*, *346*(12), 905–912.

Connor, D.J. and Sabbagh, M.N. (2008) Administration and scoring variance on the ADAS-Cog, *Journal of Alzheimer's Disease*, *15*(3), 461–4.

Creditor, M.C. (1993) Hazards of hospitalization of the elderly, *Annals of Internal Medicine*, *118*(3), 219–23.

DuBeau, C.E. (2007) Incontinence, in P. Pompei and J.B. Murphy (eds), *Geriatrics Review Syllabus: a core curriculum in geriatric medicine*, 6th edn. New York: American Geriatrics Society, 720–34.

Dubinsky, R.M., Stein, A.C. and Lyons, K. (2000) Practice parameter: risk of driving and Alzheimer's disease (an evidence-based review): report of the quality standards subcommittee of the American Academy of Neurology, *Neurology*, *54*, 2205–11.

Dyer, C.B., Connolly, M.T. and McFeeley, P. (2002) The clinical and medical forensics of elder abuse and neglect. In R.J. Bonnie and R.B. Wallace (eds), *Elder mistreatment: abuse, neglect and exploitation in an aging America* (pp. 339–81). Washington, DC: National Academic Press.

Dyer, C.B., Hyer, K. Feldt, K. *et al.* (2003) Frail older patient care by interdisciplinary teams: a primer for generalists, *Gerontology and Geriatric Education*, *24*(2), 51–62.

Dyer, C.B., Kelly, P.A., Pavlik, V.N. *et al.* (2006) The making of a self-neglect severity scale, *Journal of Elder Abuse and Neglect*, *18*(4), 13–23.

Dyer, C.B., Goodwin, J.S., Pickens-Pace, S. *et al.* (2007) Self-neglect among the elderly: a model based on more than 500 patients seen by a geriatric medicine team, *American Journal of Public Health*, *97*(9), 1671–6.

Dyer, C.B., Pickens, S. and Burnett, J. (2007) Vulnerable elders: when it is no longer safe to live alone, *Journal of the American Medical Association*, *298*(12), 1448–50.

Edelstein, B. (1999) *Hopemont Capacity Assessment Interview manual and scoring guide*. Morgantown, WV: West Virginia University Press.

Engelhardt, J.B., Toseland, R.W., O'Donnell, J.C. *et al.* (1996) The effectiveness and efficiency of outpatient geriatric evaluation and management, *Journal of the American Geriatrics Society*, *44*, 847–56.

Fernandez, H.M., Callahan, K.E., Likourezos, A. *et al.* (2008) House staff member awareness of older inpatients' risks for hazards of hospitalization, *Archives of Internal Medicine*, *168*(4), 390–6.

Fick, D.M., Agostini, J.V. and Inouye, S.K. (2002) Delirium superimposed on dementia: a systematic review, *Journal of the American Geriatrics Society*, *50*(10), 1723–32.

Fick, D.M., Cooper, J.W., Wade, W.E. *et al.* (2003) Updating the Beers criteria for potentially inappropriate medication use in older adults: results of a US consensus panel of experts, *Archives of Internal Medicine*, *163S*(22), 2716–24.

Fillit, H. and Miller, M. (1993) The geriatric evaluation and treatment unit: a model site for acute care of the frail elderly, education, and research, *Mount Sinai Journal of Medicine*, *60*(6), 475–81.

Folstein, M.F., Folstein, S.E. and McHugh, P.R. (1975) Mini-Mental State. A practical method for grading the cognitive state of patients for the clinician, *Journal of Psychiatric Research*, *12*(3), 189–98.

Freter, S., Bergman, H., Gold, S. *et al.* (1998) Prevalence of potentially reversible dementias and actual reversibility in a memory clinic cohort, *Canadian Medical Association Journal*, *159*(6), 657–62.

Fulmer, T. (2008) Screening for mistreatment of older adults, *American Journal of Nursing*, *108*(12), 52–9.

Fulmer, T., Guadango, L., Bitondo-Dyer, C. *et al.* (2004) Progress in elder abuse assessment instruments, *Journal of the American Geriatrics Society*, *52*(2), 297–304.

Gammack, J. and Paniagua, M.A. (2007) Comprehensive geriatric assessment, *Missouri Medicine*, *104*(1), 40–5.

Hamilton, M. (1960) A rating scale for depression, *Journal of Neurology, Neurosurgery, and Psychiatry*, *23*, 56–62.

Haugh, R. (2004) ACE units take a holistic, team approach to meet the needs of an aging America. A fresh model for gerontology, *Hospital Health Network*, *78*(3), 52–6.

Hendriksen, C., Lund, E. and Strømgard, E. (1984) Consequences of assessment and intervention among elderly people: a three year randomised controlled trial, *British Medical Journal*, *289*(6457), 1522–4.

Holmes, C., Boche, D., Wilkinson, D. *et al.* (2008) Long-term effects of Abeta42 immunisation in Alzheimer's disease: follow-up of a randomised, placebo-controlled phase I trial, *Lancet*, *372*(9643), 216–23.

Inouye, S.K., Bogardus, S.T. Jr., Charpentier, P.A. *et al.* (1999) A multicomponent intervention to prevent delirium in hospitalized older patients, *New England Journal of Medicine*, *340*(9), 669–76.

Islam, S. and Mannering, F. (2006) Driver aging and its effect on male and female single-vehicle accident injuries: some additional evidence, *Journal of Safely Research*, *37*(3), 267–76.

Iwarsson, S. (2005) A long-term perspective on person–environment fit and ADL dependence among older Swedish adults, *Gerontologist*, *45*(3), 327–36.

Joint Commission Resources (2009) Retrieved 6 January 2009, from www.jcrinc.com.

Katz, S. and Akpom, C.A. (1976) 12. Index of ADL, *Medical Care*, *14*(Suppl. 5), 116–18.

Kelly, P.A., Dyer, C.B., Pavlik, V. *et al.* (2008) Exploring self-neglect in older adults: preliminary findings of the self-neglect severity scale and next steps, *Journal of the American Geriatrics Society*, *56*(Suppl. 2), S253–60.

Kiely, D.K., Jones, R.N., Bergmann, M.A. *et al.* (2007) Association between psychomotor activity delirium subtypes and mortality among newly admitted post-acute facility patients, *Journals of Gerontology. Series A, Biological Sciences and Medical Sciences*, *62*(2), 174–9.

Kircher, T.T., Wormstall, H., Müller, P.H. *et al.* (2007) A randomized trial of a geriatric evaluation and management consultation services in frail hospitalized patients, *Age and Ageing*, *36*(1), 36–42.

Klausner, A.P. and Vapnek, J.M. (2003) Urinary incontinence in the geriatric population, *Mount Sinai Journal of Medicine*, *70*(1), 54–61.

Kohlman-Thomson, L. (1992) *Kohlman Evaluation of Living Skills*, 3rd edn. Bethesda, MD: American Occupational Therapy Association.

Lachs, M.S., Williams, C., O'Brien, S. *et al.* (1996) Older adults. An 11-year longitudinal study of adult protective service use, *Archives of International Medicine*, *156*(4), 449–53.

Lachs, M.S., Williams, C., O'Brien, S. *et al.* (1998) The mortality of elder mistreatment, *Journal of the American Medical Association*, *280*(5), 428–32.

Lai, J.M. and Karlawish, J. (2007) Assessing the capacity to make everyday decisions: a guide for clinicians and an agenda for future research, *American Journal of Geriatric Psychiatry*, *15*(2), 101–11.

Larson, E.B., Wang, L., Bowen, J.D. *et al.* (2006) Exercise in people 65 years and older is associated with lower risk for dementia, *Annals of Internal Medicine*, *44*(2), 1–20.

Lautenschlager, N.T., Cox, K.L., Flicker, L. *et al.* (2008) Effect of physical activity on cognitive function in older adults at risk for Alzheimer disease: a randomized trial, *Journal of the American Medical Association*, *300*(9), 1027–37.

Lawton, M.P. and Nahemow, L. (1973) Ecology and the aging process, in C. Eisdorfer and M.P. Lawton (eds), *Psychology of adult development and aging.* Washington, DC: American Psychological Association, 619–74.

Leipzig, R. (2009) Hazards of hospitalization. No longer available.

Leslie, D.L., Zhang, Y., Holford, T.R. *et al.* (2005) Premature death associated with delirium at 1-year follow-up, *Archives of Internal Medicine*, *165*(14), 1657–62.

Maly, R.C., Hirsch, S.H. and Reuben, D.B. (1997) The performance of simple instruments in detecting geriatric conditions and selecting community-dwelling older people for geriatric assessment, *Age and Ageing*, *26*(3), 223–31.

Marson, D.C., Ingram, K.K., Cody, H.A. *et al.* (1995) Assessing the competency of patients with Alzheimer's disease under different legal standards. A prototype instrument, *Archives of Neurology*, *52*(10), 949–54.

Mathias, S., Nayak, U.S. and Isaacs, B. (1986) Balance in elderly patients: the "get-up and go" test, *Archives of Physical Medicine and Rehabilitation*, *67*(6), 387–9.

McGwin, G., Jr., Sarrels, S.A., Griffin, R. *et al.* (2008) The impact of a vision screening law on older driver fatality rates, *Archives of Ophthalmology*, *126*(11), 1544–7.

Merkelj, I. (2001) Urinary incontinence in the elderly, *Southern Medical Journal*, *94*(10), 952–7.

Molander, L., Lövheim, H., Norman, T. *et al.* (2008) Lower systolic blood pressure is associated with greater mortality in people aged 85 and older, *Journal of the American Geriatrics Society*, *56*(10), 1853–9.

Monane, M., Monane, S. and Semla, T. (1997) Optimal medication use in elders. Key to successful aging, *Western Journal of Medicine*, *167*(4), 233–7.

Morley, J. (2008) Ten reasons to see a geriatrician, *Aging Successfully*, *18*(2), 8.

Morley, J.E. (2008) Successful aging or aging successfully?, *Journal of the American Medical Directors Association*, *18*(2), 8.

Morrow, M. (1985) A predictive validity study of the Kohlman evaluation of living skills. Unpublished master's thesis, University of Washington, Seattle.

Mosqueda, L., Burnight, K. and Liao, S. (2005) The life cycle of bruises in older adults, *Journal of the American Geriatrics Society*, *53*(8), 1339–43.

National Center on Elder Abuse (1998) The basics. Retrieved 23 January 2009 from www.ncea.aoa.gov/NCEAroot/Main_Site/FAQ/Basics/Types_Of_Abuse.aspx.

(2005) The basics. Major types of elder abuse. Retrieved 23 January 2009, from www.ncea. aoa.gov/NCEAroot/Main_Site/FAQ/Basics/Types_Of_Abuse.aspx.

Naylor, M.D., Brooten, D., Campbell, R. *et al.* (1999) Comprehensive discharge planning and home follow-up of hospitalized elders: a randomized clinical trial, *Journal of the American Medical Association*, *281*(7), 613–20.

Nikolaus, T., Specht-Leible, N., Bach, M. *et al.* (1995) Effectiveness of hospital-based geriatric evaluation and management and home intervention team (GEM-HIT). Rationale and design of a 5-year randomized trial, *Zeitschrift für Gerontologie und Geriatrie*, *28*(1), 47–53.

Nikolaus, T., Specht-Leible, N., Bach, M. *et al.* (1999) A randomized trial of comprehensive geriatric assessment and home intervention in the care of hospitalized patients, *Age and Ageing*, *28*(6), 543–50.

Ostrosky-Solis, F., Lopez-Arango, G. and Ardila, A. (2000) Sensitivity and specificity of the Mini-Mental State Examination in a Spanish-speaking population, *Applied Neuropsychology*, *7*(1), 25–31.

Pandharipande, P., Cotton, B.A., Shintani, A. *et al.* (2007) Motoric subtypes of delirium in mechanically ventilated surgical and trauma intensive care unit patients [electronic version], *Intensive Care Medicine*, *33*(10), 1726–31.

Pavlik, V.N., Festa, N.A., Hyman, D.J. *et al.* (2001) Quantifying the problem of abuse and neglect in adults: analysis of a statewide database, *Journal of the American Geriatrics Society*, *49*(1), 45–8.

Pickens, S., Naik, A.D., Burnett, J. *et al.* (2007) The utility of the Kohlman Evaluation of Living Skills test is associated with substantiated cases of elder self-neglect, *Journal of the American Academy of Nurse Practitioners*, *19*(3), 137–42.

Prudent, M., Dramé, M., Jolly, D. *et al.* (2008) Potentially inappropriate use of psychotropic medications in hospitalized elderly patients in France: cross-sectional analysis of the prospective, multicentre SAFEs cohort, *Drugs and Aging*, *25*(11), 933–46.

Radloff, L.S. (1977) The CES-D scale: a self-report depression scale for research in the general population, *Applied Psychological Measurement*, *1*, 385–401.

Ravaglia, G., Forti, P., Maioli, F. *et al.* (2006) Conversion of mild cognitive impairment to dementia: predictive role of mild cognitive impairment subtypes and vascular risk factors, *Dementia and Geriatric Cognitive Disorders*, *21*(1), 51–8.

Reuben, D.B. and Siu, A.L. (1990) An objective measure of physical function of elderly outpatients. The Physical Performance Test, *Journal of the American Geriatrics Society*, *38*(10), 1105–12.

Robinson, M., Novelli, W., Pearson, C. *et al.* (2007) *Global health and global aging*, Chapter 25: Creating a healthy environment for aging populations. San Francisco, CA: Jossey-Bass.

Royall, D.R., Chiodo, L.K. and Polk, M.J. (2005) An empiric approach to level of care determinations: the importance of executive measures, *Journals of Gerontology. Series A, Biological Sciences and Medical Sciences*, *60*(8), 1059–64.

Royall, D.R., Cordes, J.A. and Polk, M. (1998) CLOX: an executive clock drawing task, *Journal of Neurology, Neurosurgery, and Psychiatry*, *64*(5), 588–594.

Rubin, F.H., Williams, J.T., Lescisin, D.A. *et al.* (2006) Replicating the Hospital Elder Life Program in a community hospital and demonstrating effectiveness using quality improvement methodology, *Journal of the American Geriatrics Society*, *54*(6), 969–94.

Schimmel, E.M. (2003) The hazards of hospitalization, *Quality and Safety in Health Care*, *12*(1), 58–63.

Shugarman, L.R., Fries, B.E., Wolf, R.S. *et al.* (2003) Identifying older people at risk of abuse during routine screening practices, *Journal of the American Geriatrics Society*, *51*(1), 24–31.

Stuck, A.E., Aronow, H.U., Steiner, A. *et al.* (1995) A trial of annual in-home comprehensive geriatric assessment for elderly people living in the community, *New England Journal of Medicine*, *333*(18), 1184–9.

Tan, M.C., Felde, A., Kuskowski, M. *et al.* (2008) Incidence and predictors of post-cardiotomy delirium, *American Journal of Geriatric Psychiatry*, *16*(7), 575–83.

Tariq, S.H., Tumosa, N., Chibnall, J.T. *et al.* (2006) Comparison of the Saint Louis University Mental Status Examination and the Mini-Mental State Examination for detecting dementia and mild neurocognitive disorder – a pilot study, *American Journal of Geriatric Psychiatry*, *14*(11), 900–10.

Teri, L., Gibbons, L.E., McCurry, S.M. *et al.* (2003) Exercise plus behavioral management in patients with Alzheimer disease: a randomized controlled trial, *Journal of the American Medical Association*, *290*, 2015–22.

Tierney, M.C., Charles, J., Naglie, G. *et al.* (2004) Risk factors for harm in cognitively impaired seniors who live alone: a prospective study, *Journal of the American Geriatrics Society*, *52*(9), 1435–41.

Tinetti, M.E. (1986) Performance-oriented assessment of mobility problems in elderly patients, *Journal of the American Geriatrics Society*, *34*(2), 119–26.

Tiwari, S.C., Tripathi, R.K. and Kumar, A. (2008) Applicability of the Mini-Mental State Examination (MMSE) and the Hindi Mental State Examination (HMSE) to the urban elderly in India: a pilot study, *International Psychogeriatrics*, *21*(1), 123–8.

Toldy, A., Atalay, M., Stadler, K. *et al.* (2008) The beneficial effects of nettle supplementation and exercise on brain lesion and memory in rat, *Journal of Nutritional Biochemistry*, *20*, 974–81.

van Bemmel, T., Gussekloo, J., Westendorp, R.G. *et al.* (2006) In a population-based prospective study, no association between high blood pressure and mortality after age 85 years, *Journal of Hypertension*, *24*, 287–92.

Viggo Hansen, N., Jørgensen, T. and Ørtenblad, L. (2006) Massage and touch for dementia, *Cochrane Database of Systematic Reviews*, Oct 18;(4):CD004989.

Wei, L.A., Fearing, M.A., Sternberg, E.J. *et al.* (2008) The confusion assessment method: a systematic review of current usage, *Journal of the American Geriatrics Society*, *56*(5), 823–30.

Wieland, D. and Hirth, V. (2003) Comprehensive geriatric assessment, *Cancer Control*, *10*(6), 454–62.

Workman, R.H., McCullough, L.B., Molinari, V. *et al.* (2000) Clinical and ethical implications of impaired executive control functions for patient autonomy, *Psychiatry Services*, *51*, 359–63.

World Health Organization (2002) *Missing voices. Views of older persons on elder abuse.* Retrieved 27 January 2009 from www.who.int/ageing/projects/elder_abuse/missing_voices/en/.

(2004) *Towards age friendly primary health care.* Geneva: World Health Organization Press. Retrieved 28 December 2008 from http://whqlibdoc.who.int/publications/2004/9241592184.pdf.

(2008a) *Global burden of disease: 2004 update.* Geneva: World Health Organization Press. Retrieved 29 December 2008 from www.who.int/healthinfo/global_burden_disease/GBD_report_2004update_full.pdf.

(2008b) Age-friendly primary health centres toolkit. Retrieved 23 January 2009 from www.who.int/ageing/publications/Age-Friendly-PHC-Centre-toolkitDec08.pdf.

(2009) Ageing. Retrieved 27 January 2009 from www.who.int/topics/ageing/en/.

Yeh, S.C. and Liu, Y.Y. (2003) Influence of social support on cognitive function in the elderly, *BMC Health Services Research*, *3*(1), 9.

Yesavage, J.A., Brink, T.L., Rose, T.L. *et al.* (1983) Development and validation of a geriatric depression screening scale: a preliminary report, *Journal of Psychiatric Research*, *17*(1), 37–49.

Zeiss, A.M. and Steffen, A.M. (1996) Interdisciplinary health care teams: the basic unit of geriatric care, in L.L. Carstensen, B.A., Edelstein and L. Dornbrand (eds). *The practical handbook of clinical gerontology*. Thousand Oaks, CA: Sage, 423–50.

Zimnavoda, T., Weinblatt, N. and Katz, N. (2002) Validity of the Kohlman Evaluation of Living Skills (KELS) with Israeli elderly individuals in the community, *Occupational Therapy International*, *9*(4), 312–25.

5 Social care and older people

RAYMOND NGAN

OVERVIEW

This chapter addresses the social care and informal support networks of older people. In particular, it examines community-based home care and the needs of older people, promoting happiness in social care, Litwak's theory of shared functions applied to informal care, additional problems imposed by dementia, and the concept of effective social care.

Prologue

There is a wide consensus that participation in social networks is highly beneficial and connected with ageing that is comfortable, secure and productive. Such participation, to the extent that it means feeling valued and appreciated, is regarded as a significant component of wellbeing.

(Australian Social Policy Research Centre, 2009, p. 3)

Inadequate social support is associated not only with lower overall general health and wellbeing, but also with higher levels of emotional distress, more illness and higher mortality rates.

(WHO, 2002, p. 2)

Whilst community care has been adopted as the policy approach in developing services for the elderly in Hong Kong, it has been taken for granted that the Chinese community here would have an extended family or large kinship network to render such 'care in the community' possible. In a survey among 540 families in Hong Kong in 1989, it was found that eighty per cent of the respondents' families had a support network size of not more than four persons. The majority of the elderly respondents had, none, to very few, such family confidants. Furthermore, it was found that the more aged they were, the smaller was their support network. The smallness of these informal support networks among old people is a concern in social care for older people.

(Ngan, 1990b, p. 21)

Community care providers in Australia have found that 41 to 62 per cent of new clients are depressed and 41 per cent are lonely.

(Anderson, Karmel and Lloyd, 2008, p. 51)

Informal support networks and social care of older people

As people age, their need for informal support and social care by their families and friends increases. This is especially so in older people who have just retired and the frail and oldest old (aged 80 and above). This is the result of a change in their social networks such as fewer contacts with former colleagues and reduced social contacts as a result of their increasing frailty (e.g. following a stroke or other decrease in their mobility levels). However, despite their stronger need for increasing social support, these problems may increase, adding to their social isolation and loneliness in the community (Higgs *et al.*, 2003; Lee, 2008). Research findings from the Growing Older Programme in the UK found that

(1) older people who are living with a partner, companion or family members, are more likely to use positive strategies to promote personal optimism in old age.
(2) Maintaining contact with other people is crucial in maintaining a reasonable quality of life (QOL). But it is the quality and 'density' of contact that matters, not the frequency. Older people with lots of friends and good-quality relationships, report the best QOL. For people from ethnic minorities, whose friendships are more likely to have been disrupted by migration, contact with family members is particularly important (Walker, 2005a).

So in what ways can social care promote the notion of ageing well for older people (Bowling, 2005)? This is the focus of this chapter.

Adopting a life-course perspective that addresses role changes across the lifespan (Bengtson and Allen, 1993; Bengtson *et al.*, 1997; O'Rand, 1996), this chapter addresses the following areas: dynamics of social care and informal support networks of older people; trends in community-based home-care services and social care needs of older people; promoting happiness in social care; a discussion of Litwak's theory of shared functions in informal care and critique; difficulties in looking after elders with dementia by their family members and coping methods; and a look at the prospect of effective social care.

It is argued that in formulating long-term care services, the small informal social support networks for most older people cannot be neglected, and that a complementary partnership should be promoted in integrating formal and informal care sectors to bring about happiness and positive well-being among older people. Ngan and Kwok's study on disabled older Chinese people in Hong Kong found that 58.3 per cent of the respondents said that they had no faithful friends to share their emotional problems with, and a very high proportion (83.3 per cent) admitted that they wished to have more people for sharing their emotional and family problems (Ngan and Kwok, 1992, 1993). This finding is supported by Lee's study (2008) in the city of Guangzhou in mainland China among frail elders who are clients of the 'home-based elderly service programme'. She found that, although in urgent situations, frail elders can get immediate help from their grown-up children, usually their sons who lived apart could not spend too much time with them nor provide long-term routine care. Despite their increasing hopes of seeing their sons more, the frail elders' expectations were not met, except during their sons' longer visits at times of accidents, falls, hospitalization and similar. Frail elders in Lee's study tended to suffer from loneliness – a problem the home-based elderly service programme could not effectively deal with because it is largely a meals-on-wheels service plus limited nursing care. In addressing the merits and strengths of informal social care, constraints and limitations thus also need to be noted.

Positive dynamics of social care and informal social support networks

Positive but particularistic dynamics of social care

Researchers have found that positive social interactions between older people and their family members, relatives, friends and neighbours protect against developing difficulties with physical functions in later life (Berkman and Syme, 1979; Cape and Gibson, 1994; Seeman, 2001). Other studies have shown that being part of an extensive social network has a protective effect on elders' health (Edelbrock, 1990; Liang, 1992; Revicki and Mitchell, 1990). A UK study of older people's social engagement and health and their use of community care and medication found that those who were more socially engaged were less likely to have seen their family doctor or district nurse in the month prior to the study (Bowling, 2005). Another study (Bowling and Browne, 1991) of the association between the ability to undertake activities of daily living (ADL – see Chapter 4), disability and social ties among people over 65 in London found that social ties can help to maintain ADL in old age and even to restore them after injury or trauma.

The positive dynamics of social care are embedded in older people's social networks, which are typically composed of family members, friends and neighbours. It is thus natural for many governments to pursue a general policy of 'ageing in place', emphasizing keeping older and frail people in their home or family settings for as long as possible via the provision of home-based community support services. However, it could also be the case that increasing frailty results in older people having fewer contacts outside the home, and hence a reduction in their involvement with friends (Bowling and Browne, 1991). This particularly affects the oldest of elders (aged 80 and above) in Hong Kong and could affect their mental health and cause emotional states such as depression and loneliness (Chi and Boey, 1994; Ngan *et al.*, 1997). Informal care is also particularistic in nature as some older people could have a very small informal support network (Australian Social Policy Research Centre, 2009; Ngan, 1990a). In promoting 'ageing-in-place', strategies aimed at reducing social isolation are needed. These strategies can be planned by social workers, who mostly serve as 'care managers' in active consultation with older people and their family carers.

Social care to include formal and informal care sectors

At a conceptual level, it is necessary to delineate clearly the formal and informal sectors of care. According to Froland (1980), the formal sector of care encompasses government-mandated or sponsored services, whether state-administered or provided through chartered intermediaries such as private nonprofit organizations. As such, the formal sector also includes private market-based services (by reason of regulation or reimbursement) as well as services provided by voluntary organizations that receive governmental financial support through tax transfers. Froland (1980) refers to the informal sector of care as those sources of care and assistance provided by family members, kin, friends and neighbours, indigenous or natural helpers, and informal self-help or mutual aid activities found within networks or groups, usually on an unorganized or spontaneous basis. In terms of its nature and origin, the informal care sector is referred to as the 'natural support systems' by Baker (1977) to include family and friendship groups, local informal caregivers and self-help groups not directed by caregiving professionals in voluntary welfare organizations. Informal care is thus in the main based on informal social relationships, shared experiences, affective concern and altruism. Credibility is determined by norms of exchange within the social network whereas formal help is mostly associated with professional care in statutory, formal and voluntary welfare agencies and organizations. Figure 5.1 illustrates the schematic differences between the formal and informal care sector.

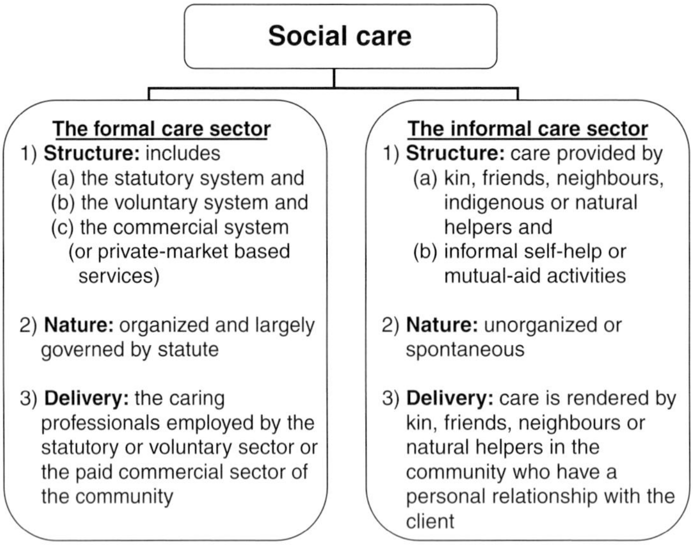

Figure 5.1 Differences between the formal and informal care sectors.

For frail older people who prefer to stay in their own residences with family members, care is typically provided by home-based support services provided by formal organizations and the bulk of tendering care by family caregivers. 'Social care' is perhaps a better term for this care pattern. As defined by Cantor (1979, 1991), social care comprises both formal and informal care networks existing side by side and providing support for activities required as part of daily living. Unlike health-related care, social care describes functional (task-oriented) and affective (emotional support) assistance in daily living, both of which constitute the predominant long-term care needs of dependent elders (Tavis, 1996). With increasing numbers of elders living alone, their emotional needs appear to be not well catered for by their grown-up sons and daughters, who often live apart. Although volunteers and home helpers might be in regular contact (e.g. through delivery of meals on wheels), few Chinese elders would wish to share their emotional problems with them (Lee, 2008). In Australia, community care providers found that 41 to 62 per cent of new clients are depressed and 41 per cent are lonely (Anderson, Karmel and Lloyd, 2008). In assessing the social care needs of frail elders who live alone or with their family members, their levels of loneliness, depression and emotional needs should be catered for properly.

Social networks, informal support networks and social support

What exactly do we mean by 'social networks'? The term dates back at least to Barnes in his 1954 study of class and committees in a Norwegian island parish.

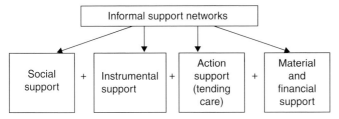

Figure 5.2 Types of informal social support.

In this he states that 'in Bremnes society, what is left is largely a network of ties of kinship, friendship and neighbourhood. This network runs across the whole of society and does not stop at the parish boundary' (Barnes, 1954). Thus, a person can have a large social network but the case might still be that he is related to his near neighbours but not every one of them is really helpful when needed. Walker, McBride and Vachon (1977) defined an individual's social networks as 'that set of personal contacts through which the individual maintains his social identity and receives emotional support, material aid and services, information and new social contacts'. This limits social networks to methods of informal support that could offer assistance to the person in need. As pointed out by Pancoast, Parker and Froland (1981), informal social networks are really no more than a term used to describe the structure within which people give and receive goodwill and good deeds in their own natural support systems, notably, family members, kin, friends, neighbours, co-workers and self-help groups.

What are the support provisions that an older person's informal support networks can render? According to Cobb (1982), informal support networks can usually perform the following four kinds of support:

(1) Social support: this has three components: emotional support, esteem support and network support leading the recipient to believe that he or she has a defined position in a network of communication and mutual obligation.
(2) Instrumental or informational support: this involves guiding persons to better coping or adaptation and to the maximization of their participation and autonomy. This is what House (1981) has called informational support – the provision of advice, experience and knowledge.
(3) Active support or tending care: this is what mothers do for infants and nurses do for patients; it reflects the kind of tending care rendered by informal carers, as, for instance, in being spontaneous and attentive to the needs of the recipients (Parker, 1981).
(4) Material support: the provision of goods, financial and material aids, and tangible aids.

These arguments are illustrated further in Figure 5.2.

Cobb (1982) remarked that social support appeared to be the most important protective function for older people, who often experienced a reduction in their supportive social networks as a result of their retirement or increasing frailty. However, among one's network of kin, friends, neighbours and co-workers, Hadley and Hatch (1978) found family members, notably spouse, sons and daughters, to be of over-riding importance in the provision of informal care to older people. In the USA, Shanas (1979) has shown how the large majority of infirm older people rely almost entirely on their families, and to a lesser extent on their friends and neighbours, for help with the housework, in preparing meals, in shopping, in bathing themselves, and when they are bedridden. Townsend (1965) in his classic study of family care of older people in London observed that those with families were far less likely to be admitted to institutions than those without, and those with very small families are more likely to be admitted than those with larger families. In Australia, the 2006 General Social Survey found that 96 per cent of older people (i.e. aged 65 and over) had some form of contact at least once a week with family and friends from outside their household, and 76 per cent had face-to-face contact with them (Australian Social Policy Research Centre, 2009). The study by Kawachi and Berman (2001) found that while social networks overall had a protective effect, networks with relatives had a particularly significant protective effect, both in delaying the onset of disability and in promoting recovery – certainly more so than networks of friends.

Limitations and constraints of informal care

Although advantageous in many respects, informal support networks are not without their limitations and weaknesses. These include the following:

(1) Not every elder has a large informal support network, ties with a neighbourhood, or an inclination to participate within a network of mutual aid in self-help groups who could be strangers to him or her. Network care is particular in nature and not universal for everyone. Moreover, not every network is helpful and caring, especially for those with less intimate ties.
(2) Continuity and reliability of care within the informal care of family, neighbours and devoted friends can also be problematic, as limited knowledge about problems and lack of resources undermine the ability to be of assistance (e.g. in cases of elders with dementia).
(3) Social and demographic trends indicate that in future there might be less family support. In addition, the increasing incidence of married women who engage in full-time jobs affects the availability of wives, grown-up daughters and daughters-in-law, who have traditionally been the major supply of informal carers.

(4) Biegel (1984) points out that existing informal support systems are often frag-
mented in their delivery. For example, there is almost always no one to coordinate the effective use of family members, kin, friends and neighbours, and
self-help groups for the well-being of frail elders.

Studies by the Australian Social Policy Research Centre (2009) found that social
contact with friends outside the home declined significantly with age. For example,
41 per cent of people aged 85 and over went out with or visited a group of
friends in the previous 3 months compared with 72 per cent of people aged 55–64.
Moreover, 66 per cent of people aged 65–74 years were actively involved in a
social or support group compared with 43 per cent of people aged 85 and over.
There are a higher number of deaths among isolated older people than among those
elders with networks of relationships and emotional support (Airling, 1987; Bath
and Deeg, 2005), while being part of a social network is a significant determinant
of longevity especially for aged men (Rowe and Kahn, 1997). Correspondingly,
in Asia, it has been found by Leung (2000) that there is an increasing trend for
older people in Hong Kong to live alone or with their spouses only. The traditional
three-generation household and extended family structure have become a rarity in
Hong Kong. With the high cost of living rising, women are increasingly required
to work to support family expenses. This trend contributes to the weakening of
support for frail older people, even in a traditional family where grandparents are
living with their children's family but are exposed to the risk of failing care and
support due to their family members' need to work out of the home (Chow, 2006;
Leung, 2000).

Family and social care of older people in post-industrial societies

From Gemeinschaft to Gesellschaft

Some sense of the direction of social change is needed so as to understand clearly
the part played by a family's informal support networks composed of the aged
person's spouse, family members, kin, friends and neighbours. As early as 1887,
the German sociologist Tönnies identified two dichotomized types of society: the
Gemeinschaft and the *Gesellschaft* (typically translated as 'community' and 'society' respectively). The former is to be found in the earlier stage of a society's development, with the social relationship being characterized by communal attachments
and small-scale interaction, and abounding with meaningful personal relationships
and intimate ties. As underlined by Tönnies, the prototype of all unions of Gemeinschaft is the family. Its three pillars, kinship, neighbourhood and friendship, are

all encompassed in the family (Bulmer, 1987; Tönnies, 1887 [1957]). However, as society undergoes social change and is transformed from a rural and agricultural to an urban and industrialized society, the close and communal attachments of the Gemeinschaft give way to the less binding and impersonal associational patterns of the Gesellschaft. In this type of industrialized society, people interact in contractual relationships for specific purposes, essentially to further their individual economic gains. People thus become much more impersonal and there are few elements of social care because of a shift towards more calculative relationships.

The importance of the above distinction is that Gemeinschaft is based upon affective and traditional ties, and Gesellschaft upon individualism, contractualism and the rational pursuit of interest (Bulmer, 1987). Certainly it appears that there are few elements of social care due to informal ties. Secondly, associated with the transition from Gemeinschaft to Gesellschaft is the idea that the primary group will eventually break down and give rise to mass society in an impersonal and rationalized urban form. Tönnies' views have been criticized because they are arguably too dichotomized. Theoretically, the idea appears sound, but empirically, as supported by the above-mentioned studies by social researchers on the prevalence of family care for older people in industrial societies, older people still receive care and aid from their friends and neighbours. They still have their close and intimate ties, though being smaller in size than in the old days in Gemeinschaft societies. Furthermore, contractual and bilateral exchanges within the pattern of urban living further necessitate informal care for stress buffering and for help in everyday and emergency situations such as illness or financial crisis (Spates and Macionis, 1987).

Although the family is alive and kicking in industrialized societies, this does not mean it is unaffected by the changing urban experience. For example, there are more dual-earner families in which both partners are obliged to work to maintain even a basic lifestyle. In post-industrialized societies (Bell, 1993), such people are often expected to work longer hours as the work is being compartmentalized to individual worker's responsibility. As noted above, this affects the availability of grown-up daughters and daughters-in-law to engage in a traditional role of caring for frail elders in the family. In addition, two key structural displacements have also had an effect:

(1) Large urban networks are not as close-knit as in smaller and rural communities. Rather, they are dispersed over the entire city areas and may even be loose-knit in having fewer regular contacts.
(2) Urban dwellers turn less frequently to kin for regular aid because their networks are composed of wider-ranging groups such as friends, neighbours and co-workers and intimate secondary groups like self-help groups (Wireman, 1984). According to Litwak and Szelenyi (1969), people usually turn to friends for

sociability and social support, co-workers for advice over work situations, kin for long-term assistance, and neighbours for emergency and easy aid.

'Convoys' and social relations in late life

Kahn and Antonucci (1980) developed the concept of *convoys* of social relations to examine social support relations and the size of informal care networks of adults. The convoy model emphasizes the importance of social relations and their longitudinal character in a lifespan perspective into old age (Antonucci and Akiyama, 1995). According to the convoy model, individuals move through their lifetimes surrounded by people who are close to them and who have a critical influence on their life and well-being. Antonucci and Akiyama (1995) point out that it is also necessary to examine how intra-individual development affects one's experiences of social care in old age. If the effects of worsening health and retirement are ignored, we cannot hope to make a realistic appraisal of the reduction in informal social support for people in late life. Thus, it is necessary to differentiate between socially close intimates and somewhat less intimate but still significant persons with whom older people are in active contact in examining the size of informal support networks. In the USA, Antonucci and Akiyama (1987) reported an average of 8.9 network members, with an average of 3.5 very close intimates, 3.5 close intimates and only 1.9 less close intimates. In their study of older adults (aged 60 and above) in Jerusalem, Auslander and Litwin (1991) found an average of 6.54 people to whom the respondent could turn for support. Ngan's study on 540 families in Hong Kong (Ngan, 1990a) found that 80 per cent of the respondents' families had a support network size of not more than four persons. A follow-up study (Ngan, 1990b) on disabled older people found that the majority of respondents had no, or very few, such family confidants. Furthermore, it was found that the older they were, the smaller their informal support networks. The smallness of these informal support networks is a concern in social care for older people, especially those frail elders who are mostly homebound due to their disabling conditions. To most elders in Hong Kong, kin networks are usually split between mainland China and the HKSAR (Hong Kong Special Administrative Region), and there is a higher tendency for married sons and daughters to move away from their aged parents' homes.

A gloomier picture of social care is found in the need for emotional support, especially for housebound and bedbound older adults. Seventy-eight per cent of the infirm respondents (aged 60 and above) in Ngan's study (1990b) reported that they did not have any co-living family members and kin to share their emotional problems, whereas another 83.3 per cent claimed that they did not have such faithful family members and kin who lived apart from them. However, a large majority

(83.3 per cent) of the respondents stated they wished to have more people to share their emotional problems. It suggests strongly that more effort is needed to enlarge the emotional sharing networks for disabled elderly people living in the community (Ngan and Kwok, 1992, 1993). Although grown-up children living apart often give money to their aged parents, their emotional support is a very important resource exchange as life-course social convoys within the family (Antonucci and Akiyama, 1995; Mancini and Blieszner, 1989). This is especially important as Lee's study (2008) found that in Guangzhou, frail elders who lived alone stated that their grown-up sons usually could not stay longer than absolutely necessary in the case of falls and unplanned hospitalization when their care could be taken up by adult daughters and doctors. These older respondents lamented that their emotional needs were not being properly matched by a son's prolonged physical availability although they tended to accept pessimistically that they could live apart from them. Furthermore, these frail elders did not like to tell their personal or family problems to neighbours, who may gossip. This is especially important to many Chinese people who have a tradition of face-saving. Lee (2008) remarked that 'as to the care from neigbours or friends, frail elders are always reluctant to trouble them. As to family care, the overriding concern is that adult children cannot spend too much time' (Lee, 2008, p. 128). Thus, although elders are basically cared for in the community, their emotional needs should not be overlooked.

The caring dilemma and caring injustice

Seen from the perspective of the caregivers, many of these people experience stress in their physical, social, financial and emotional lives (Kosberg, Cairl and Keller, 1990; Ngan and Cheng, 1992). Faced with mounting levels of stress and worry about their increasing inadequacies in looking after their declining elderly family members, caregivers will eventually face a caring dilemma (Ngan and Wong, 1995a, 1995b). This dilemma is whether they should continue the stressful family care or send their elderly relatives to institutions despite the fact that it is generally accepted in many societies as a family responsibility to look after the elderly.

Compared with earlier decades, the stress of family caregiving is particularly acute for several reasons. First, with advances in medical technology and longevity, people live longer and survive into their old age with more chronic diseases and/or with permanent disabilities which call for long-term and constant care of family members. Second, the supply of women as caregivers is reducing as more adult females join the workforce. Third, many caregivers find that they are increasingly unable to cope with the technical complexities of family care for their elderly relatives whose health conditions have deteriorated over time (MacKenzie and Beck, 1991). Indeed, in cases of senile dementia and paralytic strokes, the advice of specialized health-care professionals is required. Fourth, home-based

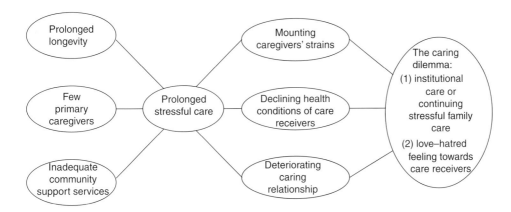

Figure 5.3 The caring dilemma.

community-care support services (notably community nursing care services and psychogeriatric home support services) often cannot keep pace with the increased demand by frustrated and stressed family caregivers. Fifth and finally, Walker (1985) argues that there is a social and cultural stereotyping expectation that the female member in the household will be the primary and usually the sole caregiver (Parker, 1981). Thus, handicapped by a lack of support and technical information on health care (e.g. fall prevention) and skills to deal with the disturbing behavioural problems of demented older people, more and more caregivers find that basic attending care patterns are inadequate. As a result, they begin to feel helpless and 'all alone' with escalating levels of anxiety (Kwan, 1991; Leung, 1989). Therefore, this increasing sense of helplessness, if not properly dealt with, might result in seeking institutional care for their frail elderly relatives. The relationships of these factors in contributing to the caring dilemma for caregivers are portrayed in Figure 5.3.

In general, women outnumber men as caregivers and their involvement in the caregiving activities is also far more intensive. Therefore, women caregivers have to bear the greater impact of the caregiving responsibilities. Thus it is understandable when Alan Walker commented that community care equals family care and family care is always women care (Walker, 1982, 1991). The Hong Kong Council of Social Service's study (1994) found that female caregivers are also more prone to psychiatric disturbances than male caregivers. Ngan and Wong (1995a) observed that a care injustice emerges when women have to shoulder most of the day-to-day caregiving of frail elderly family members as an assumed social duty without open acknowledgement and appreciation. Worse still, they have less support from other family members than their male counterparts. Similarly, Leung (1989) found that 68 per cent of his respondents surveyed reported that they had physically and psychologically abused their elderly dependants at least once when caregiving activities were provided under stressful conditions. The most common abuse was constant scolding and causing the older person to be terrified. It appears that there is a timely need for home-support community nursing and family care services to support the work of the stressed female caregivers, and that social workers should provide counselling and relevant support services to ease their emotional frustration and stress in a strained caring relationship.

The study by Ngan and Cheung (1999) on the effectiveness of home-care and support services for frail elderly people and their caregivers found that the duration of frail elderly clients' use of the services tended to contribute significantly to their family caregivers' health, knowledge of caregiving, reduced depression, perception of no life constraint, ability to take care of the elder and participation in social activities. However, a subsequent study by Ngan et al. (2001) on service use and quality perceptions in day-care centres found that although frail elderly users on average perceived high levels of the quality of care, they found a lower tendency for these centres to consult their needs (mean score = 33.4 out of a maximum 100 score) especially when family caregivers were not actively involved in their care plan since they were working in the daytime. In addition, the lack of a full-time physiotherapist in post in a typical day-care centre for older adults in Hong Kong affected their desire for more frequent personal exercise planning.

Litwak's theory of shared functions among informal carers

In discussing informal care, Litwak (1985; Litwak and Szelenyi, 1969) observed that there is a need to differentiate the types of primary-group caregivers in order to have a more realistic appraisal of their willingness and commitment to provide care (e.g. to ask for prolonged help over a considerable period from kin is not the same as asking from neighbours). Litwak described this as the *theory of shared functions* among informal carers. His theory asserts that one should turn to neighbours for handling immediate emergencies, kin for long-term care commitments and friends for emotional sharing. However, Ngan's study in Hong Kong (1990a, 1990b) found that because the size of informal support networks for families and disabled elders is small, a prerequisite is that the size of such caring networks has to be large so that people can turn to their different pools of reliable caregivers.

Thus, in the formulation of a social care plan for frail elders in need, the differing levels of care being called for should be tailored in a way that creates a realistic treatment team formed by informal carers. This calls for the use of the networking approach devised by Collins and Pancoast (1978). In this, the care manager consults their elderly clients' natural helpers (beginning with their spouse and/or grown-up children) to consolidate existing care patterns. The manager thus should act as a convenor of the elder's support networks. This promotes understanding of the existing caring commitments and, it is hoped, ensures better coordination of the caring efforts, supporting and strengthening them where necessary – for example, when it is necessary to call for the help of neighbours to buy daily necessities for homebound and frail elderly people, to mobilize kin to provide tending care, to attend to the difficulties arising from incontinence, difficulty in mobility and financial problems, and motivating a person to contact his friends for emotional support. Such a holistic treatment plan can meet the frail elder's varying social and emotional needs. It can also reduce the duplication of caring tasks and efforts, and avoid overloading the closest kin (typically the spouse or grown-up children) as caregivers.

Translating this catalysing role into practice suggests that the care manager should do 'network mapping' for clients, by identifying the number of informal carers in their social networks, the relationship with them, the types of aid which they have been providing, or are willing to provide, and the forms of support which they would need in order to provide the help on a continuing basis. The UCLA Lubben Social Networks Scale (Chi and Boey, 1992; Lubben, 1988) offers an assessment of an elder's family network, friend networks, confidant relationships and living arrangements. It is thus a useful guide in network mapping work for elderly people.

Changing concepts in ageing care

With more of their frail older citizens choosing to remain living in the community, the Australian government has been active in promoting community-based care, carer support and training, and dementia care programmes. George (2006) has observed the following changing concepts in ageing care in Australia:

(1) In mainstreaming old age and promoting a holistic approach to care of older people, there is a changing emphasis from dependence to independence, with associated questioning of the meaning of 'care' (Fine and Glendining, 2005) and the development of indicators of quality life strategies (Walker, 2006). In addition, 'vulnerability' is re-evaluated in terms of a positive approach to overcoming disabling problems in older age, rather than assuming inevitable deterioration (Schroder-Butterfill and Marianti, 2006). It is argued that formal care providers, frail elders and their families should be actively involved in formulating effective care plans.

(2) A tiered model of care and service provision was formulated in 2004. At the basic level, this includes care-link centres, providing information on locally available services. There is a basic assessment available to establish the elder's need for basic care, including respite care. At the highest level, a comprehensive assessment package determines a frail elder's need for packaged care, such as the Community Aged Care Packages (CACP) and the Extended Aged Care

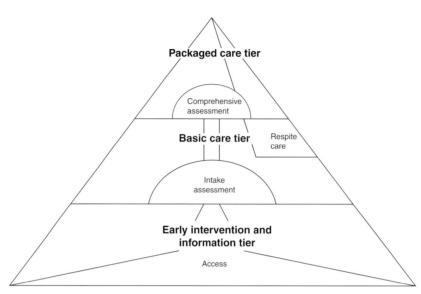

Figure 5.4 A tiered model of service provision. *Source:* George (2006). Reproduced by kind permission of the Hong Kong Association of Gerontology.

at Home (EACH). The latter is especially for those elders with mental health problems but living in their residences with family members. EACH teams serve to provide daily nursing supervision of the mentally infirm elder's medications, and the elderly client is regularly reviewed by her doctor, who coordinates her medical care, while her family coordinate her overall care at home. If deterioration necessitates a move away from the family home, the client will be able to progress to a hostel and subsequently to nursing home care (see Figure 5.4).

The system, although attractive in many respects, is not without criticism. For example, George (2006) commented that there should be a better health–aged care interface particularly with respect to coordination and transfers between hospital and community-based services. She observed that there were cases of older people being discharged at short notice without supports in place, and it was not unusual for people to wait 9 months for integrated services such as CACP. Also, some aged care services do not link well with the health-care system. For example, doctors are not always available at nursing homes at weekends, and generally staffing can be limited. Accordingly, frail/sick older residents, instead of being treated *in situ*, may find themselves sent by ambulance to an accident and emergency unit, placing pressure on an already overburdened hospital service. This is not a uniquely Australian problem. For example, in Hong Kong, the lack of nurses and psycho-geriatric trained nurses is hindering the launch of a community-wide home-based nursing care service proclaimed by the Chief Executive's Policy Address in 2007

(Tsang, 2007). Chow (2006) remarked that home-based community care services have usually been developed too late to cope with the increasing demand for nursing care in the community for frail elders living with their family carers, especially for those suffering from stroke and/or dementia.

Ageing well: social health, social capital and well-being

There is international interest in how to improve the quality of human life while extending its quantity, a concept Bowling (2005) terms 'ageing well'. It is well established that good levels of physical and mental functioning and general health status are associated with perceived well-being, morale and overall quality of life (QOL) (Bowling and Windsor, 2001). Bowling (2005) adds the caveat that it is necessary to include the state of social health in this equation. Elaborating further on WHO's (1948) definition of health as a state of complete physical, mental and social well-being, Bowling (2005, p. 31) defined social health as 'the structure, functioning and supportiveness of human relationships, the social context in which people live and integrate within society'. There is empirical support for the inclusion of social health, as several studies have found that social relationships, contacts and activities are nominated by older people as highly important for their QOL (e.g. Browne *et al.*, 1994; Farquhar, 1995).

   Social capital may be defined broadly as the resources available to individuals and groups through their social connections to their communities (Kawachi and Berkman, 2000). The term thus embraces the characteristics of older people's personal relationships and support structures, and their access to community resources. The latter notably includes periodic to prolonged visits by volunteers and participation in neighbourhood associations and the elders' own experiences of volunteerism (Putnam, 2000; Social Exclusion Unit, 2006). It seeks to promote older people's connectedness to, and integration within, society as the positive effect of strong social networks on elders' health and emotional support. This has been documented by various studies (e.g. Grundy and Sloggett, 2003; Putnam, 1993; Rochelle, Shardlow and Ng, 2009). A study of ageing in Hong Kong and the UK found that better self-reported health status was more prevalent among Hong Kong elderly respondents, with higher scores on health functioning, family-like orientation, perceived societal friendliness, favour of civic organizations, trust, mutual help, perceived social inclusion, sense of belonging, society-focused motivation (notably volunteerism), and perceived social inclusion (Rochelle, Shardlow and Ng, 2009). However, the British Chinese respondents reported significantly higher mutual help scores, reflecting the higher importance of mutual help among UK respondents compared to their Hong Kong respondents. However, this could

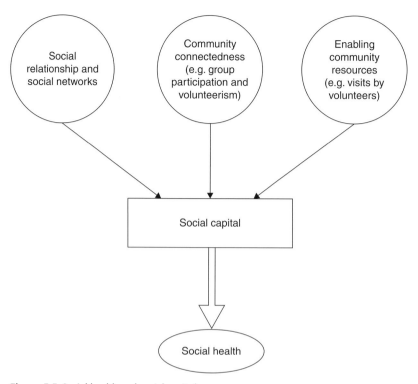

Figure 5.5 Social health and social capital.

be attributed to the fact that the British Chinese are a migrant group with fewer individuals to rely on for mutual help. Thus, the differing degrees to which social capital can promote social health among elders should be examined properly in the study of social care and subjective well-being (Figure 5.5).

The Growing Older Programme in the UK found that eleven factors affect older people's overall QOL (Help the Aged, 2005; Walker, 2005a). A slightly edited list is as follows:

(1) good social relationships with family, friends and neighbours
(2) standards of social comparison and expectations in life
(3) involvement in social and voluntary activities
(4) pursuing personal hobbies and interests
(5) good health and functional ability
(6) living in a good home in a good neighbourhood, and feeling safe
(7) a positive outlook
(8) psychological and emotional well-being
(9) adequate income
(10) easy access to affordable transport and services
(11) feeling valued and respected by others.

Although the UK study has a slightly longer list of factors, a QOL study among 3,000 elders in Hong Kong in 2003 shows more or less similar domain components with the exception of this unique item: 'eating good food' (Kwan *et al.*, 2003). The Chinese, in particular Cantonese people in southern China, place much regard and value on eating especially good food. For example, two colloquial sayings in Chinese are, 'eating is fundamental to the basic living of citizens' and 'the best food for eating is in Guangzhou [Canton City]'. A second difference between the studies is that while the UK study found that nearly three-quarters of people surveyed aged 65–69 rated their life as 'so good it could not be better' or 'very good' compared with a half and a third of those in older age groups (Help the Aged, 2005), the Hong Kong study found far lower overall QOL scores, with a variation of overall score ranging from 39.5 to 62.9 out of 100 (Kwan *et al.*, 2003; Ngan and Kwan, 2007). The mean overall QOL score was 47.9 (standard deviation (SD) of 12.52), which is significantly lower than the UK study. (The SD is a measure of how spread apart or varied the scores are – the bigger the SD, the bigger the variability.) Furthermore, it was found that the Hong Kong older respondents reported particularly low scores in the dimension of 'cultural activities' in the QOL measure. These measures included: opportunities to learn new things (mean score = 26.7 out of 100), studying (28.6) and joining interest classes (28.3). Increasing participation in social activities should thus enhance older people's community connectedness, especially when lifelong learning is being emphasized in promoting active ageing.

A major conclusion from the UK Growing Older Programme is that 'people should be encouraged to develop positive thinking and direct their perceptions upwards; they need to learn to be, and to feel, more in control of their everyday lives' (Help the Aged, 2005, p. 8). It points to the right direction in developing *active ageing* further (Walker, 2005b). The World Health Organization (WHO) defines active ageing as the process of optimizing opportunities for health, participation and security in order to enhance QOL as people age (WHO, 2002). It thus echoes the New Zealand Positive Ageing Strategy (Dalziel, 2001), which includes the following aims:

(1) empower older people to make choices that enable them to live a satisfying life and have a healthy lifestyle
(2) provide opportunities for older people to participate in and contribute to family and community
(3) reflect positive attitudes to older people
(4) ensure older people live with confidence in a secure environment and receive the services they need to do so
(5) ensure older people take responsibility for their personal growth and development through changing circumstances.

In what ways could policymakers move towards the development of 'positive ageing' or 'active ageing' strategies at a community-wide level with support from the government? This is an important policy concern in promoting social health among older people.

Quality-of-life measures

In addressing this issue, attention needs to be paid to methods of assessing QOL and similar measures. Cummins (1997) comments that commonly used QOL measurements, notably the SF-36 and the WHO-QOL scales, have a strong focus on medical symptoms and do not measure global SWB (subjective well-being). SWB refers loosely to the level of happiness, or how good people feel about their lives. The measurement of SWB is increasingly regarded as a robust and useful measure of life quality that can help monitor population wellness and identify individuals or subgroups who would benefit from interventions (Lyubomirsky, King and Diener, 2005). Such studies are useful for identifying relevant factors in promoting happiness, and early intervention programmes to help people with low SWB. The benefit of such studies, however, is greatly enhanced through the knowledge of normative population ranges.

The Personal Wellbeing Index (PWI) (The International Wellbeing Group, 2005) has been developed to measure SWB (Cummins, 2000). This is a short, generic and cross-culturally valid instrument, developed originally in Australia in 2001 by Robert Cummins. The instrument contains eight items that ask how satisfied people are with eight broad life domains. These are: standard of living, personal health, achieving in life, personal relationships, personal safety, community connectedness, future security, and spirituality/religion. Responses are made on an end-defined, 0 to 10 satisfaction rating scale. (An end-defined scale provides the respondent with definitions of what the ends of a rating scale mean (e.g. '1 = totally dislike' and '10 = totally like').) These eight domains represent the first-level deconstruction of satisfaction with 'life as a whole'. Each item is semi-abstract and together they provide a comprehensive view of subjective life quality (see Figures 5.6 and 5.7). The PWI is a reliable, valid and sensitive SWB scale which is widely used in Australia (Cummins, 2001, 2007) and other countries (International Wellbeing Group, 2005), and validation with general adult populations has shown comparable psychometric properties (Lau *et al.*, 2005; Lau, 2006).

The survey by Lau, Cummins and McPherson (2005) found that the mean PWI domain ratings from Hong Kong (range 57.5 to 72.0; SD: 14.4 to 18.9) are statistically and substantially lower on all items than those for Australia (range: 74.4 to 83.7; SD: 13.5 to 18.6). Within the PWI domains, the between-country range of

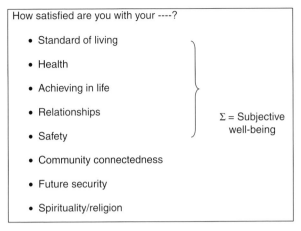

Figure 5.6 The Personal Wellbeing Index (PWI) and subjective well-being. Reproduced by kind permission of Springer Publishers.

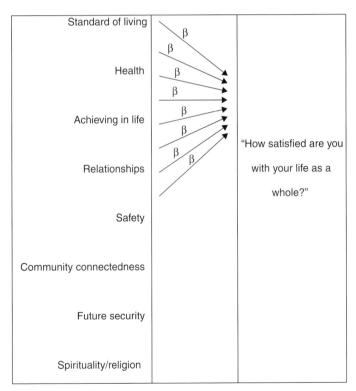

Figure 5.7 Personal Wellbeing Index: all domains must contribute unique variance. *Source:* Cummins (2000). Reproduced by kind permission of Springer Publishers.

difference is from 6.8 per cent (health) to 17.5 per cent (standard of living). An additional study by Lau *et al.* (2008) found that while elderly people living in districts suffering from severe acute respiratory syndrome (SARS) in Hong Kong showed significantly lower levels of SWB, consistent with the predictions of the theory of subjective well-being homeostasis (Cummins, 2007), these levels and those of the younger sample were found to remain within the normative range. This maintained level of SWB was due to an increased sense of community-connectedness, social networks and good health as mitigating factors. Bowling (2005) notes the need for measures of QOL to be more sensitive to differing cultural values and changes in life priorities with increasing age. This is supported by research reporting that people aged 75 and over were more likely than younger respondents to prioritize their own health, and the ability to get out and about, and were less likely to prioritize social relationships, finances and work, thus supporting the earlier discussion in this chapter on changes in convoys and social networks in later life (Kahn and Antonucci, 1980).

Social care for older people with dementia

With more older people surviving beyond their eighties, there is a higher incidence of elders with dementia. This poses increasing problems in managing their care, both by family carers and formal care staff. Common problems for family carers include elders' wandering around and getting lost, yelling and screaming, repetition of speech and disturbing behaviour, incontinence, and frequent complaints of things being lost or stolen. Mok (2009) found the following most difficult behaviours to handle for paid-care staff in elderly homes: spitting, escaping/going missing, wandering, and complaints about personal items being stolen or lost. She commented that more specialized training packages are needed to help care workers in these homes manage effectively these disturbing behaviours among dementia elders.

The late Tom Kitwood (1997) offered a *personhood* approach to train professional and family carers to adopt a holistic perspective; this, he argued, would enhance well-being through improved care of elders suffering from dementia. He urged that carers should seek to gain a holistic understanding of the person with dementia, each with their unique (and often unmet) needs for security and forgetfulness. He criticized the current medical model of dementia as an organic mental disorder because it neglects the needs and insecure feelings of the person with dementia, who is still an individual. By advancing the concept of personhood, Kitwood emphasized that the anxiety, fear, and unmet needs of older people with dementia should be recognized and addressed by care staff and their family carers (Kitwood and Woods, 1996). Thus, breakdown in communication among carers and elders with dementia (something hitherto not considered a high priority in many circles) should be avoided. Again, the needs and feelings of the person with dementia have to be recognized properly and not just as a nuisance to be controlled. For example, the message behind a person with dementia who often wanders around in the morning and afternoon in a residential home is that they are expecting family members to visit them or take them back to their former residence. Thus, reassurance from family members and/or care staff that the person is not being abandoned would be a helpful strategy emerging from Kitwood's perspective. (See Chapter 7 for further discussion of these issues.)

Another case concerns an older Chinese woman with dementia, living in Hong Kong. If not stopped, she would go to the market more than six times in a day and store excessive quantities of food in her refrigerator and kitchen. Blocking access to money was ineffective because she forgot she had no money, and as a housewife and mother for more than 50 years, she was conditioned to go to the market twice daily. If barred from leaving the house, she became restless, rude and distressed, wandering around at home and yelling at her (adult) sons and daughters. After discussion with the care manager, who adopted the personhood approach, it was eventually agreed that a small amount of petty cash would be given to her so that she could go shopping once in the morning and once again in the afternoon. If she tried to go out more frequently, family members would remind her of this, showing her the food she had bought already. This method proved effective.

However, Kitwood's personhood approach, although offering an enlightened and holistic perspective, is not a detailed, step-by-step instructional training package. It is still a value-laden approach rooted in social psychology to provide an inter-actional understanding of the needs of elders with dementia, and could appear abstract and piecemeal to family carers with low levels of education. It thus needs to be supplemented with other approaches, such as Mace's 6R behavioural management model (Mace and Rabins, 1991) and Zarit's stress management model (Zarit, 1985). These provide relatively quick methods of coping with disturbing behaviours, thus buying time to cultivate a personhood understanding. Adopting a behavioural management approach, Mace's 6R method seeks to provide a quick way to cope with the disturbing behaviours of demented elders. The *6R* is an abbreviation of *R*estrict, *R*eassess, *R*econsider, *R*e-channel, *R*eassure and *R*eview (Mace and Rabins, 1991). 'Restrict' refers to preventing the person with dementia from harming themselves or others. 'Reassess' asks caregivers to understand better the reasons for disturbing behaviours by the person with dementia. 'Reconsider' means thinking of matters from the viewpoint of the person with dementia and their fears and concerns. 'Re-channel' diverts the behaviour of the person with dementia into a safe and non-destructive form. 'Reassure' refers to giving both verbal and non-verbal recognition to the emotions of those with dementia and the caregivers themselves. 'Review' is to ask caregivers to think about what they have learnt from their experiences and how this knowledge can be transferred to other daily practices. The merit in Mace's approach is that it offers six different ways for family carers to cope with the disturbing behaviours of elderly member with dementia. However, Mace's model fails to offer a cognitive understanding of the anxiety, fear and needs of people with dementia, as it is basically a behaviourial management approach.

Zarit (1985, 1993) introduced the *stress management model* to promote a cognitive behavioural understanding of dementia to family caregivers. ('Cognitive behavioural' essentially means thinking/planning and how it shapes behaviour.) Components of the model are defined as information (content) and problem-solving (process) aspects. The purpose of intervention is to manage problem behaviours, increase social support and promote the health and well-being of caregivers. It adopts a step-by-step problem-solving process:

(1) identify the main problem
(2) generate alternative solutions
(3) select a solution: specifying pros and cons
(4) undertake cognitive rehearsal
(5) carry out the plan
(6) evaluate the outcome.

For example, an older woman with dementia attempts to phone her adult son at his office more than ten times in the morning almost every day. Zarit (1993) would suggest that the care manager identify this as the main problem and seek solutions; for example, asking her son to remind her that she has just phoned him, put a big sticker on the phone saying that her son is busy at the office, remove the phone from her reach, ask her son to call her two times each morning, etc. In a real-life instance of this problem, it was found through trial and error that the last option was the most effective solution (though her son forgets to make the second call at times). Zarit would suggest that the family carer needs to understand the message behind this frequent phoning by the mother with dementia – for example, is it because she wants to know if her son will be back in time for dinner so that she can prepare good meals in advance?

Mok (2009) demonstrated that using Mace's 6R method to train care staff in residential care homes is effective in providing quick methods to manage disturbing behaviours, at least temporarily. If followed by Zarit's stress management model, a cognitive understanding is cultivated among care workers, who become aware of the demented people's behavioural 'messages'. For example, their frequent wandering behaviour in the corridors of care homes can be interpreted as being unsure about mealtimes, uncertainty of the location of their bedrooms, forgetting the time to have a bath, and so forth. Finally, Mok (2009) found that using Kitwood's personhood method as the last training approach was effective in enhancing a holistic understanding and interaction with positive communication. The following are parts of some of the relevant verbatim in-depth interview records:

I have a deeper understanding of them [demented elders]. I have not worked in this field before. It is because of the impact from the parts of dysfunction of the brain. They don't want to be this way [disturbing behaviour] to bother us...I talk to her when I bathe her and understand her more. Now, I know how to sidetrack her when she is sad and crying for her family members. (personal care worker A)

I found she liked a singer ... So I sing for her when she looks upset and refuses to eat. Now she looks less upset. (personal care worker B)

I observed that Mrs C seems more annoyed when sitting next to the TV with the volume set high. I didn't realize this before and thought that it would be good for her to hear the sound from the TV programme. She is more stable and calm now. (personal care worker C)

Pathways of interweaving formal and informal care

In what ways could care staff enlarge the informal support networks of older people, especially those who are frail and feeble? Figure 5.8 has identified two possible pathways and three organizing roles for interweaving formal and informal care.

Pathway A is the starting point for most frail elders: having a small size of family confidants during a crisis. There are two organizing roles. First, care managers in formal welfare organizations should act as convenors to formulate a social care plan. This should first involve identifying family confidants and reliable carers. By performing network mappings in accordance with Litwak's theory of shared functions among informal carers, the assistance rendered by natural helpers can be coordinated optimally. Second, by acting as catalysts, existing support networks can be strengthened. In this regard, care managers should act as brokers to link community support services such as home help, day-care centres, home-based nursing care services, community aged-care packages and community psycho-geriatric visits to elders with mental health problems. In addition, effective links should be provided to help family caregivers join caregiver relief programmes such as respite care schemes and support groups. The aim of intervention at this level is not to overtake informal care but rather to facilitate its caring capacities by introducing community support services to ease the caregivers' burden.

Pathway B denotes the need to form an outer layer of self-help ties for older people in need. In this intervention pathway, there is a need for formal welfare professionals to act as support agents by helping survivors to form relevant self-help

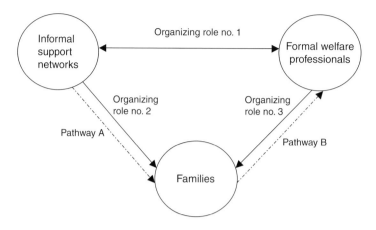

(I) <u>Pathway A</u> --- small number of family confidants during difficulties, calling for two
(II) possible organizing roles:

Organizing role no. 1 ---
(i) Convenor: social care organizer
(ii) Catalyst: strengthen existing networks

Organizing role no. 2 ---
(i) Broker: link to community support services (e.g. home help) to facilitate community care
(ii) Facilitator: facilitate informal care, e.g. caregivers' relief programmes or respite services

(II) <u>Pathway B</u> --- link to self-help peers or counterparts via forming mutual aid support groups

Organizing role no. 3---
(i) Support agent: helping to form self-help groups/ link volunteers and natural helpers in the community to clients

Figure 5.8 Pathways of interweaving formal and informal care.

mutual-aid groups. For those lone elderly people, there is a need for community empowerment. Workers in the formal welfare sector should try to facilitate visits from volunteers for constant reassurance, or should solicit the help of natural helpers in the community, such as next-door neighbours, to keep an eye on their well-being in the community should their self-care capacities become limited. These natural helpers are in effect the early alarm call to prevent family tragedies such as suicide by lonely and depressed older people, whose health conditions deteriorate quickly and who may lose hope in life. It is within such a caring context that informal care could be drawn upon through agents of community care, so that natural caregivers, support groups, volunteers and neighbourhood associations are probably the solutions to reduce social isolation among lone and frail elders living in their own residences. However, this begs the question – is the neighbourhood really caring in nature? There should be concerted attempts to promote neighbourly interaction and mutual help patterns, especially for tasks that call for proximate aid.

Conclusion: promoting happiness in old age

The primary objective of social care is to promote happiness in old age, and to enable elders to live in their residences and community as far as possible. But with increasing frailty and disabilities after stroke attacks, and with the trend for adult sons and daughters to live apart, there is an overriding concern to avoid elders living in their own houses, lonely and depressed. Although there have been attempts to promote social capital with volunteers to visit them, most frail elders prefer to have more frequent visits from their sons and grandchildren. The subjective well-being of elders living in the community and in residential care homes should be charted periodically for appropriate measures by the government to enable them to live with a happy mood bestowed by their adult children's love and concern.

Using Beck's Depression Inventory (BDI), Beck's Hopelessness Scale (BHS) and Beck's Suicide Intent Scale (BSS), Tan and Wong (2008) found that in Singapore, elderly patients who reported suicidal ideations were likely to be more severely depressed. However, in a depressed elderly person, the absence of suicidal ideations would not imply that the episode of depression was less severe.

How to promote happiness in old age through social care? We can start with the perspectives by positive psychologists like Martin Seligman (2004). He remarked that the ultimate goal of positive psychology is to make people happier by understanding and building positive emotion, gratification and meaning. He recommended that the first route to greater happiness is hedonic, increasing positive emotion by cultivating gratitude and forgiveness, by savouring and mindfulness, and by building hope and optimism. The second route is to increase the pursuit of 'gratification', which is defined as engaging in activities and pursuits that are enjoyable and fun. The third route to happiness seeks to enable one to find meaning in life: the 'pleasant life', 'the good life' and 'the meaningful life'. In what ways can we apply these three routes with depressed and very depressed older people? The most difficult part is to work with very depressed elders with strong suicidal ideations, as Shneidman's cubic model of suicide described (1987). More efforts are needed to help elders to be less preoccupied with loneliness, abandonment, uselessness and feeling a burden to family members, especially those elders with terminal illness.

In summary, expanding the effective social networks of frail elders is beneficial to their well-being. But this needs to be started with more frequent visits and concern from their adult sons and daughters. More home-based community support services should be developed to enable family caregivers to look after their infirm and frail parents at home. Care managers should seek ways to enlarge the informal caring networks of older people, and should be on the alert for their depressed moods, which increase the sense of loneliness and abandonment. Fundamentally, in discussing social care, the emotional needs and social health of lone elders should not be neglected, and social capital should be promoted to enhance integration and well-being among frail older people in the community.

Summary

Across the world, a high proportion of the care of older people is through the informal support of family and friends. How can social care best serve the goal of 'ageing well'? It can be readily established that social networks are often effective in promoting health and well-being. Differences between formal and informal care are then explored, as well as the precise definition of social networks and the levels and type of support they can offer. The limitations of informal networks are examined, such as lack of uniform or consistent provision. The effects of transition from Tönnies' Gemeinschaft to Gesellschaft on care are considered, and with it the loss of 'close-knit' communities with potentially greater and more immediate sources of aid. This leads to a discussion of Kahn and Antonucci's 'convoys' concept, and the perceived paucity of support that many older people in modern societies feel. The burden this places on caregivers, and the inequalities this often creates, are then examined, including Litwak's theory of shared functions among informal carers. This is followed by a discussion of changing official policies on promoting care. The related concepts of promoting 'ageing well' and QOL are then addressed. The effects of dementia on support both for the older adult and for the carer are examined. Finally, ways of promoting happiness in old age are discussed.

REFERENCES

Airling, G. (1987) Strain, social support and distress in old age, *Journal of Gerontology*, *42*(1), 107–13.

Alzheimer's Disease Society (2009) Information on dementia. Retrieved 5 May 2009 from www.alzheimers.org.uk/site.

Anderson, P., Karmel, R. and Lloyd, J. (2008) Movement from hospital to residential aged care. Research report. Data Linkage Series No. 6. Australian Government: Australian Institute of Health and Welfare.

Antonucci, T.C. and Akiyama, H. (1987) Social networks in adult life and a preliminary examination of the convoy model, *Journal of Gerontology*, *42*, 519–27.

(1995) Convoys of social relations: family and friendships within a life span context, in R. Blieszner and V. Bedford (eds), *Aging and the family: theory and research*. Westport, CT: Praeger Publishers, 355–71.

Auslander, G.K. and Litwin, H. (1991) Social networks, social support and self-ratings of health among the elderly, *Journal of Aging and Health*, *3*, 493–519.

Australian Social Policy Research Centre (2009) Promoting social networks for older people in community aged care. Research to Practice Briefing 2. Benevolent Society: Social Policy Research Centre, February 2009.

Baker, F. (1977) The interface between professional and natural support systems, *Clinical Social Work Journal*, *5*, 139–48.

Barnes, J.A. (1954) Class and committees in a Norwegian island parish, *Human Relations*, *7*, 39–58.

Bath, P.A. and Deeg, D. (2005) Social activity and health outcomes among older people: introduction to a special section, *European Journal of Ageing*, *2*, 24–30

Bell, D. (1993) *The coming of post-industrial society: a venture in social forecasting*. New York: Basic Books.

Bengtson, V.L. and Allen, K.R. (1993) The life course perspective applied to families over time, in P.G. Boss, W.J. Doherty, R. LaRossa *et al.* (eds), *Sourcebook of family theories and methods: a conceptual approach*. New York: Plenum Press, 469–99.

Bengtson, V.L., Burgess, E.O. and Parrott, T.M. (1997) Theory, explanation and a third generation of theoretical development in social gerontology, *Journals of Gerontology. Series B, Psychological Sciences and Social Sciences*, *52*(2), S72–88.

Berkman, L.F. and Syme, S.L. (1979) Social networks, host resistance and mortality: a nine-year follow-up of Alameda county residents, *American Journal of Epidemiology*, *109*, 186–204.

Biegel, D.E. (1984) Help seeking and receiving in urban ethnic neighborhoods: strategies for empowerment, *Journal of Prevention and Human Services*, *3*, 119–43.

Biegel, D., Shore, B.K. and Gordon, E. (1984) *Building support networks for the elderly*. Beverly Hills, CA: SAGE.

Bowling, A. (2005) *Ageing well: quality of life in old age*. Maidenhead: Open University Press.

Bowling, A. and Browne, P.D. (1991) Social networks, health and emotional well-being among the oldest old in London, *Journal of Gerontology*, *46*(1), S20–32.

Bowling, A. and Windsor, J. (2001) Towards the good life: a population survey of dimensions of quality of life, *Journal of Happiness Studies*, *2*, 55–81.

Browne, J.P., O'Boyle, C.A. and McGee, H.M. (1994) Individual quality of life in the healthy elderly, *Quality of Life Research*, *3*, 235–44.

Bulmer, M. (1987) *The social basis of community care*. London: Allen & Unwin.

Cantor, M.H. (1979) Neighbours and friends: an overlooked resource in the informal support system. *Research on Aging*, *1*, 434–63.

(1991) Family and community: changing roles in an aging society, *The Gerontologist*, *31*, 337–46.

Cape, R.D. and Gibson, S.J. (1994) The influence of clinical problems, age and social support on outcomes for elderly persons referred to regional aged care assessment teams, *Australian and New Zealand Journal of Medicine*, *24*(4), 378–85.

Chi, I. (1991) Family care of the elderly with dementia in Hong Kong, *International Social Work*, *34*, 365–72.

Chi, I. and Boey, K.W. (1992) *Validation of measuring instruments of mental health status of the elderly in Hong Kong*. Hong Kong: Department of Social Work and Social Administration, University of Hong Kong.

  (1994) *Mental health and social support of the old-old in Hong Kong*. Hong Kong: Department of Social Work and Social Administration, University of Hong Kong.

Chow, N. (2006) The practice of filial piety and its impact on long term care policies for elderly people in Asian Chinese communities, *Asian Journal of Gerontology and Geriatrics*, *1*(1): 31–5.

Cobb, S. (1982) Social support and health through the life course, in H.I. McCubbin and J.M. Patterson (eds), *Family stress, coping and social support*. Springfield, IL: Charles C. Thomas, 189–99.

Collins, A.H. and Pancoast, D.L. (1978) *Natural helping networks: a strategy for prevention*. Washington, DC: National Publishing.

Cummins, R.A. (1997) *Comprehensive Quality of Life Scale – Adult, manual*, 5th edn. Melbourne: School of Psychology, Deakin University, pp.1–51.

  (2000) Personal income and subjective well-being: a review, *Journal of Happiness Studies*, *1*, 133–58.

  (2001) The subjective well-being of people caring for a severely disabled family member at home: a review, *Journal of Intellectual and Developmental Disability*, *26*, 83–100.

  (2001–07) Reports on the Australian Unity Wellbeing Index. Retrieved from www.deakin. edu.au/research/acqol/index_wellbeing/index.htm.

  (2007) Subjective wellbeing and quality of life – a cross-cultural perspective, in K. Rao (ed.), *Mindscapes: global perspectives on psychology in mental health*. Bangalore: National Institute of Mental Health and Neurosciences, 21–31.

Dalziel, L. (2001) The New Zealand positive ageing strategy. Senior Citizens Unit, Ministry of Social Policy, Wellington, New Zealand. Retrieved from www.mosp.govt.nz.

Edelbrock, D.M. (2004) Disease, disability, service use and social support amongst community-dwelling people aged 75 years and over: the Sydney Older Persons Study. PhD thesis, School of Humanities and Human Services, Queensland University of Technology, Brisbane, Australia.

Farquhar, M. (1995) Elderly people's definitions of quality of life, *Social Science and Medicine*, *41*, 1439–46.

Fine, M. and Glendinning, C. (2005) Dependence, independence or inter-dependence? Revisiting the concepts of care and dependency, *Ageing and Society*, *25*, 601–21.

Froland, C. (1980) Formal and informal care: discontinuities on a continuum, *Social Service Review*, *54*(4), 572–87.

George, J. (2006) Changing concepts in ageing: a social policy perspective. Plenary speech presented at the 14th Annual Congress of Gerontology, Hong Kong Association of Gerontology, 25 November 2006, Programme Book, 6–12.

Grundy, E. and Sloggett, A. (2003) Health inequalities in the older population: the role of personal capital, social resources and socio-economic circumstances, *Social Science and Medicine*, *56*(5): 935–47.

Hadley, R. and Hatch, S. (1978) *Social welfare and the failure of the state*. London: George Allen & Unwin.

Help the Aged (2005) *Quality of life in older age: messages from the Growing Older Programme*. London: Help the Aged.

Higgs, P., Hyde, M., Wiggins, R. *et al.* (2003) Researching quality of life in early old age: the importance of the sociological dimension, *Social Policy and Administration*, *37*, 239–52.

Hong Kong Alzheimer's Disease Association (2009) Information on dementia. Retrieved 5 May 2009 from www.hkada.org.hk.

House, J.S. (1981) *Work stress and social support*. Reading, MA: Addison-Wesley.

International Wellbeing Group (2006) Personal Wellbeing Index and translated versions. Retrieved from www.deakin.edu.au/research/acqol/instruments/wellbeing_index.html.

Kahn, R.L. and Antonucci, T.C. (1980) Convoys over the life course: attachment, roles and social support, in P.B. Baltes and O. Brim (eds), *Life-span development and behaviour*, vol. 4. New York: Academic Press, 253–86.

Kawachi, I. and Berkman, L.F. (2000) Social cohesion, social capital and health, in L.F. Berkman and I. Kawachi (eds), *Social epidemiology*. New York: Oxford University Press, 174–90.

(2001) Social ties and mental health, *Journal of Urban Health*, *78*(3), 458–67.

Kitwood, T. (1997) *Dementia reconsidered: the person comes first*. Buckingham: Open University Press.

Kitwood, T. and Wood, R.T. (1996) Training and development strategy for dementia care in residential settings. Bradford: Bradford Dementia Group.

Kosberg, J.I., Cairl, R. and Keller, D. (1990) Components of burden: intervention implications, *The Gerontologist*, *30*, 236–42.

Kwan, A. (1991) *A study of the coping behaviour of caregivers in Hong Kong*. Hong Kong: Writers' and Publishers' Cooperatives.

Kwan, A., Cheung, C.K., Ngan, R. *et al.* (2003) *Assessment, validation and promotion for the quality of life and continuum of care of elderly people in Hong Kong*. Research Report, Hong Kong: Department of Applied Social Studies, City University of Hong Kong.

Lau, A. (2006) *Personal Wellbeing Index – Adult (PWI-A): Cantonese*, 4th edn. International Wellbeing Group. Manual 2006.

Lau, A.L.D., Cummins, R.A. and McPherson, W. (2005) An investigation into the cross-cultural equivalence of the Personal Wellbeing Index, *Social Indicators Research*, *72*, 403–30.

Lau, A.L.D., Chi, I., Cummins, R.A. *et al.* (2008) Severe acute respiratory syndrome (SARS) and the subjective wellbeing of Chinese elderly people in Hong Kong, *Journal of Aging and Mental Health*, *12*, 746–60.

Lee, W.K. (2008) Need-based community care resources for frail elders: usage and evaluation. PhD thesis. Department of Sociology, Zhungzhan University, Guangzhou, China.

Leung, E.M.F. (2000) Long-term care issues in the Asia-Pacific region, in D.R. Phillips (ed.), *Ageing in the Asia-Pacific region: issues, policies and future trends*. London: Routledge, 82–92.

Leung, W.H. (1989) An inquiry into the problem of elder abuse in Hong Kong, *Hong Kong Journal of Gerontology*, *3*(1), 6–9.

Liang, J. (1992) Social support among the aged in Wuhan, China, *Asia Pacific Population Journal*, *7*(3), 33–62.

Litwak, E. (1985) *Helping the elderly: the complementary roles of informal networks and formal systems*. New York: Guilford Press.

Litwak, E. and Szelenyi, I. (1969) Primary group structures and their functions: kin, neighbours and friends, *American Sociological Review*, *34*, 465–81.

Lubben, J.E. (1988) Assessing social networks among elderly populations, *Family Community Health*, *11*, 42–52.

Lyubomirsky, S., King, L., and Diener, E. (2005) The benefits of frequent positive affect: does happiness lead to success? *Psychological Bulletin*, *131*(6), 803–55.

Mace, N.L. and Rabins, P.V. (1991) *The 36-hour day*. Baltimore, MD: Johns Hopkins University Press.

MacKenzie, P.A. and Beck, I. (1991) Social work practice with dementia patients in adult day care, in M.J. Holosko and M.D. Feit (eds), *Social work practice with the elderly*. Toronto: Canadian Scholars' Press, 91–109.

Mancini, J.A. and Blieszner, R. (1989) Aging parents and adult children: research themes in intergenerational relations, *Journal of Marriage and the Family*, **5**, 275–305.

Mok, L. (2009) Caring for elderly people with dementia in Hong Kong: a holistic appproach. MPhil thesis, Department of Applied Social Studies, City University of Hong Kong.

Ngan, R. (1990a) The informal caring networks among Chinese families in Hong Kong. PhD thesis, Department of Social Work, University of Hong Kong.

(1990b) The availability of informal support networks to the Chinese elderly in Hong Kong and its implications for practice, *Hong Kong Journal of Gerontology*, **4**(2), 19–25.

(1993) The caring dilemma: towards effective counselling for caregivers of Chinese frail elderly, *Asian Journal of Counselling*, **2**(1), 7–16.

Ngan, R. and Cheng, I. (1992) The caring dilemma: stress and needs of caregivers of Chinese frail elderly, *Hong Kong Journal of Gerontology*, **6**(2), 21–8.

Ngan, R. and Cheung, J. (1999) A study on the effectiveness of the home care and support services for frail elderly people and their caregivers. Research report. Hong Kong: Haven of Hope Christian Service and Department of Applied Social Studies, City University of Hong Kong.

Ngan, R., Cheung, J., Ma, S. *et al.* (2001) Service use and quality perceptions in users of adult day care centres, *Hallym International Journal of Aging*, **3**(1), 115–32.

Ngan, R. and Kwan, A. (2007) Quality of life and care of older people in Hong Kong: implications for effective social services, in A. Kwan (ed.), *Promoting quality of life among older people*. Hong Kong: Cosmos Publication Press, 169–86.

Ngan, R. and Kwok, J. (1992) Informal caring networks among Chinese elderly with disabilities in Hong Kong, *International Journal of Rehabilitation Research*, **15**, 199–207.

(1993) Assisting disabled Chinese old people through informal caring networks, *Asia Pacific Journal of Social Work*, **3**(2), 90–101.

Ngan, R., Leung, E., Kwan, A. *et al.* (1997) Long term care needs, patterns and impact of the elderly in Hong Kong, *Hong Kong Journal of Gerontology*, **11**(2), 22–7.

Ngan, R. and Wong, W. (1995a) Injustice in family care of the Chinese elderly in Hong Kong, *Journal of Aging and Social Policy*, **7**(2), 77–94.

(1995b) The caring paradox: family care for Chinese elderly, *Asia Pacific Journal of Social Work*, **3**(2), 50–66.

O'Rand, A.M. (1996) The precious and the precocious: understanding cumulative disadvantage and cumulative advantage over the life course, *The Gerontologist*, **36**, 230–8.

Pancoast, D.L., Parker, P. and Froland, C. (eds) (1981) *Rediscovering self-help: its role in social care*. Beverly Hills, CA: SAGE.

Parker, G. (1985) *With due care and attention*. London: Family Policy Studies Centre.

Parker, R. (1981) Tending and social policy, in E.M. Goldberg and S. Hatch (eds), *A new look at the personal social services*. London: Policy Study Institute, 17–32.

Putnam, R.D. (1993) *Making democracy work: civic traditions in modern Italy*. Princeton University Press.

(2000) *Bowling alone: the collapse and revival of American community*. New York: Simon and Schuster.

Revicki, D.A. and Mitchell, J.P. (1990) Strain, social support and mental health in rural elderly individuals, *Journal of Gerontology*, **45**(6), S267–74.

Rochelle, T., Shardlow, S. and Ng, S.H. (2009) Ageing in Hong Kong and the UK: a comparison of the Chinese at home and abroad, *Journal of Comparative Asian Development*, *8*(1), 25–42.

Rowe, J.W. and Kahn, R.L. (1997) Successful ageing, *The Gerontologist*, *37*(4), 430–40.

Schneidman, E.S. (1987) A psychological approach to suicide, in G.R. Vandenbos and B.K. Bryant (eds), *Cataclysms, crises and catastrophes: psychology in action.* Washington, DC: American Psychological Association, 147–83.

Schroder-Butterfill, E. and Marianti, R. (2006) A framework for understanding old age vulnerabilities, *Ageing and Society*, *26*, 9–35.

Seeman, T.E., Lusignolo, T.M., Albert, M. *et al.* (2001) Social relationships, social support and patterns of cognitive aging in healthy, high functioning older adults, MacArthur Studies of Successful Ageing, *Health Psychology*, *20*, 243–55.

Seligman, M. (2004) A balanced psychology and a full life, *Philosophical Transactions of the Royal Society of London. Series B, Biological Sciences*, *359*, 1379–81.

Shanas, E. (1967) Family help patterns and social class in three countries, *Journal of Marriage and the Family*, *29*, 257–66.

(1979) The family as a social support system in old age, *The Gerontologist*, *19*(2), 169–74.

Social Exclusion Unit (2000) *Minority ethnic issues in social exclusion and neighbourhood renewal.* London: HMSO.

Spates, J.L. and Macionis, J.C. (1987) *The sociology of cities.* Boston: Wadsworth.

Tan, L.L. and Wong, H.B. (2008) Severity of depression and suicidal ideations among elderly people in Singapore, *International Psychogeriatrics*, *20*(23), 338–46.

Tavis, S.S. (1996) Families and formal networks, in R. Blieszner and V.H. Bedford (eds), *Aging and the family: theory and research.* Westport, CT: Praeger Publishers, 459–73.

Tönnies, F. (1957) [1887]. *Community and society.* East Lansing. MI: Michigan State University Press.

Townsend, P. (1965) The effects of family structure on the likelihood of admission to an institution in old age, in E. Shanas (ed.), *Social structure and the family.* Englewood Cliffs, NJ: Prentice-Hall, 163–87.

Tsang, D. (2007) Chief Executive's policy address 2007. Hong Kong: Government Printer.

Walker, A. (1982) The meaning and social division of community care, in A. Walker (ed.), *Community care: the family, the state and social policy.* Oxford: Blackwell and Robertson, 94–112.

(1985) From welfare state to caring society, in J.A. Yoder (ed.), *Support networks in a caring community.* Dordrecht: Martinus Nijhoff, 41–56.

(1991) The relationship between the family and the state in the care of older people, *Canadian Journal on Aging*, *10*(2), 94–112.

(2005a) *Understanding quality of life in old age.* Maidenhead: Open University Press.

(2005b) Active ageing: a global strategy for sustainable social protection, Hong Kong: Lingnan University Public Lecture of Vincent Woo, Distinguished Visiting Scholars Programme, 27 April 2005.

(2006) Extending quality life: policy prescriptions from the growing older programme, *Journal of Social Policy*, *35*(3), 437–54.

Walker, K.N., McBride, E. and Vachon, P. (1977) Social support networks and the crisis of bereavement, *Social Science and Medicine*, *11*(1), 35–47.

Wireman, P. (1984) *Urban neighbourhoods, networks and families.* Toronto: Lexington Books.

World Health Organization (1948) Preamble to the constitution of the WHO as adopted by the International Health Conference, New York, 19–22 June 1946. Geneva: WHO.
    —— (2002) *Active ageing: a policy framework*. Geneva: WHO.
Zarit, S.H., Orr, H.K. and Zarit, J.M. (1985) *The hidden victims of Alzheimer's disease: families under stress*. New York: New York University Press.
Zarit, S.H. and Pearlin, L.I. (1993) Family caregiving: integrating informal and formal systems for care, in Zarit *et al.*, *Caregiving systems*, 303–15.
Zarit, S.H., Pearlin, L.I. and Schaie, K.W. (1993) *Caregiving systems: formal and informal helpers*. Hillsdale, NJ: Lawrence Erlbaum Associates, Inc.

6 Cognitive processes and ageing

PAUL VERHAEGHEN

OVERVIEW

. . . .

This chapter presents a critical survey of cognitive changes in later life. It examines speed of processing, changes in cognitive skills, intelligence, assembled cognition and means of coping with cognitive limitations in later life.

. . . .

Introduction

Let me start this chapter by letting you in on a little secret. There is no such thing as the psychology of normal ageing. Allow me to illustrate this. As I write this paragraph, our 2-month-old baby son is cooing in the background. Our baby obviously has a human mind, but this mind is very different from his parents', not just quantitatively (i.e. a temporarily dimmer version of the mash-up between my wife and me), but qualitatively as well (we have no idea what his cooing signifies beyond a quiet and quite brittle delight; likewise, he doesn't have a clue what we are telling him). There is a psychology of development, and it is very much needed: a child's mind is impenetrable to an adult. There is, however, no need for a separate psychology of ageing: older adults are just like young adults, except perhaps a little slower, a little less fazed by the hassles of life and a lot more mature. Put simply, changes over the adult lifespan tend to be quantitative, not qualitative. In fact, a simple rule of thumb could be that if change in an individual appears to be qualitative – a marked shift in personality, strange changes in cognitive processing – something is wrong (e.g. Hagberg, Samuelsson, Lindberg *et al.*, 1991; Sliwinski, Lipton, Buschke *et al.*, 1996).

This of course does not mean that adulthood is marked by stability. Things do change. This is illustrated by a large-scale meta-analysis on personality and ageing by Roberts, Walton and Viechtbauer (2006). Meta-analysis is a technique by which results from many different studies are pooled and analysed as if they came from one single big study; the results summarized here were obtained from 92 studies with a total of 50,120 research participants. All these studies were longitudinal; that is, in each study a single group of people of different ages was tested repeatedly, with at least 1 year in between tests. With the exception of social vitality (i.e. sociability, positive affect and gregariousness), all personality traits show marked changes throughout adulthood. Only a few traits (social dominance, that is, dominance, independence and self-confidence, especially in social contexts; and emotional stability, which is the opposite of neuroticism) show mainly stability after age 40. Conscientiousness and agreeableness keep on rising over the lifespan; openness to experience declines after the age of 55. In sum, it seems that growing older does indeed amount to some degree of maturing – we become more self-assured, more sociable, more considerate, more dependable – perhaps at the cost of some flexibility of mind. Interestingly, this maturation process is not hard-wired in some genetic predisposition: heritability of personality change is large in childhood, but only slight in adulthood (McGue, Bacon and Lykken, 1993; Plomin and Nesselroade, 1990). Roberts *et al.* (2006) attribute their results to 'life experiences and life lessons' (p. 18); more specifically, the learning experiences and duties associated with the roles typically taken on in young adulthood – finding a long-term partner, starting a family and establishing a career. The pattern appears to be largely normative; that is, it appears to hold for most individuals: a different meta-analysis (Roberts and DelVecchio, 2000) showed that people largely maintain their rank order on personality traits over the course of adulthood – this suggests that the whole group of participants shifts up or down.

Psychologists interested in ageing are obviously concerned with describing such age-related changes, as well as examining their causes and consequences. In the next few pages I will expose my own bias, which is towards the study of cognition – how we gather, store and use information as we move through the world. Some other topics that one might consider at least in part psychological – relationships and sexuality, changing social roles, retirement, bereavement, etc. – are covered elsewhere in this book. My own bias appears to be in line with that of older adults themselves, as cognitive fitness becomes increasingly important to most people as they grow older. For instance, a 2006 survey by the MetLife Foundation found that while Americans as a whole fear getting cancer more than they fear getting any other disease, for those 55 years or older, Alzheimer's disease is the most dreaded. And while older adults often complain about memory loss (e.g. Blazer,

Hays, Fillenbaum *et al.*, 1997; Cutler and Grams, 1988), these complaints often do not correspond to actual changes in memory performance (Taylor, Miller and Tinklenberg, 1992). The association between ageing and cognitive decline is even encoded in our language. The term *senior moment*, for instance, does not refer to a revelatory flash of increased maturity but to brief memory lapses, experiences of cognitive impairment and even to functional incompetence (Bonnesen and Burgess, 2004). Even the observation that the present chapter was originally commissioned as a chapter on 'normal' ageing shows some bias: books on child rearing rarely contain chapters on the 'normal' child – in development 'normality' (whatever that is) is assumed; in ageing, it is not.

Age differences in cognitive performance

I will briefly document the basic differences observed between younger and older adults in studies of traditional aspects of cognition (speed of information processing, attention, memory and intelligence) as well as in what is sometimes called *assembled cognition* (expertise, creativity, and wisdom).

Speed of information processing

Everything we do takes time. The speed at which mental tasks are performed varies from individual to individual and from task to task. More difficult versions of the same task take longer. For example, it takes longer to read 1,000 words in this book than 1,000 words in a tabloid newspaper, just as it takes longer to process information spoken in a language or even an accent you are not completely familiar with. Psychologists measure the basic speed of information processing with tasks that are as simple as possible; for instance, by indicating with a key press on which side of a computer monitor, left or right, an X is projected. Such tasks have the advantage that they require relatively little effort and the processes used have little overlap with those implicated in higher-order cognitive tasks, such as memory or intelligence tests. A study by Lindenberger and Baltes (1997) demonstrated that these basic speed tasks (often labelled 'perceptual speed') peak early in adulthood and then show an ever-increasing decline.

One way to focus on this age-related slowing is to consider the average response time of older adults as a function of the average response time of younger adults. The resulting graph is called a Brinley plot, named after Brinley (1965). Plots are typically linear. In a meta-analysis of 92 studies representing a wide range of tasks and participants, a clear overall linear relationship was found, with an angle of slope greater than 45 degrees (Verhaeghen, 2006). A first finding from this graph (and other similar ones; e.g. Cerella, Poon and Williams, 1980) is that older adults are indeed consistently slower than younger adults. If older adults were as fast as younger adults, all data points would fall along the 45 degree diagonal. This is clearly not the case: a graph of the analysis contained 845 data points, and only 16 of those were situated on or below the diagonal.

A second conclusion is that age-related slowing is not random, but predictable. All points on the graph fell within a relatively narrow range. If ageing affected each task differently, we would expect a much less orderly pattern. Statistical analysis shows that we can explain 67 per cent of the differences between mean performance of older adult groups simply from knowing what the speed of the corresponding group of younger adults is, regardless of the nature of the task.

A third conclusion is that age-related slowing is proportional. In mathematical terms, this means that the regression line through the data points has a slope larger than 1 and an intercept close to 0. If we want to predict the average speed of a group of older adults from the average speed of a group of younger adults performing the same task, all we need do is simply multiply the average speed of younger adults by a certain value. The regression line shows this to be about 1.4; in other words, the average 70-year-old is about 40 per cent slower than the average 20-year-old. This means that older adults will be much slower on longer tasks than on tasks that are generally fast. This is best illustrated with a real-life example. In ideal circumstances, younger adults need about 2 seconds to activate the car brakes in response to an unexpected event. When circumstances are less than ideal (foggy weather, at nighttime, when talking on the cellphone, etc.) this reaction time can easily double. When younger adults need 2 seconds, older adults will need about 1.4 times 2 seconds, or 2.8 seconds. When younger adults need 4 seconds, older adults will need 1.4 times 4 seconds, or 5.6 seconds. When circumstances are ideal, older adults will be 0.8 seconds slower than younger adults, but at night, they might be 1.6 seconds slower. This could mean the difference (literally) between life and death – while driving at a relatively sedate 60 km/hour, an additional driving time of 1.6 seconds translates into a distance of 27 metres. Perhaps not surprisingly, many older adults adapt to these changes by driving more slowly or by travelling outside peak traffic hours (Charness and Bosman, 1995).

A fourth conclusion from the figures is that not all studies show the same slowing factor. Even though the band is relatively narrow and predictability is good, there is still a fan pattern to the graph, indicating variability in slowing factors. Part of that variability must be due to differences in methods across studies and to sampling error. But that is not the whole story. Further analysis revealed that there are two families of slowing factors. Some studies show smaller slowing factors (about 1.2 on average), while others show larger slowing factors (about

1.8 on average). The former studies have mostly employed two types of tasks: either sensorimotor tasks (i.e. fast reactions to the presence of simple stimuli, such as pressing a button when a light flashes) or tasks that concern simple verbal identifications (e.g. naming an object depicted on a card, reading a word out loud, determining whether a sequence of letters such as *BROP* form a word or not). These tasks show relatively little slowing. More severe slowing is observed in the second set of tasks, which have to do with spatial search processes (i.e. locating a specific item in a crowded environment) or mentally manipulating (e.g. rotating or folding) virtual objects.

Attention

Attention refers to concentrating the mind on specific aspects of the environment. Psychologists are mostly concerned with three aspects of attention: selective, divided and sustained. I will not discuss the final of the three, since data on ageing and sustained attention are sparse.

Selective attention refers to maintaining concentration on a single aspect of the environment and hence, by definition, excluding everything else. For example, at a party you might want to focus on the conversation you are having at the exclusion of all other conversations going on in the room. As everyone who has ever tried this knows, this type of attention requires effort. Psychologists often measure the ability to selectively attend by a simple but devious test called the *Stroop task*. Participants are shown a set of words printed in colour; their task is to name the colour the word is printed in. The twist is that some of the words presented are words denoting colours themselves. When the colour word is at odds with the colour it is printed in (e.g. the word *red* printed in yellow), participants are much slower than when the colour word is printed in the 'correct' colour (e.g. the word *red* printed in red) or when there is no word, but a set of Xs printed in colour. This task is difficult because reading is a quasi-automatic process, almost impossible to stop once started and this automatic reading interferes with colour naming. Surprisingly, on this task and other similar tasks, older adults are not slower than younger adults once you take into account that they are slower to name colours to begin with (see Verhaeghen and Cerella, 2002, for a meta-analysis).

Divided attention means spreading attention over more than one aspect of the situation. One example is talking on the cellphone while driving; the driver then divides her attention between keeping up with the conversation and monitoring the road. It has been found that under such circumstances the total amount of attention remains more or less constant, meaning that when you divide your attention, one or both of the tasks must suffer. In the case of chatting on the phone while driving, the cost is obvious: it takes drivers longer to brake when they are on the phone, their peripheral field of view shrinks (they get tunnel vision), and the probability of getting into an accident is increased fourfold (e.g. McEvoy *et al.*, 2005). Hence in some countries (e.g. the UK) using a cellphone while driving is illegal.

In the laboratory, psychologists measure divided attention by asking participants to perform two, typically simple, tasks at the same time – for instance, listening for a high-pitched sound while also reacting to the appearance of a visual stimulus on a computer monitor. This is called a dual-task situation. Older adults tend to do less well than younger adults, even if one takes their baseline slowing into account (Verhaeghen and Cerella, 2002). Driving while talking on the phone is never a good idea, but it would be even more disastrous for older adults. Research has shown that these dual-task costs (as they are called) also operate when participants are not aware that they are in a dual-task situation. Typically, we consider things such as walking around or simply standing up straight as effortless tasks. A German research team had participants walk around a room, tracking a particular route indicated on the floor while they were learning a list of words; the words were presented over wireless headphones (Li, Lindenberger, Freund *et al.* 2001). It turned out that people often made small missteps at the exact moment when a new word was presented. This effect was larger for older adults than for younger adults. In a different study, participants were learning a list of words while standing on a platform that simply recorded their centre of gravity (Rapp, Krampe and Baltes, 2005). Participants were wobblier during presentation of the words than in the silent pauses between words. This effect was again larger for older than for younger adults. Walking and standing turn out to be attention-demanding tasks after all, and older adults do less well on these tasks when they are additionally hit with a cognitive task to perform. Although the message from these studies appears rather glum, it was also found that older adults were quite adaptive in placing their priorities. Younger adults tend to favour the cognitive tasks (i.e. decrements were mostly in walking or balance performance) whereas older adults tended to protect their balance performance; i.e. they tended to forget more words but make fewer missteps (in the first study) or keep their centre of gravity within a safe area (second study). In later life the cost of falling is much higher than the cost of forgetting the occasional word, and older adults shift their priorities accordingly.

Another aspect of divided attention is the ability to shift attention from one task to another. A good example is an average day at the office: you switch between answering emails, fielding phone calls, actual work, dealing with visitors, making coffee, etc. Unsurprisingly, psychologists measure task-switching ability by having participants switch rapidly between simple tasks. In such studies, the stimuli are held constant, and only the task switches. For instance, participants might see a stream of digits, one at a time; on occasion, the colour of the digit switches from green to red and vice versa. Participants are trained to respond to the green digits with an odd/even judgement, and to the red ones with a size judgement (e.g. larger or smaller than 5). It has been found that every shift in task leads to a small increase in response time. The cost of switching between tasks can be calculated in two ways. One type of cost, the *global cost*, concerns the difference between the time needed during a task-switching situation and the time needed when each of the tasks is performed alone. The other type of cost, the *local cost*, is calculated during task-switching situations only, and concerns the difference between the response time during an actual shift (from odd/even to size, or vice versa) and the response time during a non-shift (two odd/even or two size judgements in a row). The global cost reflects the cost needed to keep both tasks active; the local cost reflects the need to select the correct task and repress the task no longer needed. Older adults show larger global task-switching costs than younger adults, but not larger local costs (Verhaeghen and Cerella, 2002). Older adults then have a much harder time than younger adults in keeping two tasks active at the same time, but once those tasks are active, they are as (in)flexible as younger adults in switching between them.

A final aspect of attention to consider is the size of the attentional field – the number of things or the size of the visual space that people can attend to. The attentional field is often measured by giving participants *visual search* tasks. For instance, looking for a particular target, such as the letter *F*, among a set of distractor letters, such as letters *E*. When only a single letter is present, older adults are about as fast and accurate as younger adults; but when the number of distractors increases, the age difference grows. This suggests that the attentional field shrinks with ageing. The size of the attentional field is likely to have consequences for tasks of everyday living such as driving. Karlene Ball and her colleagues (e.g. Owsley *et al.*, 1998) developed a task to measure what they call the useful field of view (UFOV). The difference between this task and traditional visual search tasks is that the UFOV tasks are dynamic: the participant has quickly and accurately to detect changes in the field of view. This is measured by asking participants to fixate the middle of a computer monitor; then, targets and/or distractors are flashed at smaller or larger distances from the point of fixation. The distance at which targets can be located with high accuracy indicates the boundary of the UFOV. Older adults do less well on this task than younger adults. To examine whether this test is indeed a good predictor of driving behaviour, Ball *et al.* (1993) studied a group of 294 drivers from Alabama, aged 55–90. The researchers measured the UFOV as well as visual acuity, contrast sensitivity, stereopsis, colour discrimination, and performance on a static visual search task. Then they investigated the participants' insurance records. The single best predictor of the number of at-fault car accidents participants were involved in was their UFOV score. Moreover, Ball and colleagues (Owsley *et al.*, 1998) conducted a 3-year follow-up with these same participants, and found again that the UFOV score was the best predictor of the probability of future accidents (the correlation was about 0.50).

Memory

This is the part of the cognitive system that manages knowledge: it extracts experience and knowledge from the environment, stores and maintains it, and (re)uses it at (it is hoped) the opportune time. The memory system is no passive registration engine, but an active system. That is, people interact in an active and dynamic way with their environment, and the information gathered along the way is rarely an exact replica of those happenings. For example, we select information depending on our interests, our motivations and our emotional state at the time of the event. Attention also plays a role: we remember things better if we pay more attention to them (and we pay more attention to things we find important). Psychologists make a difference between at least two memory registers: *working memory*, which retains information for a very brief period of time (typically less than 15 seconds), and *long-term memory*, which handles longer time spans. Working memory serves partially as the workspace of the mind and partially as a transition channel to long-term memory. This is the memory you use when you look up a number in the phone book or when you perform a mental calculation. It is not only limited in time, but also in space: its capacity is severely limited. Most people, for instance, can keep about 7 digits in their working memory, not more. One can use strategies to bypass this capacity limit, such as rehearsal, or chunking of information (essentially, grouping longer lists into conceptual 'chunks'). Working memory typically uses either an auditory or a visual code; that is, it works as an inner voice or an inner projection screen. Long-term memory contains more durable information. This is often saved in a semantic code; that is, a code associated with meaning, rather than an auditory or visual replica of reality. When you recall this text, for instance, you are unlikely to remember the sentences verbatim. Rather, you will (it is hoped) remember the gist; that is, the approximate meaning intended by the author. This has its advantages (compression) and disadvantages (lack of veracity).

One of the simplest tests for working memory is *digit span.* The participant is confronted with a series of digits, and she then recalls those she can remember. The longest series that can be remembered correctly is the memory span; it is typically between 5 and 9 items long. In a meta-analysis of 123 studies of diverse working memory measures, Bopp and Verhaeghen (2005) concluded that older adults have a span of about 7.1 digits, compared to a span of 7.6 digits for younger adults. The difference is not dramatic, but it is statistically significant. More recent span tasks take the active, dynamic nature of working memory into account. Participants are still asked to remember and then recall a set of words or digits, but now the memory items are interspersed with simple tasks such as verifying a short maths statement (e.g. *does 2 + 2 = 5?*) or checking the grammatical correctness of a brief sentence. Bopp and Verhaeghen found that younger adults can hold about 4 items in working memory, whereas older adults can retain only 3. Older adults thus seem to have more difficulty than younger adults when information needs to be actively manipulated. For example, Park *et al.* (2002) found that passive memory for digits declines less steeply than working memory. Age differences in working memory are likely to have consequences for the rest of the cognitive system. Research has consistently found that the active version of working memory correlates well with tests of intelligence (e.g. Engle, Kane and Tuholski, 1999) as well as with general language abilities (e.g. Kemper, Herman and Liu, 2004).

Long-term memory can be considered from a variety of perspectives. Psychologists often make the distinction between *implicit* and *explicit memory*. Explicit memory concerns tasks and processes that use memory in a conscious and deliberate way; implicit memory concerns tasks and processes that rely on memory, but without a conscious or deliberate attempt at retrieving information. Explicit memory can be further subdivided into *semantic memory* and *episodic memory*. Semantic memory is the memory for general facts and characteristics of things and places and people in the world, akin to an encyclopedia and dictionary in your head. Episodic memory refers to the memory for events and experiences you were part of – in effect, your autobiography. One of the fundamental differences between episodic and semantic memory is memory for context. For episodic memory, the context of the event is essential to make the memory autobiographical; for semantic memory, no context memory is necessary. To know what the word 'love' means, you do not need to know where you first encountered the word, or when you have ever used it. Autobiographically speaking, however, it is extremely important to remember when, where and to whom you have ever said, 'I love you' – misremembering can be quite dangerous. And there is a world of difference between knowing what a car is and knowing where you parked yours when you come out of the supermarket.

Brain research has shown that the temporal medial lobes, and more specifically the *hippocampus*, play a crucial role in the formation of permanent traces in explicit memory. Many of the events of the day are stored temporarily in the hippocampus. During sleep, the events are reactivated and memory codes are transferred to other areas of the brain (a process called *replay*). When this newly formed memory trace is strong enough, the original memory in the hippocampus disappears, but it leaves a form of file indicator that points at the permanent trace. The hippocampus then serves as both a control room and a library catalogue. When the hippocampus gets damaged (as happens in normal ageing but in much more extreme form in Alzheimer's disease), two forms of defects are manifest. First, new traces will be much less precise, and, second, retrieval becomes less accurate (or fails altogether). Memories that are more recent and have been reactivated less often are more likely to go first. The first form of deficit can often be observed in Alzheimer's patients. They might 'forget' your visit as soon as it is over, because it never registered; some patients may never have encoded their move to a nursing home, for instance, and keep insisting on going back 'home'. The second form of deficit could lead to the activation of routines that are no longer relevant, such as a retired Alzheimer's patient dressing for work after waking up confused. Or a patient might confuse her son with her dead husband – they may look alike, and the patient may have temporarily (or permanently) lost the memory of the husband's passing.

In contrast to explicit memory, implicit memory deals largely with information that is retrieved automatically; that is, with little or no conscious effort. Motor learning is a good example: you learn how to ride a bicycle by doing it often, and every time you get on a bike your body uses its motor memory to execute the complex set of motor patterns needed to keep your balance. When you turn on the TV and you happen upon a movie you've seen before, it takes you very little time to realize you have seen it before, and even if you don't remember the details you know it is familiar. Another example is what psychologists call *priming*; that is, a particular stimulus leads you to expect a particular other stimulus. If a friend tells you a story about something that happened during a river walk, you will spontaneously expect the word 'bank', if he uses it, to mean the side of the river, not the financial institution. Implicit memory bypasses the hippocampus and it remains often very intact, even in severe amnesic syndromes such as Alzheimer's disease or Korsakoff's disease.

Probably the best-documented finding in cognitive ageing is the large decline in episodic memory coupled with an absence of age differences in semantic memory. Park *et al.* (2002) found that the difference in episodic memory functioning between the average 70-year-old and the average 20-year-old is large; about 1.25 standard deviations. (This is a measure of variability, and in statistical terms, this is a large difference.) They also included a vocabulary test, which is a good marker for semantic memory; this variable shows an increase with age rather than a decrease. Meta-analyses confirm this picture: Verhaeghen, Marcoen and Goossens (1993) concluded that the difference between older and younger adults on memory for word lists, prose and word pairs was about 1 standard deviation (SD), and Verhaeghen (2003) found that older adults outperform younger adults on vocabulary tests by about 0.8 SD, although performance on vocabulary tests does decrease after age 90 (Singer *et al.*, 2003). One potential reason for the difference in age trajectories between the two types of memory is that semantic information is widely distributed across the cortex (Eichenbaum, 2003). For that reason alone it is less vulnerable to changes in brain volume and connectivity than episodic memory, which relies heavily on the intactness of the hippocampus.

One very important aspect of ageing in episodic memory is that the pattern of age-related loss is quantitative rather than qualitative in nature. In the Verhaeghen *et al.* (1993) meta-analysis, for instance, the most striking pattern was an across-the-board decrease in performance, with few areas of sparing or of exacerbated problems. In other words, the same principles that govern memory performance of younger adults also govern memory performance of older adults. In the memory literature, three such main principles have been distinguished: *depth of processing, encoding specificity* and *organization*. Depth of processing refers to the finding that materials are remembered better when they are processed for meaning rather than for surface characteristics (like sound or spelling). The more we understand what we are learning, the better we learn. The meta-analysis shows that when researchers help participants process material in a deeper way, both younger and older adults benefit in equal amounts. Encoding specificity refers to the finding that materials are better retrieved when the retrieval circumstances match the learning or encoding circumstances. One everyday example is what I like to call the kitchen cupboard phenomenon: you find yourself in front of, say, the kitchen cupboard with the firm conviction you came to get something, but you don't remember what. This is because the retrieval context (the kitchen) does not match the context in which you formed the intention (e.g. the garage). Simply retracing your steps, that is, going back to the encoding context, often jogs your memory (research shows that mentally retracing your steps works just as well). Another example is that it is often difficult to recognize people you only know in one context in another context – I sometimes fail to recognize one of my large-class students when they wait on me in a restaurant. The meta-analysis again shows that older adults benefit as much as younger adults from reinstatement of the original context. Organization, the third principle, is self-evident: information that can be organized is easier to remember. One example is memory for texts: we often remember the larger points better than the details. This, again, applies to older adults as well as to younger adults.

One aspect of memory testing that does influence age differences is the type of retrieval task. The findings mentioned above all concern recall; that is, memory performance when participants have to produce the correct answer themselves. Age differences are much smaller (about 0.5 SD; LaVoie and Light, 1994) when memory is tested by recognition; that is, when participants have to point out the correct answer from a number of alternatives.

Two consistent complaints often heard from older adults concern retrieval of semantic or quasi-semantic memory, namely forgetting names (or, put more accurately, retrieval of the name associated with a person about whom everything else is remembered) and word-finding problems. It is difficult to examine these two complaints in the laboratory because they appear to be uniquely tied to the retrieval situation. One method to investigate word-finding problems is to give participants a definition of a relatively rare word (e.g. 'What is another name for stamp collector?'). Sometimes the participant then finds herself in the curious state called tip-of-the-tongue: she knows the answer, but she cannot retrieve it. In tip-of-the-tongue states, incorrect alternatives sometimes keep popping up, even though the participant knows they are wrong (e.g. 'philanthropy'): often the participant has access to correct knowledge about the superficial characteristic of the word ('starts with *phil*', 'has four syllables', 'is Greek'). Studies show that older adults experience an increase in tip-of-the-tongue states, but not dramatically so. Heine, Ober and Shenaut (1999) found that older adults experience about 20 per cent more tip-of-the-tongue states than younger adults. This difference is about 0.5 SD, smaller than what is typically found in episodic memory tasks. In a second study, Heine *et al.* asked their participants to keep a diary for 28 days. Younger adults reported 5.2 tip-of-the-tongue experiences, and older adults 6.6 – again, a difference, but not a dramatic one. For both age groups, most tip-of-the-tongue states resolved spontaneously. The conclusion is that older adults do show more word-finding problems than younger adults, but that these problems are less frequent than expected on the basis of other memory problems. Perhaps these complaints are more salient to older adults because they can be spectacular, as, for instance, when one fails to retrieve a perfectly common word, or because these problems often occur in a social context and can lead to embarrassment.

Episodic and semantic memory are most often probed by looking at memories for facts and events. In real life, however, facts and events are always embedded in a context. One aspect of context that is often studied in the lab is memory for the source of a piece of information. This can be an important aspect in daily-life functioning: if you remember hearing somewhere that chocolate is a good remedy for feeling mildly depressed, it might be important also to be able to remember whether you read that in the newspaper, or whether your gossipy neighbour told you. Older adults appear to have a particular deficit in remembering context, including the source of information. Spencer and Raz (1995) conducted a meta-analysis on 46 studies. In these studies, which looked at either or both recall and recognition, the age-related difference for the content of what was learned was always smaller than the age-related difference for the learning context (0.75 versus 0.90 SD). The age difference was smaller, however, when content and context were intricately intertwined, such as words printed in a particular colour, or when words were read by either a male or female voice.

Episodic and semantic memory are retrospective forms of memory – they record the past. *Prospective memory* looks towards the future: it is the memory for intentions that need to be carried out sometime later – appointments to keep, errands to run, the mental to-do list. One method of examining prospective memory is through naturalistic studies; that is, studies that mimic the day-to-day workings of prospective memory. Typically, the participant is asked to do something in the days or weeks following an initial contact with the research team – call a particular phone number at a particular time, or mail cards at specific times. Contrary perhaps to certain expectations, older adults do much better on these tasks than younger adults. A recent meta-analysis (Henry, MacLeod, Phillips *et al.*, 2004) shows that the age difference favouring older people is about 1 SD. The reason for this age-related increase in performance may be the effective use of strategies; for instance, better use of a calendar, honed through decades of compensating for declining memory ability. Prospective memory can also be measured in the lab. Typically, the participant is engaged in a background task (e.g. a series of faces is projected on a computer screen, and the participant has to decide whether each face is famous or not); at the same time, she is also performing a prospective task (e.g. press a key when the face shown has facial hair, or turn a dial every 2 minutes). On these tasks, older adults do worse than younger adults, but the age difference, about 0.75 SD, is smaller than the deficit usually seen in episodic memory. The nature of the task covaries with the age difference: older adults are particularly disadvantaged when the characteristics one needs to react to are not very salient, when the association between the characteristic and the response is weak, and when the background task is more absorbing.

Some gerontologists make a distinction within long-term memory between *secondary* and *tertiary memory*. The latter denotes memory for facts or events that have occurred a very long time ago. This distinction resonates with many older adults. They complain that it is impossible to retain new information but that they have flawless memory for events from the distant past ('Don't ask me what I had for breakfast, but ask me anything you want about my daughter's wedding'). There are at least two problems with such assertions. First, the two events (breakfast and a wedding) are of a different nature and of unequal importance. Second, there is no way to test the correctness of the memory of the daughter's wedding day. (You, dear reader, may have learned from watching videos of such distant events from your own life that memory is indeed quite fallible.)

Tertiary memory does exist. Bahrick (1984) demonstrated that memory for Spanish vocabulary obtained from English-speaking Americans declined as a function of the number of years since they learnt the words (which was anything from circa 1 to 50 years earlier). This was greater for active knowledge (production of the correct translation) than passive knowledge (reading comprehension and word recognition). However, recall and recognition did not go to zero. Memory for Spanish vocabulary declined steeply over the first 2 years, but stabilized after that, with the remaining memories lasting 35 years or longer. Other studies using other stimuli (e.g. autobiographical events, or memory for what one has learned in a maths or psychology class) confirm this pattern: whatever information is retained 2 or 3 years after the last learning episode will last a lifetime.

There is, however, a time limit to this long-long-term memory. Bahrick, Bahrick and Wittlinger (1975) assessed memory for high-school classmates. Here, too, the active memories (producing names and recalling names prompted by photographs)

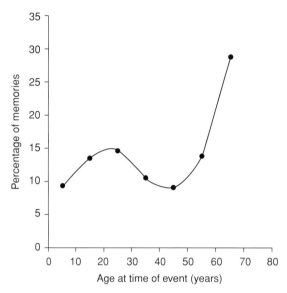

Figure 6.1 Distribution of autobiographical memories over the lifespan. The graph indicates the number of spontaneously generated memories as a function of the age at the time of the remembered event. Reproduced from Rubin, Wetzler and Nebes (1986) by kind permission of Cambridge University Press.

faded faster than the passive memories (recognizing names and faces and being able to place the right name with the correct picture). The most important new finding in this study was that there seems to be a second significant stage of decline, after 35 years of memory.

Some people believe that older adults live in the past. Research into *autobiographical memory* (memory of one's own life, as opposed to famous events taking place during one's life) does not confirm this claim. The results of one study, by Rubin, Wetzler and Nebes (1986), are reproduced in Figure 6.1. In this study, participants were given a prompt (e.g. the word 'cloud') and asked to come up with an autobiographical memory for each prompt; then they dated this memory. A first finding is that participants respond with relatively few early childhood memories (age 1–10). This is partially due to *childhood amnesia* (the phenomenon that most people have no reliable memories from before the age of 3 or 4 years). Second, most of the memories generated are not from the distant past but from recent events. Spontaneous memories are fresh, not decades old. Third, the curve shows a bump (often called the reminiscence bump) between the age of 15 and 30. The most likely explanation is that this is the age of new and exciting discoveries (first sexual experiences, gaining independence, first job, first forays into serious relationships, early parenthood, etc.). These new and emotionally salient experiences lead to better memories than routine events (which is bad news for most of us: if you aren't in the years of boredom already, you soon will be). If this hypothesis is true, the placement of the bump should shift according to the saliency of life events. This turns out to be true: people who immigrated to the USA at a late age show a bump around the time of immigration, and people who get divorced show bumps around the time of divorce and the start of a new family.

Intelligence

The study of adult age differences in intelligence is almost as old as intelligence testing itself – the earliest large-scale studies appeared in the 1930s. These studies often showed peak performance around age 20 and a steady decline after that. These studies were plagued by a number of methodological shortcomings (e.g. the participants were often illiterate or semi-literate, testing occurred in large groups in noisy rooms). The biggest problem is that these studies (like all studies on speed, attention and memory cited above) were cross-sectional in nature; that is, a sample of participants differing in age was tested at one point in time. It is thus possible that a number of the differences noted between younger and older adults are due not to age, but to generational differences, such as disparities in access to education, childhood nutrition and so on. Psychologists call such generational differences *cohort effects*; a cohort is a group of individuals growing up together within the same culture. If later-born cohorts are advantaged in terms of opportunities, cross-sectional studies will overestimate age effects because the cohort effects will favour the young.

One way to deal with cohort effects is to conduct *longitudinal research*, where one group of participants (ideally composed of people of different ages) is periodically tested and retested over a course of time (popular intervals are 3 and 7 years). The first large-scale longitudinal studies emerged in the 1950s, the best known arguably being Warner Schaie's Seattle Longitudinal Study (see Schaie, 2005, for an overview). Longitudinal research, however, has its own problems. First, even with these relatively large testing intervals retest effects can occur; that is, people score higher on the second occasion not because they have grown smarter, but because the test and the stimuli have become more familiar. Second, many longitudinal studies suffer from selective attrition: not every participant returns for a second or third testing session, and this dropout is correlated with initial ability – only the higher scorers return. Moreover, there is additional selection due to illness and death. Longitudinal research thus tends to underestimate age changes, especially in the very old.

Schaie (2005) measured longitudinal changes in six subsets of intelligence. *Inductive reasoning* is the ability to learn new concepts and the relationship between new concepts. It concerns solving logical puzzles, and measures not only insight, but also planning abilities and foresight. *Spatial orientation* is the ability to imagine spatial configurations in two or three dimensions, and to manipulate these configurations; it is also the ability to be able to assess the relationships between different objects in the same space. This ability comes in handy when getting acquainted with a new environment, when reading maps, or when assembling flat-packed furniture. *Perceptual speed* has been discussed above. *Numeric ability* concerns the understanding of the relationships between numbers; it is the ability to solve simple mathematical problems quickly and accurately. *Verbal ability* deals with the understanding of ideas as expressed in words; it is measured by the depth and breadth of passive vocabulary. *Verbal memory* concerns encoding and retrieving verbal information, such as lists of words.

Longitudinal studies generally find that although all abilities show accelerated decline after age 60 or so, peak performance for most abilities occurs much later than indicated by cross-sectional research. Only one ability (numeric ability) peaks in early adulthood. Perceptual speed peaks around age 40. Two abilities peak around age 50 – verbal ability and verbal memory. (The latter result differs from most other longitudinal studies, which show an earlier peak for memory. This is probably due to retest effects: the Seattle Longitudinal Study used the exact same list of 20 words at each measurement occasion.) There also appears to be a correlation between the time when decline becomes apparent and the size of the age effect: the abilities with the largest drop over age are perceptual speed and numeric ability. All other abilities show less drastic declines, and some even show an increase from young adulthood to early old age. A few other results from this study are noteworthy. Schaie discovered that there are no universal patterns of change. Not everyone's performance decreases on all tests. Around age 50, for instance, about half of the participants have shown a decrease on at least two abilities. At age 88, almost all participants have experienced decline on at least two abilities. But these two (or more) abilities differ across participants – there is no preordained pattern. Moreover, even at age 88, hardly any participant has experienced decline on all six measures. The group curves, then, do not generalize to the level of the individual.

Schaie also stresses that decline is no universal given. He calculated the number of participants whose scores declined, remained stable or improved over the 7-year interval between testing occasions. Over the course of adulthood, the number of participants whose scores increase declined (from 12 to 0 per cent), and the number of participants who scores decline increased (from 20 to 50 per cent). What is most striking, however, is that the majority of participants (50 to 60 per cent) show no difference in test scores. This percentage does not covary with age. In other words, most 80-year-olds experience stability in their test scores, not decline.

As expected, cohort effects turned out to be quite important in the Seattle Longitudinal Study. For almost all abilities, participants born earlier score lower, independent of age. Exceptions are verbal ability and numeric ability – those abilities peak for people born between roughly 1930 and 1950 and show a steady decline over successive cohorts. This suggests that a large part of the age-related decline observed in cross-sectional studies is not due to age at all, but to cohort differences – an indicator of a worse starting point rather than of a steep decline.

It should be noted that not everyone agrees with Schaie's (ultimately optimistic) conclusions. Salthouse (1991), for instance, observes that one factor that is not present in Schaie's analyses is historical change. The Seattle study allows one to disentangle cohort effects (related to date of birth) and historical effects (related to time of measurement). When time of measurement is taken into account, longitudinal results do not differ much from cross-sectional results: only verbal ability increases with age; all other variables decline markedly and do so from early adulthood on. Salthouse fits these results into the classical framework of *fluid* versus *crystallized intelligence* (Horn, 1970). Crystallized intelligence concerns that part of intelligence that is related to stored information, acquired over the course of the lifespan; when tested, this information is retrieved from long-term memory. Fluid intelligence concerns the manipulation of information during the course of the test itself. Verbal ability tests crystallized intelligence; all other tests in the Schaie battery tap fluid intelligence. Fluid intelligence then peaks in early adulthood; crystallized intelligence in old age.

The results of Salthouse's reanalysis have been confirmed in many other longitudinal studies (the Duke Longitudinal Study, the Berlin Ageing Study, the Bonner Längschnittstudie des Alterns, etc.). Each of those studies concludes that fluid intelligence decreases with age while crystallized intelligence rises. The two types of intelligence intersect at around age 40. It is thus tempting to conclude that younger adults are equipped with a lot of fluid resources to make up for their lack of experience. Part of Schaie's optimistic conclusions may also be tied to selection effects. Singer, Verhaeghen, Ghisletta *et al.*, (2003) analysed data from the Berlin Ageing Study and found, like Schaie, that cross-sectional age effects were larger than longitudinal age effects. When, however, only the profiles for those participants who returned for a second and third round of testing were considered, it appeared that cross-sectional and longitudinal results overlapped quite nicely. This suggests that selection is indeed a serious problem in longitudinal research – we only keep testing the fittest, and that leads to an underestimation of age effects.

Are matters different with regard to the use of intellectual skills in everyday life? Some researchers (including Schaie) argue that standard intelligence tests have little *ecological validity*; that is, the materials and tasks have little to do with older adults' daily life. The claim then is that older adults would show less decline on tests of everyday cognition. It is important to note here that standard intelligence tests have been developed precisely to have as little relevance to daily tasks as possible in order to avoid biasing towards a particular group or lifestyle. In the first half of the twentieth century, many intelligence tests (especially in the USA) used materials and questions that clearly disadvantaged particular groups (women, people of colour, non-native speakers, etc.). Modern intelligence tests therefore are as abstract as possible; the goal is to disadvantage everybody equally. In response to the perceived bias against older adults in standard tests, many researchers have developed tests for everyday problem solving. In such tests, participants work on problems that have high relevance to daily living, such as financial problems or medication-related issues. Often, these tests are presented in the form of brief vignettes (e.g. 'An older woman with no other source of income learns that, because of an administrative error, her pension cheque will be a month late. What should she do?'). These tests are obviously open-ended: there is, just as in life, no single optimal solution. Therefore, such tests are often scored by counting the number of effective and safe solutions advanced by the participant (e.g. robbing a bank would be effective, but it isn't safe). Sometimes participants are also asked how happy they are with their solution and how well they think it would work.

In a meta-analysis of 33 studies that examined age differences in these kinds of tasks, Thornton and Dumke (2005) found that older adults are still not doing quite as well as younger adults in these types of tasks, but that the difference is smaller than observed in standard tests for reasoning: 0.5 SD in the everyday problem solving tasks versus 0.9 SD for standard tests (Verhaeghen and Salthouse, 1997). When participants are asked to rate their own solutions, the age difference reverses: older adults are more pleased with their performance than younger adults are with theirs. One possibility is that older adults generate fewer solutions to problems than younger adults because they are happier with their initial solutions and do not look further, even if (at least as rated by the experimenters) older adults do not actually provide better solutions. This might be due to working-memory limitations in old age, which might preclude searching through a very large problem space until an ultimate solution is found. It is also possible to interpret the results from an expertise perspective: older adults know from experience that everyday problems do not have ideal solutions and that it is simply best to focus one's attention on a single workable solution and implement it as well as one can. An additional finding was that age differences were identical whether the problem was designed to be of concern primarily for older adults (such as the right choice of retirement plan) or for younger adults (such as decisions about an unwanted pregnancy). Age differences were, however, smaller for problems that had an interpersonal flavour (e.g. what to do when someone misbehaves at a party; 0.2 SD) than for problems that did not (e.g. what to do when your freezer breaks down in the middle of the night; 0.5 SD).

A very important domain of everyday cognition concerns medical decision making (e.g. deciding about a mastectomy or oestrogen replacement therapy). The literature on this topic is scarce, but the few studies that have been conducted indicate that, as in general everyday problem solving, older adults are faster to focus on one alternative. They also ask their doctor fewer questions and provide fewer detailed reasons for the decisions they ultimately make (Park and Hall Gutchess, 2000). Park *et al.* (2002) found that these potential deficiencies in medical decision making were linked to cognitive limitations in working memory and processing speed; prior knowledge about the specific medical problem, personal relevance of the problem, and perceived seriousness of the problem did not influence problem-solving strategies. This suggests that medical professionals who deal with older adults should be very proactive, clearly presenting the pros and cons of every solution, and should help older adults reason their way through the problems, without pushing.

Explanations for age differences in cognitive performance

Description is obviously not the only goal of gerontological research. We need explanations for cognitive changes as well. In the paragraphs above, I have already alluded to a few mechanisms that are sometimes invoked, but do not explain age-related decline very well: cohort differences and ecological validity. In this section, I will describe two approaches that are currently in vogue: cognitive-psychological explanations and biological explanations. These are not mutually exclusive: cognition is built on biology.

Cognitive-psychological explanations

Much of the research on cognitive ageing in the second half of the twentieth century has focused on micro-explanations; that is, explanations for the specific results of specific experiments without offering much in terms of an overarching framework. From the 1990s onwards, researchers seem to have been more concerned with hunting for more general principles – a limited set of variables that can indeed explain a majority of the age-related differences in cognition. The variables considered tend to be basic aspects of cognition: the idea is that deficits in these will lead to deficits in higher-order aspects of cognition as well. This hypothesis gains credibility when we consider that adult age differences in cognitive functioning are, as has been already noted, quantitative rather than qualitative. Basically three mechanisms have been posited in the literature.

The first is speed of information processing (Salthouse, 1996). As mentioned above, age-related slowing is a rather general phenomenon, which appears in even very simple tasks. The hypothesis is that this slowing of the mental clock will have two consequences. First, older adults' performance will break down when information is streaming too fast. Second, information will be lost when tasks become more complicated and require multiple steps with storage of intermediate results. This mechanism can explain age-related differences in multitasking or task switching: while one task is being performed, the other one needs to be kept more or less active in working memory. If the foreground task takes longer, it is likely that the background task may have slipped from memory (leading to cries of 'what was it again I was supposed to be doing now?').

Because slowing is so general and because the mechanism is already visible in very simple tasks, it might make sense to assume that it percolates through the whole system. This appears to be the case: in a meta-analysis Verhaeghen and Salthouse (1997) found that speed of processing can explain about two-thirds of the age-related variance in reasoning, spatial abilities and episodic memory.

A second hypothesis concerns control processes in working memory. Older adults, as noted above, have more trouble dealing with dual-task situations and with task switching – thus, processes that deal with task scheduling appear to be compromised. It is also possible that these problems are simple capacity problems: it might become harder to load more than a single task effectively in working memory. Thus, when one task is being performed, it might become harder to keep the other task equally active. Given that working memory capacity correlates with many other cognitive tasks (Engle *et al.*, 1999), it is possible that working memory plays a role in age differences in fluid cognition over and beyond the role played by processing speed.

A third hypothesis concerns sensory functioning. In the late 1990s (e.g. Lindenberger and Baltes, 1997), a group of researchers found very large correlations between age-related effects on cognition and age-related effects in very simple measures of sensory functioning. It turned out that this effect was not due to sensory limitations per se: when the visual and auditory deficits are simulated in a group of younger adults, their performance does not suffer. Additional studies demonstrated that not only sensory but also more general biological indicators correlate with cognition – measures like lung capacity, grip strength and even how many original teeth one still possesses. This makes it plausible that the causal mechanism is general biological fitness or intactness.

These three families of explanations are not mutually exclusive. Speed of processing and working memory capacity correlate with each other (e.g. Verhaeghen and Salthouse, 1997), and it is possible that speed of processing is simply an indicator for biological intactness (Salthouse, 1996). In any case, it is clear that a large part of the differences in cognitive performance between younger and older adults is due to general mechanisms that are likely to be related to brain functioning.

Biological explanations

There is no doubt that with advancing age the brain undergoes drastic changes. The brain of an average 20-year-old weighs 1,500 grams, and that of the average

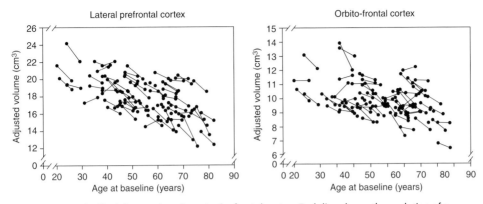

Figure 6.2 Longitudinal changes in volume in the frontal cortex. Each line shows the evolution of a single research participant. Reproduced from Raz *et al.* (2005) by kind permission of Oxford University Press and Professor N. Raz.

70-year-old 1,250 grams. Part of the weight loss is due to neuronal death, another part to shrinking of the mass of surviving neurons, and a third part to white matter loss. Not all brain structures are affected to the same degree. The frontal lobes show the largest volume loss, the temporal and parietal lobes are a little less affected, and the motor and sensory cortices are relatively spared (Raz, 2000). Figure 6.2 illustrates longitudinal changes in two specific areas of the frontal cortex – the part of the brain that is, among other things, responsible for mental coordination and cognitive control. Each of the lines in the plot is the trajectory for a single participant. It is clear that almost everybody shows a decrease in prefrontal volume, and that the rate of loss is more or less identical across participants.

Over time, the brain also gets burdened with deposits. The cytoplasm of hippocampal cells, for instance, often contains neurofibrillary tangles, loose protein segments that serve no function and in effect decrease the efficiency of signal transmission. These tangles accumulate over time and are often very obvious in Alzheimer's patients. In the interneuronal space, beta-amyloid plaques often accumulate as a result of degenerative neural structures. There are also age-related changes in the secretion and/or absorption of neurotransmitters, especially dopamine. All these changes lead to less efficient brain functioning. It appears that older adults' brains do compensate for such changes, or at least attempt to do so. One mechanism is the reduction in brain asymmetry often seen in older individuals (Cabeza, 2002). The brain's two hemispheres specialize in certain tasks; that is, some tasks are processed predominantly in one hemisphere (language, for instance, is often localized in the left hemisphere; spatial navigation in the right). Older adults appear to lose some of that asymmetry: they additionally recruit analogue structures in the opposite hemisphere. It seems that this recruitment is beneficial: older adults who have this asymmetry reduction tend to do better on cognitive tasks than older adults who do not. This recruitment is one example of how the brain adapts to the detrimental changes that come with ageing. It is important to note that these changes in brain functioning are not pathological, but a part of the normal ageing process.

Physical health plays an important role in cognitive functioning. Brain damage, hypertension and other cardiovascular disorders, thyroid disorders, stroke, hypoxaemia, medication or alcohol abuse, untreated diabetes, epilepsy and Alzheimer's disease all have a negative impact on cognitive functioning (e.g. Anstey and Christensen, 2000). Although these ailments are not part of the normal ageing process, they tend to become more prevalent with age. The effects on cognition of these illnesses are far from modest. When Verhaeghen, Borchelt and Smith (2003) examined a longitudinal sample from the Berlin Ageing Study, they found four syndromes to be related to cognitive performance: stroke, heart insufficiency, diabetes and myocardial heart infarct. Taken together, the effect on cognition was about 0.5 SD. The effect was larger for fluid intelligence than for crystallized intelligence. It is clear that prevention of cardiovascular disease can make a big difference in cognitive fitness in old age. This study also found that the effects of these ailments decreased with advancing age – after age 90, the presence or absence of these four syndromes no longer made a difference. One possible reason is that with advancing age the normal progression of brain deterioration is no longer distinguishable from the effects of cardiovascular problems and diabetes, which then have little to add to the picture.

In the USA, ethnic minority older adults fare less well on cognitive tests than non-Hispanic Whites (for an overview, see Manly, 2008), even after controlling for years of education (e.g. Bohnstedt, Fox and Kohatsu, 1994). Given that access to high-level educational opportunities for people of colour has been historically hampered in the USA and in many other countries, this variable needs to be controlled for in all analyses. Part of the Black–White difference reflects a failure to remove pro-Caucasian ethnic biases from the tests. For instance, within the African-American population the degree of acculturation (i.e. the level at which the individual participates in the values, languages and practices of her own ethnic community) still correlates negatively with test scores on fluid and crystallized intelligence even when accounting for age, education, gender and reading level (Manly, Byrd, Touradji et al., 2004). Part of this bias might be explained by stereotype threat; that is, the draining of attention away from the test itself to the concern that one's performance will confirm a negative stereotype about one's group (Steele and Aronson, 1995). Another part of the picture is health – the prevalence of several risk factors for cardiovascular disease is higher in African-Americans than in Whites, leading to higher incidences of stroke and white-matter abnormalities (Manly, 2008).

Assembled cognition

The previous paragraphs centred on cognition as it is typically defined in psychology textbooks: a set of abilities that can be measured by tests. There are, however, also forms of cognition and of intelligent behaviour that transcend the traditional definition of cognition, among other things because they are complex assemblages of different psychological aspects of performance. Here, I will briefly discuss three of such assembled types of cognition: *expertise*, *creativity*, and *wisdom*.

Expertise

A very special form of crystallized intelligence is the knowledge base an individual has acquired over a lifetime of experience in the domains of life in which she has invested most. Such accumulated knowledge can buffer or even annihilate age-related changes in basic abilities. One example is chess playing (e.g. Charness and Bosman, 1995). It seems self-evident that cognitive abilities such as speed of processing, working memory, long-term memory and reasoning ability contribute to high performance in the game. If only these were of relevance, chess players should peak in their early twenties, which is when these constituent abilities peak. That is, however, not the case: top performers in chess tend to be around 40 years of age. The reason is that peak performance in chess relies on the acquisition and use of a gigantic knowledge base of possible board positions and the best moves associated with each position. Research shows that chess grandmasters have no fewer than 50,000 of these positions stored in memory (compare this to the about 10,000 words of native-language vocabulary typically acquired by an 18-year-old college student). There is only one way to acquire that knowledge base: to play as often as possible and to spend long hours studying games from the past. There is even a correlation between the ranking of chess players and the number of chess books they own. Building up this knowledge takes many decades; after that the decline in fluid intelligence starts taking its toll.

The study of expertise has focused on the comparison of novices and experts in different domains such as musicianship, flying, graphic design, typing, baseball, crossword puzzles, chess, bridge and the game *go* (a review can be found in Hess, 2005). In each of these domains, expertise has a positive impact on performance. These effects tend to be domain-specific; that is, crossword puzzle experts are good at doing crossword puzzles, but they are not necessarily better at any other kind of memory task. Expertise does not appear to influence age differences: the differences between younger and older experts tend to be identical to those between younger and older novices. Expertise then serves to lift performance, not to stop decline. In the rare studies that do find smaller age differences for experts (graphic design in one study, flying an aeroplane in another) expertise does not make age differences disappear.

An interesting finding from a number of studies is that growing expertise, although domain-specific, can have positive consequences for those aspects of the cognitive system that the expertise relies on. For instance, Clarkson-Smith and Hartley (1990) found that bridge experts had a larger working memory, but that they did not differ from novices on speed and verbal abilities. Shimamura, Berry, Mangels *et al.* (1995) studied university professors of different ages and found the usual age-related differences in memory performance, with one exception: memory for text, which remained stable over age. Older typists (Salthouse, 1984) store more words in working memory while typing than younger typists. The conclusion is that the repeated and intensive practice of a specific ability can lead to preservation of that ability with age.

One terrain in which expertise is relevant is on-the-job performance. Even within samples of unskilled labourers there is a positive correlation between intelligence and job ratings by supervisors (e.g. Schmidt, Hunter and Outerbridge, 1986). A corollary could be that with advancing age, when abilities decline, on-the-job performance would decline as well. This is clearly not the case: meta-analyses find no relationship between age and job performance (Rhodes, 1983; Waldman and Avolio, 1986). Park (1994) offers a few reasons why this may be the case. First, the positive effects of increasing expertise might compensate for the decline in basic abilities, as explained above. Second, this effect might be enhanced because most older workers work in a stable environment, which allows them to keep using the skills they have acquired over the years. When the job requires a new skill set, as, for instance, when a new piece of information technology is introduced in the workplace, older adults tend to learn more slowly than younger adults. Research shows that lower processing speed and smaller working memory capacity are to blame for the age difference in learning rate (e.g. Echt, Morrell and Park, 1998). The same research also shows, however, that given enough time older workers can reach the same level as younger workers. Third, older workers often have more detailed knowledge about the job than younger adults. This is especially true for tacit knowledge – the kind of (often essential) knowledge that is hard to put into words and that is therefore hard to teach or train. In a study of 200 managers in a bank, Colonia-Willner (1998) found that tacit knowledge about interpersonal problems was a much better predictor of a manager's performance than any cognitive ability; this tacit knowledge also declined much less rapidly than any of the cognitive abilities tested. Fourth, older adults seek advice from other colleagues more often, they are better team players, and they often choose positions that emphasize fluid abilities less but depend much more on judgement and social skills. In this way, older workers capitalize on their strong points while avoiding their potential weaknesses.

Creativity

Creativity can be considered a special form of expertise. Although the ability to produce original ideas (one core aspect of creativity) appears to be hard-wired, time and experience are needed to elaborate on these original ideas and make them work, and those are at least partially a function of experience.

It is clear that old age does not preclude creative peak performance (see also Chapter 14). Bach composed *The Art of Fugue* at age 65; Verdi wrote *Falstaff* when he was 80; Rembrandt's later self-portraits are among his best work; Picasso kept working until he died, at age 92; Stravinsky decided to start composing in a new style, serialism, when he was 70, and delivered a few of the masterpieces in the genre (*Agon, Threni*); Goethe finished his *Faust* when he was 80. It is also clear that all of these artists, writers and composers were also very active when young; there are only a handful of examples of artists who become creative in advanced age (the writer Annie Proulx is an interesting exception; she published her first book, *Postcards*, when she was 57). The artists who stay active longest tend to be the ones who started earliest and produced their first masterpiece at an early age – creativity is a lifelong habit.

Such lifelong habits can lead to increasingly more interesting work. Painters who work a single theme for a lifetime, such as Cézanne or Degas, make their literally most valuable work late in life (Galenson, 1999). A large number of artists also produce works at the end of their lifetime that serve as a swansong. These works tend to be more popular and also simpler than the preceding works, as if the artist makes one last effort to connect to his/her audience. This phenomenon has more to do with the proximity of death than with old age – Mozart's *Requiem*, composed on the deathbed of the young composer, is a good example. Research on the age trajectory of creativity in science and the arts often finds a curvilinear association: there is an initial rise in productivity and quality, a short plateau, and then a decline (e.g. Lehman, 1953; Simonton, 1994). The placement of the peak differs across disciplines. Scientists often peak around age 35–40. Poets and mathematicians peak earlier. But philosophers and historians peak rather late: around age 60 or 70. The decline in productivity is usually steeper for artists than for scientists. There are also differences within disciplines. Within the group of classical composers, for instance, the peak for symphonic music is around age 30–35, and for operas around age 40–45. Poets peak earlier than novelists. The differences might be due to the time needed to acquire the skills and experiences necessary to make a top work: operas are more complex than purely instrumental music, novels might be invested with more life experience than poems, and philosophers and historians need a lifetime to work their way through a gigantic library. Sometimes knowledge can also hamper creativity. The pioneers of relativity theory and quantum physics were all younger than 30, unimpeded by preconceived notions about how physics 'should' work. This curvilinear association has also been found in samples that are more representative of the total population: participants in the Baltimore Longitudinal Study of Ageing (McCrae, Arenberg and Costa, 1987) showed a peak around age 40 in a standard test for creativity.

Wisdom

One of the few positive clichés about ageing is that older adults are wiser than younger adults. Most of the research on wisdom in old age has been done by the group around Paul Baltes (a review can be found in Baltes and Staudinger, 2000). Baltes defined wisdom as a system of knowledge about the meaning of life and how to be a good person – a constellation of personal characteristics that reflects a high level of cognitive, affective and behavioural maturity and reveals an unusual degree of sensitivity, openness of mind and care for humanity. In other words, no easy feat.

In Baltes' lab, wisdom is measured by confronting participants with life problems of fictitious individuals. For example, 'Someone receives a phone call from a good friend, who tells her that she cannot keep on living like this and has decided to commit suicide. What kinds of things could the caller in this situation consider and do?' Another example: 'In reflecting about life, people often realize they have not attained their dreams. What could they then do and consider?' Participants think out loud and trained observers judge their utterances on five criteria: (a) factual knowledge about the problems presented; (b) pragmatic procedural knowledge (e.g. knowing how to listen and to give advice); (c) the degree to which the problem is embedded in the life context of the fictitious person; (d) the degree to which the fictitious person's life choices and values are being accepted; and (e) the degree to which the participants understand and deal with uncertainty.

The most important finding from this line of research is that wisdom is not related to age. There are wise younger adults and wise older adults, as well as unwise youngsters and unwise seniors. A second important finding is that certain life patterns lead more easily to wisdom. Clinical psychologists, for instance, tend to score above the mean. They do not, however, score in the top range of the samples, indicating that there is more to wisdom than life experience. The third finding is that wisdom is clearly separate from cognition as traditionally defined: the correlations between wisdom and intelligence, creativity, and even personality are small. A final conclusion is that wisdom scores tend to be lower when people think about a situation alone than when they do so with a partner. Wisdom only truly blossoms in an interpersonal context.

Coping with cognitive limitations

The previous paragraphs have made it clear that ageing comes with some limitations on the functioning of the cognitive system, especially in the domains of episodic memory and fluid intelligence. What is to be done? In this final section, I describe three routes: two intervention methods (fitness training and cognitive training) and a general framework for competent ageing.

Fitness training

Colcombe and Kramer (2003) conducted a meta-analysis of 18 studies published between 1966 and 2001 in which the effects of cardiovascular fitness training on cognition was examined. The training interventions ranged from dancing to aerobic training combined with muscle training. The results of these analyses are rather surprising and encouraging: the control groups in these interventions (mostly training programmes aimed at flexibility or power) obtained a 0.2 SD increase in their cognitive functioning, whereas the cardiovascular fitness groups saw an increase in cognitive functioning of 0.5 SD. The net effect of aerobic training on cognition is therefore 0.3 SD. This is an appreciable effect: we have already noted that the difference in cognitive functioning between a 20-year-old and a 70-year-old is about 1 SD. Aerobic training then annihilates the effects of 15 years of ageing. The effect was larger in females than in males. The effect was only significant for programmes with sessions that lasted 30 minutes or longer. Short interventions (1 to 3 months) were effective, but the largest gain was observed with programmes that lasted at least 6 months. The effect was larger for individuals older than 65 than for younger older adults, and the training programmes were also effective for 70-year-olds. Demented older adults gained as much as normal older adults. The effect was largest on control processes in working memory, but there were also measurable effects on spatial ability and speed of processing.

It is plausible to assume that aerobic training impacts brain functioning directly. Colcombe *et al.* (2004) scanned the brains of 15 individuals who were part of a 45-minute/day walking programme and compared the scans with those of age-matched individuals who were part of an equally intensive programme not aimed at aerobic fitness, but at increased flexibility and musculature. The aerobic group performed better on tests of attention, and this change correlated with results from the scanner. Namely, there was heightened activation in the frontal and parietal cortex and a stronger suppression of activity in the posterior cortex. Thus, increased aerobic fitness did not result in a general effect (i.e. not all parts of the brain received enhanced blood flow). Instead, it appears to help individuals to direct activation of the areas relevant to the cognitive task at hand. The exact neuronal mechanism that underlies these changes is still unclear – it is possible that cardiovascular fitness increases the oxygen supply in the brain and thereby leads to more precise recruitment of the necessary brain areas; it is also possible that cardiovascular fitness enhances the release of particular hormones (such as neurotrophin) that have a direct impact on the number of neurons and their connections. In any case, relatively short and simple aerobic interventions appear to lead to increased cerebral fitness. These effects can be demonstrated both on standard cognitive tests and on brain activity. It is plausible that these changes will also influence everyday functioning.

Cognitive training

Cognitive performance is not merely a function of cognitive ability. Strategy use can be important as well, especially in memory functioning: how the material is studied will determine how well it will be remembered. A large number of studies have investigated what happens when older adults are instructed in new, more optimal memory strategies. The good news is that it appears to work. Verhaeghen, Marcoen and Goossens (1992) conducted a meta-analysis on 33 training studies. In these, researchers concentrate typically on a single memory strategy, such as the use of imagery, the combined use of labels and imagery to connect names to faces, or more specialized techniques, such as the method of loci (mentally placing to-be-remembered items in a visual image of a familiar scene). Memory training increased scores on a memory test by about 0.7 SD, compared with a 0.4 increase in control groups. The net gain is then about 0.3 SD, comparable to the gain obtained after aerobic training. The bad news is that the effects of strategy training, contrary to those of aerobic training, result in a *Matthew effect* ('the rich get richer, the poor get poorer'). Younger adults show larger gains than older adults, and patients with dementia show no gain at all. A second piece of bad news is that the effects are very limited. Strategy training trains a strategy, not memory (or cognition) in general. Participants who have been taught a technique to associate names and faces will do well on a face–name test, but not on a test for, say, grocery lists. Similar results were obtained in the largest cognitive training study ever conducted, the ACTIVE trial (Ball *et al.*, 2002; the study involved 2,832 older adults). Different training regimes were implemented – reasoning, memory, speed – and the effects were impressive (a net effect of about 0.5 SD for reasoning, 0.2 for memory and 1.5 for speed), but very specific: untrained abilities showed zero net gain.

The competent older adult: selective optimization with compensation

Older adults somehow need to learn to cope with their growing cognitive limitations. One framework that is often used to examine such coping behaviour is the model of selective optimization with compensation (SOC) (Baltes and Baltes, 1990). SOC is no theory (it cannot be falsified by research), but it is a good guiding principle to organize the everyday reality of ageing. The starting point of the model is that individuals guide their own development, using three principles: *selection*, *optimization* and *compensation*. Selection stands for making choices between the several alternatives life throws one's way. Selection can happen as a consequence of temporary limitations or as a shift in priorities (e.g. temporarily putting your hobbies on hold to concentrate on your career), or it can reflect a more permanent change (e.g. you decide to marry your boyfriend and stop dating). Optimization means that you try to find and apply new means to reach your goal, or that you refine the existing means (e.g. downshifting to part-time work to accommodate your new baby). Compensation operates when the means at your disposal are no longer sufficient; you then need to find alternative ways to reach your goal (e.g. hiring a nanny when there is a crunch at work). SOC is a contextual model: the concrete content of the concepts depends on the individual's context and on the specific behavioural domain, and thus is ultimately about expertise in one's own lifespan.

Baltes (1997) offered an example that might clarify these rather abstract statements. In a television interview, the then 80-year-old pianist Arthur Rubinstein was asked how he maintained such a high level of performance at such an advanced age. His response was that he did three things. First, he focused on a smaller number of pieces (selection). Second, he practised more often than he used to (optimization). Third, he used a psychological technique to compensate for the loss of physical finger speed: immediately before a fast passage, he would slow down so that the contrast made the (not-so-)fast passage sound faster than it was actually played (compensation).

Earlier in this chapter we encountered other examples of SOC in action. During dual tasking, older adults tend to protect motor tasks (balancing, walking) more than younger adults do, probably because the consequences of a fall are more severe in old age. Another example is that older adults more than younger adults use external support to compensate for memory problems. Viewed from an SOC perspective, these changes are clever ways to cope with likely permanent changes in cognitive functioning.

Research into SOC is difficult, precisely because SOC operates at the level of the individual – it is a function of an individual's highly idiosyncratic goals and means, which are hard to capture. In a recent study, Freund and Baltes (2002) therefore tried to operationalize SOC processes in a broad sense. They asked their participants rather general questions (e.g. selection: 'When I think about what is important in life, I restrict myself to one or two goals'; optimization: 'When I consider something to be truly important, I will dedicate myself to it fully'; compensation: 'When things don't go very well, I look for help or advice'). Middle-aged individuals used SOC processes the most; younger and older adults used the same number of strategies. There were, however, shifts in the type of SOC strategies favoured in each part of the lifespan. Older adults used selection strategies more often than younger adults; younger adults relied more often on compensation strategies. Competent ageing then seems to be a matter of adapting one's goals, not one's means. A second finding was that SOC strategy use did not co-vary with crystallized intelligence: expertise in one's own life course is not related to general intelligence. Third, each of the SOC processes turned out to be important for well-being: participants who indicated using SOC processes more often experienced more positive emotions and scored higher on tests for general well-being. Well-being then is not only caused by living in objectively happy circumstances, but it is also born out of the ability to creatively cope with one's limitations, and out of mastery over one's own life course.

Conclusion

As stated often throughout this chapter, the news for older adults does not appear to be good. Fluid intelligence and memory abilities decline and this decline appears to be hard-wired, linked to changes in brain functioning and in basic cognitive abilities. Only verbal abilities are spared. Looking at the picture more carefully, however, we found that older adults are not powerless vis-à-vis this decline. Living healthily and avoiding risk factors for diabetes and cardiovascular disease can counteract part of the deficit. Part of the decline can be compensated for by aerobic training. Expertise is another buffer against the negative effects of ageing. One unique type of expertise is expertise in one's own personal life course. This form of expertise, built on increasing selection as well as optimization and compensation, can help older adults to live competently and happily until a very advanced age.

Summary

Most aspects of personality are changeable in later adulthood, with a general shift towards greater affability and dependability at the cost of less flexibility.

These changes are attributable to environmental influences as compared to a much stronger genetic influence in childhood. Age differences in cognition vary according to the nature of the task. Speed of information processing, as measured by Brinley plots, indicates that in many instances there is a consistent slowing in older adults, and this tends to be greater for complex spatial skills. Attention tasks often show age-related deficits (notably divided attention). Overall, memory shows a decline in later life, but this is more marked in some areas than others. For example, passively memorizing shows less decline than the working-memory task of remembering while performing a concurrent task. Likewise, implicit and semantic memories are generally better preserved than explicit and episodic ones, largely because the neurological mechanisms controlling the former pair are less affected by ageing. Prospective memory is generally better in older than younger adults. Intelligence shows a marked ageing decline, though this can be exaggerated or underestimated depending upon the specific measurement technique used. The peak in most types of intelligence occurs before the onset of old age, and although overall there is a marked decline after 60, on an individual basis, the pattern of change and preservation is far more varied. However, viewing ageing in terms of crystallized versus fluid skills, we find a more consistent pattern of relative preservation and significant decline respectively. Practical problems (e.g. medical decision making) resulting from these changes are discussed. Explanations for age differences in cognitive performance are critically discussed. Three types of 'assembled cognition' are examined – expertise, creativity and wisdom. Finally, methods of coping with cognitive limitations (fitness training, cognitive training and selective optimization with compensation) are highlighted.

REFERENCES

Anstey, K.J. and Christensen, H. (2000) Education, activity, health, blood pressure and apolipoprotein E as predictors of cognitive change in old age: a review, *Gerontology*, *46*, 163–77.

Bahrick, H.P. (1984) Semantic memory content in the permastore: 50 years of memory for Spanish learned in school, *Journal of Experimental Psychology. General*, *113*, 1–29.

Bahrick, H.P., Bahrick, P.O. and Wittlinger, R.P. (1975) Fifty years of memory for names and faces: a cross-sectional approach, *Journal of Experimental Psychology. General*, *104*, 54–75.

Ball, K., Owsley, C., Sloane, M.E. *et al.* (1993) Visual attention problems as a predictor of vehicle crashes among older drivers, *Investigative Ophthalmology and Visual Science*, *34*(11), 3110–23.

Baltes, M. and Baltes, P.B. (1990) *Successful aging: perspectives from the behavioral sciences.* New York: Cambridge University Press.

Baltes, P.B. (1997) On the incomplete architecture of human ontogeny: selection, optimization, and compensation as foundation of developmental theory, *American Psychologist*, *52*, 366–80.

Baltes, P.B. and Staudinger, U.M. (2000) Wisdom: a metaheuristic (pragmatic) to orchestrate mind and virtue toward excellence, *American Psychologist, 55*, 122–36.

Blazer, D.G., Hays, J.C., Fillenbaum, G.G. *et al.* (1997) Memory complaint as a predictor of cognitive decline, *Journal of Aging and Health, 9*, 171–84.

Bohnstedt, M., Fox, P.J. and Kohatsu, N.D. (1994) Correlates of Mini-Mental Status Examination scores among elderly demented patients: the influence of race-ethnicity, *Journal of Clinical Epidemiology, 47*, 1381–7.

Bonnesen, J.L. and Burgess, E.O. (2004) Senior moments: the acceptability of an ageist phrase, *Journal of Aging Studies, 18*, 123–42.

Bopp, K.L. and Verhaeghen, P. (2005) Aging and verbal memory span: a meta-analysis, *Journals of Gerontology. Series B, Psychological Sciences and Social Sciences, 60*, 223–33.

Brinley, J.F. (1965) Cognitive sets, speed and accuracy of performance in the elderly, in A.T. Welford and J.E. Birren (eds), *Behavior, aging and the nervous system*. Springfield, IL: Thomas, 114–49.

Cabeza, R. (2002) Hemispheric asymmetry reduction in old adults: the HAROLD model, *Psychology and Aging, 17*, 85–100.

Cerella, J., Poon, L.W. and Williams, D.H. (1980) Age and the complexity hypothesis, in L.W. Poon (ed.), *Aging in the 1980's*. Washington, DC: American Psychological Association, 332–40.

Charness, N. and Bosman, E.A. (1995) Expertise and age, in G. Maddox (ed.), *Encyclopedia of aging*, 2nd edn. New York: Springer, 352–4.

Clarkson-Smith, L. and Hartley, A.A. (1990) The game of bridge as an exercise in working memory and reasoning, *Journal of Gerontology, 45*, P233–8.

Colcombe, S.J. and Kramer, A.F. (2003) Fitness effects on the cognitive function of older adults: a meta-analytic study, *Psychological Science, 14*, 25–130.

Colcombe, S.J., Kramer, A.F., Erickson, K.I. *et al.* (2004) Cardiovascular fitness, cortical plasticity, and aging, *Proceedings of the National Academy of Sciences of the USA, 11*, 3316–21.

Colonia-Willner, R. (1998) Practical intelligence at work: relationship between aging and cognitive efficiency among managers in a bank environment, *Psychology and Aging, 13*, 45–57.

Cutler, S.J. and Grams, A.E. (1988) Correlates of self-reported everyday memory problems, *Journal of Gerontology, 43*, 82–90.

Echt, K.V., Morrell, R.W. and Park, D.C. (1998) Effects of age and training formats on basic computer skill acquisition in older adults, *Educational Gerontology, 24*, 3–25.

Eichenbaum, H. (2003) How does the hippocampus contribute to memory?, *Trends in Cognitive Science, 7*, 427–9.

Engle, R.W., Kane, M.J. and Tuholski, S.W. (1999) Individual differences in working memory capacity and what they tell us about controlled attention, general fluid intelligence and functions of the prefrontal cortex, in A. Miyake and P. Shah (eds), *Models of working memory: mechanisms of active maintenance and executive control*. Cambridge University Press, 102–34.

Freund, A.M. and Baltes, P.B. (2002) Life-management strategies of selection, optimization, and compensation: measurement by self-report and construct validity, *Journal of Personality and Social Psychology, 82*, 642–62.

Galenson, D.W. (1999) *Quantifying artistic success: ranking French painters – and paintings – from Impressionism to Cubism*. NBER Working Papers 7407. Cambridge, MA: National Bureau of Economic Research.

Hagberg, B., Samuelsson, G., Lindberg, B. *et al.* (1991) Stability and change of personality in old age and its relation to survival, *Journal of Gerontology*, *46*, 285–91.

Heine, M.K., Ober, B.A. and Shenaut, G.K. (1999) Naturally occurring and experimentally induced tip-of-the-tongue experiences in three adult age groups, *Psychology and Aging*, *14*, 445–57.

Henry, J.D., MacLeod, M., Phillips, L.H. *et al.* (2004) A meta-analytic review of age effects on prospective memory, *Psychology and Aging*, *19*, 27–39.

Hess, T.M. (2005) Memory and aging in context, *Psychological Bulletin*, *131*, 383–406.

Holliday, S.G. and Chandler, M.J. (1986) *Wisdom: explorations in adult competence.* New York: Karger.

Horn, J. (1970) Organization of data on life-span development of human abilities, in R. Goulet and P.B. Baltes (eds), *Life-span developmental psychology: research and theory.* New York: Academic Press, 423–66.

Kausler, D.H. (1991) *Experimental psychology, cognition, and human aging*, 2nd edn. New York: Springer-Verlag.

Kemper, S., Herman, R.E. and Liu, C.J. (2004) Sentence production by younger and older adults in controlled contexts, *Journals of Gerontology. Series B, Psychological Sciences and Social Sciences*, *58*, 220–4.

LaVoie, D. and Light, L.L. (1994) Adult age differences in repetition priming: a meta-analysis, *Psychology and Aging*, *9*, 539–53.

Lehman, H.C. (1953) *Age and achievement.* Princeton University Press.

Li, K.Z.H., Lindenberger, U., Freund, A.M. *et al.* (2001) Walking while memorizing: age-related differences in compensatory behavior, *Psychological Science*, *12*, 230–7.

Lindenberger, U. and Baltes, P.B. (1997) Intellectual functioning in old and very old age: cross-sectional results from the Berlin Aging Study, *Psychology and Aging*, *12*, 410–32.

Manly, J.J. (2008) Critical issues in cultural neuropsychology: profit from diversity, *Neuropsychology Review*, *18*, 179–83.

Manly, J.J., Byrd, D.A., Touradji, P. *et al.* (2004) Acculturation, reading level, and neuropsychological test performance among African American elders, *Applied Neuropsychology*, *1*, 37–46.

McCrae, R.R., Arenberg, D. and Costa, P.T. (1987) Declines in divergent thinking with age: cross-sectional, longitudinal, and cross-sequential analyses, *Psychology and Aging*, *2*, 130–7.

McEvoy, S.P., Stevenson, M.R., McCartt, A.T. *et al.* (2005) Role of mobile phones in motor vehicle crashes resulting in hospital attendance: a case-crossover study, *British Medical Journal*, *331*, 428–32.

McGue, M., Bacon, S. and Lykken, D.T. (1993) Personality stability and change in early adulthood: a behavioral genetic analysis, *Developmental Psychology*, *29*, 96–109.

Owsley, C., Ball, K., McGwin, G. *et al.* (1998) Visual processing impairment and risk of motor vehicle crash among older adults, *Journal of the American Medical Association*, *279*, 1083–8.

Park, D.C. (1994) Aging, cognition, and work, *Human Performance*, *7*, 181–205.

Park, D.C. and Hall Gutchess, A. (2000) Cognitive aging and everyday life. in D.C. Park and N. Schwarz (eds), *Cognitive aging: a primer.* Philadelphia: Psychology Press, 217–32.

Park, D.C., Polk, T., Mikels, J. *et al.* (2001) Cerebral aging: integration of brain and behavioral models of cognitive function, *Dialogues in Clinical Neuroscience*, *3*, 151–65.

Park, D.C., Lautenschlager, G., Hedden, T. *et al.* (2002) Models of visuospatial and verbal memory across the adult life span, *Psychology and Aging*, *17*, 299–320.

Plomin, R. and Nesselroade, J.R. (1990) Behavioral genetics and personality change, *Journal of Personality*, *58*, 191–220.

Rapp, M., Krampe, R.T. and Baltes, P.B. (2005) Adaptive task prioritization in aging: selective resource allocation to postural control is preserved in Alzheimer disease, *American Journal of Geriatric Psychiatry*, *14*, 52–61.

Raz, N. (2000) Aging of the brain and its impact on cognitive performance: integration of structural and functional findings, in F.I.M. Craik and T.A. Salthouse (eds), *Handbook of aging and cognition*, 2nd edn. Mahwah, NJ: Erlbaum, 1–90.

Raz, N., Lindenberger, U., Rodrigue, K.M. *et al.* (2005) Regional brain changes in aging healthy adults: general trends, individual differences, and modifiers, *Cerebral Cortex*, *15*, 1676–89.

Rhodes, S.R. (1983) Age-related differences in work attitudes and behavior: a review and conceptual analysis, *Psychological Bulletin*, *93*, 328–67.

Roberts, B.W. and DelVecchio, W.F. (2000) The rank-order consistency of personality from childhood to old age: a quantitative review of longitudinal studies, *Psychological Bulletin*, *126*, 3–25.

Roberts, B.W., Walton, K. and Viechtbauer, W. (2006) Patterns of mean-level change in personality traits across the life course: a meta-analysis of longitudinal studies, *Psychological Bulletin*, *132*, 1–25.

Rubin, D.C., Wetzler, S.E. and Nebes, R.D. (1986) Autobiographical memory across the adult lifespan, in D.C. Rubin (ed.), *Autobiographical memory*. Cambridge University Press, 202–21.

Salthouse, T.A. (1984) Effects of age and skill in typing, *Journal of Experimental Psychology. General*, *113*, 345–71.

(1991) *Theoretical perspectives on cognitive aging*. Hillsdale, NJ: Erlbaum.

(1996) The processing-speed theory of adult age differences in cognition, *Psychological Review*, *103*, 403–28.

Schaie, K.W. (1994) The course of adult intellectual development, *American Psychologist*, *49*, 304–13.

(2005) What can we learn from longitudinal studies of adult intellectual development?, *Research in Human Development*, *2*, 133–58.

Schmidt, F.L., Hunter, J.E. and Outerbridge, A.N. (1986) The impact of job experience and ability on job knowledge, work sample performance, and supervisory ratings of job performance, *Journal of Applied Psychology*, *71*, 432–9.

Shimamura, A.P., Berry, J.A., Mangels, J.A. *et al.* (1995) Memory and cognitive abilities in academic professors: evidence for successful aging, *Psychological Science*, *6*(5), 271–7.

Simonton, D.K. (1994) *Greatness: who makes history and why*. New York: Guilford Press.

Singer, T., Verhaeghen, P., Ghisletta, P. *et al.* (2003) The fate of cognition in very old age: six-year longitudinal findings in the Berlin Aging Study (BASE), *Psychology and Aging*, *18*, 318–31.

Sliwinski, M., Lipton, R.B., Buschke, H. *et al.* (1996) The effect of pre-clinical dementia on estimates of normal cognitive function in aging, *Journals of Gerontology. Series B, Psychological Sciences and Social Sciences*, *51*, 217–25.

Spencer, W.D. and Raz, N. (1995) Differential effects of aging on memory for content and context: a meta-analysis, *Psychology and Aging*, *10*, 527–39.

Taylor, J.L., Miller, T.P. and Tinklenberg, J.R. (1992) Correlates of memory decline: a 4-year longitudinal study of older adults with memory complaints, *Psychology and Aging*, *7*, 185–93.

Thornton, W.J.L. and Dumke, H.A. (2005) Age differences in everyday problem-solving and decision making effectiveness: a meta-analytic review, *Psychology and Aging*, *20*, 85–99.

Verhaeghen, P. (2003) Aging and vocabulary scores: a meta-analysis, *Psychology and Aging*, *18*, 332–9.

(2006) Reaction time, in G.L. Maddox (ed.), *The encyclopedia of aging*, 4th edn. New York: Springer-Verlag, 114–26.

Verhaeghen, P., Borchelt, M. and Smith, J. (2003) The relation between cardiovascular and metabolic disease and cognition in very old age: cross-sectional and longitudinal findings from the Berlin Aging Study, *Health Psychology*, *22*, 559–69.

Verhaeghen, P. and Cerella, J. (2002) Aging, executive control, and attention: a review of meta-analyses, *Neuroscience and Biobehavioral Reviews*, *26*, 849–57.

Verhaeghen, P., Geraerts, N. and Marcoen, A. (2000) Memory complaints, coping, and well-being in old age: a systemic approach, *The Gerontologist*, *40*, 540–8.

Verhaeghen, P., Marcoen, A. and Goossens, L. (1992) Improving memory performance in the aged through mnemonic training: a meta-analytic study, *Psychology and Aging*, *7*, 242–51.

(1993) Facts and fiction about memory aging: a quantitative integration of research findings, *Journals of Gerontology. Series B. Psychological Sciences and Social Sciences*, *48*, 157–71.

Verhaeghen, P. and Salthouse, T.A. (1997) Meta-analyses of age-cognition relations in adulthood: estimates of linear and non-linear age effects and structural models, *Psychological Bulletin*, *122*, 231–49.

Waldman, D.A. and Avolio, B.J. (1986) A meta-analysis of age differences in job performance, *Journal of Applied Psychology*, *71*, 33–8.

7 The psychology of atypical ageing

BOB WOODS

OVERVIEW

This chapter examines types of atypical conditions probabilistically associated with ageing, including mood disorders (depression, anxiety, post-traumatic stress disorder), the dementias, mild cognitive impairment and psychological interventions in later life.

Introduction

What is 'atypical ageing'? The increased variation among older adults results, in a sense, in no one person's experience of ageing being *typical*. All are individuals, all unique, all different. Ageing challenges our concepts of normality and abnormality. For example, osteoarthritis is very common in older people, affecting half of women over 65, and so the 'normal' or typical older adult may expect to have this often painful and disabling condition. This does not stop us from seeking understanding of and treatment for this condition, and aspiring to an experience of ageing where it is less prevalent. Similarly, when we consider some of the psychological problems experienced by older people, some are very common, but we can elect to view them as outside the range of a 'typical' ageing, where the older person experiences a good adjustment to the challenges and opportunities of later life.

This chapter covers the major psychological problems of ageing, focusing on mood disorders and the dementias, which may be said to be the most frequently encountered forms of abnormal or atypical ageing in this domain. Working with older people (or 'the aged' or 'the elderly' as they were then known) has been a recognized specialism within clinical psychology practice for over 30 years. Its establishment was, in part, a reaction to the ageism inherent in mainstream clinical psychology practice at the time, which continues today in many aspects of health and social care. Older people were unlikely to receive any input from clinical psychology services, and this area of work was seen as unrewarding and less worthwhile than work with children or younger adults. In the current climate of awareness of age discrimination, the question now asked is whether having a distinct specialism in itself is a form of ageism, since an adult is an adult whether 25 or 85. It is challenging to consider what marks out clinical psychology practice with older people, apart from dates on birth certificates. The key issues appear to be:

- Prevalence of cognitive impairment – as we shall see, the dementias and related disorders become increasingly common with age.
- Experience of multiple losses, including those related to poor health and chronic health conditions as well as bereavements.
- The social context of ageing, including specialist housing, family roles, etc.
- The developmental issues being faced – retirement, proximity to death, issues of dependence and autonomy.

None of these is *directly* related to age, of course. Younger people may develop a dementia, experience a bereavement or chronic illness, live in an institution, or face the realization that life is slipping away. All are, however, more common in older people, and the task for a clinical psychology of older people is to work with people facing these and similar issues, which are often combined and inter-woven, and interact with a lifetime of experiences and opportunities, taken and missed.

It is not easy for older people and those who seek to help them to evaluate whether the changes that are being experienced might be considered as part of the typical experience of ageing, or should be seen as reflecting an abnormal process. We are limited in the comparisons we can make, since we have never experienced the ageing process before. Perhaps we look at other people of our own generation ageing, or at the experiences of our parents or grandparents as they got older. Are the changes we are aware of in ourselves similar to or greater than they experienced? Are we as aware of changes in ourselves as others are in us? For the clinical psychologist, defining 'normality' is never straightforward, and in later life the range of diversity in terms of lifetime opportunities for experi-ences, growth, development and adversity means that making comparisons simply with other people of the same age is not sufficient – the lifespan perspective of change over time must also be incorporated. The normative comparison is not how the person compares with their peer group in current adjustment and ability, but rather how their *trajectory* of change compares with that of their contemporaries.

Mood disorders

Depression

Prevalence and prognosis

Reported rates of depression in older people vary greatly according to the sample, scales and diagnostic criteria used (Blazer, 2003). A representative study is reported by Lindesay, Briggs and Murphy (1989). They surveyed nearly 1,000 elderly people in an urban area, identifying 4.3 per cent as having severe depression and a further 13.5 per cent having a mild to moderate degree of depression.

The assumption that depression must be more common in older people than in younger people cannot be tested simply by assessing all age groups on the same diagnostic instrument and comparing the prevalence rates obtained. Items on somatic symptoms (i.e. of the body) or sleep disturbance, for example, are much better indicators of depression in younger people; in older people they are likely to reflect changes in health status or sleep patterns occurring independently of mood state. Jorm (2000) reviews evidence indicating that rates of depressive disorder, anxiety and distress in older people are lower than in other age groups when other risk factors are controlled for. It should, however, be noted that there are some groups of older people who have a higher risk of mood disorders. These include older people living in care homes, older people living at home in receipt of community care services, people with dementia, and older people who are providing care for other family members.

As many as 40 per cent of care home residents without a severe cognitive impairment are reported to be depressed (Mann *et al.*, 2000; Mozley *et al.*, 2004). Around 25 per cent of older people living at home in receipt of community care also have a depressive disorder (Banerjee, 1993). Thus, it would appear that those older people with more significant needs for care are more at risk of depression, whether living at home or in a care home. Mozley *et al.* (2004) assessed depression in older people on admission to a care home, and again 5 months later. Most (71 per cent) of the residents who were depressed after 5 months had been depressed on admission, although a significant minority (29 per cent) became depressed while in the home. Thus, depression in care homes typically begins before the admission to the care home and cannot simply be attributed to the unstimulating environment and lack of activity often associated with such homes. However, these factors most likely contribute to the maintenance of depression.

Depression is common in people with dementia – around a quarter have a co-existing depression (Ballard et al., 1996). Many older people act as caregivers to other relatives or friends; caregiving is not unique to older people, of course, but rates of depression and psychological distress are high, among female carers especially (Brodaty et al., 2003; Sörensen et al., 2002).

A number of studies of the prognosis of depression in late life have been undertaken. These reflect the efficacy of the usual treatment regime, which in most cases has been antidepressant medication. As many as a third of patients with depression remain depressed 3 years later with estimates of those sustaining a complete recovery varying from 10 to 20 per cent (Denihan et al., 2000; Livingston and Hinchliffe, 1993). It is clear that a substantial number of older people with depression do not recover with the standard treatments and that relapse is a major issue.

Life events

Risk factors for developing depression in later life include bereavement, disability, prior depression, sleep disturbance and female gender (Cole and Dendukuri, 2003). In a representative sample of over 14,000 people aged 75 and over in the UK, Osborn et al. (2003) identified similar risk factors for depression, including life events, having two or more physical illnesses, and not having a confiding relationship. Kraaij and de Wilde (2001) have shown how life events over the lifespan are associated with depression in later life; life events in childhood, such as emotional abuse or neglect or difficult socio-economic circumstances, appear to increase the older person's vulnerability to subsequent life events. Stressful relationships were another important risk factor emerging from this study.

Physical health

Physical health and depression are inextricably related in later life. Older adults with physical health problems have elevated levels of depression. The most common adverse life events and difficulties relate to physical health problems. The prognosis of depression over a 3-year period is worse in those who experience physical ill health and chronic medical conditions (Denihan et al., 2000). However, distinguishing the effects of depression from physical health complaints such as fatigue, lethargy and pain can be challenging. Seeking to arrive at a single explanation for a person's presenting problems is likely to be unhelpful, as multiple pathologies are common.

There are some physical health conditions that are said to have a specific association with depressive disorders. These include Parkinson's disease and stroke. For example, a quarter of patients are found to be depressed 4 months post-stroke (Burvill et al., 1995), and, similarly, the prevalence of clinically significant depressive symptoms in Parkinson's disease is reported as 35 per cent (Reijnders et al., 2008). There have been suggestions that the increased prevalence of depression in these conditions relates to the particular types of brain changes being experienced. For example, some reports suggest that depression is more common with strokes located in particular parts of the brain, but the evidence on this is conflicting (Carson *et al.*, 2000). On the other hand, Dent *et al.* (1999) suggest that the relationship between physical health and depression is mediated by the extent of disability, rather than being attributable to the type of health problem.

A condition such as Parkinson's disease will be experienced as a dynamic process, rather than as an event. There are many problems that were encountered before diagnosis: the diagnostic assessment, the seeking to understand/accept the diagnosis and its impact on the family, the periods of the condition responding to medication, the periods when it appeared to be out of control or deteriorating rapidly, and so on. Acute onset conditions (such as stroke) present particular problems for adjustment, with a sudden, rapid loss of function. With an amputation, the person may have to adjust to a radically altered body-image, and a grief-like process appears to be frequently encountered in such a context. Some conditions, such as stroke, myocardial infarction or cancer, are perceived as especially life-threatening, alerting the person to the possibility of death, which may impact on efforts to cope. Families may become overprotective, and this in itself may add to depression, in taking away control from the individual.

The person's adjustment can only be understood in the context of what has led up to the present situation, not simply in relation to current symptoms. Coping mechanisms appropriate at one stage may not be useful at another; early on, for example, denial may have a protective function, but later it may obstruct useful interventions. In many instances, depression in the presence of physical health problems appears to reflect a difficulty in coping with and adjusting to the changed circumstances that accompany the physical health difficulty. The health problem may prevent the maintenance of roles and relationships that are central to the person's well-being and life satisfaction; pain and discomfort might mean that simple everyday activities require a major effort to complete. The person's coping resources, including their sense of mastery over their environment and their resilience, are important influences on the extent to which physical health problems do reduce well-being (Windle *et al.*, 2004).

Bereavement
Bereavement reactions in later life are discussed in detail in Chapter 15. Depression is by no means universal in bereavement, and the majority of older people adjust emotionally and socially without major mental health problems. The identification of the significant minority who do experience difficulties is complicated by the overlap between the symptoms of depression and the features of grief, such as sadness, tearfulness, loss of appetite and sleep problems. This overlap leads to elevated scores on most self-report measures of depression. Where depression

appears to be distinct is in relation to the person tending to have a negative self-image and feelings of failure and self-blame; it is where these negative thinking patterns develop that bereavement becomes a risk factor for depression. Low levels of social support and a particularly difficult or traumatic loss (such as sudden death of an adult child) are also implicated (Oyebode, 2008). Those at risk of developing depression are usually identifiable within a few months of the bereavement, using these criteria. As with other life events discussed above, there is the event of bereavement, but also the state of being bereaved, which for many who lose a spouse will involve living alone, perhaps for the first time, often leading to significant feelings of loneliness and isolation.

Suicide

There are great differences in attitudes to taking one's own life across history and between cultures. In ancient Greece, assisted suicide was available to older people who felt they no longer had anything useful to offer to society (O'Connell et al., 2004); suicide has been viewed at various times and places as an honourable act; and, in the current era, countries such as the Netherlands allow physician-assisted suicide to those for whom life has become intolerable. On the other hand, suicide was classed as a criminal act in the UK relatively recently, and assisting a person to kill themselves continues to be so.

Globally, older people are more likely than any other age group to die by committing suicide; on the other hand, they are much less likely to attempt suicide unsuccessfully (Conwell et al., 2002; O'Connell et al., 2004). However, this simple summary needs to be qualified, as rates vary greatly from area to area and internationally, reflecting in part differences in recording systems as well as cultural differences. In the 1980s, older men had the highest rates of suicide in most countries, but their place has now been taken by younger adult males in about a third of countries, including the UK. Accounting for these differences and changes is not straightforward, and, as is usual in gerontology, cohort effects, period effects and age effects must all be considered (Woods, 2008). Age effects include difficulties in coping with poor health and pain, and managing loss of income following retirement; period effects include changes in toxicity of gas supplies or of packaging and sale of painkillers, which have been shown to relate to reduced suicide rates; cohort effects may reflect differences in attitudes, perhaps related to religious affiliations, and experience of shared adversity, such as major wars. Differences between countries may reflect the greater availability of certain suicide methods with greatest risk of fatality in certain countries – firearms in particular. In the UK, drug overdose is the most common method for older women, whereas men are twice as likely to use a more violent means such as hanging, carbon monoxide poisoning, jumping from a height or drowning (Harwood et al., 2000). In the USA, in contrast, 80 per cent of older male suicides result from a gunshot, whereas guns are rarely the means of suicide in the UK, except in rural areas, where shotguns may be more accessible (Woods, 2008).

There appears to be evidence implicating life events and lack of social support, including family discord, as risk factors for suicide in older people (Conwell *et al.*, 2002). Bereavement is a particular factor for older men, who have higher rates of suicide following the death of a spouse (Cattell, 2000; O'Connell *et al.*, 2004). Around a quarter of older people who commit suicide have alcohol in their blood at post-mortem (Harwood *et al.*, 2000); its disinhibiting effects may facilitate the act, and its interaction with other drugs may potentiate their effects.

Physical health problems, and associated fear of dependency, helplessness and institutionalization have also been linked with suicide, especially in older men (Waern *et al.*, 2002). O'Connell *et al.* (2004) and Conwell *et al.* (2002) acknowledge the association of physical illness and functional impairment with suicide in older people, but conclude that this association is mediated, at least in part, through their relationship with depression. Harwood *et al.* (2001) report that nearly two-thirds of their sample retrospectively had a diagnosable depression, with as many as three-quarters of their sample thought to have had a psychiatric disorder at the time of death. Generally this had not been recognized, with only a fifth receiving care from mental health services at the time of the death, and only a quarter having had any such input in the previous year. Personality factors have also been implicated, including obsessional personality traits, reflecting reduced adaptability to change (Conwell *et al.*, 2002; O'Connell *et al.*, 2004).

While older people have relatively high rates of completed suicide, they have much lower rates of attempted suicide than younger people (Pearson and Brown, 2000). In older people the profiles of those who attempt and those who complete suicide are much less distinct than in younger people. Lebret *et al.* (2006) followed up, for at least 3 years, 51 older people who had made a suicide attempt. The original attempts had been precipitated by physical illness of the person or their partner (more common in males), relationship conflict, and loneliness or isolation. A fifth damaged their physical health further as a result of the attempt, requiring surgery or intensive care in some cases. This contributed to the increased mortality of the sample as a whole. Two-thirds were diagnosed as having depression at the time of the attempt. A relatively high proportion (38 per cent) were identified as having a memory disorder at the time of the initial attempt or during the follow-up period (although a diagnosis of dementia was only made in a third of these cases). These patients had a high risk of mortality, with a quarter dying within a year, in several cases through a further suicide attempt. Older people who attempt suicide have a relatively high risk of making further, potentially successful attempts; 6 per cent of this sample had taken their own life during the follow-up period, mainly within a year of the original attempt. 16 per cent (all female) made further unsuccessful attempts, mainly overdosing on medication.

Dennis *et al.* (2005) report a study of 76 older people referred following an episode of self-harm, and indicate high levels of suicide intent, with two-thirds having clearly wished to die when they made the attempt. Those attempting suicide were more likely to have a poorly integrated social network, and this lack of social integration was also highlighted in a qualitative study examining the experiences of 15 older people who had attempted suicide (Crocker *et al.*, 2006). Feeling invisible or disconnected from others was one of the key themes emerging in the period leading to the attempt, with feelings of loneliness and detachment being common. Crocker *et al.* (2006) draw attention to the diversity of experiences and the way in which risk factors (e.g. poor health, lack of social integration, depression) became meaningful, in part, because they were interpreted as signifying a hopeless future characterized by further decline, dependency on others and isolation.

Depression and cognitive impairment

Cervilla and Prince (1997) suggested that there are two distinct pathways to depression in later life. The first reflects the effects of adversity; as we have seen, life events and difficult life circumstances occurring in later life and earlier in the lifespan do increase the risk of depression. The second relates to changes in cognitive function, which are seen as an independent risk factor, presumably reflecting vascular changes in the brain. This form of depression is often described as *vascular depression.*

Vascular disease may be associated with depression in later life by increasing vulnerability to depression, by triggering symptoms of depression, or by maintaining depression (Alexopoulos, 2005). The pattern of depressive symptoms in older people with depression with and without vascular disease has been examined by Licht-Strunk *et al.* (2004). They concluded that the pattern of depression was similar, but people with vascular depression showed more disability. Mast *et al.* (2005) studied the relationship of cerebrovascular risk factors (hypertension, diabetes and heart disease) to depression. For older people aged less than 85, this relationship was mediated by health-related symptoms and limitations, whereas for those over 85, these risk factors had a direct effect on the symptoms of depression. In the younger old people, their depression was largely explained by their physical health symptoms and level of disability, which were in turn influenced by vascular risk factors. In the oldest age group, vascular risk factors were associated with depression, regardless of level of health problems and disability.

Vascular disease is associated with cognitive impairment, so this may be the mechanism underlying the group of older people with depression who show such impairment, have abnormal brain scans, and have a worse prognosis in terms of recovery and mortality. Over the years all manner of cognitive and physical tests of brain function were used in research studies to compare older people with dementia and older people with depression. Typically, people with depression would fall somewhere between a normal control group and those with clear-cut dementia, whatever the measure used (e.g. Jacoby and Levy, 1980; Orrell *et al.*, 1992). A group of depressed older people, with particular difficulty on cognitive tests, was identified and described as having a 'pseudodementia' or the 'reversible dementia of depression'. Neither label proved satisfactory, in that the impairments do not greatly resemble dementia (Poon, 1992), and the extent of their reversibility has been questioned (Bhalla *et al.*, 2006).

Lockwood *et al.* (2002) indicate that impairments in executive function are found specifically in older patients with depression. Younger and older patients have difficulty with sustained attention. Bhalla *et al.* (2006) report deficits in information-processing speed, delayed memory and visuospatial ability in older people who had recovered from depression; over 90 per cent of those who were cognitively impaired while depressed remained impaired when the depression had remitted, and nearly a quarter of those who were cognitively normal while depressed showed cognitive impairment after remission. Alexopoulos (2005) suggests that, in vascular depression, cognitive impairments in verbal fluency and object naming are especially prominent. Yochim *et al.* (2006) reported that verbal fluency scores were related to depression scores in a sample of older people. Depression was in turn related to the extent of vascular risk factors, but verbal fluency was not directly related to vascular risk factors.

The association between depression and dementia has been the subject of some debate, with findings such as that of Bhalla *et al.* (2006) suggesting that depression may be a precursor of dementia. Similarly, Wilson *et al.* (2004) and Gatz *et al.* (2005) suggest that depressive symptoms do predict cognitive impairment and dementia over a 5-year period. However, Vinkers *et al.* (2004), in a longitudinal study, concluded that depression is an early manifestation of Alzheimer's disease rather than a predictor of it. Similarly, Ganguli *et al.* (2006) reported that depression was associated at the time of testing with cognitive impairment, but not with subsequent cognitive decline. Thus, although depression and cognitive impairment are clearly linked, and depression is common in people with dementia, the pathways leading to their co-occurrence remain to be clarified.

Anxiety

Prevalence rates for various forms of anxiety disorder were reported from Lindesay, Briggs and Murphy's (1989) large urban community survey. Around 3.7 per cent of the 1,000 older people interviewed had a generalized anxiety disorder (anxiety without a specific cause, triggered by many diverse items and events), with a further 10 per cent having a phobic disorder (anxiety triggered by a disproportionate/irrational fear of a specific item or situation), with agoraphobia (fear of open space/public places and/or leaving home) being most common (7.8 per cent).

Co-morbidity with depression was common in relation to phobic anxiety, with 40 per cent also having significant symptoms of depression. Panic disorder was rare, when standard diagnostic criteria, requiring three panic attacks in the preceding 3 weeks for the diagnosis to be made, were applied. It is likely that older people are able to prevent such attacks by avoidance strategies, at the cost of greater dependency and disability (Livingston and Hinchliffe, 1993).

Barrowclough *et al.* (2001) highlighted the co-occurrence of anxiety and physical health problems – 80 per cent of the participants in their clinical intervention study on anxiety problems in older people had significant physical health difficulties. It is suggested that whereas younger people report more worries regarding financial problems, older people report more health-related worries. Respiratory and cardiovascular problems are often associated with anxiety symptoms (Nordhus, 2008). For example, Hynninen *et al.* (2005) reported that an anxiety condition was present in as many as 30 per cent of people with chronic obstructive pulmonary disease (COPD), which leads to severe breathing problems and is most common in older people.

Although anxiety may develop in later life, perhaps in relation to particular challenges and stressors, a significant number of older people have been living with anxiety problems for many years. Thus, Barrowclough *et al.* (2001) found that the average duration of the difficulties in their sample was 20 years. This has implications for interventions, in that the person may well have developed a lifestyle that accommodates their difficulties, and may, paradoxically, find it difficult to imagine life without them. Nordhus (2008) suggests that generalized anxiety disorder begins earlier in life in 60–70 per cent of cases, whereas phobic disorder (e.g. fear of going out or social anxiety) may develop at any time in life.

Often, presentations of phobic anxiety appear to have a fairly clear precipitant – a fall, a heart attack or a mugging in the street, perhaps. It is worth considering, then, some of the specific fears most commonly associated with older people. Lindesay (1997) reports, from a community sample, that fear of crime and phobic disorder in older people are associated. This may be mediated through the person with a phobic disorder having a greater perceived sense of personal vulnerability. Older people might have a sense of greater vulnerability to attack, in that, for them, the consequences may be more severe than for a younger person, since they might have less physical resilience and reduced social support available to aid recovery. Older people might seek to reduce their risk by avoiding going out alone at night, or by avoiding known danger areas.

Fear of falling also has a major impact on an older person's ability to go out, and can lead to the person becoming housebound. It is not based on experience of falling in every case. Howland, Peterson, Levin *et al.* (1993) report that in a sample of older people living in the community, this was the commonest fear, with rates of 40 per cent of older people often reported (Downton and Andrews;

1990; Tinetti, Mendes de Leon, Doucette *et al.*, 1994). Fear of falling is associated with self-rated health and previous falls, anxiety and depression (Downton and Andrews, 1990; Howland *et al.*, 1993; Tinetti, Richman and Powell, 1990). Tinetti *et al.* (1990) suggest that for the 50 per cent of older people whose fear of falling leads to activities being avoided, confidence is reduced and the person is likely to have less self-efficacy in avoiding falls, and indeed is at greater risk of falling (Spano and Forstl, 1992).

It is often assumed (by younger people) that older people will be fearful of death. In fact, younger people appear to be more fearful of death, while the concerns of older people focus around *dying* (McKiernan, 1996). Fears concerning the process (pain, suffocation, choking, and so on) are relatively common (Fry, 1990), and play a role in some anxiety problems. 'Minor' heart attacks, transient ischaemic attacks (in effect, short-lasting 'miniature strokes' that, although alarming, often have no lasting harm provided they are properly treated) and more chronic breathing problems may all produce sensations readily misinterpreted as being fatal. The role of hyperventilation and catastrophic cognitions in exacerbating chronic, debilitating conditions such as emphysema is poorly understood. The notion of a *catastrophic cognition* is central to the cognitive-behavioural view of panic. It occurs where the person believes they are experiencing a life-threatening illness or disastrous event, such as a heart attack, inability to breathe, a collapse, a loss of control or death. This often occurs in the context of hyperventilation, which produces a number of physical sensations readily misinterpreted, such as dizziness, tremor, chest pain and nausea. Many patients are relieved when asked to report their thoughts at such times to find that their thoughts of dying may be discussed openly and safely.

Post-traumatic stress disorder (PTSD)

As discussed above, difficult events earlier in life have an important influence on mood and well-being in older people, just as they do in younger adults (Kraaij and de Wilde, 2001). Where the event is traumatic, the older person may be considered to have PTSD. This is defined in relation to the event being outside the range of normal human experience; the event being re-experienced through flashbacks, dreams, etc.; that there are symptoms of increased arousal and avoidance of stimuli associated with the trauma; and that the problems have gone on for at least a month. This may relate to events earlier in life or to more recent traumatic experiences.

Childhood sexual abuse, exposure to traumatic incidents in wartime, rape, involvement in life-threatening accidents, and so on may all have ramifications in later life. Hunt and Robbins (2001) reported that as many as 19 per cent of 731 Second World War and Korean War veterans showed symptoms of PTSD, with even higher rates among prisoners of war (POWs) (e.g. 30 per cent of British Far East

POWs; Neal, Hill, Hughes *et al.*, 1995). Much depends, of course, on the specific experiences of combat or imprisonment. However, wartime trauma cannot simply be gauged in relation to experiencing combat, imprisonment or bombing. Foster *et al.* (2003) identified that psychological well-being was lower in older people who had been evacuated to 'safe' areas of the UK during the Second World War, with Waugh *et al.* (2007) going on to report that twice as many of this population of older people had been physically and/or sexually abused as of older people who had not been evacuated.

While some older people will have had the symptoms of PTSD ever since the traumatic event, for others the memories seem to re-emerge, perhaps reactivated through retirement or ill health. It appears as if the stress has been contained for many years, with the person coping by remaining busy and occupied. Enforced inactivity, more time to think, or perhaps a life-review process triggers memories that have been held at bay. Or, for some, the many anniversaries of events, power-fully presented through modern media, provide graphic reminders of events long forgotten (Davies, 2008). In some cases, the memories surface through nightmares initially, rather than daytime intrusive thoughts.

Older people are, of course, not immune to experiencing trauma in later life – through accidents; disasters, natural or man-made; being caught up in armed conflicts; and physical and sexual abuse. For example, Livingston *et al.* (1994) interviewed older people who had survived the Lockerbie air crash 3 years earlier. One in six still had symptoms of PTSD at that time, and a third were on medication for anxiety or sleeping. It has been suggested that trauma in later life may have more impact on someone who has previously had PTSD (Solomon and Prager, 1992), and there will, of course, be some older people who have less resilient coping mechanisms, perhaps because of difficult experiences earlier in life. The nature of the event will also influence coping; a shared natural disaster, such as a flood, will be easier to discuss and to share with others than a more personal experience, such as a sexual assault. PTSD is often missed in older people, perhaps because it may present indirectly, and, in the case of a trauma in earlier life, the person may have adjusted to the symptoms, and not find them remarkable. Often the person shows indications of depression, anxiety or physical health problems, which obscure the presence of PTSD (Davies, 2008).

The dementias

What is dementia?

The two major, internationally accepted diagnostic classification systems both define dementia as a syndrome characterized by an acquired global impairment of cognitive function, sufficient to impinge on everyday activities, occurring in clear consciousness (DSM-IV: American Psychiatric Association, 1994; ICD-10: World Health Organization, 1993). 'Global' in this context has the rather idiosyncratic meaning of 'two areas of cognitive function, one of which is memory', with memory impairment being an essential, but not sufficient, component of the diagnosis of dementia. Change from a previous level is a key part of the definition, and dementias are usually expected to show progressive deterioration. At one time, definitions would typically specify that the condition is usually irreversible, but with increased optimism regarding therapeutic strategies, this aspect has tended to be dropped.

Although cognitive changes are universal in dementia, other features, while not present in every case, are common enough to merit attention. Indeed, it is likely that it is these features which contribute more than cognitive deficits to carer strain (Donaldson et al., 1998) and placement decisions. These 'non-cognitive' features (often described as BPSD – behavioural and psychological symptoms of dementia) include depression, anxiety, hallucinations, delusions and challenging behaviours of various types (Burns et al., 1990a, 1990b, 1990c). For example, delusions – often concerning theft – were reported by Burns et al. in about a sixth of their sample of people with Alzheimer's disease, with another fifth having shown some ideas of persecution since their dementia began. Thirty per cent had misidentification syndromes, such as mistaking TV pictures or images in a picture or mirror for real people. Visual and auditory hallucinations were each noted in around a tenth of the sample.

A number of different specific types and variants of dementia have been identified. Among older people, three main disorders account for the majority of cases. The most common form is Alzheimer's disease, associated with the presence of neurofibrillary tangles and amyloid plaques in the cortex of the brain at post-mortem. Blessed, Tomlinson and Roth (1968) showed that what had until then been thought of as 'senile dementia' was characterized by these brain changes in older people; Alzheimer's disease had previously been considered as a disorder primarily occurring in younger individuals. Vascular dementia is also relatively common. In the past it has been referred to as arteriosclerotic dementia or multi-infarct dementia; the term 'vascular dementia' is preferred, as it reflects the range of ways in which the blood supply to different areas of the brain can be impaired. This may be through mini-strokes, as 'multi-infarct' implies (an infarct is death of tissue resulting from loss of blood supply), but also through disease-related damage to a variety of blood vessels. More recently, Lewy body dementia (LBD) has been identified. Lewy bodies (abnormal protein deposits found in some types of degenerating brain tissue) are found in the basal ganglia in people with Parkinson's disease; in LBD they are found in other areas of the brain also. In order to be certain of the type of dementia present, a post-mortem examination of the brain is required, and this has often been taken as the reference standard of diagnosis, although, as we shall see later, this is not always straightforward.

During life, there are some differences in presentation between the dementias; in LBD, hallucinations often occur early, there are fluctuations in performance, and memory does not stand out as the primary impairment; Alzheimer's disease has an insidious onset and gradual progression, with memory and learning especially impaired; vascular dementia shows a more step-wise decline, with periods of stability and recovery before further decline, and a patchy picture of impairment. However, these textbook presentations are sometimes difficult to discern in real life, and the likelihood of mixed presentations may make diagnosis of dementia type during life a less than precise exercise.

Although the diagnosis of a dementia syndrome (as opposed to a specific type) is generally thought to be relatively clear-cut, this applies more to the moderate/severe cases. Diagnostic uncertainty is frequent in older people, particularly where there is low mood and depression (as discussed above, where there is significant overlap), or where cognitive impairment is mild. Variants of dementia where the frontal areas of the brain show more damage early in the condition (e.g. Pick's disease, more common in younger people), where memory problems are initially less prominent, and personality changes frequently occur are often missed in the early stages.

Dementia and normal ageing

If some decline in cognitive function is to be expected in any event, then how can dementia – at least in its mild forms – be distinguished from normal ageing? The literature on the psychology of ageing is replete with examples – from longitudinal and cross-sequential studies – of age changes in cognitive function in groups of older people (e.g. Cullum et al., 2000). While it can be argued that the extent of change has been overstated at times, that changes occur cannot be refuted. There is individual variation, and a range of possible factors contributing to cognitive decline – most notably physical health problems (Elwood et al., 2002; Holland and Rabbitt, 1991). What is it that marks out the changes of dementia from those experienced by many (perhaps most) older people?

Conventionally, dementia has been seen as qualitatively as well as quantitatively distinct from normal ageing. However, it is possible to envisage normal ageing and dementia on a continuum, separated only by a necessarily arbitrary cut-off point (Cohen, 1996; Huppert, 1994). The essential distinction could perhaps be in the *rate*, rather than simply the absolute amount, of change. The argument against such a model is usually based on the qualitative differences observed in cognitive changes between Alzheimer's and normal ageing. However, such differences are less where the patients with Alzheimer's are only mildly impaired (Dawe, Procter and Philpot, 1992), suggesting there may be a continuum of change.

Such a model suggests that distinguishing between cases of early dementia may be a very difficult task, and ultimately might become a matter of definition, of setting a threshold of rate of change. Brayne (2007) points out that in epidemiological studies, overlap between normal and pathological ageing is usual. In general, a dementia develops gradually and insidiously – the point at which it is diagnosed is, in life, a matter of clinical judgement. Even at post-mortem, there are issues regarding how many plaques and tangles are needed for a diagnosis of Alzheimer's disease or how much vascular damage is needed for a vascular dementia to be identified.

The rate of change concept would account for the decline in cognitive function reported in normal ageing and would also account for the appearance (perhaps in smaller numbers) of neuropathological features, such as those associated with Alzheimer's disease, in the brains of older people who died without dementia. For example, Xuereb, Brayne, Dufouil et al. (2000) report post-mortem findings on a number of participants from a longitudinal population study of over 2,000 people aged over 75. The 101 brains studied came from older people who had been examined thoroughly on one or more occasions prior to their death; some were diagnosed as having dementia while alive, while others appeared to be ageing normally. Two main findings emerged: first, there were often present the pathologies of several forms of dementia; thus the characteristic Alzheimer's disease changes might co-occur with widespread vascular changes. Second, there was considerable overlap in the pathologies found in the people with dementia and those without. Similar findings were evident from the first 209 brains examined in the Cognitive Function and Ageing Study (CFAS) in the UK, which is following up in total over 17,500 older people (MRC CFAS, 2001). Ince (2003) concludes from these findings that 'the medical model of dementia which seeks to allocate people to distinct "diseases" becomes increasingly untenable in the face of this type of data'.

Evidently, some older people show dementia during life, with no obvious brain pathology at post-mortem, while others have significant pathology, but have been apparently unimpaired during life. In older people, the link between clinical picture and pathology appears less certain than has conventionally been claimed. Snowdon (2003), commenting on the Nun Study (an ongoing longitudinal study of a group of older nuns), describes a sister who died at the age of 85 without apparent cognitive impairment on testing, but whose brain showed large amounts of Alzheimer-type pathology. He concludes (p. 453): 'Given nearly the same location, type and amount of neuropathologic lesions, participants in our study show an incredible range of clinical manifestations, from no symptoms to severe symptoms.' Clearly, other factors also need to be considered.

Mild cognitive impairment (MCI)

If normal ageing and dementia are seen as two opposite ends of a continuum, almost inevitably an area of uncertainty between them has been labelled and become the subject of much debate. The term most often used currently is 'mild cognitive impairment' (MCI) (Tuokko and Zarit, 2003), but a number of such diagnostic terms synonymous with mild memory impairment have been utilised: these include 'benign senescent forgetfulness' (BSF), 'mild dementia', 'very mild cognitive decline', 'questionable dementia', 'limited cognitive disturbance', 'minimal dementia', 'age-associated memory impairment' (AAMI) (Dawe, Procter and Philpot, 1992), and 'age-associated cognitive decline' (AACD) (Cullum et al., 2000). MCI is characterized by subjective complaints of cognitive change, and objective evidence of cognitive impairment not sufficient to affect daily life. Typically, memory alone is impaired, but other subtypes of MCI have been described (Tuokko and McDowell, 2006).

Much of the interest in MCI stems from an interest in whether it represents a prodromal (early stage of an illness) form of Alzheimer's disease or another dementia. If it did, of course, the welcome possibility of perhaps intervening and delaying the onset of the dementia might become a reality. There is wide variation between studies, depending on the exact population studied and the criteria and tests used, but rates of conversion of between 10 and 20 per cent are typical (Tuokko and McDowell, 2006). These figures are much greater than would be expected in the age-matched general population, so there does seem to be an increased risk of dementia associated with MCI. However, it is important not to infer that because all prodromal Alzheimer's disease might be expected to look like MCI, all people with MCI will develop a dementia. A significant proportion will show improvement in cognitive function, or remain stable, or show difficulties related to other factors, such as physical health problems highlighted previously.

There is much debate regarding MCI as a 'diagnosis', as it may be seen as more of a ragbag of factors leading to cognitive impairment than a coherent entity (Visser and Brodaty, 2006). Different operational definitions continue to be used (Roberts et al., 2009), and there are concerns that normal ageing is being pathologized (Deary, 1995). Being given a 'diagnosis' of MCI is in effect being informed that the risk of developing a dementia is raised, but that the extent and severity of the current impairment does not justify the dementia label. The effects of providing this message would be worth further exploration. Does it reassure or does it increase uncertainty and anxiety? Lingler et al. (2006) identified emotional reactions in a group of people diagnosed as having MCI, including distress and anger, as well as relief at the absence of a dementia diagnosis. Some expressed satisfaction at having the cognitive impairment objectively validated. Some individuals did not acknowledge the possibility that MCI could progress to dementia, while others had developed the view that MCI would inevitably result in dementia. Lack of public awareness and information about the label of MCI may reduce attempts at coping with this situation.

Prevalence

The prevalence of the dementias has been the subject of numerous epidemiological studies internationally (e.g. Alzheimer's Disease International, 2009; Hofman, Rocca, Brayne et al., 1991). There are a number of differences between studies, but there is a broad consensus that the prevalence doubles for each increase of 5.1 years; 5 per cent of those over 65 and 40 per cent of those over 80 are widely accepted figures (Livingston and Hinchliffe, 1993). Alzheimer's Disease International (2009) have reported an authoritative meta-analysis of prevalence rates across the world. In Western Europe, 6.9 per cent of those aged over 60 are estimated to have a dementia, with 21.7 per cent of those aged 85–89 and 43.1 per cent of those aged 90 and over being affected.

In the past, there has been less certainty regarding prevalence in those over 90 and among centenarians, because large studies have not been previously feasible. If everyone who lived long enough developed a dementia, this would reinforce the concept of a continuum between normal ageing and dementia. On the other hand, survival to a certain age may mark a crossover effect, where the probability of dementia lessens, reflecting the general robust status of such survivors.

Howieson et al. (2003) report a longitudinal study of 95 healthy, community-dwelling older people who had an average age of 84 at the commencement of the study, which followed up participants for up to 13 years. Almost exactly half of the sample remained cognitively intact over the whole period or until death. Several studies have conducted population-based evaluations of centenarians. Andersen-Ranberg et al. (2001) attempted to interview every person in Denmark who reached 100 years old over a 13-month period. They report that 37 per cent had no signs of dementia, which was diagnosable in 51 per cent of the sample. A smaller study in the USA (Silver et al., 2001) reported 21 per cent having no dementia, and broadly similar findings are emerging across other countries (Antonucci, 2001). Silver et al. (2002) examined the brains of 14 centenarians from their study at post-mortem; in 10 cases the clinical picture during life and the post-mortem findings were consistent; in 2 cases, there were significant Alzheimer's disease changes despite no apparent impairments on neuropsychological tests; and in 2 cases, there had been apparent dementia during life, but no obvious neuropathological changes.

It appears that the inconsistency between brain changes and clinical presentation observed in younger samples continues into extreme old age.

Education and dementia

It has been argued that education protects against dementia (Orrell and Sahakian, 1995), with those with lower levels of education appearing to have an increased risk of developing a dementia. Some dramatic findings from the Nun Study have contributed to this view (Snowdon *et al.*, 2000). The research team was able to analyse handwritten autobiographies by the nuns at an average age of 23, some 62 years previously, and compare linguistic ability at that time with pathological brain changes observed at post-mortem. The density of expressed ideas within the autobiography was used as a measure of linguistic ability, and that correlated remarkably strongly with the severity of Alzheimer-type pathology in different brain regions. Conversely, in a larger sample from the same study, low education was not related to a diagnosis of Alzheimer's disease at post-mortem (Mortimer *et al.*, 2003).

Letenneur *et al.* (2000) report from four European follow-up studies (the EURO-DEM project) that the increased risk of developing dementia associated with fewer years of schooling was evident in women, but not in men. Women who had 7 or fewer years of education were more than four times as likely to develop dementia during the study as women with 12 or more years.

The issue is a complex one (Gilleard, 1997). Educational level is often seen as a proxy for intellectual ability (although this varies greatly across cultures and cohorts). One possibility is that a person with greater intelligence can decline for a longer time period before reaching a point where impairment is evident. Psychologists and psychometricians struggle to assess change of function over time satisfactorily, and must often rely on measures of memory and cognition that instead offer a threshold of impairment: simplistically, above-threshold scores are viewed as normal, while those below are 'in the dementia range'. Clearly, those with a lifelong relatively low intellectual and educational level require only a small degree of change to enter the range of impairment. Those with high intellectual function and education have, it would appear, more resources in reserve to maintain their function.

It does appear that those with low intellectual level are among those most often misdiagnosed as having a dementia. This may be attributable in part to the high educational loading of many of the screening tests available, such as the Mini-Mental State Examination, a widely used short questionnaire designed to assess the basic level of cognitive impairment (Orrell *et al.*, 1992). The practice in many epidemiological studies of assessing fully only those who screen positive on such a test is likely to mean that well-educated, intelligent people with dementia are excluded from the study at the outset, as they may score above the cut-off point, despite having clear impairment on more detailed neuropsychological assessment. On the other hand, family and friends of a highly intelligent person in a very demanding environment might become aware of signs of incipient dementia earlier than those supporting a person with a low intellectual level who is subject to few cognitive demands outside a well-established routine.

Tuokko *et al.* (2003) describe three models that might account for the differences in incidence of dementia between those with high education, high IQ or high occupational attainment and those with low achievement in these areas. The *brain reserve capacity model* suggests that some individuals have greater brain reserve. In other words, they can afford to lose more neurons, and can experience a higher amount of pathological changes before reaching a threshold for clinical symptoms. Education could lead to greater brain reserve capacity, with more synaptic connectivity, and brain size might be a marker of this reserve. For example, in the Nun Study, head circumference (a crude index of brain size) was related to the clinical diagnosis of dementia (Mortimer *et al.*, 2003), although not to the presence of Alzheimer's disease pathology. Those nuns with low education and small head circumference were four times as likely to show dementia as the rest of the sample.

The *cognitive reserve model* concerns itself with how effectively the remaining neural tissue is used. Intelligent, educated people have the facility to use alternative cognitive strategies, which again can result in a delay in expression of clinical and functional impairments associated with underlying brain pathology. They are more likely to continue to exercise their cognitive processes, and build their reserve further.

The third possibility relates to the *ascertainment bias* described earlier; the measures of impairment are not sensitive enough to pick up changes in this high-functioning group. From their analyses of data on the incidence of dementia from the Canadian Study on Health and Aging (a study of over 10,000 older people), Tuokko *et al.* (2003) conclude that the lower incidence of dementia for high-functioning people primarily results from ascertainment bias; the high-functioning people who developed dementia were scoring less well on tests of memory initially than those who did not develop dementia, but not within the 'impaired' range. The problem is that one threshold does not fit all, and there is a clear need for tests with normative data broken down by both age and education (Tuokko *et al.*, 2003).

Risk factors for dementia in late life

The greatest risk factor for developing dementia appears to be increasing age. However, a number of other possible factors have emerged, including genetic factors that are outside the scope of the current discussion (Howieson *et al.*, 2003; Riley *et al.*, 2000). Launer *et al.* (1999) report factors associated with the incidence of dementia from four European population-based studies. In addition to low levels of education (especially in women), female gender and current smoking (especially in men) increased the risk of dementia. History of head injury did not emerge as a factor, and there was no evidence that smoking history is a protective factor. Vascular risk factors, such as history of heart attacks, have also been shown to predict the incidence of dementia (Brayne *et al.*, 1998).

Lifestyle factors, such as cognitive stimulation and physical exercise, have been suggested to be protective, by further increasing brain reserve (Stern *et al.*, 2003). Brain reserve may offer some protection against the emergence of impairment and disability in response to neuropathology, with cognitive plasticity (essentially, flexibility of thought) compensating for neural dysfunction (Valenzuela and Sachdev, 2006), enabling some individuals to function within the normal cognitive range despite the presence of dementia-associated brain pathology. Valenzuela and Sachdev (2006) combined data from 22 studies (29,279 individuals) that had examined education, occupation, pre-morbid IQ and mentally stimulating leisure activities. They report that individuals classified as 'high reserve' had a 46 per cent lower risk of incident dementia after a median follow-up interval of 7.1 years.

A number of studies have evaluated the role of cognitive activity in protecting against the onset of dementia. For example, Wilson *et al.* (2002a, 2002b) report a longitudinal cohort study with an average follow-up of 4.5 years. At their initial interview they rated how often the study's participants engaged in a range of cognitive activities, such as reading a newspaper or books, playing card games, doing crosswords and other puzzles, watching TV and visiting museums, as well as participation in physical activities (e.g. walking for exercise). Controlling for age, gender and education, the risk of developing Alzheimer's was reduced by 33 per cent for each point increase in cognitive activity score at baseline. In contrast, number of hours of physical activity per week was not related to the risk of developing Alzheimer's disease.

The apparent superiority of cognitive activity to physical exercise needs to be examined carefully. Laurin *et al.* (2001), analysing data from the Canadian Study on Health and Aging, report that regular exercise was associated with lower risks of dementia for women. In Verghese *et al.*'s (2003) study, one form of physical exercise (dancing) was associated with lower risk of dementia, and the interaction between physical and cognitive activities must be acknowledged. Depression is, of course, also linked to reduced activity levels, and is also potentially an important risk factor, as discussed previously.

A psychological model of dementia

We may conclude the following points from the discussion so far: dementia in late life is complex, the simple disease model of dementia is untenable, brain changes are not always congruent with the clinical presentation, and multiple pathologies are more common than single disease processes.

These conclusions are a remarkably good fit with the arguments propounded by a British social psychologist, the late Tom Kitwood, who argued that the clinical presentation of dementia was not simply a manifestation of the neuropathological impairment of the damaged brain. He argued that other factors, such as the person's health, life history and personality, were also important, along with their social environment. Kitwood (1993) expressed this understanding of the variety of influences on the presentation of dementia in a simple equation:

$$D = P + B + H + NI + SP$$

where D = dementia presentation, P = personality, B = biography, H = physical health, NI = neurological impairment, and SP = social psychology.

Education and occupational attainment might be included under biography, and genetic risk factors under physical health. It is perhaps the social environment that has yet to receive full attention. Kitwood highlighted the impact of the social environment surrounding the person, suggesting that often it constituted a 'malignant social psychology', devaluing, diminishing, dehumanizing and depersonalizing the person, leading to greater disability and dysfunction. Examples of a malignant social psychology would include infantilization, disempowerment and objectification. His suggestion that the person with dementia may well appear more impaired, or to have a more severe level of dementia than is necessitated by the actual neuropathological damage that has been sustained, now appears well supported. His assertion that someone may appear to have dementia without evident neuropathological impairment also finds support, although this conclusion is diluted by the possibility that there is a form of pathology we have yet to recognize.

Kitwood was the champion of person-centred care (Woods, 1999, 2001). This model places the person with dementia at centre stage, and acknowledges their efforts to make sense of and cope with their condition. A number of studies have demonstrated the variety of coping strategies used by people with dementia to adjust to and manage their situation (Clare, 2003; Clare et al., 2006; Gillies, 2000; Seiffer et al., 2005). The development of valid and reliable self-report measures of quality of life for people with dementia (e.g. Thorgrimsen et al., 2003) has made it possible to identify factors contributing to well-being in people with dementia and to broaden the scope of potential interventions beyond simply providing support to caregivers.

Psychological interventions in later life

Which psychological interventions have proved effective for those older people who are experiencing atypical ageing? In relation to anxiety disorders in older people, there is some evidence, from randomized, controlled trials, that cognitive behavioural therapy (CBT) in group and individual formats is effective (e.g. Barrowclough *et al.*, 2001). Cognitive therapy, behaviour therapy and brief psychodynamic psychotherapy appear to be equally effective treatment modalities for depression in older people (Thompson, Gallagher and Breckenridge, 1987), with the effectiveness of cognitive therapy being comparable to that in younger people (Woods and Roth, 2005). A combined approach, using medication and monthly sessions of interpersonal psychotherapy, has been shown to be particularly helpful in preventing relapse for patients in this age group (Reynolds *et al.*, 1999). Relapse prevention, as discussed previously, is a particularly pertinent issue for older people with depression.

In essence, cognitive therapy encourages the patient to alter how they think about their problems (e.g. to think differently about an object that is at the centre of their phobia), behaviour therapy encourages the patient to alter how they behave about their problems (e.g. to learn to confront the object of their phobia), and CBT uses the aforementioned techniques in combination. Psychodynamic psychotherapy encourages the patient to address the roots of their problem, which may be unconscious (and thus is similar to psychoanalysis, but is generally shorter in treatment duration). In contrast, interpersonal psychotherapy aims to change interpersonal skills rather than the 'internal mind'.

Scogin and McElreath (1994) report a meta-analysis of psychological therapies for depression in older people, and suggest that reminiscence therapy (a general term for a variety of techniques that encourage patients to reflect on past events in their lives) appears to be as effective for depression as cognitive therapies, and a more recent meta-analysis supports the effectiveness of this approach (Bohlmeijer, Smit and Cuijpers, 2003). This is of interest in that, unlike CBT, reminiscence and life review approaches might be said to be specifically geared to the developmental position of the older person. They might readily be linked to the final phase of Erikson's lifespan developmental model (Erikson, 1963; Erikson, Erikson and Kivnick, 1986), where the task of late life is seen as involving a process of life review. The successful resolution of this stage involves a sense of integrity: accepting both what has been achieved and what will never now be possible, and balancing disappointments and regrets with successes and positive experiences and memories. This position is contrasted with a sense of despair, of a life wasted, full of regret and disappointment, and a sense of shame at the person one has become. Life review is usually undertaken on a one-to-one basis, involving the person working through their life story chronologically, with the emphasis on evaluation of events and experiences, positive and negative, rather than simply the enjoyable recall of memories (Haight, 1992).

There is a debate as to the extent to which psychological therapies, including CBT, require adaptation in their application to older adults (e.g. Laidlaw *et al.*,

2003). Woods and Charlesworth (2001) suggest that the main adaptations relate to the context of ageing, highlighting the need for therapists to be aware of issues arising from cognitive impairment and physical health problems. The problems are likely to be more long-standing than in younger adults, and so may be more deeply entrenched in the person's lifestyle. Current cohorts of older people may be less familiar with psychological therapies, and so may need more education and information regarding the collaboration that is involved. The interdependency of older people with others – family members and paid supporters – cannot be overlooked, and a more systemic approach is called for, rather than a focus simply on the individual. Finally, there needs to be recognition that some older people face considerable adversity; negative thinking is not necessarily a cognitive distortion, and the therapist needs to be sensitive to helping the person to consider ways of accepting aspects of their situation that are not amenable to change, and identifying those aspects which will make a real difference to the person's well-being.

A number of therapeutic approaches have also been developed in relation to dementia. Woods and Clare (2008) group these according to their primary focus: stimulation, cognition, behaviour and emotion. Stimulation and activity approaches cover a range from music to hand massage to aromatherapy to pets. Most recent evaluations are of multi-sensory stimulation, where a variety of types of stimulation are used, often with people with advanced dementia, to engage and calm the person, with reports of reduced depression, apathy and disturbed behaviour (Van Weert et al., 2005). Cognitive approaches include cognitive stimulation, where cognitive activities are undertaken in a group or social context; cognitive training, where the person carries out structured cognitive exercise, involving repeated practice of cognitive processes; and cognitive rehabilitation, where the person works to achieve individual goals, using a variety of means including external aids as well as targeted new learning. There is a good deal of evidence to support the effectiveness of cognitive stimulation (e.g. Spector et al., 2003) and emerging evidence for cognitive rehabilitation, but the effects of cognitive training appear to be specific to the material learned (Woods, Clare and Windle, in press). Reminiscence therapy for people with dementia has attracted relatively little empirical research to date, but some positive findings are being reported on the use of life review with people with dementia (Haight et al., 2006) and on group work (e.g. Wang, 2007).

There is a growing body of work on the effectiveness of individualized behavioural interventions and functional analysis for challenging behaviour (e.g. Cohen-Mansfield et al., 2007; Moniz-Cook et al., 2003; Teri et al., 2005). There is less evidence for emotion-focused approaches in general, including psychotherapy and validation therapy (Finnema et al., 2000; Schrijnemaekers et al., 2002). CBT for depression and anxiety in people with dementia has some support, especially when involving family caregivers (Kraus *et al.*, 2008; Teri *et al.*, 1997). There have been numerous evaluations of interventions to reduce strain in family caregivers of people with dementia (Brodaty *et al.*, 2003) and the most effective approaches appear to combine a number of elements, including peer support, psycho-education and increasing social support. For example, a programme of brief individual and family counselling for spouse caregivers, combined with peer support groups, resulted in long-standing improvements in depression for the caregivers and substantial delays in institutionalization for the person with dementia (Mittelman *et al.*, 2006).

In general, psychological therapies for older people are less well researched than those for younger people, in part because older people have been excluded systematically from treatment trials. However, there is now a good basis for suggesting that older people who do experience psychological problems in later life may benefit from a range of psychological interventions. Even in the context of dementia, there is good cause for therapeutic optimism, with the application of Kitwood's person-centred care approach itself being associated with improved outcomes for people with dementia (Chenoweth *et al.*, 2009). What is perhaps equally remarkable is that despite the challenges of later life, especially in relation to poor health and losses, many older people bring into later life sufficient resources of resilience to maintain good levels of well-being in the face of adversity (Windle *et al.*, 2009).

Summary

Although many types of atypical condition are found in older adults, several are far commoner than in, and may present differently from, younger adults. For example, older people with mood disorders such as depression often present with different patterns of symptoms. The incidence of depression in older adults and its relationship with life events, physical health, bereavement, suicide and cognitive impairment are discussed. The other common mood disorders of anxiety and post-traumatic stress disorder are also discussed, along with specific problems found in older adults with these conditions. Dementia is then addressed, first in terms of taxonomy. The differences between dementia and typical ageing and mild cognitive impairment are examined, and then the prevalence of dementia. Relatively recent research has suggested that educational level may ameliorate the effects of dementing decline, and the evidence for and against this is examined. Risk factors affecting the probability of developing dementia in later life are then discussed. It is clear that dementia has many facets, and the chapter explores Kitwood's model of dementia, which draws together the factors of personality, biography, physical health, neurological impairment and social psychology, in determining the presentation of dementing symptoms. Finally, the range of psychological interventions available to the clinician is examined.

REFERENCES

Alexopoulos, G.S. (2005) Depression in the elderly, *Lancet, 365*, 1961–70.

Alzheimer's Disease International (2009) *World Alzheimer report*. London: Alzheimer's Disease International.

American Psychiatric Association (1994) *Diagnostic and statistical manual of mental disorders*, 4th edn. Washington, DC: American Psychiatric Association.

Andersen-Ranberg, K., Vasegaard, L. and Jeune, B. (2001) Dementia is not inevitable: a population-based study of Danish centenarians, *Journals of Gerontology. Series B, Psychological Sciences and Social Sciences, 56*, 152–9.

Antonucci, T.C. (2001) Introduction to special section on centenarians and dementia, *Journals of Gerontology. Psychological Sciences and Social Sciences, 56*, 133.

Ballard, C.G., Bannister, C. and Oyebode, F. (1996) Depression in dementia sufferers, *International Journal of Geriatric Psychiatry, 11*(6), 507–15.

Banerjee, S. (1993) Prevalence and recognition rates of psychiatric disorder in the elderly clients of a community care service, *International Journal of Geriatric Psychiatry, 8*, 125–31.

Barrowclough, C., King, P., Colville, J. *et al.* (2001) A randomized trial of the effectiveness of cognitive-behavioral therapy and supportive counseling for anxiety symptoms in older adults, *Journal of Consulting and Clinical Psychology, 69*, 756–62.

Bhalla, R.K., Butters, M.A., Mulsant, B.H. *et al.* (2006) Persistence of neuropsychologic deficits in the remitted state of late-life depression, *American Journal of Geriatric Psychiatry, 14*, 419–27.

Blazer, D.G. (2003) Depression in late life: review and commentary, *Journals of Gerontology. Series A, Biological Sciences and Medical Sciences, 58*, M249–65.

Blessed, G., Tomlinson, B.E. and Roth, M. (1968) The association between quantitative measures of dementia and of senile change in the cerebral grey matter of elderly subjects, *British Journal of Psychiatry, 114*, 797–811.

Bohlmeijer, E., Smit, F. and Cuijpers, P. (2003) Effects of reminiscence and life review on late-life depression: a meta-analysis, *International Journal of Geriatric Psychiatry, 18*, 1088–94.

Brayne, C. (2007) The elephant in the room – healthy brains in later life, epidemiology and public health, *Nature Reviews Neuroscience, 8*, 233–9.

Brayne, C., Gill, C., Huppert, F. *et al.* (1998) Vascular risks and incident dementia: results from a cohort study of the very old, *Dementia and Geriatric Cognitive Disorders, 9*, 175–80.

Brodaty, H., Green, A. and Koschera, A. (2003) Meta-analysis of psychosocial interventions for caregivers of people with dementia, *Journal of the American Geriatrics Society, 51*, 657–64.

Burns, A., Jacoby, R. and Levy, R. (1990a) Psychiatric phenomena in Alzheimer's disease. I. Disorders of thought content, *British Journal of Psychiatry, 157*, 72–6.

(1990b) Psychiatric phenomena in Alzheimer's disease. II. Disorders of perception, *British Journal of Psychiatry, 157*, 76–81.

(1990c) Psychiatric phenomena in Alzheimer's disease. IV. Disorders of behaviour, *British Journal of Psychiatry, 157*, 86–94.

Burvill, P.W., Johnson, G.A., Jamrozik, K.D. *et al.* (1995) Prevalence of depression after stroke: the Perth Community Stroke Study, *British Journal of Psychiatry, 166*, 320–7.

Carson, A.J., MacHale, S., Allen, K. *et al.* (2000) Depression after stroke and lesion location: a systematic review, *Lancet, 356*(9224), 122–6.

Cattell, H. (2000) Suicide in the elderly, *Advances in Psychiatric Treatment, 6*, 102–8.

Cervilla, J.A. and Prince, M.J. (1997) Cognitive impairment and social distress as different pathways to depression in the elderly: a cross-sectional study, *International Journal of Geriatric Psychiatry, 12*, 995–1000.

Chenoweth, L., King, M., Jeon, Y. *et al.* (2009) Caring for Aged Dementia Care Resident Study (CADRES) of person-centred care, dementia-care mapping, and usual care in dementia: a cluster-randomised trial, *Lancet (Neurology), 8*, 317–25.

Clare, L. (2003) Managing threats to self: awareness in early stage Alzheimer's disease, *Social Science and Medicine, 57*, 1017–29.

Clare, L., Goater, T. and Woods, B. (2006) Illness representations in early-stage dementia: a preliminary investigation, *International Journal of Geriatric Psychiatry, 21*, 761–7.

Cohen, G. (1996) Memory and learning in normal ageing, in R.T. Woods (ed.), *Handbook of the clinical psychology of ageing.* Chichester: Wiley, 43–58.

Cohen-Mansfield, J., Libin, A. and Marx, M. (2007) Nonpharmacological treatment of agitation: a controlled trial of systematic individualized intervention. *Journals of Gerontology. Series A, Biological Sciences and Medical Sciences, 62A*(8), 908–16.

Cole, M.G. and Dendukuri, N. (2003) Risk factors for depression among elderly community subjects: a systematic review and meta-analysis, *American Journal of Psychiatry, 160*, 1147–56.

Conwell, Y., Duberstein, P.R. and Caine, E.D. (2002) Risk factors for suicide in later life, *Biological Psychiatry, 52*, 193–204.

Crocker, L., Clare, L. and Evans, K. (2006) Giving up or finding a solution? The experience of attempted suicide in later life, *Aging and Mental Health, 10*, 638–47.

Cullum, S., Huppert, F., McGee, M. *et al.* (2000) Decline across different domains of cognitive function in normal ageing: results of a longitudinal population-based study using CAMCOG, *International Journal of Geriatric Psychiatry, 15*, 853–62.

Davies, S. (2008) Psychological trauma in late life: conceptualization, assessment and treatment, in R.T. Woods and L. Clare (eds), *Handbook of the clinical psychology of ageing,* 2nd edn. Chichester: Wiley, 121–31.

Dawe, B., Procter, A. and Philpot, M. (1992) Concepts of mild memory impairment in the elderly and their relationship to dementia – a review, *International Journal of Geriatric Psychiatry, 7*, 473–9.

Deary, I.J. (1995) Age-associated memory impairment: a suitable case for treatment?, *Ageing and Society, 15*, 393–406.

Denihan, A., Kirby, M., Bruce, I. *et al.* (2000) Three-year prognosis of depression in the community-dwelling elderly, *British Journal of Psychiatry, 176*, 453–7.

Dennis, M., Wakefield, P., Molloy, C. *et al.* (2005) Self-harm in older people with depression: comparison of social factors, life events and symptoms, *British Journal of Psychiatry, 186*, 538–9.

Dent, O.F., Waite, L.M., Bennett, H.P. *et al.* (1999) A longitudinal study of chronic disease and depressive symptoms in a community sample of older people, *Aging and Mental Health, 3*(4), 351–7.

Donaldson, C., Tarrier, N. and Burns, A. (1998) Determinants of carer stress in Alzheimer's disease, *International Journal of Geriatric Psychiatry*, *13*(4), 248–56.

Downton, J.H. and Andrews, K. (1990) Postural disturbance and psychological symptoms amongst elderly people living at home, *International Journal of Geriatric Psychiatry*, *5*, 93–8.

Elwood, P.C., Pickering, J., Bayer, A. *et al.* (2002) Vascular disease and cognitive function in older men in the Caerphilly cohort, *Age and Ageing*, *31*, 43–8.

Erikson, E. (1963) *Childhood and society*, 2nd edn. New York: W.W. Norton.

Erikson, E.H., Erikson, J.M. and Kivnick, H.Q. (1986) *Vital involvement in old age*. New York: W.W. Norton.

Finnema, E., Droes, R.-M. , Ribbe, M. *et al.* (2000) The effects of emotion-oriented approaches in the care for persons suffering from dementia: a review of the literature, *International Journal of Geriatric Psychiatry*, *15*, 141–61.

Foster, D., Davies, S. and Steele, H. (2003) The evacuation of British children during World War II: a preliminary investigation into the long-term psychological effects, *Aging and Mental Health*, *7*(5), 398–408.

Fry, P.S. (1990) A factor analytic investigation of home-bound elderly individuals' concerns about death and dying, and their coping responses. *Journal of Clinical Psychology*, *46*, 737–48.

Ganguli, M., Yangchun, D., Dodge, H.H. *et al.* (2006) Depressive symptoms and cognitive decline in late life: a prospective epidemiological study, *Archives of General Psychiatry*, *63*, 153–60.

Gatz, J.L., Tyas, S.L., St. John, P. *et al.* (2005) Do depressive symptoms predict Alzheimer's disease and dementia?, *Journals of Gerontology. Series A, Biological Sciences and Medical Sciences*, *60*, 744–7.

Gilleard, C.J. (1997) Education and Alzheimer's disease: a review of recent international epidemiological studies, *Aging and Mental Health*, *1*(1), 33–46.

Gillies, B.A. (2000) A memory like clockwork: accounts of living through dementia, *Aging and Mental Health*, *4*, 366–74.

Haight, B. (1992) The structured life-review process: a community approach to the ageing client, in G.M.M. Jones and B.M.L. Miesen (eds), *Care-giving in dementia*. London: Routledge, 272–92.

Haight, B.K., Gibson, F. and Michel, Y. (2006) The Northern Ireland life review/life storybook project for people with dementia, *Alzheimer's and Dementia*, *2*(1), 56–8.

Harwood, D., Hawton, K., Hope, T. *et al.* (2000) Suicide in older people: mode of death, demographic factors, and medical contact before death in one hundred and ninety-five cases, *International Journal of Geriatric Psychiatry*, *15*, 736–43.

Harwood, D., Hawton, K., Hope, T. *et al.* (2001) Psychiatric disorder and personality factors associated with suicide in older people: a descriptive and case-control study. *International Journal of Geriatric Psychiatry*, *16*, 155–65.

Hofman, A., Rocca, W.A., Brayne, C. *et al.* (1991) The prevalence of dementia in Europe: a collaborative study of the 1980–1990 findings, *International Journal of Epidemiology*, *20*, 736–48.

Holland, C.A. and Rabbitt, P. (1991) The course and causes of cognitive change with advancing age, *Reviews in Clinical Gerontology*, *1*, 81–96.

Howieson, D.B., Camicioli, R., Quinn, J. *et al.* (2003) Natural history of cognitive decline in the old old, *Neurology*, *60*, 1489–94.

Howland, J., Peterson, E.W., Levin, W.C. *et al.* (1993) Fear of falling among the community dwelling elderly, *Journal of Aging and Health*, **5**, 229–43.

Hunt, N. and Robbins, I. (2001) The long-term consequences of war: the experience of World War II, *Aging and Mental Health*, **5**(2), 183–90.

Huppert, F.A. (1994) Memory function in dementia and normal ageing – dimension or dichotomy?, in F.A. Huppert, C. Brayne and D. O'Connor (eds), *Dementia and normal ageing*. Cambridge University Press, 291–330.

Hynninen, K., Breitve, M., Wiborg, A. *et al.* (2005) Psychological characteristics of patients with chronic obstructive pulmonary disease: a review, *Journal of Psychosomatic Research*, **59**, 429–43.

Ince, P.G. (2003) Concepts of Alzheimer's disease. *Alzheimer's Disease International: Global Perspectives*, **13**, 6.

Jacoby, R. and Levy, R. (1980) Computed tomography in the elderly. 3. Affective disorder, *British Journal of Psychiatry*, **136**, 270–5.

Jorm, A. (2000) Does old age reduce the risk of anxiety and depression? A review of epidemiological studies across the adult life span, *Psychological Medicine*, **30**, 11–22.

Kitwood, T. (1993) Towards a theory of dementia care: the interpersonal process, *Ageing and Society*, **13**, 51–67.

Kraaij, V. and de-Wilde, E.J. (2001) Negative life events and depressive symptoms in the elderly: a life span perspective, *Aging and Mental Health*, **5**(1), 84–91.

Kraus, C., Seignourel, P., Balasubramanyam, V. *et al.* (2008) Cognitive-behavioral treatment for anxiety in patients with dementia: two case studies, *Journal of Psychiatric Practice*, **14**(3), 186–92.

Laidlaw, K., Thompson, L.W., Dick-Siskin, L. *et al.* (2003) *Cognitive behaviour therapy with older people*. Chichester: Wiley.

Launer, L. J., Andersen, K., Dewey, M.E. *et al.* (1999) Rates and risk factors for dementia and Alzheimer's disease: results from EURODEM pooled analyses, *Neurology*, **52**, 78–84.

Laurin, D., Verreault, R., Lindsay, J. *et al.* (2001) Physical activity and risk of cognitive impairment and dementia in elderly persons, *Archives of Neurology*, **58**, 498–504.

Lebret, S., Perret-Vaille, E., Mulliez, A. *et al.* (2006) Elderly suicide attempters: characteristics and outcome, *International Journal of Geriatric Psychiatry*, **21**, 1052–9.

Letenneur, L., Launer, L.J., Andersen, K. *et al.* (2000) Education and the risk for Alzheimer's disease: sex makes a difference: EURODEM pooled analyses, *American Journal of Epidemiology*, **151**, 1064–71.

Licht-Strunk, E., Bremmer, M.A., van-Marwijk, H.W. *et al.* (2004) Depression in older persons with versus without vascular disease in the open population: similar depressive symptom patterns, more disability, *Journal of Affective Disorders*, **83**, 155–60.

Lindesay, J. (1997) Phobic disorders and fear of crime in the elderly, *Aging and Mental Health*, **1**(1), 81–5.

Lindesay, J., Briggs, K. and Murphy, E. (1989) The Guys/Age Concern survey: prevalence rates of cognitive impairment, depression and anxiety in an urban elderly community, *British Journal of Psychiatry*, **155**, 317–29.

Lingler, J.H., Nightingale, M.C., Erlen, J.A. *et al.* (2006) Making sense of mild cognitive impairment: a qualitative exploration of the patient's experience, *The Gerontologist*, **46**, 791–800.

Livingston, G. and Hinchliffe, A.C. (1993) The epidemiology of psychiatric disorders in the elderly, *International Review of Psychiatry*, **5**, 317–26.

Livingston, H.M., Livingston, M.G. and Fell, S. (1994) The Lockerbie disaster: a three year follow-up of elderly victims, *International Journal of Geriatric Psychiatry*, *9*, 989–94.

Lockwood, K.A., Alexopoulos, G.S. and van-Gorp, W.G. (2002) Executive dysfunction in geriatric depression, *American Journal of Psychiatry*, *159*, 1119–26.

Mann, A.H., Schneider, J., Mozley, C.G. *et al.* (2000) Depression and the response of residential homes to physical health needs, *International Journal of Geriatric Psychiatry*, *15*, 1105–12.

Mast, B.T., Azar, A.R. and Murrell, S.A. (2005) The vascular depression hypothesis: the influence of age on the relationship between cerebrovascular risk factors and depressive symptoms in community dwelling elders, *Aging and Mental Health*, *9*(2), 146–52.

McKiernan, F.M. (1996) Bereavement and attitudes to death, in R.T. Woods (ed.), *Handbook of the clinical psychology of ageing*. Chichester: Wiley, 159–82.

Mittelman, M.S., Haley, W.E., Clay, O.J. *et al.* (2006) Improving caregiver well-being delays nursing home placement of patients with Alzheimer disease, *Neurology*, *67*, 1592–9.

Moniz-Cook, E., Stokes, G. and Agar, S. (2003) Difficult behaviour and dementia in nursing homes: five cases of psychosocial intervention, *Clinical Psychology and Psychotherapy*, *10*(3), 197–208.

Mortimer, J.A., Snowdon, D.A. and Markesbery, W.R. (2003) Head circumference, education and risk of dementia: findings from the Nun Study. *Journal of Clinical and Experimental Neuropsychology*, *25*, 671–9.

Mozley, C., Sutcliffe, C., Bagley, H. *et al.* (2004) *Towards quality care: outcomes for older people in care homes*. Aldershot: Ashgate.

MRC-CFAS (Esiri, M., Matthews, F.E., Brayne, C. *et al.*) (2001) Pathological correlates of late-onset dementia in a multicentre, community-based population in England and Wales. Neuropathology Group of the Medical Research Council Cognitive Function and Ageing Study (MRC CFAS). *Lancet*, *357*(9251), 169–75.

Neal, L.A., Hill, N., Hughes, J. *et al.* (1995) Convergent validity of measures of PTSD in an elderly population of former prisoners of war. *International Journal of Geriatric Psychiatry*, *10*, 617–22.

Nordhus, I.H. (2008) Manifestations of depression and anxiety in older adults, in R.T. Woods and L. Clare (eds), *Handbook of the clinical psychology of ageing*, 2nd edn. Chichester: Wiley, 97–110.

O'Connell, H., Chin, A.-V., Cunningham, C. *et al.* (2004) Recent developments: suicide in older people, *British Medical Journal*, *329*, 895–9.

Orrell, M., Howard, R., Payne, A. *et al.* (1992) Differentiation between organic and functional psychiatric illness in the elderly: an evaluation of four cognitive tests, *International Journal of Geriatric Psychiatry*, *7*, 263–75.

Orrell, M.W. and Sahakian, B.J. (1995) Use it or lose it: does education protect against dementia?, *British Medical Journal*, *310*, 951–2.

Osborn, D.P.J., Fletcher, A.E., Smeeth, L. *et al.* (2003) Factors associated with depression in a representative sample of 14,217 people aged 75 and over in the United Kingdom: results from the MRC trial of assessment and management of older people in the community, *International Journal of Geriatric Psychiatry*, *18*, 623–30.

Oyebode, J.R. (2008) Death, dying and bereavement, in R.T. Woods and L. Clare (eds), *Handbook of the clinical psychology of ageing*, 2nd edn. Chichester: Wiley, 75–94.

Pearson, J.L. and Brown, G.K. (2000) Suicide prevention in late life: directions for science and practice, *Clinical Psychology Review*, *20*, 685–705.

Poon, L.W. (1992) Towards an understanding of cognitive functioning in geriatric depression, *International Psychogeriatrics*, **4**(Suppl 2), 241–66.

Reijnders, J.S., Ehrt, U., Weber, W.E. *et al.* (2008) A systematic review of prevalence studies of depression in Parkinson's disease, *Movement Disorders*, **23**, 183–9.

Reynolds, C.F., Frank, E., Perel, J.M. *et al.* (1999) Nortriptyline and interpersonal psychotherapy as maintenance therapies for recurrent major depression: a randomized controlled trial in patients older than 59 years, *Journal of the American Medical Association*, **281**, 39–45.

Riley, K.P., Snowdon, D.A., Saunders, A.M. *et al.* (2000) Cognitive function and apolipoprotein E in very old adults, *Journals of Gerontology. Series B, Psychological Sciences and Social Sciences*, **55**, S69-75.

Roberts, J.L., Clare, L. and Woods, R.T. (2009) Subjective memory complaints and awareness of memory functioning in mild cognitive impairment: a systematic review, *Dementia and Geriatric Cognitive Disorders*, **28**, 95–109.

Schrijnemaekers, V., van-Rossum, E., Candel, M. *et al.* (2002) Effects of emotion-oriented care on elderly people with cognitive impairment and behavioral problems, *International Journal of Geriatric Psychiatry*, **17**, 926-37.

Scogin, F. and McElreath, L. (1994) Efficacy of psychosocial treatments for geriatric depression: a quantitative review, *Journal of Consulting and Clinical Psychology*, **62**, 69–74.

Seiffer, A., Clare, L. and Harvey, R. (2005) The role of personality and coping style in relation to awareness of current functioning in early-stage dementia, *Aging and Mental Health*, **9**, 535-41.

Silver, M.H., Jilinskaia, E. and Perls, T.T. (2001) Cognitive functional status of age-confirmed centenarians in a population-based study, *Journals of Gerontology. Series B, Psychological Sciences and Social Sciences*, **56**, P134-40.

Silver, M.H., Newell, K., Brady, C. *et al.* (2002) Distinguishing between neurodegenerative disease and disease-free ageing: correlating neuropsychological evaluations and neuropathological studies in centenarians, *Psychosomatic Medicine*, **64**, 493-501.

Snowdon, D.A. (2003) Healthy aging and dementia: findings from the Nun Study, *Annals of Internal Medicine*, **139**, 450–4.

Snowdon, D.A., Greiner, L.H. and Markesbery, W.R. (2000) Linguistic ability in early life and the neuropathology of Alzheimer's disease and cerebrovascular disease: findings from the Nun Study, *Annals of the New York Academy of Sciences*, **903**, 34–8.

Solomon, Z. and Prager, E. (1992) Elderly Israeli Holocaust survivors during the Persian Gulf War: a study of psychological distress, *American Journal of Psychiatry*, **149**, 1707-10.

Sörensen, S., Pinquart, M. and Duberstein, P.R. (2002) How effective are interventions with caregivers? An updated meta analysis, *The Gerontologist*, **42**, 356-72.

Spano, A. and Forstl, H. (1992) Falling and the fear of it, *International Journal of Geriatric Psychiatry*, **7**, 149-51.

Spector, A., Thorgrimsen, L., Woods, B. *et al.* (2003) Efficacy of an evidence-based cognitive stimulation therapy programme for people with dementia: randomised controlled trial, *British Journal of Psychiatry*, **183**, 248-54.

Stern, Y., Zarahn, E., Hilton, H.J. *et al.* (2003) Exploring the neural basis of cognitive reserve, *Journal of Clinical and Experimental Neuropsychology*, **25**, 691-701.

Teri, L., Logsdon, R.G., Uomoto, J. *et al.* (1997) Behavioral treatment of depression in dementia patients: a controlled clinical trial, *Journals of Gerontology. Series B, Psychological Sciences and Social Sciences*, **52**, P159-66.

Teri, L., McCurry, S.M., Logsdon, R. *et al.* (2005) Training community consultants to help family members improve dementia care: a randomized controlled trial, *The Gerontologist*, *45*(6), 802–11.

Thompson, L.W., Gallagher, D. and Breckenridge, J.S. (1987) Comparative effectiveness of psychotherapies for depressed elders, *Journal of Consulting and Clinical Psychology*, *55*, 385–90.

Thorgrimsen, L., Selwood, A., Spector, A. *et al.* (2003) Whose quality of life is it anyway? The validity and reliability of the Quality of Life – Alzheimer's Disease (QoL–AD) Scale, *Alzheimer Disease and Associated Disorders*, *17*(4), 201–8.

Tinetti, M.E., Mendes de Leon, C.F., Doucette, J.T. *et al.* (1994) Fear of falling and fall-related efficacy in relationship to functioning among community living elders, *Journal of Gerontology*, *49*, M140–7.

Tinetti, M.E., Richman, D. and Powell, L. (1990) Falls efficacy as a measure of fear of falling, *Journal of Gerontology*, *45*, P239–43.

Tuokko, H., Garrett, D.D., McDowell, I. *et al.* (2003) Cognitive decline in high-functioning older adults: reserve or ascertainment bias?, *Aging and Mental Health*, *7*(4), 259–70.

Tuokko, H. and McDowell, I. (2006) An overview of mild cognitive impairment, in H. Tuokko and D. F. Hultsch (eds), *Mild cognitive impairment: international perspectives*. New York: Taylor & Francis, 3–28.

Tuokko, H. and Zarit, S.H. (2003) Mild cognitive impairment, *Aging & Mental Health*, *7*(4), 235–7.

Valenzuela, M.J. and Sachdev, P. (2006) Brain reserve and dementia: a systematic review, *Psychological Medicine*, *36*, 441–54.

Van Weert, J.C.M., van Dulmen, A.M., Spreeuwenberg, P.M.M. *et al.* (2005) Behavioral and mood effects of Snoezelen integrated into 24-hour dementia care, *Journal of the American Geriatrics Society*, *53*, 24–33.

Verghese, J., Lipton, R.B., Katz, M.J. *et al.* (2003) Leisure activities and the risk of dementia in the elderly, *New England Journal of Medicine*, *348*, 2508–16.

Vinkers, D.J., Gussekloo, J., Stek, M.L. *et al.* (2004) Temporal relation between depression and cognitive impairment in old age: prospective population based study, *British Medical Journal*, *329*, 881–3.

Visser, P.J. and Brodaty, H. (2006) MCI is not a clinically useful concept, *International Psychogeriatrics*, *18*, 402–9.

Waern, M., Rubenowitz, E., Runeson, B. (2002) Burden of illness and suicide in elderly people: case-control study, *British Medical Journal*, *324*, 1355.

Wang, J.-J. (2007) Group reminiscence therapy for cognitive and affective function of demented elderly in Taiwan, *International Journal of Geriatric Psychiatry*, *22*, 1235–40.

Waugh, M.J., Robbins, I., Davies, S. *et al.* (2007) The long-term impact of war experiences and evacuation on people who were children during World War Two, *Aging and Mental Health*, *11*, 168–74.

Wilson, R.S., Bennett, D.A., Bienias, J.L. *et al.* (2002) Cognitive activity and incident AD in a population-based sample of older persons, *Neurology*, *59*, 1910–14.

Wilson, R.S., Mendes de Leon, C.F., Barnes, L.L. *et al.* (2002) Participation in cognitively stimulating activities and risk of incident Alzheimer disease, *Journal of the American Medical Association*, *287*, 742–8.

Wilson, R.S., Mendes de Leon, C.F., Bennett, D.A. *et al.* (2004) Depressive symptoms and cognitive decline in a community population of older persons, *Journal of Neurology, Neurosurgery, and Psychiatry*, **75**, 126–9.

Windle, G. and Woods, R.T. (2004) Variations in subjective well-being: the mediating role of a psychological resource, *Ageing and Society*, **24**, 583–602.

Windle, G., Woods, R.T. and Markland, D.A. (in press) Living with ill health in older age: the role of a resilient personality, *Journal of Happiness Studies*.

Woods, B. (1999) The person in dementia care, *Generations*, **23**(3), 35–9.

Woods, B. and Charlesworth, G. (2001) Psychological assessment and treatment, in R. Jacoby and C. Oppenheimer (eds), *Psychiatry in the elderly*, 3rd edn. Oxford University Press, 245–63.

Woods, B. and Clare, L. (2008) Psychological interventions with people with dementia, in R. T. Woods and L. Clare (eds), *Handbook of the clinical psychology of ageing*, 2nd edn. Chichester: Wiley, 523–48.

Woods, B., Clare, L. and Windle, G. (in press) Dementia and related cognitive disorders, in P. Sturmey and M. Hersen (eds), *Handbook of evidence-based practice in clinical psychology*. Vol. II. *Adult disorders*. Hoboken, NJ: Wiley.

Woods, R. and Roth, A. (2005) Effectiveness of psychological interventions with older people, in A. Roth and P. Fonagy (eds), *What works for whom? A critical review of psychotherapy research*, 2nd edn. New York: Guilford Press, 425–46.

Woods, R.T. (2001) Discovering the person with Alzheimer's disease: cognitive, emotional and behavioural aspects, *Aging and Mental Health*, **5**(Suppl 1), S7–S16.

Woods, R.T. (2008) Suicide and attempted suicide in later life, in R.T. Woods and L. Clare (eds), *Handbook of the clinical psychology of ageing*, 2nd edn. Chichester: Wiley, 111–19.

World Health Organization (1993) *The ICD-10 classification of mental and behavioural disorders: diagnostic criteria for research*. Geneva: WHO.

Xuereb, J.H., Brayne, C., Dufouil, C. *et al.* (2000) Neuropathological findings in the very old: results from the first 101 brains of a population-based longitudinal study of dementing disorders, *Annals of the New York Academy of Sciences*, **903**, 490–6.

Yochim, B.P., MacNeill, S.E. and Lichtenberg, P.A. (2006) 'Vascular depression' predicts verbal fluency in older adults, *Journal of Clinical and Experimental Neuropsychology*, **28**, 495–508.

8 Sociological perspectives on ageing

KATE DAVIDSON

OVERVIEW

This chapter examines the sociology from several perspectives: basic concepts of ageing, a brief history of social gerontology, the interaction between gender and ageing, sexuality and ageing, and ethnicity and ageing.

Introduction

As has been discussed in other chapters of this volume, the ageing experience involves the intersection of biological, psychological and social processes. This chapter examines in more detail the last of these phenomena; that is, ageing from a sociological perspective. First, I will outline the development of social gerontology since the middle of the twentieth century. Examples will be taken from several countries but principally the UK, and unless otherwise stated, reference to the UK is intended. Then I will discuss how these early theoretical concepts were widened to accommodate greater diversity among the heterogeneous ageing populations including gender, sexuality and ethnicity. Finally, I will discuss some challenges for the future and how they might enhance our understanding of growing old in the twenty-first century.

Ageing is a sociologically interesting phenomenon because although it is a virtually universal experience – almost all of us will get old before we die – it occurs within very diverse and complex social and power dynamic contexts, including socio-economic grouping, health status, access to financial resources, gender, ethnicity and geographical location. It is paradoxical that, on the one hand, we congratulate ourselves that in our society more people live longer than at any other time in history, but on the other hand, old people are demonized for the caring and/or financial burden they impose on their family, the community and the state. Most research on older people has been grounded in problem assessing and addressing, and as such has pathologized the experience of ageing. It is only comparatively recently that gerontology has attempted to develop theoretical frameworks that seek to make sense of the social experience of ageing (following the practice of much of the rest of the book, the term 'older people' here is used to describe those over the age of 65 years). The chronology is arbitrary, but reflects the UK's statutory age for retirement, which is being equalized to 65 for women and men, phasing in the change from 2010 (Department of Work and Pensions, 2009), and it is likely that the age will ultimately be increased even further for both genders. In a large, Europe-wide survey, old people were asked what they would like to be called (Walker, 1993) and they reported that they preferred 'older people' or 'senior citizens'. What they did not want to be called is 'the elderly'. Older texts referenced in this chapter will use 'the elderly' but more recent texts will have largely stopped using the term, although it is still employed in some areas. There is frequently a time lag between individual use and general acceptance of language, and so it is still customary for the media in particular to refer to older people as 'the elderly', but I note a slow but discernible turn away from the term.

Thinking about growing old

Reflection on ageing is as old as intellectual thought itself – from ancient times, philosophers, scientists, theologians, economists, artists and writers have pondered the meanings and experiences of growing and being old. What is definitely not a phenomenon of the twentieth and twenty-first centuries is the heartfelt cry of older people that they are not treated with the respect they consider their due from younger generations – certainly not the way they respected their elders in their youth. Note the following quotation from a thirteenth-century sermon (popularly ascribed to St Peter Celestine; this sermon is sometimes ascribed to the eleventh-century Peter the Hermit):

The young people of today think of nothing but themselves. They have no reverence for parents or old age. They are impatient of all restraint...As for girls, they are forward, immodest and unwomanly in speech, behaviour and dress. (Byron, 2009)

And we have this, even older,

The children now love luxury; they have bad manners, contempt for authority; they show disrespect for elders and love chatter in place of exercise. Children are now tyrants, not the servants of their households. They no longer rise when elders enter the room. They contradict their parents, chatter before company, gobble up dainties at the table, cross their legs, and tyrannize their teachers. (attributed to Socrates (470–399 BC); quotationsbook.com 2007)

So, older people's perception of the attitudes of young people towards them can be echoed in every ageing cohort across time and cultures. One of the first seminar exercises I give to groups of both undergraduate and postgraduate students is to make two lists, one with negative stereotypes of older people, and one with positive stereotypes. Unsurprisingly, the first list is rapidly filled: *smelly, forgetful, physically and mentally sick, bad-tempered, deaf, impatient, miserable, narrow-minded* and so on. The positive stereotypes list takes longer, but mostly they come up with things like *kind, patient, wise, keepers of the family and social history, good at crosswords* (because knowledgeable), *skilled at sewing and other crafts, good gardeners and can talk over problems* (grandparents). With encouragement, it eventually dawns on the students that the negative stereotypes can and do apply to every generation but that many of the positive attributes apply almost exclusively to older people.

Reaching a great age is also not a new phenomenon: Isocrates, the Greek orator, committed suicide at the age of 98 after a very active life. Agesilaus, King of Sparta, although small, mean and lame, died in his eighties while leading a military campaign. Plato lived to the age of 91. Sophocles died at 89 having recently been alleged by his son to be of unsound mind because of his age – but the examining judges pronounced him perfectly fit. It has been almost impossible to track down the longevity of women in ancient Greece because accounts of their lives have not survived, if indeed they were documented. However, what is unprecedented is the number and proportion of people who attain old age. A particular aspect of twenty-first century demography is that people over the age of 85 are the fastest growing sector of the population. In the UK the proportion of those aged 85 and over has increased from 0.1 per cent in the early twentieth century to 2 per cent of the total population by the start of the twenty-first century (Dini and Goldring, 2008).

Changing profiles, changing lives

We are endlessly reminded in the media that we are facing an ageing apocalypse and there is a tendency to generalize and stereotype the older generation. There are, however, a few 'givens' and one is that in just about every culture women on average outlive men. However, recent data reveal that the gap in gendered

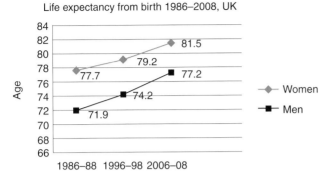

Figure 8.1 Life expectancy from birth 1986–2008, UK. From UK government data. Retrieved from www.statistics.gov.uk/STATBASE/ssdataset.asp?vlnk=9551.

life expectancy is closing. During the short period between 1986 and 2008, the difference reduced from just under 6 years to just over 4 years – a more rapid decrease than hitherto experienced.

Of note are the data which show that men in 2006–08 are living almost as long on average as did women in 1986–88 at 77.2 and 77.7 respectively (see Figure 8.1). The Continuous Mortality Investigation Report (CMIR 21) predicted that men may well outlive women by the end of this century (Ridsdale, 2004). Interpretation of extrapolating techniques for mortality (in particular from actuarial data) can be somewhat contentious and should therefore be treated with caution (see Chapter 1 for further discussion of this point). Nevertheless, if current trends continue, the mortality gap between the genders is likely to reduce and even if there is no 'crossover' as predicted, there are far-reaching implications for future generations of older men, to which I will return later.

As a result of their biological endowment of a longer life expectancy and the socially constructed propensity of women to marry men older than themselves, they are more likely to be alone when they are old, usually as a result of widowhood. Interestingly, predicted trends in marital status of people over the age of 65 reveal that in England and Wales between 2007 and 2031, the proportion of widowed women aged 65–74 will decrease from 24 per cent to 10 per cent and those aged 75+ will fall from 61 per cent to 40 per cent. In line with most of the developed world, divorce rates are increasing, and this is reflected in older generations too. For example, during this period, the percentage of divorced men aged 65–74 will increase from 9 per cent to 17 per cent and the proportion of divorced men over 75 will increase from 4 per cent in 2007 to 12 per cent in 2031 (Office of National Statistics, 2009) (Table 8.1).

The healthiest and wealthiest men are married (Gardner and Oswald, 2004); therefore, there are implications for older men facing later life without a partner that will be discussed later.

Table 8.1 Population projections by legal marital status 2007–31 (percentages)

		Married	Widowed	Divorced
Women				
65–74	2007	60	24	11
	2031	57	10	20
75+	2007	28	61	5
	2031	40	40	14
Men				
65–74	2007	76	8	9
	2031	64	4	17
75+	2007	63	26	4
	2031	61	19	12

Taken from UK government data. Retrieved from www.statistics. gov.uk/downloads/theme_population/MaritalStatusProjection06.pdf.

Regardless of gender, old age will usually bring special problems of reduced financial resources and age-related diseases. Nevertheless, recent NHS data reveal that the most intensive social and health care is given during the final 12 months of an individual's life (Department of Health, 2009). A combination of medical advances and environmental improvements in living standards and circumstances has brought about what Fries (1980) termed the *compression of morbidity* (see Chapter 3 for further discussion). In other words, more people are in better health for longer, and most illness is likely to be concentrated into a short phase at the end of life. Yet all old age continues to be viewed as a time of doom and gloom. What is not often fully understood is the extent to which society influences, and is influenced by, these attitudes to ageing.

The development of social gerontology

It was not until the twentieth century that gerontology evolved as a discipline. The term is defined in the *Concise Oxford Dictionary* as 'the scientific study of old age and the process of ageing, and of old people's special problems'. The word derives from the Greek root word meaning 'old man'. This is somewhat ironic, given that the majority of people who live to advanced years are women. Very early social gerontological theory developed during the 1930s in the USA with a flurry of intellectual activity in the 1960s and 1970s. Rather later and slower, academics in the UK contributed substantially to the discourse. One of the fundamental problems within the discipline is, as has been mentioned already, the enormous diversity in the experience of ageing. Old people are no more or less homogeneous than the rest of the population; their only unifying feature is in chronological age. There is infinite variety in how people age, according to health and financial status, marital status, gender, ethnicity, sexuality, geographical location and social support networks. Interest in this multiplicity of factors is indicated by the backgrounds of people who study ageing, from psychology, medicine, social, economic and political science, to practitioners working in private, voluntary and statutory governmental sectors. However, sociological theory on ageing evolved during the twentieth century and continues to exercise and excite researchers both in academia and the wider community.

Some of the following theories are discussed from the psychological perspective elsewhere in this book, but here I develop the societal rather than the individual perspective of the theory.

Disengagement theory was originally described by Cumming and Henry (1961) from a longitudinal study of a panel of mainly healthy, financially independent males over the age of 50 in Kansas, USA in the late 1950s. Ageing, according to Cumming and Henry, involves a gradual but inevitable withdrawal from mainstream society in preparation for death.

Aging is an inevitable mutual withdrawal or disengagement resulting in decreased interaction between the aging person and others in the social system he belongs to. The process may be initiated by the individual or by others in the situation. The aged person may withdraw more markedly from some classes of people while remaining relatively close to others. His withdrawal may be accompanied from the outset by an increased preoccupation with himself; certain institutions in society may make the withdrawal easy for him. When the aging process is complete the equilibrium which existed in middle life between the individual and his society has given way to a new equilibrium characterized by a greater distance and an altered type of relationship. (Cumming and Henry, 1961, p. 14)

Although conceived some 50 years ago, Cumming and Henry's findings continue to resonate with lay perceptions of how and why older people come to terms with withdrawal from the labour force, society and, ultimately, life.

They argued that there is a reduction in social interaction, and loss of a major role in life, usually associated with retirement, and in doing so this 'makes room' for younger generations to inhabit the social space. The main criticism of this theory is that it is (White) male-oriented, as exemplified by the wording in the above quotation. Women in mid-century, post-Second World War Midwest America were less likely to have been in long-term employment and thus did not experience the sense of disengagement brought on by retirement. Therefore, the theory does not take into account the experience of most women, who are more likely to pass retirement age without 'breaking step'; that is, whether or not they have exited the labour force, they continue to carry out the majority of the domestic respon-sibilities. They are also more likely to have worked within the service industries, frequently an extension of traditional domestic female labour, and thus experi-ence less of a disengagement from their pre-retirement existence than men (Arber, 1993). Women are also more likely to have established a social network of friends, neighbours and family, which they maintain into old age (Jerrome, 1996). Men, on the other hand, tend to lose contact with work colleagues when they retire (Thompson, 1994).

Nor does disengagement theory recognize the experience of male and female ethnic minorities, who are more likely either to leave the workforce before the retirement age because of ill health, or work beyond retirement age for financial reasons. An unintended consequence of the theory has been to legitimize age and race segregation, and has thus reinforced negative stereotypes of older people and, importantly, devalued the status and self-esteem of those people who do work with and look after older people, not to mention older people themselves.

The counterbalance to this much criticized positivistic approach to ageing were the proponents of the *activity* (Havighurst, 1963) and *continuity* (Atchley, 1971, 1987) *theories*. The basic premise of these theorists is that successful ageing involves maintaining, for as long as possible, the activities and attitudes of middle age, including social involvement. Lost roles, such as productivity (contribution to the economy) and reproductivity (childbearing/rearing), must be replaced by other activities such as voluntary work and leisure pursuits. The main criticism is that this is unrealistic and does not take into consideration (or marginalizes) the experience of women, ethnicity or disability, where role replacement, or the maintenance of middle-age values is frequently not an option. Voluntary work and leisure activities presuppose a certain amount of disposable income and a degree of physical fitness, not to mention educational and career achievements which tend to correlate with wealth and health, especially for men (Davidson and Meadows, 2009).

While there is merit in the ideological shift away from problem-based percep-tions of ageing as decline and loss, towards a more positive perspective of 'adding life to years', preventing or delaying disability, and promoting healthy or 'suc-cessful ageing', we need to be careful. Used uncritically, these ideals can set up a divide between those who are able to diversify and those who cannot, mirroring the Victorian concept of the deserving and undeserving poor; that is, the deserv-ing and undeserving old. Those worthy people who demonstrate self-control and right living will be rewarded with good health and an active life in old age. How-ever, the likelihood of 'living right' across the life course varies considerably by socio-economic circumstances and cultural norms.

We experience our social world through subjectivity (as we see ourselves) and objectivity (as others see us) – as actors and reactors. Herbert Blumer (1986) originally coined the term *symbolic interactionism* in 1969 and posited that it is through language and gestures (symbolism) as well as interaction with the physical environment that we understand and locate ourselves in society. Thus, the ageing process can be seen in terms of the relationship between individuals and their social environment and the interpretation of events which accompany old age. This is a particularly useful approach in making sense of the ageing process and takes into consideration experience at an individual level in the context of the macro, societal level (Timonen, 2008).

The paradigm shift away from the positivist, prescriptive, 'one size fits all' approach of the early theorists on ageing prompted the evolution in the USA of the *age stratification perspective* (Riley, Johnson and Foner, 1972), which was later developed as the *aging and society paradigm* (Riley, 1988) and for several decades was possibly the most cited and utilized approach in the literature on sociological aspects of ageing. Its importance lies in the recognition of ageing as a biopsychosocial dynamic over the life course; that is, a combination of biological, psychological and social factors which influence the experience of ageing. Fundamental to this perspective is the notion of *cohort flow*. Most commonly, a cohort is defined by year of birth, but it may also be defined in relation to groups of people who experience a significant historical event in different ways. In the UK, the Second World War (1939–45) is probably the single momentous experience to which people born in the 1920s and 1930s relate, whether they were children or adults at the outbreak of hostilities.

On the other hand, the children of the immediate post-war baby boom (1945–50) share a birth-cohort experience of a childhood in the newly developed welfare state, post-war education, the economic boom periods, and the social and moral revolution of the 1960s. Individuals enter and exit roles that are socially learned according to age and age-related expectations and sanctions. These will change over time according to the life-course experience, as indeed will expectations as patients and clients of health and social services, attitudes to single parenthood, same-sex relationships, race and ethnicity.

Estes (1979) identified how the commercial opportunities generated in response to the needs and expectations of older adults benefit capital and create an 'ageing enterprise'. Indeed, in the UK over the past two or three decades, we have witnessed a burgeoning of private sheltered accommodation, the business activities of Saga (holidays, motor and home insurance), and retirement villages/hotel developments in Spain and the Canary Islands offering winter sun (akin to the American experience of 'snowbirds') and so on.

Meanwhile in the 1980s in the UK, a Marxist approach was used to explain the relationship between society and older people. The *political economy of old age* was a perspective that defined the interaction between government policy, the economy and old age (Phillipson, 1982; Walker, 1981). In the political economy perspective, the state is thought to reflect the interests of the most powerful members of society and the state acts to maintain its own bureaucratic control. In other words, this is fundamentally a class struggle. The main argument is that old age is essentially structured by policy – retirement age, special benefits for older people, and so on, and is closely allied to the notion of productivity. Central to this is the issue of 'structured dependency', whereby dependency is understood in terms of the relationship between the dependent group and the labour market – the exclusion of the majority of older people from the labour market renders most of them dependent on the state for income (Townsend, 1981).

Virtually all these early theories were predicated on retirement as a marker of the commencement of 'old age'. However, Estes (1993) recognized that this perspective is rooted in the predominantly male experience of employment and economic security and does not adequately address issues of women and members of minority ethnic groups. Here, a different work pattern means they are often excluded from the labour market long before the official age of retirement. Thus, the political economy perspective expanded in the 1990s to take into account other dimensions of inequality. For example, Calasanti (1986) was among the early feminists to challenge the male paradigm of production in a formal economy by highlighting the vital, unpaid work carried out particularly by older women, and this was echoed by Arber and Ginn (1991) and Estes (1991), who pointed out how the gendered nature of the domestic division of labour is an extra causal factor in the post-retirement position of women.

Towards the end of the twentieth century there was a further development in gerontological theory, that of *critical gerontology*, which owes its evolution to mainstream critical theory (Achenbaum, 1997). It recognizes the importance of the link between theory and practice and is based on the understanding of three strands of enquiry. The knowledge gained through *measurement* – for example, health status, caregiving burden and financial resources – complemented by the *humanistic* approach, in terms of understanding the meaning of ageing through literature, personal accounts and reflexivity, together with the *political* approach, which identifies difference in effects of gender, class and race, presents a holistic view of the experience of ageing. The juxtaposition or interdisciplinarity of approaches emphasizes the notion of empowerment of older people and, in doing so, grapples with issues of social responsibility and advocacy (Wilson, 2000). Critical gerontology therefore serves to 'lift' the spectre of older people as a burden and highlights their contribution to society, not necessarily as wage earners, but as people who fulfil essential functions such as carers and volunteers, and as such are invaluable citizens in society.

More recently, Gilleard and Higgs (2005) made a serious attempt to revise critical gerontological theory, which, they argued, continues to be dominated by a political economy approach emphasizing the structural pressures and constraints associated with class, gender and ethnicity, which affect the lives of older people. Instead, they interrogated the experience of people growing older in a global world of increasing diversity, erosion of traditional values, powerful influences of consumption and changing attitudes to lifestyle choices. In so doing, they drew on a variety of disciplines and meta-theories in order to present a fresh conceptualization of ageing in the context of the twenty-first century. Drawing heavily on Ulrich Beck's distinctions between modernity 1 and 2, categorized by organized and disorganized capitalism respectively, the authors argued that, over time, class and gender conflict has become less relevant in terms of the 'haves' and 'have nots' since the majority of both working and retired people are much wealthier now than in previous generations. They note that teenagers in the 1950s and 1960s – the period of the zenith of modernity 1 – were the vanguard 'youth culture' generation, and they are today's early retired 'third agers' (Laslett, 1989), and they are experiencing the consumer culture of modernity 2. These baby boomers, they argued, will have different attitudes to authority and different aspirations for health, wealth and well-being in later life from generations whose formative years were largely characterized by economic depression, war and pre-welfare state social and health inequities.

In modernity 1, the aim of the welfare state was to 'de-commodify' old age; that is, remove the pressure of poverty and maintain equilibrium with material standards as enjoyed by the working population. Gilleard and Higgs argued that, like the working population, retired people are able to benefit from increasing consumer choice, but they are also prey to the risks and vicissitudes of modernity 2's disorganized capitalism, quoting Enron and its collapse, which affected both salaries and pensions of its present and past employees. While agreeing that it is necessary to view later life with a global, consumer-oriented perspective, I question their contention that gender, class and ethnicity have been subsumed by modernity 2's overarching emphasis on consumption. Rather, it has highlighted the gap between the haves and the have nots, and a substantial proportion of those who have less are women.

The development of gerontology with a 'gendered lens'

During the 1990s, feminist insights sought to raise awareness of the diversity of the ageing experience by examining the intersections of gender with age, race, ethnicity, sexual orientation and class (Arber and Ginn, 1995). While still remaining within a broadly political economy approach, they demonstrated the extent of structured inequalities experienced by women in later life. The numerical predominance of women in later life became identified as the 'feminization' of later life in the latter part of the twentieth century. Such feminist emphasis was placed largely on the disadvantaged position of older women in relation to their pensions, health status and access to care (Arber and Ginn, 1991; Estes, 1991). Thus, a feminist political economy approach sought to redress the earlier neglect of issues that related to women in later life, as women are more likely to face greater constraints, and have access to fewer resources (Arber and Ginn, 1991; Bernard and Phillips, 1998; Bernard, Phillips, Machin *et al.*, 2000).

Gender, age and inequality

The inception of the welfare state in the late 1940s brought about radical change in post-war society. It certainly provided the cornerstone of the improved health, education and general living standards of all generations. But, as the 1980s feminist critique of the welfare state argued, it also served to reinforce the subordination of women in a male-dominated, capitalist social structure.

It is in this context that we can see the historic achievement of the welfare state – an accommodation between capital and a male-dominated labour movement – reached its maturity in the post-war years in Northern Europe . . . this particular achievement which offered substantial gains for the working class, did so, nonetheless, at the price of the continued subordination and dependency of women. (Rose, 1986 quoted in Williams, 1991, p. 63)

This is never more apparent for the long view than with retired women whose only or principal income is a state pension, which is dependent upon National Insurance (NI) contributions either from a husband or self, or a combination. In his seminal 1942 report on *Social Insurance and Allied Services*, William Beveridge reflected the prevailing perception of a married woman's place in the home, providing 'vital though unpaid' work:

During marriage, most women will not be gainfully employed; the small minority of women who undertake paid employment or other gainful occupations after marriage require special treatment differing from that of a single woman. (Beveridge, 1942, p. 51)

Older women with interrupted employment patterns, a history of low-paid jobs, little or no access to occupational pensions, and widowed or divorced have witnessed a dramatic erosion of the proportional value of a state pension compared to national average earnings from 20 per cent in 1980, to 14 per cent in 2010 (Price and Ginn, 2003). Currently, it is estimated that a third of pensioners live in relative poverty (i.e. over 60 per cent below the national median income), and the vast majority of these are women who live alone (National Pensioners Convention, 2006). Changes to existing pension schemes have attempted to address gender inequalities, but inherent disadvantages faced by women before retirement still lead to them tending to have lower retirement income than men (Ginn, 2003), and for some the pension reforms are too late.

Although men may be better off financially when they retire, they face different challenges from women. Leaving the occupational 'breadwinner' role and the
concomitant loss of status and of co-worker relationships can serve to weaken a
man's sense of his male identity (Courtney, 2000). Moreover, Arber, Davidson and
Ginn (2003) point out:

In addition, possible loss of sexual potency, diminishing physical strength and the onset
of ill health, can further reduce his esteem both in his own eyes and those of society.
For older men, the traditional discourse of masculinity has perforce to be realigned to
accommodate the changing roles and relationships created by altered life circumstances,
particularly retirement. (p. 5)

In comparison to younger men, then, an older man's status is much diminished
within society whereas, as mentioned above, women pensioners are more likely to
have entered retirement without breaking step, since they were less likely to have
enjoyed high employment status in the first place (Calasanti and Slevin, 2001).

Nevertheless, an area in which older people have benefited financially over the
last three decades or so has been the increased value of home ownership. But
even this benefit can be a double-edged sword. It has produced the phenomenon
of some people who are 'equity rich but income poor' (Leather, Littlewood and
Munroe, 1998) whereby older people are living in valuable property, but a low
income or loss of savings as a result of the recession means they cannot afford
repairs and maintenance. This is particularly relevant to older widows, and to a
lesser extent, widowers, who now lack a partner who carried out domestic and
property-oriented tasks. Widowers are more likely to be able to afford, or still do
the more major home maintenance, but bringing in paid help for domestic tasks
can be costly. Additionally, living alone is a predisposing factor for entry to a care
home – following discharge from hospital, for example.

Despite media and public perception, in England only a relatively small percentage of *all* people over the age of 65 are in residential care (5 per cent) (Wanless,
2006). However, for the oldest old, that is, those over the age of 85 and the fastest
growing section of the UK population, the proportion is nearer 50 per cent, and
the vast majority of these are widows (Grundy and Murphy, 2006). The value of
the 'now empty' owner-occupied home is included in the means-tested assessment
of their care costs. This could mean that the previous family home has to be sold
in order to cover these costs, thus eroding all or a large part of an inheritance, a
result that can be problematic within a family, and between siblings.

Gender, health and social trends

While women generally live longer than men, they experience more years of limiting, long-standing illness (LLSI); hence the adage, 'women are sicker but men

die quicker' (Annandale and Hunt, 2001). Whereas men tend to suffer from 'catas-trophic' conditions such as pulmonary and cardiovascular diseases, women suffer more chronic disease and disability such as arthritis and type 2 diabetes. Health is a life-course issue and, critically, men present with life-threatening diseases ear-lier than do women and are thus compromised at a younger age. Nevertheless, as noted above, the mortality gap is narrowing: men's life expectancy is increasing while women's is remaining relatively stable. There are several explanations put forward for this catch-up phenomenon. Only a relatively small proportion of men now work in the highly dangerous occupations in heavy industry, such as coal mining and ship building, which used to claim many lives either while they were working or in early retirement as a result of adventitious disease or injury.

The two world wars brought down the average age of survival for men during the first seven decades of the twentieth century. Lifestyle changes as a result of health education have improved men's morbidity and mortality rates of cardiovascular disease in late middle age (Riska, 2006). Middle-aged women, on the other hand, are experiencing lifestyles quite different from the majority of previous generations and which can be deleterious to health (e.g. working in stressful occupations and unsafe alcohol consumption). But, crucially, middle-aged men are developing a more health-oriented rather than sickness-oriented approach to help-seeking from medical practitioners (Courtney, 2000). For men who matured in the middle of the twentieth century, seeking help for illness was principally done as a last resort as they maintained their sense of 'manliness' with a mixture of stoicism, scepticism and fear of finding out the truth (Davidson and Arber, 2003). Gender differences in morbidity and mortality have long been on the agenda in biomedical research and publications (Annandale and Hunt, 2001). But only comparatively recently has there been interest in the social aspects of the health behaviours of older men, which include the life-course experiences of marital status, (previous) occupation, sexuality and ethnicity.

Refocusing the gender lens

Gender refers to both men and women, but this dyadic concept was somewhat lost until comparatively recently. 'Gender studies' in the 1980s and 1990s hijacked the term to become synonymous with women and feminism. Slower to develop were studies on men, and the term 'masculinities' came late into the sociological lexicon. While the twenty-first century has witnessed an explosive growth of sociological research on masculinity, it has largely omitted the lives of older men (Meadows and Davidson, 2006). Rather, it has concentrated on masculinities with reference to race, sexuality, sport, violence, fatherhood and so on. This gap in the literature is crucial, simply because, as theorized by Thompson (1994), Davidson and Meadows (2009) and others, age facilitates changes in masculinities. Some groups of older men may have to face their own particular challenges arising from changes that occur through the loss of normative roles and relationship status, which usually emphasize masculine autonomy and power, but for some the changed status may bring some compensations. For example, it has been argued that the ending of men's need for breadwinning has resulted in an increased capacity for a less self-serving, more caring, style of interacting with others, especially apparent when they become grandfathers (Mann, 2007).

Most older men are married, have children and grandchildren, and enjoy better health and greater wealth than previous cohorts or never married peers (Gardner and Oswald, 2004). Analysis of the General Household Surveys 1993, 1994, 1995, 1996 and 1998 by Davidson and Arber (2004) revealed that most men who live alone have fewer financial resources, poorer health and fewer social networks than partnered men. Divorced and single men were less likely than those married or widowed to talk to neighbours or to visit or host family or relatives. Davidson, Daly and Arber (2003) researched the social participation of older men, in particular divorced and never married men, who are more likely to be socially isolated and to have poorer health than those who remain married in later life. They found that men who lived on their own were reluctant to join local community groups such as day centres and luncheon clubs, unlike lone females, largely because such centres were perceived as being aimed at very old people, and at older, bossy, gossiping women, with whom their respondents claimed they had absolutely nothing in common. Many of the divorced men in their study reported that they had very little contact with adult children as a result of an acrimonious dissolution of their marriage, whereas widowed men reported increased contact with adult children since the death of their wife. As noted in Table 8.1, it is projected that there will be a substantial increase in the proportion of divorced men, trebling by 2031 for those over the age of 75, and this is likely to have serious implications for the quality of life for these men in advanced years.

The sexuality lens refocused

Another group of previously or never married people receiving scant attention has been older non-heterosexuals, which includes the lesbian, gay and bisexual (LGB) relationships in later life (Heaphy, Yip and Thompson, 2004). While there has been increasing mainstream attention from psychology, sociology and the biomedical sciences, gerontology has virtually ignored this area. However, as Pugh (2002) points out, within the UK, ageing as experienced and negotiated by LGB communities has been neglected, too, in non-heterosexual research and literature. A methodological problem encountered by Heaphy et al. (2004) in their research was that their respondents were self-selected and tended to be in higher educational and higher-income groups than the general population. The men were more likely than the women to have been recruited through interest groups, newsletters and Internet-based networks run for and by older gay men. Older lesbians were recruited through informal groups and snowballing; that is, by word of mouth in friendship networks, which is likely to produce a more homogeneous sample of like-minded people. Davidson (1999) found similar gendered patterns in her recruitment of older widows and widowers, and it could be argued that there are parallel experiences in social networking for heterosexual and non-heterosexual older men and women. However, there are additional issues that pertain specifically to the LGB communities. For example, as Cronin (2004) found, lesbian or gay older adults are more likely to live on their own, are less likely to receive social support from family members, but are more likely to have stronger social networks of friends who provide support.

More research on non-heterosexual elders has been carried out in North America, which has shown how well older non-heterosexual people manage and negotiate age and ageing (Quam and Whitford, 1992). But as Heaphy *et al.* (2004) point out, these early studies examined middle-aged (in their forties and fifties) gay and lesbian people, who were maturing in a much more liberal society than had been experienced by much older non-heterosexuals, many of whom rendered themselves invisible or masked their sexuality in a homophobic climate of disapprobation. There is no doubt that there has been a substantial thaw in attitudes to non-heterosexual relationships, spearheaded by celebrity admission to, and celebration of, their 'gayness' (e.g. Alan Turing has recently received a posthumous apology). Still, for some, as experienced recently by a young, formerly married Welsh rugby player, the decision to 'come out' was very difficult and only taken after the zenith of his career in a testosterone-laden, machismo sport. It is only too easy to understand how an 'ordinary person' born before or during the Second World War might have found it impossible. Even today, we have no idea who hides their sexuality because of their job or profession – male and female schoolteachers, politicians, sports people, for example – but retirement may offer them release from their secrecy and duplicity, and old age allows them freedom at last (Jones and Pugh, 2005).

Love the body you're in?

From ancient to modern times, alchemy has been called upon to find a 'cure' for the deleterious physical processes of ageing, from a potion of the 'fountain of youth' to the 'wonder sweetie to end wrinkles' (Rogers, 2009, p. 1). None, except in mythology and fiction, have so far been successful, which begs the question: why fight against the inevitable? To a large extent, it is understandable that people do not wish to relinquish their beauty, strength, skills, and mental and physical performance to the ravages of a crumbling body (Jackson, 1990). However, there is a larger picture than the individual loss of physical attraction and prowess. We live in a society which is fundamentally youth-oriented and age discriminatory; thus, older people become 'other' (than young) and socially marginalized. Ageist views are held by young and old people alike and permeate almost all our lives from comic birthday cards to insults (e.g. 'you are playing like a load of old women!'), let alone a rich vocabulary to describe older people: *wrinklies*, *crumblies*, and far more offensive terms such as *coffin dodgers*. There are distinct gender differences, but no less important to each, is how older men and women both perceive themselves, and are perceived within a youth-dominated culture.

Susan Sontag (1978, p. 73) depicted the 'double standard of ageing' and argued that 'Getting older is less profoundly wounding for a man...Men are "allowed" to age, without penalty, in several ways that women are not.' There is no doubt that there are heavy pressures on women to 'stay' young and 'look' young that are less pronounced for men as they age (Featherstone and Hepworth, 2000). With the discourse negatively focusing on ageing women's bodies, it is no surprise that, generally, women express greater dissatisfaction with their ageing bodies than do men. Feminist analysis has argued that the pressure on women to look younger in the face of the negative aspects of ageing means they are more likely to adopt various forms of anti-ageing strategies, from, on a low level, dyeing hair to cosmetic surgery, on a more drastic level (Ballard, Elston and Gabe, 2005). As Gilleard and Higgs (2005) point out, there is a vast and lucrative commodity market for anti-ageing products.

Taking a horizontal age view, that is, comparing older men with older women, men do appear to fare better. Grey hair, for example, is a signifier of stateliness, wisdom and distinction in older men but is often viewed with horror by women themselves and others as a sure sign of old age and 'letting themselves go' (Arber and Ginn 1991). Men, though, are not immune to pressure to disguise greying hair in middle age when they should still be considered 'Young Turks' in the prime of their lives (Arber *et al.*, 2003). Slevin (2008) found that both older heterosexual and gay men attempt to retain or regain notions of youthful manhood by disciplining their bodies through exercise and diet. However, as discussed above, we know that when the body starts 'breaking down', men are less likely to seek professional medical help (Kaye, Crittenden and Charland, 2008).

Many of the older men but few women in Heaphy *et al.*'s (2004) study reported that a youth-oriented gay culture made them conscious of their ageing. The women, especially those with politicized feminist identities, had fewer problems with coming to terms with their changing bodies. Interestingly, Slevin (2008) found that although the lesbians in her study generally expressed satisfaction with their bodies, their ambivalence about weight was a dominant issue, not unlike heterosexual women. Paradoxically, women face pressure from feminists, on the one hand, being urged to reject age-resisting activities in order to 'grow old gracefully' and, on the other hand, to take hold of the increasing opportunities available to them and reject an ageing identity (Ballard *et al.*, 2005).

From a vertical age perspective (i.e. from young to old), men fare less well than women, who are more likely to report compensations in release from the pressure as sexual beings in competition with younger women (Gott and Hinchliff, 2003). One of the greatest, and often hidden, losses for men is their sexual potency and with it their core sense of masculinity. About a third of the remaining 556 men (average age 62 years) of the Massachusetts Male Aging Study 8-year follow-up (1995–97) reported moderate or complete erectile dysfunction (ED) (in Kalache, 2000, p. 24). The discovery of the efficacy of Viagra alerted middle-aged and older men to the possibility of revitalizing their libido and their sense of male identity. Nevertheless, the commonest reason for lack of sexual intimacy (which does not necessarily involve penetration) is the lack of a partner.

The fundamental need for companionship does not wane with age or generation so we might speculate on the alternative social interaction dynamics which have accompanied, and will be influenced by, demographic change. One such development has been the blossoming of older people looking for partners through dating sections in magazines, in newspapers and on Internet sites. A cursory glance at any site reveals that older men, whether straight or gay, almost always advertise for partners younger, sometimes much younger, than themselves (Phua, 2002). Even older women seeking male companionship will opt for an older man, but reassure the reader she is 'young at heart', although the age difference is likely to be narrower than for men seeking women. Once a relationship has been established, an interesting choice for older people has been identified as a living apart together (LAT) relationship (de Jong Gierveld, 2002; Ghazanfareeon Karlsson and Borell, 2002).

The 'couple' maintain separate homes but visit each other, including overnight with or without sexual intimacy; socialize; carry out daily routine activities such as shopping, cooking and eating; and go on holidays. Levin and Trost (1999) found that women, in particular, choose to remain independent and do not wish to have the responsibility of 'keeping house' for anyone else, especially if they have been previously married. It is likely that LAT relationships will become increasingly common, as women may desire a new relationship but also wish to maintain their domestic and financial independence. The financial independence of both men and women in such an arrangement may allay fears of loss of inheritance from adult children. Interestingly, adult children are more willing to accept that their father has found 'a lady friend' who brings him happiness but are often less accepting of their mother's 'gentleman friend' and may view her as being 'unfaithful' to their late father (Davidson, 1999). However, current societal changes in attitudes towards sexuality will undoubtedly impact upon later generations and their notions of appropriate, non-maritally based sexual behaviour.

Nevertheless, older women, whether widowed, divorced or never married, are much less likely than men to desire or seek another romantic partner. Certainly, not all men want a new partner, as they do not feel they could ever find happiness with another woman (Davidson, 2002). Demographic realities are such that women who are single again outnumber available men in later life. Even if these women do desire a new partner, they might encounter men seeking a younger woman, or men too old, poor or sick to be perceived as attractive.

It has not been until comparatively recently that the study of gender has included the meaning of masculinity within what has been termed the 'feminization of old age' (Arber and Ginn, 1991). Although older men may no longer be able to compete with younger men in terms of physical strength, earning ability and sexual prowess, their sense of male identity is not diluted, but altered. I would argue that masculinities are elastic, stretching and shrinking within the social context: off the rugby pitch to cuddle a baby daughter, or still in control of the family finances despite having suffered a stroke. It is this elasticity which enables men to maintain their sense of manliness, and it is only when the stretch is too great, the elastic too thin, that they lose this sense of self.

Although gender or rather older men are now on the agenda, there is another area which has been difficult to study until comparatively recently – difficult mainly because of their relatively sparse population and their social 'invisibility' – the area of ethnic elders (Nazroo, Bajekal, Blane et al., 2004). The 1991 and 2001 censuses were the first to include questions on ethnicity to reflect the growing racial and ethnic diversity experienced in UK. They also revealed the small but increasing proportion of ethnic elders. In the general population, people over the age of 60 comprised 20 per cent in the UK. The England census 2001 showed that the ethnic/migrant population comprised 13 per cent – and 9 per cent if only non-White groups are considered. For the vast majority of Black elders, the UK is their second homeland. For example, in London, over 90 per cent of non-White people over the age of 65 were born outside the UK, and for over 60 per cent, English is not their first language (Lowdell, Evandrou, Bardsley et al., 2000).

Ethnic elders and society

There are two main groups of non-White elders: Black Caribbean, who migrated to the UK mainly in the 1950s in response to a call for labour for the post-war reconstruction of Britain, and Indian, who migrated mostly in the 1960s for both economic and socio-political reasons. Within these two groups, the proportions of people over the age of 65 are 11 per cent and 6 per cent respectively. More recent migrants, from Pakistan, Bangladesh and Africa, including those people of Asian origin expelled from Uganda by Idi Amin in the 1970s, have a much younger profile. Those under 16 comprise about 37 per cent of these groups (compared with 20 per cent of the White population), and only 4 per cent are over the age of 65. Another anomaly of the newer migrants is a result of the pattern of economic migration: because the group principally comprises men who came for employment, men outnumber women approximately 3:2 in the older population. Progressive ageing of the non-White ethnic groups is anticipated in the future, but this will depend on fertility levels, mortality rates and future net migration (ONS, 2004).

Much of the research conducted on ageing, race and ethnicity has been problem-based, concentrating on social inequality and health differentials (Nazroo et al., 2004). Early research on race from the USA examined the 'double jeopardy' of growing old and Black in a youth oriented, primarily White society (Dowd and Bengtson, 1978). Alison Norman (1985) identified a 'triple jeopardy' of being female, Black and old. The emphasis on social disadvantage has contributed to the perception of life of an ethnic elder as one of unrelenting deprivation. Scholars who study ethnic minorities, however, point out that these studies frequently ignore the many strengths in their communities (Minkler, 1996). As with the general population, an ageing ethnic population is not heterogeneous. Nazroo et al. (2004) employed a research methodology which was sensitive to the diverse cultural experience of ageing within the context of personal history, family and community. They argued that despite significant inequalities in health and financial resources, most marked in those over the age of 60, there are strong family and community ties inextricably bonded with their sense of culture and religion. Particularly in the South Asian groups, the grandparents' role involved teaching their grandchildren the 'old ways'.

The imperative of maintaining an attachment to traditional, social, language and cultural links with a homeland, even if that homeland is rarely if ever visited, is universal: the British in their colonies, the Chinese in Soho, the Italians in New York, the Turks in Berlin – the list is endless. South Asian migrants are no exception. Trans-national networks, primarily based on kinship ties, provide the cultural continuity which gives meaning to their lives within an alien environment. Communities living half a world away from their origins engage in collectively familiar practices which generate a 'social glue' of solidarity in facing hostility often experienced within the host country. In contrast to the settlers, their locally born and raised offspring have a much more complex relationship with their ancestral roots. However, different migratory patterns within the South Asian population, diverse traditional attitudes to marriage and intermarriage, geographical origins from the subcontinent, attachment to the home nation, and integration with the host nation have meant that both the experience of the grandparent generation and that of the grandchild generation differ substantially between migrant South Asian communities.

In Nazroo *et al.*'s (2004) study, older ethnic minority people were found to be heavily involved in voluntary work for, and beneficiaries of, their church, temple, mosque or community centre (p. 56). It would be easy, therefore, to say, 'Well, they look after their own, so we don't need to interfere.' But health and welfare delivery is primarily directed at the indigenous UK population and is not always responsive to cultural diversity such as diet, hygiene protocols, language and power relations. An explicit challenge is to translate rhetoric to reality in empowering a group of people ageing in a second homeland and in an alien culture.

Conclusion

Ageing is a life-course issue: those of us who reach advanced years will do so with an individual physical, psychological and social history that influences our experience of the ageing process. Gerontological theory has developed from the positivistic concept of 'this is what old age means' through the prescriptive 'this is how old age should be' eventually to the recognition of a heterogeneous population that negotiates later life through the lens of class, gender, sexuality and ethnicity. Nevertheless, it is possible to comment on some trends which will impact upon our 'greying society'.

Marriage rates and fertility are falling at all ages except in the minority South Asian communities, and changing social norms surrounding divorce and marital separation are leading to an increasing number of women and men without some sort of family support in later life (Kneale and Joshi, 2008). Asian grandchildren born in the host country may eschew the cultural norm of young, arranged marriage and larger families. Among the childless, there may be older LGB couples who have not felt the need to conform to marriage before declaring their true sexuality. However, it is important to point out that an increase in the number of unmarried or childless older people may also have positive rather than solely negative implications. For example, retired childless couples may potentially have greater income and therefore more wealth in retirement than couples with children because they have not experienced the cost of raising children (Plotnick, 2009).

Even so, there are obvious implications for state provision of health and social support services for the burgeoning population of lone older people, both in care-home and community-care settings, especially those over the age of 85. It is predicted by some commentators that half the children born at the beginning of the twenty-first century will live on average to be 100 (Boseley, 2009), thus swelling the ranks of the 'oldest old'. There will be a need for an increase in paid carers, who, if current trends continue, are likely to be migrant workers from lower-income countries (Staines, 2009). There are also implications for the country of origin in terms of loss of young, skilled workers, children left behind to be cared for by grandparents, and the lack of carers in their own families and institutions.

Clews (2009) suggests that the recession around the end of the first decade of the present century in the UK has meant that employment income is not as attractive to overseas employees as in the first years of the century and that unless working conditions and remuneration are improved, recruitment of both domestic and overseas care staff will not keep pace with the employment needs. Nursing older people has been addressed in other sections of this volume, and so there is no need to expand on the major implications here, but just to say that there are global ramifications for formal in informal caring in an ageing society.

This chapter has discussed a wide range of sociological aspects of gerontology and older people's role in society, and as such will have overlapped with others in this volume. It is hardly surprising, since ageing is indeed experienced within a wide variety of physical, psychological and social contexts, and it is almost impossible to unpick the tapestry upon which our lives have been embroidered.

Summary

The chapter begins by considering the concept of ageing and growing old, and it is demonstrated that many attitudes and opinions have been consistent across recorded time. The population changes in ageing are considered. The chapter then proceeds to examine the development of social gerontology, including disengagement, activity and continuity theories of ageing, moving through to the aging and society paradigm, political economy of old age, critical gerontology, and models based on the concept of modernity 1 and 2 (organized and disorganized capitalism). The issue of gender and ageing, and the at times complex interaction between these factors, is examined along with the interrelated issues of health and social trends. The discussion leads into an extended examination of sexuality and ageing, relationships, and the changing outlook engendered by societal shifts in attitude. The chapter concludes with a critical discussion of the issue of ethnic elders and society.

REFERENCES

Achenbaum, W.A. (1997) Critical gerontology, in A. Jamieson, S. Harper and C. Victor (eds), *Critical approaches to ageing and later life*. Buckingham: Open University Press, 16–26.

Annandale, E. and Hunt, K. (eds) (2001) *Gender inequalities in health*. Buckingham: Open University Press.

Arber, S. (1993) Inequalities within the household, in D. Morgan and L. Stanley (eds), *Debates in sociology*. Manchester University Press, 118–39.

Arber, S., Davidson, K. and Ginn, J. (2003) Changing approaches to gender and later life, in S. Arber, K. Davidson and J. Ginn (eds), *Gender and ageing: changing roles and relationships.* Maidenhead: Open University Press/McGraw-Hill Education, 1–14.

Arber, S. and Ginn, J. (1991) *Gender and later life: a sociological analysis of resources and constraints.* London: Sage.

(eds) (1995) *Connecting gender and ageing: a sociological approach.* Buckingham: Open University Press.

Atchley, R. (1971) Retirement and leisure participation: continuity or crises?, *The Gerontologist* *11*(1), 13–17.

(1987) *Aging: continuity and change.* Belmont, CA: Wadsworth.

Ballard, J., Elston, M.A. and Gabe, J. (2005) Beyond the mask: women's experiences of public and private ageing during midlife and their use of age-resisting activities, *Health*, *9*, 169–87.

Bernard, M. and Phillips, J. (eds) (1998) *The social policy of old age: moving into the 21st century.* London: Centre for Policy on Ageing.

Bernard, M., Phillips, J., Machin, L. *et al.* (eds) (2000) *Ageing women.* London: Routledge.

Beveridge, W. (1942) *Report of the Committee on Social Insurance and Allied Services.* London: HMSO.

Blumer, H. (1986) *Symbolic interactionism: perspective and method.* Berkeley, CA: University of California Press.

Boseley, S. (2009) Great expectations: today's babies are likely to live to 100, doctors predict, *The Guardian*, 2 October. Retrieved from www.guardian.co.uk/society/2009/oct/02/babies-likely-to-live-to-100.

Byron, T. (2009) We see children as pestilent, *The Guardian*, 17 March. Retrieved from www.guardian.co.uk/education/2009/mar/17/ephebiphobia-young-people-mosquito.

Calasanti, T. (1986) The social creation of dependence, dependency ratios, and the elderly in the United States: a critical analysis, *Social Science and Medicine*, *23*(12), 1229–36.

Calasanti, T. and Slevin, K. (2001) *Gender, social inequalities and aging.* Walnut Creek, CA: AltaMira Press.

Clews, G. (2009) Is the overseas nursing market recession proof?, *Nursing Times.net* (26 May 2009). Retrieved from www.nursingtimes.net/whats-new-in-nursing/acute-care/is-the-overseas-nursing-market-recession-proof/5001969.article.

Courtney, W.H. (2000) Constructions of masculinity and their influence on men's well-being: a theory of gender and health, *Social Science and Medicine*, *50*, 1385–1401.

Cronin, A. (2004) Sexuality in gerontology: a heteronormative presence, a queer absence, in S.O. Daatland and S. Biggs (eds), *Ageing and diversity: multiple pathways and cultural migrations.* Bristol: Policy Press, 107–22.

Cumming, E. and Henry, W. (1961) *Growing old: the process of disengagement.* New York: Basic Books.

Davidson, K. (1999) Gender, age and widowhood: how older widows and widowers differently realign their lives. Guildford, UK, University of Surrey (unpublished thesis).

(2002) Gender differences in new partnership choices and constraints for older widows and widowers, *Ageing International*, *27*(4), 43–60.

Davidson, K. and Arber, S. (2003) Older men's health: a lifecourse issue?, *Men's Health Journal*, *2*(3), 72–5.

(2004) Older men, their health behaviours and partnership status, in A. Walker and C. Hennessy (eds), *Growing older: quality of life in old age.* Maidenhead: Open University Press/McGraw-Hill, 127–48.

Davidson, K., Daly, T. and Arber, S. (2003) Older men, social integration and organisational activities, *Social Policy and Society*, *2*(2), 81–9.

Davidson, K. and Meadows, R. (2009) Older men's health: the role of marital status and masculinities, in B. Gough and S. Robertson (eds), *Men, masculinities and health: critical perspectives*. London: Palgrave, 109–24.

de Jong Gierveld, J. (2002) The dilemma of repartnering, *Ageing International*, *27*(4), 61–78.

Department of Health (2009) Integrated care. Retrieved from www.dh.gov.uk/en/Healthcare/IntegratedCare/index.htm.

Department of Work and Pensions (2009) The Social Security (Equalisation of State Pension Age) Regulations 2009. Retrieved from www.dwp.gov.uk/docs/equalisation-state-pension-age.pdf.

Dini, E. and Goldring, S. (2008) Estimating the changing population of the 'oldest old'. Office for National Statistics. Retrieved from www.statistics.gov.uk/articles/population_trends/PT132OldestOldArticle.pdf.

Dowd, J. and Bengtson, V. (1978) Ageing in minority populations: an examination of the double jeopardy hypothesis, *Journal of Gerontology*, *33*(6), 338–55.

Estes, C. (1979) *The aging enterprise*. San Francisco, CA: Jossey Bass.

(1991) The new political economy of aging: introduction and critique, in M. Minkler and C. Estes (eds), *Critical perspectives on aging: the political and moral economy of growing older*. New York: Baywood, 1–22.

(1993) The aging enterprise revisited, *The Gerontologist*, *33*(3), 292–8.

Featherstone, M. and Hepworth, M. (2000) Images of ageing, in J. Bond, P. Coleman and S. Peace (eds), *Ageing in society: an introduction to social gerontology*. London: Sage, 143–57.

Fries, J. (1980) Aging, natural death and the compression of morbidity, *New England Journal of Medicine*, *303*(3), 130–5.

Gardner, J. and Oswald, A. (2004) How is mortality affected by money, marriage and stress?, *Journal of Health Economics*, *23*(6), 1181–1207.

Ghazanfareeon Karlsson, S. and Borell, K. (2002) Intimacy and autonomy, gender and ageing: living apart together, *Ageing International*, *27*(4), 11–26.

Gilleard, C. and Higgs, P. (2005) *Contexts of ageing: class, cohort and community*. Cambridge: Polity.

Ginn, J. (2003) *Gender, pensions and the lifecourse: how pensions need to adapt to changing family forms*. Bristol: Policy Press.

Gott, M. and Hinchliff, S. (2003) Sex and ageing: a gendered issue, in S. Arber, K. Davidson and J. Ginn (eds), *Gender and ageing: changing roles and relationships*. Maidenhead: Open University Press/McGraw-Hill, 63–78.

Grundy, E. and Murphy, M. (2006) Marital status and family support for the oldest-old in Great Britain, in J.-M. Robine, E.M. Crimmins, S. Horiuchi *et al.* (eds), *Human longevity: individual life duration and the growth of the oldest-old population*. Dordrecht: Springer, 415–36.

Havighurst, R. (1963) Successful aging, in R. Williams, C. Tibbitts and W. Donahoe (eds), *Process of aging*. University of Chicago Press, 311–15.

Heaphy, B., Yip, A. and Thompson, D. (2004) Ageing in a non-heterosexual context, *Ageing and Society*, *24*(6), 881–902.

Jackson, D. (1990) *Unmasking masculinities: a critical autobiography*. London: Unwin Hyman.

Jerrome, D. (1996) Continuity and change in the study of family relationships, *Ageing and Society*, *16*(1), 91–104.

Jones, J. and Pugh, S. (2005) Ageing gay men: lessons from the sociology of embodiment, *Men and Masculinities*, *7*(3), 248–60.

Kalache, A. (2000) Men, ageing and health, *The Aging Male*, *3*(1), 3–36.

Kaye, L., Crittenden, J. and Charland, J. (2008) Invisible older men: what we know about older men's use of healthcare and social services, *Generations*, *32*(1), 9–14.

Kneale, D. and Joshi, H. (2008) Postponement and childlessness: evidence from two British cohorts, *Demographic Research*, *19*(Article 58), 1935–68.

Laslett, P. (1989) *A fresh map of life*. London: Weidenfeld & Nicolson.

Leather, P., Littlewood, M. and Munro, M. (1998) *Make do and mend? Explaining homeowners' approaches to repair and maintenance*. Housing Repair and Maintenance Series. Bristol: Policy Press.

Levin, I. and Trost, J. (1999) Living apart together, *Community, Work and Family*, *2*, 279–94.

Lowdell, C., Evandrou, M., Bardsley, M. *et al.* (2000) *Health of ethnic minority elders in London*. London: Directorate of Public Health, 222.

Mann, R. (2007) Out of the shadows?: grandfatherhood, age and masculinities, *Journal of Ageing Studies*, *21*(4), 271–81.

Meadows, R. and Davidson, K. (2006) Maintaining manliness in later life: hegemonic masculinities and emphasized femininities, in T. Calasanti and K. Slevin (eds), *Age matters: realigning feminist thinking*. New York: Routledge, 295–311.

Minkler, M. (1996) Critical Perspectives on ageing: new challenges for gerontology, *Ageing and Society*, *16*(4), 467–87.

National Pensioners Convention (NPC) (2006) *The Message*, Spring Issue. London: NPC.

Nazroo, J., Bajekal, M., Blane, D. *et al.* (2004) Ethnic inequalities, in A. Walker and C. Hennessy (eds), *Growing older: quality of life in old age*. Maidenhead: Open University Press, 35–59.

Norman, A. (1985) *Triple jeopardy: growing old in a second homeland*. London: Centre for Policy on Ageing.

Office of National Statistics (2004) *Ethnicity and identity*. Retrieved from www.statistics.gov.uk/cci/nugget.asp?id=456.

  (2009) *2006-based marital status projections for England and Wales*. Retrieved from www.statistics.gov.uk/downloads/theme_population/MaritalStatusProjection06.pdf.

Phillipson, C. (1982) *Capitalism and the construction of old age*. London: Macmillan.

Phua, V.C. (2002) Sex and sexuality in men's personal advertisements, *Men and Masculinities*, *5*(2), 178–91.

Plotnick, R. (2009) Childlessness and the economic well-being of older Americans, *Journals of Gerontology. Series B, Psychological Sciences and Social Sciences*, *64*(6), 767–76.

Price, D. and Ginn, J. (2003) Sharing the crust: gender, partnership status and inequalities in pension accumulation, in S. Arber, K. Davidson and J. Ginn (eds), *Gender and ageing: changing roles and relationships*. Maidenhead: Open University Press, 124–47.

Pugh, S. (2002) The forgotten: a community without a generation: older lesbians and gay men, in D. Richardson and S. Seidman (eds), *Handbook of lesbian and gay studies*. London: Sage, 161–81.

Quam, J. and Whitford, G. (1992) Adaptation and age-related expectations of older gay and lesbian adults, *The Gerontologist*, *32*, 367–74.

QuotationsBook.com (2007) Socrates. Retrieved from http://quotationsbook.com/quote/44998/.

Ridsdale, B.C. (2004) *CMIR (Continuous Mortality Investigation Report)*, 21. London: Institute of Actuaries and Faculty of Actuaries.

Riley, M. (1988) On the significance of age in sociology, in M. Riley, B. Huber and B. Hess (eds), *Social structures and human lives*. Newbury Park, CA: Sage, 24–45.

Riley, M., Johnson, M. and Foner, A. (1972) *Aging and society*. Vol. 3. *A sociology of age stratification*. New York: Russell Sage.

Riska, E. (2006) *Masculinity and men's health: coronary heart disease in medical and public discourse*. Lanham, MA: Rowman & Littlefield Publishers.

Rogers, L. (2009) Wonder sweetie to end wrinkles, *The Sunday Times*, 20 December, 1–2.

Slevin, K. (2008) Disciplining bodies: the aging experiences of older heterosexual and gay men, *Generations*, *32*(1), 36–42.

Sontag, S. (1978) The double standard of ageing, in V. Carver and P. Liddiard (eds), *An ageing population*. Milton Keynes: Open University Press, 72–80.

Staines, R. (2009) UK will need 3000 overseas care workers per year, says report, *Nursing Times.net* 25 June. Retrieved from www.nursingtimes.net/whats-new-in-nursing/management/uk-will-need-3000-overseas-care-workers-per-year-says-report/5003251.article.

Thompson, E. (1994) Older men as invisible men, in E. Thompson (ed.), *Older men's lives*. Thousand Oaks, CA: Sage, 1–21.

Timonen, V. (2008) *Ageing societies: a comparative introduction*. Maidenhead: McGraw-Hill.

Townsend, P. (1981) The structured dependency of the elderly: a creation of social policy in the twentieth century, *Ageing and Society*, *1*(1), 5–28.

Walker, A. (1981) Towards a political economy of old age, *Ageing and Society*, *1*(1), 74–94.

(1993) Age and attitudes: main results from a Eurobarometer survey. AC Commission (DG5/CEC).

Wanless, D. (2006) *Securing good care for older people*. London: The Kings Fund.

Williams, F. (1991) *Social policy: a critical Introduction*. Cambridge: Polity Press [first published 1989].

Wilson, G. (2000) *Understanding old age: critical and global perspectives*. London: Sage.

9 Retirement

LYNN McDONALD

OVERVIEW

. . . .

This chapter examines key facets of retirement, including the institutionalization of retirement, definitions of retirement, the scope of retirement, the age of retirement, the length of retirement, retirement theories, reinventing the concept of retirement, health and wealth, the timing of retirement, and families and retirement.

. . . .

Introduction

Retirement, as a social institution, emerged in modern industrialized societies at the beginning of the twentieth century. Scholarship into retirement began in earnest in the late 1940s and early 1950s, but because of its rapid evolution, there is always some doubt about the relevance of research conducted in earlier times to retirement today. Just as social scientists think they have a clear picture of the transition from work to retirement, its causes and consequences, the picture shifts, presenting different economic conditions, policies and individual preferences that require new explanations. For example, while retirement may have been initially developed as a reward for loyal older workers to encourage lifelong attachment to employers, in a recession, retirement may be used as a mechanism to trim older workers from the labour force as quickly as possible. These variations on retirement are founded on the underlying idea that retirement was designed to move the older worker out of the labour force in a systematic manner without causing undue financial upset, while solving the societal problem of what to do with an ageing labour force. In light of this aim of retirement, not only must the impact of retirement on the individual be examined but so must the impact on society as a whole, and no less so, the synergies between both.

As the retirement process grows ever more complex, it requires our close attention, perhaps more so than at any other time in history. In the first instance, because the purpose of retirement is to move older workers out of the labour force, retirement became the last phase of the life course and contributed to our definition of old age as the last segment of a person's life that followed their education and work. Indeed, retirement is the principal bridge to later life and helps to define the circumstances of old age since it links the institutional structures of work and non-work mainly through a pension, the generosity of which contributes to well-being in old age. In the second instance, labour force withdrawal has serious consequences not only for the welfare of the individuals involved but also for determining the actuarial requirements of public and private pensions, the size and composition of the future labour force, and the overall formulation of public and private pension policies. The intent of this chapter, then, is to examine retirement today in economically developed countries, its brief history, current patterns, explanations of retirement and the major controversies.

The institutionalization of retirement

Retirement did not exist in most countries prior to industrialization and most people adapted their work to their changing capacities by working until they were no longer capable. The historian Andrejs Pakans (1989) argues that people stepped down from their work in traditional Europe, but the process of withdrawal was informal and could be long or short depending on the person's health and/or wealth. For example, a farmer could slowly diminish his workload by delegating the more demanding tasks to his sons or sons-in-law and still maintain control of the process because he owned the land which the children wished to inherit. Because the history of retirement is primarily one of men's retirement, little is known of women although they probably stepped down in tandem with their husbands. If the male worker was a non-property owner in the employ of others, the tendency was to continue work until physically impossible. At the time, the relations of labour were characterized as paternalistic, a more personal type of relationship between employer and employee which preceded the more impersonal relationships of industrial capitalism (Pentland, 1981, p. 26). According to historical accounts of the nineteenth-century workplace, older workers were reassigned to jobs that suited their abilities so they could work as long as possible (Macnicol, 1998; Snell,

1996). If women worked in waged labour, they were most likely to be employed in 'natural' female jobs as domestic servants, midwives, washerwomen, laundresses, and teachers (Cohen, 1988, p. 166).

Pensions were unheard of for the majority of older people but did exist for some specific groups. Chinese bureaucrats in thirteenth-century China received small stipends once they left work while in England they could sell their office to generate income during the seventeenth century, and later the pension of an existing officer was paid for by his successor (Achenbaum, Weiland and Haber, 1996; Titmuss, 1968). In Canada in the eighteenth century, the Hudson Bay Company made some provision for 'the servants in case of sickness and old age' and allowed a pension in 'any case that was deserving' (Simpson, 1975, pp. 182–7). Older soldiers in far-flung outposts like those in the British garrison in Canada were paid pensions which served to attach them to Canada, while the younger soldiers deserted to the USA. The historians Morton and McCallum note, 'Such men would endure the privations and discipline of military life in return for a secure old age' (Morton and McCallum, 1988, p. 6). As countries became more industrialized, private pension plans began to grow for many groups and were initially a gift designed to ensure that ageing male workers did not jeopardize their relations with the employer (e.g. going on strike), in return for a secure old age. Contributory pensions also ensured that the norm of thrift was preserved because pensions were recompense for saving. Public pensions, offered at a defined age and as a citizen's right, were introduced in Great Britain in 1908, in Canada in 1927, and in the USA with the passage of the Social Security Act in 1935 (McDonald, 2002). These developments received impetus from the German Reichstag with its adoption of the Old Age Insurance Law in 1889. Bismarck, relying on a military metaphor, called for state pensions for working-class men in a rapidly industrializing Germany:

The State must take the matter into its own hands, not as alms giving but as the right that men have to be taken care of when, from no fault of their own, they have become unfit for work. Why should regular soldiers and officers have old age pensions, and not the soldier of labour? (quoted in Donahue, Orbach and Pollack, 1960, p. 351)

At the outset, state pensions were meagre but with adjustments over time became more generous in many countries, but not all. For example, in Britain, the first state pension, which was means-tested, paid 5 shillings (£0.25 – in real terms approximately £100 by 2010 prices) a week at the post office to men and women who had reached age 70, but a hundred years later it is in real terms slightly less generous, and is about a quarter of the mean national wage.

As would be expected, there are as many histories of retirement as there are developed countries with retirement programmes and pensions. All the histories have, however, several commonalities. Retirement is a social construction that took root in modern industrialized societies near the beginning of the twentieth century and became a well-established social institution in Western societies following the Second World War (Achenbaum, 1978; Atchley, 1982; Fischer, 1978; Graebner, 1980; Haber, 1978; Haber and Gratton, 1994; Phillipson, 1999; Snell, 1996). Two historical models are used to explain how retirement came to be, the 'impoverishment model, evident in the history of welfare' (Haber and Gratton, 1994, p. 88), sometimes called the industrialization hypothesis, and the competing model, the 'social security model' developed in the USA where the establishment of social security is argued to have led to mass retirement (Haber and Gratton, 1994). A version of these two models is proposed by Macnicol's (1998, 2008) supply and demand accounts of retirement and their combination in which he favours the decline in the demand for older workers in advanced industrial economies, and provides evidence for this process in Britain that started in the 1890s.

In the impoverishment model, with the advent of industrialization and urbanization in the late nineteenth century and early twentieth century, older people underwent a dramatic and revolutionary displacement in the home and in the workplace. Industrialization pushed older people to the sidelines of the paid labour force and deprived them of lucrative work because they were 'worn out' (a popular theory of ageing at the time), causing them undue hardship from poverty (McDonald and Wanner, 1990). In the modern era, the skills of older adults were considered to be obsolescent in light of the new faster technologies in the workplace; they were relegated to a low socio-economic status and were subject to ageism. The accompanying demographic changes ushered in the small nuclear family and undermined older people's once powerful position in the family and served to detach them from family resources. Out of work and set adrift from extended family, it became difficult to ignore the plight of the elderly. Proponents of this perspective argued that the poverty of older people was the impetus for the establishment of social security, a benevolent response on the part of most policymakers in Western societies (Haber and Gratton, 1994, p. 15). In bold strokes, the catalyst causing mass retirement was industrialization.

In contrast, Gratton (1993) and Gratton and Haber (1994), based on an analysis of American historical wealth indices, American census data, labour and pension statistics, and household size, show that the aged have always been more wealthy than the young and that their economic viability improved from 1890 to 1930 when industrialization was at its height. During this time, the economic well-being of older people was contingent on family economic strategies as opposed to individual strategies to create the family 'fund' to which all family members, including children, contributed their wages and from which all family expenditures were drawn. Older people did suffer some job insecurity during industrialization because of a job market sometimes hostile to older workers, and no one ever was certain of the long-term value of their assets or of their longevity. Income from the wages of grown children helped to preserve or increase family savings to protect the family against unemployment, sickness, or death of the head of the household. The co-residency and family-based economic strategies created life-cycle security, but at the cost of intergenerational friction in both working-class and middle-class families. Conflict over lines of family authority and the pressure on adult children to contribute their wages to the family economy and their subsequent loss of educational opportunities weighed against the need of the family to support their older members. A logical response to these problems, made possible only by the growing average industrial wage, was the sentiment that separate dwellings supported by an independent income would relieve the internal pressures resulting from the family fund. However, this view had barely taken hold in the 1920s before the economic devastation of the Great Depression forced families, once again, to rely on family economic strategies and co-residency to survive. Haber and Gratton (1994) argue that the introduction of Social Security for the old in America was embraced by all age groups because it offered a more secure alternative to the family fund and allowed the old to retire and the young to establish independent, separate households (Gratton, 1993, pp. 46–66).

A significant addendum to these explanations is the invention of mandatory retirement. In America, the innovation of the Ford Motor Company of rewarding seniority through annual bonuses and the introduction of the wage ladder became particularly attractive during labour strikes in the early twentieth century. Having deskilled the worker with the introduction of scientific management, which divided the production process into small repetitive operations that emphasized efficiency and speed (Taylor, 1947), the discipline attached to the crafts disappeared, causing the continuous turnover of uncommitted workers. By creating a complex set of graduations among indistinguishable jobs within the factory, Ford provided semiskilled workers with an artificial hierarchy to climb, one that was tied to seniority rather than skill. With the creation of the internal labour market the seniority schemes necessitated a cut-off point. Older workers became inefficient because they received considerably more money than younger workers for doing the same work and, as a result, an important reason for mandatory retirement was invented (Haber and Gratton, 1993, p. 109). Haber and Gratton argue that these innovations worked for and against older workers, on the one hand protecting the long-term employment of some and, on the other hand, preventing older workers, like women, from breaking into 'internal markets' and causing unemployment. Mandatory retirement, although abolished in the USA, is still evident in some form today in countries like Canada and in European Union countries where older workers can be forced to retire at age 65 according to a recent ruling by the European Court of Justice in Luxembourg (*The Times*, 23 October 2007).

Without a doubt, the history of retirement will be context-specific depending on the country in question and most likely is more nuanced beyond an amalgamation of both views. While Europe leans toward the function of public policies in creating and sustaining retirement (European Commission, 2007; Kohli and Rein, 1991; OECD, 1995; Phillipson, 2004; Platman and Taylor, 2004), North America has a propensity for favouring individual behavioural explanations and the roles of policies in corporations (Atchley, 1976; Hardy *et al.*, 1996; Marshall and Marshall, 2003; McDonald and Wanner, 1990; Quinn, Burkhauser and Myers, 1990). For the purposes of understanding retirement today, it is important to note that the development of retirement is synonymous with the life-course institutionalization hypothesis (O'Rand and Henretta, 1999, p. 181). This hypothesis suggests that, over the long term, individual lives have become increasingly organized by institutions of the state and of the workplace. In this process, individuals have been freed from the ties of family and the earlier paternalistic relationships of the workforce, as noted above. The bureaucratic structures of firms linked to industrialization, which favoured specialized divisions of labour, hierarchical chains of command and centralized authority, are age-based, so, for example, permission from an employer to continue to work into old age is replaced by age as the criterion for retirement (Graebner, 1980). Similarly, the availability of public or private/occupational pensions at a specific age encourages exit from the labour force at that age and tends to reduce individual discretion in the decision (Chappell, McDonald and Stones, 2008, p. 330). Why this matters is because the debates about retirement today are related to the potential unravelling of some aspects of this institutional model, depending upon the research reviewed, the country under consideration and the factors reviewed, such as changes in the age of retirement or the pathways to retirement (Kohli, 2007).

Retirement today

Definitions of retirement

Modern-day retirement research in the social sciences does not share a common definition of retirement, although at first glance the issue seems simple enough. Although retirement generally refers to late-life separation from waged labour, there are still many variations in the definitions and confusion along the continuum from paid to unpaid labour (Denton and Spencer, 2008; Quadagno and Hardy, 1996). For example, how do housewives or the disabled retire if they have never had an attachment to the labour force, or how is an individual classified who has numerous exits from and entrances into the labour force (Quadagno and Hardy, 1996, p. 326; Szinovacz, 1982)? From a conceptual perspective, retirement has been characterized as an institution (noted above), an event, a process, a social role and a life phase (Kohli, 2007; Kohli and Rein, 1991; McDonald and Wanner, 1990; O'Rand and Henretta, 1999; Stone and Nouroz, 2006). Generally, the conceptual definition chosen by a researcher is a function of a specific feature of retirement that is of interest such as policy or the behaviour of retirees.

As described above in the discussion of the history of retirement, retirement is usually seen as a social institution by those interested in broader societal issues, rather than as an individual's specific retirement. Kohli (2007) notes that institutions are 'stable insofar as they reproduce themselves through routine self-activating processes. Institutions may start as purposive social constructions but gradually become self-evident as they turn into second nature, be it in terms of a shared belief system or of a taken-for-granted structural reality' (Kohli, 2007, p. 257). As an institution, retirement functions to remove older workers from the labour force in a timely and orderly fashion, which is beneficial for the individual and society. Kohli and Rein (1991), for example, focus on institutionally based pathways, such as state policies and work regulations that define the life course and retirement. A number of researchers have examined the problem of 'structural lag' (Riley, Kahn and Foner, 1994), wherein institutional retirement regulations and policies are argued to be mismatched with the changing demographics, women's work trajectories and the economy because the model is based on the male bread-winner model of the nineteenth century (Chappell et al., 2008, Moen, 2003). As an illustration, the fact that life expectancy is longer today in most countries than it was in the nineteenth century opens up the possibility that workers could remain in the labour force to older ages without undue hardship in order to be consistent with these changes in longevity.

Retirement, as a single event or ritual, usually refers to the formal end of employment, which, most of the time, is accompanied by some rite of passage, such as a party and the giving of a gift to honour and say goodbye to the individual (McDonald and Wanner, 1990). The celebration of retirement as a one-of-a-kind event has rarely been studied even though it represents one of life's most significant transitions. The contemporary celebration of retirement, according to historian Achenbaum (2006), p. 50, is 'awkward' because people have lost a shared vision in the last few decades of what retirement is or ought to be, and no one really knows what life will be like after work (2006, p. 50). The proverbial gold watch of the past – that not all retirees actually received – originally stood for the continuous passage of years spent with one employer and the golden time yet to come. As the research shows, this is a state of affairs that no longer exists for many employees because the post-work years can go in many directions including a return to the labour force (Achenbaum, 2006; McDonald, 1997).

With the rising significance of a life-course approach within the study of ageing and retirement in the last 25 years, the transition into retirement, as a process, has become one of the main focal points for researchers (Burtless, 2009; Ebbinghaus, 2006; Fasang, 2009; Stone and Nouroz, 2006). The transition to retirement generally involves multiple movements between designated positions on the way to a state of being retired (Stone and Nouroz, 2006, p. 294). The specific sequence of positions that comprise an individual's transition into retirement is usually called a trajectory. An example of this type of research is found in the work of Fasang (2009), who compares Germany and Britain to assess how social policies interact to shape individual retirement patterns and economic inequality. Retirement as a social role was probably the earliest version of a 'process approach' when scholars tried to determine exactly the nature of the retiree role, the rights and obligations of the retiree, and, as a process, how the role was approached, assumed, and relinquished (Atchley, 1976, 1980; Riley, Johnson and Foner, 1972). Retirement as a phase of life with stages is a formulation most closely associated with Atchley (1976) but is rarely used today.

An assessment of the variety of measures of retirement concluded that there was no optimal measure of the concept, since all definitions have flaws (Denton and Spencer, 2008; O'Rand and Henretta, 1999). The way retirement is measured, however, is crucial because the measure determines who will or will not be included in research and policy, whose perception of retirement matters, and why research findings on the same issue may be contradictory. Some of the more common measures include the labour force participation rate, the economic activity rate, inactivity rates, number of hours worked in the past year, non-participation in the labour force, a reduction in work responsibilities, age at which the person left his or her career job, receipt of social security benefits, receipt of a private pension, a self-definition of retirement, and any combination of the preceding indicators. Most standard measures of retirement have some inadequacies especially when a life-course perspective of retirement is used and in cases where there has never been an attachment to the labour force. New longitudinal techniques are being used to study life-course trajectories and there is a move to more cross-country comparisons to understand these trajectories (Mayer, 2008).

Scope of retirement

The major reason for inactivity among older people is retirement, accounting for 55 per cent of all of the inactive population aged 55 to 64 (Employment in Europe, 2007). In the UK in 2008, 78 per cent of men aged 55 to 59 years remained active compared to 94 per cent in 1970. For men aged 60 to 64 the pattern was similar with 58 per cent in the labour force in 2008 compared to 74 per cent in 1970. The activity rate for men age 65 and over was 19 per cent in 1970 compared to only 9 per cent in 2008. In the USA, 77 per cent of men aged 55 to 59 were active in 2008 compared to 88 per cent in 1970; 59 per cent aged 60 to 64 in 2008 compared to 74 per cent in 1970; and 20 per cent aged 65 plus in 2008 compared to 26 per cent in 1970. The data underscore three trends in the retirement data that have occurred in a number of Organization for Economic Cooperation and Development

(OECD) countries. Although there has been a decline for all age groups, declines for men have been greater for those younger than 65 in both countries through the 1970s and 1980s; the decline after age 65 appears to have remained fairly stable but there is a slight upward trend in all ages that starts in the mid-1990s and accelerates after 2000, a situation found in many OECD countries (European Commission, 2007). The acceleration is attributed to differences in labour markets for older workers across various countries, although more research on this issue is required.

The trend for women is quite different from men because the rates represent the increase in women's labour force participation that started in the 1960s (McDonald, 2006). The increasing midlife participation of women is evident in both countries. In the UK, while 46 per cent of women aged 55–59 in 1970 were active, 69 per cent were active in 2008, and for those 60 to 64, 22 per cent were active in 1970 compared to 32 per cent in 2008. Over time, the activity rate of women over 65 only grew a little from 4 to 5 per cent. In the USA, the growth is far more dramatic with 48 per cent of women aged 50 to 59 active in 1970 compared to 67 per cent in 2008; 35 per cent aged 60 to 64 in 1970 versus 49 per cent in 2008, and for those over age 65, 9 per cent were active in 1970 compared to 12 per cent in 2008. For women, higher activity rates in younger cohorts are associated with participation at older ages, meaning that the growing participation of prime-age women (25–49) is subsequently shifting through into higher rates for older women. The rates, therefore, represent a general increase in women's labour activity over age groups and across countries (OECD, 2006).

Women's increased participation has narrowed the gender gap at all ages, which leads experts to argue that women's retirement will look very similar to men's retirement in the near future (McDonald, 2006). However, in the USA there has been a slowing of the long-term upward trend for prime-age women through the 1990s and falls in participation in the 2000s, foretelling perhaps different conditions for retirement (OECD, 2005a). It could be argued that because of women's later entry into the labour market their individual histories with retirement are only about to begin. One thing is for certain and that is some cohorts of women are playing 'pension catch-up' to men, who have been in the market for most of their lives (Moen, 1996).

An international comparison of activity rates shows participation rates among people in the European Union (EU) are comparatively low compared to other countries. The average activity rate for the EU-27 is lower than Australia, Canada, Japan, China and the USA. For example, the EU-27 is 17 percentage points below the USA, 21 percentage points below Japan, and 12 points behind Canada (European Commission, 2007, p. 72). The activity rate for older women in the USA is quite remarkable since the rate is higher than the rate for men in the EU (European Commission, 2007, p. 72). Although participation rates for older people in the USA are higher than on average across OECD countries and in Europe, they are not the highest. A range of countries such as Denmark, Japan, South Korea, New Zealand, Norway, Sweden and Switzerland have higher rates for either men or women or both. For example, Iceland has consistently higher rates across all groups where close to 90 per cent of the population was participating in the labour force in 2004 (OECD, 2006).

In light of the demographic ageing and its impact on employment in Europe, especially increases in disability-free longevity, it is not surprising that the EU set itself two objectives to increase the employment of older workers in a multi-pronged approach to promoting 'active ageing'. The Stockholm European Council (2001) and the Barcelona European Council 2002 targeted employment for older workers, the former setting a goal that by 2010 at least half of workers aged 55–64 should be in employment, and the latter hoping to raise the actual or 'effective' retirement age by 5 years by 2010 (European Commission, 2007; Jolivet and Lee, 2004; OECD, 2006). Reports from the USA estimate that, at best, labour force participation of older workers could be increased by about 6 per cent and Canada could make even higher adjustments to include the older worker in the labour market (OECD, 2005b).

Age of retirement

While labour force participation and activity rates are helpful in understanding the extent of older worker involvement in the labour market and, by definition, their inactivity, a more precise account of retirement is available when examining trends over time in the age of retirement. North America does not utilize the term 'average effective age of retirement' commonly used in Europe and focuses more on whether a retirement was early (before the 'normal' age of retirement at age 65) or late (after age 65). In Europe, the average effective age of retirement refers to the average age at which older workers leave the labour force completely, usually compared to the official age of retirement, when a full old-age pension is taken up by a recipient.

The age of retirement has declined sharply over time for both men and women from over age 68 in the late 1960s to well under age 65 in the 1990s, indicating why there is considerable alarm in many EU countries about the costs of an inactive population that will affect the size and cost of pensions, the productivity of the labour force, and the social and psychological costs of exclusion (European Commission, 2007; Jolivet and Lee, 2004; Macnicol, 2008; Marshall, 2009; OEDC, 2006; Phillipson and Smith, 2005). In the majority of OEDC countries, the age of retirement is lower than the official age for receiving a full pension and represents what North Americans would label 'early retirement' (Chappell *et al.*, 2008). Japan and South Korea are notable exceptions where the effective age of retirement is close to 70 for men despite an official retirement age of 60. In other countries, men, on average, are still in the workforce at age 65 in Denmark, Iceland, Ireland, Portugal and Switzerland, but have left work by age 60 in Austria, Belgium, France, Hungary, Luxembourg and the Slovak Republic. Women in all OECD countries tend to retire 1–2 years earlier than men (OECD, 2006, p. 31).

Length of retirement

To exacerbate concerns about older workers and the economy, the long-term decline in the retirement age, together with increases in longevity, have produced a rise in the number of years that workers can expect to spend in retirement (Hicks, 2003). Data from the OECD indicate that men, on average, could expect to spend fewer than 11 years in retirement in 1970, compared with 18 years in 2004. The corresponding increase for women has been from approximately 14 to 23 years (OEDC, 2006, p. 32). As would be anticipated, there are substantial country differences in the OECD figures, which continue to rise with time. It is quite remarkable that men in France retiring in 2004 could expect to spend more than 21 years in retirement while in the same year, retiring South Korean men could expect to spend fewer than 12 years. According to the OECD, in 1970, the difference between the two countries was only 1 year (OECD, 2006, p. 32). Although the evidence that human life is approaching a finite limit is inconclusive, the number of years that workers can expect to spend in retirement is likely to rise further until these limits are met (National Institute on Aging, 2006). Although contestable in some academic circles (Brückner and Mayer, 2005), the data on retirement suggest that overall, there may be a need to rethink the meaning of retirement or at least reduce the structural lag between a nineteenth-century model of retirement to be aligned with twenty-first century lifestyles (Stone, 2006).

Retirement theory

Theories explicitly designed to explain retirement are scarce and are little more than rejigged theories found in mainstream gerontology. Most theories either focus on the micro-level of individual actors or the macro-level of structure and policy in explaining retirement (Estes *et al.*, 2001). Those theories that attempt to link both micro- and macro-perspective usually represent some version of a life-course perspective.

Individual level theories

At the micro-level of theory development, the early theories were structural functional in nature wherein any phenomena were considered to be functional to society. Grounded in this perspective is the view that retirement enables employers to remove more highly compensated workers from the labour force and make way for younger workers to be hired at lower wages. *Disengagement, activity* and *continuity* theories shared the underlying premises of ageing at the time that took for granted the inescapability of physical, social and psychological decline, the importance of scripted roles, and how people adjusted to these roles. In disengagement theory, retirement was considered a part of a normal, mutual and beneficial withdrawal of the individual and society from each other (Cumming and Henry, 1961; see also Chapters 1 and 8). Retirement in this view is not socially constructed but considered to be a natural part of life. Activity theory, developed in opposition to the assumptions of disengagement theory, considered retirement a version of a healthy activity that replaced work following withdrawal from the labour force. Continuity theory treated retirement as a factor that generated a discontinuity in activities that had to be replaced with other forms of social activity (Costa and McRae, 1980). In all three instances retirement was seen to be a natural event, totally in the hands of the individual retiree, so if retirement did not pan out in a positive fashion it was the fault of the individual. There was no thought given to the possibility that retirement might be affected by social, political or economic structures (McDonald and Wanner, 1990). A contemporary rendering of these theories is evident in the *successful ageing* (Rowe and Kahn, 1997) and *productive ageing* frameworks (Estes, Mahakian and Weitz, 2001; Holstein, 1992). Successful ageing provides lists of the risk factors for unsuccessful ageing and describes the successful choices to be made by the individual, which, presumably, would include retirement. Productive ageing seeks to reverse the 'decline and deficit' view of ageing and replace it with the perspective that older people produce many goods and services that provide direct benefits to society. Although both frameworks seem attractive, it is never quite clear what form a successful or productive retirement might take. Both frameworks focus on activities and individual responsibility, and pay no heed to structural factors, such as the economy, ethnicity or social class. The end result is that these perspectives are in danger of 'blaming the victim' if retirement does not proceed in the most beneficial way (Chappell *et al.*, 2008).

Another individually focused social science theory relevant to retirement is rational *decision-making theory* in micro-economics. In this theory, patterns of behaviour, such as retirement, reflect the choices made by individuals as they try to maximize their benefits and minimize their costs (Simon, 1997). Retirement is frequently treated like a simple economic issue (Courchene, 1994) where people make rational decisions that maximize their savings for and their income in retirement. While it is a mainstay theory in economics used to explain retirement, the problem with this theory is that most of the assumptions are unrealistic in application (Burtless, 2004).

Societal theories

One of the theories that directly addresses retirement is very similar to Macnicol's (2008) demand-side explanation of retirement. In brief, *modernization theory* explains how the status of older people has declined over time with the modernization of society and how retirement facilitated this process (Cowgill and Holmes, 1972). With the growth of an ageing population due to better health technologies, the intergenerational competition for jobs increased, and the new jobs were technologically innovative and favoured younger workers who were more technically skilled. As a consequence, there were fewer suitable jobs for older workers, who were living longer, so retirement was invented to resolve the unemployment problem. Retirement, in turn, led to lower incomes, and lower incomes produced lower social status for the aged (Chappell *et al.*, 2008). It is not surprising that modernization theory has few followers today because there is little empirical support for the theory, the history of modernization does not match the timing of the marginalization of the elderly, and the universality of the process is questionable given the variety of world cultures.

Riley, Johnson and Foner (1972) proposed *age stratification theory* that envisions life as a series of roles linked together on the basis of age strata. As people age, they move from one stratum to another and each stratum has age-related capacities that depend both on biology and social definitions. According to Riley *et al.* (1972), behaviour is explained by the role occupancy of a cohort (people grouped by a common feature; in this case, date of birth) as they move through the linked roles. In the domain of retirement, the linked roles were education, work and retirement, which subsequently has been called the 'lockstep of the life course'. When this theory was applied in an earlier era, retirement was seen as a role with an age criterion for entrance and exit that applied to a specific cohort of people. When the theory was created in the USA, the age norms were so powerful that if people did not retire *exactly* at age 65 years, they were labelled 'age deviants' (Nelson and Nelson, 1972). More recently, the theory has been criticized as relying on a static concept of social structure (Quadagno and Reid, 1999). A newer paradigm has been introduced today called the *ageing and society paradigm* (Riley, Foner and Riley, 1999), which essentially argues that age-based distinctions will be removed in society in the near future so that we live in an age-integrated society where all people, no matter what their age, interact freely together (Riley, 1997). In the case of retirement, age criteria would no longer be relevant.

The *political economy of ageing theory* has undergone a number of iterations but at base is a structural theory that emerged in the late 1970s and early 1980s with the work of Estes (1979), Guillemard (1980), Walker (1981), Phillipson (1982) and Myles (1984). The theory proposes that the experience of ageing is better understood within the context of the economy (e.g. economic sectors like core, periphery and state), social policy (and the state responsible for it), and the social structure, namely the intersection of age, gender, class and ethnicity (Estes, Gerard, Zones *et al.*, 1984). When retirement is examined within this perspective, it is seen as a marginal and dependent status occupied by older people, that is the culmination of the effects of social, economic, and political processes prior to retirement. More recently, the spotlight of political economy has been cast on ageing in a global context (Phillipson, 2003). For example, the contention that the World Bank and the World Trade Organization have attempted to create a world political environment that diminishes the role of the welfare state would without doubt be detrimental to many older people contemplating retirement or already retired (Walker, 2005; Yeats, 2001).

Critical theory, a close cousin of political economy theory, has its roots in the Frankfurt school (neo-Marxism), postmodernism, the humanities and feminism. Critical theorists are normative in approach since they critically evaluate existing social and economic structures and how ageing and the aged are socially constructed within these structures (Phillipson and Walker, 1987). Even though critical theory was evident earlier in Europe, where there was a long tradition of critiquing retirement as an institution, Atchley (1993) in the USA was the first to propose a 'critical gerontology of retirement', which would expose the hidden power struggles and patterns of domination influencing retirement. Atchley (1993), a celebrated scholar in retirement research, publicly reversed his analytical views on retirement and reinterpreted his own institutional view of retirement in a more negative light. He changed the focus of his research to show how removing older workers from the labour force serves the interests of capitalists and is of questionable value to society. He claims that retirement, as an institution, ensures that society has no obligation to provide a job for an older worker who may wish to be gainfully employed. Given the current pension troubles in most advanced societies where the struggle is to keep older workers in the labour force, this is a rather serious contention (OESCD, 2006). Furthermore, he postulated that the institution of retirement reinforces the erroneous view that older workers are less productive. Phillipson (1999, 2003), from the USA, maintains that the changes in work and retirement today reflect the trends associated with the emergence of postmodern societies. With this postmodern turn, the replacement of mass production with flexible forms of work, the globalization of social life, and the weakening of social security policies that govern the retirement transition generate a different type of retirement that has little social protection and is characterized by individual risk (Phillipson, 2005). Mayer (2005) and more recently Kohli (2007) both give short shrift to the 'de-standardization' hypotheses about the life course, and retirement specifically, because, according to them, there is not enough evidence to make the case either way.

Integrating micro- and macro-perspectives

The *life-course perspective* emerged over the last 40 years as part of a trend toward a contextual understanding of human developmental processes and is often considered the pre-eminent perspective in social gerontology (Dannefer and Uhlenberg, 1999; Elder, Johnson and Crosnoe, 2003; Settersten, 2003). The value of the theory lies in the potential it has to integrate the individual and structural aspects of most issues, including retirement. There are basically two primary forms that life-course study has taken: a focus on the life course itself and the incorporation of the life course into existing substantive theories (George, 2003, p. 673). There is a possible third form where substantive theories could be transposed into a life-course perspective but this has received little attention. In the first form the emphasis has been on describing the contours of the life course, the historical emergence of the life course as a recognizable pattern, the way historical events alter the life course, and the diversity found in the life course. The second tradition integrates life-course principles into other theoretical traditions. Initially, researchers grounded their understanding in individual or group-specific life courses studied over time (Kohli, 2007). However, in the past two decades, theorists have enhanced the perspective at the macro-level by suggesting that social institutions, 'by their very nature provide a structural basis for ordering people's lives' (Marshall, 2009, p. 574).

The sociologist Glen Elder (1998) is one of the main architects of a life-course perspective and has developed five paradigmatic principles that provide a concise map of the life course: development and ageing as lifelong processes, lives in historical time and place, social timing, linked lives and human agency (Elder *et al.*, 2003). All principles can be applied to retirement but the most common ones employed have been the use and study of trajectories as to how people move from work to retirement and the steps along the way (Stone and Nouroz, 2006), the influence of social policies on retirement patterns (Fasang, 2009) the timing of retirement (Mutchler *et al.*, 1997), the problems of dual-career couples and families who wish to retire but share linked lives (Schellenberg, Turcotte and Ram, 2006; Szinovacz, 2006), and an overwhelming amount of research on human agency that examines almost every aspect of retirement behaviour from planning for retirement, through the decision to retire and the aftermath of retirement in terms of health, wealth and satisfaction (cf. Chappell *et al.*, 2008).

One of the more interesting aspects of the life-course framework is that it is not a genuine theory but rather a perspective or framework within which theories can be nested (Ferraro, Shippee and Schafer, 2009) or from which principles can be drawn and incorporated into other theories (Flippen and Tienda, 2000) depending on what is being studied and the proclivities of the researcher (Ferraro, Shippee and Schafer, 2009). Historical events influence the social structure, the economy and social policy. In turn, social structure, social policies and differences across the economy shape the life course to which the individual brings his or her own traits and capabilities. At the same time, the individual belongs to a specific age group, an age cohort such as the baby boomers, which can influence experiences and views of retirement over time. For example, dual economy theory could be used to study rates of retirement in different economic sectors as could the cumulative disadvantage/advantage hypothesis where the inequalities created by work histories prior to retirement are perpetuated after retirement and become amplified by cumulative effects over time. The approach has many limitations, the most obvious being that the perspective is representative of life in Western industrialized nations, a condition that does not apply to all people and countries (Dannefer, 2003).

Issues in retirement

In recent years, the importance of older workers and their retirement have shot to the top of the policy hierarchy in most economically advanced OECD countries. The primary reason can be attributed to unprecedented population ageing and the growing consensus that older workers should be encouraged to remain in the workforce longer to help promote economic growth and reduce the burden of future public expenditures on social security and health care (European Commission, 2007; GAO, 2009; HRSDC, 2006; OECD, 2006). Anticipating the ageing of the population, many countries took early action by introducing pension change. The common elements to these reforms include reductions of pension replacement rates – in other words, the degree to which the pension replaces what was earned prior to retirement (Mexico, Portugal), increasing the official and earliest ages of retirement (e.g. Denmark, Germany, Iceland, Norway, the UK and the USA), and introducing or changing actuarial adjustments in pension benefits for early and late retirement (Spain, USA). Recognizing that pension change alone was not enough, the focus has been expanded to the older worker and how to enhance his or her labour force participation. Within this changing context there are a number of issues that have captured more attention than others. Here we touch on a few of the enduring issues that have taken on new forms and that will continue to shape the retirement of tomorrow.

Reinventing retirement

With the changes associated with economic restructuring and the retrenchment of the welfare state in some countries, scholars began to question the 'education-work-retirement lockstep' of the life course. On one side of the debate it has been argued that the life course is 'coming undone' (Guillemard, 1997, p. 455); it is becoming 'longer and fuzzier' (Kohli and Rein, 1991, p. 22), blurred (Mutchler *et al.*, 1997), more variable in timing (Henretta, 1992) and less standardized (Marshall, 2009, p. 580). On the other side of the debate are those who disagree with the 'disorder' hypothesis mainly because the research on changing life patterns remains inconclusive (cf. Brückner and Mayer, 2005; Fasang, 2009; Kohli, 2007; Mayer, 2004). According to the naysayers, undergirding these observations is the lack of conceptual clarity of concepts like de-standardized, or de-institutionalized without a clear definition of the processes to which they refer (Fasang, 2009). Whatever the outcomes of the debate (subject to further research), it has certainly affected recent ideas about retirement. It is difficult to avoid the idea that there have been modest changes in the temporal order of the stages in the life course, if not changes in time spent in the various stages. As Phillipson (2004) argues, there may be a 'broadening in the institution of retirement', referring to the many ways to make the retirement transition (Phillipson, 2004, p. 161).

At its height in the 1950s (USA), 1960s and 1970s (EU), retirement was a taken-for-granted labour force exit at age 60 or 65 (depending on the country), with few options and very few choices for the individual. Retirement was normatively expected in combination with income supports from occupational and social security pensions and was a fundamental dimension of the organization of the life course for most workers. It was a single status passage with few reversals. Today, retirement can be a process with no distinct beginning or end, it is a multi-layered process, it can involve multiple exits, or it may never happen at all. It may be governed by more than several institutional timetables but also by diverse individual biographies that interact with these schedules.

Certainly, retirement is no longer defined by a single chronological age since most people retire between ages 50 and 62, not the conventional age 65, and well before physical decline. At its pinnacle, retirement was seen as a right of citizenship as well as a positive social act, but today a substantial number of people are involuntarily forced into retirement by supposedly voluntary early retirement packages (Hardy, Hazelrigg and Quadagno, 1996), poor health (Turcotte and Schellenburg, 2007), unemployment (McMullin and Marshall, 2001; Tompa, 1999), caregiving responsibilities (McDonald, 2002), or the retirement of a spouse (Szinovacz, 2006). The retirement transition is also less likely to be circumscribed by state pension policies, since growing numbers of people take alternative routes into retirement through other programmes like disability pensions (OECD, 2004). The devolution of state responsibility to the individual for retirement income increases individual risk and loosens the ties that bind the individual to the state (Gilleard and Higgs, 2005; Vickerstaff and Cox, 2005; Wolff, 2003). The shift from defined benefit plans to defined contribution plans in the USA would be an example. Finally, retirement does not always constitute a one-time event representing an abrupt transition from work to retirement. Retirement can be gradual through part-time work, and it can involve temporary bridge jobs between main career jobs and non-work, it can involve multiple exits from the labour force, and it may never happen at all (McDonald, 2006). For example, among Canadians 45 years of age and over in 2002, 30 per cent report they had no intention of retiring, while a study in the USA found that close to 50 per cent of workers use bridge jobs to move into retirement (Quinn, 1999). Within these changes, Moen (2003) goes so far as to suggest a new stage in the life course that she calls the new *midcourse life stage*, which falls between the end of career building and growing old and represents the plurality of passages noted above (Moen, 2003, p. 270).

These modifications to the retirement transition herald considerable future uncertainty for many people as they contemplate their retirement. 'More choice' may really mean less choice as corporate and public policies are adjusted to increase the working life of the older worker, pensions are ratcheted back in generosity to sustain social security systems, and the current global economic downturn places more stress on older workers who want to but are hesitant to leave their jobs for retirement (AARP, 2008). What will transpire for more vulnerable groups, like women (e.g. the divorced and separated, caregivers) and ethnic minorities or new immigrants, remains to be seen.

Health and wealth

Researchers have grappled with the issue of what drives the majority of workers to retire prior to the effective age of retirement, as noted earlier. Investigators have generally limited their questions to whether it is the involuntary push of poor health or the voluntary pull of unearned income from pensions and assets that leads to early retirement (McDonald, 1997; McDonald and Wanner, 1990). The answers offered by scholars depend on the historical context, the orientation of the researcher, and the country in question, to underscore just a few delimiting factors. In the early retirement research, ill health was found to be a very important predictor of early retirement (e.g. Guillemard and Rein, 1993, Quinn and Burkhauser, 1990; Reno, 1971). With the introduction of early retirement plans in the 1980s that were devised to quickly remove older workers from the labour market in recessionary times, the focus swung to pension income (both public and private) as a more important predictor of retirement (Wise, 1993). At this time, the recognition of the retirement effects on social security was so clear that a number of countries, like Germany, the USA and Italy, upped their ages of retirement (Chen, 1994; Guillemard and Rein, 1993; Sheppard, 1991). The1990s saw the mounting costs of pensions for a rapidly growing older population and longer retirements, so the kaleidoscope shifted slightly to the alteration of pension schemes to stem the tide of early retirement (Martin and Whitehouse, 2008). The renewed interest in the health of older workers in the last decade is related to increases in longevity, disability-free life expectancies, and the decline in the arduousness of work which make early retirement all the more perplexing to many (Fries, 2003; Turcotte and Schellenberg, 2007).

Currently, there are a number of studies that confirm that the financial incentives embedded in public and private pension schemes are significant but modest in determining retirement decisions (Blöndal and Scarpetta, 1998; Burniaux et al., 2003; Coile and Gruber, 2000; Duval, 2003; Gruber and Wise, 1999, 2004; Gustman and Steinmeier, 2005; McDonald, Donahue and Marshall, 2000; Schils, 2005). Depending on the country, retirement decisions will also be influenced by the age at which early retirement benefits can be first accessed, the generosity of replacement rates, and the costs of continuing to work in terms of changes in the present value of net pension wealth from working an additional year (Cremer and Pestieau, 2003; OECD, 2006).

Researchers also continue to confirm that poor health plays an important role in the individual retirement decision (Bound et al., 1997; Dwyer and Mitchell, 1998; Kerkhofs et al., 1997; McNair et al., 2004; OECD, 1998; Schellenberg et al., 2006). It comes as no surprise that several researchers have found retirement decisions to be a combination of both sets of factors (Alcock et al., 2003) while others have shown that health problems influence retirement plans more strongly than do economic factors (Dwyer and Mitchell, 1998; Humphrey et al., 2003). In a number of countries, almost 30 per cent of older workers retire because of ill health (Phillipson, 2005; Schellenberg and Silver, 2004) highlighting the size of the task ahead for governments and firms who hope to find ways to maintain these workers in the labour force (OEDC, 2006; Phillipson and Smith, 2005). For those older workers already retired due to poor health, the probabilities of re-entering the labour market are small, and decline rapidly as the length of unemployment increases (Alcock et al., 2003; McNair et al., 2004).

Work and the timing of retirement

With the new interest in older workers and their work environment, the existing investigations of these factors have taken on a new weight. As would be expected, the characteristics differ across countries and are sometimes open to dispute. Overall, however, the research indicates that unmarried men have a greater probability of retiring before age 65 years than married men (Schellenberg, 2003; Whiting, 2005). Men with higher personal incomes or financial security (Arthur, 2003; Humphrey et al., 2003; Smeaton and McKay, 2003) and previous jobs in the core industrial sector of the economy (where jobs are the most stable and high paying) also tend to retire earlier (McDonald, 2006). Generally, women tend to retire earlier than men (Eckefeldt, 2008; Schellenberg, 2003) although the gap is closing.

The level of a woman's household income, as opposed to her personal income, decreases the age of her retirement, highlighting the important place of marriage in women's economic security in later life (McDonald, 1997, 1996; Peracchi and Welch, 1994; Szinovacz, 2006). The findings on the presence of dependants in the family indicate that when children live at home, both men and women in the family are less likely to retire early (Pienta, 2003).

Research about the effect of ethnicity on retirement is almost non-existent, as is that on the influence of race and ethnicity on the timing of retirement. While some studies do exist, most of these are nation specific. In the USA the findings apply to the differences between African, Hispanic and Caucasian Americans (Flippen and Tienda, 2000; Green, 2005; Hayward, Friedman and Chen, 1998). For example, Honig (1996) found, when comparing the retirement plans of African-American, Hispanic, and White married men and women, that retirement expectations accurately forecast retirement behaviour and that they differed by race and gender. An early Canadian study found that the chances of being retired are uniformly lower for all foreign-born groups in Canada, compared with the Canadian-born, after age and gender are taken into account. People from Asia, Africa, and Latin America have the least chance of retiring early and tend to retire later than the general Canadian population (Wanner and McDonald, 1989). More recent research clearly shows the precarious position of visible minorities in Canada. According to the 2001 Census in Canada, 7.2 per cent of the total Canadian population 65 and older were part of a visible minority group, and this group received significantly less income from public and private pensions in retirement than mainstream older Canadians, women faring the worst in all ethnic groups (McDonald, 2006). The differences could possibly reflect such factors as length of time in Canada, facility with official languages, educational credentials and barriers in the labour market. Even worse is the economic situation of Aboriginal peoples, whose total dependency on government retirement pensions bespeaks a lifetime of racial discrimination and inequality (Chappell et al., 2008).

The type of employment at the time of retirement can affect the timing of retirement. A number of studies find that blue-collar workers and low-skilled workers are likely to retire earlier than white-collar workers and more highly skilled workers (Blöndal and Scarpetta, 1998). Some studies have demonstrated that workers who were highly committed to their work or liked their work delayed retirement, while those with opposite views retired earlier (Duchesne, 2004; Hansson, DeKoekkoek, Neece et al., 1997; Reitzes, Mutran, Fernandez, 1996; Vickerstaff, Baldock, Cox et al., 2004). Stress and strain in the workplace also play a role in the timing of retirement. A Norwegian study found that older workers who took early retirement because of a disability experienced more job strain (Blekesaune and Solem, 2005), while a Canadian investigation found that older workers with high job strain in managerial, professional or technical jobs retired earlier than those with low strain in their jobs. Strain was not related to early retirement for older workers in sales, services, clerical or blue-collar occupations (Turcotte and Schellenberg, 2005). Most recently, a few studies have highlighted the importance of changing working hours in times of recession that result in fewer employees, which in turn fosters early retirement for older workers (e.g. Gustman and Steinmeier, 2004; OECD, 2006).

On the flip side of the retirement coin are those who retire 'late' or after the statutory retirement age in a given country. The numbers in this group continue to grow at a rapid rate. For example, in the USA, the labour force participation of those over age 65 is over 20 per cent for men and over 12 per cent for women, and the proportion is growing faster than the working-age population (Bureau of Labor Statistics, 2008). Those who work past official retirement ages are likely to be men, immigrants, be well educated, with higher occupational status, and to be self-employed. The single most important predictor of late retirement is level of education (Duchesne, 2004; McNair et al., 2004; Monette, 1996). Women with the same education as men are much less likely to be working (Duchesne, 2004).

The quest to retain older workers in the labour force will have to take into consideration unemployment. An old practice may re-emerge in the midst of the latest economic global crisis. During recessions unemployment rates are higher for older workers and a large portion of retirement during these periods is really unemployment (McMullin and Marshall, 2001; OECD, 2006; Rowe and Nguyen, 2003; Tompa, 1999). New studies also show that the earlier investigations that found the probability of being displaced declines with age are no longer applicable (Farber, 2005). With the world economic recession under way, older workers may be faced with a double-edged sword. A recent study in the USA has clearly shown that if the economy does not improve appreciably, 6 in 10 workers age 45 or over will delay retirement and work longer (AARP, 2008). On the one hand, unemployment rates are beginning to rise in many countries (e.g. USA, UK, France, Germany, Spain) and on the other, older workers, at least in America, want to prolong work out of economic necessity (Munnell, Muldoon and Sass, 2009). It is highly unlikely that older workers will come out of the recession unscathed, especially in light of current reductions in wages and salaries, time redistributions and massive lay-offs if past practices are any indication.

Families and retirement

Women's increased labour force participation, larger contributions to household income, increased pension coverage, and increased presence in professional and managerial occupations make retirement relevant to them today. In recognition of women's changing roles, scholars have created new models of family retirement that are grounded in a life-course perspective (Pienta, 2003; Szinovacz, 2006).

When considering age, wives with much older husbands are less likely to retire early, as are married men with younger wives (Szinovacz, 2002), although most couples apparently want to retire at the same time. Tompa (1999) found that both men and women tend to make joint retirement decisions with their spouses, a finding supported in recent research where almost one-half of dual career couples plan to retire together even though only one-third manage this coordination (Schellenberg, Turcotte and Ram, 2006). The age differences between spouses and the qualifying ages for official pensions do not align, so one spouse may have to retire before the other, stay in the labour force longer, or take a reduced pension.

The research further indicates that the transition from work to retirement is more likely to be associated with a decline in marital quality from the perspective of the retired partner who has a working spouse (Moen, Kim and Hofmeister, 2001). In the USA, Szinovacz and Davey (2005) found that retired husbands have a difficult time staying home alone when their wives still work, harking back to the 'housewife' retirement studies in the 1950s (Keating and Cole, 1980). Finally, in terms of the quality of the relationship, there appears to be some evidence that spouses in close relationships, those with joint interests, and those wishing to spend more time together are inclined to retire whereas couples in conflict-ridden relationships may delay retirement (Henkens, 1999; Szinovacz and Schaffer, 2000). Another study reports that satisfaction with retirement was lower for those retirees whose decision to retire was strongly influenced by their spouse (Smith and Moen, 2004).

The marital history of the couple may also have some bearing on retirement, since remarried widowers are less likely to retire, and remarried widows are more likely to retire (Szinovacz and DeViney, 2000). Since the inception of retirement as an institution, the most important predictor of women's age of retirement has been marital status because it determined income in retirement and satisfaction with retirement (McDonald, 1996; McDonald and Robb, 2004). Today, the pensions of both spouses are important in the retirement decision because of the longer and stronger presence of women in the labour force (Schellenberg, Turcotte and Ram, 2006). When marital support disappears, however, women's secondary poverty becomes all too evident in retirement. There is considerable evidence in industrialized nations that older unattached women, namely the divorced, separated and widowed, are the poorest of the poor in old age (Bonnet and Geraci, 2009; McDonald and Robb, 2004).

Finally, family care obligations also impinge on retirement decisions, usually for women, who provide the bulk of family care (Chappell et al., 2008). Although there is considerable research on the effects of caregiving on employment, there is only preliminary research on the relationship between caregiving and retirement. Initial research indicates that caregiving does lead to very early retirement for women and, when the caregiving is over, women are left financially weakened, unable to rejoin the labour force because of obsolescent skills and few financial and psychological resources (McDonald *et al.*, 2007).

The ageing of the population and the burgeoning ranks of baby boomers moving into retirement are about to generate newer versions of retirement that are likely to alter the institution of retirement further. The baby boomers will be the first female cohort in history whose labour force participation will span most of their adult lives (Statistics Canada, 2000). These women will have the opportunity for the first time of defining their own retirement because of their strong presence in the labour force, their higher levels of educational attainment, and their increased occupational prestige (McDonald, 2006, p. 155). It is likely that the reformulations will take into account the fact that marriage will not be as central to women's retirement as it once was given the declines in the prevalence and stability of marriage in several countries. In addition, women will find themselves in the position of double caregiving, looking after their own children and ageing parents simultaneously. Despite the merging of male and female labour force patterns, women's pensions will still not be equal to men's pensions in old age. To the degree that private and semi-private components of many pension systems replicate the inequality in the labour market, and as long as women have interrupted work histories due to family responsibilities, their abilities to save and accumulate pension benefits will be different and will likely affect the timing and nature of their retirement.

Conclusions

This chapter has provided an overview of retirement from its inception to the present day. The brief journey has illustrated that retirement is an ever-changing institution that is a product of the history and of personal agency but context bound by country. In most advanced economies, retirement evolved from a process of stepping down within the confines of the family into an age-based, society-wide institution, supported by a national pension system. The form for retirement, as we know it today, is predicated on a male, nineteenth-century life-course model, where a woman's place was in the home, supported by the husband as sole breadwinner. Retirement, despite its short history, clearly became a normative aspect of the life course as older workers left the marketplace in droves at ever younger ages until the turnaround in the late 1990s. While there are a few theoretical attempts to explain retirement, most have serious limitations, requiring innovative thinking. The four retirement issues addressed here are only a sampling of many potential concerns of researchers and policymakers but were chosen because they are long-standing challenges with new twists that will have serious repercussions for society in the years to come.

Summary

Retirement has been a majority experience in industrialized countries since the early twentieth century; the history of concepts of retirement, before and after the introduction of state pensions, is examined and the effects on workers and their families are compared across countries. The institutional view that these dynamics have created is then examined for its applicability and utility in the current climate. Definitions of 'retirement' are critically discussed. Level of retirement, as measured by activity rates, compared across time, gender and countries, reveals significant differences. The related issues of age of retirement and length of retirement are then discussed. Theories of retirement can be categorized as micro (aimed at the individual) or macro (aimed at structure and policy) levels. These are discussed, before the possibility of integrating micro- and macro-perspectives is critically examined. In practice, several key practical issues influence discussions of retirement issues and subsequent decision-making. These include a need to redefine the basic concept of retirement, the interaction of health and wealth, the relationship between type of work and the planning of retirement, and the interaction between familial circumstances and retirement.

REFERENCES

Achenbaum, W.A. (1978) *Old age in a new land*. Baltimore, MD: Johns Hopkins University Press.

(2006) Retirement before social security, in W.H. Crown (ed.), *Handbook on employment and the elderly*. Westport, CT: Greenwood Press.

Achenbaum, W.A., Weiland, S.J. and Haber, C. (1996) *Key words in sociocultural gerontology*. New York: Springer.

Alcock, P., Beatty, C., Fothergill, S. *et al.* (2003) *Work to welfare: how men become detached from the labour market*. Cambridge University Press.

American Association of Retired Persons (AARP) (2008) Retirement security or insecurity? The experience of workers aged 45 years and older. Retrieved from http://assets.aarp.org/rgcenter/econ/retirement_survey_08.pdf.

Arthur, S. (2003) *Money, choice and control*. Bristol/York: Policy Press/Joseph Rowntree Foundation.

Atchley, R.C. (1976) *The sociology of retirement*. New York: Wiley.

(1982) Retirement as a social institution, *Annual Review of Sociology*, **8**, 263–87.

(1993) Critical perspectives on retirement, in T.R. Cole, W.A. Achenbaum, P.L. Jakobi *et al.* (eds), *Voices and visions of aging: toward a critical gerontology*. New York: Springer, 3–19.

Bilefsky, D. (2007) Top EU court backs mandatory retirement age of 65, *New York Times*, 16 October. Retrieved from www.iht.com/articles/2007/10/16/africa/retire.php.

Blekesaune, M. and Solem, P. (2005) Working conditions and early retirement, *Research on Aging*, **27**(1), 3–30.

Blöndal, S. and Scarpetta, S. (1998) *Falling participation rates among older workers in the OECD countries: the role of social security systems*. Paris: Economic Department, Organization for Economic Co-operation and Development (OECD).

Bonnet, C. and Geraci, M. (2009) Correcting gender inequality in pensions: the experience of five countries, *Population and Societies*, *453*, 1–4.

Bound, J., Schenbaum, M., Stinebrickner, T. *et al.* (1997) Measuring the effects of health on retirement behaviour. Paper presented at the International Health and Retirement Surveys Conference, Amsterdam.

Brückner, H. and Mayer, K.U. (2005) The de-standardization of the life course: what it might mean? And if it means anything, whether it actually took place?, *Advances in Life Course Research*, *9*, 27–53.

Bureau of Labor Statistics (2008) *Older workers*. Retrieved from www.bls.gov/spotlight/2008/older_workers/data.htm.

Burniaux, J.M., Duval, R. and Jaumotte, F. (2003) *Coping with ageing: a dynamic approach to quantify the impact of alternative policy options on future labour supply in OECD countries*. Paris: Economics Department, Organization for Economic Co-operation and Development (OECD).

Burtless, G. (2004) *Social norms, rules of thumb, and retirement: evidence for rationality in retirement planning*. Boston: Brookings Institution, Retirement Research Center, Boston College.

   (2008) *The rising age at retirement in industrial countries*. Chestnut Hill, MA: Center for Retirement Research at Boston College.

Butler, R. and Schechter, M. (2001) Productive aging, in G. Maddox (ed.), *Encyclopedia of aging*, 3rd edn, vol. II. New York: Springer, 824–5.

Chappell, N.L., McDonald, L. and Stones, M. (2008) *Aging in contemporary Canada*, 2nd edn. Toronto: Pearson.

Chen, Y.P. (1994) 'Equivalent retirement ages' and their implications for Social Security and Medicare financing, *The Gerontologist*, *34*(6), 731–5.

Cohen, M. (1988) *Women's work, markets and economic development in nineteenth-century Ontario*. University of Toronto Press.

Coile, C. and Gruber, J. (2000) *Social security and retirement*. Cambridge, MA: National Bureau of Economic Research.

Costa, P.T. and McRae, R.R. (1980) Still stable after all these years, in P.B. Baltes and O.G. Brim (eds), *Life span development and behaviour*, vol. 3. New York: Academic Press, 65–102.

Courchene, T. (1994) *Social Canada in the millennium: reform imperatives and restructuring principles*. Toronto: C.D. Howe Institute.

Cowgill, D.O. and Holmes, L.D. (1972) *Aging and modernization*. New York: Appleton-Century-Crofts.

Cremer, H. and Pestieau, P. (2003) The double dividend of postponing retirement, *International Tax and Public Finance*, *10*, 419–34.

Cumming, E. and Henry, W. (1961) *Growing old: the process of disengagement*. New York: Basic Books.

Dannefer, D. (2003) Whose life course is it, anyway? 'Linked lives' in global perspective, in R.A. Settersten, Jr (ed.), *Invitation to the life course: toward new understandings of later life*. New York: Baywood, 143–57.

Dannefer, D. and Uhlenberg, P. (1999) Paths of the life course: a typology, in V.L. Bengston and K.W. Schaie (eds), *Handbook on theories of aging*. New York: Springer, 306–26.

Denton, F.T. and Spencer, B.G. (2008) *What is retirement? A review and assessment of alternative concepts and measures.* Hamilton, ON: SEDAP, McMaster University.

Donahue, W., Orbach, H. and Pollack, O. (1960) Retirement: the emerging social pattern, in C. Tibbitts (ed.), *Handbook of social gerontology.* University of Chicago Press, 330–406.

Duchesne, D. (2004) More seniors at work, *Perspectives on Labour and Income, 16*(1), 55–67.

Duval, R. (2003) *The retirement effects of old-age pension and early retirement schemes in OECD countries.* Paris: Economics Department, Organization for Economic Co-operation and Development (OECD).

Dwyer, D.S. and Mitchell, O.S. (1998) *Health problems as determinants of retirement: are self-rated measures endogenous?* Cambridge, MA: National Bureau of Economic Research.

Ebbinghaus, B. (2006) *Reforming early retirement in Europe, Japan and the USA.* Oxford University Press.

Eckefeldt, P. (2008) Pension reform in the European Union: how to cope with ageing populations. Cicero Foundation Great Debates Seminar, Paris.

Elder, G.H., Jr (1998) The life course as developmental theory, *Child Development, 69*(1), 1–12.

Elder, G.H., Jr, Johnson, M.K. and Crosnoe, R. (2003) The emergence and development of life course theory, in J.T. Mortimer and M.J. Shanahan (eds), *Handbook of the life course.* New York: Plenum, 3–19.

Estes, C.L. (1979) *The aging enterprise.* San Francisco: Jossey Bass.

Estes, C.L. and Associates. (2001) *Social policy and aging.* Thousand Oaks, CA: Sage.

Estes, C.L., Gerard, L., Zones, J.S. *et al.* (1984) *Political economy, health, and aging.* Boston: Little Brown.

Estes, C.L., Mahakian, J.L. and Weitz, T.A. (2001) A political economy critique of "productive aging", in C.L. Estes and Associates (eds), *Social policy and aging: a critical perspective.* Thousand Oaks, CA: Sage, 187–200.

European Commission (2007) *Employment in Europe 2007.* Brussels: Employment Analysis Unit, European Commission.

Farber, H.S. (2005) *What do we know about job loss in the United States? Evidence from the Displaced Workers Survey, 1984–2004.* Chicago: Federal Reserve Bank of Chicago.

Fasang, A.E. (2009) *Social policy and temporal patterns of retirement: evidence from Germany and Britain.* New Haven, CT: CIQLE, Yale University.

Ferraro, K.F., Shippee, T.P. and Schafer, M.H. (2009) Cumulative inequality theory for research on aging and the life course, in V.L. Bengston, M. Silverstein, N. Putney *et al.* (eds), *Handbook of theories of aging,* 2nd edn. New York: Springer, 413–34.

Fischer, D.H. (1978) *Growing old in America.* New York: Oxford University Press.

Flippen, C. and Tienda, M. (2000) Pathways to retirement: patterns of labor force participation and labor market exit among the pre-retirement population by race, Hispanic origin, and sex, *Journals of Gerontology. Series B, Psychological Sciences and Social Sciences, 55*(1), S14–27.

Fries, J.F. (2003) Measuring and monitoring success in compressing morbidity, *Annals of Internal Medicine, 139*(5 Pt 2), 455–9.

GAO (2009) *Older workers: enhanced communication among federal agencies could improve strategies for hiring and retaining experienced workers.* Washington, DC: Government Accountability Office (GAO).

George, L. (2003) Life course research: achievements and potential, in J.T. Mortimer and M.J. Shanahan (eds), *Handbook of the life course.* New York: Kluwer Academic Publishers, 671–80.

Gilleard, C. and Higgs, P. (2005) *Contexts of ageing.* Cambridge: Polity Press.

Graebner, W. (1980) *A history of retirement.* New Haven, CT: Yale University Press.

Gratton, B. (1993) The creation of retirement: families, individuals, and the social security movement, in K.W. Schaie and W.A. Achenbaum (eds), *Societal impact on aging: historical perspectives.* New York: Springer, 45–68.

Green, F. (2005) *Understanding trends in job satisfaction: final report.* Swindon: Economic and Social Research Council.

Gruber, J. and Wise, D. (eds) (1999) *Social security and retirement around the world.* University of Chicago Press.

(eds) (2004) *Social security and retirement around the world: micro-estimation.* University of Chicago Press.

Guillemard, A.M. (1980) *La Vieillesse et l'état.* Paris: Presses Universitaires de France.

(1997) Rewriting social policy and changes in the life-course organization: a European perspective, *Canadian Journal on Aging, 16*(3), 441–64.

Guillemard, A.M. and Rein, M. (1993) Comparative patterns of retirement: recent trends in developed societies, *Annual Review of Sociology, 19,* 469–503.

Gustman, A.L. and Steinmeier, T.L. (2004) *Personal accounts and family retirement.* Cambridge, MA: National Bureau of Economic Research.

(2005) The social security early entitlement age in a structural model of retirement and wealth, *Journal of Public Economics, 89*(2–3), 441–63.

Haber, C. (1978) Mandatory retirement in nineteenth-century America: the conceptual basis for a new work cycle, *Journal of Social History, 12*(1), 77–96.

Haber, C. and Gratton, B. (1994) *Old age and the search for security: an American social history.* Bloomington, IN: Indiana University Press.

Hansson, R.O., DeKoekkoek, P.D., Neece, W.M. *et al.* (1997) Successful aging at work, annual review, 1992–1996: the older worker and transitions to retirement, *Journal of Vocational Behaviour, 51,* 202–33.

Hardy, M.A., Hazelrigg, L.E. and Quadagno, J.S. (1996) *Ending a career in the auto industry: 30 and out.* New York: Plenum Press.

Hayward, M.D., Friedman, S. and Chen, H. (1998) Career trajectories and older men's retirement, *Journals of Gerontology. Series B, Psychological Sciences and Social Sciences, 53*(2), S91–103.

Henkens, K. (1999) Retirement intentions and spousal support: a multi-actor approach, *Journals of Gerontology. Series B, Psychological Sciences and Social Sciences, 54,* S63–74.

Henretta, J.C. (1992) Uniformity and diversity: life course institutionalization and late life work exit, *Sociological Quarterly, 33,* 265–79.

Hicks, P. (2003) New policy research on population aging and life-course flexibility, *Horizons, 6,* 3–6.

Holstein, M. (1992) Productive aging: troubling implications, in M. Minkler and C.L. Estes (eds), *Critical gerontology: perspectives from political and moral economy.* Amityville, NY: Baywood, 359–73.

Honig, M. (1996) Retirement expectations: differences by race, ethnicity, and gender, *The Gerontologist, 36*(3), 373–82.

HRSDC (Human Resources and Skills Development Canada) (2006) *Targeted initiative for older workers.* Retrieved from www.hrsdc.gc.ca/eng/cs/sp/hrsd/eppd/tiow.shtml.

Humphrey, A., Costigan, P., Pickering, K. *et al.* (2003) *Factors affecting the labour market participation of older workers.* London: Department of Work and Pensions.

Jolivet, A. and Lee, S. (2004) *Employment conditions in an ageing world: meeting the working time challenge.* Geneva: Conditions of Work and Employment Series, No. 9, International Labour Force.

Keating, N.C. and Cole, P. (1980) What do I do with him 24 hours a day? Changes in the housewife role after retirement, *The Gerontologist, 20*(1), 84–9.

Kerkhofs, M., Lindeboom, M., Theeuwes, J. *et al.* (1997) Age related health dynamics and changes in labour market status. Paper presented at the International Health and Retirement Surveys Conference, Amsterdam.

Kohli, M. (2007) The institutionalization of the life course: looking back to look ahead, *Research in Human Development, 4*(3–4), 253–71.

Kohli, M. and Rein, M. (1991) The changing balance of work and retirement, in M. Kohli, M. Rein, A.M. Guillemard *et al.* (eds), *Time for retirement: comparative studies of early exit from the labour force.* Cambridge University Press, 1–35.

Macnicol, J. (1998) *The politics of retirement in Britain, 1878–1948.* Cambridge University Press.

(2008) Older men and work in the twenty-first century: what can the history of retirement tell us?, *Journal of Social Policy, 37*(4), 579–95.

Marshall, V.W. (2009) Theory informing public policy: the life course perspective as a policy tool, in V.L. Bengston, D. Gans, N. Putney *et al.* (eds), *Handbook of theories of aging.* New York: Springer, 573–93.

Marshall, V.W. and Marshall, J.G. (2003) Ageing and work in Canada: firm policies, *Geneva Papers on Risk and Insurance, 28*(4), 625–39.

Martin, J.P. and Whitehouse, E. (2008) *Reforming retirement-income systems: lessons from the recent experiences of OECD countries.* Paris: Directorate for Employment, Labour and Social Affairs, and Organization for Economic Co-operation and Development (OECD).

Mayer, K.U. (2004) Whose lives? How history, societies and institutions define and shape life courses, *Research in Human Development, 1*, 161–87.

(2005) Life courses and life chances in a comparative perspective, in S. Svallfors (ed.), *Analyzing inequality: life chances and social mobility in comparative perspective.* Palo Alto, CA: Stanford University Press, 17–55.

(2008) *New directions in life course research.* New Haven, CT: CIQLE, Yale University.

McDonald, L. (1996) *Transitions into retirement: a time for retirement.* Toronto: Centre for Applied Social Research, University of Toronto.

(1997) The link between social research and social policy options: reverse retirement as a case in point, *Canadian Journal on Aging/Public Policy, 23*(S1), 90–113.

(2002) The invisible retirement of women. Social and Economic Dimensions of Aging Paper 69. Retrieved 1 July 2006 from http://ideas.repec.org/s/mcm/sedapp1.html.

(2006) Gendered retirement: the welfare of women and the "new" retirement, in L. Stone (ed.), *New frontiers of research on retirement.* Ottawa: Statistics Canada, 137–64.

McDonald, L., Donahue, P. and Marshall, V. (2000) The economic consequences of unexpected early retirement, in F.T. Denton, D. Fretz and B.G. Spencer (eds), *Independence and economic security in old age.* Vancouver: University of British Columbia Press, 267–92.

McDonald, L. and Robb, A.L. (2004) The economic legacy of divorce and separation for women in old age, *Canadian Journal on Aging, 23*(Suppl 1), S83–97.

McDonald, L., Sussman, T. and Donahue, P. (2007) *When bad things happen to good people: the economic consequences of retiring to caregive.* Hamilton, ON: SEDAP, McMaster University.

McDonald, L. and Wanner, R.A. (1990) *Retirement in Canada.* Toronto: Butterworths.

McMullin, J.A. and Marshall, V.W. (2001) Ageism, age relations, and garment industry work in Montreal, *The Gerontologist*, *41*(1), 111–22.

McNair, S., Flynn, M., Owen, L. *et al.* (2004) *Changing work in later life: a study of job transitions.* Surrey: Centre for Research into the Older Workforce, University of Surrey.

Moen, P. (1996) Gender, age, and the life course, in R. Binstock and L. George (eds), *Handbook of aging and social sciences*, 4th edn. San Diego, CA: Academic Press, 174–87.

— (2003) Midcourse: navigating retirement and a new life stage, in J.T. Mortimer and M.J. Shanahan (eds), *Handbook of the life course.* New York: Kluwer Academic/Plenum Publishers, 269–91.

Moen, P., Kim, J. and Hofmeister, H. (2001) Couples' work/retirement transitions, gender, and marital quality, *Social Psychology Quarterly*, *64*, 55–71.

Monette, M. (1996) *Canada's changing retirement patterns: findings from the General Social Survey.* Ottawa, ON: Statistics Canada.

Morton, D. and McCallum, M.E. (1988) *Superannuation to indexation: employment pension plans.* Toronto: Queen's Printer for Ontario.

Munnell, A.H., Muldoon, D. and Sass, S.A. (2009) *Recessions and older workers.* Chestnut Hill, MA: Center for Retirement Research at Boston College.

Mutchler, J.E., Burr, J.A., Pienta, A. M. *et al.* (1997) Pathways to labor force exit: work transitions and work instability, *Journals of Gerontology. Series B, Psychological Sciences and Social Sciences*, *52*(1), S4–12.

Myles, J. (1984) *Old age in the welfare state: the political economy of public pensions.* Boston: Little Brown.

National Institute on Aging and Population Reference Bureau (2006) *The future of human life expectancy: have we reached the ceiling or is the sky the limit?* Washington, DC: National Institute on Aging and Population Reference Bureau.

Nelson, N.E. and Nelson, E.E. (1972) Passing in the age stratification system. Paper presented at the Annual Meeting of the American Sociological Association, New Orleans.

OECD (1995) *The transition from work to retirement.* Paris: Organization for Economic Co-operation and Development (OECD).

— (1998) *The retirement decision in OECD countries.* Paris: Organization for Economic Co-operation and Development (OECD).

— (2004) *Employment outlook.* Paris: Organization for Economic Co-operation and Development (OECD).

— (2005a) *Ageing and employment policies: Canada.* Paris: Organization for Economic Co-operation and Development (OECD).

— (2005b) *Ageing and employment policies: United States.* Paris: Organization for Economic Co-operation and Development (OECD).

— (2006) *Live longer, work longer.* Paris: Organization for Economic Co-operation and Development (OECD).

O'Rand, A.M. and Henretta, J.C. (1999) *Age and inequality: diverse pathways through later life.* Boulder, CO: Westview Press.

Pakans, A. (1989) Stepping down in former times: a comparative assessment of retirement in traditional Europe, in D.I. Kertzer and K.W. Schaie (eds), *Age structuring in comparative perspective.* Hillsdale, NJ: Lawrence Erlbaum Associates, 175–95.

Pentland, H.C. (1981) *Labour and capital in Canada, 1650–1860.* Toronto: James Loremont.

Peracchi, F. and Welch, F. (1994) Trends in labour force transitions of older men and women, *Journal of Labour Economics*, *12*(2), 210–42.

Phillipson, C. (1982) *Capitalism and the construction of old age*. London: Macmillan.

(1999) The social construction of retirement: perspectives from critical theory and political economy, in M. Minkler and C.L. Estes (eds), *Critical gerontology: perspectives from political and moral economy*. New York: Baywood, 315–18.

(2003) Globalization and the reconstruction of old age: new challenges for critical gerontology, in S. Biggs, A. Lowenstein and J. Hendricks (eds), *The need for theory: critical approaches to social gerontology*. Amityville, NY: Baywood, 163–79.

(2004) Work and retirement transitions: changing sociological and social policy contexts, *Social Policy and Society*, *3*(2), 155–62.

(2005) The political economy of old age, in M.L. Johnson, V.L. Bengston, P.G. Coleman *et al.* (eds), *The Cambridge handbook of age and ageing*. Cambridge University Press, 502–9.

Phillipson, C. and Smith, A. (2005) *Extending working life: a review of the research literature*. Norwich: Department of Work and Pensions.

Phillipson, C. and Walker, A. (1987) The case for a critical gerontology, in S. DeGregorio (ed.), *Social gerontology: new directions*. London: Croom Helm, 1–15.

Pienta, A.M. (2003) Partners in marriage: an analysis of husbands' and wives' retirement behaviour, *Journal of Applied Gerontology*, *22*(3), 340–58.

Platman, K. and Taylor, P. (2004) Age, employment and policy, *Social Policy and Society*, *3*(2), 143–4.

Pyper, W. (2006) Aging, health and work, *Perspectives on Labour and Income*, *18*(1), 48–58.

Quadagno, J.S. and Hardy, M.A. (1996) Work and retirement, in R. Binstock and L. George (eds), *The handbook of aging and the social sciences*. New York: Academic Press, 325–45.

Quadagno, J.S. and Reid, J. (1999) The political economy perspective in aging, in V.L. Bengston and K.W. Schaie (eds), *Handbook of theories of aging*. New York: Springer, 344–58.

Quinn, J.F. (1999) Retirement patterns and bridge jobs in the 1990s, *EBRI Issue Brief*, *206*, 1–22.

Quinn, J.F. and Burkhauser, R.V. (1990) Work and retirement, in R. Binstock and L. George (eds), *Handbook of aging and the social sciences*, 3rd edn. New York: Academic Press, 307–27.

Quinn, J.F., Burkhauser, R.V. and Myers, D.L. (1990) *Passing the torch: the influence of economic incentives on work and retirement*. Kalamazoo, MI: W.E. Upjohn Institute for Employment Research.

Reitzes, D.C., Mutran, E.J. and Fernandez, M.E. (1996) Preretirement influences on postretirement self-esteem, *Journals of Gerontology. Series B, Psychological Sciences and Social Sciences*, *51*(5), 8242–9.

Reno, V. (1971) *Why men stop working at or before age 65*. Rockville, MD: US Department of Health, Education and Welfare, Social Security Administration, Office of Research and Statistics.

Riley, M.W. (1997) Rational choice and the sociology of age: heuristic models, *American Sociologist*, *28*(2), 54–60.

Riley, M.W., Foner, A. and Riley, J.W., Jr (1999) The aging and society paradigm, in V.L. Bengston and K.W. Schaie (eds), *Handbook of theories of aging*. New York: Springer, 327–43.

Riley, M.W., Johnson, M.E. and Foner, A. (1972) *Aging and society. Vol. 3: A sociology of age stratification*. New York: Russell Sage.

Riley, M.W., Kahn, R.L. and Foner, A. (eds) (1994) *Age and structural lag*. New York: Wiley.

Rowe, G. and Nguyen, H. (2003) Older workers and the labour market, *Perspectives on Labour and Income*, *15*(1), 55–8.

Rowe, J.W. and Kahn, R.L. (1997) Successful aging, *The Gerontologist*, *37*(4), 433–40.

Schellenberg, G. (2003) Retirement transitions in Canada: evidence from the 2002 General Social Service. The 2003 Symposium on New Issues in Retirement. Ottawa, ON.

Schellenberg, G. and Ostrovsky, Y. (2008) *2007 General Social Survey report: the retirement plans and expectations of older workers*. Ottawa, ON: Canadian Social Trends, Statistics Canada.

Schellenberg, G. and Silver, C. (2004) *You can't always get what you want: retirement preferences and experiences*. Ottawa, ON: Canadian Social Trends, Statistics Canada.

Schellenberg, G., Turcotte, M. and Ram, B. (2006) The changing characteristics of older couples and joint retirement in Canada, in L. Stone (ed.), *New frontiers of research on retirement*. Ottawa: Statistics Canada, 199–218.

Schils, T. (2005) *Early retirement patterns in Europe: a comparative panel study*. Amsterdam: Dutch University Press.

Settersten, R.A., Jr (Ed.) (2003) *Invitation to the life course: toward new understandings of later life*. New York: Baywood.

Sheppard, H. (1990) The "new" early retirement: Europe and the United States, in I. Bluestone, R. Montgomery and J. Owen (eds), *The aging of the American workforce*. Detroit, MI: Wayne State University Press, 158–78.

Simon, H.A. (1997) *Administrative behavior: a study of decision-making processes in administrative organizations*, 4th edn. New York: Free Press.

Simpson, R.L. (1975) Review Symposium on Work in America, *Sociology of Work and Occupations*, *2*: 182–7.

Smeaton, D. and McKay, S. (2003) *Working after state pension age: quantitative analysis*. London: Department of Work and Pensions.

Smith, D. and Moen, P. (2004) Retirement satisfaction for retirees and their spouses: do gender and the retirement decision-making process matter?, *Journal of Family Issues*, *25*(2), 262–85.

Snell, J.G. (1996) *The citizen's wage: the state and the elderly in Canada, 1900–1951*. University of Toronto Press.

Statistics Canada (2000) *Women in Canada, 2000: a gender-based statistical report*. Ottawa, ON: Statistics Canada.

Stone, L. (ed) (2006) *New frontiers of research on retirement*. Ottawa, ON: Ministry of Industry.

Stone, L. and Nouroz, H. (eds) (2006) *New frontiers of research on retirement: technical annex*. Ottawa, ON: Statistics Canada.

Szinovacz, M. (1982) *Women's retirement: policy implications of recent research*. Beverly Hills, CA: Sage.

(2002) Couple retirement patterns and retirement age, *International Journal of Sociology*, *32*(2), 30–54.

(2006) Families and retirement, in L. Stone (ed), *New frontiers of research on retirement*. Ottawa, ON: Statistics Canada, 165–98.

Szinovacz, M. and Davey, A. (2005) Retirement and marital decision-making: effects on retirement satisfaction, *Journal of Marriage and the Family*, *67*, 387–98.

Szinovacz, M. and DeViney, S. (2000) Marital characteristics and retirement decisions, *Research on Aging*, *22*(5), 470–98.

Szinovacz, M. and Schaffer, A.M. (2000) Effects of retirement on marital conflict management, *Journal of Family Issues*, *21*, 367–89.

Taylor, F. (1947) *Scientific management*. New York: Harper.

The Times (2007) National employment policy justifies age bias, *The Times*, 23 October, p. 98.

Titmuss, R.M. (1968) *Commitment to welfare*. London: Allen and Unwin.

Tompa, E. (1999) *Transition to retirement: determinants of age of social security take up.* Hamilton, ON: SEDAP, McMaster University.

Turcotte, M. and Schellenberg, G. (2005) Job strain and retirement, *Perspectives on Labour and Income*, *17*(3), 35–9.

(2007) *A portrait of seniors in Canada, 2006.* Ottawa: Statistics Canada.

Vickerstaff, S., Baldock, J., Cox, J. *et al.* (2004) *Happy retirement? The impact of employers' policies and practice on the process of retirement.* Bristol: Policy Press.

Vickerstaff, S. and Cox, J. (2005) Retirement and risk: the individualisation of retirement and experiences?, *Sociological Review*, *53*, 77–95.

Walker, A. (1981) Towards a political economy of old age, *Ageing and Society*, *1*, 73–94.

(2005) Towards an international political economy, *Ageing and Society*, *25*, 815–899.

Wanner, R.A. and McDonald, L. (1989) Ethnic diversity and patterns of retirement, in J. Frideres (ed), *Multiculturalism and intergroup relations.* New York: Greenwood Press, 89–106.

Whiting, E. (2005) The labour market participation of older people, *Labour Market Trends*, *113*, 285–96.

Wise, D. (1993) Firms pension policy and early retirement, in A.B. Atkinson and M. Rein (eds), *Age, work, and social security.* New York: St. Martin's Press, 51–88.

Wolff, E.N. (2003) The devolution of the American pension system: who gained and who lost?, *Eastern Economic Journal*, *29*(4), 477–90.

Yeats, N. (2001) *Globalization and social policy.* London: Sage.

10 Sexuality and ageing

REBECCA FLYCKT AND SHERYL A. KINGSBERG

OVERVIEW

This chapter examines the topic of sexuality in older adults: sexual behaviours and attitudes about ageing; types of sexual dysfunction and their prevalence; physiology and pathophysiology of the male and female sexual response; medical conditions affecting sexuality; endocrinological, psychiatric and psychosocial factors; female and male sexual dysfunctions and disorders; assessment and treatment considerations.

Introduction

In this new millennium, the topic of sexuality in older adults has finally come of age. Whereas conversations about the sexual behaviours of mature men and women were once whispered and private, it is now acceptable openly to discuss these matters in magazines and newspapers, on television, and even at dinner parties. The psychological and physiological impact of ageing on sexuality is particularly timely for a variety of reasons. The first reason has been labelled the 'Viagratization of America', a phenomenon that has expanded worldwide (Kingsberg, 2002). The development of phosphodiesterase type-5 (PDE-5) inhibitors, beginning with Viagra (sildenafil) in 1998, sparked a renewed interest in exploring the sexual activities of older people. Once men had a non-invasive method for treating the inevitable sexual effects of ageing, the topic took the media world by storm. Previously a matter of patient reticence, older men began to present to their physicians anticipating the provision of particular therapies to enhance sexual performance. Viagra became a household name. Even a former American presidential candidate, Bob Dole, became a spokesperson for Viagra and discussed his erectile dysfunction (ED) in television ads. Although some criticize PDE-5 inhibitors for disrupting the sexual equilibrium among older couples or focusing attention too heavily on the mechanical aspects of sex, the growth of these medications on the market has clearly refocused attention on the sexual beliefs and practices of mature adults.

Second, and almost as apparent a reason, is that American baby boomers have become what Western culture now calls 'the young old'. This generation, who in its youth held the mantra, 'don't trust anyone over 30', is known for rejecting the lifestyle models of previous generations. Despite the fact that many people, including mature men and women, still hold a belief that 'sex is for the young', research has shown that interest in an active sexual life remains high in our older years. The myths of sexuality in mature people described by Henry and McNab (2003), such as lack of desire, fragility and inability to accomplish sex, and physical unattractiveness, are being broken down by a second sexual revolution. Robust, vivacious and sexy men and women in popular media, such as Tina Turner, Catherine Deneuve and Harrison Ford, have overturned cultural stereotypes of older people as withered, weak and asexual.

Third, research in the fields of sexual medicine and sociology is beginning to focus specifically on sexuality in the elderly. In the past, studies of sexuality have largely overlooked older adults. Clearly, there is an age-related decline in sexual behaviour and function; however, a satisfying sexual life is still a priority among older adults and is often achieved within this context. Newer studies have helped to identify rates of sexual dysfunction in older men and women, and physiological research is characterizing normal and abnormal changes observed in mature adults. Whereas it may be tempting to focus on easily quantified variables, such as how many successful episodes of coitus are achieved in a period of time or the presence or absence of ED, many researchers advocate exploring other relevant characteristics of sexual behaviour, such as interest in sex, satisfaction or enjoyment of sexual life, and sexual expectations and beliefs with ageing (Schiavi, 1999). Perhaps including these measures in our enquiries can offer a more multidimensional perspective on ageing and sexuality. Research into this topic has also begun to focus on the importance of redefining roles and expectations in an ageing population that still has interest and capability for an active and satisfying sexual life.

What follows is a discussion of normal and abnormal changes with ageing as well as information necessary for the evaluation and treatment of the most common male and female sexual dysfunctions. A key point to keep in mind in distinguishing normal age-related changes from true pathology should be the presence of patient and/or partner distress, not a quantified decrease in the frequency of or desire for sex. Additionally, what is described in this chapter should translate to older men and women regardless of sexual orientation, and heterosexual relationships should not be assumed in the elderly. Any and all therapies should be provided in a relevant social and cultural context, with sensitivity to diverse attitudes, beliefs, backgrounds and orientations among mature men and women.

Sexual behaviours and attitudes about ageing

The process of ageing, as with most aspects of life, produces significant changes in our sexuality. Most notably, sexual behaviour and function show clear and con-sistent age-related declines. Despite these, the majority of older people strongly disagree with statements like 'older people no longer want sex' or 'older people no longer have sex' (Nicolosi et al., 2004). Data from this same survey, the multi-national Global Study of Sexual Attitudes and Behaviors, which included 27,500 men and women between the ages of 40 and 80, demonstrated that 83 per cent of men and 63 per cent of women rated sex as being moderately to extremely important in their lives overall. The majority of these respondents had experienced intercourse in the past 12 months, and most had intercourse at least once per week (Laumann et al., 2006). These statistics reinforce the notion that well into our older years, adults both prioritize and engage in sexual activities.

The fact that older men and women retain an active interest in their sexual lives may initially seem at odds with data on changes in sexual behaviour and ageing. Although there is considerable individual variability in sexual activity with advancing age, most studies have demonstrated a steady, progressive decline in mature men and women (with women showing more significant declines than men). These trends in ageing were initially documented by Kinsey (Kinsey, Pomeroy and Martin, 1948) and reinforced by more recent studies (Lindau et al., 2007). For example, the Baltimore Longitudinal Study of Aging showed that as men and women age, the frequency of sexual intercourse and sexual activity collectively decreased and, to a lesser extent, sexual interest also decreased (Martin, 1975). Another study documented that the frequency of intercourse gradually diminished from an average of once per week in men aged 30–39 to once per year in men aged 90–99 (Mulligan and Moss, 1991). There is a noteworthy gender gap, as mature women at all ages are less likely than mature men to have an intimate relationship and to engage in sexual activities (Lindau et al., 2007). Other non-intercourse sexual behaviours have been shown to decline in older men and women as well, including activities like oral sex, masturbation, and touching and caressing. Similarly, sexual thoughts, fantasies and dreams tend to be less.

In contrast, there are some studies that show that, if sexual activity is retained in later years, the frequency of sexual events is similar to that observed in younger populations. For example, a national survey of thousands of older adults showed *if they remained sexually active*, the amount of sexual activity was similar to that observed in adults 18–59 years old in another comprehensive, population-based study (Lindau *et al.*, 2007; Laumann, Paik and Rosen, 1999). The concept of 'use it or lose it' seems to apply to sexuality among mature men and women; active and fulfilling sexual lives in our younger years are predictive of continued interest and engagement in sexual activities in older age.

Prevalence of sexual dysfunction and ageing

In addition to diminished frequency and interest, most studies have clearly shown that difficulties with sex are common with advancing age. However, the influence of ageing on sexual dysfunction can only be understood within the greater context of adult sexuality. At all ages, sexual dysfunction is highly prevalent in both men and women. The National Health and Social Life Survey (NHSLS) surveyed 1,410 and 1,749 American men and women, respectively, between the ages of 18–59, and reported that 31 per cent of men and 43 per cent of women had experienced a sexual problem within the past year (Laumann, Paik and Rosen, 1999). In 2007, the National Social Life, Health, and Aging Project reproduced these findings in ageing populations, reporting that among the 3,000 older American men and women surveyed, approximately half of all respondents had at least one 'bothersome' sexual problem (Lindau *et al.*, 2007). Despite the high prevalence of 'bothersome sexual problems' in both men and women between 57–85 years of age, the majority remained sexually active.

Dating back to the original data on prevalence of sexual dysfunctions described by Kinsey (Kinsey *et al.*, 1948; Kinsey, Pomeroy, Martin *et al.*, 1953) and the classic works on sexuality from Masters and Johnson in the 1960s and Helen Singer Kaplan in the 1970s, the sex lives of older adults have been infrequently addressed. Fortunately, several larger studies have been subsequently conducted to help clarify the nature and prevalence of male and female dysfunctions in older populations. For example, the Massachusetts Male Aging Study (Feldman, Goldstein, Hatzichristou *et al.*, 1994) reports significantly higher rates of ED than were previously acknowledged, with 40 per cent of men experiencing ED by age 40 and 67 per cent by age 70. It should be noted that all degrees of ED were included in this study, ranging from minimal ED to complete ED, and that complete ED appeared to be relatively uncommon in this sample. The multinational Men's

Attitudes to Life Events and Sexuality (MALES) study showed a similar trend for increasing frequency and severity of ED with advancing age (Rosen *et al.*, 2004). In the 20–29 age group, the rate was reported as approximately 8 per cent. However, men aged 60–69 had a rate of 30 per cent and men aged 70–75 reported rates as high as 37 per cent. These data were collected from almost 28,000 men across eight countries including the USA and UK, a sample representing one of the broadest and most comprehensive studies of ED to date. Statistics regarding prevalence of ED are in stark contrast to male interest in sexual activity with advancing age. Despite the high rates of ED cited above, 50 per cent of men over age 80 report having interest in sexual activity (Gentili and Mulligan, 1998).

Mature women also face their share of sexual difficulties, although they seem less likely to engage in conversations with health-care providers about their sexual well-being. Data from the National Social Life, Health and Aging Project showed that women were almost half as likely as men to have discussed sex with their doctor after age 50 (Lindau *et al.*, 2007). Similarly, women are less likely than men to look for treatments for sexual problems (AARP, 1999). A web-based survey of almost 4,000 women found that a striking 40 per cent of women did not seek help from a health-care provider for sexual function complaints, but 54 per cent said that they wanted to (Berman *et al.*, 2003). Although women may not be discussing problems with sex, studies show that female sexual dysfunctions are highly prevalent in older age. In fact, most studies demonstrate that sexual dysfunctions are *more* frequent in women than men at all ages (Walsh and Berman, 2004). Data from the 29 countries included in the Global Study of Sexual Attitudes and Behaviors showed that men reported consistently higher levels of subjective sexual well-being than women regardless of their socio-cultural context (Laumann *et al.*, 2006), a finding that contrasts with previous reports that women experience greater happiness and describe more intense positive emotions than men (Nolen-Hoeksema and Rusting, 1999). This same study also stated that women are more likely than men to rate sex as an unimportant part of life and to report lack of pleasure with sex.

The exact prevalence of female sexual dysfunctions in both younger and older women is unclear. The PRESIDE (Prevalence and Correlates of Female Sexual Disorders and Determinants of Treatment Seeking) trial, a large, USA-based study, reported the overall prevalence of sexual disorders to be 12 per cent for subjects meeting the 'distress' criteria for a true diagnosis and over 40 per cent for subjects reporting a sexual problem (Shifren, Monz, Russo *et al.*, 2008). Other studies of mature adults reporting 'problems' (not necessarily diagnoses) reinforce rates as high as 43 per cent for low desire, 39 per cent with poor lubrication, and 34 per cent with orgasm (Lindau *et al.*, 2007). Interestingly, the PRESIDE data indicated that sexual dysfunctions associated with distress were more common between the ages of 45–65 (versus both younger and older women). It may be that older women may

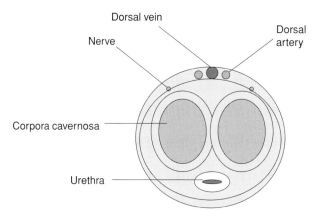

Figure 10.1 Cross-section of the penis.

have adjusted expectations about sexual function and can therefore experience greater satisfaction in their sexual lives despite the ineluctable consequences of an ageing body (Shifren *et al.*, 2008).

The National Council on the Aging (1998) survey of 1,300 Americans over age 60 confirmed that sexual activity plays an important role in relationships among ageing men and women. The majority of men and women agreed that sex was an important component of their relationship with their partner and about half reported being sexually active (at least once per month). Interestingly, 74 per cent of the sexually active men and 70 per cent of the sexually active women reported being as satisfied or *even more* satisfied with their sexual lives than they were in their forties. Despite the high prevalence of sexual dysfunction among older adults and the clear and significant decline in the frequency of their sexual interest and activity, sex and sexuality continues to be an important component in the lives of mature men and women. It is fair to state that when older people are completely sexually abstinent, it is almost always due to lack of an available partner or because of health problems. It is also important to highlight that natural changes of ageing do not necessarily correlate with perceptions of intimacy, pleasure or sexual satisfaction in older adults.

Physiology and pathophysiology of the male sexual response

The physiology of the male sexual response requires an understanding of male anatomy and function. The penis is composed of two parallel, sponge-like tissues, called the corpora cavernosa (Figure 10.1). Blood vessels run between the corpora cavernosa and control blood flow to and from these tissues. Under the influence of the parasympathetic nervous system, a vasodilator is released which causes the muscle in the walls of the blood vessels to relax. (The autonomic nervous system controls involuntary actions of the body over which we have little conscious control. It is divided into two components – the sympathetic and parasympathetic. In the main, the sympathetic instructs the body to change activity in one direction (*inter alia*, increase heart rate, raise blood pressure, suppress activities in glands and intestines), while the parasympathetic does the opposite.) Blood then leaks from the vessels and fills the corpora cavernosa, thereby achieving an erection (Meston and Frohlich, 2000). Once the corpora cavernosa are engorged with blood, the pressure blocks off the normal outflow of blood and the erection is maintained for sexual activity. While input from the parasympathetic nervous system dominates during erection, the sympathetic nervous system prevails in ejaculation. Sympathetic input induces the release of noradrenaline, which causes seminal fluid to move into the urethra (Schiavi, 1999). During orgasm, sexual pleasure peaks and a reflex is initiated. Rhythmic contractions of the reproductive organs and muscles propel the ejaculate through the urethra. Subsequently, tone in the blood vessels of the corpora cavernosa is restored to normal, and blood is allowed to flow away from the penis, returning the organ to its non-erect state.

In older men, normal physiological changes produce notable differences in sexual function. As men age, it takes longer to achieve an erection and the orgasm experienced generally takes longer, is weaker and has less volume of semen (Ginsberg, 2006). For example, in one study of men who reported good health, participants who were 48–65 years old had nearly a six times longer erectile response time while watching an erotic film than younger men (Solnick and Birren, 1977). In similar studies, although sexual interest by self-report remained high, there are documented significant age-related losses in both erectile capacity and time to erection (Rowland, Greenleaf, Dorfman *et al.*, 1993). Additionally, the refractory period (time between erections) has been shown to be longer in older men. Older men manifest changes in sexual function during rapid eye movement (REM) sleep as well. For example, the frequency, duration and degree of nocturnal penile tumescence decrease as men age. Even in men who reported regular intercourse with a partner and good sexual function, most men older than 60 did not achieve a full erection during sleep (Schiavi and Schreiner-Engel, 1988). This is in contrast to younger men under similar circumstances. These age-related changes are in keeping with physiological data that show older men have less sensation and vascular reactivity to stimuli in their extremities. Most likely, the pathophysiology manifest in the genitalia is reflective of global changes occurring throughout the body with normal ageing.

Generally speaking, ED results from either insufficient blood flow into the erectile tissues or from blood flowing too easily out of the erectile tissues. As mentioned earlier, muscle relaxation within the blood vessels is crucial in maintaining an erection, and the pathophysiology of ED is characterized by impairments in smooth muscle relaxation. One hypothesis of ED is that excessive input from the sympathetic nervous system overpowers the parasympathetic tone necessary to achieve erection. Alternatively, the endothelium (the inner lining of the blood vessel wall) may not respond appropriately to input from the parasympathetic nervous system. It is known that patients with medical conditions such as high blood pressure, high cholesterol or diabetes do not oxygenate their endothelium well, and perhaps the relaxation of endothelial smooth muscle in these populations is impaired. Venous incompetence may also play a role in the pathophysiology of ED in mature males. As venous vessels throughout the body become fragile with ageing, veins in the penis may allow leakage of blood from the penis during a stage when engorgement is critical to maintaining tumescence (Mulligan and Katz, 1989).

Physiology and pathophysiology of the female sexual response

Compared to that of males, the female sexual response remains poorly understood. Efforts have often been made to transform traditional sexual response models, such as the model originally described by Masters and Johnson in 1966, to better fit the complexities of women's sexuality. This primary model posited four sequential stages (excitement, plateau, orgasm and resolution), with desire preceding arousal. Helen Singer Kaplan and Harold Leif each revised this model to include the concept of desire as the first stage of the sexual response (Kaplan, 1977; Leif, 1977) However, more recent studies on sexual behaviour in women show that women's motivations for sex are complex and variable, and alternative non-linear cycles have been developed for the female sexual response (Basson, 2000). Feelings of desire are not necessarily what triggers sexual behaviour in women, and Basson has suggested that sexual behaviours in women tend to be more responsive than initiative (Basson, 2001). In this way, arousal is often present before desire in women.

The physiology of the female sexual response seems similar to the male, and results from the interplay of the sympathetic and parasympathetic nervous systems and the blood supply to the female sexual organs. The blood and nerve supplies to the vagina are similar to those of the penile shaft. The cycle of arousal begins with increased blood flow to the vagina and vulva. Consequently, the vulva swells, the vagina lengthens and dilates, and the clitoris enlarges and becomes more prominent and receptive to stimulation. More blood flow forces fluid to pass through the vaginal walls to lubricate the vagina. Orgasm occurs with rhythmic contractions of the muscles of the pelvic floor followed by the contraction of the uterus and vagina. Following orgasm, the muscles relax and blood flow decreases,

Table 10.1 Changes in female sexual physiology with ageing

- Atrophy of bladder and vagina mucosa
- Diminished vasocongestion and vaginal lubrication
- Narrowing and shortening of vagina
- Decreased oestrogenization of pelvic tissues
- Reduced muscle tone and tension
- Diminished elasticity of vagina
- Shrinking clitoral size
- Fewer uterine contractions with orgasm
- Increase in vaginal pH
- Decreased sensation and response to stimulation

allowing the vagina to relax and the uterus and cervix to return to their normal positions. This process can take up to 30 minutes in some women.

There appears to be a normal, gradual decrease in sexual interest and the sexual response in women as they enter menopause and older age (see Table 10.1 for a list of the physiological changes associated with ageing and female sexual function). Some of these changes have the potential to interfere with normal sexual functioning and cause significant distress. Notably, the decline in oestrogen levels during perimenopause as well as diminished blood flow to the vagina can cause symptomatic vaginal dryness. The decreased blood supply makes engorgement and lubrication for normal intercourse more difficult. As oestrogen levels decrease, the epithelial lining of the vagina can change quite rapidly from soft, pliant, elastic tissue to thin, weak, fragile tissue. These atrophic tissues are more prone to irritation and infection. Additional vascular, muscular and connective tissue changes occur over time. Decreased muscle tone in the pelvis can cause increased time to orgasm and diminished peak of orgasms.

Clitoral changes from ageing include shrinkage, a decrease in perfusion (swelling with blood), diminished engorgement during the desire and arousal phases, and a decline in the neurophysiological response, including slowed nerve impulses and a decrease in touch perception, vibratory sensation and reaction time. Decreased muscle tension may increase the time it takes for arousal to lead to orgasm, diminish the peak of orgasm, and cause a more rapid resolution. Additionally, the uterus typically contracts with orgasm, and with advancing age those contractions may become painful. Despite all of these ominous physiological findings, female sexual satisfaction does not appear to decline appreciably with ageing (Avis, Stellato, Crawford *et al.*, 2000; Laumann *et al.*, 1999). In fact, it should be noted that recent studies indicate that variables such as a woman's feelings about her partner, the presence of a partner with sexual problems, and overall feelings of well-being have greater effect on mature female sexuality than hormonal changes

(Avis, 2000; Hartmann, Philippsohn, Heiser *et al.*, 2004). Female sexuality is influenced by multiple factors, and data from the Massachusetts Women's Health Study II showed that mental health, smoking, marital status and general health had a more significant relationship with sexual functioning than menopausal status (Avis, 2000). In addition, interpersonal factors such as a partner's health, attractiveness and ability to communicate can have a significant impact on sexuality. This multidimensional model is likely to fit the experience of older women, whose desire levels have also diminished over time.

Medical conditions affecting sexuality

Not only does the ageing body experience problems with sexual functioning, but also the likelihood of developing other health problems increases in older age, with a subsequent impact on relationships and sexuality. Sexual problems can be due to physical limitations, lack of energy, side effects of medications or issues with self-image as a 'sick person'. From minor concerns such as decreased energy or strength to major illnesses such as cardiovascular disease, diabetes or cancer, the physical decline of the ageing body must be acknowledged and accommodated. Good coping skills in relation to ageing bodies can help to maintain a satisfying sexual life. The balance of a couple's emotional relationship also changes when one or both partners become ill or develop chronic health problems. As the primary caregiver, one partner may need to make considerable sacrifices of freedom and independence to provide for the continual needs of their partner. To look after an ill partner full-time, even functioning sometimes as a nurse, could result in an imbalance of roles with one or both people losing desire.

In populations of older men and women, medical conditions and prescription medications commonly relate to sexual difficulties. The presence of any disease entity, even a minor one, can dramatically impact sexual life. In the National Social Life, Health, and Aging Project, sexuality was closely tied with health, in men more so than in women. Subjective reports of 'poor health' have been associated with up to forty times the incidence of sexual dysfunction in men over age 70 (Mulligan *et al.*, 1998). Similarly, it has been shown that women with good health are more likely to have interest in sexual activities and to engage in sex (Avis, 2000). The relationship between health and sexual well-being either can be direct or can occur as the result of a complex interaction of physiological and psychosocial factors. Table 10.2 presents an illustrative list of conditions linked to sexual dysfunction.

Any illness that causes pain, limited mobility, malaise or weakness can have a negative effect on sexual functioning. However, of all of the medical co-morbidities, those that impair the proper functioning of blood vessels are the

Table 10.2 Medical conditions known to be related to sexual dysfunction (Phillips, 2000)

Cardiovascular
- Coronary artery disease
- Hypertension
- Dyslipidaemia
- Stroke

Haematogical
- Cancer/leukaemia
- Sickle cell disease

Endocrine
- Diabetes

Neurological
- Head injury
- Multiple sclerosis
- Epilepsy
- Spinal cord injury

Psychiatric
- Anxiety
- Depression
- Substance abuse

Other
- Chronic renal disease
- Chronic liver disease/hepatitis
- Chronic pulmonary disease
- Urinary dysfunction
- Degenerative disease

most likely to produce sexual dysfunctions, commonly ED in men and lubrication difficulties in women. Diseases such as diabetes, hypertension, coronary artery disease, stroke, peripheral vascular disease and hyperlipidaemia (excess lipids in the blood) have the clearest association with sexual dysfunction. Chronic renal or hepatic disease has been linked to difficulties with sexual desire and/or arousal, probably through multiple mechanisms. Alcohol use and abuse, which are common in older men especially, are known to contribute to difficulties with sex. Additionally, tobacco use is known to induce injury to the lining of blood vessels, and erectile difficulties are twice as common in smokers versus nonsmokers (Nakagawa, Watanabe, Ohe *et al.*, 1990). It should be noted that most diseases that are associated with sexual dysfunction are treatable, but that these treatments may not resolve the sexual problems (Mulligan *et al.*, 1998). For example, improvement in haemoglobin A1C levels in diabetics does not necessarily correlate with reduced ED (Yaman, Akand, Gursoy *et al.*, 2006). In addition, although there is evidence for a vascular origin for sexual dysfunction in the elderly, there are still no arterial or venous corrective surgeries that have been proven to restore normal functioning.

Diabetes is among the most frequent medical conditions associated with sexual dysfunction, with ED occurring in roughly 25–60 per cent of men with diabetes (Schiavi, Stimmel, Mandeli *et al.*, 1993), and worsening with age. In addition to ED, men with diabetes also demonstrated markedly decreased rates of desire, arousal, activity and satisfaction. For female patients, diabetes can cause decreased vaginal lubrication and possible lessening of libido (Ginsberg, 2006). The relationship between diabetes and sexual dysfunction is likely due to the vasculopathy and neuropathy commonly found in long-standing diabetics. There is also often associated high blood pressure, high cholesterol and peripheral vascular disease, which can negatively impact both male and female sexual functioning.

It should be noted that men presenting with erectile difficulties should be assessed for other underlying medical illnesses. ED appears to be a marker of poor blood flow throughout the body, and these patients are likely to need evaluation for additional vascular diseases. Potentially, the early detection and treatment of other vascular problems in patients with ED can lower their risk of stroke, heart disease or peripheral vascular disease.

Medications are another possible contributor to sexual dysfunction, and in the USA elderly men and women take an average of six medications per day, with inhabitants of other industrialized countries not far behind (Henry and McNab, 2003). Medications that have been implicated in sexual dysfunction include antidepressants, particularly SSRIs (selective serotonin reuptake inhibitors), neuroleptics and antihypertensives. Up to 10 per cent of older people take an antidepressant, and SSRIs have been associated with some degree of sexual dysfunction in up to 80 per cent of patients (Rosen, Lane and Menza, 1999). Patients with a medication-induced problem will classically present with more sudden onset of the dysfunction, associated with starting a new medication. Discontinuation often results in the restoration of normal sexual functioning. See Table 10.3 for a list of medications that have been linked to sexual dysfunction.

Lastly, cancer and cancer treatments are often associated with sexual dysfunction. Prostate hyperplasia (abnormal increase in number of cells) and malignancy occur commonly in older men. Male sexual dysfunction attributable to prostate disease is usually due to the presence of a new lesion or the result of treatments. Local radiation and decreased innervation due to surgery are both known risk factors for the development of sexual dysfunction. For women, breast cancer and gynaecological malignancies can have a tremendous impact on self-image and feelings of sexuality. Vaginal dryness, post-surgical discomfort, lymphoedema (swelling due to accumulation of lymph fluid) and the side effects of chemotherapy can hinder both a woman's desire for sex and her ability to engage in sexual activities (Ginsberg, 2006; Kaiser, 2003).

Table 10.3 Medications known to have sexual side effects (Kingsberg and Janata, 2007)

Psychotropic medications
- **Antidepressants**
  - SSRIs (selective serotonin reuptake inhibitors)
  - MAOIs (monoamine oxidase inhibitors)
  - TCAs (tricyclic antidepressants)
  - Trazodone
- Mood stabilizers
  - lithium
- Antipsychotics
- Benzodiazepines
- Barbiturates
- Antiepileptics
  - phenytoin
- Amphetamines

Antihypertensive and cardiovascular medications
- Beta blockers
- Alpha blockers
- Diuretics (thiazides and spironolactone)
- Lipid-lowering medications
- Digoxin
- Methyldopa
- Clonidine

Other
- Antihistamines
- Narcotics
- Indomethacin
- Ketoconazole
- Hormonal preparations
  - Oral contraceptives
  - Oestrogens and progestins
  - Antiandrogens
  - GnRH agonists
  - Danazol
  - Steroids

Endocrinology of sexuality and ageing

Hormones play an important role in normal sexual functioning, regardless of age, for both men and women. Additionally, hormone imbalances have been implicated in sexual dysfunction. In men, testosterone deficiency or hypogonadism (underactive sex organs) may underlie hypoactive sexual desire and, less frequently, ED. Only approximately 5 per cent of cases of ED are attributable to low circulating levels of the testosterone (Mulligan, 1989). Hypothyroidism or elevated prolactin (a hormone) levels have also been found to contribute to male sexual dysfunction, although this aetiology is far less common than hypogonadism. High prolactin levels can be the result of medications, hypothalamic-pituitary tumours, or chronic renal disease. These elevations can be associated with depressed testosterone levels and may impair sexual desire and erectile capacity. Note, however, that in this scenario testosterone supplementation has not been shown to correct the dysfunction.

In recent years, a lively debate has arisen regarding the role of androgens (mainly testosterone) and androgen replacement for postmenopausal women. The importance of androgens in female sexual drive has been acknowledged for over 50 years (Greenblatt, 1942). Several recent large placebo-controlled, double-blind clinical trials have shown the efficacy and short-term safety of transdermal testosterone treatment for hypoactive sexual desire disorder (HSDD) (Braunstein *et al.*, 2005; Buster *et al.*, 2005; Davis *et al.*, 2008; Shifren *et al.*, 2006). However, although the data to date are encouraging, the long-term safety of testosterone supplementation is still unknown, particularly in relation to the risk of breast cancer and cardiovascular disease (Braunstein, 2007).

It is well understood that women achieve peak androgen production in their mid-twenties. Half of androgens are produced in the ovaries and the remaining 50 per cent comes from peripheral conversion of precursors produced by the ovaries and adrenal glands (Kingsberg, Simon and Goldstein, 2008). Healthy premenopausal women produce approximately 300 μg of testosterone per day, about 5 per cent of the daily production in men. Beginning in their early thirties, women gradually lose circulating testosterone and the adrenal preandrogens (androstenedione and dehydroepiandrosterone (DHEA)) in an age-related fashion (Davis, 2001). By the time most women reach their sixties, their testosterone levels are half of what they were before age 40. Testosterone, along with the metabolite dihydrotestosterone (DHT), is the most powerful endogenous androgen in both sexes. Testosterone travels through the body bound to albumin and sex hormone-binding globulin (SHBG). During the transition to menopause, women experience a decrease in SHBG alongside a decrease in oestrogen. Due to the decline in the binding protein, more active testosterone may be circulating through the body. Some perimenopausal women will notice an initial increase in sexual desire and activity around this time, perhaps because of the changes in SHBG production.

Besides normal ageing, androgen levels in women can also decline due to surgical removal of the ovaries (oophorectomy), premature ovarian failure, adrenal insufficiency, hypopituitarism, corticosteroid use and oestrogen replacement. Women who have their ovaries removed, even if they are removed postmenopausally, will experience a significant decline in total testosterone. Even a postmenopausal ovary is still producing approximately 40 per cent of a woman's testosterone (Buster *et al.*, 2005). Some women may notice this sudden decline in testosterone and may experience a loss of sexual desire.

Psychiatric factors

Research in the psychology of ageing reinforces that marked cognitive impairment and depression, although commoner, are nonetheless *not* normal aspects of becoming older (see Chapters 6 and 7). However, psychological problems are common contributors to sexual dysfunction and should be screened for, evaluated and treated if present. Dementia, characterized by a global deficit in memory and cognitive function, is also common and can contribute to a wide range of sexual difficulties. Alcohol abuse is a frequently encountered entity for men in later life, especially in conjunction with psychiatric illness. Older men are up to six times more likely than older women to have problems with alcohol abuse (Schiavi, 1999). Other drugs of abuse such as heroin or cocaine are much less commonly encountered, but questions regarding illicit drug use should not be omitted simply because of a patient's age.

Although sexual dysfunction is often described as either organic or psychogenic, it is often difficult to separate the two, and this distinction may be more of theoretical interest than clinical utility. It is clear that the mind has both excitatory and inhibitory effects on sexual arousal and response, and problems like anxiety and depression may interact with physiological causes of sexual dysfunction in ageing adults. For example, the association between ED and depression is high, with cause and effect probably moving in both directions. ED alone has been associated with depression rates as high as 50 per cent (Shabsigh *et al.*, 1998). In the Massachusetts Male Aging Study, the degree of depression rose in direct relation to the severity of the ED (Feldman *et al.*, 1994). Depression in women has a negative association with sexual satisfaction and frequency of sexual activities, and women with depression are more likely to endorse feelings of low desire (Avis, 2000; Hartmann *et al.*, 2004). Whereas sound mental health is associated with greater satisfaction with sex, increasing stress or anxiety are related to reduced sexual interest and function (Laumann, 2008).

Psychosocial factors in sexuality and ageing

Multiple interrelated factors can play a role in how sexual a person feels. Included among these are changes in careers/retirement, financial concerns, life stressors, physical or mental fatigue, excessive food or alcohol consumption, availability of a partner, or sexual difficulties (Lenahan and Ellwood, 2004). Many of these issues pertain to adults of any age, but some are unique to older men and women.

Sexual activity is strongly tied to the context of a person's relationship with their partner (if they even have a partner). However, we cannot use age as a reliable predictor of relationship status. Mature adults may be involved in a passionate new relationship, a long-term intimate relationship, a long-term non-intimate/distant relationship or no relationship at all. Adults of all ages would benefit from recognizing that the expectations about sexuality in long-standing relationships will differ from expectations that are about ageing bodies. David Schnarch (1997) contends that most of us are best able to achieve our 'sexual potential' later in life, e.g. our forties, fifties, and sixties. Discriminating between what he calls 'genital prime' and 'sexual prime', he contends that sexual peak is correlated less with age than with who one is as a person. True sexual intimacy is only attainable by individuals who have the capacity for emotional intimacy, and who trust and respect their partners. Although a long-term relationship does afford this kind of intimacy, there are also some undeniable sexual advantages to a new relationship. However, these exciting new relationships are as likely to occur in later life, after divorce, or after the death of a spouse, as they are in young adulthood (Kingsberg, 2002).

Social psychology theories can also help us to understand desire and sexuality in older adults. One concept that is particularly relevant to sexuality is *self-perception theory* (SPT). SPT proposes that people make attributions about their own attitudes, feelings and behaviours by relying on their observations of external behaviours and the circumstances in which those behaviours occur (Bem, 1965). As an example, imagine a 55-year-old woman who has been married for decades. Throughout her marriage she has had the drive to be sexual about once per week. Her husband, on the other hand, has had the drive to be sexual far more often, which has resulted in a sexual relationship where he is always the initiator. Through observations of her own behaviour, the woman begins to see her sexual role as the recipient, only engaging in sexual activities when asked. Although she may have been receptive to her husband's advances and enjoyed the encounters, the woman's self-perception is that her desire is minimal and that she is not a sexual person. Her self-perception is that of a person that hardly ever thinks of sexual activity on her own and certainly never initiates it. Another example of SPT is the self-perceptions that occur as a result of long-term relationships. In this case, both partners observe a lack of passion in their relationship. In the early stages of the sexual relationship, sex was exciting. Their passion was fed by novelty, mystery, challenge or even danger. But, as with all long-term relationships, passion gradually shifts to a dynamic of comfort, security and partnership. Many couples do not understand this normal progression and mourn the loss of excitement and passion, interpreting the change as a flaw in the relationship. In other words, they observe their own lack of passion and interpret this as meaning that they no longer have adequate desire for their partner.

Another useful social psychology concept is called the *overjustification hypothesis*. This argues that when an external reward is given to a person for performing an intrinsically rewarding activity, the person's intrinsic interest will decrease (Lepper, Greene and Nisbett, 1973). Imagine that our same 55-year-old woman responds to her husband's sexual initiation and experiences a reward, such as relief from guilt (a form of negative reinforcement) or from the demands of an unsatisfied husband, or alternatively, gratitude from her husband and more chores performed the next day. Subsequently, the true enjoyment of the sexual encounter may decline for her. The woman in this scenario now interprets her enjoyment as being primarily from the outside reward instead of the actual activity of sex.

It is clearly important to recognize how women perceive and interpret their own behaviours in relation to sex. Many women, due to self-perceptions and overjustification, perceive sex as a task or an obligation rather than an enjoyable experience and consider themselves sexually inadequate. In addition, people in long-standing relationships can interpret the natural decrease in excitement and passion as a failure of the couple rather than a normal adjustment. Therefore, even if health-care providers improve drive and overall desire, treatments can be undermined if they do not address and then alter these long-held misattributions.

The importance of context in understanding mature sexuality cannot be overstated, and one of the most significant psychosocial or contextual variables that affect older adults is the presence of partner sexual dysfunction. ED is often the cause of a decline or even cessation in sexual activities among older heterosexual couples or male homosexual couples. Many postmenopausal women are abstinent because of their male partner's erectile difficulties or his decline in libido. Conversely, mature women with a diminished interest and/or ability to engage in sexual activities may find that their partners ultimately abandon efforts within the context of their partnership, and may choose abstinence, masturbation or other relationships.

As a male partner begins to experience one sexual dysfunction, he may find that a vicious cycle results. For example, men with erectile difficulties may develop anxiety related to the sexual event. Anxiety can cause premature ejaculation (in an effort to quickly complete the sexual act before loss of erection) or can lead to the man focusing his attention on non-erotic stimuli, which exacerbates his ED. Both premature ejaculation and ED can cause depression and/or performance anxiety, which could then affect desire adversely. This negative feedback loop unfortunately occurs quite commonly in middle-aged and older men. The demands of the sex act create an environment of anxiety and fear, which is often followed by embarrassment or shame due to performance difficulties. The cycle is then perpetuated if no interventions are provided.

Although Viagra can help to ameliorate some of the physiological and mechanical problems of sex, the presence of the PDE-5 inhibitors can create a shift in the sexual equilibrium maintained within a couple. Women who initially adjusted to having a partner with a sexual limitation must once again adjust to a relationship that involves increasing demands for sexual activity. This scenario poses a challenge. Older people in more established relationships might need more time to accommodate the accompanying cognitive shift, and a new mindset about a sexual relationship. More importantly, mature women need more time for their bodies to readjust to a partnered sexual life. In contrast, once the male partner can achieve a reliable erection, he typically wants to use it immediately (unless there are other psychogenic factors contributing to avoidance of intercourse or low desire). Unfortunately, if intercourse has not been attempted for a long time, the woman's atrophic vagina has probably narrowed and become less elastic and will not be able instantly to accommodate a penis. The pain or injury associated with an abrupt resumption of sexual activity can lead to a secondary female sexual dysfunction of dyspareunia or vaginismus (respectively, painful intercourse and severe contraction of the vagina – see below). Heterosexual postmenopausal women who have been sexually abstinent should begin by slowly stretching their vaginas. This can be accomplished by using a finger or dilator gradually to enlarge the vagina so that it might ultimately accommodate a penis. In this scenario, sexual intercourse cannot be resumed immediately.

Culture also influences both men and women's perceptions of ageing and sexual behaviour. Pharmacia Corporation recently surveyed 1,200 women to see how ethnicity impacted perceptions of menopause. African-American women appeared to be the most optimistic about their menopausal transition, whereas Caucasian women were found to be the most anxious, Asian women were more muted about symptoms, and Hispanic women were the most stoic (Pharmacia Corporation, 2001). Some older people may also harbour more conservative beliefs and a narrower understanding of sexual life. During the first half of the twentieth century, sexual education and discussions of sexuality were often omitted in schools and homes. Older men and women may have internalized stereotypes that the elderly are uninterested and incapable of engaging in sex, that sex among older people is inappropriate and distasteful, and that older adults are physically unattractive and sexually undesirable (Riportella-Muller, 1989). Of course, individual backgrounds (including variables such as religion, educational level, sexual history, personality and marital status) can influence the wide range of sexual attitudes and knowledge found in ageing adults. Studies have demonstrated that not only younger adults, but older adults, too, often view mature men and women as less knowledgeable, less desirous, and less capable in matters of sex. Mature males may not be educated regarding normal age-related changes in sexual function, and may be concerned that changes they observe in their performance are abnormal, and reflective of decreased strength and virility. Simply providing sexual education therapy and reassurance about what is normal to these patients can lead to enhanced sexual activity and satisfaction ratings (White and Catania, 1982).

Feelings of sexual inadequacy must also be taken in context of a pervasive fear in ageing populations that they are becoming less capable in both mental and physical endeavours. Along with ageing comes retirement and illness, and mature men and women are concerned with continuing to be useful and worthwhile in the home and in society. Individuals who develop effective coping skills are able to adapt to new circumstances while preserving feelings of self-esteem, self-worth and satisfaction. Therapies in ageing adults with feelings of sexual inadequacy must be targeted towards putting into practice such coping mechanisms, which can reaffirm sexual self-worth and identity during the transition to later life.

Female sexual dysfunctions

Decreased vaginal lubrication is the most widespread and bothersome problem for older women, usually related to a lack of oestrogen stimulation in the reproductive tissues. In addition to this common concern, female sexuality can be affected by the presence of a variety of sexual disorders. The *Diagnostic and Statistical Manual of Mental Disorders* (DSM-IV-TR) (American Psychiatric Association, 2000) lists six female sexual dysfunctions: hypoactive sexual desire disorder (HSDD), sexual aversion disorder, female sexual arousal disorder (FSAD), female orgasmic disorder, dyspareunia and vaginismus. The three most common for mature women among these will be discussed below.

Hypoactive sexual desire disorder

HSDD is defined as 'absent or diminished feelings of sexual interest or desire, absent sexual thoughts or fantasies, and a lack of responsive desire' (Basson *et al.*, 2003). It is the most prevalent female sexual dysfunction for women of all ages (Laumann *et al.*, 1999; Shifren *et al.*, 2008). In the National Health and Social Life Survey, about one-third of women aged 18–60 experienced a loss of desire in the last year, a finding which has been shown to increase with time, especially after 60 years of age (Anastasiadis, Salomon, Ghafar *et al.*, 2002; Kingsberg, 2002). HSDD is also the sexual dysfunction that has often been associated with menopause because of diminishing testosterone levels. A study of over 2,000 pre- and postmenopausal women showed rates of low desire ranging from 26.7 per cent in premenopausal women to 52.4 per cent in postmenopausal women (West *et al.*, 2008). However, recent large-scale studies do not support the long-held belief that it is the menopause itself that causes HSDD. Instead, it appears to be age much more than menopausal status that is related to decreased sexual drive. In fact, decreased sexual drive is one of the most common and noteworthy changes that occur with normal ageing. The misattribution that menopause automatically results in loss of sexual drive is deep-rooted and can result in misguided and misdirected treatments by health-care providers. In fact, many health-care providers and even women themselves have difficulty in understanding the deceptively complex nature of sexual desire.

'Desire' refers to one's interest in being sexual and is determined by the interaction of three distinct but interrelated components: (1) drive; (2) beliefs/values; (3) motivation (Levine, 1992). Drive is spontaneous sexual interest, or the biological element of desire. It is characterized by sexual thoughts, feelings, and fantasies or dreams. It can also manifest as erotic attraction to others in proximity, seeking out sexual activity (alone or with a partner), and genital tingling or increased genital sensitivity. Drive is the component that is affected by declining testosterone levels. The second component of desire is based on an individual's expectations, beliefs and values about sexuality. People will have greater desire if their beliefs and values about sexuality are positive. The third component of desire is the psychological and interpersonal motivation. Motivation is guided by emotional or interpersonal factors and is characterized by the willingness of a person to engage in sexual activities with a given partner (Levine, 1992). This component is complex and elusive, but can have the greatest influence overall on desire.

Distinguishing drive from desire is very important when assessing sexual problems, as treatments vary widely based on which component or components of desire are compromised. For example, a woman might have a very strong sexual drive but if she is not motivated to be sexual (e.g. if there is conflict with her partner, if she is stressed at work, or if she has depression or anxiety), she will not act on that drive. Conversely, even if a woman has lost some of her biological drive but retains a strong interest in being close and intimate with her partner, she will still seek out and enjoy sexual encounters despite a lack of physical cues or interest. This differentiation of drive from desire is particularly important in understanding female sexuality. It also highlights gender differences in the sexual response cycle and is in keeping with Basson's model of a non-linear female response cycle (Basson, 2000). As previously described, for many women, particularly postmenopausal women, drive fades and is no longer the initial step in the response cycle. For many women, drive may have never been the first stage of being sexual. Instead, desire grows along with or after arousal and accompanies a shift from a point of sexual neutrality. Arousal may occur as a conscious decision, or it can come from a physical or emotional stimulus. Often arousal is the result of seduction or suggestion from a partner (receptivity). Older women should be counselled that decreases in the initial drive to be sexual are normal consequences of ageing and not the sign of a sexual dysfunction unless there is associated distress. This reality of ageing must be normalized for mature women to provide comfort and reassurance as well as to avoid a self-fulfilling prophecy.

Decreased desire has been linked to interpersonal issues (such as a predictable, boring sexual routine that develops over time, conflict within a relationship, or stress), medical problems, medication use or natural consequences of ageing. Before treating patients with this disorder, a full history should be explored to clarify whether an interpersonal cause rather than a biological cause could be at the root of the problem. Treatments include counselling (either alone or as a couple), treating medical or psychological conditions that can affect desire, adjusting medications known to decrease desire, and testosterone supplementation if decreased desire is thought to be related to the declining testosterone levels associated with ageing.

Female sexual arousal disorders

Many women at some point in their lifetimes experience difficulties in initiating or maintaining adequate lubrication for sexual activities. As women age, they often require more time and stimulation to become aroused than they did in their younger years. This can be due to medical conditions that can decrease blood flow to the genital area, or to decreased sensation that occurs globally with ageing and that can lessen response to stimulation. Atrophy of the vulva and surrounding tissues can also decrease sensation (Bachmann and Leiblum, 2004). Arousal disorders can interact with desire disorders as well, as arousal often precedes desire in older women. An important distinction in this category is between subjective sexual arousal, where women report a lack of sexual pleasure or excitement (but may still experience normal lubrication), and impaired genital arousal, where typical vulvar swelling or lubrication in response to stimulation is lacking. There is also a combined genital and subjective arousal disorder, where neither sexual excitement nor genital arousal is present. This last dysfunction is the most common clinical presentation for female arousal disorders.

Treatments for sexual arousal disorders consist of individual and couples counselling, vaginal lubricants and topical (applied to a specific part of the body) oestrogens. Couples therapy should be directed towards education about normal changes with ageing, and should encourage longer and more focused sexual stimulation as part of sexual activities. Sexual partners should also be encouraged to experiment and become creative in their sexual practices, thereby avoiding the pitfalls of a repetitive sexual routine (which can dampen desire and arousal). A variety of over-the-counter vaginal lubricants are available to facilitate genital comfort and stimulation. Once stimulation becomes less uncomfortable and more pleasurable to older women, both desire and arousal may increase. Additionally, exercising the vagina through regular activity seems to increase lubrication and reduce vaginal irritation with intercourse (Bachmann and Leiblum, 2004). Oestrogen, which is available through a wide range of delivery methods, may well be the best treatment for women who have vulvovaginal atrophy due to menopause, and can restore genital tissue and increase lubrication in postmenopausal women. However, systemic oestrogen use should be prescribed with caution given recent findings from the Women's Health Initiative (Rossouw *et al.*, 2002), and should be used at the lowest possible dose for the shortest possible duration. Fortunately, topical oestrogen (i.e. creams, pill, suppository or rings with an oestrogen reservoir) can often successfully resolve vulvovaginal atrophy and does not seem to carry the same risks as the systemic administration of oestrogen therapy. Finally, vacuum devices designed to improve blood flow to the clitoris have been developed and approved for use in the USA as a treatment for arousal disorders.

Dyspareunia

Dyspareunia is characterized by pain with penetration of the vagina or during intercourse. It is important for assessment and treatment to distinguish if the pain is localized to the entrance of the vagina ('superficial') or if the pain is experienced as deep in the pelvis or lower abdomen. Dyspareunia should also be distinguished from vaginismus, which is described as involuntary and unwanted contractions of the outer third of muscles in the vagina, which cause difficulties with vaginal penetration. Vaginismus is often the result of dyspareunia and is better characterized as a reflexive anxiety response to anticipated pain. Both disorders are common in older women as a result of vaginal atrophy secondary to declining oestrogen levels. In one survey of postmenopausal women, almost 30 per cent of subjects reported vaginal dryness, soreness or dyspareunia (van Geelen, van de Weijer and Arnolds, 1996). Oestrogen replacement therapy, unless medically contraindicated, will often prevent genital atrophy and preserve the integrity of female tissues (Freedman, 2000). Topical oestrogen cream or a vaginal oestradiol ring may help to act locally to prevent genital atrophy and vaginal dryness (Berman and Goldstein, 2001; North American Menopause Society, 2007).

Dyspareunia is a common finding in older women who attempt to resume intercourse after an extended period of abstinence due to their partner having a renewed interest in sexual activity (often as the result of treatment for ED). It can also occur when the vagina has atrophied (for example, after the death of a spouse), and sexual activity has resumed with a new partner. In addition to lubricants and low-dose vaginal oestrogens, counselling and behavioural exercises using vaginal dilators and progressive muscle relaxation can provide significant benefit.

Male sexual dysfunctions

As with women, DSM-IV-TR (American Psychiatric Association, 2000) lists several male sexual dysfunctions (MSDs), including premature ejaculation, delayed ejaculation, ED, HSDD and sexual aversion. The following discussion will focus on the two most common MSDs in older men: ED and HSDD. Although treatments for both are readily available, many older men do not gain access to available therapies due to communication barriers with health-care providers. Many men feel that, unlike other medical problems, sexual difficulties represent personal failure. Psychologically, this is associated with anxiety and feelings of low self-worth and inadequacy. Men with a sexual problem may see themselves as less masculine and less virile, and this shame can result in avoidance of the topic with health-care professionals. In addition, clinicians may themselves feel uncomfortable or uncertain broaching the topic of MSD with their patients, and may not ask the necessary questions to uncover a history of MSD. Because few male patients spontaneously express concerns regarding MSD with their providers, it is important that screening for MSD occurs at routine visits.

Erectile dysfunction (ED)

ED is the most common MSD in older males. It is defined as the persistent inability to achieve or maintain an erection sufficient for intercourse or masturbation. ED was previously called 'impotence', a term which is now avoided due to its obvious negative connotations. A key component of this diagnosis is its perseverance across time and situations, as many men experience transient ED at some point in their lives. For assessment and treatment purposes, ED is typically identified as either organic ED or psychogenic ED, although, most likely, difficulties attaining or maintaining an erection are due to multiple causes. If a purely psychogenic basis is suspected, several indicators can help to make the diagnosis. Psychogenic sexual dysfunction often appears suddenly, often in conjunction with an event of significance. Additionally, psychogenic problems are often present only in certain situations. For example, men with psychogenic ED may note that morning erections or nocturnal tumescence/ejaculation continue normally.

There have been several treatments employed in the treatment of ED prior to the proliferation of PDE-5 inhibitors on the market. In addition to medications, there are other options, including counselling and behavioural therapies, penile injection or urethral suppositories of medications that induce erections, external vacuum devices, topical creams and, as a last resort, penile implants. The patient, ideally along with his partner, should be presented with an array of options, rather than immediate prescribing of a PDE-5 inhibitor. It is important to ensure the right treatment fit for the patient as well as to attempt to engage a receptive partner prior to initiating treatment.

Penile injections and suppositories have existed for decades and provide results with minimal discomfort. These treatments work by introducing prostaglandins into the corpora cavernosa, which then leads to smooth muscle relaxation and ultimately erection.

Another less invasive option is the external vacuum device, perhaps one of the oldest and least expensive methods of achieving erection. Vacuum pumps help to fill the penis with blood and subsequently a tight-fitting band can be placed around the organ to help prevent premature venous drainage. Vacuum devices help to improve erectile function in the majority of men with ED. However, the discontinuation rate for this treatment is high due to discomfort in using the devices and dissatisfaction with the quality of the erections.

Notwithstanding these alternatives, oral PDE-5 inhibitors now represent the standard of care in the treatment of ED. These include sildenafil (Viagra), tadalafil (Cialis) and vardenafil (Levitra). The mechanism of PDE inhibitors is blockage of cyclic guanosine monophosphate (cGMP) degradation, which enhances smooth muscle relaxation and blood flow to the penis. All of the PDE-5 inhibitors have similar success rates of about 70 per cent (Gresser and Gleiter, 2002). These medications are less likely to benefit patients who have severe vascular disease or who have undergone prostate surgery. More importantly, they are contraindicated in men who are taking nitrates for cardiovascular illnesses, as the combination can produce severe hypotension and even death.

Interestingly, despite quoted efficacy rates as high as 82 per cent with sildenafil (Gresser and Gleiter, 2002) and documented improvements of quality of life and mood following treatment, many older men treated with medications for ED do not continue therapy. In fact, many men who seek treatment for ED do not even fill their prescriptions, and some who fill their prescriptions never attempt a trial of the medication. In the Men's Attitudes to Life Events and Sexuality (MALES) study, only 58 per cent of the men surveyed sought treatment for ED (Rosen et al., 2004). Of those who did, 34 per cent tried their prescription only once, 25 per cent filled their prescription but did not use it, and 29 per cent received a prescription but did not fill it. Only 16 per cent of men who had sought treatment for ED received a prescription, filled it, and were actively using it at the time of the survey. One easily correctible reason for the surprisingly high discontinuation rate is the lack of appropriate education around proper use. For example, it is important for both patients and clinicians to understand that, while these medications assist in achieving and maintaining erection, desire is a necessary prerequisite.

Despite the existence of proven therapies, lingering notions of sexual health as separate from physical health prevent some men who seek help from obtaining treatment. In the USA, although many insurance plans do pay for medications to address ED, some offer little to no coverage. The rationale is that ED is not a medical disorder, but a psychological or electively treated disorder. However, it is clear from studies focusing on quality of life that both the patient and the partner's quality of life are significantly improved after initiation of treatment for ED. In addition, self-esteem and emotional well-being have been shown to be significantly lower at 10 weeks after the initiation of treatment with sildenafil (Steidle, Stecher, Pace *et al.*, 2006).

Low sexual desire/HSDD

The most common hormonal cause of sexual dysfunction in older men is hypogonadism. It is known that there is a direct connection between androgens and sexual desire, and circulating testosterone levels decline with age. In fact, as men age, there is a normal decrease in serum circulating testosterone of about 1 per cent per year to an average of approximately 30 per cent lower testosterone levels in older men (Gray, Feldman, McKinlay *et al.*, 1991). It should be noted, however, that men with lower levels of testosterone often achieve erections without difficulty. In patients who do complain of loss of desire, testing of testosterone levels can be accomplished with a simple blood test. Studies of men with hypogonadism and subsequent HSDD have helped to establish normal serum blood levels for testosterone in males, below which dysfunction in desire and arousal can occur. In addition to waning levels of testosterone, cerebral monoamines, endorphins and luteinizing hormone-releasing hormone show age-related declines, and may play a role in sexual desire and functioning.

Primary HSDD without concomitant ED, although the second most reported MSD in ageing men, represents only a fraction of cases of MSD. It is much more typical for HSDD to present with secondary ED. Therefore, the key to assessment and treatment in this case is to determine whether the HSDD is the primary disorder or whether ED is the primary disorder. Treatment may be quite different based on whether HSDD is the cause or the result of ED.

As with other MSDs, low desire can be associated with medical illnesses. The illnesses most commonly found in conjunction with low desire are those that hinder mobility, such as arthritis, paralysis and neurological disorders. In addition, older males with cardiovascular disease often fear that sexual activity will precipitate a cardiac event, a fear that causes both low libido and ED. Multiple reports have demonstrated that men who have suffered a heart attack have fewer sexual events and less enjoyment of sex. Depression is also often found in patients with HSDD. Although HSDD can certainly interfere with a patient's quality of life to the extent that depression results, more often HSDD is a symptom of a depressive episode. Furthermore, depression and HSDD are often correlates of underlying serious medical conditions, including hypogonadism and cardio-vascular disease. It is important to note that the side effects of medications commonly prescribed for depression may cause both ED and HSDD. Other medications commonly linked to HSDD are the thiazide diuretics used to treat high blood pressure.

Testosterone supplementation, when administered appropriately to men with a documented deficiency, can quickly restore sexual drive and normal erectile functioning.

Older men with HSDD who have subnormal levels of testosterone for their age may achieve enhanced desire as well as non-sexual benefits with testosterone ther-apy. Men who took testosterone for underlying hypogonadism also had improved maintenance of bone density as well as better energy levels and an enhanced sense of well-being (Wang *et al.*, 1996). Careful diagnosis of which MSD is the primary sexual problem is important. Supplementing testosterone in patients with ED that is unrelated to the HSDD may increase desire for or frequency of sexual events, but is unlikely to assist strength of the erection. Testosterone can be administered in oral, parenteral and transdermal forms. Of all delivery routes, transdermal testos-terone (gels and patches) has the most promising side-effect profile and appears to mimic most closely normal physiology.

As with female patients, pharmacological agents are only one component of therapy, and male HSDD can also be ameliorated with psychological and behavioural interventions. As stated earlier, older couples can fall into predictable schedules and habits of sexual behaviour and may experience boredom and loss of desire as a result. Behavioural therapies can be targeted to enhance communi-cation, creativity and pleasure, and expand the range of sexual activities. Often redirecting the focus away from concerns about an unreliable penis and diffi-culties with penetration can allay anxieties about sexual performance in older couples.

Assessment and treatment considerations for the older patient

Although ageing may contribute to changes in the sexual dynamics of a rela-tionship, a number of treatment modalities are available, both psychological and medical. Training as a sex therapist is not necessary to effectively address many of the sexual problems of ageing patients. Instead, counsellors and health-care providers can easily provide a basic assessment and evaluation. If necessary, with minimal education they can provide helpful treatments or, alternatively, know when to refer. The most valuable step towards treating older adults can be taken just by initiating a discussion about sexual concerns. By asking about sexuality, the patient receives a message that it is appropriate to discuss sexual problems, and this validates a person's self-perception as a sexual being. No sexual dysfunction can be treated if it is not first assessed or acknowledged.

In addition simply to asking about matters of sexuality, the detection of sexual dysfunction hinges on good clinical procedures, including a sound medical and sexual history, a detailed physical examination, and sometimes basic laboratory testing. Taking a sexual history can be performed either directly or through indirect patient questionnaires. It is important in these discussions to use basic and candid language that will make the patient feel more comfortable. The use of clinical terms should be tailored to the patient's own choice of words or to terms that can be understood regardless of educational level. Open-ended questions can be useful at the outset to allow the patient room to bring up topics that may feel uncomfortable. Ideally, the partner is also interviewed. Evaluation of both men and women must take into account that there is a wide range of what constitutes 'normal' sexual behaviour in ageing adults. According to the DSM-IV-TR, a dysfunction is associated with patient and/or partner distress or dissatisfaction rather than an objective quantification of what is 'normal' frequency, desire or duration of sexual activity.

A thorough history should include the onset of the disturbance, whether the dysfunction began in conjunction with other medical co-morbidities or medication use, and whether normal sexual function still occurs in other contexts (e.g., with ED, do erections occur during masturbation, during sleep or in the morning?). The history should also include a survey of factors that make the condition better or worse. Patients with clear evidence of psychopathology, such as depression or dementia, can be offered further psychological counselling or therapy.

In mature men and women, health-care providers often overlook asking about, screening for and treating sexually transmitted infections. As people are living longer and often adding one or more new sexual partners in their older years, their likelihood increases of contracting gonorrhea, chlamydia, herpes, trichomoniasis or even more serious sexually transmitted infections such as syphilis or HIV/AIDS. In fact, postmenopausal women are even more likely than their younger counterparts to contract HIV infection after an exposure, due to lessened lubrication and atrophic vaginal walls (Senior, 2005). Older women with a new sexual partner should also be screened with Pap smears to detect abnormal cells related to human papillomavirus infection.

A physical exam should be conducted when a dysfunction is investigated. In men, the exam should look for evidence of endocrine disorders that have been associated with MSD, such as hypogonadism or hypothyroidism. In addition to the gonads, the penis should be carefully examined for structural abnormalities. Most importantly, the neurological and vascular systems should be investigated. In women, the external genitalia should be examined for atrophy, and an internal exam should evaluate for pelvic organ prolapse or vaginismus with entry into the vagina. For both sexes, a full neurological exam can identify deficiencies in sensation, reflexes and blood flow. In males, the cremasteric and bulbocavernosus reflexes should be intact, even into old age. (In the cremasteric reflex, a pointed object run along the thigh should cause the testis on the same side of the body to rise; in the bulbocavernosus reflex, there is a muscular contraction of the rectum when the tip of the penis or clitoris is squeezed.)

Laboratory testing should include a hormone profile. Although endocrine assessment (including total and bioavailable testosterone, prolactin and thyroid measurements) seems clearly indicated when low libido is present in males, there is considerable debate regarding the utility of laboratory testing in investigations of ED. Some would suggest that a minimum of testosterone level testing is necessary with ED, while others argue that this testing is only necessary in cases related to male hypogonadism. Additional testing for both sexes can include correlates of underlying vascular and/or neuropathic dysfunction, such as serum glucose (for diabetes), serum lipids (for hyperlipidaemia), creatinine (for renal dysfunction), and prolactin and thyroid tests (for endocrine causes). In men, prostate function can be assessed with a (prostate-specific antigen) PSA level.

If a problem is identified, in addition to the medical and psychological treatments outlined in previous sections, health-care providers can provide basic sex education and encourage patients to expand or change their sexual repertoire. For example, many couples are unaware of the fact that, despite ED, men are still able to experience desire, arousal and orgasm. Even within a sexually enlightened culture, older couples may still retain fairly restrictive and conservative views of what is 'appropriate' and 'normal'. In this case, treatment can be tailored to help older women and couples redefine what 'normal' sexual activity involves. Couples struggling with ED or genital atrophy may find great relief in knowing that sexual intercourse need not be the 'main event', and that sexual and/or sensual activities can help achieve mutual satisfaction and intimacy. Teaching older couples to vary their sexual positions from the standard 'missionary' approach may be difficult, but could ultimately help to achieve more comfort with intercourse. Mature men and women may benefit from less strenuous positions and alternate methods of stimulation (e.g. increased use of oral sex, manual stimulation, sexual aids and sensual non-genital activities like bathing together, massage or erotic movies/literature – see Leiblum, 1991). Small adjustments can result in notable improvement in sexual fulfilment. A small change can be as simple as suggesting that couples make love in the morning when energy is higher for ageing men and women rather than late in the evening when fatigue can be significant. Furthermore, improved communication, both in and out of the bedroom, is imperative in older couples, even with partners that have been together for decades. A couple needs to be able to communicate effectively in order to navigate smoothly a change in sexual repertoire. In addition, discussion and communication about sex itself can be seductive, enticing and sexual. Effective communication in everyday life can enhance the quality of the overall relationship, which will provide additional benefit to the sexual dynamic of the couple.

Conclusions

Sexual interest and expression remain high in older adults despite normal, age-related changes in sexual activity and physiology. Chronic illness, which is widespread in both mature men and women, can interact with hormonal, vascular and endocrine causes to produce sexual dysfunctions. Although sexual dysfunctions are often a topic of both patient and clinician reticence, common disorders such as HSDD in women or ED in men do respond to intervention. A thorough history involving the patient and, ideally, their partner, a physical exam, and a limited laboratory assessment are indicated. Psychological and relationship factors should be taken into account when assessing and providing appropriate treatments for sexual difficulties. Treatments should be multidisciplinary and should address both individual and partner goals and expectations. Sexual satisfaction, rather than performance, should be emphasized in ageing populations. Education regarding normal ageing, which can provide reassurance and emphasize coping mechanisms, can be invaluable when counselling mature patients about their sexual concerns. Prioritizing sexual health as a component of overall health must be a goal for today's health-care providers to ensure good quality of life for older adults.

Summary

The topic of sexuality in later life has arguably come of age in the last few years, and the continuation of sexual activity of some description into old age is the norm. However, the incidence of sexual dysfunction increases in later life. The forms dysfunction can take are discussed in detail, beginning with pathophysiological changes in the male sexual response, followed by female sexual response. Medical conditions common to later life that can affect sexual functioning are then examined, along with unwanted side effects from common methods of treatment of these conditions. Particular attention is paid to the endocrinology of the ageing body and its effects on sexual functioning. It is noted that, in addition to physical causes, psychiatric and psychosocial factors can also have a profound influence, and these are discussed. Gender-specific dysfunctions (including gender-related types of HSDD such as hypogonadism, dyspareunia and ED) and their treatments are critically considered. Finally, assessment and treatment considerations for the older patient are addressed.

REFERENCES

AARP/Modern Maturity Sexuality Survey (1999) Washington, DC: National Family Opinion (NFO) Research.

American Psychiatric Association (2000) *Diagnostic and statistical manual of mental disorders*, 4th edn, text revision (DSM-IV-TR). Washington, DC: APA.

Anastasiadis, A.G., Salomon, L. and Ghafar, M.A. *et al.* (2002) Female sexual dysfunction: state of the art, *Current Urology Reports*, 3(6), 484–91.

Avis, N.E. (2000) Sexual function and ageing in men and women: community and population based studies, *Journal of Gender-Specific Medicine*, 37(2), 37–41.

Avis, N.E., Stellato, R., Crawford, S. *et al.* (2000). Is there an association between menopause status and sexual functioning?, *Menopause*, 7, 297–309.

Bachmann, G.A. and Leiblum, S.R. (2004) The impact of hormones on menopausal sexuality: a literature review, *Menopause*, 11(1), 120–30.

Basson, R. (2000) The female sexual response: a different model, *Journal of Sex & Marital Therapy*, 26(1), 51–65.

(2001) Human sex-response cycles, *Journal of Sex & Marital Therapy*, 27(1), 33–43.

Basson, R., Leiblum, S., Brotto, L. *et al.* (2003) Definitions of women's sexual dysfunction reconsidered: advocating expansion and revision, *Journal of Psychosomatic Obstetrics and Gynaecology*, 24(4), 221–9.

Bem, D. (1965) An experimental analysis of self-persuasion, *Journal of Experimental Social Psychology*, 1, 199–218.

Berman, J.R. and Goldstein, I. (2001) Female sexual dysfunction, *Urology Clinics of North America*, 28(2), 405–16.

Berman, L., Berman, J., Felder, S. *et al.* (2003) Seeking help for sexual function complaints: what gynecologists need to know about the female patient's experience, *Fertility and Sterility*, 79(3), 572–6.

Braunstein, G.D. (2007) Management of female sexual dysfunction in postmenopausal women by testosterone administration: safety issues and controversies, *Journal of Sexual Medicine*, 4(4 Pt 1), 859–66.

Braunstein, G.D., Sundwall, D.A., Katz, M. *et al.* (2005) Safety and efficacy of a testosterone patch for the treatment of hypoactive sexual desire disorder in surgically menopausal women; a randomized, placebo-controlled trial, *Archives of Internal Medicine*, 65(14), 1582–9.

Buster, J.E., Kingsberg, S.A., Aguirre, O. *et al.* (2005) Testosterone patch for low sexual desire in surgically menopausal women: a randomized trial, *Obstetrics and Gynecology*, 105, 944–52.

Davis, S.R. (2001) Testosterone treatment: psychological and physical effects in post-menopausal women, *Menopausal Medicine, 9*(2), 1–6.

Davis, S.R., Moreau, M., Kroll, R. *et al.* (2008) Testosterone for low libido in postmenopausal women not taking estrogen, *New England Journal of Medicine, 359*(19), 2005–17.

Feldman, H.A., Goldstein, I., Hatzichristou, D.G. *et al.* (1994) Impotence and its medical and psychosocial correlates: results of the Massachusetts Male Ageing Study, *Journal of Urology, 151*(1), 54–61.

Freedman, M. (2000) Sexuality in post-menopausal women, *Menopausal Medicine, 8*, 1–4.

Gatz, M., Kasl-Godley, J.E. and Karel, M.I. (1996) Ageing and mental disorders, in J. Birren and K.W. Schaie (eds), *Handbook of the psychology of ageing*, 4th edn. San Diego, CA: Academic Press, 365–82.

Gentili, A. and Mulligan, T. (1998) Sexual dysfunction in older adults, *Clinics in Geriatric Medicine, 14*, 383–93.

Ginsberg, T.B. (2006) Ageing and sexuality, *Medical Clinics of North America, 90*(5), 1025–36.

Gray, A., Feldman, H.A., McKinlay, J.B. *et al.* (1991) Age, disease, and changing sex hormone levels in middle-aged men: results of the Massachusetts Male Ageing Study, *Journal of Clinical Endocrinology and Metabolism, 73*(5), 1016–25.

Greenblatt, R.B. (1942) Hormone factors in libido, *Journal of Clinical Endocrinology and Metabolism, 3*, 305.

Gresser, U. and Gleiter, C.H. (2002) Erectile dysfunction: comparison of efficacy and side effects of the PDE-5 inhibitors sildenafil, vardenafil and tadalafil – review of the literature, *European Journal of Medical Research, 7*(10), 435–46.

Hartmann, U., Philippsohn, S., Heiser, K. *et al.* (2004) Low sexual desire in midlife and older women: personality factors, psychosocial development, present sexuality, *Menopause, 11*(6 Pt 2), 726–40.

Henry, J. and McNab, W. (2003) Forever young: a health promotion focus on sexuality and ageing, *Gerontology and Geriatrics Education, 23*(4), 57–74.

Kaiser, F.E. (2003) Sexual function and the older woman, *Clinics in Geriatric Medicine, 19*(3), 463–72.

Kaplan, H.S. (1977) Hypoactive sexual desire, *Journal of Sex & Marital Therapy, 3*, 3–9.

Kingsberg, S.A. (2002) The impact of ageing on sexual function in women and their partners, *Archives of Sexual Behavior, 31*(5), 131–7.

Kingsberg, S.A. and Janata, J.W. (2007) Female sexual disorders: assessment, diagnosis and treatment, *Urology Clinics of North America, 34*, 497–506.

Kingsberg, S.A., Simon, J.A. and Goldstein, I. (2008) The current outlook for testosterone in the management of hypoactive sexual desire disorder in postmenopausal women, *Journal of Sexual Medicine, 5* (Suppl 4), 182–93; quiz 193.

Kinsey, A.C., Pomeroy, W.B. and Martin, C.E. (1948). *Sexual behavior in the human male.* Philadelphia: W.B. Saunders.

Kinsey, A.C., Pomeroy, W.B., Martin, C.E. *et al.* (1953) *Sexual behavior in the human female.* Philadelphia: W.B. Saunders.

Laumann, E.O., Paik, A. and Rosen, R.C. (1999) Sexual dysfunction in the United States: prevalence and predictors, *Journal of the American Medical Association, 281*(6), 537–44.

Laumann, E.O., Paik, A., Glasser, D.B. *et al.* (2006) A cross-national study of subjective sexual well-being among older women and men: findings from the Global Study of Sexual Attitudes and Behaviors, *Archives of Sexual Behavior, 35*(2), 145–61.

Laumann, E.O. and Waite, L.J. (2008) Sexual dysfunction among older adults: prevalence and risk factors from a nationally representative U.S. probability sample of men and women 57–85 years of age, *Journal of Sexual Medicine*, **5**(10), 2300–11.

Leiblum, S.R. (1991). The midlife and beyond. Presented at the 2th Annual Postgraduate Course of the Psychology Professional Interest Group of the American Fertility Society, 'Sexual dysfunction: patient concerns and practical strategies', October, Orlando, FL.

Leif, H.I. (1977) Inhibited sexual desire, *Medical Aspects of Human Sexuality*, **7**, 94–5.

Lenahan, P. and Ellwood, A. (2004) Sexual health and ageing, *Clinics in Family Practice*, **6**(4), 17–39.

Lepper, M., Greene, D. and Nisbett, R. (1973) Undermining children's interests with extrinsic rewards: a test of the 'overjustification hypothesis', *Journal of Personality and Social Psychology*, **28**, 129–37.

Levine, S.B. (1992) *Sexual life*. New York: Plenum Press.

Lindau, S.T., Schumm, L.P., Laumann E.O. *et al.* (2007) A study of sexuality and health among older adults in the United States, *New England Journal of Medicine*, **357**(8), 62–74.

Martin, C.E. (1975) Marital and sexual factors in relation to age, disease, and longevity, in R.D. Wirdt, G., Winokur and M. Roff (eds), *Life history research in psychopathology*, vol. 4. Minneapolis, MN: University of Minnesota Press, 326–47.

Masters, W.H. and Johnson, V.E. (1966) *Human sexual response.* New York: Bantam Books.

Meston, C.M. and Frohlich, P.F. (2000) The neurobiology of sexual function, *Archives of General Psychiatry*, **57**(11), 1012–30.

Mulligan, T. and Katz, P.G. (1989) Why aged men become impotent, *Archives of Internal Medicine*, **149**(6), 1365–6.

Mulligan, T. and Moss, C.R. (1991) Sexuality and ageing in male veterans: a cross-sectional study of interest, ability, and activity, *Archives of Sexual Behavior*, **20**(1), 17–25.

Mulligan, T., Retchin, S.M., Chinchilli, V.M. *et al.* (1998) The role of ageing and chronic disease in sexual dysfunction, *Journal of the American Geriatrics Society*, **36**, 520.

Nakagawa, S., Watanabe, H., Ohe, H. *et al.* (1990) Sexual behavior in Japanese males relating to area, occupation, smoking, drinking and eating habits, *Andrologia*, **22**(1), 21–8.

National Council on the Aging (1998) *Healthy sexuality and vital aging.* Washington, DC: National Council on the Aging.

Nicolosi, A, Laumann, EO, Glasser, DB. *et al.* Global Study of Sexual Attitudes and Behaviors Investigators' Group (2004) Sexual behavior and sexual dysfunctions after age 40: the Global Study of Sexual Attitudes and Behaviors, *Urology* **64**(5), 991–7.

Nolen-Hoeksema, S. and Rusting, C. (1999) Gender differences in well-being, in D. Kahneman, E. Diener and N. Schwarz (eds), *Well-being: the foundations of hedonic psychology.* New York: Russell Sage Foundation, 330–50.

North American Menopause Society (NAMS) (2007) The role of local vaginal estrogen for treatment of vaginal atrophy in postmenopausal women: 2007 position statement of the North American Menopause Society, *Menopause*, **14**(3), 355–69.

Ofman, U., Kingsberg, S.A. and Nelson, C.J. (2008) Sexual problems and cancer, in V.T. DeVita, S. Hellman and S.A. Rosenberg (eds), *Cancer: principles and practice of oncology.* Philadelphia: Lippincott Williams and Wilkins, 2804–15.

Pharmacia Corporation (2001) New research on menopause and sexuality finds women are not seeking medical help for chronic symptoms affecting intimate relationship. Press release, 15 November. Peapack, NJ: Pharmacia.

Phillips, N.A. (2000) Female sexual dysfunction: evaluation and treatment, *American Family Physician*, *62*, 127–36, 141–2.

Riportella-Muller, R. (1989) Sexuality in the elderly: a review, in K. McKinney and S. Sprecher (eds), *Human sexuality: the societal and interpersonal context*. Norwood, NJ: Ablex, 210–36.

Rosen, R.C., Lane, R.M. and Menza, M. (1999) Effects of SSRIs on sexual function: a critical review, *Journal of Clinical Psychopharmacology*, *19*(1), 67–85.

Rosen, R.C., Fisher, W.A., Eardley, I. *et al.* (2004) The multinational Men's Attitudes to Life Events and Sexuality (MALES) study. I. Prevalence of erectile dysfunction and related health concerns in the general population, *Current Medical Research and Opinion*, *20*(5), 607–17.

Rossouw, J.E., Anderson, G.L., Prentice, R.L. *et al.* Writing Group for the Women's Health Initiative Investigators (2002) Risks and benefits of estrogen plus progestin in healthy postmenopausal women: principal results from the Women's Health Initiative randomized controlled trial, *Journal of the American Medical Association*, *288*(3), 321–33.

Rowland, D.L., Greenleaf, W.J., Dorfman, L.J. *et al.* (1993) Ageing and sexual function in men, *Archives of Sexual Behavior*, *22*(6), 545–57.

Schiavi, R.C. (1999) *Ageing and male sexuality.* Cambridge University Press.

Schiavi, R.C. and Schreiner-Engel, P. (1988) Nocturnal penile tumescence in healthy aging men, *Journal of Gerontology*, *43*(5), M146–50.

Schiavi, R.C., Stimmel, B.B., Mandeli, J. *et al.* (1993) Diabetes mellitus and male sexual function: a controlled study, *Diabetologia*, *36*(8), 745–51.

Schnarch, D. (1997) *Passionate marriage.* New York: Henry Holt.

Senior, K. (2005) Growing old with HIV, *The Lancet Infectious Diseases*, *5*(12), 739.

Shabsigh, R., Klein, L.T., Seidman, S. *et al.* (1998) Increased incidence of depressive symptoms in men with erectile dysfunction, *Urology*, *52*(5), 848–52.

Shifren, J.L., Davis, S.R., Moreau, M. *et al.* (2006) Testosterone patch for the treatment of hypoactive sexual desire disorder in naturally menopausal women: results from the INTIMATE NM1 study, *Menopause*, *13*(5), 770–9.

Shifren, J.L., Monz, B.U., Russo, P.A. *et al.* (2008) Sexual problems and distress in United States women: prevalence and correlates, *Obstetrics and Gynecology*, *112*(5), 970–8.

Solnick, R.L. and Birren, J.E. (1977) Age and male erectile responsiveness, *Archives of Sexual Behavior*, *6*(1), 1–9.

Steidle, C.P., Stecher, V.J., Pace, C. *et al.*; the SEAR Study Group (2006) Correlation of improved erectile function and rate of successful intercourse with improved emotional well-being assessed with the Self-Esteem and Relationship questionnaire in men treated with sildenafil for erectile dysfunction and stratified by age, *Current Medical Research and Opinion*, *22*(5), 939–48.

van Geelen, J.M., van de Weijer, P.H. and Arnolds, H.T. (1996) Urogenital symptoms and their resulting discomfort in non-institutionalized 50-to-75-year-old Dutch women, *Nederlands tijdschrift voor geneeskunde*, *140*(13), 713–16.

Walsh, K.E. and Berman, J.R. (2004) Sexual dysfunction in the older woman: an overview of the current understanding and management, *Drugs & Aging*, *21*(10), 655–75.

Wang, C., Alexander, G., Berman, N. *et al.* (1996) Testosterone replacement therapy improves mood in hypogonadal men – a clinical research center study, *Journal of Clinical Endocrinology and Metabolism*, *81*(10), 3578–83.

Wang, C., Eyre, D.R., Clark, R. *et al.* (1996) Sublingual testosterone replacement improves muscle mass and strength, decreases bone resorption, and increases bone formation markers in hypogonadal men – a clinical research center study, *Journal of Clinical Endocrinology and Metabolism*, *81*(10), 3654–62.

West, S.L., D'Aloisio, A.A., Agans, R.P. *et al.* (2008) Prevalence of low sexual desire and hypoactive sexual desire disorder in a nationally representative sample of US women, *Archives of Internal Medicine*, *168*(13), 1441–9.

White, C.B. and Catania, J.A. (1982) Psychoeducational intervention for sexuality with the aged, family members of the aged, and people who work with the aged, *International Journal of Aging & Human Development*, *15*(2), 121–38.

Yaman, O., Akand, M., Gursoy, A. *et al.* (2006) The effect of diabetes mellitus treatment and good glycemic control on the erectile function in men with diabetes mellitus-induced erectile dysfunction: a pilot study, *Journal of Sexual Medicine*, *3*(2), 344–8.

11 Policies on ageing

SUZANNE WAIT

OVERVIEW

. . . .

After defining policies on ageing, historical and cross-cultural perspectives are presented. Issues relevant to the formulation/implementation of ageing policies are discussed. Three case studies are presented: age equality, malnutrition and human resources for health. Drawing on these, the chapter concludes by examining future challenges.

. . . .

Introduction

Italy has one of the lowest birth rates and highest levels of life expectancy in Europe. As a result, the traditional multi-generational home with 'Mamma' at the centre is not necessarily as common as it may have been decades ago. A significant number of older people have resorted to taking on immigrant women as live-in carers, who effectively assume the role traditionally played by a daughter, daughter-in-law or niece. This trend has become so common that a special term has been created to designate these women: *badanti*. Moreover, the Italian government has introduced special concessions in immigration law to secure legal residence status for the *badanti*. The growth of the *badanti* population, however, raises several concerns. There is a chronic shortage of care workers trained to work with older people and *badanti*, like other care workers, require training and skills development. As single immigrant women, *badanti* are socially isolated and often lack proper social protection and social networks of their own. There is the need for communication and coordination between home care provided by *badanti* and community services. And most importantly: who will care for the *badanti* when they, in turn, grow old?

This particular example illustrates the complexity and multifaceted nature of policies on ageing. It also serves as a note of caution about this chapter. First, the reader should be aware that to present a review of all policies related to ageing would be both impossible and unwieldy given the breadth of topics to be addressed. Such a review would also rapidly become obsolete as policies evolve continually. The second caveat is that policies on ageing are specific to their national and cultural context.

To counter these risks, this chapter steers away from discussing actual policies in great detail and instead frames discussions around the issues that arise in existing policies on ageing and the factors that need to be taken into account in their implementation. However, specific case studies in three chosen areas of policy are provided to help focus discussions. Also, examples are drawn mostly from the region with which this author is most familiar, namely the UK and Europe.

What are policies on ageing?

Before defining policies on ageing, it is worthwhile considering why policies on ageing have emerged so prominently on international and national political agendas in the last few decades. A realistic perspective is that much of the impetus has been financial – fears about the financial sustainability of pensions and social protection systems and of the shrinking workforce that will support an ageing population. The need to foster 'healthy', 'active' and 'productive' ageing is also a strong political motivator, as governments and society in general want to ensure that older persons remain healthy, active, financially secure and able to live independently in their homes for as long as possible. Cynics may claim that this political will is driven simply by fear that older people will become a drain on social resources. However, this author would advance the more positive view that there is increased social consciousness of the realities of ageing and a growing recognition that we have a responsibility to 'make it right' for future generations of older people.

Let us move on to define the scope of policies on ageing. Walt and Gibson (1994) suggested that policies are defined in terms of the processes, boundaries, underpinning values, and objectives that guide them. They identify four key components of policy: content, actors (individuals and groups), processes needed to implement change, and the context for such processes (social, political, cultural, economic and historical) which may explain why policy outcomes are or are not achieved. They also state that policies cannot be divorced from the context within which they are formulated and implemented (Walt and Gibson, 1994).

The content of ageing policies varies significantly as ageing affects every facet of society. As was iterated on a UN website, ageing is 'such a global demographic transformation [that it] has profound consequences for every aspect of individual, community, national and international life. Every facet of humanity will evolve: social, political, cultural, psychological and spiritual' (UN Programme on Ageing, 2002). It is also important to recognize that 'policies on ageing' is not equivalent to 'policies for older people', in terms of devising programmes and services for a discrete group of beneficiaries within society. Ageing is a dynamic process that affects every one of us. Thus, to be successful, policies on ageing cannot take an 'us and them' approach and must instead look at the implications of ageing for all generations, present and future. Similarly, they must take into account a broad range of actors, including all levels of government, the population at large, and the private and non-profit sectors.

However, policies on ageing are mostly centred on the following areas: health and social care, pensions, income and finance, human rights, social inclusion, community development and regeneration, housing, transport, education and lifelong learning. In each of these areas, different approaches have been tried and tested in different countries and policies have evolved with their own successes and failures.

Another aspect of policies on ageing that is important to consider is the distinction between policy formulation and implementation (Lane, 1997). Policies on ageing have been formulated at an international level (e.g. by the UN), at regional levels (e.g. by the European Commission) and at national levels (e.g. in government strategy, programmes and legislation). Implementation depends on the area of policy being targeted – for policies affecting public service provision (for example, health and social care), devolution of budgetary and administrative responsibility to local authorities and communities is a common feature in many countries. Thus, policies are usually set centrally but implemented locally. This dichotomy brings about tensions that have been articulated elsewhere in the literature on decentralization and devolution (Greer and Trench, 2008).

An historical perspective

It is always difficult to define a starting point for the development of given policies. However, it is fair to say that the impetus for policies on ageing arose from the first World Assembly on Ageing in Vienna in 1982. This set the ground for the rights of older persons to be adopted in 1991 in the UN Principles for Older Persons.

Table 11.1 Objectives arising from the recommendations for action from the Madrid International Plan of Action on Ageing, 2002

Priority direction I: older persons and development
- Recognition of the social, cultural, economic and political contribution of older persons
- Participation of older persons in decision-making processes at all levels
- Employment opportunities for all older persons who want to work
- Improvement of living conditions and infrastructure in rural areas
- Alleviation of the marginalization of older persons in rural areas
- Integration of older migrants within their new communities
- Equality of opportunity throughout life with respect to continuing education, training and retraining as well as vocational guidance and placement services
- Full utilization of the potential and expertise of persons of all ages, recognizing the benefits of increased experience with age
- Strengthening of solidarity through equity and reciprocity between generations
- Reduction of poverty among older persons
- Promotion of programmes to enable all workers to acquire basic social protection/social security, including, where applicable, pensions, disability insurance and health benefits
- Sufficient minimum income for all older persons, paying particular attention to socially and economically disadvantaged groups
- Equal access by older persons to food, shelter and medical care and other services during and after natural disasters and other humanitarian emergencies
- Enhanced contributions of older persons to the reestablishment and reconstruction of communities and the rebuilding of the social fabric following emergencies
- Reduction of the cumulative effects of factors that increase the risk of disease and consequently potential dependence in older age
- Development of policies to prevent ill health among older people
- Access to food and adequate nutrition for all older persons

Priority direction II: advancing health and well-being into old age
- Universal and equal access to health-care services
- Elimination of social and economic inequalities based on age, gender or any other ground, including linguistic barriers, to ensure older persons have universal and equal access to health care
- Development and strengthening of primary health-care services to meet the needs of older persons and promote their inclusion in the process
- Development of a continuum of health care to meet the needs of older persons
- Involvement of older persons in the development and strengthening of primary and long-term care services
- Improvement in the assessment of the impact of HIV/AIDS on the health of older persons, both for those who are infected and those who are caregivers for infected or surviving family members
- Provision of adequate information, training in caregiving skills, treatment, medical care and social support to older persons living with HIV/AIDS and their caregivers
- Enhancement and recognition of the contribution of older persons to development in their role as caregivers for children with chronic diseases, including HIV/AIDS, and as surrogate parents
- Provision of improved information and training for health professionals and para-professionals on the needs of older persons
- Development of comprehensive mental health-care services ranging from prevention to early intervention, the provision of treatment services and the management of mental health problems in older persons

Table 11.1 (*cont.*)

- Maintenance of maximum functional capacity throughout the life course and promotion of the full participation of older persons with disabilities

Priority direction III: ensuring enabling and supportive environments

- Promotion of 'ageing in place' in the community with due regard to individual preferences and affordable housing options for older persons
- Improvement in housing and environmental design to promote independent living by taking into account the needs of older persons, in particular those with disabilities
- Provision of a continuum of care and services for older persons from various sources and support for caregivers
- Support for the caregiving role of older persons, particularly older women
- Elimination of all forms of neglect, abuse and violence against older persons
- Creation of support services to address elder abuse
- Enhancement of public recognition of the authority, wisdom, productivity and other important contributions of older persons

Reproduced by kind permission of the United Nations.

The latter provided guidance on areas such as independence, participation, care, self-fulfilment and dignity of older people. The year 1999 was the International Year of Older Persons and had as its core theme 'a society for all ages'. In addition to raising awareness of the issues surrounding population ageing, it seeded the idea that these issues should be taken into consideration in all sectors and policy areas (UN Programme on Ageing, 2002).

In 2002, the Madrid International Plan of Action on Ageing (MIPAA) was adopted at the Second World Assembly on Ageing. The Plan was signed by 160 countries who committed themselves to create a society for all ages and to consider ageing in social and economic development plans and policies (UN Programme on Ageing, 2002). The plan was accompanied by a Regional Implementation Strategy that provided a road map for individual governments to draft their own national strategies and define clear objectives for implementation. The novelty of the MIPAA is that it was the first international agreement to underline the role of older people as positive contributors to society, while promoting dignity and security in ageing, defending older people's rights, and encouraging their full participation in all aspects of society (Age – the Older People's Platform, accessed 31 December 2008). The plan called for 'changes in attitudes, policies and practice at all levels in all sectors so that the enormous potential of ageing in the twenty-first century may be fulfilled' (UN Programme on Ageing, 2002).

The recommendations of the MIPAA are centred on three main themes: (1) ageing and development, (2) advancing health and well-being into old age, and (3) ensuring enabling and supportive environments. The list of recommendations is extensive and this chapter cannot begin to do justice to them all. Table 11.1 presents an outline of the main priority directions and objectives advanced in

MIPAA. This list has, in essence, formed the basic framework for many national policies on ageing that have been developed since.

MIPAA also puts forth several very powerful themes that have been echoed in national policies on ageing developed since (for examples from the UK, the reader is referred to Age Concern, 2008; HM Government, 2005, 2008). One such theme is the human rights of older people, the importance of age equality and the need to eliminate discrimination on the basis of age. Another major theme is the need for governments to mainstream ageing; that is, to incorporate ageing within social, economic and cultural strategies, policies and programmes. The objective is to create truly integrated policy responses to ageing that bridge across different governmental departments and sectors of society. A final theme is the need to include older people as important stakeholders in the planning of social and economic structures and programmes. In addition, MIPAA stresses the links between old age and poverty and the importance of taking into account the concerns and needs of older people in national development frameworks and poverty eradication programmes (UN General Assembly, 2003).

Since the Second World Assembly on Ageing, a number of institutions have monitored the implementation of MIPAA objectives and recommendations within national frameworks. Although it would be misleading to suggest that national policies on ageing have been guided entirely by the MIPAA, it did provide a significant steer for policy development in the field of ageing across the world.

An international dimension

Population ageing represents a major social achievement: the manifestation of progress and improvement in the human condition. It also remains an issue of global concern that requires concerted, well-focused and forward-looking policy measures at the national, regional and international levels. (UN Economic and Social Council, 2006)

It is often erroneously assumed that the gains in life expectancy observed over the past few decades have arisen mostly in richer countries. In fact, much of the increase in longevity in the past 50 years has come from poorer countries, not from more developed economies (see Chapter 1). Of course, gaps in average life expectancy prevail globally and life expectancy is closely correlated with the GDP of nations. However, these gaps are projected to narrow in the future – with the only notable outlier being Africa on account of pervasive poverty and the impact of HIV/AIDS (UN Economic and Social Council, 2006).

In Asia, Latin America and Oceania, population ageing is occurring at a rapid and unprecedented pace. The old age dependency ratio (defined as the ratio of persons over 65 per 100 adults of working age) is expected to double in 50 years in several middle-income nations. It took between 150 and 200 years for this doubling to occur in richer countries. Similarly, developing countries will see a fourfold increase in the number of people over 65 between 2000 and 2050, whereas the corresponding increase in wealthier nations is 1.7 (UN Economic and Social Council, 2006).

There are a number of differences between the challenges posed by ageing in developed versus less developed countries. Developed nations are mostly concerned about the sustainability of their social protection systems, whereas less developed countries have to deal simultaneously with the challenges of population ageing and those of development. Older people in developed countries are concentrated mostly in urban areas, whereas, in poorer nations, up to half of the population, including many older people, reside in rural areas. Older people in developing countries often reside in multigenerational homes, whereas this is less the case in developed countries.

The need to mainstream ageing into other policies and programmes is also par-ticularly important in developing countries. Ageing should be included alongside poverty eradication programmes to include poor older people; a multigenerational perspective is needed when looking at intergenerational issues; ageing needs to be coupled with policies on the advancement of women when looking at older women; rural development agendas need to think about ageing in rural and remote areas and the risk of social exclusion and isolation; and HIV/AIDS policies need to think about older persons who act as caregivers of family members affected by or orphaned by HIV/AIDS (UN General Assembly, 2003). The MIPAA advocates that ageing should be integrated into internationally agreed goals such as the Millen-nium Development Goals. An important obstacle in implementing this in practice is that age-disaggregated data are rarely available, particularly from developing countries, to both inform and allow for the evaluation of the impact of differ-ent programmes and policies. Data collection by age and gender is thus urgently needed to enable policy planning, monitoring and evaluation and to contribute to the development of effective policies in these countries (UN Programme on Ageing, 2002).

Finally, it is very important to point out that awareness of ageing issues and public perception of older people are at very different levels of development across countries. Cultural attitudes towards older people and towards ageing vary con-siderably from one culture to another (see Chapter 12) and have a huge bearing on the role that older people play in communities, the barriers that they may face in accessing services, their inclusion or exclusion within their communities, and the supportiveness of their environments to help them maintain independence in their homes. These variations may be seen within the region covered by the European Union (EU). In many of the former communist nations of Central and Eastern Europe, community services and social care are poorly developed, and health care is still dominated by a hospital-centric culture. As a result, social, health and home care to help foster the independence of older people is significantly lacking. Yet, intense migration of younger generations threatens the informal care support networks upon which many older people are reliant on a daily basis. Moreover, a culture of early retirement prevailed until very recently, and thus the notion of productive engagement of older people remains anathema both politically and socially. Finally, notions of age discrimination, understanding of the implications of ageing for all of society, and empathy for the multiple barriers that older people may face in every aspect of their lives have not yet reached the public, let alone the political, conscience (HelpAge International, 2002). These cultural attitudes must be taken into account in the development of 'European' policies. It also follows that any policy development must be accompanied by awareness campaigns about the realities of ageing, efforts to transform negative stereotypes into more positive images of ageing, and concrete actions to help promote age-inclusiveness within society. These recommendations are by no means confined to any country in particular and are of equal relevance to all nations, regardless of the strength of their culture on ageing.

Issues arising in setting policy agendas on ageing

Though policies on ageing may cover topics as diverse as pensions and social exclusion, there are a number of issues facing all policies on ageing. Some of the more salient ones are discussed in the following section.

Heterogeneity within the ageing population

As noted in Chapter 1, 'old' has traditionally been defined as anyone over the age of 60 or 65. Yet, as the population ages and a greater proportion of the population enters into the 'older people' category, the sheer law of numbers implies that we will be seeing increased diversity within the older population, in terms of socio-economic status, ethnicity, culture, health status, functional ability, preferences and expectations. Indeed, it may be said that to lump all people over 60 into a single category is as meaningless as lumping together all people over the age of 40. Moreover, generalizations and stereotypes about older people are somewhat meaningless and former assumptions need to be revised. As was once iterated by Grimley Evans, any individual 65, 70 or 75 years old is unlikely to present as the 'average' 65-, 70- or 75-year-old (Grimley Evans, 2001).

There has been a growing literature pointing to socio-economic inequalities within many industrialized countries. Within the city of London alone, life expectancy covers a range of 8 years. Manual workers in their fifties have similar health status and levels of disability to people in their seventies from professional classes (Wilkinson and Marmot, 2003). Until recently, it was thought that socio-economic inequalities were somehow nullified by age. However, a number of studies have demonstrated that inequality persists (Huisman *et al.*, 2004). Socio-economic disadvantage has been linked to an increased risk of disability (Grundy and Glaser, 2000), chronic disease, depression and decline in cognitive function in later life (SHARE, 2005). Poorer older people are also at greater risk of social exclusion and exclusion from public services. This can also have an ethnic and cultural dimension. For example, in the UK, 17 per cent of pensioners overall live in poverty, yet this proportion is 42 per cent among the Pakistani and Bangladeshi communities (Department of Work and Pensions, 2008).

Policies on ageing are gradually responding to these data and specifically targeting vulnerable groups within the older population, including older women, older people living in rural communities, older members of ethnic and cultural minorities, older people with disabilities, and older people who lack social networks. Indeed, policies on ageing must take into consideration the diversity of socio-economic and other circumstances affecting the older population and ensure that policies are equitable across the whole population. They should contain targeted actions and programmes and make efforts to reach out to vulnerable groups, to remove barriers in access to services and programmes, and empower vulnerable older people to become engaged in improving their well-being. Finding culturally and socially appropriate solutions to address the needs of each vulnerable group is paramount to ensuring that these groups are not forgotten in policy initiatives and programmes. Moreover, age should be considered an intrinsic factor in the social inequalities debate (Wait and Harding, 2006).

The feminization of ageing

It is a well-known fact that women live longer than men and that as a result, there are more older women than men. What is less appreciated is that this is particularly true in the 'oldest-old' segment of the population. Worldwide, nearly twice as many women are over 80 than men. Older women also have more chronic health conditions, multiple morbidities, disability and depression than men (SHARE, 2005). In fact, there is a saying that 'men die quicker but women are sicker' (Lahelma *et al.*, 1999). The implication for policy is that a greater number of older persons will be women and they are at greater risk of presenting with disability and morbidity.

Policies on ageing need to address the special needs of older women. In addition to increased risk of disability, women are at greater risk of social isolation as they age. In industrialized countries, the current generation of older women has had access to less education and professional training than older men. Having had to reconcile work with caregiving responsibilities, women have often had limited ability to build pensions for retirement, thus putting them at greater risk of poverty. In poorer countries, illiteracy and lack of employment among older women is common, thus creating the risk of social isolation in later years. The MIPAA in particular underlines the need for policies on ageing to recognize that although women make significant unpaid contributions to the community, they often lack financial independence in older age and have little control over property and financial resources. It recommends that institutional linkages be strengthened at the national level between organizations responsible for the advancement of women and government bodies involved in ageing-related policies and programmes (UN General Assembly, 2003).

An important consideration with regard to older women is also the fact that women – and particularly older women – often neglect their own health needs and focus on those of their families. For example, cardiovascular disease is the greatest killer of women; however, it affects them later in life than men. This fact, however, is seldom known by women themselves, their physicians or society in general. There is very little awareness among older women of the risks of heart disease in their demographic group, and older women often do not engage in preventive behaviours to mitigate their risk. Several studies have also demonstrated that cardiac prevention and care services are less often offered to women and the quality of services is lower for women than for men (Shaw *et al.*, 2004). To redress these imbalances and decrease the risks of heart disease in women, a number of national and international heart disease charities in North America and Europe have launched targeted campaigns to sensitize women to the risks of cardiac disease and encourage them to take proactive steps to limit their risks (see European Heart Network, 2005). This example illustrates the need for policies on ageing not only to empower older women but also to sensitize them to their ability to act proactively to affect their health, well-being and social circumstances.

Dedicated versus age-inclusive services

Many policies on ageing are focused on ensuring that public services are adapted to the needs and expectations of older people. In many cases, this requires making adaptations to existing practices, structures and programmes to make them suitable for older people. In other cases, it may be deemed appropriate to create dedicated services specifically for older people. This has, for example, been the rationale behind the creation of geriatric wards and day centres. This approach is not, however, without its risks. Take the example of geriatric mental health wards, to which every person over 65 is referred. An otherwise healthy 65-year-old suffering from depression may find it disheartening to be treated in a ward dominated by people in their eighties suffering from dementia. There is no single solution to this dilemma. Caution is required to recognize the diversity of situations that arise within the older population and to find sensitive solutions tailored to the needs of the population being targeted.

The sustainability of social protection systems

A common assumption – often echoed by the media – is that the ageing of the population will bankrupt health-care systems. In fact, there is growing evidence that future increases in the demand for care may be offset, to a certain degree, by reduced disability levels and improved health status of older populations. Predictions for long-term care are less optimistic. For example, it is estimated that the costs of long-term care would need to rise in the UK by up to 315 per cent by 2051 to meet the needs of the ageing population (Wittenberg *et al.*, 2004). Thus, most industrialized countries are engaged in reforms to adapt the capacity and resources of existing health and social care systems to make sure that they can meet the needs of an ageing population. Fears about the sustainability of social protection systems have also led governments to encourage individuals to take more direct responsibility for preparing for later life. In the UK, the current government has adopted the concept of 'progressive universalism': state support should be available to everyone; however, individuals' economic situations should determine the appropriate balance of contributions between individuals and the state for the cost of services (Age Concern, 2008). A policy initiative reflecting this approach is the creation of 'personal accounts' as an alternative to employer-sponsored pension schemes. Employees and employers both contribute on a matched-funding basis and all eligible employees are automatically enrolled into either scheme. It is hoped that this policy will help overcome current reticence towards saving and ensure that individuals contribute sufficiently to their pension funds over the course of their working lives (Age Concern, 2008). Germany and Japan introduced mandatory care insurance in 1994 and in 2000, respectively, in an effort to limit the risks of exploding social care costs for families and society in general. In Germany, the insurance is intended to contribute to (but not cover entirely) care received in the home as well as nursing home costs. It is financed through employer and employee contributions as well as pensions, alongside other social security contributions. Dependants are included in working family members' insurance policies.

The issue of the sustainability of social protection programmes is particularly pertinent to the situation of older people in developing countries, where universal coverage for health care and other services is a rarity rather than the norm. The argument is often made that social protection is a luxury that cannot be afforded in low-income countries. However, several studies have refuted this belief. In particular, the International Labour Organization has published studies that show that basic non-contributory pensions and health care can be delivered for a cost representing a very small percentage of GDP (International Labour Organization, 2005). International donor agencies have also started to invest in social protection programmes in poorer countries, guided by the belief that the right to social protection is a basic right enshrined in the Universal Declaration of Human Rights (UN Economic and Social Council, 2006). Promisingly, a number of lower-income countries have also developed their own social protection programmes. Some have introduced so-called social pensions which ensure that a minimum subsistence income is paid to older persons of lower income. Other benefit programmes include old age allowances and widow's allowance programmes, which have been successfully implemented in parts of Asia (UN Economic and Social Commission for Asia and the Pacific, 2007).

The governance of policies on ageing

Improvement of public services (health, social care and others) remains a key focus of many policies on ageing. However, adjustments to such services must take into account the increasing complexity of ownership and governance over all so-called 'public' services. In reality, in most industrialized (and increasingly in developing) countries, services such as health and social care are seeing a growing penetration by the private and voluntary sector, and service provision is rarely managed by a single central structure. As a result, policy reforms aimed at improving the age-friendliness of such services must affect the non-public participants in service provision as well as state-run ones. Efforts have been made in many countries to ensure that overseeing regulatory bodies in given sectors have accountability for private as well as public sector service providers. However, proper coordination of all actors on the ground and clear lines of accountability need to be drawn if reforms are to be successfully pushed through the entire pathway of services that older people encounter.

The need for better data

A critical issue facing all policy areas related to ageing is the lack of reliable, disaggregated data on the older population. Most international and national databases group data into a single category of 'over 60' or 'over 65'. With the population of persons over 65 now representing close to a quarter of the population, it is time to introduce a more sophisticated collection and presentation of demographic, social, economic and health statistics on older people. Better stratification of data will help strengthen the evidence base for policy planning and programme development, and subgroup analyses will permit greater understanding of the diversity within the older population. There is also the need to select appropriate indicators of the well-being (economic, physical and otherwise) of older persons in order to monitor progress of given policies and programmes over time. A promising example in the UK is that, since 2007, healthy life expectancy at 65 is one of the key indicators collected by government at national and local levels (Age Concern, 2008). Efforts have also been made internationally to develop indicators to help monitor the ability of policies to mainstream ageing and meet the needs of older populations (Marin and Zaidi, 2007).

These issues are among the many that confront policies on ageing, in terms of their formulation, appropriateness and feasibility in different cultural contexts. What follows is a snapshot of three policy areas – age equality, malnutrition and human resources for health.

Policy focus: age equality

In recent years, one of the most prominent areas of policy development in the field of ageing has been with regard to age discrimination and age equality. Age discrimination may be described as any 'action which adversely affects older persons because of their chronological age alone' (Department of Health, 2001). There is mounting evidence, and increased awareness, from several countries, of the pervasiveness of age discrimination or 'ageism' in all aspects of our society; e.g. upper age restrictions (not necessarily stated explicitly) on travel insurance, car insurance, and financial aid; barriers in access to surgical procedures or specialist care; barriers of entry into continuing education or civic society, such as volunteering; limited career advancement or impossibility of finding a job after a given age (Age Concern, 2008). Examples abound, yet age discrimination still remains somewhat of an elite discourse and probably the most unacknowledged of prejudices in our society.

In Europe, discussions of age discrimination first entered the policy realm in the area of employment. Employment rates among older European workers are on average 20 per cent lower than in Japan or the USA – and 10 per cent lower than the OECD average. As a result, Europe has set legislative and policy measures to encourage workers to stay active for longer and to stop discrimination of workers on the basis of age. In 2001, the European Council of Stockholm set a target rate of 50 per cent employment for older workers. At the Barcelona European Council meeting in 2002, an increase of about 5 years in the effective retirement age was advocated for the EU by 2010. And most importantly, in 2003, the European Equal Treatment Directive made discrimination on the basis of age effectively illegal in all aspects of employment practice. Member states had until 2006 to transpose the directive into national legislation. Transposition has been 'patchy at best', and it is doubtful whether many nations will reach the target employment rates for older workers by 2010 – for a full review of implementation, the reader is referred to the Age Platform Europe (www.age-platform.org). Nonetheless, this European leadership in policy has created a cascade of national policy initiatives aimed at keeping older workers at work for longer and encouraging the age-inclusiveness of work environments.

The above is an exciting area of policy development. Some of the actions and policies taken to tackle age-related barriers have included:

- discouraging early retirement in cultures where early exit from employment was used in an effort to counter young unemployment (though never successfully)
- allowing for the combination of pension and employment income after a given age, in order to safeguard the financial security of older people even if they keep on working
- eliminating the use of sickness or disability benefits as a way out of unemployment (this has been common practice in several European countries and is fraught with abuse)
- allowing for more flexible working conditions
- promoting age-sensitivity training for employers and employees in all sectors.

The implementation of these employment policies is at its early stages and much work remains to be done. However, this is an interesting testing ground for the need to converge political will, private sector actions, public attitudes and social mores. Probably the biggest debate, which is still ongoing in most countries, is whether to ban mandatory retirement age. This has already been done in New Zealand, Australia, and the USA. The European agenda includes a potential extension of age discrimination legislation to the area of goods and services. For further reading on this topic, the reader is referred to Walker and Taylor (1998) and Elgar and Taylor (2006).

From age discrimination to age equality

The policy landscape and language surrounding age discrimination has recently moved away from age discrimination towards a more positive notion of age equality. In many ways, age equality may be viewed as the antithesis of age discrimination. The difficulty facing policymakers is to make a decision as to what 'equality' really means. As was eloquently voiced by a UK legal expert: 'Any discussion of equality must have a dual emphasis. It must reveal and challenge the prejudicial nature of assumptions that old people have failing health and capability. But at the same time, those who do face ill health must be treated fairly and equitably' (Fredman, 2001, p. 9). Age equality does not mean everyone is the same, but it does imply that everyone should be treated the same regardless of age and that policies must accommodate the different facets of old age.

The notion of age equality is also central to efforts to mainstream ageing. Age should be considered alongside the other defining characteristics of individuals – or, put differently, ageism needs to be tackled alongside other 'isms' such as racism and sexism. The UK has provided interesting and bold leadership in this domain by creating, in 2007, the Equality and Human Rights Commission. This non-departmental public body arose from the dismantling of the former commissions for Racial Equality, Equal Opportunities, and Disability Rights. Its key tasks are to promote equality, tackle discrimination, protect human rights and promote good relations between these different groups. It has the onerous task of seeking and protecting equality on the basis of race, ethnicity, gender, age, sexual orientation, and religion or belief. Not surprisingly, the new commission has met with some serious challenges. It must achieve the appropriate balance between different stakeholder group interests without diluting individual group agendas. It is also expected to find common ground among the laws and regulations that were developed initially with the interests of one of these stakeholder groups in mind (Age Concern, 2008). In the next few years, it will be interesting to see whether this all-encompassing equality is achievable in practice.

Policy focus: malnutrition

In 2005, excerpts from the internationally acclaimed playwright Alan Bennett's memoirs, *Untold Stories*, were published. In one section, he described the following scene at a nursing home:

The turnover of residents is quite rapid since whoever is quartered in this room is generally in the later stages of dementia. But that is not what they die of. None of these lost women can feed themselves and to feed them properly . . . demands the personal attention of a helper, in effect one helper per person. Lacking such one-to-one care, these helpless creatures slowly and quite respectably starve to death. This is not something anybody acknowledges, not the matron or the relatives (if, as is rare, they visit), and not the doctor who makes out the death certificates. But it is so. (Bennett, 2005, p. 134)

Bennett's poignant account echoed the calls to action of a number of academics, think tanks and charities on the urgent need to tackle malnutrition in the older population. Malnutrition constitutes a significant, and in most part avoidable, problem of public health (see also Chapters 3 and 4). Fifty per cent of hospitalized older patients are malnourished on admission. Ten per cent of older people living in the community are thought to be malnourished. In nursing homes, the prevalence of malnutrition is thought to reach 60–100 per cent (European Nutrition for Health

Alliance, 2005; Stratton *et al.*, 2003). The costs of malnutrition are equal to, if not greater than, those of obesity (BAPEN, 2005). Malnutrition remains poorly recognized, undetected and undertreated by clinicians, particularly GPs, who may be the first port of call for older people living in the community. How has this been allowed to happen in our wealthy societies? The root causes of malnutrition are as much social as clinical. Poor appetite and dentition, and loss of taste and smell may play a role; however, lifestyle and social factors (isolation, loneliness, poverty, inability to shop or prepare food) and psychological factors (confusion, depression, bereavement) are equally important (European Nutrition for Health Alliance, 2005).

Until recently, malnutrition was simply absent from the policy agenda, but advocacy and campaigning led to huge advances in policy over the past few years. Policy responses must reflect the multi-causal nature of malnutrition, and offer solutions that use a combination of approaches, such as the following:

- raising awareness among society, older people and their families of the risks of malnutrition and ways to prevent it
- dedicated training of all professionals who come into contact with older people on the risks, manifestations and prevention of malnutrition (social care workers, GPs, hospital staff, nurses and community care workers)
- instituting standardized screening of malnutrition in older people (this is now the policy in nursing homes in many European countries as well as hospitals upon admission)
- creating accountability and ownership for the management of malnutrition within the health service and social care.

The last policy response is the most complex to enact. Unlike a strictly clinical problem such as heart disease, the issue of 'who owns malnutrition' and thus, who is responsible for preventing, managing and treating it, is a difficult one. The responsibility lies with older people themselves and all persons involved in their care and well-being – which, in the case of dependent older people still living in their homes, usually encompasses a myriad of social care workers from private and public agencies, health visitors, nurses, GPs, hospital specialists, relatives, community services and volunteer agencies. The coordination of these players is at best remiss, as policies advancing the need for integrated care solutions consistently bemoan (Lloyd and Wait, 2005). The question of who should pay for these solutions is also a difficult one in countries where social and community care typically are resource-poor and heavily decentralized and where national health-care systems have very ring-fenced budgets that allow little room for manoeuvre.

The solution lies in making the prevention and management of malnutrition a central priority within all settings of care where it may be detected and treated.

Moreover, clear pathways for the prevention and management of malnutrition need to be identified and sufficient resources allocated at the community level (European Nutrition for Health Alliance, 2006).

Policy focus: human resources in health

One of the most important concerns of policymakers is the question of who will care for older people in the future. The need for appropriate planning of human resources in health has only recently come to the attention of policymakers at national and international levels. In fact, it is fair to say that human resources for health have been poorly managed and scarcely planned, at least across Europe, for the past several decades. Possibly the most urgent challenge is how to adapt human resources to rapid changes occurring in the environment for care. Of these, ageing of the population and technological advances and changing expectations of care are certainly the most prominent.

The most obvious impact of the ageing of the population is on the need for more geriatrics-trained physicians and clinicians. Dedicated training on how to detect and treat disease in older patients is needed across all medical specialties, particularly general practice. However, the ageing of the population will affect human resources in other ways as well. First, the management of chronic illness, common in older age, is at odds with the traditional acute-care, hospital-based model of care. In order effectively to manage chronic conditions over time, individuals must be offered person-centred, integrated care that allows them to age within their homes and meets their needs in a cohesive way in terms of maintaining health, fostering independence and mitigating the impact of disability. Policies advocating integrated care have been advanced across a number of industrialized countries. However, implementation poses challenges. It calls for new models of care that render the traditional boundaries between professions obsolete, and it calls for a change to the current hierarchy of professions within health and social care (Leichsenring, 2003; Lloyd and Wait, 2005). It also has ramifications for resourcing of health and social care: integrated care cannot be achieved if we do not have more health-care workers at the interface between health and social care – home-care workers, nurses, community health/district health nurses, physiotherapists and rehabilitation specialists (Dubois *et al.*, 2006).

Ageing also affects the health workforce intrinsically – the latter, too, is ageing. Denmark, the UK, France and Sweden are all seeing the greying of their nursing workforce (International Council of Nurses, 2002). In the UK, one nurse in five is over 50 and 25 per cent of consultant physicians will reach the age of 65 and retire over the next decade (Federation of the Royal Colleges of Physicians, 2007). Although aggressive policies for both training new doctors and nurses and recruiting foreign clinicians have been implemented in several countries (especially the UK), the time lag needed to train health professionals fully is at least 10 years. Severe imbalances between supply and demand of health-care labour are thus both inevitable and imminent (Dubois *et al.*, 2006).

And finally, a dilemma affecting all countries is whether the current role of informal care will continue with future generations. Currently, 60–80 per cent of older people are cared for by their relatives. Older women play the greatest role in informal care, as spouses, mothers, and grandmothers. As family structures evolve, it may be dangerous to take for granted that this unpaid care workforce will be available in the future. Moreover, policies that provide support and financial security to carers of older people are urgently needed.

Discussion

In the introduction to the policy report *A Better Government for Older People,* a UK politician wrote, 'Preparing a strategy is the beginning of a process, not the end of it' (HM Government, 2005, p. 1). These are, undoubtedly, exciting times for policies on ageing. But a number of challenges continue to face their implementation.

First, it is important that society, governments, the media and all generations adopt realistic expectations about old age. The term 'active ageing' has become a popular slogan for how we wish to see our older population (and indeed, ourselves) in later years. Yet this concept does not recognize that a balanced perspective on ageing is needed, one where later life is not one-dimensional but a fluid, complex and heterogeneous phenomenon (Lloyd-Sherlock, 2004). We may not all be jumping out of parachutes or running marathons at the age of 94, but we may not all be bedridden and frail either. Growing diversity and socio-economic inequalities within the older population also suggest that old age may indeed present many different faces. In light of this diversity, policies aimed at achieving active or healthy ageing must accommodate the different sets of circumstances facing older individuals as they age. Older people can only age well within their communities if their independence is fostered, if they are provided with sufficient information and support to meet the demands of daily life, if barriers in access to services of all kinds – health, housing, care, community involvement – are removed, and if their health status permits it. Thus it is not sufficient for policies to strive for active ageing; they must also help create supportive environments to enable older people to remain active and healthy for as long as possible. However, as in many areas of policy, there is often a gap between the ambitious goals for reform set out in ageing policy reports and the realities of implementation on the ground. Policy formulators too rarely take into account or make explicit the resources needed to implement changes, the training requirements, and the processes and structural adaptations needed to implement reform. With increased decentralization in most public services, the need for dialogue between policy formulators and implementers becomes that much more urgent.

Another important challenge facing policymakers is the need to ensure the sustainability of social protection systems for future generations. Many governments are attempting to push the onus for responsibility onto older people themselves in order to encourage them to prepare adequately for old age. This philosophy is behind the creation of personal (pension) accounts in the UK, for example, or long-term care insurance in Germany and Japan. Yet an equitable balance between government support and individual responsibility must be found. In particular, information, advice and support must be made available to vulnerable individuals who may not have the skills and willingness to take on this responsibility at different points in their lives. Otherwise, such initiatives may exacerbate existing social inequalities and contribute further to the social exclusion and financial insecurity of more disadvantaged older individuals.

Another challenge is to create responsive services and information that correspond to the needs, expectations and wishes of people as they grow old. Genuine efforts are needed to take older people's needs and aspirations into account systematically in the design of new buildings, the configuration of websites, the drafting of consumer information materials, and the design of local services to ensure that they are not only age-friendly but also age-appropriate (HM Government, 2008). These efforts must be extended to all services and information – whether provided by the public, private or non-profit sector.

There remain a number of unknowns about the ageing of the populations. Demographic projections are corrected over time as more recent and accurate information becomes available. Policies on ageing formulated now need to be pertinent to future older generations – and these generations may have different behaviours, needs, and social or family circumstances from those of current generations of older people. Will older generations be more demanding than current generations of older people? Will they want to take responsibility for their well-being and independence? Will they still prefer to age within their homes and communities? Answers to these critical questions will emerge gradually through research and population studies.

Another important question relates to age discrimination. What is the practical alternative to making decisions on the basis of age? In the field of employment, campaigners urge that age should not enter into decisions related to hiring or promoting workers, and that individual ability should instead be the arbiter. This may be feasible in the field of employment, but less so in fixing policies about who is entitled to a driver's licence or eligible to join the military. In such cases where a threshold is needed, the use of age is so embedded in practice that one struggles to think of a characteristic that may be less arbitrary and a better candidate to achieve social justice. These are important questions to address if one wishes to persuade people to move away from age-based barriers and thresholds.

Finally, there is an ongoing debate within the literature on whether we will be able to enjoy the social, economic and health benefits brought about by the extension of healthy life – the so-called longevity dividend (Olshansky *et al.*, 2006). The rise of obesity, and in particular childhood obesity, is posing such a threat to current demographic projections that there is a serious risk that current generations may live shorter and less healthy lives than previous generations (Olshansky *et al.*, 2005). We may need to wait a few decades more to see whether this threat will be realized or not.

I would like to conclude this chapter with the following question: *what will make policies on ageing work?* Successful implementation will require the confluence of political leadership and commitment, social consciousness and engagement, economic feasibility, local action and implementation, and cultural and attitudinal changes. It is this last factor that is likely to prove the most challenging and that may take the longest to transform. Ageing may be high on the policy agenda, but age discrimination and fear of ageing are still pervasive throughout society. We remain, somehow, ambivalent about old age, approaching it with a mixture of 'admiration' and 'contempt' (Minois, 1989). For policies on ageing fully to achieve their goals, huge efforts must be made to face up to our prejudices, reverse adverse imagery of older people, mitigate fears about the sustainability of our social protection systems, avoid the social exclusion of older people within our communities, and genuinely recognize older people as positive contributors to our societies. This is a tall order but it is, and society must believe it is, achievable for the sake of all generations, present and future.

Summary

Taking the Italian home workers ('badanti') phenomenon as an example, the chapter illustrates the complexity of discussing policies on ageing. The nature and range of what 'policies on ageing' actually mean are discussed, and their historical development is examined. Cross-country comparisons are then offered to illustrate the key factor of cultural norms and attitudes. Further factors that shape policies (their creation and effectiveness) are examined – heterogeneity within the ageing population, the 'feminization' of ageing, dedicated versus age-inclusive services, the sustainability of social protection systems, and the governance of policies on ageing. The need for better data stratified by age is then raised. Three policy areas are then highlighted – age equality, malnutrition and human resources for health.

The chapter concludes with a detailed discussion of the matters raised earlier in the chapter, leading to a key final question – namely, what will make policies on ageing work?

REFERENCES

Age Concern (2006) Hungry to be heard. The scandal of malnourished older people in hospital. London: Age Concern.

(2008) *The age agenda. Public policy and older people.* London: Age Concern.

Bennett, A. (2005) The candlewick way of death. An excerpt from *Untold stories*. London: Faber & Faber. Excerpt reprinted in *The Sunday Telegraph*, 24 September 2005. Retrieved from www.telegraph.co.uk/news/uknews/1499070/The-candlewick-way-of-death.html?pageNum=3.

Department of Health (2001) National Service Framework for Older People. Retrieved from www.dh.gov.uk/assetRoot/04/07/12/83/04071283.pdf.

Department of Work and Pensions (2008) *Households below average income, 2005/6.* London: HMSO.

Dubois, C.A., McKee, M. and Nolte, E. (2006) *Human resources for health in Europe.* European Observatory on Health Care Systems. Maidenhead: Open University Press.

Elgar, E. and Taylor, P. (2006) *Employment initiatives for an ageing workforce in the EU-15.* Luxembourg: Office for Official Publications of the European Communities.

Elia, M., Stratton, R., Russell, C. *et al.* (2005) *The cost of disease-related malnutrition in the UK and economic considerations for the use of oral nutritional supplements in adults.* London: British Association of Parenteral and Enteral Nutrition.

European Heart Network (2005) *A healthy heart for European women.* Brussels: European Heart Network.

European Nutrition for Health Alliance (2005) *Malnutrition within an ageing population: a call for action.* Retrieved from www.european-nutrition.org/files/pdf_pdf_34.pdf.

(2006) Malnutrition among older people in the Community Policy Recommendations for Change. A report by the European Nutrition for Health Alliance, BAPEN (British Association for Parenteral and Enteral Nutrition), the International Longevity Centre-UK in collaboration with the Associate Parliamentary Food and Health Forum, May 2006. Retrieved from www.european-nutrition.org/files/pdf_pdf_54.pdf.

Federation of the Royal Colleges of Physicians of the United Kingdom (2007) *Census of consultant physicians in the UK, 2006. Data and commentary.* Edinburgh: author.

Fredman, S. (2001) What do we mean by age equality? Paper presented at the Institute for Public Policy Research Seminar, Nuffield Foundation. Retrieved from www.bapen.org.uk/pdfs/malnut_in_the_community.pdf.

Greer, S.L. and Trench, A. (2008) *Health and intergovernmental relations in the devolved United Kingdom.* London: Nuffield Trust.

Grimley Evans, J. (2001) Age discrimination. Implications for the ageing process. London: Institute of Public Policy Research.

Grundy, E. and Glaser, K. (2000) Socio-demographic differences in the onset and progression of disability in early old age: a longitudinal study, *Age and Ageing, 29*, 149–57.

Haveman-Nies, A., De Groot, L. and Van Staveren, W. (2003) Dietary quality, lifestyle factors and healthy ageing in Europe: the SENECA study, *Age and Ageing, 32*(4), 427–34.

HelpAge International (2002) *A generation in transition. Older people's situation and civil society's response in East and Central Europe.* Retrieved from www.helpage.org/ publications/?adv=1&ssearch=&filter=f.yeard&type=3/&region=&topic=&language= &page=7.

HM Government (2005) *Opportunity age. Meeting the challenges of ageing in the 21st century.* Retrieved from www.dwp.gov.uk/publications/dwp/2005/opportunity_age/opportunity-age-volume1.pdf (accessed on 12 January 2009).

(2008). *Preparing for an ageing society: a discussion paper.* Retrieved from www.dwp.gov.uk/ docs/ageingstrategy.pdf.

Huisman, M., Kunst, A.E., Andersen, O. *et al.* (2004) Socioeconomic inequalities in mortality among elderly people in 11 European populations, *Journal of Epidemiology and Community Health*, *58*, 468–75.

International Labour Organization (2005) *Can low income countries afford basic social protection? First results of a modeling exercise.* Issues in Social Protection, Discussion paper 13, June.

Lahelma, E., Martikainen, P., Rahkonen, O. *et al.* (1999) Gender differences in ill health in Finland: patterns, magnitude and change, *Social Science and Medicine*, *48*, 7–19.

Lane, J.-E. (1997) Implementation, accountability and trust, in Michael Hill (ed.), *The policy process: a reader*, 2nd edn. London: Prentice-Hall, 296–313.

Leichsenring, K. (2003) *Providing integrated health and social care for older persons – a European overview.* Dortmund: European Centre for Social Welfare Policy and Research.

Lloyd, J. and Wait, S. (2005) *Integrated care: a guide for policymakers.* Alliance for Health and the Future and International Longevity Centre-UK. Retrieved from www.ilcuk.org.uk/files/ pdf_pdf_7.pdf.

Lloyd-Sherlock, P. (2004) Ageing, development and social protection: generalizations, myths and stereotypes, in P. Sherlock (ed.), *Living longer: ageing, development and social protection.* London: UNRISD and Zed Books, 1–20.

Major developments since the Second World Assembly on Ageing (2006) Report of the Secretary-General of the United Nations to the Commission on Social Development, *International Social Science Journal*, *58*(190), 667–80.

Marin, B. and Zaidi, A. (eds) (2007) Mainstreaming ageing: indicators to monitor sustainable policies. Vienna: Ashgate.

Minois, G. (1989) *History of old age: from antiquity to the Renaissance.* Oxford: Blackwell.

Olshansky, J., Perry, D., Miller, R.A. *et al.* (2006) In pursuit of the longevity dividend, *The Scientist*, *20* (March), 28–36.

Olshansky, S.J., Passaro, D.J., Hershow, R.C. *et al.* (2005) A potential decline in life expectancy in the United States in the 21st century. *New England Journal of Medicine*, *352* (11), 1138–45.

Pirlich, M., Schutz, T., Kemps, M. *et al.* (2003) Prevalence of malnutrition in hospitalized medical patients: impact of underlying disease, *Digestive Disorders*, *21*, 245–51.

SHARE (Survey of Health, Ageing and Retirement in Europe) (2005) Retrieved from www. share-project.org.

Shaw, M., Maxwell, R., Kees, K. *et al.* (2004) Gender and age inequity in the provision of coronary revascularisation in England in the 1990s: is it getting better?, *Social Science and Medicine*, *59*, 2499–2507.

Stratton, R. Green, C. and Elia, M. (2003) *Disease-related malnutrition: an evidence-based approach to treatment.* Wallingford: CABI Publishing.

United Nations (2002) *Report of the Second World Assembly on Ageing.* Madrid, 8–12 April. New York: United Nations.

United Nations Economic and Social Council (2006) *Major developments in the area of ageing since the Second World Assembly on Ageing.* Report of the Secretary-General. Geneva, 21 November.

United Nations Economic and Social Council (2007) *World Economic and Social Survey 2007: development in an ageing world. Overview.* New York: United Nations.

United Nations General Assembly (2003) *Follow-up to the Second World Assembly.* Report of the Secretary-General, 17 July.

United Nations Programme on Ageing (2002) *Report of the Second World Assembly on Ageing, Madrid, 8–12 April.*

United Nations Economic and Social Commission for Asia and the Pacific (2007) High-Level Meeting on the Regional Review of the Madrid International Plan of Action on Ageing (MIPAA), 9–11 October. Retrieved from www.unescap.org/esid/psis/meetings/ageingmipaa2007/Bangladesh.pdf.

Wait, S. and Harding, E. (2006) *The state of ageing and health in Europe.* International Longevity Centre-UK and the Merck Company Foundation, June. Retrieved from www.ilcuk.org.uk/files/pdf_pdf_4.pdf.

Walker, A. and Taylor, P. (1998) *Combating age barriers in employment – a European portfolio of good practice.* Luxembourg: Office for Official Publications of the European Communities.

Walt, G. and Gilson, L. (1994) Reforming the health sector in developing countries: the central role of health policy, *Health Policy and Planning, 9*(4), 353–70.

Wilkinson, R. and Marmot, M. (eds) (2003) *Social determinants of health: the solid facts,* 2nd edn. Geneva: World Health Organization.

Wittenberg, R., Comas-Herrera, A., Pickard, L. *et al.* (2004) *Future demand for long-term care in the UK. A summary of projections of long-term care finance for older people to 2051.* York: Joseph Rowntree Foundation.

12 Cross-cultural differences in ageing

SANDRA TORRES

OVERVIEW

This chapter is conceived as an introduction to the study of cross-cultural differences in ageing and old age. As such it summarizes some of the major trends observed in the three areas of gerontological enquiry that focus on the study of culture and ethnicity's impact on the way in which ageing is experienced and understood: anthropo-gerontology, cross-cultural gerontology and ethno-gerontology. The chapter summarizes some of the work done on the impact that culture has on the way in which the construct of successful ageing is understood and presents some of the challenges that the globalization of international migration is expected to have in the way in which gerontologists study culture and ethnicity.

Introduction

This chapter examines the impact that ethnicity and culture have on the manner in which ageing and old age are experienced and understood. It draws upon the disciplines of anthropo-gerontology, cross-cultural gerontology and ethno-gerontology, and some of the key concepts used in these will be defined in the opening section of this chapter. These introductions will be followed by a critical consideration of one of social gerontology's most debated constructs; namely, *successful ageing*. This will be done to demonstrate what the fields in question have contributed to this debate. The chapter will end with a discussion of the challenges to research, policy and practice that are posed by globalization, the hybridization of cultures that this phenomenon poses, the contemporary increase in international migration flows and trans-national communities, and the implications that all of these trends have for the study of culture/ethnicity, migration, inequality and 'the periphery' since these are all themes with which cross-cultural and ethno-gerontologists are concerned.

Cross-cultural gerontology: the anthropology of ageing comes of age

Cross-cultural gerontology examines how different cultures conceptualize the process of ageing, and the social position that old age holds. The field is also about the impact that different cultural backgrounds, value orientations and/or cultural values exert on the experience of ageing and old age. As such, cross-cultural gerontology has its roots in an anthropological understanding of the world even though not everybody that conducts cross-cultural gerontology research is, in fact, trained as an anthropologist. This means that culture is at the very core of cross-cultural gerontology. By 'culture' we mean the way in which a society's values, attitudes and norms being passed from one generation to the next makes what happens in these societies meaningful, and/or how these values, attitudes and norms impact on the way in which people make sense of their surroundings. Culture is, in other words, about what is 'constituting the way of life of an entire society' (Jary and Jary, 1991, p. 101). This is why Sokolovsky (1997) stresses the need to study ageing and old age in a culturally appropriate manner by stating that 'each cultural system creates a perceptual lens composed of potent symbols through which a particular version of reality is developed' (p. xiv). Hence, at the very core of cross-cultural gerontology's endeavours lies an interest in questioning the universal manner in which ageing and old age are regarded by culture-unaware gerontologists.

Having clarified what cross-cultural gerontologists share as their common interest, it seems appropriate to move on to an abridged presentation of the types of research questions with which they are concerned. Summarizing the vast amount of research that has been generated over the years in this area is an impossible task in the confines of a short chapter. Pedagogically sound introductions to the anthropology of ageing – which is often referred to as the field that lay the ground for what we now call cross-cultural gerontology – can be found in the edited collections by Myerhoff and Simić (1978), Amoss and Harrell (1981), Fry (1981) and Rubinstein (1990) as well as in the chapter on the history of anthropology's

concern for ageing and old age written by Holmes (1980) and the articles written
by Keith (1980) and Fry (1980). (For a critical discussion of how the anthropology
of ageing and old age has evolved, see Cohen (1994), who questions whether this
subfield of gerontological enquiry is as critical as it prides itself on being.) This
history – which spans over eight decades – is filled with numerous contributions
to theory development in gerontology (Climo, 1992). These include, among others, showing that although 'every known society has a named category of people
who are old – chronologically, physiologically or generationally... this group is
defined differently in different places' (Amoss and Harrell, 1981, p. 3). One of
anthropology's main contributions to the study of ageing and old age is, therefore,
the vast array of studies that have shown that the status and roles accorded to older
people and the way in which old age is regarded are determined by societal, cultural, historical, economic and political factors or a combination of these (Arnhoff,
Leone and Lorge, 1964; Clark, 1967; Clark and Anderson, 1967; Cowgill, 1974a,
1974b; Cowgill and Holmes, 1972; Fry *et al.*, 1997; Keith *et al.*, 1994; Maxwell
and Silverman, 1970; Press and McKool, 1972; Simmons, 1945, 1946, 1960).

Two of the seminal works with which this field of enquiry is associated demand
special attention since they paved the way for gerontology's culture-specific awareness. The first is Simmons' (1945) synthesis and comparison of existing ethno-
graphic information about older people in different societies in the book titled *The
Role of the Aged in Primitive Society*. Simmons explored how 71 non-Western
societies accorded status to older people and what the determinants of favourable
and unfavourable conditions were for them in these 'primitive' societies. His analysis focused on formal social status as related to economic, social and cultural
variables and showed, *inter alia*, that the status accorded to older people differed
in different societal structures. Through his work we learned, for example, that
older people tend to be accorded higher status in societies where, among others, their traditional skills and knowledge are valued, where security of property
rights, and civil and political status exists, and where the types of routine services
often performed by older people (such as cooking, babysitting and the mending
of broken things) guarantee general welfare that cannot be accessed otherwise (cf.
Simmons, 1946). In a later study, Simmons (1960) suggested that although there
are differences in the manner in which old age and ageing play out in different
societies, there are also some universals that older people share regardless of which
culture they come from. These are that older people wish to live as long as possible, to hide their diminished energy, to keep on sharing in the affairs of life, to
safeguard their seniority rights, and to have a dignified death.

Cowgill and Holmes' (1972) seminal work *Ageing and Modernization* is also
worthy of being mentioned because of the enormous inspiration it has been to
numerous cross-cultural gerontologists through the years. Its main focus was older
people's vulnerability and the impact that societal change and modernization has
on this. In this study, 14 different societies were compared in order to examine the

impact that industrialization, urbanization and modernization have on the societal status accorded to older people. The results showed that the status of older people tended to be high in preliterate societies and lower and/or ambiguous in modern ones. Moreover, societal change – especially if it occurs rapidly and involves modernization – was shown to have an adverse effect on the position of older people. The reasons why this is the case were explored by Maxwell and Silverman (1970), who showed that the type of knowledge that older people typically possess becomes obsolete once societies change. Press and McKool (1972) augmented this argument, demonstrating that older people are at a disadvantage in societies that can be characterized by economic heterogeneity, diversity, discontinuity in father–son relationships and an early turnover of family resources, as well as in societies where ascriptive roles and nuclear family dependency are of little importance. These results sparked numerous arguments (see Albert and Cattell's (1994) and Palmore and Manton's (1974) critique of modernization theory) when first published, primarily because they tended to be misinterpreted as arguing that old people in traditional societies are always highly regarded, when, in fact, they are not. According to Keith (1980, p. 342), 'this point seems worth stress[ing] because the insidious consequence of missing it is an assumption that good treatment for the aged is part of a vanishing lifeway and impossible in the modern world'. With reference to this, Palmore and Manton (1974) have shown – through their study of 31 countries – that as societies move beyond the transitional stage of rapid modernization, status discrepancies between the young and the old tend to decrease. The status devaluation that older people experience in societies that change from a 'primitive' state to a more modern one is therefore transitional and should be understood against the backdrop that other cultural, religious and political factors bring about. Hence, Cowgill and Holmes (1972, p. 87) stressed something that seems to have been lost along the way; namely that

how a society develops and changes under the impact of modernizing forces depends to a great extent upon the values it held previously. A society whose major religion is Buddhism may be quite differently affected by industrialization and urbanization than one operating under a Judeo-Christian tradition. The same is true for traditional differences in political and economic philosophy.

With respect to the contributions that the anthropology of ageing has made to understanding how cultural change impacts on the lives of older people, Holmes and Holmes (1995) have proposed a number of generalizations that have implications for how cross-cultural gerontologists think about the impact of cultural, societal, economic, religious and political factors on old age and ageing. These are as follows:

(1) Modernization affects the way in which we conceptualize old age.
(2) Longevity is directly related to the degree of modernization.

(3) Modern societies have a relatively high proportion of older people in their population.

(4) Older people are accorded more respect in societies where they constitute a low proportion of the total population.

(5) Societies in the process of modernizing tend to favour the young (while the old are at an advantage in more stable societies).

(6) Respect for older people tends also to be greater in societies in which the extended family has not lost its importance (especially when the extended family functions as the household unit).

(7) In pre-industrial societies the family is typically responsible for the economic security of older people, whereas in industrial societies the responsibility falls partially or totally on the state.

(8) The proportion of older people who retain leadership roles is lower in modern than in pre-industrial societies.

(9) Religious leadership is more likely to be a role one can continue with once one becomes older in a pre-industrial society.

(10) Retirement is a modern invention found only in modern and highly productive societies.

These considerations guide most cross-cultural and/or anthropo-gerontological enquiries.

Ethno-gerontology: employing the ethnic lens to study ageing and old age

The generalizations mentioned above have also had an impact on how we think about ageing and old age when we employ an *ethnic lens*. By this, we mean an approach that is ethnicity-sensitive as well as aware of what ethnic minority status means to the way in which we conceive and experience ageing and old age. These issues are also relevant to the ageing of migrants (especially those that have migrated between societies that have varying modernization levels), adding to the allure of ethnicity as an important point of departure for studies of ageing and old age. It is important to add that 'ethnicity' is a term often used interchangeably with 'culture' since the former includes the latter and the latter could sometimes be interpreted differently because of the various ethnic groups that may co-exist within a society. Ethnicity is, however, the term utilized to denote the attachments between people that are based on common descent, and this is why Jary and Jary (1991, p. 151) define it as 'the shared (whether perceived or actual) racial, linguistic, or national identity of a social group'. As such, and when aiming to differentiate between ethnicity and culture, it may be helpful to think of ethnicity as a background variable denoting the social group to which a person 'belongs' and to think of culture as the diverse ways that make this type of 'belonging' meaningful. The word 'belongs' is placed in inverted commas because ethnic identity is always a situationally determined subjective matter. This is why Wallman (1979, p. ix) claims that the idea of perception is pivotal to our understanding of ethnicity since 'ethnicity refers generally to the perception of group difference... and the sense of difference which can occur when members of a particular cultural... group interact with non-members'. Those interested in deepening their understanding of ethnicity as an important aspect of social stratification are recommended Jenkins (1997) and Cornell and Hartmann (1998), who offer an excellent introduction to this area. The relationship between ethnicity and identity is explored by Jenkins (1996).

Studies of ageing and old age that use an ethnic lens are generally concerned with ethnic differences and the social inequality that is often associated with ethnic minority status. There is still some confusion as to how the terms 'anthropo-gerontology', 'cross-cultural gerontology' and 'ethno-gerontology' are used (cf. Sokolovsky, 1997). There are, however, some differences in what these fields focus on, which is why we will here treat cross-cultural gerontology and ethno-gerontology as separate fields of enquiry. The latter is the field of gerontological enquiry that has – at least in the USA – succeeded in putting the needs of minority older people into the gerontological agendas of research, policy and practice. This has been done through improving the understanding that issues such as economic security, health care, health status and well-being might be defined differently across racial and ethnic subgroups of older people. Green (1989), p. 377 argued that 'ethnicity has come into ageing research primarily as a concern with a social problem'. Certainly, most ethno-gerontological research is concerned with measures of coping, adjustment, adaptation and satisfaction and with the issue of social inequality (cf. Burton *et al.*, 1992). In this respect (and because this chapter is meant to work as an introduction to these fields), it seems necessary to mention that just as with cross-cultural gerontology, there are two theoretical perspectives which ethno-gerontology is particularly associated with. These are the *double jeopardy* and *age-as-levelling* hypotheses. Double jeopardy argues that being an ethnic/racial minority and being old constitute two sets of disadvantages with which ethnic older minorities must reckon (cf. Burton and Bengtson, 1982; Dowd and Bengtson, 1978; Jackson, Kolody and Wood, 1982). In contrast, age-as-levelling proposes that older age exerts a levelling effect on the ethnic differences found to a more marked extent at younger ages (cf. Kent, 1971). Both these perspectives have been disputed because it is almost impossible to study them empirically (Blakemore and Boneham, 1994). However, these two hypotheses (especially double jeopardy) still permeate the majority of ethno-gerontological research, which is why they are mentioned here. A current consensus opinion is that although double jeopardy may exist with regard to income and physical health (cf. Dowd and Bengtson, 1978; Jackson *et al.*, 1982), minority elders' mental health, mortality and family relations are areas the hypothesis fails to explain. Nazroo (2006) studied some of these issues in the British context and found similar patterns with regard to what the double jeopardy hypothesis can and cannot explain.

Having examined the main perspectives of enquiries in ethno-gerontology, it is important to address when and how this field has developed. This is, after all, how we can delineate where we have been and where we should be heading. In this regard, it is important to remember that as a distinct field of enquiry, ethno-gerontology is relatively new. Although there have been gerontologists interested in raising the discipline's ethnicity-awareness for more than four decades, it was not until the establishment of the Gerontological Society of America (GSA)'s Task Force on Minority Issues in Gerontology in 1987 that one could begin to speak of ethno-gerontology as being an area of enquiry of its own. Of interest here is also that the GSA's Informal Interest Group on International Migration and Ageing was established in 1993, attesting to American gerontologists' awareness that migration also has an impact on the way in which ageing and old age are experienced and understood. The establishments of these groups are sometimes used as points of departure when speaking of the development of an ethno-gerontological tradition, which is why we acknowledge them here. This research area is, in other words, not as old as cross-cultural gerontology (and the anthropology of ageing that paved the way for that field). It is perhaps because of this that ethno-gerontology is still relatively underdeveloped as far as research traditions go. It was not until the late 1980s and the establishment of the task force in question that the ethnicity and/or minority-oriented tradition of gerontological research started to differentiate itself from the anthropology of ageing tradition and the field of cross-cultural gerontology presented earlier. Thus, although we have been applying the ethnic lens for some decades now, the fact remains that this is still a relatively underdeveloped field of gerontological enquiry as far as theory is concerned.

The reason for this underdevelopment has been debated over the past two decades (cf. Burton *et al.*, 1992; Kramer and Barker, 1994; Torres, 2001a, 2009; Usui, 1989). Burton *et al.* (1992) have, for example, blamed the field's ways of thinking and the ever-present focus on social inequality for dooming them to theoretical stagnation. Torres (2001a) and (2009) has expanded on their assessment by arguing that part of the problem has been caused by the field's focus on single-nation/culture studies and the failure to recognize the migrant life course as a theoretically profuse point of departure from which gerontological studies can be launched. Usui (1989) and Kramer and Barker (1994) followed another line of argumentation when proposing that the reason why ethno-gerontology has failed to develop theoretically is that there is a lack of conceptual clarity in the way in which ethnicity is handled. Kramer and Barker (1994) have shown, for example, that although numerous advancements have been made in the way in which ethnicity is understood in the social sciences, gerontologists who apply the ethnic lens tend to do so in the relatively deterministic manner that was characteristic of the essentialist/ primordial understanding of ethnicity rampant in the first half of the twentieth century. In one of the most insightful book review essays about ethno-gerontological literature ever written, they write that in research

on the elderly, ethnicity is presented largely as a fixed, static, invariant characteristic of individuals in homogeneous social groups... All too often 'ethnic' research and analysis rely on this type of dated definition... In contrast to functionalist approaches where ethnicity is a static, stable, personal or group attribute, the concept of ethnicity as used in contemporary social science theories is one of a dynamic, fluid, situationally-invoked phenomenon. Ethnicity is an idea, an identity, that is always under construction and re-construction by individuals who actively monitor and change their social environment... [contemporary] research into ethnicity examines not outcomes but processes. (Kramer and Barker, 1994, p. 412)

As an explanation of this state of affairs, they suggest that it is probably the problem of the orientation of the field (which Burton *et al.*, 1992 referred to as the ways of thinking of the field and the focus on social inequality that is at their core) that has led to ethno-gerontology's constant promotion of consensual models to improve the quality of life of minority elders. However, it must be mentioned that in addressing ethnicity in the fixed manner that Kramer and Barker (1994) describe, we are failing to recognize what Green (1989, p. 383) argues so poignantly, namely that 'a more powerful ethnogerontology would be one in which the emergent quality of ethnicity, its salience rather than its givenness, would be the starting point'.

Here it may be interesting to note that this is a field that began out of North American gerontologists' growing awareness that their societies were characterized by ethnic diversity and an ethnicity-informed gerontology was needed if they were to design research, practice and policies that met the needs of minority elders. In relation to this, Blakemore and Boneham (1994, p. 138) suggest that

it is understandable that in societies where 'ethnic politics' matters, or where there are much larger minority communities than those in Britain, commentators have sought to define a separate field of ethnogerontology.

With regard to Britain's lack of an ethno-gerontological tradition of its own, Blakemore (1997), states that compared to other multicultural societies, Britain has yet to develop an understanding of ageing and old age that is ethnicity-informed. Boneham (2002) suggests, in turn, that the neglect of research in this area is based on the assumption that there are few ethnic 'others' in Britain – an assumption that could easily be questioned. As Blakemore (1997) himself argued, although ethnic minorities constitute a small proportion of the British population, there is evidence that older people from these communities are marginalized and so there is a need to consider ethnic and cultural influences in how ageing and old age are experienced and understood in this part of the world as well. Hence, he proposes that the lack of British gerontologists' interest in ethnicity lies not necessarily in the assumed lack of numbers that Boneham (2002) refers to, but rather in the 'understandable concern . . . that reliance on "culturalist" explanations can problematize or pathologize minority groups' (Blakemore, 1997, p. 29). This explains perhaps why both of them argue against working towards establishing a British ethno-gerontological imagination of its own since they see such a pursuit as risking 'cutting off minority studies in a "research ghetto", while making it more difficult to incorporate ethnic and cultural comparisons in "mainstream" gerontological research' (Blakemore and Boneham, 1994, pp. 138–9). Regardless of whether or not we think that ethno-gerontological enquiries should 'segregate themselves' into a field of their own, the fact remains that there is – at least in the USA – a field of gerontological research that is concerned with ethnicity and minority-related issues, a field that an introduction to the study of cross-cultural differences in ageing such as this one must acknowledge. With regard to the current status of this field and where it should be heading, it is important to note what Kramer and Barker (1994) have already stated, but which is still a challenge; namely, that for advancements to be made we need to stop simplifying ethnic groups into large homogeneous population blocks since this can lead to a confusion of ethnicity with minority status, a conflation of ethnicity with the experience of being an immigrant, and a disregard for the kind of cohort, sex, class, historical and regional differences that are at the very core of what the study of culture – understood as context – is actually about.

The study of successful ageing: an example of what a cross-cultural approach can unveil

After this introduction to how the fields in question have developed and what the issues debated the most have been, it seems important to exemplify what the cross-cultural approach to the study of ageing and old age has meant for one of social gerontology's guiding principles (cf. Fisher, 1995), the successful ageing paradigm. The reason why this paradigm was chosen is that this is a theme identified as a potentially fruitful area of enquiry for comparative research. Daatland and Motel-Klingebiel (2007, p. 345) write, for example, that all the models of 'good ageing'

tend to be (explicitly and implicitly) normative. They are in fact assumed to have general, even universal, relevance, and thus invite an evaluation of their cross-cultural validity. Comparative studies may then help us separate the possibly universal from the culturally distinct forms of a good old age.

With regard to the universality that is often taken for granted when culture-unaware gerontologists discuss what constitutes a good old age, Scheidt *et al.* (1999) write that successful ageing has become a powerful paradigm in the culture of gerontology. As such, notions of what it means to age well have been debated quite intensively in our field because of the lack of culture relevance that tends to characterize 'mainstream' gerontology's research in this respect (cf. Cohen, 1998; Scheidt *et al.*, 1999; Thomas and Chambers, 1989; Torres, 2001b), as well as on the basis of the exclusive focus on native groups that has been characteristic of successful ageing enquiries (cf. Torres, 2004). Gerontologists who are anthropologically aware have, for example, enquired into the validity of this construct when the cultural settings of the older people being studied have been disregarded (e.g. Keith *et al.*, 1990). They have also questioned the focus on ageing well that is characteristic of what Cohen (1998) calls 'the internationalist (read American) gerontological epistemology' for having impeded mainstream gerontologists from understanding that neither the ageing process as such nor midlife is in fact the universal given that they assume them to be (cf. Ikels *et al.*, 1992 and Wray, 2006). Hence, the concept of ageing well is restrictively contingent upon 'the value system of the inquirer or their social construction of reality' (Bowling, 1993, p. 449).

In this respect it seems important to draw attention to the most comprehensive study of culture and ageing that has been conducted within the last decade, Project AGE, since this study explored, among other things, how the construct of successful ageing is understood in different cultural settings. Research in seven communities and four cultural sites (the !Kung and the Herero in Botswana, Clifden and Blessington in Ireland, Momence and Swarthmore in the USA, and Hong Kong) was undertaken in order to investigate how different communities shape the experience of ageing and pathways to well-being for their elderly populations (see, among others, Keith *et al.*, 1990, 1994 and Ikels *et al.*, 1995). As such, this project showed, among other things, that older people's understandings of successful ageing are contingent upon their culture of origin and that 'intercommunity variation interacts with cultural systems to influence how people define successful ageing' (Sokolovsky, 1997, p. xv). Thus, there was consistency in the factors assumed to produce a good old age and/or to lead to a difficult one. The four major factors mentioned by the informants in Project AGE were physical health and functioning, material security, family and sociality. Consistency does not, however, mean that there was uniformity in the manner in which the construct of successful ageing was understood since the importance accorded to these factors, as well as the implications that these were assumed to have, differed across the sites (cf. Fry *et al.*, 1997). Thus, although decline in physical health and functioning were mentioned when discussing what poses difficulty in old age in all sites, it was mostly in the US sites that the health status of individuals assumed to be having a good old age was discussed. In a similar manner, although family was thought to contribute to a good old age, it was clear that families play a less central role in providing economic and physical support in Ireland and the USA. The issue of sociality differed also since sociality was found to be most important in large-scale societies whereas it was less so in small-scale societies where people were seen as members of a collective rather than as individual personalities. Clear cultural differences regarding living arrangements in old age were also documented by Project AGE. Their results show, for example, that Americans associate successful ageing with self-sufficiency and independent living, while older people in Hong Kong could not understand why one would want to be self-sufficient in later life (cf. Ikels *et al.*, 1995).

Other culture-specific studies of successful ageing also attest to the powerful determining force of cultural values. In a phenomenological study of British and Indian elders' understandings, Thomas and Chambers (1989) found, for example, that religious beliefs and practices constitute a major theme in Indians' understandings of what it means to age well whereas this religious aspect did not play a central role in the manner in which this construct was understood by the British men interviewed. For the Canadian Inuit community, the important thing is not physical health per se but rather how declining health is managed. Hence, Collings (2001) argues that the most important determinant of successful ageing is not material but ideological since it is an individual's attitudes toward life, and in particular their willingness to pass on accumulated wisdom to the younger generation, that determines if an older person is deemed to be ageing successfully or not. Willcox *et al.* (2007), who studied what ageing well means to a group of older women weavers who come from the Okinawa region, found that weaving is part of the culture's identity in this region (known for having the longest average life expectancy for men and women in the world as well as the highest concentration of centenarians within Japan). Hence, remaining productive and socially engaged is central to ageing well for Okinawan women.

Torres' (1999) formulation of a culturally relevant theoretical framework from which studies of understandings of successful ageing can be launched can also be mentioned when presenting cross-cultural gerontologists' contributions to the debate on the successful ageing paradigm. This framework posits that there is congruence between the value orientation that people prefer and the understanding of successful ageing they uphold. In the preliminary testing of this framework, Torres (2001b, 2003) found that this seems to be the case. For example, those that had value orientations promoting mastering nature were the same people who thought of ageing well in terms of delaying the ageing process. In contrast, those that had value orientations promoting surrendering to nature were people who thought of successful ageing in terms of acceptance of and/or relinquishment to the debilitating aspects of later life. Hence, Torres (2003) suggests that understandings of successful ageing need not be based only on the value orientations underpinning some of the currently popular ageing paradigms. Other value orientations can be *and are* used as points of departure for conceptualizing what ageing well entails. Departing exclusively from the value orientations that we gerontologists uphold is problematic, as this is almost always synonymous with a disregard for other ways of making sense of this notion. Hence, Torres argues that the term 'successful ageing' is problematic only if we accept the ethnocentric manner in which it is handled by mainstream gerontologists – that is, if only Western understandings in this respect permeate the literature and are allowed to guide our practices. If the construct of successful ageing were to be seriously regarded as the cultural construction it actually is, then the 'problem with the paradigm of successful ageing', as Scheidt *et al.* (1999) refer to it, is that it excludes the variety of ways in which understandings concerned with it are constructed. Moreover, Torres' (2006a) study (the only study on successful ageing so far that has focused on migrants) showed that considerable variation exists in the manner in which Iranian immigrants to Sweden think about successful ageing. This suggests that there is not only intercultural variation in the manner in which this construct is understood but also intracultural variation. The Iranian immigrants interviewed claimed also to have reformulated the manner in which they thought about this construct since moving to Sweden and coming into contact with other ways of thinking about ageing well besides the ones they were accustomed to in their country of origin. Hence, Torres (2004) argues that findings such as these are important for raising not only gerontology's culture relevance with respect to what constitutes successful ageing but also the field's awareness of how theoretically profuse the migrant life course can be.

Regardless of whether the focus has been on single cultures or in-between cultures, the fact remains that successful ageing is one of the areas of studies to which cross-cultural and ethno-gerontologists have contributed by showing that established gerontological constructs are, in fact, far more culturally malleable than mainstream gerontologists seem willing to acknowledge. Great cultural differences exist in the manner in which the construct of successful ageing is understood, and this is why cross-cultural gerontologists have argued that the successful ageing paradigm is not culture-sensitive enough (Thomas and Chambers, 1989).

International migration and globalization: the challenges ahead

Despite the numerous contributions that the anthropology of ageing and the field of ethno-gerontology have made over the past decades, Daatland and Motel-Klingebiel (2007, p. 343) have claimed that 'gerontology has not invested seriously in comparative studies' even though these studies are very well suited to testing theoretical hypotheses. Related to this assertion is Tesch-Römer and von Kondratowitz's (2006) assessment that most of today's comparative studies are not as theory-driven as they should be. They have argued that 'the potentials of comparative ageing research are not fully realized for the time being. In many cases, there is little theorizing as to whether there should be differences (or similarities) in ageing processes across countries, societies and cultures' (p. 155). This provocative statement started a debate in the *European Journal of Ageing* about the pros and cons of comparative studies and, among others, the level of analysis that these depart from; that is, whether they are concerned with the comparisons of countries, societies or cultures. Although the debate in question is interesting in its own right, and relevant to studies of cross-cultural differences, it is this very issue about what it means to have culture as the preferred level of analysis and the specific challenges that globalization and international migration pose to that one level that will be addressed in this final section. The rationale for doing this is that this is likely to be a key issue for future research. Tesch-Römer and von Kondratowitz (2007, p. 104) state that 'today's reality in a world of globalizing social relations must be described as a mixture of cultures. Through travelling, migration, and the mass media, modern societies are not characterized by a "pure" monoculture, but by the coexistence, cooperation or conflict between various cultures.' Hence, it seems appropriate to end a chapter on cross-cultural differences in ageing with a section that addresses the implications of globalization and international migration for the fields that have been in focus here.

In one of the latest books published on the implications of globalization for gerontology, Torres (2006b) addresses the specific challenges that this phenomenon poses to the study of culture, migration, inequality and the periphery, which are some of the central issues often tackled by anthropo- and ethno-gerontologists. In that book, she lists some of the constitutive features of globalizing processes (such as the geographical expansion and increased density of international trade, relations, media, communities and exchanges of different kinds) and argues that globalization is bound to have 'a tangible impact not only on the world as we know it but on the way in which we acquire knowledge about that world' (Torres, 2006b, pp. 231–2). Globalization is, in other words, altering the contexts in which meaning construction takes place and is affecting people's sense of identity as it relates to place (cf. Giddens, 1994). Phillipson (2006) addresses the implications of globalization for the study of ageing in general and claims that this phenomenon has produced

a distinctive stage in the history of ageing, with tensions between nation-state-based policies concerning demographic change and those formulated by global actors and institutions. Social ageing can no longer be viewed solely as a national problem or issue, but one that affects individuals, groups, and communities across the globe. Local and national inter-pretations of ageing had substance where nation states (at least in the developed world) claimed some control over the construction of welfare policies. They also carried force where social policies were being designed with the aim or aspiration of leveling inequali-ties and where citizenship was still predominantly a national issue. The changes affecting all of these areas, largely set in motion by different aspects of globalization, are generating significant implications for work in the field of gerontology. (pp. 43–4)

It is for reasons such as these that Torres (2006b) set out to explore the specific challenges that globalization poses not only to the study of culture in general but also to the way in which we think about the impact that cultural values have on the manner in which we understand and experience ageing and old age. Tomlinson (1999, p. 27) argues, for example, that 'globalization disturbs the way we conceptualize "culture" for culture has long had connotations tying it to the idea of fixed locality', and this is one of the issues implicitly raised by Phillipson when he addresses – as he does in the quotation above – the relevance that national boundaries have had for the manner in which we think about societies and policies. To this end, globalization theorists interested in the specific implications of this phenomenon for the study of cultural values have argued that culture used to be conceived as a point of reference that was essentially territorial and 'belonged' to specific localities (cf. Gille and Riain, 2002; Kearny, 1995; Neverdeen Pieterse, 1994). This is why we used to think of cultural values as ideas that were taught through socialization within specific geographical localities. In global times such as ours, it has been suggested that culture must be thought of as 'general human software' that is not necessarily learned in a specific and easily discernible geographic locality (Swindler, 1986). Hannerz (1992, p. 261) suggests, for example, that 'the autonomy and boundness of cultures must nowadays be understood as a matter of degree'. Hence, Gille and Riain (2002) have argued that assessing the social by going to the local is not as easy a task as it used to be. King (1991, p. 6) suggests, in turn, that globalization complicates the study of culture not just because 'increasingly, many people have no roots; it's also that they have no soil'. It is because of these considerations that Torres (2000) has argued that although anthropo- and ethno-gerontologists have yet to develop a postmodern ethno-gerontology of their own, the time has come to address the impact that globalization will have on the manner in which we address culture and ethnicity in these fields (cf. Torres, 2006b).

Specifically of relevance to ethno-gerontology is Torres' (2008) discussion of the implications that the so-called 'age of migration' has for social gerontology in general, and the theoretical profuseness embedded in the study of the migrant life course in particular. With respect to the latter she argues (just as Blakemore (1999) argued before her although from the perspective of the fruitfulness embedded in studying ethnic differences per se) that the discontinuity that characterizes the migrant life course is an interesting source of information about how older people adapt to ageing. According to Blakemore (1999, p. 767), 'theorizing about old age tends to assume a stable society as a background to change'. It is because of this that Warnes *et al.* (2004) have argued that the globalization of international migration is bound to make an impact on the manner in which we study ageing and old age. When urging social gerontologists to consider this phenomenon as a future challenge to be reckoned with, they drew attention to the fact that the heterogeneity of older migrants is far larger in globalized times such as ours. It used to be the case – or rather we used to assume – that older migrants differed from their ethnic majority counterparts in clear-cut and distinctive ways (the double jeopardy hypothesis mentioned in a previous section is evidence of this). Nothing can be further from the truth these days. This is why Richmond (2002) argues that the globalization of international migration is weakening the oft-assumed distinction between 'typical sending' and 'typical receiving' countries and is questioning the stereotypical assumptions about migrants that we often make. Warnes *et al.* (2004, pp. 310–11) point out, for example, that 'in European countries today, older migrants include people who are among the most deprived and excluded in our societies . . . and others who are in the vanguard of innovative, developmental and positive approaches to later life'. With respect to the issue of heterogeneity they have suggested that there are at least four different groups of older migrants. One comprises those that have migrated late in life for amenity-seeking purposes, such as those that are often referred to as international retirement migrants. The other group that has also migrated late in life but which often has a different situation altogether is the group comprising older migrants that have migrated for family reunification purposes. The third group is those who have migrated earlier in life because of political and/or religious prosecution. Last but not least, there is the group consisting of those that have migrated for work (who tend to migrate earlier in life). Warnes *et al.*'s (2004) typology of older migrants distinguishes, in other words, between those that migrate young and age as migrants and those that migrate in old age. This typology differentiates also between different countries of origin and suggests that affinity between the cultures from which these older migrants came and the cultures to which they have migrated is bound to have an impact on how old age and ageing are experienced as a migrant. On the basis of all of these distinctions and what previous research has shown about these different groups, they suggest that older migrants' future welfare eligibility and health-care rights will be different for these different groups, and that is why European ethno-gerontologists need to pay attention to the implications that different welfare positions will have for the well-being of older migrants.

Thus, one of the challenges faced by ethno-gerontologists today concerns gaining an understanding of the causes of the heterogeneity of older migrants and the ways in which these affect the migrant life course in general and the manner in which ageing and old age are experienced and understood depending on different prior and post-migration conditions. In globalized times such as ours, for example, the sampling of migrant populations becomes a challenge since the interesting issue may no longer be how migrants fare in comparison to their native counterparts, but how different types of migrants fare compared with one another. Torres (2008) argues also that the age of migration is challenging social gerontologists to abandon what could be referred to as the traditional driving force of gerontological studies that focus on migrants (i.e. the idea that differences in culture of origin and host culture are what is interesting about them) for a migrant life-course focus that puts the actual process of migration and the post-migration situation of migrants at the very core of older migrants studies. Moreover, it must be noted that the heterogeneity of older migrants poses challenges not only to how research that is sensitive to this heterogeneity is going to be conducted, but also to how gerontological practice that can address this diversity in a culturally appropriate manner is to be designed and delivered.

Another challenge that the globalization of international migration and the state of affairs known as the 'age of migration' poses to ethno-gerontology is the phenomenon known as transnationalism. This phenomenon refers to the variety of multi-stranded social ties established and sustained by some migrants across national borders and the life-course linkages between countries of origin and host countries that these bring about (cf. Glick-Schiller, Basch and Szanton-Blanc, 1992, 1995). When describing what characterizes the lives of transnational migrants, Portes, Guarnizo and Landolt (1999, p. 217) write that these are people who 'live dual lives: speaking two languages, having homes in two countries and making a living through continuous regular contact across national borders'. The group of older migrants known as international retirement migrants belongs, in other words, to the transnational migrant group (cf. Gustafson, 2001; King, Warnes and Williams, 2000). The late-in-life amenity-seeking behavioural patterns that characterize these older migrants are bound to become an interesting source of information about, among other things, adaptation in later life and the way in which a successful old age is pursued. This is why it seems important to acknowledge that transnationalism is bound to be addressed by cross-cultural and ethno-gerontologists in the future. One of the challenges facing these gerontologists will be how to formulate and implement policies that cater for these migrants' needs, not to mention how to design health and social care services that suit their lifestyles. The work of Ackers and Dwyer (2002) and Dwyer (2000, 2001) is particularly interesting in this respect since it shows how entrepreneurial older migrants (particularly international retirement migrants who move from northern to southern Europe for amenity-seeking purposes) can be in navigating the welfare systems of the countries in which they live. With specific regard to research, transnationalism opens up new research questions, such as how does this phenomenon affect, for example, intergenerational relationships and intergenerational solidarity, and quality of life and well-being in old age, as well as the political economy of informal care. The way in which research is conducted is also affected by transnationalism since transnational communities challenge the one-culture/one-nation research design and one-culture/one-nation research teams that are typical of cross-cultural and ethno-gerontological enquiries now.

An additional consideration with respect to globalization and the age of migration is that these phenomena are expected to intensify the existing gaps in wealth and resources between the rich and the poor nations, between the First and the Third Worlds, and between what sociologists tend to refer to as 'the centre and the periphery' (i.e. the West and the rest) (cf. Bauman, 1998 and Mittleman, 2000). Richmond (2002, p. 715) argues, for example, that 'in a global economy based on unregulated free market principles, the rich is bound to get richer and the poor relatively poorer'. This is why globalization theorists tend nowadays to distinguish between the 'winners' and the 'losers' of globalization. Beck (2000) argues that older people in the 'losing' nations will suffer especially badly. This has implications for ethno-gerontologists – especially in the USA – whose ways of thinking are characterized by an emphasis on social inequality, discrimination, and racism (cf. Burton *et al.*, 1992) and for anthropo-gerontologists who focus on the Third World. With respect to the latter, it seems necessary to draw attention to Polivka (2001), who has argued that older people in developing countries will not only outnumber their counterparts in the developed world but become sicker and poorer in years to come. Globalization, it has thus been argued, challenges the study of 'the periphery' and hence in turn Third World-interested gerontologists to expand their research agendas to include issues concerning the implications that lack of economic resources and financial well-being have for ageing and old age. With respect to this, Torres (2006b) argues that in globalized times such as ours, we must make sure that non-Western older people do not end up being relegated both to 'the periphery' of the world and to the periphery of the gerontological imagination.

Conclusions

Having presented some of the challenges that globalization and international migration pose to the fields of enquiry with which this chapter is concerned, it seems propitious to bring this section to an end by suggesting that cross-cultural gerontologists' main concern used to be raising mainstream gerontology's understandings of how cultural values affect the way in which we make sense of, and experience, the process of ageing and old age. Ethno-gerontological enquiries seemed, in turn, to have been mostly preoccupied with calling attention to the inequalities that older ethnic minorities face and the fact that culturally and ethnically sensitive research, policy and practice are needed if we are to meet the needs and exploit the opportunities that diversity creates. In globalized times such as ours, the research agendas of these fields are being challenged in numerous ways to go back to their roots and engage even more in comparative endeavours since it is these that have led us to understand that the behaviour and attitudes of and about older people are (although diverse because of class, racial/ethnic, religious, occupational, educational, income and family differences) always understandable within the socio-cultural contexts that have given them their meaning (cf. Climo, 1992). Without them, cross-cultural and ethno-gerontology stand little chance of further developing a globalization and international migration-aware gerontological imagination of their own.

Summary

The study of ethnicity and culture's impact on the way in which ageing and old age are experienced and understood began with anthropological enquiries to unveil the position that older people were accorded in different societies. Hence, this chapter begins with an abridged presentation of the work that the founding fathers of anthropo-gerontology – Simmons, Cowgill and Holmes – did to pave the way for gerontological enquiries into cross-cultural differences. After presenting the way in which the anthropology of ageing developed, we move on to present another line of enquiry into cross-cultural differences in ageing and old age – ethno-gerontology. At the core of this section are the concepts of double jeopardy and age as levelling since these are central to the way in which ethnicity's impact on ageing and old age is understood. In this section we touch upon both the way in which an 'ethnic lens' to gerontology has developed in the USA and the British scepticism in relation to developing an ethno-gerontological imagination of their own. This we do in order to give the reader some insight into how the study of cross-cultural and ethnic differences can be approached. The chapter moves on to shed light on empirical research on one of the most debated concepts in gerontology – successful aging. This is done in order to show how malleable this concept is when examined across different cultures, and how adopting a single cultural stance can lead to distorted interpretations. The chapter concludes with a detailed critical review of the challenges that international migration and globalization pose to the way in which we study culture and ethnicity's impact on the experience of ageing and old age. This is done in order to give the reader a bit of insight into one of the debates that preoccupy ethnicity and culture-aware gerontologists now. This chapter aims, finally, not only to introduce readers to the roots of this line of enquiry but also to give them a bit of insight into where the field is heading.

REFERENCES

Ackers, L. and Dwyer, P. (2002) *Senior citizenship? Retirement, migration and welfare in the European Union.* Bristol: Policy Press.

Albert, S.M. and Cattell, M.G. (1994) *Old age in global perspective.* New York: G.K. Hall.

Amoss, P.L. and Harrell, S. (1981) Introduction: an anthropological perspective on aging, in P.L. Amoss and S. Harrell (eds), *Other ways of growing old: anthropological perspectives.* Stanford, CA: Stanford University Press, 1–24.

Arnhoff, F.N., Leone, H.V. and Lorge, I. (1964) Cross-cultural acceptance of stereotypes toward aging, *Journal of Social Psychology, 63,* 41–58.

Bauman, Z. (1998) *Globalization: the human consequences.* New York: Columbia University Press.

Beck, U. (2000) *What Is globalization?* Cambridge: Polity Press.

Blakemore, K. (1997) From minorities to majorities: perspectives on culture, ethnicity and ageing in British gerontology, in A. Jamieson, S. Harper and C. Victor (eds), *Critical approaches to ageing and later life.* Buckingham: Open University Press, 27–38.

(1999) International migration in later life: social care and policy implications, *Ageing and Society, 19*(6), 761–74.

Blakemore, K. and Boneham, M. (1994) *Age, race and ethnicity: a comparative approach.* Buckingham: Open University Press.

Boneham, M. (2002) Researching ageing in different cultures, in A. Jamieson and C. Victor (eds), *Researching ageing and later life: the practice of social gerontology.* Buckingham: Open University Press, 199–210.

Bowling, A. (1993) The concepts of successful and positive ageing, *Family Practice, 10*(4), 449–53.

Burton, L. and Bengtson, V.L. (1982) Research in elderly minority communities, in R.C. Manuel (ed.), *Minority aging.* Westport, CT: Greenwood Press, 282–303.

Burton, L.M., Dilworth-Andersson, P. and Bengtson, V.L. (1992) Creating culturally-relevant ways of thinking about diversity and ageing: theoretical challenges for the twenty-first century, in E. Percil Stanford and F.M. Torres-Gil (eds), *Diversity: new approaches to ethnic minority aging.* New York: Baywood, 6–21.

Clark, M. (1967) The anthropology of aging: a new area for studies of culture and personality, *The Gerontologist, 7,* 55–64.

Clark, M. and Anderson, B. (1967) *Culture and aging: an anthropological study of older Americans.* Springfield, IL: Charles Thomas.

Climo, J.J. (1992) The role of anthropology in gerontology: theory, *Journal of Aging Studies, 6*(1), 41–55.

Cohen, L. (1994) Old age: cultural and critical perspectives, *Annual Review of Anthropology, 23,* 137–58.

(1998) *No aging in India: Alzheimer's, the bad family, and other modern things.* Berkeley, CA: University of California Press.

Collings, P. (2001) 'If you got everything, it's good enough': perspectives on successful ageing in a Canadian Inuit community, *Journal of Cross-Cultural Gerontology, 16*(2), 127–55.

Cornell, S. and Hartmann, D. (1998) *Ethnicity and race: making identities in a changing world.* Thousand Oaks, CA: Pine Forge Press.

Cowgill, D. (1974a) Aging and modernization: a revision of the theory, in J.F. Gubrium (ed.), *Late life: community and environmental policy.* Springfield, IL: Charles Thomas, 124–46.

 (1974b) The aging of populations and society, *Annals of the American Academy of Political and Social Sciences*, *415*, 1–18.

Cowgill, D. and Holmes, L.D. (eds) (1972) *Aging and modernization.* New York: Appleton-Century-Crofts.

Daatland, S.-O. (2007) The comparative ambition, *European Journal of Ageing*, *4*, 93–5.

Daatland, S.-O. and Motel-Klingebiel, A. (2007) Separating the local and the general in cross-cultural aging research, in H.W. Wahl, C. Tesch-Römer and A. Hoff (eds), *New dynamics in old age: individual, environmental and societal perspectives.* Amityville, NY: Baywood Publishing, 343–59.

Dowd, J.J. and Bengtson, V.L. (1978) Aging in minority populations: an examination of the double jeopardy hypothesis, *Journal of Gerontology*, *33*, 427–36.

Dwyer, P. (2000) Movements to some purpose? An exploration of international retirement migration in the European Union, *Education and Ageing*, *15*(3), 353–77.

 (2001) Retired EU migrants, healthcare rights and European social citizenship, *Journal of Social Welfare and Family Law*, *23*(3), 311–27.

Fisher, B.J. (1992) Successful aging and life satisfaction: a pilot study for conceptual clarification, *Journal of Aging Studies*, *6*, 191–202.

 (1995) Successful aging, life satisfaction and generativity in later life, *International Journal of Aging & Human Development*, *41*, 239–50.

Fry, C.L. (1980) Toward an anthropology of aging, in C. Fry (ed.), *Aging in culture and society: comparative viewpoints and strategies.* New York: Praeger Publishers, 139–236.

 (eds) (1981) *Aging, culture and health.* New York: Praeger Publishers.

 (1996) Age, aging and culture, in R.H. Binstock and L.K. George (eds), *Handbook of ageing and the social sciences.* New York: Academic Press, 117–36.

Fry, C.L., Dickerson-Putman, J., Draper, P. *et al.* (1997) Culture and the meaning of a good old age, in J. Sokolovsky (ed.), *The cultural context of aging: worldwide perspectives.* Westport, CT and London: Bergin & Garvey, 99–123.

Giddens, A. (1994) Living in a post-traditional society, in U. Beck, A. Giddens and S. Lash (eds), *Reflexive modernization.* Cambridge: Polity Press, 16–49.

Gille, Z. and Riain, S.O. (2002) Global ethnography, *Annual Review of Sociology*, *28*, 271–95.

Glick-Schiller, N., Basch, L. and Szanton-Blanc, C. (eds) (1992) *Towards a transnational perspective on migration: race, class, ethnicity and nationalism reconsidered.* New York: New York Academy of Science.

 (eds) (1995) From immigrant to transmigrant: theorizing transnational migration, *Anthropological Quarterly*, *68*(1), 48–63.

Green, J. (1989) Aging and ethnicity: an emergent issue in social gerontology, *Journal of Cross-Cultural Gerontology*, *4*, 377–83.

Gustafson, P. (2001) Retirement migration and transnational lifestyles, *Ageing and Society*, *21*(4), 371–94.

Hannerz, U. (1992) *Cultural complexity: studies in the social organization of meaning.* New York: Columbia University Press.

Holmes, E.R. and Holmes, L.D. (1995) *Other cultures, elder years.* Newbury Park, CA: Sage.

Holmes, L.D. (1980) Trends in anthropological gerontology: from Simmons to the seventies, in J. Hendricks (ed.), *In the country of the old*. New York: Baywood Publishing Company, 35–44.

Ikels, C., Dickerson-Putman, J., Draper, P. *et al.* (1995) Comparative perspectives on successful aging, in L. Bond, S.J. Cutler and A. Grams (eds), *Promoting successful and productive aging*. Thousand Oaks, CA: Sage, 304–23.

Ikels, C., Keith, J., Dickerson-Putman, J. *et al.* (1992) Perceptions of the adult life course: a cross-cultural analysis, *Ageing and Society*, *12*, 49–84.

Jackson, M., Kolody, B. and Wood, J.L. (1982) To be old and black: the case for double jeopardy in income and health, in R.C. Manuel (ed.), *Minority aging*. Westport, CT: Greenwood Press, 95–100.

Jary, D. and Jary, J. (1991) *The HarperCollins dictionary of sociology*. New York: HarperPerennial.

Jenkins, R. (1996) *Social identity*. London and New York: Routledge.

   (1997) *Rethinking ethnicity: arguments and explorations*. Thousand Oaks, CA: Sage.

Kearney, M. (1995) The local and the global: the anthropology of globalization and transnationalism, *Annual Review of Anthropology*, *24*, 547–65.

Keith, J. (1980) 'The best is yet to be': toward an anthropology of age, *Annual Review of Anthropology*, *9*, 339–64.

Keith, J., Fry, C.L., Glascock, A.P. *et al.* (1994) *The ageing experience: diversity and commonality across cultures*. London: Sage.

Keith, J., Fry, C.L. and Ikels, C. (1990) Community as context for successful aging, in J. Sokolovsky (ed.), *The cultural context of aging*. New York: Bergin & Garvey Publishers, 245–61.

Kent, D. (1971) The elderly in minority groups, *The Gerontologist*, *11*, 26–9.

King, A.D. (ed.) (1991) *Culture, globalization and the world-system: contemporary conditions for the representation of identity*. Binghampton, NY: State University of New York Press.

King, R., Warnes, A.M. and Williams, A.M. (2000) *Sunset lives: British retirement to the Mediterranean*. Oxford: Berg.

Kramer, J.B. and Barker, J.C. (1994) Ethnicity in the elderly: book review essay, *Journal of Cross-Cultural Gerontology*, *9*, 403–17.

Maxwell, R.J. and Silverman, P. (1970) Information and esteem: cultural considerations in the treatment of the aged, *Aging and Human Development*, *1*, 361–92.

Mittleman, J.H. (2000) Globalization: captors and captive, *Third World Quarterly*, *21*(6), 917–29.

Myerhoff, B. and Simić, A. (eds) (1978) *Life's career ageing: cultural variations on growing old*. Thousand Oaks, CA: Sage Publications.

Nazroo, J. (2006) Ethnicity and old age, in J.A. Vincent, C.R. Phillipson and M. Downs (eds), *The futures of old age*. London: Sage Publications, 63–73.

Nederveen-Pieterse, J. (1994) Globalization as hybridization, *International Sociology*, *9*(2), 161–84.

Palmore, E.B. and Manton, K.M. (1974) Modernization and status of the aged: international correlations, *Journal of Gerontology*, *29*, 205–10.

Phillipson, C. (2006) Ageing and globalization: issues for critical gerontology and political economy, in J. Baars, D. Dannefer, C. Phillipson *et al.* (eds), *Aging, globalization and inequality: the new critical gerontology*. Amityville, NY: Baywood Publishing Company, 183–204.

Polivka, L. (2001) Globalization, population, aging and ethics, *Journal of Aging and Identity*, **6**(3), 147–63.

Portes, A., Guarnizo, L.E. and Landolt, P. (1999) The study of transnationalism: pitfalls and the promise of an emergent research field, *Ethnic and Racial Studies*, **22**, 217–37.

Press, I. and McKool, M. (1972) Social structure and status of the aged, *Aging and Human Development*, **3**, 297–306.

Richmond, A.H. (2002), Globalization: implications for immigrants and refugees, *Ethnic and Racial Studies*, **25**(5), 707–27.

Rubinstein, R.L. (ed.) (1990) *Anthropology and ageing: comprehensive reviews*. Dordrecht: Kluwer Academic Publishers.

Scheidt, R.J., Humpherys, D.R. and Yorgason, J.B. (1999) Successful aging: what's not to like, *Journal of Applied Social Gerontology*, **3**, 277–82.

Simmons, L. (1945) *The role of the aged in primitive society*. New Haven, CT: Archon Books.
  (1946) Attitudes toward aging and the aged: primitive societies, *Journal of Gerontology*, **1**, 72–94.
  (1960) Aging in primitive societies: a comparative survey of family life and relationships, in C. Tibbetts (ed.), *Handbook of social gerontology*. University of Chicago Press, 62–91.

Sokolovsky, J. (ed.) (1997) *The cultural context of ageing: worldwide perspectives*. Westport, CT and London: Bergin & Garvey.

Swindler, A. (1986) Culture in action: symbols and strategies, *American Sociological Review*, **51**, 273–88.

Tesch-Römer, C. and von Kondratowitz, H.J. (2006) Comparative ageing research: a flourishing field in need of theoretical cultivation, *European Journal of Ageing*, **3**, 155–67.
  (2007) Unique as well as universal – complexities of comparative ageing research, *European Journal of Ageing*, **4**, 103–6.

Thomas, L.E. and Chambers, K.O. (1989) Successful aging among elderly men in England and India: a phenomenological comparison, in L. Eugene Thomas (ed.), *Research on adulthood and aging: the human science approach*. Albany, NY: State University of New York Press, 183–203.

Tomlinson, J. (1999) *Globalization and culture*. University of Chicago Press.

Torres, S. (1999) A culturally-relevant theoretical framework for the study of successful ageing, *Ageing and Society*, **19**(1), 33–51.
  (2000) A postmodern ethnogerontology: why not?...what for?, *Contemporary Gerontology*, **6**(4), 114–17.
  (2001a) Understandings of successful ageing in the context of migration: the case of Iranian immigrants to Sweden, *Ageing and Society*, **19**(1), 33–51.
  (2001b) Understandings of successful ageing: cultural and migratory perspectives. Uppsala, Sweden: Dissertation defended at the Department of Sociology, Uppsala University.
  (2003) A preliminary empirical test of a culturally-relevant theoretical framework for the study of successful ageing, *Journal of Cross-Cultural Gerontology*, **18**, 73–91.
  (2004) Making sense of the construct of successful ageing: the migrant experience, in S.O. Daatland and S. Biggs (eds), *Ageing and diversity: multiple pathways and cultural migrations*. Bristol: Policy Press, 125–39.
  (2006a) Different ways of understanding the construct of successful aging: Iranian immigrants speak about what aging well means to them, *Journal of Cross-Cultural Gerontology*, **21**, 1–23.

(2006b) Culture, migration, inequality and 'periphery' in a globalized world: challenges for the study of ethno- and anthropo-gerontology, in J. Baars, D. Dannefer, C. Phillipson *et al.* (eds), *Aging, globalization and inequality: the new critical gerontology*. Amityville, NY: Baywood Publishing Company, 231–51.

(2008) The age of migration: what does it mean and why should European social gerontologists care?, *Retraite et Société*, *16*, 67–90.

(2009) Vignette methodology and culture-relevance: lessons learned from a study on Iranians' understandings of successful aging, *Journal of Cross-Cultural Gerontology*, *24*(1), 93–114.

Usui, W. (1989) Challenges in the development of ethnogerontology, *The Gerontologist*, *29*(4), 566–8.

Wallman, S. (ed.) (1979) *Ethnicity at work*. London: Macmillan.

Warnes, A.M., Friedrich, K., Kellaher, L. *et al.* (2004) The diversity and welfare of older migrants in Europe, *Ageing and Society*, *24*(3), 307–26.

Willcox, D.C., Willcox, B.J., Sokolovsky, J. *et al.* (2007) The cultural context of successful ageing among older women weavers in a northern Okinawan village: the role of productive activity, *Journal of Cross-Cultural Gerontology*, *22*, 137–65.

Wray, S. (2006) Women making sense of midlife: ethnic and cultural diversity, *Journal of Aging Studies*, *21*, 31–42.

13 Technology and ageing

ANTHEA TINKER

OVERVIEW

This chapter examines how technology can enhance and compensate in the lives of older adults. It critically examines the scope and value of technology, and its use in specific circumstances (including dementia, care, transport), special considerations (e.g. gender, ethics), and future directions and policy.

Introduction

Technology is developing at a very rapid pace. These developments allied to an ageing population make 'technology and ageing' an exciting topic to study. Technology covers a wide range of meanings including 'the application of scientific knowledge for practical purposes' and 'machinery and equipment developed from such scientific knowledge', which is the definition in the *Oxford English Dictionary* (Soanes, 2005). *Gerontechnology* is the embracing term which covers technology for older people.

This chapter will start by considering the scope of technology and the people for whom it is designed. The focus is on ageing, which necessitates a life-course approach. People do not become 'old' on a particular birthday although for purposes of services, such as pensions, a chronological threshold date is often chosen (see Chapter 1). The experience of people before they reach a defined date is crucial when considering the use of technology. Those for whom a handwritten note or typewriter is the most modern form of communication are very different from those who use computers with ease. It is, therefore, important to look at both the current and future generations of older people, and it is useful to start by examining the scope of technology.

The scope of technology

As stated above, the general term for technology for older people, although not a familiar expression in countries such as the UK, is *gerontechnology*. Before 1990 there were many different ways of describing the subject including 'ergonomics for old people' and 'aids for the handicapped' (Bouma, 2007). Others in their research merely described the types of technology such as alarms or communication aids without necessarily using a generic term (Tinker, 1984). In 1997 the International Society for Gerontechnology (ISG) was established. This came about as a result of a series of international conferences on ageing and technology. The journal *Gerontechnology* was founded by the ISG in 2001. The journal states that its objectives are 'devoted to the fundamental aspects of technology to serve the ageing population'. Herman Bouma, one of the founders, describes it as being at the cross-fertilization matrix between gerontology (the study of ageing) and technology (understanding innovation) (Bouma, 2007). The most comprehensive account of the development of gerontechnology is in the paper 'Gerontechnology in Perspective' (Bouma, Fozard, Bouwhuis *et al.*, 2007). The key element, according to some, is 'consumer pull as opposed to technology push' (Clarkson, Coleman, Keates *et al.*, 2003, p. 601). In other words, the growth in gerontechnology is actually being more influenced by what consumers want rather than real innovations in the technology.

A simpler way of looking at gerontechnology is to consider the ways it may be needed (Tinker, 1999). These include (1) the need for contact (e.g. for information, reassurance, medication, social and practical purposes); (2) help with personal, domestic and mobility problems (e.g. nutrition, hygiene, mobility, environmental); and (3) medical (for diagnosis, treatment and rehabilitation).

Bouma expands this to consider technology to address the problems of physical and psychological restrictions – in other words to address the gradual slowing of functions (Bouma, 2007). These include the following:

- mobility – walking and equilibrium
- sensory – vision (acuity, field of view) and hearing (noisy environments, speech, directional bearing)
- motor – trembling (writing, fine motor skills) and declining strength
- memory – short-term, working, long-term
- multiple (i.e. the ability to carry out more than one task at a time) tasks.

| Gerontechnology impact matrix | | | | |
| Life domain | | | | |
Goal	Health Self-esteem	Housing Daily living	Mobility Transport	Communication Governance	Work Leisure
Enhancement Satisfaction	*Telemedicine* *Internet/www*	*Wireless/remote* *(e.g.phone)*	*GPS navigation* *Info publ. transp.*	*Mobile phone* *Internet/www*	*Digital* *camera* *Internet/* *www*
Prevention Engagement	*Healthy diet* *Home trainer*	*Smart ventil.* *Safety illumin.*	*Car automation* *Traffic info*	*Video links*	*Focused* *lighting*
Compensation Assistance	*Passive/active* *alarms*	*Smart IADL*	*Pedelec* *Battery* *wheelchair*	*Hearing aids*	*Power* *tools* *Robot pet*
Care support organization	*Smart intake* *Control-PDA*	*Electronic keys*	*Powered lifting*	*Care networks* *Video links*	*Robots*

Figure 13.1 Gerontechnology impact matrix. GPS: Global Positioning System; IADL: instrumental activities of daily living; PDA: personal digital assistant. *Source:* reproduced by kind permission of Professor Bouma (2007).

Technology can also be considered as fixed (such as housing adaptations, e.g. a walk-in shower), portable (such as bath seats, wheelchairs), and electronic (such as smoke detectors, alarms).

A third way of looking at technology is to consider the varied involvement of professionals: where a professional uses equipment in the home; where a professional uses equipment in a situation that is not domestic (e.g. in the doctor's surgery); and some monitoring where the older person, professional and family may respond to certain events. Yet another perspective, which contributes to a theoretical approach, is that of the goals of gerontechnology. Bouma describes these as enhancement and satisfaction, prevention and engagement, compensation and assistance, and care support and organization (see Figure 13.1). The latter definitions are useful ones by which to measure the value of technology.

Bouma also suggests that another conceptual way of looking at technology is to consider the purposes it might have. This is interesting because it also involves one of the essential elements of the subject which is its multidisciplinarity. He divides the purposes as follows:

- supporting the ageing body (nutrition, such as healthy food, and physiology, such as regular exercise)
- supporting the ageing mind (psychology, such as mental activities)
- supporting social relations and interest in society (social psychology, such as contacts with family, friends, etc.)

- supporting an enabling society (sociology)
- supporting health (medicine, such as combating disease and rehabilitation).

Under 'supporting an enabling society' other social sciences could be added, including social policy, economics and sociology.

There is need for caution when considering findings about technology and older people because of the relative absence of robust research. In general, good-quality studies about technology are still scarce and the generalizability of most findings is somewhat limited (Hailey, Roine and Ohinmaa, 2002; Hailey, Ohinmaa and Roine, 2004). For older people there is very little in the way of large trials.

A section later in this chapter describes in more detail the kinds of technology and the needs they are designed to meet. However, the growth in papers given at ISG conferences (for example, nearly 200 in June 2008, which ranged from a step machine to help with osteoarthritis to a hand-held game console as a companion for older people) demonstrates the range of research which is going on.

Some factors affecting demand from older people for technology

Differing definitions of older age

As noted in Chapter 1, ageing takes place from birth, and how this is defined may be biological, social or psychological. People will age at different rates and in different circumstances. The age at which a person is considered 'old' depends on factors that include chronological age, how they look, how they are perceived by others, the cultural context, and, sometimes, an arbitrary definition for the sake of providing services. It is also possible to define older people by cohorts, but there may be differences here too. The key factor when considering ageing is to recognize the changing demographic profile of older people. This can be summed up as an increase in the numbers and proportion of older people. This is paralleled by an increase in the numbers and proportions of very old people and the decline in support ratios. All of these together with other factors will be examined in turn to see what the impact is likely to be on technology. A note of caution should be sounded. There is uncertainty about birth rates, mortality, emigration and immigration, not only in terms of projecting current trends but also because there are local differences.

A changing demographic profile

There are a number of important demographic factors to take into account. These include an increase in numbers and proportions of older people, an increase in

Table 13.1 Percentage of total population aged 60 and over in 2006 and projections for 2050

	2006	2050
World total	11	22
More developed regions*	20	32
Less developed regions**	8	20
Least developed regions***	5	10
Example of regions/UK		
UK	21	29
Asia	9	24
Africa	5	10

Source: UN Population Division, 2006 (9).
* All regions of Europe and North America, Australia/New Zealand and Japan.
** All regions of Africa, Asia (excluding Japan), Latin America and the Caribbean, and three other regions.
*** Includes 48 countries of which 33 are in Africa, 9 in Asia and 5 in Oceania.
Reproduced by kind permission of the United Nations.

numbers and proportions of very old people, more older people living alone, a decline in support ratios, and an ageing workforce.

An increase in numbers and proportions of older people

Table 13.1 shows the projected increase in both numbers and proportions of older people. The definition of an older person here is that given by the United Nations; that is, aged 60 and over (United Nations Population Division, 2006). A varied picture is presented with a projected doubling of proportions in the world from 2006 to 2050, but with much larger increases in less developed regions. Table 13.2 shows that there will be large increases in the numbers and proportions of very old people as a proportion of old people. In most cases the increases will be dramatic. Again the definition of very old is arbitrary – in this case aged 80 and over.

The reasons for an ageing population include falls in fertility rates and low mortality. The fall in the birth rate was the original principal reason for an ageing population, and this is still the case for some developing countries. But in countries with already high proportions of older people where there is low fertility and low mortality, it is falls in mortality at older ages that are now a major determinant of continued population ageing.

One of the important reasons for an increased role for technology within an ageing population is that there is a strong association between age and disability (Office for National Statistics, 2008). This means that older people will need more

Anthea Tinker

Table 13.2 Percentage of population aged 80 and over as a percentage of all aged 60 and over in 2006 and projections for 2050

	2006	2050
World total	13	20
More developed regions*	19	29
Less developed regions**	10	18
Least developed regions***	7	10
Example of regions/UK		
UK	21	30
Asia	11	19
Africa	8	10

Source: UN Population Division, 2006 (9).
*, **, *** as Table 13.1.
Reproduced by kind permission of the United Nations.

help with tasks in the home and for their personal care either from humans or technology. The increased risk of dementia, which rises to one in five of the population of those aged 80 and over, will also bring potential challenges for technology as will end-of-life strategies. At the same time family sizes are dropping and more couples are deciding not to have children or to have one child only. This will mean that any informal help has to come from a declining pool of people.

More older people living alone

The above problems are magnified by an increase in the proportion and number of older people living alone. In 2006, 8 per cent of older men and 19 per cent of older women lived alone in the world (United Nations Population Division, 2006). If technology can help, there may be less need for dependence on human support.

A decline in support ratios

Support ratios are defined as the number of people aged 15-64 per older person aged 65 and older (United Nations Population Division, 2006). Across the world, if present trends continue, there will be a decline in support ratios. In other words, there will be fewer people of working age (that does not necessarily mean that they will all be in paid work, of course) in relation to older people (Table 13.3). While the support ratios will decline everywhere, this will be most marked in Asia and Africa.

An ageing workforce

The other side of the picture of an increase in numbers and proportions of older people is that it is projected that there will be a decline in numbers of younger

Table 13.3 Potential support ratio in 2006 and projections for 2050$^+$

	2006	2050
World total	9	4
More developed regions*	4	2
Less developed regions**	11	4
Least developed regions***	17	10
Example of regions/UK		
UK	4	3
Asia	10	4
Africa	16	10

Source: UN Population Division, 2006 (9).
*, **, *** as Table 13.1.
+ The number of people aged 15–64 per older person aged 65 and older.
Source: Reproduced by kind permission of the United Nations.

workers. For example, in the UK it is projected that while the percentage of people of working age will decline from 61.9 per cent in 2004 to 56.7 per cent the percentage of pensioners will rise from 18.6 to 27.5 per cent in the same period (Government Actuary's Department, 2004). One of the effects of an ageing workforce is that older people may be either encouraged to remain in paid employment or persuaded to return to the workforce. The latter might be to a new kind of job. Technology may have a role to play in the design of either the workplace or the equipment that is used in workspaces. However, any modifications likely to be made (such as better lighting) would benefit all employees.

Using technology: differences between current and future generations

As already indicated there will be many differences between generations that will affect their use of technology. Those who were born before the Second World War may not have experienced modern technology, but they were the generation who went through a war and saw rapid developments during that time. It also gave many women the experience for the first time of working in factories and with machinery, thus giving them an insight into the vast potential of technology. People who are approaching old age now have lived through very different experiences from their parents and grandparents. Many will have direct experience of computers, mobile phones and other gadgets at work. This kind of technology also reduces the physical demands of day-to-day living – which may mean that current generations of older people have more energy for work (Charness and Czaja, 2005).

In summary, what the previous sections have shown is that an increasingly old generation, some of whose members will be physically and mentally impaired, will look for help with their personal and domestic tasks. With a greater number of older people living alone and the growing reduction in the size of families together with a lack of people in the workforce, families may well turn to technology to try to solve their problems. There may, of course, be other solutions such as cheap labour from other countries, but for many the answer may be technology.

Types of technology and the needs they are designed to meet

The most rapid development of technology has occurred in the last 150 years where new products, new services, mass production and mass distribution, together with new materials and globalization, have accelerated changes in life for most people (Bouma, 2007).

The use of computers varies according to age. In the USA, a large (2,000 participants) representative sample of older adults was studied (Charness, 2008). It was found that increased use was associated with positive attitudes about technology, level of higher education and being in work, but older age was associated with decreased technology use independently of these other factors. There may be age-related problems with using computers for some older people. These include vision, hearing, motor ability and cognition. One way of making computers easier is to customize features that can be set to meet individual needs (Hanson, Snow-Weaver and Trewin, 2006). In the UK in 2006, 63 per cent of people of all ages had used the Internet in the past 3 months, but the figure for people aged 65 and over was only 20 per cent. In the European Union (EU) in 2004, 8 per cent of those aged 65–74 had used the Internet (Whitney and Keith, 2006).

The absence of robust research in this field has already been mentioned. One exception to this is the European Seniors Watch Survey in 2000 on new technologies, which focused on computers (Ekberg, 2002). This was a study of 9,600 older people in the EU. One of the most interesting things about this survey was the way the researchers classified their participants. These were as follows:

- the *digitally challenged* – those with no experience and no interest in computers
- the *technologically open-minded* – non-users but keen on learning about technology and/or wishing to gain computer skills
- the *old-age beginners* – users with fewer computer skills using computers less than once a week
- the *experienced front-runners* – users with advanced computer skills using computers at least once a week.

There was a steady drop in interest according to age but 53 per cent of those over 70 were still keen to learn about new technologies.

It is easy to assume that the experiences of younger and older adults are different partly because today's younger generations have in general grown up with computers and they will therefore be more comfortable with them in old age. However, as Xie (2003) has pointed out, there are complex cultural and social contexts to take into account. He also argues that if, for instance, 'future prices of computer equipment and Internet access are too high for future generations of older adults who have limited financial resources in retirement, then it is likely that those older adults, even though they might have had proper experience with and interest in ICTs [information and communication technology], would have to reduce or even eliminate their use of computers and the internet later in life' (Xie, 2003, p. 300).

Before about 1990, the focus of technology for older people was on *assistive technology* (AT) for people with disabilities (often referred to then as 'handicapped'). Some of the terms used for technology are used interchangeably. These terms include *AT*, *aids and adaptations*, *telecare* and *telemedicine*. The World Health Organization (WHO) defined *AT* as 'an umbrella term for any device or system that allows an individual to perform a task they would otherwise be unable to do or increases the ease and safety with which the task can be performed' (World Health Organization, 2004, p. 10). They defined an assistive device as 'equipment that enables an individual who requires assistance to perform the daily activities essential to maintain health and autonomy and to live as full a life as possible' (p. 10). AT can be fixed (e.g. adaptations), portable (e.g. bath seats, wheelchairs) or electronic (e.g. some detectors, alarms). Research for the Royal Commission on Long-Term Care showed the potentiality of AT in meeting the needs of older people on the margins of institutional care (Cowan and Turner-Smith, 1999; Tinker, Wright, McCreadie *et al.*, 1999).

Alarms are among the oldest forms of AT both in mainstream and specialist housing. There are several different ways of activating them (wrist, pendant, pull cord, wall-mounted intercom, telephone, etc.). Their main purpose is to enable a response to be made in emergencies and to provide reassurance (Fisk, 2003). Research shows that alarms are both underused and misused (Fisk, 2003; Tinker, Wright, Hanson *et al.*, 2007). An example of the latter is in a study of remodelled sheltered housing where the alarm was used for internal communications (Tinker *et al.*, 2007). When this happened it was found that there was no distinction between real emergencies and routine calls (e.g. to ask whether a prescription has arrived). This system (where the alarm call goes to people outside the scheme) left residents with no means of contacting the staff or one another. Incorporating a hotel-like telephone system could be one of the technological solutions to this problem.

Aids and adaptations are another form of technology often incorporated under 'AT'. There is good research evidence, especially from the UK, about the value of repairs, improvements and adaptations in the home (Tinker *et al.*, 1999). Home Improvement Agencies (HIAs) have been set up in most parts of the country. They are non-profit-making bodies to provide help, mainly to elderly owner occupiers, with improving, adapting and repairing their homes. They are a feature of UK policies that were highlighted in the main Housing Strategy Paper where stress was laid on their key role to enable householders to exercise choice about their home environment (Department for Communities and Local Government, 2008). In the 1970s they had a clear client focus of older owner occupiers living in poor or unsuitable housing but this has widened to other vulnerable sections of the public. Other services have developed including the 'handyperson' services (Care and Repair, 2006). These are people who can provide a wide variety of small but important tasks in and around the home to enable people to maintain and improve their living environment. Technology does not necessarily mean computerized equipment – it also includes application of practical/novel solutions, such as grips to open bottles and jars.

There are two branches of gerontechnology that include the prefix *tele* ('at a distance'). They are *telemedicine* and *telecare*. Telemedicine has been defined by the WHO as 'the employment of communication technology to provide assistance in the diagnosis, treatment, care and management of health conditions in remote areas' (World Health Organization, 2004, p. 54). Other definitions include these phrases, 'the delivery of health care at a distance' and 'the remote exchange of physiological data between a patient at home and medical staff at hospitals'. The assumption is that there is a health professional at one or both ends of the communication, thus allowing conditions to be monitored and/or second opinions to be sought. Telehealth is another description for the use of devices such as those described above. They include devices for measuring weight, blood pressure, blood glucose and oxygen saturation. Units can be tailored to measure, for example, diabetes, hypertension, congestive heart failure and chronic obstructive pulmonary disease. One of the leaders in the field of telemedicine (and currently editor of the journal *Telemedicine and Telecare*) is Richard Wootton. The book he co-edited with John Craig (*Introduction to Telemedicine*) in 1999 has stood the test of time with its descriptions of the services covered and how these can be developed and evaluated (Wootton and Craig, 1999).

'Telecare' is a collective term for information and communications technology (ICT) used to provide care remotely in people's homes. For example, it can be used to monitor health-related daily activities, as well as providing automatic detection and notification of emergencies (see Department of Health, 2005). Hanson and colleagues describe the types of sensors as those which monitor security and safety of the domestic environment, personal safety, vital health signs and daily activities in lifestyle (Hanson, Osipovič, Hine *et al.*, 2006). The researchers state that the rationale behind this is an assumption that in the long run it will allow older people and people with long-standing health conditions to live independently in their homes for longer and at the same time there will be a saving of public resources. However, they point to the following challenges:

- technological, not just about re-engineering existing services but also moving on from adding to the available social alarm technology to an intelligent sensor system
- organizational, diverse and complex service involving a range of stakeholders with a need for clear policy and strategy
- cost-effectiveness, which requires tools for evaluation
- ethical, because it touches on issues of surveillance, empowerment and control with a need for obtaining informed consent and activating response protocols (Hanson *et al.*, 2006).

Lifestyle monitoring can be considered part of telecare or telemedicine. This has been described as a way in which people's habitual domestic movements can be monitored and then someone can be alerted if there are deviations from this (Hanson *et al.*, 2006). The concept of lifestyle monitoring, according to Hanson *et al.* (2006), was developed in the late 1990s as a non-intrusive, low-cost technological solution to enhance care to older people. It was a proactive rather than reactive service to large numbers of geographically dispersed clients, thus cutting the time needed to detect potentially serious problems, and (it was hoped) reassuring carers.

Underpinning some of these concepts is that of information communications technology (ICT), which covers products that store, manipulate, transmit or receive information electronically in a digital form. It can include computers, television and robots. The combination of the terms *information technology* and *communications technology* took place in the 1980s to emphasize the merging of both technologies.

A number of researchers have argued that the increased availability of ICT should increase both the quality of life and the independence of older adults (Damadoran and Olphert, 2008). They maintain that a significant number of older people already regularly use ICT with enthusiasm, and that those over 65 are the fastest growing sector of Internet users. However, they quote the UK Digital Inclusion Panel 2004 as stating that 'there is a real risk that in the medium to long term, significantly more citizens will migrate from being digitally engaged to being unengaged than the other way round, as their capabilities change' (Damadoran and Olphert, 2008 p. 79). It is argued that 'cellular telephones probably will develop into the main control devices of ICT-based services. They have emerged as the new fully networked computer, and currently exceed the computing power of desk-top personal computers in 2001' (van Bronswijk, Kearns and Normie, 2007, p. 129). Specific developments such as the smart phones with touch screens are user-friendly and powerful. However, it must also be remembered that older people are among the poorest members of society and many have no access to ICT.

The challenge of dementia

An increasing number of older, especially very old, people in the population means a growth in those with dementia (see Chapter 7). There is a real challenge for families and for services in providing care and support for those both at home and in institutions.

There are a number of ways in which technology can help older people with dementia and their carers. A growing field is monitoring so that cameras and other devices can be used to check what the person with dementia is doing. For example, if they try to wander out of the home, a device may tell them to go back inside. Some devices will take action but are little different from what people without dementia may use. For example, turning the tap off when the bath is nearly full or turning the kettle off when it boils. Computer-generated interactive devices are another way in which people can exchange experiences with others. A more radical approach is tagging. The older person has a device attached to them so that their whereabouts are known and, if they wander, they can be found. Unless explicit consent is given for this, it can be held to be unethical. Decisions about which parts of a person's living environment should be monitored (e.g. stairs or bathroom) would need careful consideration so that the needs of the individual and the carer are met and that privacy is balanced by other factors.

As Tondu and Bardou point out, some of the behaviour exhibited by people with dementia has traditionally been met by physical or pharmacological methods of restraint that can have serious drawbacks (Tondu and Bardou, 2008). If a safe environment can be created, then these drawbacks may be decreased. As has been well documented, older people with dementia are vulnerable to abuse, and these technologies should help to protect their rights rather than leave them open to possible violations.

It should also be noted that some technology can help carers. For example, the Internet can provide support at the same time as affording a degree of privacy and accessibility that other user groups cannot.

Technology, institutions and the home environment

Across the world the trend is towards 'staying at home options' and away from institutional care. In the UK most people aged 65 and over live in their own homes and this proportion is rising (Table 13.4).

There are challenges in providing services in these different environments. There may be greater economies of scale in providing technology in institutions. However, one of the challenges when considering the implementation of technology in people's homes is to ensure that they do not look like institutions. The strong

Table 13.4 Where people aged 65 and over live

	1991 (Great Britain)		2001 (England and Wales)	
%				
	Own home	Institution	Own home	Institution
65+	95	5	98	2
85+	75	25	80	20
95+	52	48	58	42

Source: UK Census 1991 and 2001.

association between age and disability means that appropriate designs and technology are needed in both environments.

Design that is appropriate for everyone is sometimes called 'inclusive design' and sometimes 'design for all' or 'universal design'. The use of the latter originated in the USA in relation to both design of products and the built environment. It is described as 'the design of products and environments to be usable by all people, to the greatest extent possible, without the need for adaptation or specialised design' (Whitney and Keith, 2006, p. 125). This kind of design for everyone avoids stigmatization and considers the needs of the widest possible range of people. However, an opposite case is put by Newell, who argues that people without disabilities can find adapted items harder to use (Newell, 2006). He cites the example of a 'text-only' web that can be an ideal solution for blind people but might provide challenges for people with poor literacy skills. He also says that designing for older and disabled people may help others. He cites the example of the design of a large-button telephone for people with sight and dexterity impairments that became a best-seller.

Lifetime homes is another concept that embraces technology. It describes homes that are built to be adaptable enough to meet the changing needs over a lifetime. Key features include a gentle or sloping approach to the property, doors wide enough to allow wheelchair access, living room at entrance level, entrance level lavatory, walls able to take adaptations, low window sills, and electric sockets and controls at convenient heights. The design should include future-proofing features to enable them to be adapted when needed.

Smart housing is a term used to describe the electronic and computer-controlled integration of many devices within the home. It allows the integration of environmental controls either by personal control or automatically. This includes door and window openers, curtains and blinds, heating, lighting, security devices including motion sensors and video surveillance, telephone and communication, and controls for water taps and cookers. Monitoring of activities can even be extended to daily health checks. For example, an instrumented lavatory pan has been developed to measure heart rate, temperature, and nutrition (Tamura, Togawa, Ogawa *et al.*, 1998). Smart housing consists of a number of features which would also help people with disabilities. Recommendations from research on remodelling sheltered housing and residential care homes to extra care housing included the installation of automatic light switches to illuminate the path between bed and lavatory at night (Tinker *et al.*, 2007). If this light was triggered by a motion detector, it could help prevent falls. As an alternative, a night light at floor level can also be used but if there is a visual impairment, a higher level of illumination may be needed than is provided by a night light. Additionally, the following AT may provide help: a shower chair, a mobile hoist, over-bed tables, an adjustable bed and raised toilet seats of different heights.

However, there is a practical problem with smart housing. If such technology is fitted, someone must take responsibility for it, and statutory bodies are often unwilling to take on novel and potentially costly commitments (Cowan and Turner-Smith, 1999).

For all these forms of technology, research shows the value of a multidisciplinary approach both to the provision of services and research. An illustration of this is the REadingKIng's (REKI) project (Lansley, McCreadie and Tinker, 2004; Lansley, McCreadie, Tinker *et al.*, 2004; Tinker and Lansley, 2005). The research question was, 'how far and at what cost, can the housing stock be modified to accommodate the assistive technology that can enable older occupants to remain in their homes?' The study covered both mainstream and sheltered housing. This found that appropriately selected adaptations and AT can make a significant contribution to the provision of living environments which facilitate independence. They can both substitute for traditional formal care services and supplement these services in a cost-effective way.

Technology, health and social care

Fozard has discussed the impact of technology on health and focused on self-esteem (Fozard, 2005). He considers that there are four components to this impact. The first is prevention and engagement, where technology can help or delay age-associated physiological and behavioural changes that restrict functioning. This can be done by measuring gait through sensors to consider susceptibility to falls. The second is compensation and assistance, which can compensate for loss in strength and motor functioning with examples from wheelchairs to hip protectors. The third is care, support and organization, including products such as those that monitor the use of medication or equipment that provides information about physiological functioning. The fourth is enhancement and satisfaction where evidence about technology supports the range of activities from comfort and education to communications.

The European Seniors Watch Survey in 2000 found interest in information about health issues on the Internet was highest among those who were 'the experienced front-runners' where 61 per cent were interested (Ekberg, 2002). This compared with 'the old-age beginner' (45 per cent), 'the technologically open-minded' (38 per cent) and 'the digitally challenged' (15 per cent). This survey also found that not only were nearly half of 'the experienced front-runners' interested in information about medical treatment displayed on computers or TV screens but so were one-third of the 'the old-age beginners' and the 'technologically open-minded'. And well over 20 per cent of these groups were interested in getting a doctor's advice on a health problem via video telephone. Information can also be given to carers via computers and the latter may also be used to access support groups. Advocacy groups such as the (UK) Alzheimer's Society have been at the forefront of providing help and information via the Web.

As noted above, telemedicine is one way in which technology can be harnessed to provide a service for older people. For example, robots may provide post-stroke rehabilitation (Accoto, Zollo, Formica et al., 2008), and numerous studies show the value of fall monitors. Perhaps one of the most exciting developments has been the use of mobile phones to monitor health. Patients can record details about their condition and its treatment on their phones. Data (e.g. about blood sugar levels or blood pressure) are then collected and sent automatically to a central monitoring service, which can alert a professional to potential problems in the condition of the patient. Automated messages may also be sent to remind patients to take medication or go for an appointment. Video-conferencing allows patients and professionals to interact without the need for travel. It also allows professionals, such as a doctor, to consult a specialist in a hospital or other location, to ask for advice.

The ways in which technology can help in the social care of older people include the provision of sensors in the older person's home, which can alert carers or staff to a problem. Alarms which the older person can use to obtain help are another form of telecare. However, they may not be used for fear of causing unnecessary fuss, or older people may feel that there is a stigma attached to their use.

Technology, leisure mobility and transport

Leisure pursuits are another way in which technology can be used by older people. In Japan a sharing of experiences of television programmes between generations is one way in which this can happen (Tachashima and Umemuro, 2008). The objectives of technology in the areas of mobility and transport 'should not only stimulate, preserve and prolong mobility, but they should also contribute to the safety of mobility' (Huson, Oomens and Sauren, 1992, p. 212). The authors also make the point that it is important to look at low-tech solutions before looking to high-tech ones. Another way in which mobile phones have been used successfully has been to help older people navigate around places (McCreadie, 2005). Way-finding technology such as this has to be easy to use.

There is growing interest in older people as drivers. Summing up the issues, Ball and Wahl stated that 'Maintaining driving competence in the later years of life can be integral to an individual's health, independence and quality of life. As we age, however, our driving skills may become compromised or called into question. Driving cessation can lead to negative consequences such as reduced access to social, religious, employment and health-care activities; increased dependence on others; and feelings of depression, isolation and helplessness. A balance must be struck between society's concern for individual autonomy – represented for many older adults by access to the car keys – and its equally legitimate concern for public safety. Achieving this balance calls for technological advances in the evaluation of driving risks, development of effective driver rehabilitation programmes, vehicle design advances that support the needs of older drivers, improvements in road and signal design that can accommodate subtle, age-related declines in visual and cognitive functions, and the identification of transportation alternatives to promote independence among non-drivers' (Ball and Wahl, 2002, p. 217). There is no doubt that in industrialized countries, an adequate transport service is in most cases essential. Lack of access to suitable transport can lead to social isolation and suitable public transport is essential for those older people who do not have access to a car (House of Lords, 2005).

Ethical issues

There are some key ethical issues connected with technology. These include consent, privacy of information and person/place, equality of access, autonomy versus independence, paternalism, patient and provider relationships and medicalization of the home. Taipale has recently commented on the way human beings are being monitored and measured 24 hours a day and how ethical issues will emerge more powerfully in the context of new innovations (Taipale, 2008). As well as these, other issues came out of an EU-funded project which discussed raised expectations and subsequent withdrawal of new technology from participants which had occurred during the research (Magnusson and Hanson, 2003). In a thoughtful analysis of ethical issues and privacy van Hoof and colleagues have distinguished between devices in the home which are connected to a network and those that are not (van Hoof, Kort, Markopoulos et al., 2007). In the case of the latter there may be connections to a call centre that includes medical staff and carers along with assistance, security and maintenance services. They warn that 'in practice,

Table 13.5 Percentages of people aged 65 and over unable to manage certain tasks without help

| | 1998–9 Great Britain | |
	Men	Women
Domestic tasks	24	41
Self-care	23	38
Mobility	9	19

Source: Office for National Statistics (2000, p. 67).

governments, family and yet unknown parties cold also be linked to the data and have access to data' (van Hoof *et al.*, 2007, p. 156). They make the important point that miniaturization and concealment of devices may make a home less like a hospital environment and be less intrusive than visits from staff. However, 'In the home environment that is considered to be a safe haven, one might forget about the implications of data collection and transmission' (van Hoof *et al.*, 2007, p. 157). They also claim that there may be issues for people with dementia and their partner/carers concerning the misuse of data.

Gender issues

In most countries women outnumber men in old age. The significance of this is that on average women experience worse health (Table 13.5). For example, the prevalence of long-standing health conditions is higher and, as important for technology, women's ability to perform certain tasks without help is higher than for men. Women are also more likely to have fewer resources than men in old age. On the other hand, women live longer than men (see Chapters 1 and 2).

Usability issues

One of the two founders of the ISG, Vappu Taipale, has pointed to the importance that they placed on user involvement (Taipale, 2008). She quotes the objectives of the ISG when it was founded in 1997, which included 'to promote cultural and scientific, international exchanges between researchers and engineers of all disciplines, designers and architects, related industries, organisations and professionals in the field of comfort, welfare and health for the ageing and the aged, and to involve the older citizen in all relevant activities'. She maintains that the voice of older people has to become stronger and that a real partnership has developed with them in the field. Charness and Czaja also claim that the full potential of technology has not been realized because 'designers of most systems have not considered older adults as active users of technology and thus many interfaces are designed without accommodating the needs of this population' (Charness and Czaja, 2005, p. 668). Not only are user needs and preferences to be taken into account but also training and support are necessary. The non-use of technology is something which also needs to be taken into account. An overview of the research relating to this field found that there were complex reasons for non-use (Wessels, Dijcks, Soede *et al.*, 2003).

There is growing evidence regarding the views of older people themselves about the usability of technology. Housing studies of older people in the UK have found that technology helps independence but must work efficiently and be reliable, safe and simple (McCreadie and Tinker, 2005). However, these studies have also shown that older people are diverse and pragmatic, and feel they know best and that there must be a 'felt' need for devices. Mountain sums up the research which shows that technology must be compact, simple to operate and maintain; be useable, preferably without the assistance of the carer; complement the contribution of health professionals; and be capable of giving encouraging feedback even when progress is slow (Mountain, 2008). There are many ways of involving users, from unstructured interviews through focus groups, observation and using critical user forums. However, there may be problems, apart from lack of awareness of need, and these include the lack of time and money (Goodman, Langdon and Clarkson, 2006). The issue can rapidly become a complicated and time-consuming exercise.

There is also the issue of whether older people can learn to use technology. A number of studies have examined this (cf. Charness and Czaja, 2005). They indicate that while older people may be able to use technology for a variety of tasks they may be slower to acquire new skills and require more help and practice. The research does, however, indicate that training interventions can be successful.

A key to user involvement is the need for information for older people, their carers and professionals. A study, 'Improving the provision of information about assistive technology for older people', has built on previous research (Wright, McCreadie and Tinker, 2005). For older people a number of barriers were identified concerning their lack of awareness about the devices combined with not knowing whom to approach, as well as problems with written information. For professionals this was summarized as follows:

Firstly, it is apparent that professionals often lack a comprehensive picture of the available national and local services and potential support. Secondly, professionals are often not well served by their agency's inadequate database of information. Not only do the databases fail to contain up to date information, they tend to be restricted to information relevant to that agency's remit rather than to the subject as a whole. Thirdly, these studies draw similar conclusions about common professional behaviour of deliberately withholding relevant information. A fourth factor affecting professionals' behaviour may be economic constraints. (Wright *et al.*, 2005, p. 13)

The conclusions of the research were that there are a variety of ways of giving information, and some innovatory methods were discussed including greater use of television and computers. Guidebooks or handbooks which give information can help (Pain, McLellan and Gore, 2003).

Costs

There is growing, but still insufficient, evidence about the costs and benefits of technology. However, evidence from the USA shows that technology has the potential to confer improved quality of life for older people and their carers and that there are cost savings (Agree and Freedman, 2000). In this study a distinction was made between technology which could substitute for personal care (such as canes and walkers and devices which enabled a person to go to the toilet alone, or a bath seat and grab bars which enable a person to shower) and those which could supplement the help of a carer (e.g. wheelchairs). A subsequent study of devices to be used at home found that canes and crutches reduced the need for care and were associated with lower costs for formal help (Allen, Foster and Berg, 2001). Also in the USA, William Mann and colleagues have undertaken a number of studies focusing on cost savings. In one randomized control trial they found that the functional rate of decline among the older samples could be slowed and the costs of some home-care interventions could be reduced through a systematic approach to providing AT (Mann, Ottenbacher, Fraas *et al.*, 1999). As has been seen above, a UK study also found that AT could both substitute for traditional formal care services and supplement these services in a cost-effective way. Research for the Office of Disability found that there could be savings (Heywood and Turner, 2007). The report authors stated: 'Not all adaptations save money. But where they are an alternative to residential care, or prevent hip fractures or speed hospital discharge; where they relieve the burden of carers or improve the mental health of a whole household, they will save money, sometimes on a massive scale' (Heywood and Turner, 2007, p. 14). In a further study, one of the authors provides examples of where this has happened and other research has also shown the value of housing adaptations (Heywood, 2001).

Emerging markets

Industry has responded to both the demand and the potential demand for technology by creating new products. Butler describes these as 'silver industries' or 'the mature market' (Butler, 2008). He itemizes these as financial services, legal services, health-care services, housing and living arrangements and travel and hospitality. It is telling that a recent book *Ageing in a Consumer Society* has as its subtitle *From Passive to Active Consumption in Britain* (Jones, Hyde, Victor *et al.*, 2008). The development of markets has been helped by the increased availability of resources to the population. In the UK in the first part of the twentieth century, 'food alone consumed over half the costs of living, and for the working classes, 95% of family expenditure was devoted to purchasing the necessities of food, housing, fuel and clothing'. By contrast, in the early twenty-first century, food accounts for only 16 per cent of household expenditure. For older people patterns of consumption as expressed in the ownership of goods has become very similar to the rest of the population.

Linking technology to other services

It is increasingly being realized that technology alone cannot provide an adequate service for frail older people as a stand-alone component. The need for the back-up of personal care, whether provided by informal carers or professionals, is crucial. A clear message in the UK about telecare is the need to integrate it with domiciliary care. However, the position is becoming more complicated with the introduction of personalized care. Personalized care is a development from individual budgets where people are allocated a certain sum of money and allowed to spend it themselves on services rather than having them provided. There is increasing focus on individualism and independence together with citizenship and consumer rights. For example, pilot schemes to allow older people to set up individual budgets (devolved budgets allowing the older person to choose and control the services they get) has been followed by personal budgets (Vallelly, 2008). While strictly being for social care, the term is increasingly being used for all schemes that allow older people to make the choices about the services themselves.

Future technological developments

It is important to think about future proofing for homes and the environment. For example, the development of the automatic or smart toilet, which combines the functions of a toilet and a bidet with warm air for drying, can give users their independence, privacy and dignity while freeing carers from having to toilet the older person. The automatic provision of other 'smart homes' technology could be provided. For example, intelligent taps in bathrooms and kitchens that turn themselves off when the bath, basin or sink is full can counter the risk of flooding when taps are left on. Similarly, gas and heat detectors can be used to provide an alert when gas is escaping or a pan has been left to boil dry. Intelligent cookers that turn themselves off would be a more forward-looking solution.

Since Internet access provides a means for shopping, handling finances, entertainment and staying in touch with a social network for house-bound people, provision of broadband Internet access is needed in all sheltered (supported housing) schemes with at least one Internet-ready computer in a communal area (Tinker *et al.*, 2007).

When considering future developments, it is not just new devices that may feature but the more widespread use of existing ones. Who, for example, could have foreseen the spread of relatively inexpensive video recorders or mobile phones (including the facility to send messages by text) when they first became available? But for some people of all ages it is the simple solution that would help, such as devices to open jars and bottles as well as so-called 'childproof' medicine containers.

There is some evidence that the potential for new developments is not being realized and that one reason may be the failure to engage meaningfully with older people themselves (House of Lords, 2005, p. 63). One chapter of this report on ageing and technology by the House of Lords Science and Technology Committee was headed *Industry and Commerce: The Missed Opportunity*, which sums up what they found (House of Lords, 2005, p. 67).

It has been argued that the fourth-generation systems (from 2010–2020) will involve a move from monitoring users and detecting emergency situations to more sophisticated ones (Brownsell and Bradley, 2003). This could include implanting sensors under the skin and providing robotic assistance to help with cleaning, retrieving articles from the floor, etc.

Policy developments

One of the most influential and long-standing programmes in Europe is COST, which was set up at a ministerial conference in 1971 to lay the foundations for scientific and technical cooperation at a European level. There have been many programmes of research since then which have focused on different aspects of technology. Many have had older people at the centre of the research. Technology is mentioned in a number of recent documents. A survey of assistive technology in the EU showed that, while there were great variations across Europe there were consistent findings that older users had problems in selecting devices, evaluating them and finding the most appropriate one at an acceptable cost (Marx, 2003). Subsequently the European Commission described 'A new health care delivery model based on a preventative and person-centred health system. This new model can only be achieved through proper use of ICT, in combination with appropriate organisational changes and skills' (Mountain, 2008).

Some countries have made significant investment in technology for older people and the UK is a good example. A number of reports had highlighted the contribution that technology could make to the lives of older people. For example, the Audit Commission report had stressed this role (Department of Health, 2006). In their 2000 report they maintained that investment in equipment could deliver high-quality care and enable people to remain in the community and out of institutions. The influential report produced in 2005 by the Lords Science and Technology Committee was mentioned in the previous section. Despite telecare, especially alarms and sensors, being high on the government's agenda, research is increasingly showing the low level of provision of all kinds of technology (Mountain, 2008).

In the UK, in 2006 the Department of Health in the policy document *Our Health, Our Care, Our Say* argued that self-management of long-term conditions using technological innovations could provide care to older people in their own homes including the use of technology (Department of Health, 2006). At a conference to discuss these findings, it was held that there were no or very few policies focused on assisting older people to age in place safely (Kinsella, 2006).

Conclusion

Technology offers many possibilities for older people in the future and some of these ways have been identified. However, while it may improve the quality of life of older people, it is unlikely to be able to meet all their needs. As part of a package of measures which includes help from other people (paid and informal) and medical help, it has great potential. For academic purposes it is interesting that there is a lack of much theoretical framework. Concepts which might be applicable such as autonomy, a life-course approach, activity and disengagement and well-being are notable by their absence. Much research seems to be quite pragmatic. Nevertheless, technology can provide better information (especially access to expert advice) for older people and their carers, and enable better communications with professionals.

Ultimately, will technology replace family care? There is evidence of strong family care (especially from adult children to their older parents) in many instances (Glaser, Stuchbury, Tomassini *et al.*, 2006). However, government policy cannot assume that the availability of children or other family members will reduce the use of, or demand for, publicly funded health and social care services.

Summary

The chapter begins by examining the scope of what is meant by technology for older people, before examining factors affecting older people's demand for technology, such as contrasting definitions of old age, changing demographics and generational differences in the use of technology. It then critically discusses the types of technology that are available and the needs they are designed to meet. The particular challenges that dementia poses are then examined. The fact that not everyone lives in the same type of environment is explored, with consideration of the effects of housing type. This leads to a discussion of the role of technology in health and social care, leisure, mobility and transport, before matters are placed in perspective by considerations of ethical, gender and usability issues, and costs. In addition, the effects of future needs are considered in addressing emerging markets and future technological developments. The chapter concludes with a consideration of policy developments.

REFERENCES

Accoto, D., Zollo, L., Formica, D. *et al.* (2008). Design of a planar robotic machine for telerehabilitation of elderly patients, *Gerontechnology*, *7*, 65–78.

Acheson, D. (1998) *Inequalities in health report*. London: The Stationery Office.

Agree, E. and Freedman, V.A. (2000) Incorporating assistive devices into community based long-term care: an analysis of the potential for substitution and supplementation, *Journal of Aging and Health*, *12*, 426–50.

Allen, S.M., Foster, A. and Berg, K. (2001) Receiving help at home: the interplay of human and technological assistance, *Journals of Gerontology. Series B, Psychological Sciences and Social Sciences*, *64B*, 374–82.

Audit Commission (2000) *Fully equipped*. London: Audit Commission.

Ball, K. and Wahl, H. (2002) Driving in old age, *Gerontechnology*, *1*, 217–19.

Bouma, H. (2007) Gerontechnology in perspective. Paper presented to the Eindhoven Master's Workshop, Eindhoven, 2007.

Bouma, H., Fozard, J.L., Bouwhuis, D.G. *et al.* (2007) Gerontechnology in perspective, *Gerontechnology*, *6*, 190–216.

Brownsell, S. and Bradley, D. (2003) *Assistive technology and telecare*. Bristol: Policy Press.

Butler, R.N. (2008) The longevity revolution. Paper given to UK Age Research Forum, 2 October 2008.

Care and Repair (2006) *Small things matter – the key role of handyperson services*. Nottingham: Care and Repair.

Census 1991 and 2001. www.statistics.gov.uk.

Charness, N. (2008) Computer and Internet use in the USA: influence of age, attitudes, employment status and education, *Gerontechnology*, *7*, 92–7.

Charness, N. and Czaja, S.J. (2005) Adaptations to new technologies, in M.L. Johnson (ed.), *The Cambridge handbook of age and ageing*. Cambridge University Press, 662–9.

Clarkson, J., Coleman, R., Keates, S. *et al.* (2003) *Inclusive design: design for the whole population*. Berlin: Springer.

Cowan, D. and Turner-Smith, D. (1999) The role of assistive technology in alternative models of care for older people, in A. Tinker, F. Wright, C. McCreadie *et al.* (eds), *Alternative models of care for older people*. Royal Commission on Long Term Care: Research Volume 2. London: The Stationery Office, 325–46.

Damadoran, L. and Olphert, W. (2008) Sus-IT: sustaining IT use by older people to promote autonomy and independence. Paper given to UK Age Research Forum, 2 October 2008. www.ukarf.org.uk/1.html.

Department for Communities and Local Government, Department of Health, Department for Work and Pensions (2008) *Lifetime homes, lifetime neighbourhoods: a national strategy for housing in an ageing society.* DCLG, www.communities.gov.uk.

Department of Health (2005) *Building telecare in England.* London: HMSO. www.dh.gov.uk/prod_consum_dh/groups/dh_digitalassets/@dh/@en/documents/digitalasset/dh_4115644.pdf.

Department of Health (2006) *Our health, our care, our say.* London: The Stationery Office.

Ekberg, J. (ed.) (2002) *European Seniors Watch Survey.* Helsinki: Stakes.

Fisk, M. (2003) *Social alarms to telecare.* Bristol: Policy Press.

Fozard, J.L. (2005) Impacts of technology on health and self-esteem, *Gerontechnology,* **4,** 63–76.

Glaser, K., Stuchbury, R., Tomassini, C. *et al.* (2006) The long term consequences of partnership disruption for support in later life in the UK, *Ageing and Society,* **28,** 329–51.

Goodman, J., Langdon, P. and Clarkson, P. (2006) Equipping designers for inclusive design, *Gerontechnology,* **4,** 229–33.

Government Actuary's Department (2004) *Population projections 2004–2074.* www.gad.gov.uk.

Hailey, D., Ohinmaa, R. and Roine, R. (2004) Study quality and evidence of benefit in recent assessments of telemedicine, *Journal of Telemedicine and Telecare,* **10,** 318–24.

Hailey, D., Roine, R. and Ohinmaa, A. (2002) Systematic review of evidence for the benefits of telemedicine, *Journal of Telemedicine and Telecare,* **8**(S1), 1–7.

Hanson, J., Osipovič, D., Hine, N. *et al.* (2006) *Lifestyle monitoring as a predictive tool in telecare. Telemed and eHealth. Transforming the patient experience.* London: Royal Society of Medicine Press.

Hanson, V.L., Snow-Weaver, B.S. and Trewin, S. (2006) Software personalization to meet the needs of older adults, *Gerontechnology,* **5,** 160–9.

Heywood, F. (2001) *Money well spent.* Bristol: Policy Press.

Heywood, F. and Turner, L. (2007) *Better outcomes, lower costs: implications for health and social care budgets of investment in housing adaptations, improvements and equipment.* Bristol: Office for Disability Issues/University of Bristol.

House of Lords (2005) *Ageing: scientific aspects.* Volume 1. Report: House of Lords Science and Technology Committee. First report of session 2005–06. London: The Stationery Office.

Huson, A., Oomens, C. and Sauren, A. (1992) Introduction to and summary on mobility, transport and motor performance, in H. Bouma and J. Graafmans (eds), *Gerontechnology.* Oxford: IOS Press, 209–14.

Jones, I.R., Hyde, M., Victor, C.V. *et al.* (2008) *Ageing in a consumer society.* Bristol: Policy Press.

Kinsella, A. (2006) Switched on to telecare: providing health and care support through home-based telecare monitoring in the UK and the US. World conference on Systemics, Cybernetics and Informatics, 16–19 July 2006, Orlando: Florida, USA.

Lansley, P., McCreadie, C. and Tinker, A. (2004) Can adapting the homes of older people and providing assistive technology pay its way?, *Age and Ageing,* **33,** 571–6.

Lansley, P., McCreadie, C., Tinker, A. *et al.* (2004) Adapting the homes of older people: a case study of costs and savings, *Building Research and Information,* **32,** 468–83.

Magnusson, L. and Hanson, E.J. (2003) Ethical issues arising from a research, technology and development project to support frail older people and their family carers at home, *Health and Social Care in the Community, 11*, 431–9.

Mann, W.C., Ottenbacher, K.J., Fraas, L. *et al.* (1999) Effectiveness of assistive technology and environmental interventions in maintaining independence and reducing home care costs for the frail elderly, *Archives of Family Medicine, 8*, 210–17.

Marx, F. (2003) Access to assistive technology in the European Union, in G.M. Craddock, L.P. McCormack, R.R. Reilly *et al.* (eds), *Assistive technology – shaping the future.* Amsterdam: IOS Press, 98–102.

McCreadie, C. (2005) Older pedestrians, mobile phones and new way-finding technology, *Gerontechnology, 4*, 51–4.

McCreadie, C. and Tinker, A. (2005) The acceptability of assistive technology to older people, *Ageing and Society, 25*, 91–110.

Mountain, G. (2008) Potential of technology in the self management of long term conditions. Paper given to UK Age Research Forum, 2 October 2008. www.ukarf.org.uk/1.html.

Newell, A. (2006) Older people as a focus for inclusive design, *Gerontechnology, 4*, 190–9.

Office for National Statistics (2000) *People aged 65 and over.* London: Office for National Statistics.

(2007) *Social trends 37.* Basingstoke: Palgrave Macmillan.

(2008) *Social trends 38.* Basingstoke: Palgrave Macmillan.

Pain, H., McLellan, L. and Gore, S. (2003) *Choosing assistive devices: a guide for users and professionals.* London: Jessica Kingsley.

Riseborough, M. (1997) *Community alarm services today and tomorrow.* Oxford: Anchor Trust.

Soanes, S. (ed.) (2005) *Oxford English Dictionary.* Oxford University Press.

Tachashima, K. and Umemuro, H. (2008) Activating communications among family members living far apart by sharing common topics through television, *Gerontechnology, 7*, 219–24.

Taipale, V. (2008) User perspective and the development of gerontechnology, *Gerontechnology, 7*, 218.

Tamura, T., Togawa, T., Ogawa, M. *et al.* (1998) Fully automated health monitoring in the home, *Medical Engineering and Physics, 20*, 573–9.

Tinker, A. (1984) *Staying at home.* London: The Stationery Office.

(1999) Helping older people to stay at home: the role of supported accommodation, in A. Tinker, F. Wright, C. McCreadie *et al. Alternative models of care for older people.* Royal Commission on Long Term Care: Research Volume 2. London: The Stationery Office, 265–98.

Tinker, A. and Lansley, P. (2005) Introducing assistive technology into the homes of older people: feasibility, acceptability, costs and outcomes, *Journal of Telemedicine and Telecare, 11*, 1–3.

Tinker, A., Wright, F., McCreadie, C. *et al.* (1999) *Alternative models of care for older people.* Royal Commission on Long Term Care: Research Volume 2. London: The Stationery Office.

Tinker, A., Wright, F., Hanson, J. *et al.* (2007) *Remodelling sheltered housing and residential care homes to extra care housing.* London: King's College London and University College London.

Tondu, B. and Bardou, N. (2008) A systematic approach applied to the design of a strolling corridor for elderly persons with Alzheimer's-type dementia, *Gerontechnology, 7*, 223–38.

United Nations Population Division (2006) *Population ageing.* New York: United Nations.

Vallelly, S. (2008) *Building choices: personal budgets and older people's housing – broadening the debate.* London: Housing 21.

van Bronswijk, J., Kearns, W.D. and Normie, L.R. (2007) ICT infrastructures in the ageing society, *Gerontechnology*, *6*, 129–34.

van Hoof, J., Kort, H., Markopoulos, P. *et al.* (2007) Ambient intelligence, ethics and privacy, *Gerontechnology*, *6*, 155–63.

Wessels, R., Dijcks, B., Soede, M. *et al.* (2003) Non-use of provided assistive technology devices, a literature overview, *Technology and Disability*, *15*, 231–8.

Whitney, G. and Keith, S. (2006) Active ageing through universal design, *Gerontechnology*, *5*, 125–8.

Wootton, R. and Craig, J. (1999) *Introduction to telemedicine.* London: Royal Society of Medicine Press.

World Health Organization (2004) *A glossary of terms for community health care and services for older persons.* Kobe: WHO. http://whqlibdoc.who.int/wkc/2004/WHO_WKC_Tech.Ser._04.2.pdf.

Wright, F., McCreadie, C. and Tinker, A. (2005) *Improving the provision of information about assistive technology for older people.* Report to the Helen Hamlyn Trust. London: King's College London.

Xie, B. (2003) Older adults, computers and the Internet: future directions, *Gerontechnology*, *2*, 289–305.

14 Literary portrayals of ageing

DIANA WALLACE

OVERVIEW

· ·

This chapter examines the artistic representations of ageing and old age, concentrating upon literary portrayals. The subject is examined through key topics, including old age as motif and metaphor, changing representations of ageing in post-1970s fiction, creativity and the life course, life writing, gender and ageing, anthologies, theorizing age, and new directions in the literature of ageing.

· ·

Artistic representations of older people both shape and have the potential to counter our ideas about age and ageing. Old age may be conceived of as 'Other' in youth-obsessed Western culture, 'a foreign country with an unknown language' in May Sarton's suggestive phrase (1973, p. 17), but it is an/other country in which most people will, barring accidents, eventually come to live. A novel, poem, play, painting or photograph, film or television series, or, less obviously, a piece of music may allow us imaginatively to engage with the fact of our own ageing. It may also help us to recognize the subjectivity of those who are already 'older' (since age is often understood relationally) and to understand the ways in which age and ageing are culturally constructed.

This essay is dedicated to my parents: my mother, who at 70 cycled 500 miles across France, and my father, who at 68 began a university course in his second language, Welsh.

In her still neglected study, *Old Age* (1972, first published as *La Vieillesse* and translated as *The Coming of Age* in the USA), Simone de Beauvoir set out to break the 'conspiracy of silence' around what she called this 'forbidden subject' (1972, p. 21). And she called for an imaginative act of empathy which recognizes the self in the Other:

> If we do not know what we are going to be we cannot know what we are: let us recognise ourselves in this old man or in that old woman. It must be done if we are to take upon ourselves the entirety of our human state. And when it is done we will no longer acquiesce in the misery of the last age; we will no longer be indifferent, because we shall feel concerned, as indeed we are. (1972, p. 5)

Beauvoir's book identifies many of the key issues which concern those who study representations of ageing: old age as 'Other' when seen from outside (p. 284); the notion of ageing as 'decline' (p. 17); the notion that age is 'not solely a biological, but also a cultural fact' (p. 13); the 'disgust' aroused by evidence of sexuality in the old, especially in women (p. 150); the disjunction between inner feelings and outer appearance (p. 292); crucial gender differences – that women, for instance, live longer and are more vulnerable to poverty (as well as to expectations about youth and beauty) yet also cope better (p. 261); and the role of memory (p. 363).

Old Age can now be seen as one of the earliest and most important contributions to the emergence of what Thomas R. Cole in the introduction to the first edition of the *Handbook of the Humanities and Aging* calls 'a whole new field of interdisciplinary knowledge – humanistic gerontology', which developed from 1975 onwards (Cole *et al.*, 1992, p. xii). Humanistic gerontology asks: 'What does it mean to grow old?' (p. xvi). Artistic representations of ageing offer one important way of addressing that question, and literary gerontology as described by Anne M. Wyatt-Brown in the first and second editions of the *Handbook* (1992, pp. 331–51; 2000, pp. 41–59) has developed since the 1970s in a variety of extremely fruitful ways, although its influence on mainstream literary criticism is still peripheral compared with issues of, say, class, race or gender.

The imaginative engagement Beauvoir calls for can be enabled through literary representations of ageing and old age. Voice and point of view can be manipulated in a literary text so that we see through the eyes of, for instance, the 76-year-old first-person narrator of May Sarton's novel *As We Are Now* (1973) and identify with her desperation at being trapped in a 'concentration camp for the old' (1973, p. 3). This capacity to evoke empathetic response together with the sheer range of representations of ageing in literature – from Chaucer's cuckolded old husband in the May–January story of *The Merchant's Tale* through Shakespeare's maddened Lear to T.S. Eliot's lyric assertion that 'Old men ought to be explorers' (1974,

p. 203) – may be one reason why the field of literary gerontology is comparatively more developed than the study of ageing in some other areas of the arts and humanities.

While this chapter will focus on the representation of ageing in literature, this is not to imply that there has not been important work in other areas. It is one of the strengths of work on representations of ageing that it is so often inter-disciplinary. Essays on literature sit alongside those on art, history, philosophy, world religions and performance in the ground-breaking *Ageing and the Elderly: Humanistic Perspectives in Gerontology* (1978) edited by Stuart F. Spicker, Kathleen M. Woodward and David D. Van Tassel, and in both editions of the *Handbook of the Humanities and Aging* (1992, 2000). Several of the collections of essays cited here include work on film, television, painting or photography (e.g. Deats and Lenker, 1999; Jansohn, 2004; Jamieson *et al.*, 1987; Woodward, 1999), while theorists like Kathleen Woodward and Margaret Gullette are interested in visual as well as literary images of ageing. Work in other areas often faces similar issues and deploys similar theoretical paradigms, and the connections between them are extremely valuable. Similarly, while this chapter is divided into sections for ease of reading, these categories overlap and work by one scholar may appear in more than one area.

Old age as motif and metaphor

'Ageing is a missing category in current literary theory,' Anne M. Wyatt-Brown wrote in 1993 (Wyatt-Brown, 1993a, p. 1). English literature has always, of course, offered representations of ageing and old age, but criticism has tended to focus on them as a motif, metaphor or symbol of something else: love, time, creativity, memory, mortality. Shakespeare's King Lear, self-proclaimed a 'poor old man / As full of grief as age; wretched in both' (Act II, scene iv, ll. 275–6) after rejection by his 'ungrateful' daughters, is probably the most famous portrait of old age in the English literary canon. The concept of life as a series of 'ages' or 'stages' is perhaps most familiar to us through Jaques' 'All the world's a stage' speech in *As You Like It*, which ends with 'second childishness and mere oblivion, / Sans teeth, sans eyes, sans taste, sans everything' (Act II, scene vii, ll. 165–6). Shakespeare's sonnets return repeatedly to the questions of time and mortality and contain some of our best-known treatments of age as a poetic motif, including sonnets number 22, 'My glass shall not persuade me I am old', and number 73, 'That time of year thou may'st in me behold' (1999, pp. 87, 113).

The *carpe diem* theme of much sixteenth- and seventeenth-century poetry explicitly invokes ageing and mortality. Robert Herrick's admonishment to virgins to 'Gather ye rosebuds while ye may / Old Time is still aflying' is based on the argument that things can only get worse:

> That age is best which is the first,
> When youth and blood are warmer;
> But being spent, the worse, and worst
> Times still succeed the former.
>   (Quiller-Couch, 1939, p. 274)

Ageing here is seen explicitly and inevitably as decline. The elegant ironies of Marvell's 'To His Coy Mistress', with its assertion that 'The grave's a fine and private place, / But none, I think, do there embrace' (Quiller-Couch, 1939, p. 400), make more obvious the constructed nature of this picture of ageing and mortality as part of an elaborate and conventionalized argument to entice a young woman into bed. Alongside this there is a tradition of male poets lamenting their own physical decline. Ben Jonson's 'My Picture Left in Scotland' recounts the visible signs of ageing in his body which make his love deaf to his pleadings:

>   . . . she hath seene
> My hundred of gray haires,
> Told seven and fortie years,
> Read so much waste, as she cannot embrace
> My mountaine belly, and my rockie face,
> And all these through her eyes, have stopt her eares.
>   (Gardner, 1957, p. 92)

Yet, while the flesh may decay and 'passions are no more', as Edmund Waller puts it in 'Old Age', there may be spiritual compensations with the popularly supposed coming of wisdom in later life: 'Stronger by weakness, wiser men become / As they draw near to their eternal home' (Quiller-Couch, 1939, p. 319). In the twentieth century W.B. Yeats' famous rage against the depredations of ageing was set against the imperatives of art, rather than religion, in 'Sailing to Byzantium':

> An aged man is but a paltry thing,
> A tattered coat upon a stick, unless
> Soul clap its hands and sing, and louder sing
> For every tatter in its mortal dress.
>   (Cole and Winkler, 1994, p. 323)

This tradition can be traced down to Philip Larkin, whose 'On Being Twenty-six' locates the decline associated with the ageing process surprisingly early: 'I feared these present years, / The middle twenties, / When deftness disappears' (1988, p. 24).

These images of ageing from the traditional canon of English literature are some of those which are most familiar in Western culture, to the point of cliché in some cases. Given this tradition, as Helen Small comments, 'it is the more surprising that so few critics have read these works *for* what they have to say about old age' (2007, p. 5). What we have lacked, as Wyatt-Brown indicates, are theories of ageing that allow us to read such representations with the same kind of attention we give to other categories of social difference – race, class or gender. The development of literary gerontology from the 1970s onwards, however, has drawn our attention to a much wider field of representations of age and ageing, and offered us increasingly sophisticated ways of interrogating and theorizing them.

New genres: representing ageing in post-1970 contemporary fiction

The development of humanistic gerontology can be closely linked to the emergence in the early 1970s of a body of new fiction which self-consciously interrogated the processes of ageing, and which, in Thomas R. Cole's words, 'offered older people as complex and exciting protagonists' (1994, p. 4). This work can be seen as in part a response to the changing demographics that meant that the majority of the population could expect to become old (see Chapter 1). Initial attention to representations of ageing in literature, such as Richard Freedman's examination of canonical English literature from 1700 to 1900 (1978), suggested that these were uniformly negative. Similarly, although Celeste Loughman noted a growing interest in centralizing old age in novels by Kingsley Amis, Muriel Spark, Saul Bellow and Junichiro Tanizaki, she argued that 'the literature of senescence focuses . . . on the inevitable process of degeneration and decay [presenting] a dark, unlovely picture of old age' (1977, p. 80).

Later critics, however, coined new terms to reflect their sense that new fictional genres were emerging which challenged such notions of ageing as decline. 'About 1975,' writes Margaret Morganroth Gullette in *Safe at Last in the Middle Years: The Invention of the Midlife Progress Novel* (1988), 'it was observable that culture was giving its writers permission to overthrow the traditional decline view that the middle years are a time of devolution' (1988, p. xiii). Gullette's actively polemical study of four novelists – Saul Bellow, Margaret Drabble, Anne Tyler and John Updike – argued for the development of a new genre, the 'midlife progress novel' (or *midlife Bildung*, from *Bildungsroman*, the 'novel of development'), which counters the 'corrosive, powerful, negative ideology of ageing' (p. xiii) with plots which affirm the possibility of progress and development during the middle of the life course. By reading comparatively across each writer's *oeuvre*, she traces a pattern whereby characters emerge from the 'dangerous' years of early adulthood to a point where Updike's Harry Angstrom can aver in *Rabbit Is Rich* (1981), 'Midlife age is a wonderful country, all the things you thought would never happen are happening' (in Gullette, 1988, p. 56).

With more emphasis on later life, Barbara Frey Waxman in *From the Hearth to the Open Road: A Feminist Study of Aging in Contemporary Literature* (1990) coined the term *Reifungsroman* (or 'novel of ripening'), inspired by May Sarton's 'optimistic concept of "ripening towards death in a fruitful way"' (1990, p. 2). Waxman's study examines some of the most important novels of ageing, including May Sarton's *As We Are Now*, Doris Lessing's *The Summer Before the Dark* (1973) and *The Diaries of Jane Somers* (1984), Elizabeth Taylor's *Mrs Palfrey at the Claremont* (1971), Paule Marshall's *Praisesong for the Widow* (1983), Barbara Pym's *Quartet in Autumn* (1978), and Margaret Laurence's *The Stone Angel* (1964). Although they do not offer a uniformly rosy picture of ageing, Waxman identifies important characteristics which they have in common: a narrative structure which focuses on a journey or quest for self-knowledge; a narrative voice, either first person or third person omniscient, which draws the reader into the ageing protagonist's world; the use of dreams or flashbacks for life review; a concern with the physical body and illness; and a sense that, even in frail old age, there is the possibility of an opening up of life.

In Lessing's *The Diaries of Jane Somers*, for instance, the relationship between middle-aged Janna Somers and 90-year-old Maudie Fowler is transformative for both women. Janna's diary includes an extraordinarily powerful section where she thinks herself into Maudie's consciousness, imagining her daily struggle to maintain her increasingly frail body. Lessing's searing depiction of the humiliations brought by an ageing body – it is 'terrible, terrible, terrible' (1985, p. 137) for Maudie that Janna has to wash Maudie's private parts after she has soiled herself – is balanced by the sense that both women, in Waxman's term, 'ripen' through their friendship. First-person narrative and the dependency brought by a physical frailty are also central to Sarton's *As We Are Now*, where Caro Spencer, immured against her will in a nursing home she calls a 'concentration camp for the old' (1973, p. 3), insists that 'I am not mad, only old' (p. 3). 'Old age,' Caro recognizes, 'is not interesting until one gets there, a foreign country with an unknown language to the young, and even the middle-aged' (p. 17). These novels challenge the 'othering' process that Beauvoir identified and insist that we engage with that 'foreign country' by presenting it through the eyes of those who inhabit it.

Constance Rooke proposes a slightly different term for this new genre – '*Vollendungsroman* (from the German for "winding up")' (1992, p. 245). As she sees it, the *Vollendungsroman* focuses on 'disengagement' or the 'deconstruction of ego' in old age (1992, p. 245). This question of the advantages and penalties of disengagement is, she reminds us, at the heart of Shakespeare's *King Lear*, but the task of the *Vollendungsroman* is to discover 'some kind of affirmation in the face of loss' (p. 248). Laurence's *The Stone Angel* is the text she offers as 'a classic example of the genre', where the use of first-person narrative allows the cantankerous 90-year-old Hagar to tell her own story and counters the 'invisibility or marginalisation of old people, their reduction to stereotype' (p. 249). Through Hagar's recognition of her mistakes and attempt at atonement the novel finally offers the reader a hard-won affirmation. In this suggestive essay, Rooke draws attention to the importance of speech and memory in depicting the story of a life, and also notes how certain images recur in these texts in a way that suggests archetypes: mirrors, the fall and the circle, the child and images associated with birth, animals, the house and water.

In naming and thus making visible these new genres (and the older people they depict), these critics offer us a different way of reading representations of ageing. But they also point towards the importance of historicization and the way in which any representation of ageing is always intimately connected to its historical moment.

Late style: creativity and the life course

Closely related to questions about the representation of age and ageing is the issue of creativity and its relationship to the life course: does old age bring a new way of thinking? If so, is its effect positive (achievement) or negative (decline)? Critics often distinguish between the early, middle or late work of writers, artists and musicians; the 'late plays' of Shakespeare (*The Tempest* and *The Winter's Tale*), for instance, have been seen as demonstrating the wisdom and serenity of older age. In contrast, Theodor Adorno, the first to use the term 'late style' in a 1937 essay, saw Beethoven's last works, in Edward Said's words, as 'a form of exile from [Beethoven's] milieu' (Said, 2004, p. 2). Beauvoir was one of the earliest to discuss the effects of ageing on creativity, while Elliott Jacques' 1965 essay on the effects of midlife crisis on creativity in the work of 'great men' (1965, p. 502), was influential on early work, but both had an essentially pessimistic view. Debates about potential definitions of 'late style' reach across the arts as Julius S. Held's discussion of artists demonstrates. His conclusion is that '[t]here is not, and cannot be, one set of criteria that would do for all artists and all periods to define the style of old age. Yet questioning what kind of transformations of their art took place as they got older remains . . . a valid historical study' (1987, p. 129), is echoed in other disciplines.

The development of humanistic gerontology enabled a more theorized approach to these questions in literary criticism. Kathleen Woodward's early study, *At*

Last, the Real Distinguished Thing: The Late Poems of Eliot, Pound, Stevens, and Williams (1980), had its roots in her interest in the late poems of Wallace Stevens and their place in our culture as 'an old man's poems' (1980, p. x). Woodward extended her study to T.S. Eliot's *Four Quartets*, Ezra Pound's *Pisan Cantos*, and William Carlos Williams' *Paterson*, looking not for stereotyped images of ageing but for connections or similarities of style, tone or perspective. Her conclusion was that 'a new way of thinking (and thus being in the world), a new mode of cognition, may emerge in old age' (1980, p. xii). Despite the obvious differences between the poems, Woodward suggested that they were all marked by four characteristics: the central image of what Eliot in *Burnt Norton* calls 'the still point'; a new meditative mode of reflection; a new hero – the wise old man; and a dedication to tradition, creation and life review as a stay against chaos (1980, p. 6). Her central concern was with the nature of wisdom, which she saw as 'intuitively connected with age' (1980, p. 118). There are problems with Woodward's account, as she recognizes: *Four Quartets*, for instance, was written when Eliot was middle-aged rather than 'old'.

Examining the attitudes towards ageing in the work of four later American poets – Robert Penn Warren, Langston Hughes, Gwendolyn Brooks and Elizabeth Bishop – Carolyn H. Smith found both ambivalence and a wisdom which 'involves stoic courage in encounters with role loss, physical decline and death' (1992, p. 219). Smith reads images of the aged in these poems as 'projections of the poets' concerns for their own ageing and dying' (p. 219). Her essay is especially valuable because it introduces the differentials of both race and gender. Both Warren and Hughes' views on ageing had their roots in their relationships with a grandparent, for instance, but Warren's desire for individual freedom contrasts with Hughes' desire for freedom for 'all blacks' (p. 226). Moreover, both Hughes and Brooks themselves have come to be seen as emblems of wisdom for later generations. Smith's essay offers an important argument for reading poems 'not as single, separate artifacts but together as collective representations' (p. 236), so as to encompass the varied feelings about ageing which may be present even in different poems by the same poet.

In order to think about the effect of ageing on creativity, we need to consider the whole lifespan of an artist, rather than just its ending. Anne M. Wyatt-Brown, another critic who has consistently maintained and demonstrated that gerontologists and literary critics have much to gain from each other, has looked at continuity and change across the lifespan in essays on Barbara Pym and Penelope Mortimer (1988), Anita Brookner (1989a), and Virginia Woolf and E.M. Forster (1989b). As she points out, drawing on Erik Erikson's model of ageing (1964), writers and artists develop identity themes early, but 'the shock of old age, ill health, and unaccustomed vulnerability can force them to develop new perceptions' (1988, p. 835). While this can prevent creativity, 'for some, even the unpleasant aspects of ageing can be inspiring' (p. 835). As examples of increased creativity in old age, Penelope Mortimer and Barbara Pym also demonstrate what Wyatt-Brown calls 'an important paradox about the nature of late style: there is as much evidence of continuity as of change' (1988, p. 839). The grimness of Pym's *Quartet in Autumn* was a response to the rejection of her work and an enforced retirement and move to the country following a bout of cancer and a stroke, for instance, but her final novel, *A Few Green Leaves* (1980), written when she knew she was dying of cancer, has 'a new note: the mature acceptance of death as part of the life cycle' (1988, p. 837).

Reading fiction in relation to autobiography and theories of life cycles can reveal that some writers experience a radical shift in midlife: E.M. Forster stopped writing fiction altogether, while Virginia Woolf experienced a 'surprising period of near serenity' which produced *To the Lighthouse* (Wyatt-Brown, 1989b, p. 61). In contrast, Anita Brookner actually started writing in her early fifties in response to a sense of dissatisfaction with her career as an art historian and '"a terrible feeling of powerlessness"' (Wyatt-Brown, 1989a, p. 176). Drawing on gerontological work, Wyatt-Brown suggests that Brookner was responding 'to the same forces which, according to David Gutmann, cause many middle-aged mothers to switch their roles from being caretakers of small children to executive managers of their adult extended family' (Wyatt-Brown, 1989a, p. 176).

Differences of gender are central here. Thinking of Woolf, Doris Grumbach, Stevie Smith and May Sarton among others who found greater freedom or fame as older women, Carolyn Heilbrun in *Writing a Woman's Life* (1988) suggests that women's lives follow a different trajectory or pattern from men's: 'It is perhaps only in old age, certainly past fifty, that women can stop being female impersonators, can grasp the opportunity to reverse their most cherished principles of "femininity"' (1988, p. 126). Heilbrun's work is an influence on the essays in Anne M. Wyatt-Brown and Janice Rossen's edited collection, *Aging and Gender in Literature: Studies in Creativity* (1993b), which foreground gender as well as class, sexual orientation and the writer's psychology in their discussion of issues of literary creativity and psychological development. Wyatt-Brown's essay on May Sarton, for instance, uses her initial disappointment with Sarton's *The Education of Harriet Hatfield* to generate three models of late-life writing: of continuity (drawing on Erikson's theory of life cycles); of liberation or revival; and of an unexpected 'politics of old age' (1993, p. 53). In Sarton's case, the emergence of the last mentioned is only recognizable when her entire *oeuvre* is considered. The variety of writers discussed here encourages comparative reading. Louise Bogan's sense of her poetic vocation was so shaped by an ideology of youthful romantic love, Marcia Aldrich argues, that she was unable to write after her early forties (1993, pp. 105–20). In contrast, the ageing Colette, Bethany Ladimer argues, rejected the romance plot in favour of an 'erotic satisfaction in the process of writing itself' (1993, p. 242).

Life writing: auto/biography, memory and reminiscence

Life writing (autobiography, memoir, biography) is both a source of information for studies of creativity and a source of representations of ageing which has itself generated a body of work, particularly in relation to memory and reminiscence. Beauvoir herself repeatedly returned to the theme of ageing in both her memoirs and autobiographically influenced fiction. While *Old Age* has been criticized for its unremittingly dark portrait of ageing, reading it against Beauvoir's other writings, as Kathleen Woodward (1988) has shown, offers a more complex and often surprisingly positive picture.

Life writing can offer an immensely valuable representation of age and ageing from inside, rather than as imagined from the outside by a younger writer. May Sarton's journals – among them *Journal of a Solitude* (1973); *Recovering* (first published in 1980), which tells of her recovery from breast cancer in her sixty-sixth year; and *At Seventy: A Journal* (1984) – are an extraordinary record of the ageing process with its associated frailties as well as a testament to the importance of friendships, love and gardening as ways of making meaning. A poet who was also the author of one of the most important novels of ageing, *As We Are Now*, Sarton was one of the most tireless challengers of stereotypes about old age, repeatedly exploring the transformative possibilities of the later years: 'The pure joys, the joy of a wild flower or a bird, or simply the silence of trees is there in old age because we are less distracted by personal emotion. Is that it?', she speculates in *Recovering* (1986, p. 87).

Connected to this area of life writing is another relatively new genre, the memoir of a parent, such as Philip Roth's *Patrimony* (1991), Blake Morrison's *And When Did You Last See Your Father?* (1993), or *Driving My Father* (1995) by Susan Wicks. These often deal with the issues raised by looking after an ageing and increasingly dependent parent – 'It's terrible to be so helpless,' Wicks' father sobs at one point (1995, p. 120). The tension between documenting the difficulties of coping with a parent suffering from dementia and preserving their dignity has also been admirably recorded by Ros Coward in her newspaper series, *Looking After Mother*, which ran in *The Guardian* from January 2007 to October 2008. Recognizing the taboos against being explicit about the processes of ageing, Coward writes that 'It will take another revolution like feminism to make society accept that [caring for the elderly] is something that can't be hidden away, needing as much respect and support as childcare' (2008, p. 2).

However, these texts, unlike Sarton's journals, are actually forms of what we can call, following Kathleen Woodward's rethinking of Robert Butler's work, 'midlife review'; that is, they possibly tell us more about the midlife ageing of the writer than the old age of their parent. Butler's ground-breaking essay, 'The Life Review:

An Interpretation of Reminiscence in the Aged' (1963), provided a re-evaluation of reminiscence as an important process rather than merely aimless wandering. Using literature and film together with case histories, he argued for the 'universal occurrence in older people of an inner experience or mental process of reviewing one's life' (1963, p. 65). This process of dealing with earlier unresolved conflicts, which is triggered by impending death, could lead either to depression or to the evolution of candour, serenity and wisdom (1963, p. 65). It is, of course, precisely the process enacted in Sarton's *A Reckoning* (first published in 1978) or in Vita Sackville-West's *All Passion Spent* (1931) and provides a useful way of interpreting these novels, as well as life writing. Critiquing Butler's essay through memoirs as well as fiction, however, Woodward contends that 'meaning is always produced within a specific tradition and historical context and that we must always be especially heedful of accounts of the experience of the elderly produced by a younger generation' (1986b, p. 143). This is true, Woodward suggests, of Butler himself who was in his thirties when he wrote 'The Life Review'.

The work of Margaret Gullette has been especially innovative in the way it reaches across gerontology, feminism, literary criticism and life writing. Her *Declining to Decline: Cultural Combat and the Politics of the Midlife* (1997) developed her earlier discussion of the revisionist midlife progress novel by combining it with what she calls 'age autobiography' (p. 11), personal essays about herself and her parents which function as cultural critique, and enable a wide-ranging analysis of what it means to be 'aged by culture' (pp. 6–7). As she puts it:

The basic idea we need to absorb is that whatever happens in the body, human beings are aged by culture first of all ... Age ideology is my shorthand term for the system that regulates it all. (1997, p. 3)

The question she explores here is *how* that process operates, in part through narratives of decline/progress. It is in representations of ageing in women's midlife progress novels by Lessing, Drabble, Tyler and others, including the '"post-maternal" novel' (p. 94), that she finds a model of resistance, asking, 'How is it, though, that growing numbers of women's novels can resist the dominant culture and model this complex kind of progress?' (p. 87). Ironically, the very visibility of negative representations of women's ageing – in, for instance, the presentation of the menopause as cataclysmic, '*the* change' (p. 103) – provides one reason for the development of such discourses of resistance. By contrast, Gullette suggests, 'That men age is a truly taboo subject' (p. 106). Gullette's use of age autobiography to explore cultural narratives of decline/progress and what she terms 'age socialisation' has been developed further in *Aged by Culture* (2004), which begins with an account of the reactions of children visiting a face-ageing exhibition in the Boston Museum of Science. Increasingly moving into the realm of cultural studies, Gullette here lays out an agenda for what she has come to call 'age studies'.

Gender and ageing: a 'female phenomenon'?

As the work of Gullette and others suggests, one of the most energetic motors behind literary gerontology has been feminist theory. It is no accident that Beauvoir, author of *The Second Sex* (1949), should also have written on old age. As she noted in both texts, women are especially vulnerable to what we now call 'ageism' – the coin termed by Robert Butler in the 1960s (Bytheway, 1995) – because they live longer and are subject to particularly brutal expectations about youth, beauty and sexuality. As Susan Sontag so starkly put it in 'The Double Standard of Aging': 'That old women are repulsive is one of the most profound aesthetic and erotic feelings in our culture' (1972, p. 37). In 'Ageing as a Feminist Issue' (1987), Cherry Russell drew attention to the bias towards male models of ageing in gerontology, and the neglect of the issue within women's studies, and summarized the issues thus:

Ageing is a substantially female phenomenon and old women face a range of special problems including greater poverty, higher rates of aloneness, institutionalisation and loneliness, disadvantages in work and remarrriage, ill health and medicalisation, symbolic denigration, and increased burden of care for others. (1987, p. 129)

However, just as novelists such as Margaret Drabble have turned their attention to the issue of age as they grew older, so have the leaders of second-wave feminism themselves. Two especially influential texts have been Germaine Greer's *The Change: Women, Ageing and the Menopause* (1991) and Betty Friedan's *The Fountain of Age* (1993).

The relationship between women's studies, gerontology and literary studies has worked in several different directions. Fiction was an important resource for several of the early feminists who addressed issues of ageing: both Jane Ford and Ruth Sinclair (1987) and Barbara McDonald with Cynthia Rich (1983), for instance, refer to May Sarton's *As We Are Now*. On the other hand the focus on 'images of women' in early feminist literary criticism provided a model for work on stereotypes of ageing in literature. Such stereotypes – the witch, hag or crone – have also been interrogated in other media such as Karen M. Stoddard's *Saints and Shrews: Women and Aging in American Popular Film* (1983) or Joanna Frueh's work on women artists. Frueh (1994) draws attention to the paradoxical relationship between the 'visible' nature of signs of ageing and the 'invisibility' of the older woman in our culture. She notes that while Germaine Greer may argue that such invisibility can bring freedom to the post-menopausal woman, it creates difficulties for the woman artist whose art is neither recognized nor bought (1994, p. 270).

Attention to gender is crucial because it throws into relief the differences in both experience and representations of age and ageing. Questioning the work of Freedman and Loughman as well as the overriding negativity of Beauvoir's *Old Age*, Emily M. Nett suggested that, given their focus on texts by men, 'the gerontophobia they encounter represents *male* impressions of growing old' (1990, p. 177; emphasis added), where the 'tragedy of being old is the decline of potency – sexual power above all' (p. 179). Contrasting these with novels written by women, including *The Stone Angel*, *Mrs Palfrey at the Claremont*, and Sarton's *Mrs Stevens Hears the Mermaids Singing* (1965), and rereading Spark's *Memento Mori* (1959) against these, Nett found a very different depiction of ageing as 'an exciting adventure' (p. 179) which, although it encompasses very real difficulties, leads to some kind of 'spiritual transcendence' (p. 183). Memory is central to this journey. In Sarton's novel, for instance, Hilary Stevens has three encounters with her mirror which allow her to integrate her present image as an 'Old crone, with hardly a wisp of hair left and those dewlaps and those wrinkles' (Sarton in Nett, p. 186) with that of her earlier youthful self, and to understand that 'one does not become less oneself with the years, but more so' (p. 186). By repositioning the stereotype of the crone as a pre-Christian mythic archetype, Nett argues, we can read it as only one manifestation of feminine being within a cyclical rhythm which enables the women protagonists to be reborn rather than '"end[ing] up" (as in Kingsley Amis' title)' (p. 187).

Issues of gender are foregrounded by Sara Munson Deats and Lagretta Tallent Lenker, in their edited volume, *Aging and Identity: A Humanities Perspective* (1999), through the inclusion of sections on both the ageing male *and* the ageing female in literature, as well as sections on ageing in the community (including African-American and Native American writers), and ageing in the fine and popular arts. The collection builds on previous work (particularly that of Betty Friedan), both to interrogate stereotypes of ageing and think about the ways in which they can be deconstructed. Its wide range embodies what the editors call, borrowing Thomas Moody's term, a 'dialectical gerontology', reading work which inscribes 'both the strong and weak faces of age' (1999, p. 7). Thus, Kirk Combe and Kenneth Schmader's clinical consideration of Shakespeare's Lear and Prospero as 'case studies in aged heterogeneity' (pp. 33–46), can be read against Christine McCall Probes' discussion of the 'good counsel' offered by two European princesses, Marguerite de Navarre and Madame Palatine (pp. 149–59), or Norman N. Holland's reader-response discussion of two viewings, 32 years apart, of Fellini's film *8½* (pp. 213–27). The portrait of age which emerges from these essays is in Friedan's terms, 'two-faced', embodying an old age characterized by 'heterogeneity, diversity, balance of contraries, wisdom' rather than traditional stereotypes (1999, p. 7).

Writing in 2004, Roberta Maierhofer called for the development of what she termed 'anocriticism' (from the Latin *anus*, 'old woman'); that is, criticism which links theories of gender and ageing to 'search for a specific female culture of ageing in the tradition of Elaine Showalter's "gynocriticism"' (2004, p. 156). Arguing for a distinction between chronological age and the cultural stereotypes associated with age, she draws on Ursula K. Le Guin's notion of the 'third pregnancy' (menopausal change) in *The Space Crone* (1976) to discuss texts which show how women can repudiate stereotypical notions in order to change and define themselves in their own terms, despite societal pressures.

Signs of the emergence of such an 'anocriticism' can be seen in Zoe Brennan's *The Older Woman in Recent Fiction* (2005), and the collection of essays edited by Phyllis Sternberg Perrakis, *Adventures of the Spirit: The Older Woman in the Works of Doris Lessing, Margaret Atwood, and Other Contemporary Women Writers* (2007). Brennan's book, which focuses on representations of women over 60, is one of the most detailed and thoughtful considerations of the representation of women's ageing in literature. In a chapter on 'Paradigms of Ageing and Ageism', she compiles a useful survey of hypotheses about senescence from a range of disciplines including gerontology, feminism and psychoanalysis. These are then deployed and interrogated in chapters on the 'Angry and Frustrated Older Woman', the 'Passionate and Desiring Older Woman', the 'Contented and Developing Older Woman', and the 'Wise and Archetypal Older Woman'. The texts discussed include novels by Lessing, Sarton, Pym, Angela Carter and Molly Keane, as well as, more surprisingly, detective fiction. Brennan's work is underpinned by a Foucauldian understanding of discourse to show how these novels 'not only depict subversive acts, but also themselves are reverse discourses that challenge and perhaps supplant, more dominant and restrictive models of senescence' (2005, p. 9).

The essays on recent women's fiction in *Adventures of the Spirit* return to the metaphor of the journey to explore 'a new kind of midlife and older woman's narrative, one that is spiritual in nature' (Perrakis, 2007, p. 1), and frequently includes a retrospective reassessment which can lead to a new sense of self. Over half of these essays focus on the work of Doris Lessing and Margaret Atwood, affirming the importance of their work in this area, but the inclusion of essays on other texts – especially Susan Berry Brill de Ramírez's discussion of storytelling by elder Native American women – demonstrates the variety of women's representations of ageing.

Anthologies: enabling cross-cultural/cross-historical readings

One of the benefits of the critical attention to age and ageing has been the production of anthologies such as Elizabeth Cairns, edited, *Singing in Tune with Time:*

Stories and Poems About Ageing (1993a), and Thomas R. Cole and Mary G. Winkler, edited, *The Oxford Book of Aging* (1994), which make visible a wider spectrum of writing and illuminate the culturally constructed nature of ageing. *Singing in Tune with Time* focuses on twentieth-century writing by women from a range of cultures, including Colette, Margaret Laurence, Grace Nichols, Ismat Chugtai, Muriel Spark and Paule Marshall. The story from which the anthology's title comes, Cairns' own 'Echoes' (1993b, pp. 195–208), offers a depiction of a grandmother's sexual re-encounter with a man she loved as a student but didn't then have the courage to go to bed with. In its whole-hearted validation of active sexuality in an older woman, it offers a positive counter to the assumptions about youth and desirability in the *carpe diem* poems discussed earlier.

Cole and Winkler's *Oxford Book of Aging* offers an even broader cross-cultural and cross-historical selection of texts from Cicero, Confucius, the Bible, the Koran and Native American stories, through to Florida Scott-Maxwell, Ursula K. Le Guin, and 'Frances, a nursing home resident'. The thematic arrangement of the anthology foregrounds a multiplicity of experience and aspiration across boundaries of time, ethnicity, race, nationality and gender. Here, for instance, Shakespeare's account of the 'seven ages' of man can be compared with the traditional Ojibway story 'The Four Hills of Life' (Cole and Winkler, 1994, pp. 20–3), which places its emphasis on the achievement of those who reach old age (the fourth hill) and live life 'in its entirety' (p. 23), rather than on a decline into 'second childhood'. Moreover, the voice of the 'medicine man' who interprets the story draws our attention to what David Erben has called the 'rich, vital role of elders as storytellers and educators' in Native American culture (1999, p. 130).

'Many of our most troubling dilemmas,' Cole has suggested, 'are linked to the fact that Western culture offers few convincing ways to make sense of physical decline and the inevitability of death' (1994, p. 4). In the introduction to the second edition of *Handbook of the Humanities and Aging*, Cole and Ray noted the continuing absence of coverage of ageing in the 'diverse populations in the United States and Europe or in the countries of Africa and Latin America' (2000, p. xii). Work on a wider range of cross-cultural representations of ageing is developing. In addition to the work of Smith, Ramírez and Erben already cited, Charles J. Hegler and Annye L. Refoe, for instance, have discussed the work of Ernest J. Gaines, pointing to the wealth of African-American literature which demonstrates the '"emancipatory possibilities of late life"' (1999, p. 139). More recently, Ira Raja (2004) discusses a shift to the use of older women's bodies to signify the nation in the post-independence Hindi short story as the Westernization of young women's changing roles make them problematic figures. However, while many of these areas still remain under-explored, the kinds of cross-cultural comparisons enabled by anthologies at least draw attention to other ways of conceptualizing age and ageing.

The uses (and abuses) of literature: a resource for gerontologists?

Anthologies also offer important resources for what Anne Wyatt-Brown has called 'our original audience, clinicians in gerontology' (2000, p. 41). Much of the work on representations of ageing has been inspired or informed by their uses for those working in gerontology: as case studies, as evidence for theoretical models, as inspiration or consolation for older people, and as aids to empathy and understanding for those who work with them.

Both writers and theorists have been aware of the potential of representations of age, ageing and, indeed, death for those immediately facing these issues. May Sarton noted with pleasure the appeal of her novel, *A Reckoning*, in which Laura, told she is dying, reviews her life in search of the 'real connections' (1984, p. 11). Sarton commented:

It's been used in the hospices and nursing homes, and often read by people who are dealing with the dying. It has been useful, there is no doubt, and that is a wonderful feeling. (Brennan, 2005, p. 68)

From a critical perspective, Robert N. Wilson in an essay on Leo Tolstoy's 'The Death of Ivan Ilyitch', discusses the educative possibilities of literature as 'case studies', arguing that artists can give us 'models of coping and incompetence' (1995, p. 123). If Ivan Ilyitch is 'a model of unhealthy living and agonized dying' (p. 117), poets such as Edmund Waller, Wilson suggests, can offer consolation: 'Poetry reminds us that in meeting death we are not alone' (p. 124). There are issues with this approach, which will be discussed below, but Sarton and Wilson usefully remind us of the emotional power of literature.

Fiction, Constance Rooke argues, 'contextualises and particularises the problems of gerontology' (1992, p. 254). Thus, it can offer a particularly rich source of examples for use by carers or clinicians working with older people. As Jill Manthorpe notes, 'Claims for the benefits of reading about old age are overwhelmingly positive' (1995, p. 5). She cites Lisette N. Kautzmann's work (1992), suggesting that such representations can help educate students, sensitizing them to the values and concerns of older people. Literature can also provide ethically acceptable '"perfect" case studies' to illustrate, for instance, family dynamics (Manthorpe, 1995, p. 5). Less discussed is the way in which fiction, Manthorpe maintains, can assist in debates about 'policy and service development' (p. 5). The example she gives is the historical depth which can be provided by a consideration of representations of 'private residential homes', usually seen as a creation of the 1980s, but depicted in earlier fiction such as Paul Bailey's *At the Jerusalem* (1967) or Bernice Rubens'

A Five Year Sentence (1978), while Margaret Forster's *Have the Men Had Enough?* (1989) offers a comparison of private and public provision. Through the use of alternating first-person narratives, Forster's novel also depicts the practical and ethical difficulties faced by the relatives who care for an older woman increasingly incapacitated through dementia. Like Lessing's *Jane Somers*, it foregrounds the gender issues which mean that both the elderly and those who care for them are usually female.

Gerontologists have also used literature as what Deats and Lenker call 'a well-stocked laboratory' (1999, p. 11) for the study of ageing. An early example is Robert Butler's influential article on 'The Life Review' (1963), discussed above, which uses examples from literature and film – notably a detailed reading of Henry James' *The Beast in the Jungle* (1903), but also references to Bergman's *Wild Strawberries*, Aristotle, Somerset Maugham and Samuel Beckett's *Krapp's Last Tape*. This article, however, demonstrates some of the problems with using literature unproblematically as evidence. Rereading James' story – which deals with John Marcher's recognition that he has failed to live his life fully because of a secret conviction that 'something rare and strange' would sooner or later happen to him – Woodward (1986b) points out that Marcher is, in fact, in the *middle*, rather than the end of his life and that the story therefore tells us more about 'those who live their lives in *prospective* time' than those concerned with a retrospective life review (1986b, pp. 156, 155). There are key differences, Woodward's essay demonstrates, between the processes of creating fictions and of making meaning out of ageing, between 'literature' and 'life'.

The problems involved in any use of literature in the study of older people have been further explored by Hannah Zelig (1997), who warns of the dangers of extrapolating from literature without bearing in mind the individuality of any text as the imaginative product of a particular individual located in a specific cultural context. Returning to Tolstoy's 'Ivan Ilyitch', she points out that Ivan's death 'was peculiar to circumstances of his time and place', and Wilson's essay demonstrates the dangers of ignoring these in order to make a text 'stand for certain "timeless" lessons or values' (1997, p. 45). Too often, Zelig argues, literature is used to make '*a priori* generalisations' or to furnish 'glittery anecdotes' to enliven gerontological studies (p. 47). Only if it is 'carefully contextualised in terms of its literary specificity (its genre and complete narrative) and historical background', she rightly warns, can literature be 'an invaluable means of enriching gerontology' (p. 47).

The complex interface between gerontology and literature needs to be handled in an informed and sensitive way, then, but it has the potential to enrich both fields. Teresa Mangum's article 'Literary History as a Tool of Gerontology' (2000), despite its title, actually pushes in both directions, aiming to persuade fellow literature teachers to consider the issue of ageing *and* to persuade social scientists and the health-care system to 'take literary history seriously' (2000, p. 63). Her emphasis here is on literary *history*, and the way in which a reading of the past can inform understandings of the present. To answer the question of why old age is often portrayed as 'childlike', she turns to nineteenth-century children's literature and the work of Dickens. Her project here is not so much to find the origins of our beliefs but to juxtapose past and present to generate comparativist views which can jolt or shift our assumptions and suggest alternatives.

Although it is presented as exploring the 'potential of literature as a geronto-logical resource' the sociologist Mike Hepworth's *Stories of Ageing* (2000) also has much to interest literary scholars. Hepworth's interest is in the potential of litera-ture as an imaginative resource that can 'engage our interest and concern' (2000, p. 6) in understanding variations in the meaning of the experience of ageing. To this end he uses a 'symbolic interactionist' framework within which the self is seen as emerging out of interaction with others, and shaped by an ongoing imaginative awareness of how others see us. Reading itself is, Hepworth suggests, 'a process of symbolic interaction where the reader has some freedom to interpret the text according to his or her own ideas, emotions and consciousness of self' (p. 5). The texts Hepworth discusses are 'popular' fiction, particularly crime fiction, from the 1930s onwards – by writers including Agatha Christie, Pat Barker, Simon Brett, James Herriot, Penelope Lively, Julian Rathbone and Joanna Trollope – chosen to be familiar and accessible. With chapters focused round key issues to do with the relationship between body, self and society, Hepworth shows how age iden-tity through the life course is shaped through 'stories' in various different ways. Fictions are especially 'adept at describing and expressing the *emotions* associated with growing older' (p. 65), he suggests, so those stories can 'help us feel as well as think' (p. 28).

Theorizing age: psychoanalysis to postmodernism

'Literary gerontology, like gerontology in general, is not rich in theory', Anne Wyatt-Brown noted in 1993 (1993a, p. 3). Yet the need for age theory, not least as a weapon of 'cultural combat', has been emphasized by Gullette among others: 'To me theory has to be practical, plain-speaking, personal, poetic, speculative, passionate – theory for all of us... It needs to be everywhere' (1997, p. 11). Psy-choanalysis proved a rich ground for some of the most interesting early work, but more recently theorists have turned to postmodern and poststructuralist ideas.

An initial exploration of the potential of psychoanalysis is offered in the essays in Kathleen Woodward and Murray M. Schwartz, edited, *Memory and Desire: Aging–Literature–Psychoanalysis* (1986), which drew on an eclectic range of approaches from Freud, Winnicott, Lacan, Kristeva, and Erikson, and ranged over texts from *King Lear* to those of Marguerite Duras. Key essays included Norman N. Holland's reading of one of Freud's most famous case studies against a memoir written by 'Little Hans' himself when a 68-year-old opera director; Ellie Ragland-Sullivan's Lacanian reading of *The Picture of Dorian Gray* to suggest that Wilde translated the issue of homosexuality into a monstrous picture of ageing; and Diana Hume George's discussion of contemporary women poets and their engagement with images of their parents, especially their mothers. The most influential essay here, Kathleen Woodward's 'The Mirror Stage of Old Age', brought together Freud, Lacan, and Beauvoir in a reading of Proust to posit the existence of a phase of old age which is the obverse of Lacan's mirror stage in infancy. Woodward's theorization offers a particularly sophisticated way of reading the mirrors which so often appear in representations of ageing. However, the use of psychoanalytic and literary theory in these essays raises a question of audience. As Wyatt-Brown pointed out, most of these critics (with the exception of Woodward) were unfamiliar with the work of gerontologists and wrote for literary specialists (1999, p. 340). Calling for more communication between the two groups, Wyatt-Brown asked for a combination of 'gerontological and literary theories in language that is accessible to all' (p. 340).

It is perhaps Kathleen Woodward's ability to draw on and write for both disciplines which has made her work so influential. A study of representations of old age through psychoanalysis and twentieth-century fiction, her *Aging and Its Discontents: Freud and Other Fictions* (1991) further developed her analysis of the gerontophobia of Western culture. This negative view of ageing, she argued, is reinforced by Freudian psychoanalysis with 'its emphasis on castration, narcissism, mourning and anxiety' (1991, p. 17). Woodward's method is to take a psychoanalytic concept in each chapter and read it against a fictional scene: the mirror stage and Proust; narcissism, aggression and Woolf's *The Years*; generations and Eva Figes' *Waking*; mourning, melancholia and Barthes' *Camera Lucida*; masquerade and Thomas Mann's *Death in Venice*. Recognizing the cultural specificity of her texts, she appends a 'counter-text' to each chapter, without comment, as a reminder of 'other representations and traditions' (p. 18). Reading Freud's own anxieties about ageing, she shows how psychoanalysis, 'made as it is out of the stuff of Freud's life and writing, has worked to avoid if not repress the *theorization* or *analysis* of old age' (p. 37). Anxieties about ageing are displaced onto those about death, which are covered in turn by sexual anxieties.

Woodward's methods produce a series of bravura readings of which it is perhaps her theorizations of the mirror stage of old age and youthfulness as masquerade which have proved the most ground-breaking. The latter draws on Joan Riviere's theorization of womanliness as 'masquerade' but reworks it to argue that 'In a culture which so devalues age, masquerade with respect to the ageing body is first and foremost a denial of age, an effort to erase or efface age and put on youth'

(p. 148). In *Death in Venice* Aschenbach, in love with a young boy, feels disgust for his own ageing body and attempts, through make-up, youthful clothes and dyed hair, to appear younger. But this masquerade, Woodward suggests, does not hide but makes more grotesquely visible the old age it attempts to mask. Paradoxically, 'A mask may express rather than hide a truth. The mask may itself be one of multiple truths' (p. 148). While Woodward discusses male-authored masquerade her theorization has proved fruitful for critics of women's writing. Cynthia Port, for instance, develops the idea to look at 'the 'dual masquerade of femininity and youth' which must be performed by female characters in the novels of Jean Rhys if they are to 'maintain value in the sexual marketplace' (2001, p. 213). Woodward's own work has gone on to develop its connections with feminism in, for instance, her work on the older woman as a 'missing person' in Freudian psychoanalysis (1995).

The turn to postmodern and poststructural theories (Judith Butler, Foucault, Baudrillard, Lyotard), which posit identity, particularly gender and sexual identity, as 'performative' and the body itself as culturally constructed and discursively produced, has important implications for our understandings of age and ageing. A disjunction between visibly ageing appearance (as in Proust's mirror scene) and a 'youthful' inner self is a common motif in representations of ageing and focuses attention on the body. 'I don't *feel* old', as the cliché puts it. Situating this disjunction within the context of postmodern consumerist culture with its emphasis on lifestyles and youthfulness, Featherstone and Hepworth (1991) have developed the concept of the *mask of ageing*. The external appearance of ageing is seen as a 'mask', represented as pathological or deviant, which conceals the 'normal' inner essential self. However, as the hotel barber's argument in *Death in Venice* – 'We are all as old as we feel, but no older, and grey hair can misrepresent a man worse than dyed' (Mann, 1955, p. 77) – suggests, this is a dangerous line to tread. 'How does age resistance differ from age denial?', as Julia Twigg asks (2004, p. 63), and she notes that some feminist theorists have been unhappy about a potential separation of body and self in Featherstone and Hepworth's theorization (pp. 63–4). Women tend to have particularly fraught relationships with their mirror images, in part as Diana Tietjans Meyers has pointed out, because 'women's ageing features have been shanghaied as figurative vehicles for decline and demise' (1999, p. 38).

Postmodern and poststructural theorizations also inform the essays in Kathleen Woodward, edited, *Figuring Age*: *Women, Bodies, Generations* (1999), which address 'the cultural discourses and social practises that construct the meaning of ageing for us' (p. xvi). As part of their project to make older women 'visible', they cover a range of representations from the literary to visual and performance media, including personal photographs and mirror images, fashion and consumer culture, Charcot's work on hysteria, film, body-building, the performance art of

Rachel Rosenthal, illustrations from children's books, and Jacqueline Hayden's photographs. Many of these essays (notably those by Nancy Miller and Margaret Gullette) engage with theory through personal autobiographical reflections, often (like Woodward's own essay) focusing on intergenerational paradigms, which foreground and problematize our understanding of the relational and the subjective nature of age and ageing. These kinds of cultural critiques, Julia Twigg has argued, can help to recover the 'important territory' (2004, p. 61) of the body for a traditional gerontology which has found it difficult to engage with. Twigg herself uses Foucauldian ideas to explore the 'body work' (2004, p. 67) of caring for those in deep old age.

Feminism has again led the way in much of this theoretical work but feminists have also used theories of age for self-reflection. The essays in a special issue of the journal *Studies in the Literary Imagination* (2006) edited by Victoria Bazin and Rosie White examine representations of ageing in texts as varied as French films, the ageing Simone Signoret, post-feminist 'chick lit', 1960s fashion and Sarah Waters' *Affinity*, to raise key questions about the relationship of age and history. They develop Woodward's questioning of models of generational relation (1999) to interrogate the historical construction of the ageing 'body' of feminism itself, often represented in the popular media in generational terms, as tired, old 'second-wave' feminists are superseded by the glamorously youthful charms of 'third-wave' feminism.

New directions: the future

The continuation of a fertile interdisciplinarity and theorized self-reflexivity is evident in recent work by established age critics. Kathleen Woodward's (2006) recent essay on representations of the older woman in film and the work of contemporary artists such as Louise Bourgeois builds on and reviews her own earlier work further to explore the in/visibility of the older woman. Similarly, Margaret Gullette (2008) has reflected on her own journey from literary criticism to a more inclusive 'age studies', within which she positions herself as an 'age critic'. The question of the relationship between ageing and creativity was revisited in the late Edward Said's *On Late Style: Music and Literature Against the Grain* (2006), a project driven by his own personal circumstances, which focuses on lateness as a kind of deliberate 'going against' rather than any kind of final serenity.

However, there are also signs of interest from within mainstream history and literary criticism. While much of the early work was American in origin, British scholars are increasingly contributing to this area. Within history, Pat Thane's landmark study, *Old Age in English History: Past Experiences, Present Issues*

(2000), starts by looking at representations of old age from classical, medieval and seventeenth- and eighteenth-century literature in order to try to distinguish facts from fantasy. 'Old age cannot simply be a social construct, artifice of perception, or fashioned through discourse – unquestionably bodies age, change, decay,' she argues (2000, p. 5). Nevertheless, as she shows, the 'meaning of old age is not fixed and it has different meanings in different contexts' (p. 5). Indeed, what has been consistent across time is the variety and contradictory nature of representations of old age, meaning that '"Old people" are not and never have been a single, simple category' (p. 459), but have always been divided by class, income, gender, race, and age itself. Thane's work provides a wealth of invaluable material for the scholar interested in historicizing representations of age and ageing. Interdisciplinary historicization is also the keynote of Nina Taunton's *Fictions of Old Age in Early Modern Literature and Culture* (2007), which returns to Shakespeare and other early modern writers to position them within the diversity of writings on age – classical, philosophical, Biblical, medical, legal, moral, scientific – during this period. Complex and contradictory views of old age, epitomized by the opposing influences of Cicero's idealized *De Senectute* and Bacon's emphasis on decay in *Historie of Life and Death*, contributed to an ambivalence about the subject, which Taunton unpicks by reading, for instance, *The Comedy of Errors* in the light of dietary advice and *King Lear* in relation to laws on inheritance.

With the exception of Cicero, old age has tended to be a marginal issue in philosophy, as Helen Small acknowledges in her 'deliberately essayistic' study, *The Long Life* (2007), which attempts to redress this lack and show 'what might be required if we are to become more seriously philosophical about old age' (2007, p. 18). Small stages a series of dialogues between key philosophical and literary texts – Plato and *Death in Venice*, Aristotle and *King Lear*, Alastair Macintyre and Saul Bellow's *Ravelstein*, Adorno and Dickens' *The Old Curiosity Shop*, and so on – to argue that in order to think about old age we also have to think about wider issues, such as what constitutes a 'good life', what it means to be a person, or what it means for a society to be just. Small's readings are erudite and illuminating but given that, as Pat Thane among others has pointed out, 'Old age has long been a predominantly female experience' (2000, p. 3), the fact that she includes among her admittedly eclectic choice of texts only one by a woman (a short poem by Stevie Smith) means that there is only half a story here. Similarly, among the philosophers, Beauvoir and Martha Nussbaum are acknowledged as influences but they are not given the detailed discussion of their male counterparts.

This caveat notwithstanding, in such recent work there are clear indications that work on representations of age and ageing can continue to draw strength from its interdisciplinarity. Small's refusal to conclude with any 'grand pronouncements' is itself heartening. As she puts it, 'One of the problems with and for old age is that, while there has been too little thinking about it over the years, there have been quite enough pronouncements' (2007, p. 265).

Summary

Consideration of Simone de Beauvoir's *Old Age* leads into a critical examination of literary treatments of old age and ageing, beginning with its perhaps most often encountered form as a motif and metaphor for decay and mortality. The next section, which addresses new genres of post-1970s fiction, challenges many of the traditional portrayals, and finds sources of enrichment and hope in representations of older adults and the ageing process. Moving from the written word to the writer, the concept of 'late style' and the influences of ageing on the writing process are critically considered. The related issue of life writing – of evaluation through biography and autobiography – is then examined. The discussion leads into an examination of gender and ageing, and of anthologizing literature on old age. The use of literature in enhancing gerontologists' understanding of ageing is examined, and although a complex interface is identified, it points to the use of literature and writing as a 'gerontological resource'. The chapter concludes with an analysis of the theoretical underpinnings of literary gerontology, and this in turn leads to a discussion of potential new directions for future studies.

REFERENCES

Aldrich, M. (1993) Lethal brevity: Louise Bogan's lyric career, in Wyatt-Brown and Rossen (eds), *Aging and gender in literature: studies in creativity*, 105–20.

Bazin, V. and White, R. (eds) (2006) Special issue on 'Women, age and difference', *Studies in the Literary Imagination*, **39**(2).

Beauvoir, S. de (1972) *Old age*. Trans. Patrick O'Brian. London: André Deutsch and Weidenfeld and Nicolson.

   (1983 [1949]) *The second sex*. Trans. H.M. Parshley. Harmondsworth: Penguin.

Brennan, Z. (2005) *The older woman in recent fiction*. Jefferson, NC and London: McFarland.

Butler, R.N. (1963) The life review: an interpretation of reminiscence in the aged, *Psychiatry*, **26**, 65–76.

Bytheway, B. (1995) *Ageism*. Buckingham and Philadelphia: Open University Press.

Cairns, E. (ed.) (1993a) *Singing in tune with time: stories and poems about ageing*. London: Virago.

Cairns, E. (1993b) 'Echoes', in Cairns, *Singing in tune with time*, 195–208.

Cole, T.R. (1992) The humanities and aging: an overview, in Cole *et al.* (eds), *Handbook of the humanities and aging*, xi–xxiv.

Cole, T.R., Van Tassel, D.D. and Kastenbaum, R. (eds) (1992) *Handbook of the humanities and aging*. New York: Springer.

Cole, T.R., Kastenbaum, R. and Ray, R.R. (eds) (2000) *Handbook of the humanities and aging*, 2nd edn. New York: Springer.

Cole, T.R. and Winkler, M.G. (eds) (1994) *The Oxford book of aging.* Oxford University Press.

Combe, K. and Schmader, K. (1999) Shakespeare teaching geriatrics: Lear and Prospero as case studies in aged heterogeneity, in Deats and Lenker, *Aging and identity: a humanities perspective*, 33–46.

Coward, R. (2008) Have I done enough?, *The Guardian*, Family section, 18 October, 1–2.

Cumming, E. and Henry, W. (1961) *Growing old: The process of disengagement.* New York: Basic Books.

Deats, S.M. and Lenker, L.T. (eds) (1999) *Aging and identity: a humanities perspective.* Westport, CT and London: Praeger.

Eliot, T.S. (1974 [1963]) *Collected poems, 1909–1962.* London: Faber and Faber.

Erben, D. (1999) The sacred ghost: the role of the elder(ly) in Native American literature, in Deats and Lenker, *Aging and identity: a humanities perspective*, 130–8.

Featherstone, M. and Hepworth, M. (1991) The mask of aging and the postmodern life course, in M. Featherstone, M. Hepworth and B.S. Turner (eds), *The body: social process and cultural theory.* London: Sage, 371–89.

Ford, J. and Sinclair, R. (1987) *Sixty years on: women talk about old age.* London: Women's Press.

Forster, M. (2004 [1989]) *Have the men had enough?* London: Vintage.

Freedman, R. (1978) Sufficiently decayed: gerontophobia in English literature, in S.F. Spicker, K. Woodward and D.D. Van Tassell (eds), *Aging and the elderly: humanistic perspectives in gerontology.* Atlantic Highlands, NJ: Humanities Press, 49–82.

Friedan, B. (1993) *The fountain of age.* New York: Simon and Schuster.

Frueh, J. (1994) Visible difference: women artists and aging, in J. Frueh, C.S. Lanyer and A. Raven (eds), *New feminist criticism: art, identity, action.* New York: Icon, 264–88.

Gardner, H. (ed.) (1957) *The metaphysical poets.* Harmondsworth: Penguin.

George, D.H. (1986) Who is the double ghost whose head is smoke?: women poets on aging, in Woodward and Schwartz (eds), *Memory and desire*, 134–53.

Greer, G. (1992 [1991]) *The change: women, ageing and the menopause.* London: Penguin.

Gullette, M.M. (1988) *Safe at last in the middle years: the invention of the midlife progress novel: Saul Bellow, Margaret Drabble, Anne Tyler and John Updike.* Berkeley, CA: University of California Press.

(1997) *Declining to decline: cultural combat and the politics of the midlife.* Charlottesville, VA and London: University Press of Virginia.

(2004) *Aged by culture.* University of Chicago Press.

(2008) What exactly has age got to do with it?: my life in critical age studies, *Journal of Aging Studies*, 22, 189–95.

Hegler, C.J. and Refoe, A.L. (1999) Aging and the African-American community: the case of Ernest J. Gaines, in Deats and Lenker, *Aging and identity: a humanities perspective*, 139–47.

Heilbrun, C.G. (1989 [1988]) *Writing a woman's life.* London: Women's Press.

Held, J.S. (1987) Commentary on style and the aging artist, Special issue on 'Style and aging', *Art Journal* (Summer), 127–33.

Hepworth, M. (2000) *Stories of ageing.* Buckingham and Philadelphia: Open University Press.

Holland, N.N. (1986) Not so little Hans: identity and ageing, in Woodward and Schwartz (eds), *Memory and desire*, 51–75.

(1993) $8^{1}/_{2}$ and me: the thirty-two-year difference, in Deats and Lenker, *Aging and identity: a humanities perspective*, 213–27.

Jacques, E. (1965) Death and the mid-life crisis, *International Journal of Psychoanalysis*, **46**, 506–14.

Jamieson, A., Harper, S. and Victor, C. (eds) (1997) *Critical approaches to ageing and later life*. Buckingham and Philadelphia: Open University Press.

Jansohn, C. (ed.) (2004) *Old age and ageing in British and American culture and literature*. Studien zur englischen Literatur, 16. Munster: LIT Verlag.

Kautzmann, L.N. (1992) Using literature to educate students: images of caregivers in poetry and prose, *Educational Gerontology*, **18**, 17–26.

Ladimer, B. (1993) Colette: rewriting the script for the aging woman, in Wyatt-Brown and Rossen (eds), *Aging and gender in literature: studies in creativity*, 242–57.

Larkin, P. (1988) *Collected poems*. Ed. Anthony Thwaite. London: Marvell Press and Faber and Faber.

Laurence, M. (1993 [1964]) *The stone angel*. University of Chicago Press.

Lessing, D. (1985 [1984]) *The diaries of Jane Somers*. Harmondsworth: Penguin.
   (2002 [1973]) *The summer before the dark*. London: Flamingo.

Loughman, C. (1977) Novels of senescence: a new naturalism, *The Gerontologist*, **17**, 79–84.

Maierhofer, R. (2004) Third pregnancy: women, ageing and identity in American culture. An anocritical approach, in Jansohn, *Old age and ageing in British and American culture and literature*, 155–71.

Mangum, T. (2000) Literary history as a tool of gerontology, in Cole *et al.*, *Handbook of the humanities and aging*, 62–76.

Mann, T. (1955 [1928]) *Death in Venice, Tristan, Tonio Kröger*. Trans. H.T. Lowe-Porter. Harmondsworth: Penguin.

Manthorpe, J. (1995) The private residential home in fiction, *Generations Review*, **5**(1), 5–6.

Marshall, P. (1984 [1983]) *Praisesong for the widow*. New York: Plume.

McDonald, B. with Rich, C. (1983) *Look me in the eye: old women, aging and ageism*. London: Women's Press.

Meyers, D.T. (1999) Mirror, mémoir, mirage: Appearance, aging and women, in M.L. Walter (ed.), *Mother time: women, aging and ethics*. Lanham, MD: Rowman and Littlefield, 23–41.

Morrison, B. (2007 [1993]) *And when did you last see your father?* London: Granta.

Nett, E.M. (1990) The naked soul comes closer to the surface: old age in the gender mirror of contemporary novels, *Women's Studies*, **18**, 177–90.

Perrakis, P.S. (ed.) (2007) *Adventures of the spirit: the older woman in the works of Doris Lessing, Margaret Atwood, and other contemporary women writers*. Columbus, OH: Ohio State University Press.

Port, C. (2001) 'Money, for the night is coming': Jean Rhys and gendered economies of ageing, *Women: A Cultural Review*, **12**(2), 204–17.

Probes, C.M. (1999) Aging and the continental community: good counsel in the writings of two mature European princesses, Marguerite de Navarre and Madame Palatine, in Deats and Lenker, *Aging and identity: a humanities perspective*, 149–59.

Pym, B. (1994 [1980]) *A few green leaves*. London: Flamingo.
   (2004 [1978]) *Quartet in autumn*. London: Pan.

Quiller-Couch, A. (ed.) (1939) *The Oxford book of English verse, 1250–1918*. Oxford University Press.

Ragland-Sullivan, E. (1986) The phenomenon of ageing in Oscar Wilde's *Picture of Dorian Gray*: a Lacanian view, in Woodward and Schwartz (eds), *Memory and desire*, 114–33.

Raja, I. (2004) Signifying the nation: identity, authenticity and the ageing body in the post-independence Hindi short story, *Journal of Commonwealth Literature*, *39*(3), 25–43.

Ramírez, S.B.B., de (2007) Surviving the colonialist legacy of the Klondike Gold Rush: a nature woman elder's liberatory and integrative storytelling turn, in Perrakis, *Adventures of the spirit*, 241–69.

Rooke, C. (1992) Old age in contemporary fiction: a new paradigm of hope, in Cole *et al.*, *Handbook of the humanities and aging*, 241–57.

Roth, P. (1996 [1991]) *Patrimony*. London: Vintage.

Russell, C. (1987) Ageing as a feminist issue, *Women's Studies International Forum*, *10*(2), 125–32.

Sackville-West, V. (1983 [1931]) *All passion spent*. London: Virago.

Said, E. (2004) Thoughts on late style, *London Review of Books*, *26*, 15 (5 August). Retrieved from www.lrb.co.uk/v26/n15/print/said01_.html.

  (2006) *On late style: music and literature against the grain*. London: Bloomsbury.

Sarton, M (1973) *As we are now*. New York and London: Norton.

  (1984 [1978]) *A reckoning*. London: Women's Press.

  (1985 [1973]) *Journal of a solitude*. London: Women's Press.

  (1986 [1980]) *Recovering: a journal*. New York and London: Norton.

  (1989) *The education of Harriet Hatfield*. New York and London: Norton.

  (1993 [1965]) *Mrs Stevens hears the mermaids singing*. New York and London: Norton.

  (1993 [1984]) *At seventy: a journal*. New York and London: Norton.

Shakespeare, W. (1999) *The sonnets and A lover's complaint*. Ed. John Kerrigan. London: Penguin.

Small, H. (2007) *The long life*. Oxford University Press.

Smith, C.H. (1992) Images of aging in American poetry, 1925–1985, in Cole *et al.* (eds), *Handbook of the humanities and aging*.

Sontag, S. (1972) The double standard of aging, *Saturday Review*, *23*, 37.

Spicker, S.F., Woodward, K.M. and Van Tassel, D.D. (eds), (1978) *Ageing and the elderly: humanistic perspectives in gerontology*. Atlantic Highlands, NJ: Humanities Press.

Stoddard, K.M. (1983) *Saints and shrews: women and aging in American popular film*. Westport, CT and London: Greenwood Press.

Taunton, N. (2007) *Fictions of old age in early modern literature and culture*. New York and London: Routledge.

Taylor, E. (1982 [1971]) *Mrs Palfrey at the Claremont*. London: Virago.

Thane, P. (2000) *Old age in English history: past experiences, present issues*. Oxford University Press.

Twigg, J. (2004) The body, gender, and age: feminist insights in social gerontology, *Journal of Aging Studies*, *18*, 59–73.

Waxman, B.F. (1990) *From the hearth to the open road: a feminist study of aging in contemporary literature*. New York, Westport, CT and London: Greenwood Press.

Wicks, S. (1995) *Driving my father*. London: Faber and Faber.

Wilson, R.N. (1995) The case of Ivan Ilyitch, *Ageing and Society*, *15*, 115–24.

Woodward, K. (1980) *At last, the real distinguished thing: the late poems of Eliot, Pound, Stevens and Williams*. Columbus, OH: Ohio State University Press.

(1986a) The mirror stage of old age, in Woodward and Schwartz (eds), *Memory and desire*, 97–113.

(1986b) Reminiscence and the life review: prospects and retrospects, in T.R. Cole and S.A. Gadow (eds), *What does it mean to grow old? Reflections from the humanities*. Durham, NC: Duke University Press, 135–78.

(1988) Simone de Beauvoir: aging and its discontents, in S. Benstock (ed.), *The private self: theory and practice of women's autobiographical writings*. Chapel Hill, NC and London: University of North Carolina Press, 90–113.

(1991) *Aging and its discontents: Freud and other fictions*. Bloomington and Indianapolis, IN: Indiana University Press.

(1995) Tribute to the older woman: psychoanalysis, feminism, and ageism, in M. Featherstone and A. Werrick (eds), *Images of aging: cultural representations of later life*. London: Routledge, 79–96.

(1999) *Figuring age: women, bodies, generations*. Bloomington and Indianapolis, IN: Indiana University Press.

(2006) Performing age, performing gender, *NWSA Journal*, *18*(1), 162–89.

Woodward, K. and Schwartz, M.M. (eds) (1986) *Memory and desire: aging–literature–psychoanalysis*. Bloomington, IN: Indiana University Press.

Wyatt-Brown, A.M. (1988) Late style in the novels of Barbara Pym and Penelope Mortimer, *The Gerontologist*, *28*(6), 835–9.

(1989a) Creativity in midlife: the novels of Anita Brookner, *Journal of Aging Studies*, *3*(2), 175–81.

(1989b) The narrative imperative: fiction and the aging writer, *Journal of Aging Studies*, *3*(1), 55–65.

(1992) Literary gerontology comes of age, in Cole *et al.*, *Handbook of the humanities and aging*, 331–51.

(1993a) Introduction: aging, gender, creativity, in Wyatt-Brown and Rossen (eds), *Aging and gender in literature: studies in creativity*, 1–15.

(1993b) Another model of the ageing writer: Sarton's politics of old age, in Wyatt-Brown and Rossen (eds), *Aging and gender in literature: studies in creativity*, 49–60.

(2000) The future of literary gerontology, in Cole *et al.*, *Handbook of the humanities and aging* (2nd edn), 41–61.

Wyatt-Brown, A.M. and Rossen, J. (eds) (1993) *Aging and gender in literature: studies in creativity*. Charlottesville, VA and London: University Press of Virginia.

Zelig, H. (1997) The uses of literature in the study of older people, in Jamieson, *Critical approaches to ageing and later life*, 39–48.

15 Palliative care for older adults

LYNN O'NEILL AND SEAN MORRISON

OVERVIEW

In modern industrialized societies, the experience of death is often preceded by lengthy illness. This chapter therefore commences with a study of palliative care and key aspects, including pain and symptom management and advance care planning. It proceeds to examine caregiver burden and settings of care before a final section on grief and bereavement.

Introduction

Any textbook on gerontology would not be complete without a chapter on the topic of death, dying and bereavement. Indeed, that was the intended title of this section of the book. However, a brief discussion of the context in which many older adults live today, and eventually die, will help explain the alternative title as it appears above.

In 1900, the leading causes of death in the USA were pneumonia, tuberculosis and intestinal infections. This pattern was true across much of the developed world. These three diseases are all infectious, all resulted in rapid death due to lack of effective treatments, and all affected individuals of all ages. With modern advances, first in sanitation and later in antibiotics and other medical treatments, some people with these ailments survived and others were prevented from contracting the illnesses in the first place. One of the consequences of these advances is what Robert Butler (2008) has coined *the longevity revolution*. In his book of the same name, Butler describes the unprecedented gains in life expectancy of more than 30 years that have been observed in the industrialized world since the beginning of the twentieth century (see Chapter 1). With this increase in life expectancy comes an increase in chronic disease and a frame shift in the leading causes of death. In 2001, five of the top seven causes of death in the USA for people 65 and older fell firmly into the category of chronic disease: heart disease, cerebrovascular diseases, chronic lower respiratory disease, diabetes mellitus and Alzheimer's disease (Centers for Disease Control, 2003).

What is hidden in these statistics is the fact that many older adults will live for years with one or more of these chronic illnesses. Although the combination of these chronic illnesses may be life-limiting, patients' deaths are often preceded by long periods of slow physical decline and functional impairment. Their course may be punctuated by multiple, unpredictable exacerbations of disease requiring hospitalization and a more rapid decline in function (Liao, McGee, Cao et al., 2001). While these exacerbations may be followed by attempts at rehabilitation, older adults rarely return to their previous level of function and will inevitably return to the slow decline that preceded the exacerbation of disease. This pattern of chronic disease, slow physical decline and functional impairment is a far cry from the pattern of a century ago when, typically, people were well, contracted an infection, and died. Thus, a chapter about death, dying and bereavement for older adults must encompass not just the immediate end-of-life period for the patient and the bereavement period which follows for the family, but the entire chronic disease trajectory.

Palliative care addresses all of the concerns which arise during this chronic disease trajectory and thus will be the focus of this chapter. After defining palliative care, the chapter will focus on aspects of palliative care at the forefront of caring for older adults with serious illness including (1) pain and symptom management, (2) advance care planning including decision-making and establishing goals of care, (3) caregiver burden and settings of care, and (4) bereavement.

Palliative care

Palliative care is transdisciplinary, focusing on preventing and relieving suffering in order to support the best possible quality of life for patients with serious illness and their families. Palliative care includes enhancing quality of life for patients and family members, helping with decision-making, and providing patient and family-centred care coordination (National Consensus Project for Palliative Care, 2004). Although in some countries the term 'palliative care' is still synonymous with end-of-life care, the World Health Organization (WHO) recently published a broader definition that includes provision of palliative care to those early in

Table 15.1 Tenets of palliative care

Palliative care:
- Provides relief from pain and other distressing symptoms
- Affirms life and regards dying as a normal process
- Intends neither to hasten nor postpone death
- Integrates the psychological and spiritual aspects of patient care
- Offers a support system to help patients live as actively as possible until death
- Offers a support system to help the family cope during the patient's illness and in their own bereavement
- Uses a team approach to address the needs of patients and their families, including bereavement counselling, if indicated
- Will enhance quality of life, and may also positively influence the course of illness
- Is applicable early in the course of illness, in conjunction with other therapies that are intended to prolong life, and includes those investigations needed to better understand and manage distressing symptoms

---

Source: World Health Organization, Definition of Palliative Care (2008).
Reproduced by kind permission of the World Health Organization.

the course of illness and in conjunction with other therapies that are intended to prolong life (WHO, 2008). This is illustrated in Table 15.1. Indeed, palliative care is provided in conjunction with all other appropriate treatments to patients living with serious and advanced illness.

Pain and symptom management

A major focus of palliative care is the relief of physical suffering through the recognition and treatment of symptoms. The prevalence of symptoms in older patients with chronic illness is high and often under-recognized. In a study of community-dwelling elders aged 60 or older with advanced chronic obstructive pulmonary disease (COPD), congestive heart failure (CHF), or cancer, 86 per cent reported at least one symptom as moderate or severe. The most commonly reported symptoms included limited activity (61 per cent), fatigue (47 per cent), and physical discomfort (38 per cent) (Walke *et al.*, 2004). The high prevalence of cognitive impairment in this population can present challenges to symptom assessment and management. However, in patients who are verbal, patient self-report remains the reference standard of assessment. A study of 750 nursing home residents found that although patients with cognitive impairment may under-report pain, the self-reports of these patients were as valid as those without cognitive impairment (Parmelee, Smith and Katz, 1993). That is, a patient's report of pain is valid whether they are cognitively impaired or not. However, because the cognitively impaired under-report pain, close attention must be paid to mood disturbances, functional decline and changes in behaviour that may herald unreported pain (Ferrell, Ferrell and Rivera, 1995).

In patients with severe cognitive impairment who are non-verbal, pain and other symptoms often are difficult to identify and may present atypically as agitation, increased confusion or decreased mobility (Pautex, Michon, Guedira *et al.*, 2006). In this situation, the clinician should attempt to assess pain and other symptoms by direct observation and by obtaining history from caregivers. In addition, it is important to look for evidence of pain-related behaviours during ambulation, transfers and personal care (AGS Panel on Persistent Pain in Older Persons, 2002).

Advance care planning

Providing medical care for older people typically involves medically and ethically complex decision-making across various care settings and requires consideration of patients' multiple co-morbid conditions, quality of life, family support, financial capacity, and their wishes regarding treatments. Highlighting the challenges of providing palliative care to older adults is a study comparing patients aged 80 and older to younger patients, all of whom were referred to an academic palliative care service for consultation (Evers, Meier and Morrison, 2002). Patients aged 80 and older had a higher prevalence of dementia and incapacity to make decisions. This finding has immediate bearing on the process of decision-making and establishing goals of care in older adults and highlights the importance of advance care planning.

Establishing goals of care

Advance care planning is making decisions about the type of care you want to receive in the event that you become unable to speak for yourself. These decisions are also commonly referred to as one's *goals of care*. Early in the course of a patient's chronic illness, be it dementia, congestive heart failure, COPD, or a combination of diseases, the physician should engage the patient in a discussion of goals of care. The values and belief systems of each individual patient will inform how these goals are defined. Early in chronic disease, goals may include, but not be limited to, preserving autonomy, maintaining quality of life, prolonging life and reducing burden on family caregivers. Later in the disease course, these discussions may shift to decisions about the benefits and burdens of life-sustaining treatment and identifying conditions or circumstances which a patient might consider a 'fate worse than death' or under which 'life wouldn't be worth living'.

A priority during early discussions should be assisting patients to identify and appoint a primary decision-maker in preparation for a time when they are unable to make decisions themselves. This designee is sometimes referred to as the *health-care proxy* or *durable power of attorney for health care*. Patients should be encouraged to involve their designee in future conversations regarding advance care planning, as this may reduce stress associated with surrogate decision-making later in the course of the disease, especially if decisions to withdraw life-sustaining treatment are made (Tilden, Tolle, Nelson *et al.*, 2001).

After patients identify goals for their current treatment and a preferred surrogate decision-maker, the discussion should then focus on advance treatment directives. In the case of dementia, where a decline in cognitive and functional status is expected, involving patients in these discussions while they are still able to participate is of utmost importance. Often overlooked, however, is the importance of similar advance discussions involving patients with other chronic conditions such as congestive heart failure or COPD. In these disease processes, it is not uncommon for exacerbations to increase in frequency and severity. Under such circumstances, mechanical ventilation and intensive care may be offered to patients and their families in an effort to prolong life. For some patients, maximal efforts to prolong life may be the goal and, as such, mechanical ventilation and intensive care are appropriate treatments. For others, such life-prolonging treatments may be unacceptable under any circumstance. Still others might consider a trial of therapy with the stipulation that such treatment be discontinued if it became clear that the patient would not be able to return to a quality of life that is acceptable to him or her. In a study aimed at understanding the treatment preferences of seriously ill older adults, Fried and colleagues (2002) found that preferences change in response to changes in the burden of treatment, its outcomes and the likelihood of the outcomes. Furthermore, the possibility of cognitive or functional impairment after a given treatment plays a particularly important role in patients' preferences and should be explicitly considered when discussing advance care planning.

Reassessing goals of care

Once established, goals of care often change. Discussions should be frequently revisited as a patient's outlook and goals may change as their disease progresses and as they experience increasing functional decline. It also may be necessary to extend the discussion over the course of several visits, as the complexity and seriousness of the decisions facing them may overwhelm patients and families.

Establishing goals of care for patients without decision-making capacity

Often health-care professionals become involved in a patient's care later in the course of their chronic illness. In these cases, prior advance care planning including discussions with the patient, family and health-care professionals may or may not have taken place. Therefore, with each new patient, goals of care should be addressed. Although the patient may not be able to participate fully in such discussions, it is important to recognize that even patients with moderate dementia may be able to make some statements regarding their values, such as the importance of quality of life, being free of pain, or remaining at home as long as possible.

When patients with dementia no longer have decision-making capacity, clinicians must rely on the patient's surrogate or proxy to make decisions and judgements based on the patient's previously stated wishes and/or knowledge of the patient's long-held beliefs and values. However, the values and goals of these surrogates may conflict with those of the patient and with those of other family members. Every effort should be made to identify the main participants in the decision-making and to assemble all of these people for a meeting. When beginning these discussions with family members, a consensus-building approach is useful, first allowing the family to narrate how the patient has come to this stage of illness, followed by a dialogue between the physician and decision-makers about prognosis (Karlawish, Quill and Meier, 1999). This allows the family members to reflect positively on the life of the patient and to describe the type of person they were prior to their functional and cognitive decline. In cases where specific advance care planning discussions did not take place directly with the patient, hearing about the patient as a person and about their values and preferences will allow the clinician to refer to these statements when later addressing the overall goals of care and specific decisions about withholding or withdrawing therapies.

Withholding and withdrawing life-sustaining therapies

Once a consensus is achieved regarding the patient's diagnosis, prognosis, and overall goals and values, the next step is to utilize that framework to develop a plan of care. In the case of a patient with dementia, the clinician should educate the surrogate decision-makers on the fact that dementia is a terminal illness. With that in mind, it may be appropriate to discuss potentially life-sustaining therapies that the patient would or would not have wanted in this situation.

Potential candidates for discussion include cardiopulmonary resuscitation (CPR), mechanical ventilation, dialysis, artificial nutrition and hydration, antibiotic therapy and hospitalization. The decision to withhold or withdraw any of these therapies is difficult, and surrogates often have feelings of guilt (Prendergast and Puntillo, 2002). Clinicians can assist the surrogate by defining his or her role as helping clinicians to understand what treatments align best with the patient's goals. In so doing, the clinician is not asking the surrogate to assume the responsibility for treatment decisions but to represent the patient's values and preferences (Vig, Starks, Taylor *et al.*, 2007). Once consensus seems to have been reached regarding the patient's wishes, the clinician may choose to recommend a plan of care that is concordant with these wishes (Lang and Quill, 2004, Winzelberg, Hanson and Tulsky, 2005). Depending on the situation, the recommendation may be for a time-limited trial of the therapy in question or, alternatively, for withholding or withdrawing the therapy. By recommending a plan of care commensurate with the patient's wishes, the clinician in part removes the burden often felt by family members who must make such difficult decisions.

As part of the recommendation to withhold or withdraw a specific treatment, a plan outlining exactly what *will* be done to help and treat the patient will allow family members to feel that they are acting in a manner that will promote the patient's dignity and relief of suffering, and will demonstrate the medical team's continuing commitment to the care of the patient. The clinician should stress that the focus of the patient's care will be on aggressive symptom management and on providing social support for the family. *Symptom management* is the attempt to improve the quality of life in patients by treating the symptoms of the illness and unpleasant side effects of treatment. In *aggressive symptom management*, alleviating suffering may override treatment of the underlying causes of the symptoms because there is no realistic expectation of recovery. It is *not* synonymous with euthanasia, since aggressive symptom management aims at relieving suffering prior to death and *not* hastening death. As surrogates may experience continued internal questioning and regret related to the decision to withdraw a specific treatment, offering reassurance that surrogates made a good decision for the patient may help bring closure to the process for them (Vig *et al.*, 2007).

Artificial nutrition and hydration

Consideration of artificial nutrition and hydration is common in seriously ill older patients, particularly those with dementia. Dysphagia, or difficulty in swallowing, is an expected consequence of end-stage dementia and other chronic neurological illnesses. This swallowing dysfunction can cause patients to aspirate their own saliva and/or food and liquids into their lungs, predisposing them to develop aspiration pneumonia, an often fatal infection. Also common in the late stages of dementia are behaviours such as food refusal, clamping the mouth shut or holding the food without swallowing. As patients begin to lose weight due to inability to meet their caloric needs or when recurrent episodes of aspiration have occurred, physicians often offer provision of artificial nutrition and hydration through placement of a percutaneous endoscopic gastrostomy (PEG) tube. PEG tubes allow liquid nutrition to be delivered directly to the stomach through a tube in the abdominal wall.

For many families, much significance is ascribed to the provision of nutrition. Concerns may arise that their loved one will suffer hunger or thirst if no nutrition or hydration is provided. Although no studies have examined the experience of hunger in patients with advanced dementia, evidence from terminally ill, cognitively intact patients with anorexia (profound loss of appetite) demonstrates that they do not suffer hunger (McCann, Hall and Groth-Juncker, 1994). There is no evidence that artificial nutrition and hydration prolongs life, relieves suffering, reduces aspiration or pneumonia, or improves quality of life in patients with advanced dementia (Finucane, Christmas and Travis, 1999; Fisman, Levy and Gifford, 1999; Gillick, 2000; Meier, Ahronheim, Morris *et al.*, 2001). Artificial saliva, sips of water or ice chips, and good oral hygiene can help alleviate the symptom of dry mouth if it is present.

Difficult decisions regarding artificial nutrition and hydration that must be made late in the course of a family member's illness can be eased by discussing these issues with the patients themselves while they are still able to express their opinions.

Settings of care and caregiver burden

With the functional decline that accompanies worsening serious illness, many older adults will experience an increased dependence on others for basic daily activities. Loss of independence in one's instrumental activities of daily living (IADLs), including shopping, meal preparation, managing finances, transportation, and housekeeping, is often the first sign of functional decline. Patients may soon also require assistance with the activities of daily living (ADLs) including bathing, dressing, toileting, transferring, and eating. More than 6 million people aged 65 and older in the USA require some type of long-term care (Feder, Komisar and Niefeld, 2000), and the majority of this care occurs at home (National Alliance for Caregiving and AARP, 2004). In fact, about 80 per cent of care recipients aged 65 or older live at home or in community-based settings, while the remainder reside in nursing facilities (US Department of Health and Human Services, 2004). Of those who live at home, 80 per cent receive their care exclusively from family, friends and volunteers. Among the remaining 20 per cent who pay for a caregiver, an additional two-thirds also receive informal assistance from family or friends.

The economic burden of caregiving on society is great. Informal caregivers' unpaid contribution to American society is in the hundreds of billions of dollars annually (Arno, 2002), a figure reflected worldwide (e.g. in 2005 the cost of just informal care for dementia alone was estimated at US\$315.4 billion (Wimo, Winblad and Jonsson, 2009)). This figure does not take into account the wages and benefits sacrificed when people reduce their hours at work or, in fact, quit their jobs in order to provide care for a family member.

Caregiving also affects the health of the caregivers themselves. The Nurses' Health Study found an 80 per cent increased risk of heart attack or cardiac death for those caregiving greater than 9 hours per week for an ill spouse (Lee, Colditz, Berkman *et al.*, 2003). In a separate study, caregivers reporting emotional strain had a 63 per cent increased risk of death when compared with non-caregiving controls (Schulz and Beach, 1999).

Given the growing number of caregivers as well as the physical, emotional and economic burden of caregiving, importance should be placed on identifying caregivers' needs. In a survey of 475 family members who had recently experienced the death of a loved one, researchers identified a list of changes that family members felt would improve care of the dying. Included were having the loved one's wishes honoured; being included in the decision process; and providing for support and assistance at home with practical matters such as transportation, medicines and equipment, and with personal care needs such as bathing, feeding and toileting. Family members also wish to be provided with honest information, to be listened to, to have their privacy respected, and to be remembered and contacted after the death (Tolle and Tilden, 1999).

Grief and bereavement

This last wish of family members – to be remembered and contacted after the death – leads to another important aspect of palliative care: bereavement. Throughout most of a patient's disease course, the clinicians must focus primarily on the patient: diagnosis, treatment, response to treatment and symptoms. As a patient nears death and after the patient's death, however, equal attention must be paid to the caregivers. Both caregiver stress and the extent to which caregivers are prepared for the death of a loved one can impact the psychological well-being of the caregivers after the death.

Bereavement is defined as the experience of losing a loved one to death, and grief is the emotional distress associated with that loss (Zhang, El-Jawahri and Prigerson, 2006). Deaths of loved ones are common life experiences shared by many, but research has demonstrated that these occurrences are among life's most stressful experiences (Osterweis, 1984) and that bereaved persons are at increased risk of many adverse physical, mental and social outcomes (Zhang *et al.*, 2006). However, normal, uncomplicated grief reactions are experienced by approximately 80–90 per cent of bereaved individuals (Prigerson, 2004). Therefore, the negative outcomes associated with bereavement are concentrated in a minority of bereaved persons (Zhang *et al.*, 2006).

The process of bereavement and the morbidity associated with it begins before the death of a loved one. Upon hospice admission, more than half of the caregivers of patients had clinically significant levels of depression, with rates of depression more than three times that of demographically matched controls (Haley, LaMonde, Han *et al.*, 2001). After the death of a spouse, the prevalence of major depression among widows/widowers was found to be 20 per cent 2 months after the death of a spouse and 15 per cent one year after the death (Zisook and Shuchter, 1991). Distinct from the symptoms of bereavement-related depression and anxiety, approximately 10 per cent of widows/widowers suffer from the symptoms of prolonged grief (Prigerson, Bierhals, Kasl *et al.*, 1996).

Experts in the field have yet to agree upon a definition for prolonged grief, but Zhang and colleagues (2006) have proposed a description and diagnostic criteria for *prolonged grief disorder*. The symptoms include yearning for the deceased, trouble accepting the death, inability to trust others since the death, excessive bitterness or anger about the death, difficulty in forming new relationships, feeling emotionally numb, feeling life is empty, feeling the future holds no meaning, and feeling on edge. To meet the proposed criteria for prolonged grief, these symptoms must last at least 6 months and must cause marked dysfunction in social, occupational or other important domains. These same symptoms are common in normal grief reaction, but generally persist for less than 6 months.

One of the modifiable risk factors of morbidity associated with terminal caregiving is the extent to which the caregiver is prepared for the death of their loved one. The task of preparing caregivers for the death is necessary but often neglected. In a national sample, 23 per cent of bereaved caregivers contacted reported that the death in question was 'extremely' unexpected (Teno, Clarridge, Casey *et al.*, 2004). When this task is neglected, bereaved caregivers suffer from worse mental health. In a study of 112 spouses of deceased cancer patients, more depressive symptoms and more severe grief were observed among those who were not prepared for the death (Houts, Lipton, Harold *et al.*, 1989). Other investigators have demonstrated that the relationship between preparedness and psychiatric morbidity is dose-dependent; that is, the less prepared bereaved persons felt, the higher the risk of psychiatric complications including anxiety and tranquilliser use up to 5 years after the death (Valdimarsdóttir, Helgason, Fürst *et al.*, 2004).

Contributing to lack of death preparedness is uncertainty in illness. When inadequate information is provided, a situation is unpredictable, or insecurity in one's understanding exists, caregivers and patients often experience uncertainty (Mishel, 1988). In one study examining the association between uncertainty and health in spousal caregivers of patients with advanced cancer, a higher level of caregiver uncertainty was found to be negatively associated with health (Stetz, 1989).

Death preparedness, despite its importance in impacting morbidity in caregivers, has never been fully defined (Rabow, Hauser and Adams, 2004). Other topics including prognostication, death acceptance and anticipatory grief are related to, but not synonymous with, preparedness (Hebert, Prigerson, Schulz *et al.*, 2006). Through conducting focus groups of patients, families and health-care providers, Steinhauser and colleagues (2001) demonstrated that preparedness is multidimensional and includes medical dimensions such as knowing what signs and symptoms to expect during the last hours of life, the psychological realm including discussing grief and emotions, spiritual concerns including prayer and discussing the meaning of death, and practical issues such as funeral arrangements.

Palliative care aims to address many of these modifiable risk factors of morbidity associated with terminal caregiving by providing expert communication with patients and their families about their illness, prognosis and disease trajectory. Palliative care also provides support during the bereavement period through various methods including intentional follow-up phone calls with families, support groups and referral to additional community resources.

Future directions and conclusion

As a result of the longevity revolution, older adults comprise the majority of patients who are approaching the end of life. Despite this, the majority of research on dying patients has focused on a younger population. For instance, the SUPPORT study, which is the largest study of adult hospital deaths in the USA, had a median age of 66 (SUPPORT Principal Investigators, 1995). By 2030, 20 per cent of the USA population will be aged 65 or older, and the fastest growing demographic group, those aged 85 and older, is predicted to more than double in size from 3.5 million to 8.5 million over the next 30 years (National Center for Health Statistics, 2001). As our population continues to age at increasing rates, care of the older adult will become an increasingly acute concern for governments and health-care organizations alike, as well as for practising clinicians, patients and their caregivers. Additional research is needed to further define the experience of older adults living with and dying from chronic illness, so that we as a society can best respond to the needs of both the patients and their caregivers.

Palliative care practitioners aim to address the many potential sources of suffering for patients and families living with serious illness. By providing expert pain and symptom management, guidance in decision-making, support for caregivers and solace for the bereaved, palliative care teams are integral partners in the care of older adults with serious illness.

Summary

Although the study of death, dying and bereavement is a key part of gerontology, the current experience of death often involves a prolonged end of life period, necessitating an examination of palliative care in this final phase. The chapter examines the concept of palliative care, drawing upon its transdisciplinary nature, and critically discusses some of its key aspects, including pain and symptom management, advance care planning (with particular emphasis upon goals of care and their establishment in patients of all types, including those lacking decision-making capacity because of e.g. dementia). The ethically challenging topic of withholding and withdrawing life-sustaining therapies is discussed, as is the provision of artificial nutrition and hydration. In a different perspective on the same processes, the settings of care and caregiver burden are considered, before a critical discussion of grief and bereavement. The chapter concludes with a discussion of possible future directions for research.

REFERENCES

AGS Panel on Persistent Pain in Older Persons (2002) The management of persistent pain in older persons, *Journal of the American Geriatrics Society, 50*(6 suppl), S205–24.

Arno, P.S. (2002) Economic value of informal caregiving: 2000. Presentation before the American Association for Geriatric Psychiatry, Orlando, FL.

Butler, R.N. (2008) *The longevity revolution: the benefits and challenges of living a long life.* New York: PublicAffairs.

Centers for Disease Control and Prevention (2003) *Births, marriages, divorces and deaths data for 2001.* Hyattsville, MD: Division of Vital Statistics.

Evers, M.M., Meier, D.E. and Morrison, R.S. (2002) Assessing differences in care needs and service utilization in geriatric palliative care patients, *Journal of Pain and Symptom Management, 23*, 424–32.

Feder, J., Komisar, H.L. and Niefeld, M. (2000) Long-term care in the United States: an overview, *Health Affairs, 19*(3), 40–56.

Ferrell, B.A., Ferrell, B.R. and Rivera, L. (1995) Pain in cognitively impaired nursing home patients, *Journal of Pain and Symptom Management, 10*(8), 591–8.

Finucane, T.E., Christmas, C. and Travis, K. (1999) Tube feeding in patients with advanced dementia, *Journal of the American Medical Association, 282*, 1365–70.

Fisman, D.N., Levy, A.R., Gifford, D.R. *et al.* (1999) Survival after percutaneous endoscopic gastrostomy among older residents of Quebec, *Journal of the American Geriatrics Society, 47*, 349–55.

Fried, T.R., Bradley, E.H., Towle, V.R. *et al.* (2002) Understanding the treatment preferences of seriously ill patients, *New England Journal of Medicine, 346*(14), 1061–6.

Gillick, M.R. (2000) Rethinking the role of tube feeding in patients with advanced dementia, *New England Journal of Medicine, 342*, 206–10.

Haley, W.E., LaMonde, L.A., Han, B. *et al.* (2001) Family caregiving in hospice: effects on psychological and health functioning among spousal caregivers of hospice patients with lung cancer or dementia, *Hospital Journal, 15*, 1–18.

Hebert, R.S., Prigerson, H.G., Schulz, R. *et al.* (2006) Preparing caregivers for the death of a loved one: a theoretical framework and suggestions for future research, *Journal of Palliative Medicine, 9*, 1164–71.

Houts, PS., Lipton, A., Harold, A. *et al.* (1989) Predictors of grief among spouses of deceased cancer patients, *Journal of Psychosocial Oncology, 7*, 113–26.

Karlawish, J.H.T., Quill, T. and Meier, D.E. for the ACP-ASIM End-of-Life Care Consensus Panel (1999) A consensus-based approach to providing palliative care to patients who lack decision-making, *Annals of Internal Medicine, 130*, 835–40.

Lang, F. and Quill, T. (2004) Making decisions with families at the end of life, *American Family Physician*, *70*(4), 719–23.

Lee, S., Colditz, G.A., Berkman, L.F. *et al.* (2003) Caregiving and risk of coronary heart disease in U.S. women: a prospective study, *American Journal of Preventative Medicine*, *24*(2), 113–19.

Liao, Y., McGee, D.L., Cao, G. *et al.* (2001) Recent changes in the health status of the older U.S. population: findings from the 1984 and 1994 supplement on aging, *Journal of the American Geriatrics Society*, *49*, 443–9.

McCann, R.M., Hall, W.J. and Groth-Juncker, A. (1994) Comfort care for terminally ill patients. The appropriate use of nutrition and hydration, *Journal of the American Medical Association*, *272*, 1263–6.

Meier, D.E., Ahronheim, J.C., Morris, J. *et al.* (2001) High short-term mortality in hospitalized patients with advanced dementia: lack of benefit of tube-feeding, *Archives of Internal Medicine*, *161*, 594–9.

Mishel, M.H. (1988) Uncertainty in illness, *Image – the Journal of Nursing Scholarship*, *20*, 225–32.

National Alliance for Caregiving and AARP (2004) *Caregiving in the United States*. Retrieved from http://assets.aarp.org/rgcenter/il/us_caregiving.pdf.

National Center for Health Statistics (2001) Centers for Disease Control: National Vital Statistics Report. 9 October 2001.

National Consensus Project for Quality Palliative Care (2004) Clinical practice guidelines for quality palliative care. Retrieved from www.nationalconsensusproject.org.

Osterweis, M., Solomon, F. and Green, M. (eds) (1984) *Bereavement: reactions, consequences, and care.* Washington, DC: National Academy Press.

Parmelee, P.A., Smith, B. and Katz, I.R. (1993) Pain complaints and cognitive status among elderly institution residents, *Journal of the American Geriatrics Society*, *41*, 517–22.

Pautex, S., Michon, A., Guedira, M. *et al.* (2006) Pain in severe dementia: self-assessment of observational scales?, *Journal of the American Geriatrics Society*, *54*, 1040–5.

Prendergast, T.J. and Puntillo, K.A. (2002) Withdrawal of life support: intensive caring at the end of life, *Journal of the American Medical Association*, *288*(21), 2732–40.

Prigerson, H.G. (2004) Complicated grief: when the path of adjustment leads to a dead-end, *Bereavement Care*, *23*, 38–40.

Prigerson, H.G., Bierhals, A.J., Kasl, S.V. *et al.* (1996) Complicated grief as a disorder distinct from bereavement-related depression and anxiety: a replication study, *American Journal of Psychiatry*, *153*, 1484–6.

Rabow, M.W., Hauser, J.M. and Adams, J. (2004) Supporting family caregivers at the end of life: "they don't know what they don't know", *Journal of the American Medical Association*, *291*, 483–91.

Schulz, R. and Beach, S.R. (1999) Caregiving as a risk factor for mortality: the Caregiver Health Effects Study, *Journal of the American Medical Association*, *282*(23), 2215–19.

Steinhauser, K.E., Christakis, N.A., Clipp, E.C. *et al.* (2001) Preparing for the end of life: preferences of patients, families, physicians, and other care providers, *Journal of Pain and Symptom Management*, *22*, 727–37.

Stetz, K.M. (1989) The relationship among background characteristics, purpose in life, and caregiving demands on perceived health of spouse caregivers, *Scholarly Inquiry for Nursing Practice*, *3*, 133–53.

SUPPORT Principal Investigators (1995) A controlled trial to improve care for seriously ill hospitalized patients: the Study to Understand Prognoses and Preferences for Outcomes and Risks of Treatment (SUPPORT), *Journal of the American Medical Association, 274,* 1591–8.

Teno, J.M., Clarridge, B.R., Casey, V. *et al.* (2004) Family perspectives on end-of-life care at the last place of care, *Journal of the American Medical Association, 291,* 88–93.

Tilden, V.P., Tolle, S.W., Nelson, C.A. *et al.* (2001) Family decision-making to withdraw life-sustaining treatments from hospitalized patients, *Nursing Research, 50,* 1–11.

Tolle, S.W. and Tilden, V.P. (1999) *The Oregon report card: improving care of the dying.* Portland, OR: Oregon Health Sciences University.

US Department of Health and Human Services, Health Resources and Services Administration (2004) *Nursing aides, home health aides, and related health care occupations—national and local work-force shortages and associated data needs.* www.directcareclearinghouse. org/download/RNandHomeAides.pdf.

Valdimarsdóttir, U., Helgason, A.R., Fürst, C.J. *et al.* (2004) Awareness of husband's impending death from cancer and long-term anxiety in widowhood: a nationwide follow-up, *Palliative Medicine 18,* 432–43.

Vig, E.K., Starks, H., Taylor, J.S. *et al.* (2007) Surviving surrogate decision-making: what helps and hampers the experience of making medical decisions for others, *Journal of General Internal Medicine, 22*(9), 1274–9.

Walke, L.M., Gallo, W.T., Tinetti, M.E. *et al.* (2004) The burden of symptoms among community-dwelling older persons with advanced chronic disease, *Archives of Internal Medicine, 164,* 2321–4.

Wimo, A., Winblad, B. and Jonsson, L. (2009) An estimate of the total worldwide societal costs of dementia in 2005, *Alzheimer's and Dementia, 3,* 81–91.

Winzelberg, G.S., Hanson, L.C. and Tulsky, J.A. (2005) Beyond autonomy: diversifying end-of-life decision-making approaches to serve patients and families, *Journal of the American Geriatrics Society, 53*(6), 1046–50.

World Health Organization (2008) WHO definition of palliative care. Retrieved, from www.who. int/cancer/palliative/definition/en/.

Zhang, B., El-Jawahri, A., and Prigerson H.G. (2006) Update on bereavement research: evidence-based guidelines for the diagnosis and treatment of complicated bereavement, *Journal of Palliative Medicine, 9*(5), 1188–1203.

Zisook, S. and Shuchter, S.R. (1991) Depression through the first year after the death of a spouse, *American Journal of Psychiatry, 148,* 1346–52.

16 Conclusions

IAN STUART-HAMILTON

OVERVIEW

This chapter first notes that changes in individuals might vary from those of groups. It then addresses how changes in one area of gerontology can have a significant effect on others, leading to a need constantly to maintain a broad knowledge of the subject.

The purpose of a concluding chapter in an edited volume is typically to draw together the themes raised and create a grand overview, preferably one filled with sage wisdom. I have no pretentions of being able to do such a thing, not least because trying to find a unifying theme, beyond a bland platitude, such as 'more must be done', in a subject as diverse as gerontology would be a fool's errand. In support of this I cite the words of the historian H.A.L. Fisher, who wrote the following, largely as a riposte to the then-fashionable view of history as an inevitable process towards a particular ideological system of government:

Men wiser and more learned than I have discerned in history a plot, a rhythm, a predetermined pattern. These harmonies are concealed from me. I can see only one emergency following upon another as wave follows upon wave, only one great fact with respect to which, since it is unique, there can be no generalizations, only one safe rule for the historian: that he should recognize in the development of human destinies the play of the contingent and the unforeseen. (Fisher, 1935, p. vii)

It is important to remember that for much of this book we have talked about older adults as a group, and how they act and feel on average or en masse. But of course on an individual level, they are far more variable. This was neatly illustrated in Paul Verhaeghen's masterful analysis of intellectual changes in Chapter 6, where it was demonstrated that although different types of intelligence reliably decline as a cohort average as people get older, the pattern of change within each individual in the group is different. And thus, much of what H.A.L. Fisher wrote about history can be adapted to gerontology. In spite of any grand themes that people can see in an *overview* of the ageing process, from the viewpoint of a single person experiencing ageing, it is far more likely to seem to be a scattering of events, experiences and changes, and not something following a rigid timetable. The contingent and the unforeseen play a greater role in our individual experiences of age and ageing than theoretical models and statistical summaries based on groups make it appear. Of course, these are hardly new criticisms, and nearly every academic subject has at some point been accused of creating work that applies to everyone in general and no one in particular. But it is a point worth stressing, nonetheless. Whereas errors in treatment, applications of policy, etc., can often be corrected in earlier adulthood, in old age, there is no possible future date for restitution.

In the search for better understanding of gerontological issues, it will not have escaped readers' attention that there seems to be an insatiable search for theories to explain findings. Almost always, one of the most damning criticisms of an academic topic is that it is 'theory light'. Without theorizing and models, the argument runs, all we have is a collection of uninterpreted facts, and these neither guide nor inform. This is a valid point, but it can be questioned whether the argument can be pushed too far so that the search for a better theory blinds us to more important facts. The perennial problem with improving a theory is that the theory rather than the phenomenon it was originally intended to examine becomes the centre of attention. In short, we end up pursuing research for its own sake, forgetting why the research question was asked in the first place.

In discussing this problem, I am perennially reminded of a scene from that great classic of English literature, *Winnie the Pooh* (Milne, 1926). In an early chapter in the book, our beloved but rather stupid bear has been walking in the snow in a circle round a group of trees, when he sees a set of paw tracks in the snow ahead of him. Convinced that there is a dangerous animal (which he names a *woozle*) ahead of him, he cautiously sets off on the same circular route again, aided by Piglet, who has had the misfortune to arrive at just the wrong time. So Piglet and Pooh track the woozle together. Having walked round the trees a full circuit, they haven't found the woozle, but now see *more* tracks in the snow that indicate there are two woozles ahead of them, and also the tracks of a much smaller, third animal, which Pooh names a *wizzle*. And so Pooh and Piglet once more track their elusive prey, and again don't find either a woozle or a wizzle, but on returning to their starting point discover there are now yet more animals ahead of them. Of course, all that has happened is that Pooh and Piglet have been tracking their own footprints, and with every circuit of the trees they have convinced themselves that there are more and more animals ahead of them, whereas in fact they have created the whole problem for themselves.

I am not claiming that gerontological research as a whole has turned into a giant woozle hunt, but, nonetheless, we should be mindful of pursuing some topics in too great a depth, distracting ourselves, to adopt Newton's famous phrase, with a few pebbles on the beach while the ocean of truth lies before us. For although this book has demonstrated that we already have discovered much about ageing, and are more certain in our knowledge than 20 years ago, nonetheless there are still profound gaps in our knowledge. For example, one of the key instructions to authors preparing their individual chapters was that they should try where possible to include a significant cross-cultural element in their writing. In many cases this proved difficult, simply because research has been almost exclusively concentrated in a limited number of Western industrialized cultures. Of course, not all topics will benefit equally from a multi-cultural analysis. For example, most biological and psychological ageing changes are likely to be the same the world over. But as soon as factors such as family, financial situation and social status are raised, there could be profound differences between cultures, and the findings of a body of studies based in one culture will not automatically apply to another. There is a clear need for this anomaly to be resolved.

Similarly, there are key gaps in knowledge within specific disciplines. For example, within the psychology of ageing, there is surprisingly little known about what happens to people with atypical childhood disorders such as autism when they reach old age (Stuart-Hamilton, Griffith, Totsika *et al.*, 2009). It would be unreasonable to expect that every single topic that could conceivably be addressed by gerontologists should have been covered in depth. Since by definition gerontology can be applied to anything where old age and ageing could play a role, this would be an extremely long list. However, arguably, some prudence and foresight are needed in the future to ensure that the more important topics are addressed and not simply the ones that currently have attracted funding and have an impressive set of theoretical models. Indeed (with tongue only slightly in cheek), there might be an argument made that if a topic already has more than a hundred theoretical publications to its name, all research should be suspended until other topics have been examined in greater depth. There are only so many times we can go round the same copse of trees.

Does this mean that gerontology is in poor shape? Of course not – it is vibrant in its diversity. Research is being increasingly funded as governments realize that the population is growing older and research is needed as a practical necessity (something, incidentally, that gerontologists have been telling them for decades, had politicians bothered to listen). And a little controversy and variance of opinion is a sign of health, not disorder. As classical musicians are wont to comment, if there is a single definitive performance of a piece, then it is not worth playing.

However, no matter how vibrant and active the research, no matter what the findings point to, they are of no value unless they are acted upon. Practitioners and policymakers need to heed the findings, which are not always intuitively obvious. Time and again through this book, we have seen that suppositions about ageing and older adults go against the grain of conventional wisdom and popular belief. An individual reader might not feel that they can do much to change the situation, but they can act within their sphere of influence, and collectively, the experience of older adults can be improved.

What, then, should our goals for improvement be? This is an easy question to answer in general, but a hard one to answer in specific, concrete and thus measurable terms. As noted at the start of this chapter, it is easy to produce platitudinous statements like 'something must be done', and similarly it is easy to pander to understandable but vague aspirations of a better deal for older people and talk of improved experiences for older adults, longer life, better health, greater access to care and so forth. The problem is that such goals become harder to establish in practice. How do we define significantly 'better health', for example? As we have seen, increasing how long someone lives does not in and of itself constitute improvement, if the person's additional life has been bought with suffering. How do we define better access to care? As several chapters have argued with great persuasiveness, it is not simply a matter of providing more care services (though this is desirable) – it is the nature of the care that is offered, and whether it is timely and appropriate for the specific needs of the recipients. And what constitutes a good level of health care in one culture might appear very inadequate in another country with a higher level of economic development. Nor can we assume that living longer in and of itself should be seen as desirable in all circumstances. Aside from the Tithonus myth, just as much as this book has addressed the issue of a better quality of life, so there must be a better quality of dying. In many topics in gerontology, the elephant in the room is death. Because what follows old age is the same for everyone (debates of what happens *after* death are, thankfully, not the preserve of this book), there is at times more than a whiff of a feeling that we are discussing how best to look after the inmates on death row. It is entirely appropriate, as noted in Chapter 14, that we should celebrate ageing, and look at it squarely in the face, not just see it as a metaphor for our mortality. But we equally cannot ignore the fact that old age is, for all its manifest blessings, the departure lounge for the voyage to the undiscovered country; and all of us have a guaranteed ticket. A good leaving of life is arguably as key as the consideration of prolonging life (or, if you prefer, putting off the inevitable).

Therefore, although many gerontologists are opposed to this notion, we must face the fact that old age and death are strong associates. This questions, therefore, how much attention we should pay to the needs of gerontology. After all, even if we were to improve the lives of older adults (and as we have seen, that in itself is a vague concept), what use is there in this if older people then die? Well, actually, there is rather a lot of use. Even on the grounds of years of remaining life, the argument is often spurious. To take a single simplistic example, medical practitioners regularly revive and treat hardened drug addicts, and to do otherwise would break every ethical principle. But medical staff do this, knowing that an addict's remaining life expectancy is in many instances less than that of a moderately healthy 70-year-old. Care cannot be apportioned purely on the grounds of the time left to the recipient. Of course, there is a danger of sophistry in such arguments, and we must be wary of overstretching them. The addict example is in some respects a poor one, since there is no competition for resources. However, suppose the issue were whether the recipient of a much-needed replacement kidney should go to a 60-year-old, clean-living, much-loved grandfather or a 20-year-old, reformed drug addict. The question is now much less clear-cut, but, arguably, ultimately boils down to the issue of age. Do we reward older adults for what they have done, rather than what they are likely to do from now on, or do we reward younger adults, not for what they have done but for their future potential? The answers to such questions lie outside gerontology, and are more suitable for medical ethics or philosophy. But we cannot assume that, because there is a list of things that we should like to see changed in order to improve the lot of older adults, they automatically will, in a world of limited resources.

Which brings us back to the question we have already sidetracked once – namely, what *do* we want for older people? Without clear goals, how can a convincing argument be made? As just noted, demands for older adults are demands for scarce resources that others often have a claim on too. We are not in a position to demand everything that is, at least in theory, desirable – others have needs that must be met as well. And even when a demand is met, this may have effects that are not always advantageous. Take the following example, widely reported in the UK news media. On 1 July 2007, England introduced a ban on smoking in public places. A study demonstrated that, 15 months later, emergency admissions to hospital for heart attacks were significantly lower than in the 5-year period prior to the ban (Sims, Maxwell, Bauld *et al.*, 2010). In the case of men and women aged over 60, there was a drop of 3.07 and 3.82 per cent respectively, and there was a drop of 3.46 per cent in men under 60. All three figures were statistically significant (in other words, they are unlikely to be due to chance fluctuations in the data), but the drop of 2.46 per cent in women under 60 was not significant (i.e. it *could* be a chance result). These figures indicate that cutting out smoking saves lives, and in its own terms, this can only be seen as good. It can also be seen that the effect is especially pronounced in older people. But it does have implications for other aspects of later-life care. We know, for example, that dementia increases in frequency past the age of 60. Therefore, of the 3+ per cent of people saved, the smoking ban has probably meant that a significant proportion of them now will live long enough to experience dementia before they die (see Chapter 7). Again, higher survival rates mean that more people claim pensions, creating a greater financial burden on an already overstretched system. None of this is an argument to encourage people to smoke, but it does illustrate how tinkering with one aspect of life expectancy and the ageing process can have unforeseen consequences down the line. If we re-examine the chapters on atypical ageing and retirement in this light, we can see that simply increasing life expectancy is not automatically good. And, as other chapters have observed (e.g. Chapters 2, 3, 4 and 15), it is not enough to increase life at all costs.

Should we therefore prevent piecemeal attempts such as this to improve the lives of older people? Of course not – we cannot block improvements to health and welfare because there *might* be knock-on effects. And again, there is a danger that if we judge issues by the eventual balance sheet, the most extraordinary things might be asked for. An interesting case in point is the El Niño storms of 1997–8. These caused their usual trail of destruction – in this case, costing an estimated $4 billion. But what was less appreciated is that in fact El Niño eventually created a net saving of $15 billion. This is because, although El Niño causes damage, it brings with it higher winter temperatures, less spring flooding and milder winds elsewhere in the USA. This resulted in lower heating costs, less storm damage from other wind systems – and about 800 fewer cold-related deaths, mostly among older people. The gross saving brought about by El Niño was an estimated $19 billion (Lomborg, 2001). Of course this does not mean that we should argue that severe storms are a good thing because on a statistical basis they result in fewer deaths among vulnerable older people. Nor should we argue that global warming is a good thing because, if the summers do become markedly hotter, the increased deaths from heatstroke and related conditions among older people will be more than offset by fewer deaths from hypothermia during the milder winters (see Maccabee, 2010). The argument still holds even if the number of lives saved (or more accurately, prolonged) is on a remarkable scale. For example, one estimate is for 170 *million* fewer deaths by 2100 because of global warming (Lomborg, 2007). It should be added that some of these figures are drawn from the work of a somewhat controversial environmental researcher, but, nonetheless, the main point is valid – just the fact that life can be extended does not automatically justify the means.

But this even more stresses the need for clear goals. And it means in particular that policymakers need to gain a clear idea that changes in one policy will affect another. This goes beyond the relatively simple knock-on effects of a ban on smoking in public places. There is little point in trying to cut rates of childhood and early adult obesity, discouraging teenagers from taking drugs, and telling the whole nation to eat their five portions of fruit and/or vegetables a day and exercise five times a week, if at the other end of the age spectrum there is woefully inadequate planning for the resulting increase in the number of pensioners and the disproportionate increase in burdens on the health and social care services.

And here we reach the essence of what our goals should be. Each subdiscipline within gerontology will have its own set of desiderata. These will in many cases differ from culture to culture and across time. That is practically inevitable, though it does mean that trying to create firm figures in the context of this chapter is impossible. But one thing can be firmly stated; namely, whatever desiderata are created, others need to know about them. As I hope I have demonstrated, tinkering with life expectancy and the experience of ageing just a little bit can have considerable repercussions for others involved in the health and welfare of older people. And this ultimately is why we need the discipline of gerontology. Many of the individual fields have little in common – they are drawn from radically different academic and practical traditions, and other than a shared interest in old age and ageing, practitioners in their specialist fields have very little shared background. But the output of their work *does*. If we want changes in the experience of ageing to be optimally effective, we need to communicate with each other, so that one group can plan optimally given the changes introduced by other groups. Research in *any* topic connected with gerontology cannot judge its success purely in terms of its own field – there can be no woozle hunting. Alter one part of the ageing experience and it is all affected, sometimes slightly, and sometimes in a major manner. But in every case, everyone needs to know.

I ended Chapter 1 with the following statement:

Should we therefore view old age as a heroic summation of all that has passed, or as an agonized brooding on all that has been lost? It is the responsibility of gerontology to address this question and ensure that in the future there is only one possible answer.

This still holds true. But having considered a wider range of approaches to ageing and old age, we can now surely appreciate that answers to this issue must form part of a matrix. To quote John Donne, 'No man is an island, entire of itself.' Although gerontology is a diverse subject, we of necessity must be aware of its varied constituent parts if we are to have an effective understanding and hence better care provision for older people.

Summary

The chapter begins by noting that although many of the chapters address changes in age groups, the experiences of individuals might considerably vary from this and follow a less predictable pattern. The chapter then considers the danger of over-concentration on specific theoretical questions. It then critically discusses the effects of changes in one area of gerontological practice on others, taking as an example the diminution in heart attacks among older adults in the UK following a public smoking ban. It is noted that setting clear goals for future research and development is thus an extremely difficult task. However, the need for researchers across subdisciplines in gerontology to be kept informed of each other's work, so that appropriate planning can be made, is stressed as a key factor in ensuring the continued improved experience of older people.

REFERENCES

Fisher, H.A.L. (1935) *A history of Europe.* Glasgow: Collins.

Lomborg, B. (2001) *The skeptical environmentalist: measuring the real state of the world.* Cambridge University Press.

(2007) *Cool it: the skeptical environmentalist's guide to global warming.* New York: Knopf.

Maccabee, H. (2010) Direct health effects of climate change: an overview, *Journal of American Physicians and Surgeons,* **15**, 38–41.

Milne, A.A. (1926) *Winnie the Pooh.* London: Methuen.

Sims, M., Maxwell, R., Bauld, L. *et al.* (2010) Short term impact of smoke-free legislation in England: retrospective analysis of hospital admissions for myocardial infarction, *British Medical Journal,* **340**, 2161.

Stuart-Hamilton, I., Griffith, G., Totsika, V. *et al.* (2009) *The circumstances and support needs of older people with autism.* Report for the Welsh Assembly Government. Cardiff: Welsh Assembly.

Index